AF361294

# MAKING WORLDS: GLOBAL INVENTION IN THE EARLY MODERN PERIOD

# MAKING WORLDS

## Global Invention in the
## Early Modern Period

*Edited by Angela Vanhaelen and Bronwen Wilson*

Published by the University of Toronto Press in association with the
UCLA Center for Seventeenth- and Eighteenth-Century Studies and
the William Andrews Clark Memorial Library

ISBN 978-1-4875-4493-5 (cloth)
ISBN 978-1-4875-4495-9 (EPUB)
ISBN 978-1-4875-4496-6 (PDF)

---

**Library and Archives Canada Cataloguing in Publication**

Title: Making worlds : global invention in the early modern period / edited by
Angela Vanhaelen and Bronwen Wilson.
Names: Vanhaelen, Angela, editor. | Wilson, Bronwen, editor.
Series: UCLA Clark Memorial Library series.
Description: Series statement: The UCLA Clark Memorial Library series |
Includes bibliographical references and index.
Identifiers: Canadiana (print) 20220268673 | Canadiana (ebook) 2022026886X |
ISBN 9781487544935 (cloth) | ISBN 9781487544959 (EPUB) |
ISBN 9781487544966 (PDF)
Subjects: LCSH: Civilization, Modern. | LCSH: Globalization – History.
Classification: LCC CB357.M35 2022 | DDC 303.48/209–dc23

---

We wish to acknowledge the land on which the University of Toronto Press
operates. This land is the traditional territory of the Wendat, the Anishnaabeg,
the Haudenosaunee, the Métis, and the Mississaugas of the Credit First Nation.

This book has been published with the help of a grant from the UCLA Center
for Seventeenth- and Eighteenth-Century Studies.

University of Toronto Press acknowledges the financial support of the
Government of Canada, the Canada Council for the Arts, and the Ontario Arts
Council, an agency of the Government of Ontario, for its publishing activities.

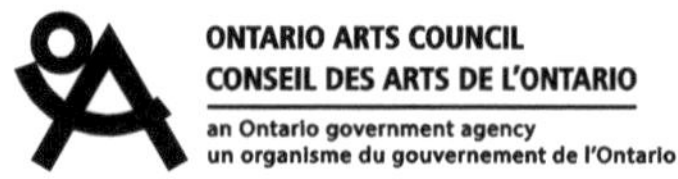


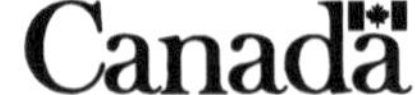

# Contents

**Part II: In-Between Spaces**

**Part III: Other Worlds**

# Illustrations

# Acknowledgments

The attempt to change our approach to early modern culture – a shift in focus that considers multiple global viewpoints – is necessarily a collaborative endeavour. This volume developed out of "Making Worlds: Art, Materiality, and Early Modern Globalization," a series of three interdisciplinary conferences held at the UCLA William Andrews Clark Memorial Library at the University of California, Los Angeles in 2018 and 2019, which brought together an impressive group of international scholars with stimulating results.[*] We are grateful to the Center for Seventeenth- and Eighteenth-Century Studies and the Clark Library for this partnership opportunity. The collegiality, intellectual generosity, and organizational support were extraordinary. Sincere thanks to Helen Deutsch, Kathy Sanchez, Candis Snoddy, Erich Bollman, Jeanette LaVere, Alastair Thorne, and many others who made these events and their planning such a success and also a pleasure. The *Making Worlds* initiative has been generously funded by the Social Sciences and Humanities Research Council of Canada. We want to thank the numerous graduate students who have played a crucial role in the project as we developed our ideas together by sharing research, leading discussion groups, organizing and chairing sessions at conferences, and contributing entries on key terms to our project website. We warmly acknowledge the contributions of the Clark Library's Ahmanson-Getty postdoctoral fellows, Payton Phillips Quintanilla and Elisa Antoinetta Daniele. Finally, we are grateful to Mark Thompson and Christine Robertson at the University of Toronto Press, copy editor Dylan Reid, the two insightful readers of the manuscript, and Cynthia Fang for her superb assistance and steering of the book through these stages.


[*] See http://www.1718.ucla.edu/core-program-2018-19/. The three individual conferences were titled "In Between Spaces" (October 12–13, 2018), "Material Flows" (February 1–2, 2019), and "Other Worlds" (May 3–4, 2019).

MAKING WORLDS: GLOBAL INVENTION
IN THE EARLY MODERN PERIOD

# chapter one

# Introduction

ANGELA VANHAELEN AND BRONWEN WILSON

This volume advocates an approach to early modern studies that is reoriented to consider the worldmaking potential afforded by the fluctuating dynamics of global mobility. The essays together interrogate historical narratives and theoretical frameworks that have shaped our understanding of the cultural impacts of globalization in the early modern period (c. 1500–1700). A dominant view characterizes early modernity as "the age of exploration" and tracks the massive annihilation of cultures worldwide as a result of expanding trade routes, religious missions, wars, invasion, transatlantic slavery, disease, resource extraction, monoculture, and settler colonialism, among other historical factors. Attentiveness to the effects of this significant escalation of European global conquest has generated theoretical approaches structured by binaries of centre and periphery or self and other. Such theories tend to assert the powers of empire, colonialism, capitalism, and religious institutions as the main drivers of globalization and cultural change, and associate the early modern period with the start of the Anthropocene and new perceptions of the world as human-made.[1] Complicating these explanatory frameworks are numerous recent studies that take into consideration cultural encounters, exchanges, and entanglements that occurred across geographical borders and bodies of water.[2] This type of transcultural approach puts pressure on the notion that identities and practices are circumscribed by pre-existing national, imperial, and continental frontiers or prescribed in a top-down manner by institutions like church, nation, or empire.[3] The term "mondialization" has been deployed to differentiate aspects of early modern globalism, foregrounding creativity, resilience, subversion, resistance, and the "survivance" of oppressed and beleaguered cultural groups, forms, and practices.[4] "Mondialization," with its emphasis on "monde" and worlding, also acknowledges the vital role of materials and the earth itself in every process of worldmaking and in the face of environmental destruction.[5] Taking into account the destructive powers of globalization as well as the transcultural operations of "mondialization," our volume considers how the making of worlds and the devastation of worlds worked in tandem in early modernity. We investigate these complex interactions as constant, ongoing practices that continue to shape how we make – and make sense of – the world today.

Bringing together a series of interdisciplinary studies based on close analysis of diverse creative forms and practices, this volume is structured in terms of three interrelated realms of early modern worldmaking: the material, the spatial, and the imaginative, which are examined in the sections "Material Flows," "In Between Spaces," and "Other Worlds." This tripartite division confronts a significant challenge for global cultural studies today and for early modern cultural producers in the past, which is the irresolvable problem of how to conceive of the global.[6] It is important to acknowledge that we can only see the world from our own limited position within it; we can never comprehend the totality, imagine every other possible position, or impose a single perspective or approach to encapsulate the complex variety of all peoples and cultures. To study global dimensions of early modern cultures is necessarily to embark on an open-ended endeavour, one that disrupts and redefines our fields of study by taking into account the limits of our knowledge and the inevitable failure of any attempt to order the world according to fixed viewpoints, categories, boundaries, theories, or approaches. Recognizing the impossibility of devising a comprehensive methodology or theoretical framework inclusive of all peoples, places, and cultural forms, we nonetheless underline the importance of asking new questions, and we contend that these questions often are raised by close study of early modern artefacts, texts, objects, images, and practices. By attending to local specificity, we can gain insight into global cultural dimensions and begin to discern multiple interconnections between small parts and an imagined global whole. Our volume accordingly is reoriented towards those activities and interactions that manifest creativity and imagination in ways that unsettle and upset expectations regarding where the local ends and the global begins.

By asking new questions about the local specificity of early modern images, objects, texts, and practices, the authors bring into view the vast webs of global interconnectivity that characterized the early modern world. In keeping with this approach, we take as our starting point a

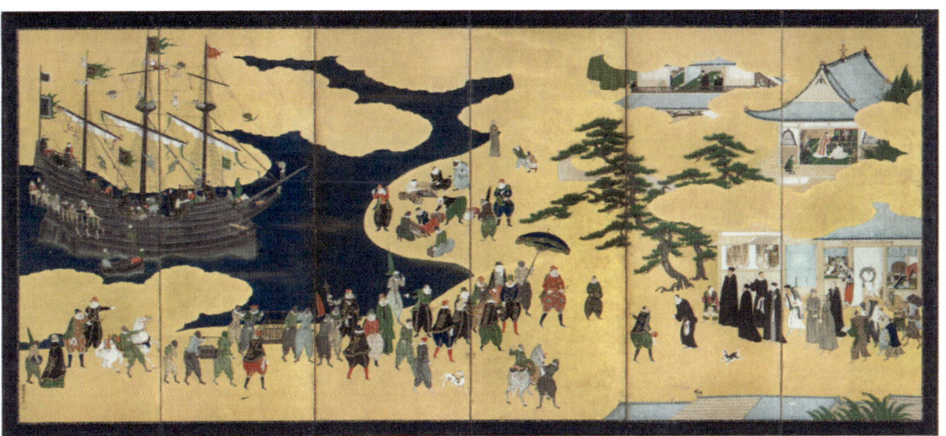

Figure 1.1. Kanô Naizen, *Arrival of the Southern Barbarians, nanban* ("southern barbarian") screen, early seventeenth century. Colour and gold leaf on paper, 363.2 x 154.5 cm. Kobe City Museum, Kobe. Photograph courtesy of Kobe City Museum

particular artefact – an early seventeenth-century Japanese *nanban* folding screen – to see how it envisions global practices and other worlds from a local perspective and how it illuminates the spatial, material, and imaginative processes of worldmaking that are the focus of our volume. *Nanban* screens were produced in pairs for Japanese patrons, often from the merchant class involved in Iberian trade, and for export by foreigners. These folding screens decorated business offices or homes, and they typically represent, and possibly celebrate, according to Yukio Lippit, the departure and arrival of foreign ships in the harbour of a Japanese port city (fig. 1.1).[7] A view of global connectedness unfolds in artworks like these, which showcase transoceanic travel, describing its means as well as motives. *Nanban* screens present the increasing mobility of a group called the *nanban-jin*, "southern barbarian peoples," mainly designating Iberian merchants and missionaries who came to trade and to convert. Made by Japanese artists, *nanban* screens depict the infiltration of the *nanban-jin* using a Japanese pictorial format and idiom: traditional craft techniques are stretched both to incorporate new subject matter and to expedite acquisition by foreign traders. The striking use of gold foil creates a sparkling luminous ground, which can be seen to operate on a symbolic level, evoking nebulous other worlds beyond the local, and highlighting the imaginative work of representing visible and invisible places on the surface of the screen. The undulating edges of the gold ground suggest the swelling waves of the ocean, rolling cloud formations, and faraway locales as yet unknown. The expanding frontiers of the world are thus imagined from an insular shore.

Both material and representational, the presence of gold leaf might also signal how precious metals were drivers of global trade. Together with the calligraphic lines that animate swirling waves, the incorporation of shimmering gold enlivens the image. As David Kim has recently argued, the use of gold ground in early modern artistic production makes us consider the particular material qualities of gold, its ductility and malleability, its propensity to be hammered into thin sheets, stretched in various directions, and shaped to create forms.[8] Our term "material flows," then, can refer to the movement of people and things around the globe and also indicate how the reworking of materials and resources is integral to creative processes of making, and also unmaking, worlds.[9] Materials flow across the surface of the screen as well as across oceans. Not visible – but playing a foundational role in the production of these mobile luxury objects – are the brutal practices of mining for precious metals, labour often undertaken by enslaved persons. The unrepresented devastation of lifeways thus contributes to this golden vision of an interconnected world.

Global trade created burgeoning markets for goods from all parts of the world. Disembarking from the Portuguese carrack anchored in the harbour is a group of sailors whose diverse origins are suggested by the attention paid to their varying skin tones. They parade examples of textiles, ceramics, chests, furniture, and exotic animals transported from China and South Asia. Similar things are for sale in the city shops, and the detailed rendering of these shop interiors allows another glimpse of world-destroying processes, with animals reduced to the exotic furs and feathers trafficked in a local marketplace. In the arrival panel, a Jesuit priest and Japanese Christians holding rosaries come out to greet the cargo-bearing crew (fig. 1.2). The ambitious religious missions of the Jesuits clearly have taken hold, with a significant impact on local identities, practices, and belief systems. Rendered with gold, Roman Catholic liturgical metalwork adorns the newly established churches that alter more than the architectural fabric of the Japanese city. Here the screen's golden glimmer marks the influx of both material wealth and religion, drawing attention to new luxury objects as well as new world views.[10] As

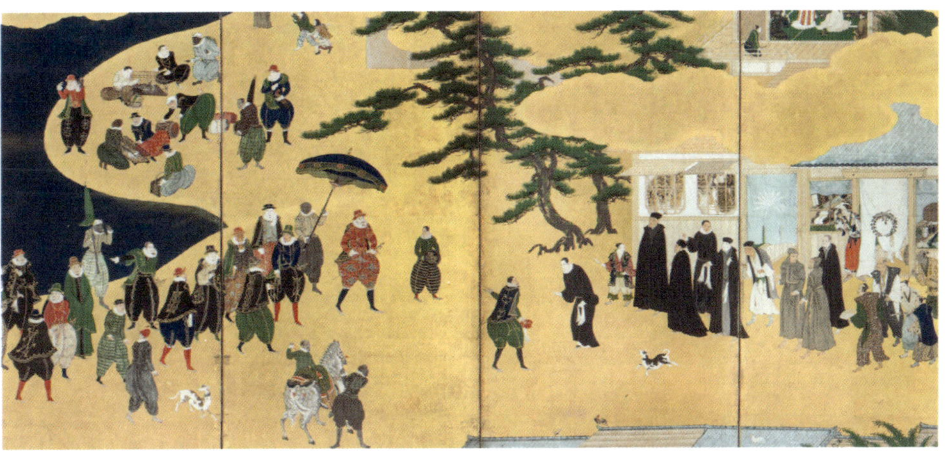

Figure 1.2. Detail of the *nanban* screen (fig. 1.1)

the *nanban* screen indicates, and a number of the essays in this volume show, trade and religion, while in tension, also worked in tandem.

The convergence of disparate peoples, creatures, and things in the port city indicates multiple ways that the powerful forces of globalization were experienced locally and inflected on indigenous histories and traditions. The Japanese harbour depicted on the screen represents what we are calling an in-between space – a cosmopolitan locale, in this instance, where local understandings and representations of the global are produced and where transcultural encounters occur. As the essays in this volume demonstrate, in-between spaces reveal the porous boundaries of early modern worlds, allowing us to move away from categorizing cultural forms and practices in terms of circumscribed regions or nationalities and to consider instead the complex interactions afforded by contact zones. A partial list of significant early modern in-between spaces would include cities, harbours, ships, trading posts, markets, churches, temples, collections, gardens, menageries, taverns, shops, business offices, company headquarters, and domestic interiors. We are thinking about such places as provisional points of intersection for mobile elements with multiple vectors of direction, varying intensities, and complex relations. These are spaces that are open to becoming something new. As the *nanban* screen suggests, in-between spaces can provoke assertions of boundaries and distinctions, where cultural identities are imposed and enforced by religious, political, and economic systems and authorities. Even so, and in spite of glaring asymmetries of power, the mobile fluctuations and the coexistence of diverse peoples and perspectives in the same space can simultaneously generate opportunities for creative, unpredictable, and performative reinventions.

We contend that different vantage points are necessary for apprehending the power dynamics involved in making worlds, as inventions resulting from crossing geographies are often inherently contradictory and can serve a range of interests. For this, the *nanban* screens are also illuminating as they offer unique insights into the conditions of their own production. As Samuel Luterbacher has recently argued, it is crucial that the glittering surfaces of the *nanban* screens not be seen as reflecting too smooth and seamless an image of the global flows and exchanges from which they emerged.[11] Consider again the representation of a variety of dark-skinned peoples on ship and shore. The parade of cargo is led by the European captain, shadowed by a figure who likely represents an enslaved African man, who is shielding the captain's lighter skin with a parasol (fig. 1.2). Notably, the figures who carry the freight clearly indicate Iberian reliance on the servitude and bodily labour of legions of non-European peoples worldwide. The screen shows us that materials never just flow from place to place easily and on their own, but are extracted, transported, and physically hauled by bodies. When confronted with the image of these labourers, we have to imagine that each worker could offer a distinctive and divergent point of view and thus was in some sense an active participant in the worldmaking endeavours that are depicted. Our term "material flows," then, can be seen as movement propelled by collaborations and imaginative creativity as well as coercion and violence, so that a single, finalized, and agreed-upon vision of the world never fully emerges. The making of new worlds usually involves the destruction of old worlds, and a cobbling together of contingent fragments from other worlds. When we are attentive to these processes, counter-histories of globalization come into view, challenging the influential narratives and prevailing modes of historical thought crafted by dominant groups.[12] Here we might conclude that the close study of made things can reveal what grand narratives of globalization sometimes conceal, providing opportunities for a finer-grained analysis of the ambivalent dynamics of early modern worldmaking.

There is burgeoning interest in the study of material culture and mobility as means to approach global histories, and our volume is in dialogue with a number of recent publications that consider global interactions and the circulation of artefacts and practices. Related in theme is *The Global Lives of Things: The Material Culture of Connections in the Early Modern World*, which poses a foundational question: "what can we learn about the early modern world by studying its objects?"[13] The theoretical framework of this collection of essays situates it within recent scholarship on colonialism and consumption and offers a significant rethinking of the role of the commodity in early modernity. Also important is the edited collection *Objects in Motion in the Early Modern World*, which focuses on phenomena that were made to travel. Drawing on theories about the social lives of things, the essays especially explore practices of collecting, gift exchange, and diplomacy. This volume pays particular attention to how transcultural exchanges often transformed meanings and uses of artefacts that were made in one place and then taken up in a different cultural and geographical context.[14] As Paula Findlen sums up this vital process, "the early modern period was repeatedly defined and redefined by episodes in which different societies became familiar with each other's things."[15] The pivotal role of religion in the mobilization of artefacts is underscored in *The Nomadic Object: The Challenge of World for Early Modern Religious Art.* Debates about religion and art in Europe and their impacts are pursued along global trajectories and through conversion attempts.[16] Other significant interventions include *The Globalization of Renaissance Art*, which advocates a less Eurocentric approach to writing about and teaching Renaissance art history, while acknowledging ongoing disciplinary entrenchment in nationalistic institutions and values.[17] These and other volumes together emphasize how the study of any local culture must take into account the influences of global mobility, and the authors convincingly demonstrate how the close analysis of material objects and their uses can provide new ways of understanding the interconnectedness of the early modern world, exposing stark and often violent inequalities as well as creative and resistant practices.

Building from these studies, our book considers global mobility as a worldmaking process.[18] Instead of following individual human actors or objects, contributors accentuate activities and interactions, as well as reinventions and translations. The chapters elucidate how mundane and spiritual worlds cohabit, sometimes so naturally as to be overlooked, while in other cases the profane and sacred collide, their impact manifested conspicuously. With essays by scholars of history, literary studies, theatre and performance, art history, and anthropology, a strength of this collection is that it departs from discipline-specific studies of globalization in order to examine the interdisciplinary phenomenon of making worlds.

The geographical expanse of the case studies gathered here – while not comprehensive – is varied, and the aim of the thematic structure of the volume is to forge fresh connections among disparate geographical regions and fields of study. Our three sections on the material, spatial, and imaginative aspects of global interconnectivity provide opportunities to reassess early modern processes of worldmaking from various disciplinary and interdisciplinary vantage points. As many of the case studies show, the imposition of European economic, religious, political, and military models on other parts of the world paradoxically unleashed unprecedented forces of invention as institutionalized powers came up against the creativity of peoples and the comingling of practices, materials, and techniques of making. The chapters in this volume accordingly advance questions about histories of globalization by attending to how the unprecedented expansion of global transit offered possibilities for interactions that included the testing of local identities and inventive experimentation with new and various cultural forms. In reorienting the discussion away from categories of self and other, local and foreign, nation and colony, the authors consider the potential of resourcefulness and imagination without losing sight of exploitation and devastation. As the *nanban* screens indicate, and as our volume argues, the multifaceted forces of globalization inconsistently generated an ongoing dynamics of making, unmaking, and remaking worlds.

The first section of the volume, "Material Flows," considers the circuitry and transformations of materials, motifs, styles, artistic vocabularies, and practices across geographical boundaries. Demonstrating a shift away from area studies, state formation, and fixed borders, these chapters take into account the expansion of routes of transit by tracing the paths of early modern artefacts and rituals to discern the larger implications of materials that circulate and interweave.

The opening chapter, by Kristopher Kersey, develops the idea of the implicated image by pursuing the role of folded and pleated media in Japan's encounter with Europe from the mid-sixteenth to the early seventeenth century. Kersey significantly extends our introductory discussion of *nanban* folding screens to include other folded formats such as fans, maps, and documents in order to grapple with the fact that implication itself was a defining feature of Japanese visuality in early modernity. The chapter devotes critical attention especially to the most marginalized of all folded media: the folding fan. A Japanese invention purportedly devised in the early Heian period (794–1192), it achieved widespread global diffusion in early modernity. After tracing the provisional paths the technology took on its journey from east to west Eurasia, the analysis turns to a discussion of how the distinguishing material qualities of such objects – paper, tactility, portability, and especially convergent fold-lines – impacted the construction of virtual space in Japanese pictorial culture. While the Deleuzean *pli* once defined a certain discourse on the European Baroque, this essay shows that an expanded view of the early modern world will require a reassessment of such popular tropes, with the fold itself serving as a prime metaphor for global encounters.

The next chapter, by Carrie Anderson, investigates the key role played by Dutch West India Company (WIC) ships in facilitating the inhumane transportation of enslaved people between Africa, South America, and North America. Often overlooked is the fact that enslaved peoples were forced to travel with an abundance of essential goods and commodities destined for the Dutch colonies and trading posts, including food, tools, and – importantly – textiles. The textiles carried on these ships ranged from coarse to fine, each serving a different purpose along the trans-Atlantic trade routes: blue-and-white textiles called Guinea cloths were traded for subjugated peoples on the African coast; a variety of European linens were presented as diplomatic gifts to Indigenous peoples of Brazil; and a wide range of textiles were made into clothing, to be worn by WIC officers and other inhabitants of the colonies, but also by the people who were forcibly brought there. The cargo lists of slave ships indicate that textiles travelled next to – but were not worn by – the often naked shackled people with whom they shared a space in the hold. By bringing together visual and archival material related to the overseas activities of the Dutch West India Company, this essay importantly reconsiders the impact of such documents, which callously sever human "cargo" from the textiles that have long played a role in the formation of social identities.

The following chapter, by Elisa Daniele, also brings documentary and visual evidence to bear on the early modern understanding of the specific material qualities and the transport of a particular trade good. Focusing on a commemorative album created for *Il Tabacco*, a ballet staged as part of Turin's 1650 carnival at the court of the Duchess of Savoy, Christine of France, the essay analyses the album's ink and watercolour drawings, which take the viewer on a journey that follows the global transit of tobacco. The vivid imagery indicates how the dancers in the ballet performed the story of tobacco, enacting how it was grown, prepared, and consumed according to diverse geographically specific customs. Putting the album's imagery in dialogue with travel literature, pamphlets, and medical treatises, Daniele's analysis brings to light a host of anxieties and ambiguities surrounding the introduction of an ingestible product from the "New World" to Europe. A semantically unstable commodity, tobacco was considered as both a panacea for all ills and as a dangerous threat to individual health and national wealth.

In the fourth chapter in this section, Benjamin Schmidt explores a particular type of art used in Tokugawa Japan, focusing on *fumi-e* or "stepping-on pictures." Modestly-sized, low-to medium-relief plaquettes, typically cast in bronze or brass and bearing religious iconography, *fumi-e* were enlisted chiefly for the performance of *e-fumi*, a ceremony in which the Japanese were asked to tread on Christian art – to stomp on images of the Virgin, the Pietà, the Crucifixion, and other religious scenes – in order to demonstrate their indifference to Christianity and allegiance to the Tokugawa shogunate. As art objects that were cast, disseminated in multiples, desecrated, and distressed, *fumi-e* present an especially vivid narrative of early modern global flows, offering an opportunity to think about the radically different ways that religious artefacts were used outside of Europe; about the various ways non-Europeans engaged with and appropriated European forms and aesthetics; and, not least, about how both the creation and the destruction of art were integral to processes of making worlds.

The final essay in this section, by Helen Smith, demonstrates how European efforts at worldmaking were characterized by a tension between the quest for an all-encompassing cosmic viewpoint and localized experiences and ways of knowing the world.[19] What does it mean, asks Smith, to look at the products of the dairy and to see other worlds? What is it about the mundane egg that prompted early modern natural philosophers in England and beyond to ruminate on foundational questions about the creation of the world? Eggs were both extraordinary – acquired from far-away places and collected in curiosity cabinets of the kind described by Daniela Bleichmar in chapter 7 – and yet also ordinary, even universal in their constituent parts. Accordingly, the egg, and also cheesemaking – on account of the coagulation of its parts – provided everyday conceptual tools for imagining the transformation of chaos into the orderly form of the world. Such analogies in the work of Francis Bacon, René Descartes, and William Harvey, who dissected eggs, were countered by the polymath Margaret Cavendish, for whom the kitchen was a laboratory for thinking. Cavendish, who contemplated women's work, and the flow and suspension of matter and natural forces such as heat, identifies sympathies instead of mere analogies for understanding the making of worlds. Visual imagery of women's labour and foodstuffs – eggs, as a medium and subject for still life painting, and making cheeses, which in turn generate worms – round out Smith's account of natural philosophy's material flows. In the cases that Smith examines, domestic know-how is central to early modern European efforts to understand how the world was formed.

The chapters in part 2, "In-Between Spaces," consider movement, migration, and invention through, between, and within early modern spaces. As seen on the *nanban* screen picturing a Japanese port city, in-between spaces could be transitional, both isolated and connected, and open to unpredictable forms of traffic from other worlds. As such, these spaces have much to teach us about the commingling of materials, media, motifs, practices, and people across and between cultures in the early modern world as well as the unequal relations that structured such entanglements. Contributors uncover new uses for, practices in, and configurations of sites such as curiosity cabinets, collections, and libraries. They also inspect things like albums, games, inventories, and folios to determine how certain types of objects can create an in-between space for the exploration of global relations. The essays together show how interactions between spaces, objects, and people gave rise to often unanticipated and new ways of crafting and understanding global connectivity.

In the opening chapter, Daniela Bleichmar takes up the early modern curiosity cabinet – a key site where new understandings of the world were forged in dialogue with a far-flung variety of material objects. Bleichmar confronts a puzzling aspect of such collections, whose inventories show how artefacts and materials were routinely misidentified and misattributed in spite of the fact that their origins were mostly known. Close analysis of these inventories reveals how cultural and geographical confusion was a purposeful means to order and reorder the material fragments of other worlds, facilitating the worldmaking and remaking activities of the collector. This study thus describes curiosity collecting as a spatial practice that encapsulated the global aspirations of the period within the in-between space of the cabinet.

In chapter 8, Ting Chang examines a group of card games, toys, and maps produced in France in the seventeenth and eighteenth centuries that set in motion imagined contacts with distant lands. Activating the player's physical and cognitive capacities, in many cases these games, which were made mainly for ruling elites, facilitated rehearsals for combat and military plotting. As in the curiosity cabinet, interactions with these types of world-dominating objects created a space that gathered people with a similar mental outlook around a table. Fostering competition, these games developed strategic thinking, visual acumen, and also haptic knowledge so that players became participants in and even co-creators of imperial history. Early modern games and toys of the simplest materials thus offered immersive experiences, allowing players to re-invent the world from the in-between space of play.

Emine Fetvacı's chapter also describes the mobile dynamics and worldmaking potential of works on paper, focusing on the seventeenth-century collection called the *Album of the World Emperor*, made for the ruler Sultan Ahmed I (r. 1603–17) by his courtier Kalender Pasha (c. 1614–16). Like the curiosity cabinet, albums were a means to create a microcosm of the world by gathering and comparing artworks in multiple genres from varied historical and geographical contexts. The album contains a world that Sultan Ahmed I claimed for himself. It includes images that reference the actual territory of Ottoman lands as well as regions beyond the Ottoman Empire, especially Iran, Western Europe, and India. Focusing on hitherto unexplored relationships between the Ottomans and Mughals, Fetvacı shows how the artisan, in the process of cutting, assembling, and pasting paintings of costumed figures, flora and fauna, European devotional prints, and the ornamental paper of the album, conjoined parts of the early modern world. With its manifold visual styles and traditions, and its figures sometimes oriented to encompass multiple viewers situated around the pages, the album gathers a different kind of world, one that is composite and heterogeneous.

The final chapter in this section considers the long history of collecting by examining the academic library as an in-between space for showcasing and preserving material objects. Insisting on the ongoing worldmaking abilities of early modern things, Patricia Badir's essay examines the permanent loan of four seventeenth-century folios of Shakespeare's works – including a remarkably valuable First Folio – from the Folger Shakespeare Library to the University of British Columbia (UBC) Library in 1960. Only two such loans were ever made and UBC, surprisingly, was chosen because of "its growing significance for humanistic education in the Pacific Northwest." Twenty-five years later, the books were recalled by the Folger trustees. Badir's chapter elucidates the fraught dynamics of this loan and its retraction, particularly in connection with institutional history and the history of English studies in the context of Cold War nation-building, and Vancouver's specific history and location as part of a former British colony at the very western edge of the North American continent. In studying the afterlife of an object that is emblematic of the early modern world, Badir shows how the First Folio was valued as much more than a record of Shakespeare's writings. Its material presence in an academic library in British Columbia made it an active participant in the postcolonial culture wars of the twentieth century. The Folger loan thus provides a means to think through canonicity and disciplinarity in a manner that revises familiar narratives of early modern empire and colonization to which the study of Shakespeare is often attached.

Having examined the potential for creative interaction to which "material flows" and "in-between spaces" gave rise, the final section turns to "other worlds." These are imaginary places, such as paradises, wildernesses, or the cosmos itself, evoked by forms such as paintings, performances, and representations of terrestrial and astronomical imagery. Chapters consider ways in which literary, artistic, theatrical, theological, and cartographic forms became *loci* for imagining and inventing other worlds.

The desert is the other world of the opening essay, by Lyle Massey, which considers how artistic representations of settings perceived as desolate show the force of an environment and the entwining of the earthly and spiritual realms. In Massey's analysis, the desert is both an actual terrestrial ecosystem and an imaginary otherworldly space. Focusing on Giovanni Bellini's paintings of Saint Jerome in the wilderness, the essay tracks how the background setting of the saint's deprivation becomes more than a symbolic reflection of his inner state, as in earlier paintings of the theme. Taking an eco-critical approach, the chapter investigates early modern understandings of the desert as an animate place imbued with the organic and lively qualities of natural elements like stone, and indicates how environmental and religious experience – the worldly and the otherworldly – were profoundly interconnected. Bellini's artistic rendering of a singular figure in the wilderness thus traces the changing place of the individual in a world that was perceived as both imminent and transcendent.

Identifying a similar tension between worldliness and holiness, Gavin Hollis takes up the display of maps in the households of post-Reformation England. Hollis's chapter inspects three sites of cultural production: map matter (planar maps, views, and globes), literary texts, and household decor. In Shakespeare's tragedy *Richard III*, the lyric poetry of Robert Herrick, and Thomas Middleton's comedy *The Puritan*, map-reading and display is situated as a fraught domestic practice – one which might connote worldly hubris as much as reverence for the otherworldly. Contemporaneously with these literary works, elite householders wove map matter into their household designs – in textiles and hangings, in stone- and woodwork, and through carefully positioned maps, views, and globes. Across these literary, dramatic, and material contexts emerges an understanding of maps as publications of a household's global reach and secular ambition that was tempered, at times uneasily, by assertions of piety and reminders of the fleeting nature of earthly achievements. In the post-Reformation household, and through the material practices of mapping, the English simultaneously made the world, recoiled from it, and performed their spiritual detachment even as they celebrated their worldliness.

Challenging historical narratives that celebrate the sudden emergence of modern, secular, scientific-naturalistic understandings of the cosmos, J.B. Shank emphasizes a slow, tangled movement towards secular scientific naturalization and the Enlightenment during the eighteenth century. Shank's chapter shows the persistence of ancient pagan cosmological understandings and the continuing presence and power of Judeo-Christian scriptural accounts in published works by European scholars that offered accounts of the primordial origins of the cosmos. This assemblage of old and new understandings is situated in relation to shifting institutional authority, where clerics and university professors competed for scientific authority alongside men of letters, artists, engravers, antiquarian scholars, bookmakers, and collectors. Especially important was the changing print-media environment where the new prevalence of large, lavishly illustrated books allowed for a multi-media engagement with cosmology that could produce transformative consequences. As Shank demonstrates, these new ways of mediating scientific discussion were just as important in bringing about the modernizing changes of the period as any secularizing rupture or "crisis of the European mind," to cite Paul Hazard's famous formulation.

Providing a different perspective on cosmic origins is chapter 14, by John Pohl and Danny Zborover, which takes as its starting point one of the most enduring forms of Indigenous pageantry performed throughout southern Mexico, the Danza de la Pluma – a festival rooted in pre-Hispanic creation stories, heroic histories, and dynastic accounts painted in screenfold books or codices. Through performative re-enactments, Mixtec rulers irrefutably fixed their role as society's mediators with the supernatural and maintained proprietary claims by divine right through claims of descent from various parts of a personified landscape. This chapter examines how the Indigenous peoples of southern Mexico today continue to use performance to document their historical experiences on their own terms and through the entwining of chronicled events with myth. In studying a Pacific coastal festival, Pohl and Zborover have discovered that the Chontal of San Pedro Huamelula present a variant dance festival that combines the creation story with an alternate history that celebrates an alliance with the Dutch rather than the Spanish. The opening of the Manila Galleon had effectively cut Dutch merchants out of trade in the Pacific, and they countered by establishing special trade relationships with Indigenous peoples antagonistic to Spanish interests, ranging from Brazil to Oaxaca to Japan. The Huamelula festival of coastal Oaxaca therefore explains why this area continued to prosper even after the Manila Galleon moved to Acapulco, and provides new insights into a contraband economy that was just as important for conveying transnational culture globally as the Galleon itself.

The final chapter, by Thijs Weststeijn, also investigates the complex dynamics of Dutch trade relations and, like Massey, Hollis, and Shank, presents evidence that challenges received historical narratives of secularization. In *The Embarrassment of Riches* (1987), Simon Schama famously argued that Dutch urban merchants were initially hesitant to showcase wealth that they believed had been predestined by God; it was only towards the end of the seventeenth century that this pious embarrassment made way for a more open kind of secular bourgeois consumerism, shared by large swathes of society. Focusing on the burgeoning market for Chinese goods in particular, the chapter first discusses celebratory accounts of trade, and then moves to texts that expressed cultural unease with the desire for luxury imports from other worlds. A key critique was that unfettered trade ran counter to the global division of goods and peoples that had been ordained by the Divinity. As Weststeijn shows, these sentiments of cultural and spiritual anxiety were formulated throughout the century and, if anything, intensified with the increasingly regular consumption of foreign wares around 1700.

In conclusion, what the essays in our volume together show is that attentiveness to the early modern mobility of peoples, materials, objects, ideas, and formats across physical and cultural boundaries unsettles familiar ground and incites us to move in new directions. Through close examination of material things, imaginative representations, and spatial practices and interactions, each chapter focuses on the real and imaginary labour of making and unmaking worlds. The various kinds of global invention explored by the authors often challenge familiar geographical, chronological, and conceptual frameworks and terms of reference. Scholarship that is guided by the boundary-crossing aspects of transcultural creativity entails being receptive to unexpected forms and practices that thwart efforts to categorize objects of knowledge or to accumulate them into a canon. In many of our case studies, singular and local details give rise to global questions and to multiple perspectives that require acknowledging differences rather than assimilating them. The global inventiveness we are exploring involves both experimentation and failure, and it shows how worldmaking is often simultaneously creative and destructive. To see these contradictions requires grappling with what is unfamiliar to us and travelling in unpredictable directions on a journey that does not finally arrive at meanings but moves continuously between encounters with incomplete processes of making, unmaking, and remaking. We are proposing that this kind of transcultural research matters for the future because it forces us to contend with the limits of our knowledge and thus to rethink our methods.

**NOTES**

1  Michael Hardt and Antonio Negri, *Empire* (Cambridge, MA: Harvard University Press, 2000); Antonio Negri, *Reflections on Empire* (Cambridge, UK: Polity Press, 2008); Bruno Latour, *An Inquiry into Modes of Existence: An Anthropology of the Moderns* (Cambridge, MA: Harvard University Press, 2013); Bruno Latour, "Agency at the Time of the Anthropocene," *New Literary History* 45 (2014): 1–18; Bruno Latour and Catherine Porter, *Facing Gaia: Eight Lectures on the New Climatic Regime* (Cambridge, UK: Polity Press, 2017); Erle C. Ellis, *Anthropocene: A Very Short Introduction* (Oxford: Oxford University Press, 2018); Jane Bennett, *Vibrant Matter: A Political Ecology of Things* (Durham, NC: Duke University Press, 2010); Ayesha Ramachandran, *The Worldmakers: Global Imagining in Early Modern Europe* (Chicago: University of Chicago Press, 2015); Allison Kavey, "Think you there was, or ever could be a world such as this I dreamed," in *World-building and the Early Modern Imagination,* ed. Allison Kavey (New York: Palgrave, 2010), 1–4; Roland Greene, "World," in *Five Words: Critical Semantics in the Age of Cervantes and Shakespeare* (Chicago: University of Chicago Press, 2013), 143–72.
2  Nicholas Thomas, *Entangled Objects: Exchange, Material Culture, and Colonialism in the Pacific* (Cambridge, MA: Harvard University Press, 1991); Steven Mullaney, "Imaginary Conquests: European Material Technologies and the Colonial Mirror Stage," in *Early Modern Visual Culture: Representation, Race, and Empire in Renaissance England,* ed. Clark Hulse and Peter Erickson (Philadelphia: University of Pennsylvania Press, 2000), 15–43; Kumkum Chatterjee

and Clement Hawes, *Europe Observed: Multiple Gazes in Early Modern Encounters* (Lewisburg, PA: Bucknell University Press, 2008); Ian Hodder, *Entangled: An Archaeology of the Relationships between Humans and Things* (Malden, MA: Wiley-Blackwell, 2012); Ralph Bauer and Marcy Norton, "Introduction: Entangled Trajectories: Indigenous and European Histories," *Colonial Latin American Review* 26, no. 1 (2017): 1–17; Sebastian Conrad, *What is Global History?* (Princeton, NJ: Princeton University Press, 2016); Peter Burke, Luke Clossey, and Felipe Fernández-Armesto, "The Global Renaissance," *Journal of World History* 28, no. 1 (2017): 1–30; and Carina L. Johnson and Ayesha Ramachandran, eds., "Multiplicities: Recasting the Early Modern Global," special issue, *Modern Philology,* 119, no. 1 (2021), especially their "Introduction— The Jaguar's Beer: Critical Approaches to Multiplicity in the Early Modern World," 1–12, and Zoltán Biedermann, "(Dis)Connected History and the Multiple Narratives of Global Early Modernity," 13–33.

3  On transculturation, see Fernando Ortiz, *Cuban Counterpoint: Tobacco and Sugar,* trans. Harriet de Onís (New York: Alfred A. Knopf, 1947); also Monica Juneja, "'A Very Civil Idea ...' Art History, Transculturation, and World-Making – with and Beyond the Nation," *Zeitschrift für Kunstgeschichte* 81 (2018): 461–85; and Astrid Erll, "Circulating Art and Material Culture: A Model of Transcultural Mediation," in *Mediating Netherlandish Art and Material Culture in Asia, ed.* Thomas DaCosta Kaufmann and Michael North (Amsterdam: Amsterdam University Press, 2014), 312–28.

4  There has been much recent discussion of terminology. See especially: Jean-Luc Nancy, *Creation of the World or Globalization* (Albany: SUNY Press, 2007); Serge Gruzinski, *Les quatre parties du monde: histoire d'une mondialisation* (Paris: Martinière, 2004); Arjun Appadurai, *Modernity at Large: Cultural Dimensions of Globalization* (Minneapolis: University of Minnesota Press, 1996); Serge Gruzinski, "Art History and Iberian Worldwide Diffusion: Westernization/ Globalization/Americanization," in *Circulations in the Global History of Art,* ed. Thomas DaCosta Kaufmann, Catherine Dossin, and Béatrice Joyeux-Prunel (Burlington, VT: Ashgate, 2015), 47–58; Carolyn Dean and Dana Leibsohn, "Hybridity and Its Discontents: Considering Visual Culture in Colonial Spanish America," *Colonial Latin American Review* 12, no. 1 (2003): 5–35; and Victor Li, "Elliptical Interruptions: Or, Why Derrida Prefers *Mondialisation* to Globalization," *The New Centennial Review* 7, no. 2 (Fall 2007): 141–54.

5  Bruno Latour, *Down to Earth: Politics in the New Climatic Regime* (Cambridge, UK: Polity Press, 2018), 40–2.

6  Ramachandran, *Worldmakers,* 1–18; Peter Sloterdijk, *In the World Interior of Capital* (Cambridge, UK: Polity Press, 2006), 28–32; Peter Sloterdijk, *Spheres* (Los Angeles, CA: Semiotext(e), 2011).

7  Yukio Lippit, "Japan's Southern Barbarian Screens," in *Encompassing the Globe: Portugal and the World in the 16th and 17th Centuries*, ed. Jay A. Levenson (Washington, DC: Smithsonian Institute, 2007), 3:244–53. We are especially indebted to the article by Samuel Luterbacher, "Surfaces for Reflection: Nanban Lacquer in the Iberian World," *Journal of Early Modern History* 23, no. 2–3 (2019): 152–90.

8  David Kim, "Points on a Field: Gentile da Fabriano and Gold Ground," *Journal of Early Modern History* 23, no. 2–3 (2019): 191–226; see also Lauren Jacobi, "Reconsidering the World-system: The Agency and Material Geography of Gold," in *The Globalization of Renaissance Art*, ed. Daniel Savoy (Leiden: Brill, 2017), 131–57; Anne Dunlop, "On the Origins of European Painting Materials, Real and Imagined," in *The Matter of Art: Materials, Practices, Cultural Logics, c.1250–1750*, ed. Christy Anderson, Anne Dunlop, and Pamela H. Smith (Manchester: Manchester University Press, 2014), 68–96; and Carrie Anderson, "Between Optic and Haptic: Tactility and Trade in the Dutch West India Company's Gold Box," *Oud Holland* 133, no. 2 (2020): 127–43.

9  For example, see Byron Ellsworth Hamann, "The Mirrors of *Las Meninas*: Cochineal, Silver, and Clay," *The Art Bulletin* 92, no. 1/2 (2010): 6–35.

10  See Luterbacher's evocative analysis of this screen in "Surfaces for Reflection," 158–60.

11  Luterbacher, "Surfaces for Reflection," 187.

12  On counter-histories, see Catherine Gallagher and Stephen Greenblatt, "Counter-History and the Anecdote," in *Practicing New Historicism* (Chicago: University of Chicago Press, 2001), 49–74; and Saidiya Hartman, "Venus in Two Acts," *Small Axe* 26 (June 2008): 1–14.

13  Anne Gerritsen and Giorgio Riello, eds., *The Global Lives of Things: The Material Culture of Connections in the Early Modern World* (London: Routledge, 2016), i. See also Paula Findlen, "Afterword: How (Early Modern) Things Travel," in *The Global Lives of Things*, 241–6.

14  Daniela Bleichmar and Meredith Martin, eds., *Objects in Motion in the Early Modern World* (Hoboken, NJ: Wiley-Blackwell, 2016); on mobility, see Stephen Greenblatt, ed., *Cultural Mobility: A Manifesto* (Cambridge, UK: Cambridge University Press, 2010).

15  Paula Findlen, "Early Modern Things: Objects in Motion, 1500–1800," in *Early Modern Things: Objects and their Histories, 1500–1800*, ed. Paula Findlen (New York: Routledge, 2012), 8.

16  Christine Göttler and Mia Mochizuki, eds., *The Nomadic Object: The Challenge of World for Early Modern Religious Art* (Leiden: Brill, 2017).

17  Daniel Savoy, "Introduction," in *The Globalization of Renaissance Art: A Critical Review*, ed. Daniel Savoy (Leiden: Brill, 2017), 1–13, and Claire Farago,

"The 'Global Turn' in Art History: Why, Where, and How Does It Matter," in *The Globalization of Renaissance Art*, 299–313. We want to flag the inherently Eurocentric nature of the term *global Renaissance* for scholars whose primary areas of research are not in Europe.

18  This volume also builds upon our earlier special issue: Angela Vanhaelen and Bronwen Wilson, "Introduction: Making Worlds: Art, Materiality, and Early Modern Globalization," *Journal of Early Modern History* 23, no. 2–3 (2019), 103–20.

19  On this tension between the local and the global in early modern European thought, see Ramachandran, *The Worldmakers*.

# PART I

# MATERIAL FLOWS

# chapter two

# The Early Modern Fold: Pleated Media in Japan's Encounter with Europe

KRISTOPHER W. KERSEY

This chapter scrutinizes the implications of doubled, folded, and pleated media in the context of Western Europe's attempt from the sixteenth to the early seventeenth century to bring archipelagic East Asia into its economic and ecclesiastical fold. The theme here is inevitably contentious, as the era coincides with the advent of the Baroque, a style if not an epistemic mode that the theorist Gilles Deleuze (1925–1995) famously characterized as having been defined by the fold (*le pli*).[1] Yet, as the opening pun demonstrates, the problem takes on a different timbre in English. This is not to mention Japanese, a language in which "folding" has far broader connotations: temporal (*ori*, lit. "occasion"), social (*oriau*, lit. "to reach an agreement"), and even violent (*oru*, lit. "to break"). If *implication* is to be a useful global framework for describing the cultural production of early modernity, then that framework must be able to travel outside of a Latinate semantic field. Even if one turns from language to materiality, the European focus on volute forms and draped textiles overshadows the presence of folded East Asian artefacts in contemporaneous global circulation. For a historian of Japan, this flattening of the narrative seems all the more problematic given that folded pictorial surfaces – books, screens, and especially fans – were among the most prominent vehicles for the global transmission of knowledge about Japan, its geographical emplacement, its people, and its pictorial culture throughout this historical era. In fact, the direct Japan–Europe encounter itself was enabled by material and navigational technologies (printing on paper and long-range sea travel) that made possible the contact of points far removed from one another: geographical folds, if one will. As such, it would seem that the global turn may require a reassessment of the relationship of "the fold" to early modernity. To open up consideration of this issue, the task of this chapter will be to explore the implications of Japanese folded media in the context of the sixteenth-century encounter of the easternmost and westernmost cultures of Eurasia.

We will approach the question from several angles. First, whereas Japanese folding screens have been the focus of significant critical attention in this context, this focus has been at the expense of other folded media – chief among them folding fans. This oversight likely has to do with the historiographical error whereby the nineteenth century overshadows and skews one's understanding of the earlier moment. As is well known, the folding fan was emblematic of Japan in the nineteenth-century Euro-American imaginary. Such fascination is often attributed to novelty, yet this was far from the case. In fact, Europe had already been in possession of the folding fan as a technology, accessory, and pictorial medium for more than three centuries by that point. One key difference, however, was that the object in the nineteenth-century Euro-American imagination was strongly gendered as feminine. Once framed as women's fashion accessories, moreover, a predominantly male and often misogynistic community of historians was preconditioned to dismiss these objects as highly frivolous, whereas the folding fan in Japan enjoyed a status as a pictorial support that was in no way inferior to paintings on silk or paper scrolls.[2] The differing statuses of these objects in the Euro-American sphere and in Japan in the nineteenth century demands its own extensive analysis, but the central point for our purposes is that one must attempt to bracket nineteenth-century Japonisme in order to understand the place of such objects in earlier centuries. To that end, we seek to know the initial reaction to such objects, the way in which they made their way to Europe, and the features of these objects that were lost or denatured in the European appropriation.

### The Barbarian Temple

An obvious place to begin is with the genre of Japanese screen painting known as *nanban byōbu*.[3] Such objects typically present genre scenes of Iberian traders and ecclesiasts (the so-called *nanban*, or "southern barbarians") distributed across two folding screens, with the foreigners either having just arrived or just departed the shores of Japan (or sometimes their home nations). As a token of exotica, it is not surprising that much pictorial attention was paid to the foreigners' physiognomy and clothing. The fantastical ships themselves were a favoured subject, with eye-catching and amusing acrobatic feats depicted within the crow's-nests and sails. The dating for the hundred or so extant *nanban* screens spans perhaps the late sixteenth to the eighteenth century, a long run during which the genre continued to evolve.[4] Dozens of figures might occupy the surface of such a screen, many of whom would have folding fans in hand. Given the prevalence of fans in Japan at this time, it seems only natural that the Iberian visitors would immediately adopt this nimble and practical technology. Yet the images on *nanban* screens do not reflect this: in examining the extant corpus, fans appear in foreign hands in only a single case.[5] Then again, despite what one might imagine, recent scholarship reveals that *nanban* ship screens are less novel and less documentary than they are sometimes taken to be; they were, in the words of Yukio Lippit, "mediated by a separate tradition of alienism" in that they borrowed heavily from the pre-existing conventions of depicting East Asian treasure ships.[6] Moreover, as a species of Occidentalist exoticism, it only makes sense that the screens might omit any trace of acculturation and appropriation in order to make the Europeans seem as foreign as possible.

As it happens, the earliest extant Japanese depiction of European proselytization is found not on a *nanban* screen but on the surface of a folding fan (fig. 2.1). Attributed to Kano Sōshū (1555–1601), the younger brother of the celebrated painter Kano Eitoku (1543–90), it portrays an urban streetscape centred upon the Church of Our Lady of the Assumption (*Hishōten no seibō kyōkai*), a Christian complex constructed in 1576 in Kyoto.[7] The multi-storied "southern barbarian temple" (*nanbandera*) – as it was popularly known – is depicted according to a Japanese architectural idiom.[8] Within the compound are some two dozen figures, six of whom stand in an inner courtyard wearing black ecclesiastical robes. One of the more fascinating details in this scene is the curious presence of a small shop in a street just outside the temple that appears to be in the business of selling hats, if not other items, in a *nanban* style.[9] Were this actually the case, the church would seem to have been as much a site for the propagation of fashion as of faith.[10] Indeed, crucifixes and rosaries were sometimes used during the "Christian century" as fashion accessories rather than pious implements; famously, the progenitrix of Kabuki theatre, Izumo no Okuni, was said to have worn a rosary around her waist while performing the salacious and gender-bending riverside acts that gave birth to this theatrical form.[11] The misappropriation reminds us that material culture often moves in ways that are independent of any original ideological or pragmatic framing.

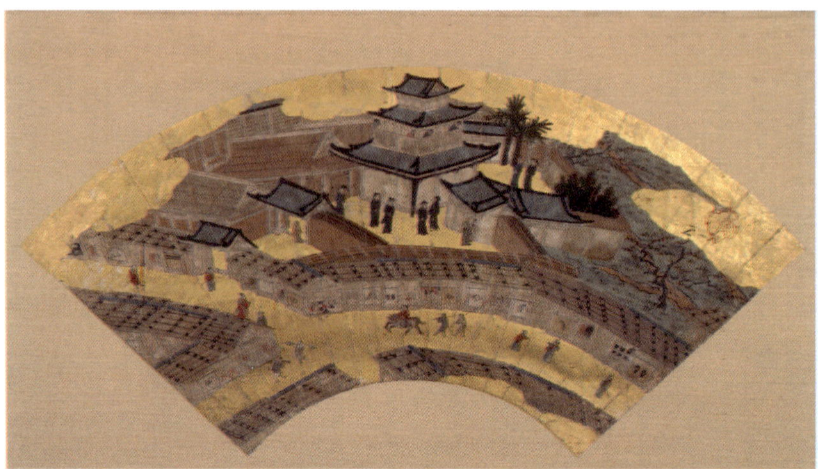

Figure 2.1.  Kano Sōshū, *Fan Painting of the Metropolitan Southern Barbarian Temple*, late sixteenth century. Gold and pigments on paper, 50.6 cm (fan at maximum width). Kobe City Museum, Kobe. Photograph courtesy of Kobe City Museum

The *nanbandera* fan is presumed to have been designed as part of a series of sixty-one fan paintings depicting famous places within the capital.[12] These famous-places fans would likely have been affixed to the surface of a set of folding screens in order to form a folded cityscape panorama. The resultant work would have been a deluxe and clever version of the well-established genre of cityscape screens (*rakuchūrakugai-zu*, literally, "scenes within and without the capital").[13] In such compositions, the cityscape of the capital (or other cities) is depicted by concatenating vignettes of city life depicted according to a common aerial perspective, with scenes joined by the use of golden clouds billowing between the vignettes to provide spatial and sometimes temporal ellipses. Contemporaneous with such cityscape screens were screens bearing folding fans – either pasted on or in trompe-l'oeil – arranged on a gold background, against a landscape setting, or seen as if floating down the surface of a river.[14] Hence the *nanban* fan was perhaps intended for use in a clever conflation of the two genres, with the landmarks of the metropolis rendered on folded, modular media before then being arranged onto a larger folding artefact.

Useful for our purposes are a set of such "capitalscape" screens dated to 1615 and now in the collection of the Tokyo National Museum. Known as the Funaki screens, the metropolitan panorama provides an impossibly rich overview of the capital, replete with figures from all walks of society, Iberian traders included. One also finds within its folds a detailed depiction of a fan vendor's shop – clearly indicated by a fan-shaped icon on the curtain hanging before its door. With deep visual access into the atelier, one is able to see a nearly complete production chain: painting, the mounting of fans, the carving of the ribs, various designs on display, and a series of boxes of completed fans ready for transport. Such transparency itself would have made a visit to a fan shop a visually arresting experience. Although the Funaki screens only depict one shop on this street, a 1593 registry of the city of Kyoto lists no fewer than eleven, while a separate screen of this genre in the collection of the National Museum of Japanese History depicts nine.[15] While this number of fan shops may at first seem surprising, one must bear in mind that these workshops had to meet a high volume of demand. Japan's urban population had doubled between 1450 and 1590 (with a national population estimate of approximately sixteen million persons at the turn of the seventeenth century).[16] Kyoto's population had fallen after the Heian period (794–1192), but soared from 1570 on to reach a peak population of 400,000 by the mid-seventeenth century; meanwhile, the new city of Edo (present-day Tokyo) would reach one million inhabitants by 1700.[17] It is likely that a significant portion of this urban population would have been in possession of folding fans, ephemeral objects that would have been in need of regular replacement. Seen in this light, whether fans were in the hands of Europeans in Japan or not is immaterial given the fact that fans would have been omnipresent within their visual environment.

**Striking Contrasts**

Another place to look for the presence of folded media in this encounter is in the documentary record. One prominent European in Japan during this moment was the Jesuit missionary Luís Fróis (1532–1597), who had arrived in the archipelago in 1563. Fróis was the author, in 1585, of the earliest European analysis of Japanese culture based upon first-hand experience: *Striking Contrasts in the Customs of Europe and Japan* (*Tratado em que se contêm muito sucinta e abreviadamente algumas contradições e diferenças de costumes entre a gente de Europa e esta província de Japão*).[18] Fans figure several times within his text, which was curiously structured as a

series of six hundred distichs, following a "for us ... while for them ..."
structure. As the compositional form itself reveals, the entire text is structured around opposition, difference, and even polarity, thus precluding
at a formal level the possibility of noteworthy common ground.[19] When
fans do appear in *Striking Contrasts*, gender is the contrast, with Fróis surprised to see them in the hands of men. Fróis finds it important to mention materiality, too, with the goldenness of the fans being noteworthy.
Even in a much earlier text, written just two years following his arrival,
he mentions passing by a fan shop such as the one described above,
wherein artisans were at work making (again) "golden fans."[20] Despite
the widespread prevalence of the gold ground in medieval European
painting – especially in Christian contexts – its use in the manufacture
of fans seemed somehow astounding. This was likely due to the material
nature of contemporaneous European fan leaves, which might be constructed of a wide variety of materials including skins, textiles, lace, or
even precious materials such as ivory. Last, Fróis seems surprised to see
fans used in Buddhist contexts for what he terms "preaching." This likely
returns to the feminine valence of such objects in his mind, which would
have made the notion of a European using a fan in a religious context
(excepting flabella) a ludicrous notion.

Fróis omitted, however, an important distinction, one of which he was
likely aware: fans were not only used in Japan as handheld implements,
but also deboned and remounted as objects of display. In such display
contexts, fans might serve as vehicles for the visual manifestation of collected social capital, a power that fans accrue by virtue of inscriptions or
even the simple trace of possession from a previous celebrated owner.
Perhaps the most complex extant example of such a use of fans is a set
of four celebrated pairs of folding screens in the collection of the Zen
temple Nanzenji in Kyoto. Each screen within this set bears thirty fans
evenly distributed across a field of gold. While fans might be immediately pasted onto folding screens without ever being folded, these fans
bear traces of use, meaning they were collected and repurposed for the
screens. From thirty-five encomia inscribed on the fans, it is possible to
date the assemblage: the earliest to 1534 and the latest to 1622. Many of
these fans are ornamented with gold paint and gold leaf, making them
precisely contemporaneous to those Fróis commented upon – golden
fans from the hands of Japanese religious figures. Okudaira Shunroku
has conducted a revealing analysis of the fans' encomia, which indicate that the Nanzenji screens index complex homosocial relationships
between several generations of monks.[21] The screens thus operated,

among other things, as a tool for the ostentation of social capital, as they diagrammed lineage, network, and pedigree through a spatialized assemblage. As Okudaira's research makes clear, the beguiling fans in the hands of the monks Fróis saw were not mere rhetorical props, but powerful markers of subjectivity and significant vehicles for the intergenerational transfer of social capital.

Fróis was witness to the Momoyama period (1573–1600), a tumultuous if culturally efflorescent era that saw the violent unification of the majority of the archipelago under a series of ruthless warlords. Just after Fróis's death, in 1603, the last of these unifiers, Tokugawa Ieyasu (1543–1616), would establish his new capital in Edo (present-day Tokyo), from which the Tokugawa family would rule for the next two and a half centuries. As the unifying warlords grew wise to the political dangers of Christian proselytization, the fledgling community's fate dramatically turned. Beginning with an anti-Christian edict in 1587 and punctuated by the martyrdom in 1597 of twenty-six Christians in Nagasaki (a sensational event visually propagated throughout the Christian world), several decades of persecution succeeded in the virtual eradication of the religion. Concomitant with unification and stability was a stark diminution in the volume of direct European trade. The English abandoned their faltering attempts in 1623, the Spanish the following year, and the Portuguese were expelled in 1639. Thereafter, the Dutch would be the sole European nation allowed to trade with the Japanese until the mid-nineteenth century. Here begins the period of Japanese history problematically known as the "locked nation" (*sakoku*), during which direct exchange with the outside world was severely regulated. Yet one must take this notion of isolation with a grain of salt. As Ronald P. Toby has demonstrated, the term *sakoku* itself only dates to the nineteenth century.[22] That Japan successfully resisted implication within Eurocentric networks of capital flow did not mean that Japan was isolated from East Asia, nor did it mean that Japan was unaware of what was happening in the rest of the world. In other words, independence should not be mistaken for hermeticism, just as globalism should not be defined by the degree of integration into Eurocentric networks of capital flow. Nevertheless, the prevalence of this isolationist narrative enables a historiographical fold (indeed, all typological and analogical structures might be conceived as species of folds), such that the 1853 arrival of the American Commodore Matthew C. Perry (1794–1858) is cast as somehow analogous to the 1543 arrival of the Portuguese, with the triumphant Perry "opening" a "closed"

Japan to "global" trade.[23] Recent scholarship, by contrast, has ventured an inversion of this paradigm, with the sixteenth and seventeenth centuries cast as the time when Japan "discovered Europe," bringing Western Europeans into its fold and integrating them into its economic, social, and cultural practices.[24]

Regardless of how one frames the situation, it was during this period, in the late 1630s, that the folding fan would come to ground the European exchange with Japan in a very concrete way. As the Japanese government would no longer allow the European traders to occupy Japanese land, the traders were relegated to Dejima (or Deshima), a fan-shaped, artificial island located just metres off the coast of Nagasaki. Initially constructed with the Portuguese in mind, following their expulsion in 1639 the small island came to host and contain the Dutch from 1640. This territorial prosthesis would be the sole contact point for direct European trade for more than two centuries, its surface marked by the structures and small gardens that patterned their confined lives. Throughout early modernity, the morphology of the fan literally mediated the direct geospatial interface of Japan and Western Eurasia.[25]

## Importation without Import

Let us move now from morphology and historiography to the folded media themselves. Given the prominence of fans within early modern European culture, one might imagine that the means by which they came to Europe would be well known, but the exact conduits remain contested.[26] Most early scholarship straightforwardly assumed that this originally Japanese technology must have been imported via direct Japanese-European trade: either via the Dutch (from 1640) or the earlier Portuguese (1543–1639).[27] But as folding fans already appear in European portraits and catalogues of costume by the mid-sixteenth century, neither hypothesis is early enough. Indeed, direct European trade is likely immaterial. Given the burgeoning network of Portuguese entrepôts throughout South and Southeast Asia in the early sixteenth century, the format was likely introduced to Europe piecemeal and over several centuries by way of fan makers and traders throughout East and South Asia.[28] Pre-existing terrestrial and littoral routes would have made the transfer feasible as early as the Song dynasty (960–1279). Concatenated interregional trade, in other words, should not be discounted in the face of the small, if impressive, long-distance routes that were newly emergent in the sixteenth century.

The motivation for the fan's spread was likely not a matter of cultural appropriation or exotica alone; there are certain physical features of the fan that incentivize its transmission independent of these factors. First, consider the tight conformity (the ergonomics, so to speak) of the fan in relationship to the anatomy of the grasping hand. In the right hand, a rightward torque of the thumb spreads the closed fan open against the resistance of the fingers on the opposite side – running from the outer to the index finger. The size and angle of the circular section of the fan are likewise delimited by the span of the palm, and the fanning motion itself is chiefly the result of the supination and pronation of the wrist. The fan acts in lieu of and as an extension of the hand, making it a prosthesis by definition. When fanning, moreover, the fan closes the circuit between face and hand, arguably the two most charged and expressive loci of the body. Fans hence occupy a relationship with the sensorium that is eminently immediate; that is, unlike many other pictorial media, they are not just extensions of the visual imaginary into space, but physical prostheses that remain in contact with the body. As this immediacy makes clear, these objects evolved to be fitted to human social habits of fashion, ostentation, and cooling, such that they readily engender proliferation – like pictorial burrs. Their light weight and small size made them ideal tokens of trade. They are, in this sense, coevolved with human anatomy and visuality such that they transformed their beholders into agents for propagation and proliferation.

However folding fans made their way to Europe, they seem to have quickly lost any association with Japan. Remember that Fróis commented on the particularities of their use, but not their existence, for these implements were already a feature of upper-class feminine attire when he left for the archipelago. This is clearly evident in the then-emergent genre of pictorial costume compendia.[29] For instance, in one early costume book, the *Recueil de la diversité des habits, qui sont de présent en usage, tant es pays d'Europe, Asie, Affrique & isles sauvages* (Paris, 1567) of François Desprez (1525–1580), a single figure is represented as "a woman of Asia" (*la femme d'Asie*), but no fan is in her hands.[30] Likewise, in the expanded edition of Cesare Vecellio's (c. 1531–c. 1601) landmark survey of world costume, *Habiti antichi et moderni di tutto il mondo* (*Ancient and Modern Clothing of the Entire World*) of 1598, folding fans appear in the hands of European noblewomen (e.g., the "young Roman woman" ["Giovani Gentildonne Romane"] and the "Noble Pisan" ["Nobili Pisane"]), but not in the hands of the East Asians. Given that such costume histories, like maps, are one of the arenas in which the early modern European ethnographic impulse made an early appearance, if fans were seen as "Japanese" it seems odd not to find them here.[31] In fact, the sole Japanese exemplar within Vecellio's *Habiti* is a young man incongruously dressed in a suit of heavy brocades.[32]

As Bronwen Wilson has noted, the source for Vecellio's image was most likely one of the members of the so-called "Tenshō Embassy": four Japanese Christian young men whom Alessandro Valignano (1539–1606), Father Visitor of the Jesuit mission in Japan, sent on a grand public relations tour of Europe from 1582–90.[33] Their highest-profile audiences were with Pope Gregory XIII (1502–1585) and King Phillip II of Spain (1527–1598), but the voyagers were feted in dozens of European cities along the way, creating a veritable "Japan boom" in Europe.[34] One might expect that this would have been a spectacle of racialized exoticism, yet as Wilson has argued, the racial identity of the Japanese boys was often confounding for European eyes: "the Japanese visitors tested the representational system of Europeans because they fell between existing categories of identity."[35] Analogies varied widely, with some seeing them as African and others seeing the Japanese as white. Valignano himself averred that the Japanese were "all white ... surpass[ing] all the other known races of the world."[36] The Tenshō mission, moreover, was expressly designed to show equality, mimicry, and assimilation – a successful transmission of Catholic culture – hence sartorial signs of difference, including the use of folding fans, might have been downplayed.[37] The four "ambassadors" were selected and instructed for this particular public relations spectacle. Yet despite the impact they had on establishing the image of the Japanese in the European imagination, their visit was less a genuine encounter with Japanese culture and more an occasion for European powers to celebrate a successful instance of cultural and religious conversion.

During their European tour, the Venetian Senate commissioned Jacopo Tintoretto (1518–1594) to make portraits of the young men.[38] Left unfinished upon his death, the likeness of only a single visitor, that of Itō Mancio (né Sukemasu), was salvaged and completed by a later painter, likely Jacopo's son and heir Domenico (fig. 2.2). Only rediscovered in 2014, it is among the earliest European depictions of a Japanese subject in the prestige medium of oil on canvas. Tintoretto's treatment of Itō's physiognomy seems to corroborate Wilson's point – a delineation of similar humanity rather the exaggerated expression of difference that would often characterize the Euro-American depiction of Japanese bodies well into the twentieth century. Radiography has revealed that the frill around

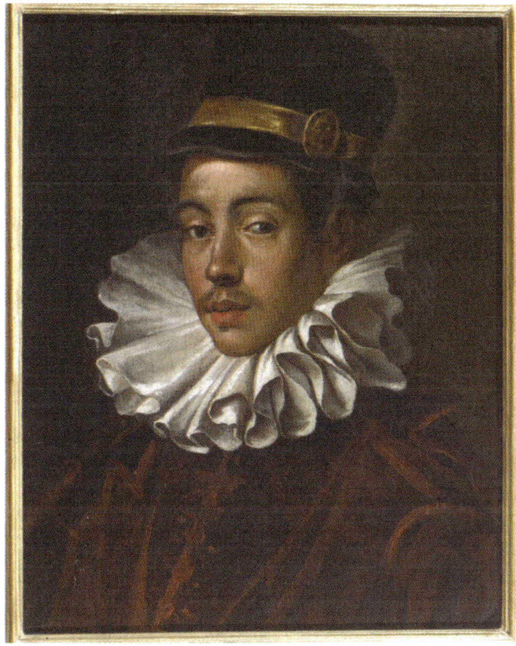

Figure 2.2. Domenico Tintoretto, *Portrait of Itō Mancio*, 1585. Oil on canvas, 54 x 43 cm. Fondazione Trivulzio, Milan. Photograph courtesy of Fondazione Trivulzio

Itō's neck was much enlarged by a later painter – a curious decision that made the portrait not only less foreign but less antiquated as well.

In contrast to the Tenshō iconography, one finds in an illustration published in 1600 a very different image of the Japanese.[39] It appeared in a published account of the journey of the first Netherlander to circumnavigate the world, Olivier van Noort (1558–1627). The engraving depicts the crew of a Japanese ship that Van Noort encountered travelling from the Philippines to Borneo. Labelled as "dressed in the Polish fashion," one can see immediately the work of apperception, as a foreign encounter is made analogous to that already known.[40] Yet unlike the Tenshō images, the hairstyles here are in keeping with those current in Japan at the time; the weapons they carry – curved swords, pikes, longbows, and guns – are likewise somewhat more accurate. Most telling of all, of course, is the presence of two folding fans in the men's hands. The simple scene reminds us not only that fans were used by men – likely even by seafaring men far from Japan – but also that Japanese traders were active in East and Southeast Asia during this period via Japan's "red seal" ships.[41] This latter fact rarely gets mentioned in framing the place of Japan in early modernity. Likewise, Japanese objects, including folding fans and folded screens, also travelled *eastwards* – across the Pacific – where they propagated themselves just as readily. For clear evidence of this, one need look no further than the genre of *biombo*, large folding screens produced in New Spain whose very name (from the Japanese *byōbu*) alerts one to the genre's Japanese origins.[42] The encounter with Europe, in other words, is just one aspect of the much larger narrative of the agency of Japanese folded media in global modernity.

## Second Comings

How fans such as those found in the hands of these seafaring men made their way to Europe, however, is a different question. Through more than two decades of research on Habsburg portraiture, Annemarie Jordan Gschwend has produced a robust and compelling thesis concerning the advent of imported Japanese fans in European courts.[43] Her account centres tightly on Lisbon in the mid-sixteenth century. For instance, in 1552, the painter Antonis Mor (1516/20–c. 1576) along with his student Alonso Sánchez Coello (1531/32–88) travelled from the Brussels court of Maria of Hungary (1505–1558) to the Lisbon court of her sister Catherine of Austria (1507–1578), wife of John III (1502–1557), in order to paint portraits of the court.[44] One resultant portrait, now in the collection of the Convent of Las Descalzas Reales in Madrid, depicts Maria of Portugal (1527–1545), daughter of Catherine's eldest sister Leonor of Austria, holding in her lap an object that appears to be a Japanese or Ryūkyūan paper folding fan.[45] An even earlier portrait of Catherine's daughter, the short-lived María Manuela (1527–1545), contains a similar object. This latter portrait is lost, but Antoine Trouvéon, an artist who accompanied a French embassy in 1542, made a copy that survives (fig. 2.3).[46] In this full-length portrait, María Manuela holds in her hands a folding fan, one that Jordan Gschwend purports to be Japanese, as such objects were available in the Portuguese court from 1540.[47] Thereafter, when Maria Manuela married Phillip II of Spain in 1542, she took the "Portuguese custom of coquettishly using Asian folding fans" with her to the court in Madrid, out from which, one presumes, the use spread to other courts

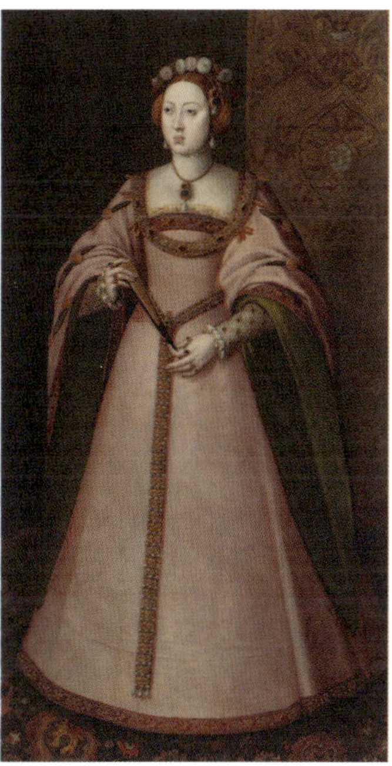

Figure 2.3. *María Manuela de Portugal*, sixteenth century. Oil on canvas, 193 x 102 cm. Museo Nacional del Prado, Madrid. Photograph courtesy of the Museo Nacional del Prado

in Europe.[48] Indeed, the Habsburg dynasty was in control of much of the European continent at the time, making a wide and rapid courtly diffusion unsurprising. Accordingly, it would have been from the Iberian Peninsula that the use of fans of East Asian origin would have spread to the rest of Europe, travelling counter-intuitively eastward.[49] Even though much is made of the early seventeenth-century Japanese pivot away from Iberian traders in favour of the Dutch, one must bear in mind the Netherlands had, until that time, been under Spanish Habsburg rule. In fact, the Eighty Years War (1568–1648), which resulted in definitive Dutch independence from the Habsburgs, runs in the background throughout the timeline of this narrative. All things considered, Jordan Gschwend's thesis seems rather compelling.

In speaking of Japanese folding fans in Europe, one must be careful to distinguish the technology from the nation, since the technology could spread independent of its Japaneseness. The technology spread throughout East Asia soon after its invention in Japan. By the early sixteenth century, well before the arrival of the Portuguese in Japan, folding fans were being manufactured even in Venice.[50] Such early Italian manufacture helps to explain the long-prevailing theory that it was Catherine de Medici who introduced the use of folding fans in European court culture, having brought fans with her from Italy to the French court in 1533.[51] Indeed, this would explain why the use of fans seems proper to Italy but not Asia according to the costume histories of the Italian writer Vecellio and the Frenchman Desprez.

Yet what concerns us here, however, is not so much the technology as the association with Japan. This specificity is all the more telling since this is an era in European history when Japanese and Chinese objects were rarely distinguished (even sometimes subsumed into the larger category of "Indian") .[52] This period is also prior to the tight association of Japan with lacquerwork (e.g., "japanning"). Yet folding fans identified *as Japanese* began to circulate in Europe almost precisely at the same moment as direct European trade with Japan. Fans made in Japan had perhaps also made their way into Europe much earlier through concatenated, indirect trade, yet the crucial difference – as Jordan Gschwend notes – is that in the context of the Lisbon court, their Japaneseness mattered, since such objects indexed the court's uniquely global trade network that allowed for long-distance importation.[53] Hence the attribution of a specific locality of manufacture was surely motivated by a desire to highlight the far reach of Portuguese mercantilist power.

A crucial factor here is the role played by women in this encounter. In Jordan Gschwend's research, it was through the explicit agency of Catherine of Austria, the women at her court, and the women to whom she was connected that the East Asian folding fan became identified as a luxury import good appropriate to women of their station.[54] Although folding fans would have been a prominent part of male attire in East Asia – as we saw in Van Noort – these originally ungendered objects became gendered as feminine in the European context. This gender assignment would have far-reaching consequences, since it would structure the way in which Japanese fans were received when they began to flow into Europe again in large numbers in the nineteenth century.

In discussing the reach of the Habsburg trade network, one should be wary of positing something particularly modern or even early modern about the fledging Iberian entry into this market, for these objects had served as pictorial vehicles for the global export of Japanese visual culture for nearly five centuries before Europe's interest.[55] In the centuries before the Portuguese arrival, hundreds – and sometimes thousands – of fans were exported as a part official East Asian diplomatic and trade missions; large numbers must have been exchanged through illicit trade networks, as well.[56] Nor was the connection to courtliness new. One hundred luxury folding fans were gifted to the Ming emperor as part of every official "tributary" mission from Japan.[57] In addition to the one hundred official gift fans, the emissaries would also bring supplementary fans to sell, with the number of such fans peaking at 2,200 in 1453.[58] One must bear in mind that these fans fulfilled the imperative to present representative items that were performatively exported, imported, and utilized with a degree mindfulness of the metonymy for Japan itself. Such tribute missions, far from being burdensome shows of obeisance, were pro forma excuses to conduct highly profitable trade. In fact, so vigorous was this trade that the Ming protested against the rowdiness, frequency, and unabashed commercialism of such Japanese missions.[59] Coincidentally, the last of these missions was in 1547, just four years after the arrival of the Portuguese in Japan. Seen in this light, the export of fans to Europe in the sixteenth century – and then to wider North Atlantic markets in the nineteenth century – was merely an extension of a long-established regional economy of haptic, radial pictures. It serves to remind us that the flow of goods into Europe in early modernity was not as neatly centripetal as is sometimes imagined; instead, we find complex networks of interregional encounters that sometimes had little to do with Europe directly. In other words, when it comes to the history of this particular medium, it was perhaps Europe and not Japan that was brought into the fold.

Regardless of the exact conduits for the fan's arrival into Europe, robust markets soon developed. Indeed, fans would become a mainstay commodity for the various East India companies.[60] Just as with netsuke, fans were similarly small, lightweight, resilient, and easily marketable. It is no wonder that East Asian fans would so quickly and readily flood the market.[61] And flood they did. As early as 1695, England's fan makers found themselves in dire financial straits, purportedly due to this competition, such that they filed a grievance with the House of Commons requesting a ban on the import of fans of Asian manufacture.[62] The grievance claimed that over 130,000 fans had been imported (no timeframe is given), which had led to much unemployment: "great Numbers of Men, Women and Children, used to be constantly Employed, some in making the Sticks, Papers, Leathers, and in Ordering and Stiffning of the Silks, others in Painting, Varnishing, and Japanning, and in preparing other Materials wherewith Fanns are made." The grievance also mentions the "great Quantities of Silk, Paper, Leather, Wyer, and several Tunns of Whale-bone, Tortoise-shell, Ivory, Box, Ebony, and other sorts of Wood, which were Imported from Turky, Russia, and other Foreign Parts." The document is telling, since it demonstrates that these seemingly trifling objects were the result of the collaborative labour of remarkably diverse craftspersons whose work relied upon and fuelled wide-reaching networks of trade.[63]

While the figure of 130,000 may seem hyperbolic, the actual number may have been even greater. A manifest from the contemporaneous *Macclesfield*, a ship in transit from Guangdong to England in 1699, listed a hundred thousand fans in a single shipment.[64] Not all of these fans were pictorial, nor were they necessarily similar to items that would have been produced for the domestic markets within East Asia (in fact, they likely were not), yet the sheer volume of these exports alerts us to the fact that despite the emphasis placed on ceramics during this period, folding fans played a role far larger than presently imagined as vehicles for the pictorial transmission of East Asian visual culture. Indeed, until the rise of polychrome xylography in the late eighteenth century, one is hard-pressed to imagine a more dynamic vehicle for the export of Japanese visual and material culture abroad.

**Pleated Vision**

Aside from the sheer volume of pleated media exported by Japan in early modernity, a more theoretical question concerns their consequence: the relationship of folded media to the ways in which geographical and virtual space were schematized, diagrammed, and transmitted. The first step in pursuing this question is to note the role of angle and aspect in pictorial perception, as folds dramatically impinge on the stability of one's perception of any marked surface. For example, with a mounted fan, each of the thin, conjoined planes sits at a separate angle to the eye, such that a single hand-held fan produces a vast array of mercurial "images" depending on the motion of the hand. The designer of such a pleated image must negotiate the interplay of virtual (painted) and embodied (aspectual) perspectives. While this holds true for folding screens as well, with screens one must move one's body or physically rearrange the screen into a changeable but relatively stable series of angles in order to shift the embodied perspective. The scale and physical instability of the folding fan, however, renders its images all the more unstable and multifaceted, hence making such dynamism far more prominent.[65]

Beyond pleatedness, the convergence of the fold lines into a single point further distinguishes the folding fan. Fans "fan out," with profound consequences for the way in which they inflect the images on their surfaces. This effect has led some, such as Kazuko Mende, to posit that fan-painting represents its own species in the history of linear perspective.[66] Indeed, as early as the twelfth century, Japanese fans incorporated the material folds into the depiction such that the virtual space likewise diminished at the bottom and was enlarged the top.[67] This was a function of not only the arc-like shape of the fan, but also its folds, the lines of which structure the semiotic ground of the painted surface, thus complicating any perspectival attempt to convey spatial illusion.[68] Using digital software, Mende has been able to distort the fan-shaped image in order to "correct" it into a familiar rectilinear arrangement; and the wild resultant distortions underscore her point. Accordingly, the longstanding, stable nature of the folding fan as a medium seems to have supported the development and maintenance of sophisticated pictorial treatments of space that were proper to the medium. This raises the stakes for the story of the fan's European adoption, since pictorial fans may represent an important vehicle for the transmission of this complex and pleated species of picturing to westernmost Eurasia.

As the early fan historian Percival MacIver noted, however, even after Europeans had adopted the material format, only rarely did they attempt to grapple with the medium's complexity.[69] The reason for this reticence was that European perspective systems, especially those with a straight horizon line, were often at odds with the curvilinear format. A clear way to demonstrate this disjunction is through a European-style etching by the Japanese painter, theorist, and Occidentalist of sorts, Shiba Kōkan (1747–1818), who early advocated for the adoption in Japan of European pictoriality (fig. 2.4). The impression, printed on the surface of a folding fan, is after his painting *The Leathermakers* – itself after the engraving of Jan Luyken (1649–1712) and Caspar Luyken (1672–1708) from their *Het Menselyk Bedryf* (*Human Industry*, Amsterdam, 1694).[70] One is immediately struck by the rectangularity of the impression, which jars with the curvilinear fan. Once folded, moreover, the vanishing lines of the etching's composition must compete with the radial lines of the folds. Kōkan is an extreme example, and certainly some Euro-American painters did attempt to work with the folded surface, but they were the exception rather than the rule. For instance, when European-made fan

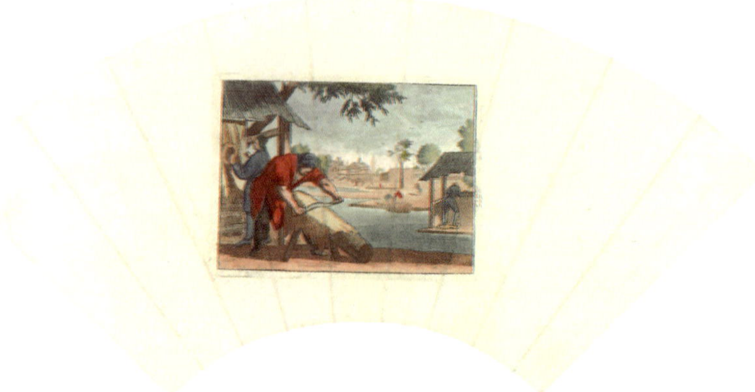

Figure 2.4. Folding fan bearing an impression of *The Leathermakers* by Shiba Kōkan. Hand-coloured etching, ink and pigment on paper. Private collection, Japan

leaves were mounted and framed – literally flattened – artists might be called upon to fill in the composition in order to create a fully rectilinear composition. That this was even possible reveals that foldedness was often incidental to the internal structure of the image. In fact, sometimes the infill is so successful that it is difficult to perceive any trace of the original fan-shaped composition at all.

Thinking of the fan surface in this way, as a perspectival space, likewise complicates the relationship of linear perspective to the human body. Linear perspective is often diagrammed as a conical projection radiating from the embodied eye of a beholder to the surface of a picture; it further entails a particular standpoint at which the illusion obtains and from which the picture seems to replace the visual field. In the case of the fan, however, the point of convergence is found quite literally in the palm of the hand, as the pivot itself operates, by definition, as the point where the convergent fold lines meet. In that regard, one might even go so far as to posit that fans represent a haptic form of perspective. The lines of convergence are material and indelible, thus making their attendant perspectival system almost inherent. As such, this tight interplay of medium and materiality made fans one of the media proper to East Asia that was most strongly resistant to Euro-American appropriation. By contrast, Euro-Americans might lift freely from the pictorial conventions found in woodblock prints, as their rectilinearity posed no problem; the material and morphological features of a fan painting, however, made such images less easy to adapt.

## Terrestrial Implications

Be that as it may, the way in which the fan format bends space was not without European analogues. In the context of the sixteenth century, the most similar contortions of space were found not in the pictorial arts so much as in the various cartographic projections devised in order to depict the earth's spherical surface as a planar, graphic object. Various cartographic projections competed, of course, with varying degrees of fidelity and distortion. Most germane for our purposes are conic projections such as those employed in Ptolemaic cartography, the prevailing European schema for the conception of the Earth's surface from antiquity until early modernity.[71] One can see this clearly in the earliest extant early modern edition of the oldest extant Latin text on geography, the *Cosmographia* of Pomponius Mela (fl. 37–42 CE), published in Venice in 1482.[72] Arresting is the fact that the woodblock print that accompanied this publication – the second-oldest woodblock map created in Italy – depicts the world as an enormous fan, one canopied by a grand architectural enclosure (fig. 2.5).

Maps and atlases were, of course, both tools for enabling encounter and emblems of possession, as geographical images allowed one not only to navigate but also to display a mastery of the shape, location, and features of the depicted land. Through such images, the entire Earth was systematically made perusable, presentable, and portable. Predictably, the fold figures prominently here, as maps were often folded, with the fold lines themselves producing a rectilinear grid over the entire surface of the map (irrespective of the lines of the virtual projection). The notion of the folded map becomes even more acute when one considers the codex atlas, wherein the gutter of the binding brings its own material entailments to bear. If one turns, for instance, to the *Geographia* (1511) of Bernardus Sylvanus (act. 1490–1511) – the first European atlas to place Japan correctly – the symmetry of the heart-shaped world means that upon closing the book, the edges of the world line up, effectively making the binding a mechanism for collapsing and completing the image.[73] The projection employed by Abraham Ortelius (1527–1598) in his groundbreaking *Theatrum orbis terrarum* (*Theatre of the World*, 1570)

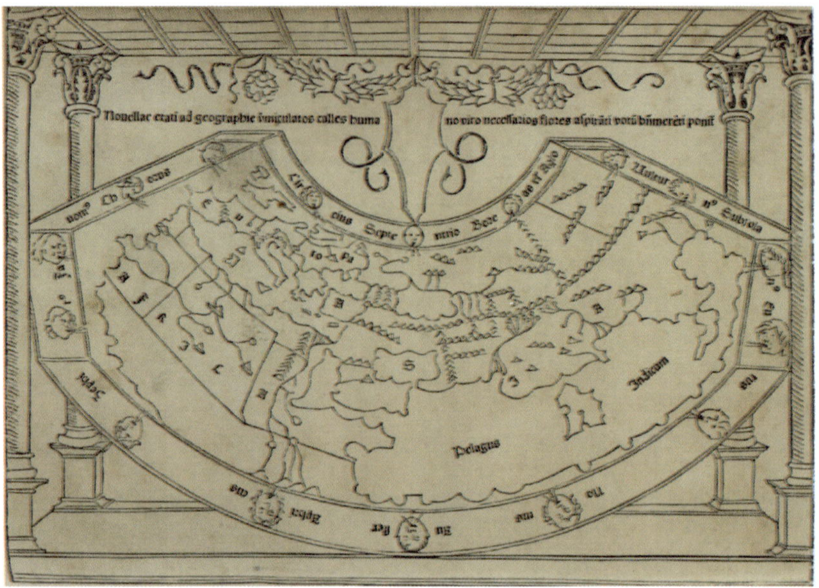

Figure 2.5. Pomponius Mela, *Cosmographia, sive de situ orbis* (Venice: Erhard Ratdolt, 1482). Woodcut, ink on paper. Texas Collection, Baylor University. Photograph courtesy of Baylor University

likewise preserved this symmetry in its iconic global conspectus, the *Typus orbis terrarum*, where the vertical central fold again closes the world upon itself, creating a sort of flattened anti-globe, with the entire surface of the Earth pressed upon another point (but not its antipode) when closed.[74] In a similar sense, the folded materiality of maps and atlases seems to index the spatial collapse afforded by the navigational practices that were enabled by and constituent of such images.

Even beyond collapse, the projection of the *Theatrum* meant that as one turned within the atlas to the more detailed sheets, the latitudinal and longitudinal lines would clearly trace a fan-like structure over the surface of the earth.[75] Nowhere was this relationship between the fan shape and cartography more apparent than in the gigantic world map made by Urbano Monte (1544–1613), which showed the entire surface of the Earth spread across three square metres according to a north polar azimuthal projection.[76] This massive circular image of the world required some sixty independent manuscript sheets. The four closest to the centre formed perfect quadrants, whereas those further away from the centre appeared more like fan leaves.[77] The treatment of Japan here is especially detailed, a situation that perhaps reflects Monte's incorporation of knowledge he obtained directly from the Tenshō mission, with whom he was able to meet personally.[78] Indeed, the encounter with the Japanese youths was the direct impetus for Monte's own foray into cartography, which began with an attempt to map the Japanese archipelago.[79] As this monumental map reveals, cartographers grappling with the problem of how to project a spherical shape onto a rectilinear place often found themselves constructing images that behaved according to patterns of distortion similar to those used in East Asian fan painting.[80]

It is important to bear in mind that, in the sixteenth century, Europeans and Japanese had limited cartographic knowledge about one another. As Angelo Catteneo has well demonstrated, the period is defined by an exchange of geographical and cartographic knowledge between the two edges of the Eurasian continent, as each attempted to fit the other into its prevailing paradigm.[81] When the Jesuits arrived, for instance, it remained unclear to Europeans that Korea was a peninsula, that Japan comprised several main islands, that Hokkaidō existed, and that a vast ocean separated the Japanese islands from the West Indies. While atlases such as Ortelius's hold a privileged place in European cartographic history, their most celebrated Japanese counterparts are doubtless cartographic folding screens.[82] Such objects folded, typically along five folds between six panels, to present a pliable image of the world that might be architecturally arranged for a sort of cartographic inhabitation – a literal immersion within the image of the world.[83] To borrow Fróis's oppositional rhetoric, these screens were, in a sense, concave surrounds that consumed the viewer, in contrast to the convex globe and the hand-held atlas. But one would not want to take the opposition too far: as Lach notes, at the turn of the fifteenth century, wall maps were installed in the ducal palace in Venice; between 1563 and 1575, Cosimo I de' Medici (1519–1574) had Ignazio Danti (1536–1586) create atlas wall panels for the Sala della Guardaroba (Palazzo Vecchio); and Pope Gregory XIII (1502–1585) commissioned similar maps for the Vatican not a decade later.[84] Giovanni Raneri has argued that such European "mural map cycles" impressed the Tenshō emissaries, and may thus have influenced the development of *nanban* cartographic screens in Japan.[85] These European examples, however, were often monumental and planar – neither portable nor as intimately immersive as Japanese cartographic screens. Here again, *folded* virtual space failed to gain traction in the European context.

This resistance to folded space is spectacularly illustrated by the recent discovery of a seventeenth-century Japanese screen of the aforementioned cityscape genre found dissected and embedded within the walls of one of the "Indian cabinets" at Schloss Eggenberg in Graz, Austria.[86] Rather than embrace the folded, bird's-eye, cartographic space, the object was disassembled panel by panel, with each panel then centred within its own elaborate trompe-l'oeil frame – not dissimilar to gilded mounts for porcelain – such that the pictorial legibility of the Japanese screens, not to mention their folded materiality, was completely effaced. It was an attempt to fold one system into another, with the result being an aesthetic of encasement rather than engagement. The frontality common to many European technologies of virtuality was ill-suited to interface with such strongly pleated pictorial space.

On a final note, however, when looking for European analogues to East Asian folding fans, pleated media may not necessarily be the best place to look when, on purely morphological grounds, there are far more immediate and tactile analogues. For instance, in terms of shape, one cannot help but note the striking similarity between the folding fan and the altitude quadrant: both handheld, nearly identical in scale, with lines converging in the palm.[87] Indeed, it is easy to mistake a quadrant for a fan in reading the cartographic and navigational iconography one finds in the frames and along the margins of European maps. As such, one wonders whether the shape of the folding fan might not have had a particular appeal during an era when the navigational instrument that allowed for one's positioning within the world was so superficially similar. Despite their common tactility as handheld technologies, the handling itself was distinct, with the quadrant used by placing it up to the eye, hence closing the theoretically freighted hand–eye circuit in one of the most direct ways imaginable. The two technologies had complementary investments in quadratic thought – one squaring the round surface of the Earth, the other de-squaring the rectilinearity of the pictorial field. One was a technology for navigating the map's pictorial field, while the other was a technology for making images themselves into tactile and mobile units.

If one favours tactility and handling over morphology, one finds an even stronger analogue in the common compass – not the magnetic dial, but the tool comprised of two sticks joined by a single hinge – used in the process of mapmaking, distance-measuring, plotting, and navigating. As with the folding fan, a compass was held in a single hand and pivoted open and closed with the hinge in the cradle of the palm. One might even cast the compass as a simple, instrumentalized fold, with the resultant angle made to index any number of computational outputs. The hinge itself operates as a metaphor for navigation, as it is the trigonometric convergence where two disparate plotted points are made to meet. For want of textual corroboration, the analogy to such navigational tools must remain speculative, but it seems highly improbable that mariners would not have observed at least some degree of similarity between their fan-shaped and hinged navigational tools and the fans that globally proliferated in their lifetimes.

Mere decades following the direct European contact with Japan, the distant and largely unknown archipelago had become a site of arguably unrivalled European fascination.[88] Central to this process were a variety of folded media. Our attention here has been limited to image-bearing folded media – fans, screens, maps, and bound atlases; absent from our discussion, however, were the most pedestrian but most prominent folded media of early modernity: documents themselves.[89] Whether document or picture (or amalgam thereof), the fold afforded privacy, permitted condensation, and enabled protection (of the marked surface), such that it engendered portability, dislocation, and exchange.

Of all folded media, however, it was the folding fan that most concerned us here. A poorly understood medium, it should be clear now that fans deserve greater analysis due to their bodily immediacy, social modalities, trans-cultural fluidity, and pictorial complexity. This is not to mention, of course, the sheer volume of such objects in circulation. While Japanese fans remain emblematic of nineteenth-century Japonisme, we have seen how this tired trope obscures the long-lived agency of these objects. The role of European aristocratic women in the European adoption of this medium – and the object's attendant gendering – also deserve more focus, as does the agency of the wide networks of non-European agents responsible for the global proliferation of the technology. Last, the most speculative hypothesis here is that fans may exhibit formal parallels with European cartographic visuality; and they may have tactile commonality with European navigational tools. All told, if we are to write a more truly global history of global modernity, then its various implications must be taken far more literally.

**NOTES**

1 Gilles Deleuze, *Le pli: Leibniz et le Baroque* (Paris: Minuit, 1988).

2 In fact, as vehicles for calligraphic inscription, fans were supports for the highest of all East Asian brush arts, hence removing any doubt as to the esteem in which they were held.

3 For an analysis of the genre, see Yukio Lippit, "Japan's Southern Barbarian Screens," in *Encompassing the Globe: Portugal and the World in the 16th & 17th Centuries*, ed. Jay A. Levenson (Washington, DC: Arthur M. Sackler Gallery, Smithsonian Institution, 2007), 244–53; Narusawa Katsushi, "Two Streams of Namban Painting," in *Japan Envisions the West: 16th-19th Century Japanese Art from Kobe City Museum*, ed. Yukiko Shirahara (Seattle: Seattle Art Museum, 2007), 57–73; and Joseph F. Loh, "When Worlds Collide – Art, Cartography, and Japanese Nanban World Map Screens" (PhD diss., Columbia University, 2013), 62–9.

4 The number of extant works is approximately ninety-two. For the catalogue raisonné, see Sakamoto Mitsuru, ed., *Nanban byōbu shūsei* (Tokyo: Chūō kōron bijutsu shuppan, 2008). On the trajectory of *nanban* screens, see Lippit, "Southern Barbarians."

5 See the screen in the private collection of an anonymous "Y" in Sakamoto, *Nanban byōbu shūsei*.

6 See Lippit, "Southern Barbarians," 247–53; Loh, "Worlds Collide," 62–9.

7 The attribution is based on both style and the presence of a gourd-shaped seal impression on the right side of the fan. *Majiwaru bunka tsunagu rekishi musubu bi – Kōbe shiritsu hakubutsukan meihinsen* (Kobe: Kobe City Museum, 2019), 154–5. Narusawa Katsushi, "Kinsei shoki zokuga toshite no nanban byōbu: sono tanjō kara henbō made," in Sakamoto, *Nanban byōbu shūsei*, 298.

8 On such *nanban* architecture, see Lippit, "Southern Barbarians," 250–1.

9 Narusawa, "Kinsei shoki zokuga toshite no nanban byōbu," 298.

10 I thank Anton Schweizer for pointing out that *nanban* or *nanban*-style objects sometimes had a talismanic valence, as these objects were related to an exotic new religious sect. Here we see how the nineteenth-century phenomenon of wearing the costumes of another culture – "cultural cross-dressing" as Christine Guth has termed it – had early roots. See Christine Guth, "Charles Longfellow and Okakura Kakuzo: Cultural Cross-Dressing in the Colonial Context," *Positions: East Asia Cultures Critique* 8, no. 3: 605–36; and her later *Longfellow's Tattoos: Tourism, Collecting, and Japan* (Seattle: University of Washington Press, 2004); see also Lippit, "Southern

Barbarian," 253. The phenomenon was not limited to Japan. A prominent example is the pleasure taken by the Yongzheng Emperor (r. 1723–35) in cross-dressing to appropriate numerous subject-positions, including that of a European. We see here perhaps the origins of the Occidentalism (or the later "Hollandism") present in early modern Japanese visual and material culture.

11 For more on the fashionability of European dress and Christian implements, see Loh, "Worlds Collide," 10–11.

12 Narusawa, "Kinsei shoki zokuga toshite no nanban byōbu," 298.

13 The earliest record of such paintings appears in an entry dated 1506 in the diary of the courtier Sanjōnishi Sanetaka (1455–1537), yet the oldest extant exemplar – the so-called Machida Version – dates to some three to four decades later. For a monograph-length treatment of the genre, see Matthew Philip McKelway, *Capitalscapes: Folding Screens and Political Imagination in Late Medieval Kyoto* (Honolulu: University of Hawai'i Press, 2006).

14 Patricia Graham, "Fans Afloat: Samurai Taste in *Yamato-e* Design," *Orientations* 34 (2003): 20–9.

15 Okudaira Shunroku, "Fans of the Zen Community: A Study of the Nanzen-ji Screens," in *Ink and Gold: Art of the Kano,* ed. Felice Fischer and Kyoko Kinoshita (Philadelphia: Philadelphia Museum of Art, 2015), 13.

16 William Wayne Farris, *Japan to 1600: A Social and Economic History* (Honolulu: University of Hawai'i Press, 2009), 171. For more on pre-modern demographic trends, see William Wayne Farris, *Japan's Medieval Population: Famine, Fertility, and Warfare in a Transformative Age* (Honolulu: University of Hawai'i Press, 2006).

17 The Kyoto figure is from Conrad Totman, *Japan: An Environmental History* (London: I.B. Tauris, 2016), 162.

18 For an English translation, see *The First European Description of Japan, 1585: A Critical English-Language Edition of* Striking Contrasts in the Customs of Europe and Japan *by Luis Frois, S.J.,* trans., ed., and ann. Richard K. Danforth, Robin D. Gill, and Daniel T. Reff, intro. Daniel T. Reff (London: Routledge, 2014).

19 Fróis seems to have established an influential precedent in this regard. Later commentators, such as François Solier (1558–1628) and Luis de Guzmán (1543–1605) would follow this pattern of contrastive commentary. Donald F. Lach and Edwin J. Van Kley, *Asia in the Making of Europe, Volume III: A Century of Advance, Book Two: South Asia* (Chicago: Chicago University Press, 1993), 1829 and 1845–6.

20 Cited in Guida Carvalho and Cristina Castel-Branco, *Luis Frois: First Western Accounts of Japan's Gardens, Cities and Landscapes* (Singapore: Springer

Singapore, 2019), 70; and Conrad Totman, *A History of Japan*, 2nd ed. (Malden, MA: Blackwell, 2005), 242.

21  Okudaira, "Fans of the Zen Community," 14–17.

22  For a thorough deconstruction of the "locked nation" trope, see Ronald P. Toby, *State and Diplomacy in Early Modern Japan: Asia in the Development of the Tokugawa Bakufu* (Princeton: Princeton University Press, 1984), especially the introduction.

23  Onoda Kazuyuki, "The Reception of Maps between Japan and the West," in *Japan Envisions the West: 16th-19th Century Japanese Art from Kobe City Museum*, ed. Yukiko Shirahara (Seattle: Seattle Art Museum, 2007), 33; Lippit, "Southern Barbarian," 253.

24  Narusawa argues the Japanese encountered Europe "on their own terms"; see "Two Streams," 58. "When Japan Discovered Italy" was the title of an exhibition at the MUDEC (Museo delle Culture) in Milan: Marisa di Russo, ed., *Quando il Giappone scoprì l'Italia: Itō Mancio e le "ambascerie" giapponesi, 1585–1615* (Milan: 24 Ore Cultura, 2019).

25  This is frequently noted by early historians, the earliest perhaps being S. Blondel, *Histoire des éventails chez tous les peuples et à toutes les époques* (Paris: Librairie Renouard, 1875), 28. See also Ugo Alfonso Casal, "The Lore of the Japanese Fan," *Monumenta Nipponica* 16 (1960): 103. The latter was by far the most extensive, rigorous, and exhaustive scholarship in English published at its time.

26  Some contest a Japanese origin altogether, preferring an independent European origination. See Nancy Armstrong, *Fans in Spain* (London: Philip Wilson, 2004), 17 and passim.

27  A bibliography and précis of these theories are given in Ariel Beaujot, *Victorian Fashion Accessories* (London: Berg, 2012), 66–7. The earliest Japanese historian of the fan, Nakamura Kiyoe, argued that the fan came to proliferate throughout European courts following the marriage of Catherine of Medici to Henry II of France in 1533. Nakamura does not give a source. As he later notes, Europeans did not have access to Japanese paper, thus they used other materials. Yet it is not clear how the technology would have made its way into the Medici court in the first place. Nakamura Kiyoe, *Nihon noōgi* (Kyoto: Kawara shoten, 1942). Bennet gives a similar history, but with more agency given to Henry III; see Anna Gray Bennett, *Unfolding Beauty: The Art of the Fan* (New York: Thames and Hudson, 1988), 12–13; see also her earlier *Fans in Fashion* (Rutland, VT: Tuttle, 1981), especially 8–9.

28  Casal, "Lore," 111, 115. An early popular account of the history of the fan was that of Louisa Parr, "The Fan," *The Harpers Monthly*, August 1889, 399–409. Parr suggests the folding fan was introduced to Europe in the

fifteenth century from Chinese folding fans. The scholar Annemarie Jordan Gschwend suggests that fans from East Asia began to enter European courts following the Portuguese passage through Malacca in 1511. See Johannes Beltz and Annemarie Jordan Gschwend, *Elfenbeine aus Ceylon: Luxusgüter für Katharina von Habsburg (1507–1578)* (Zürich: Museum Rietberg, 2010), 54.

29 The first to research from the perspective of European costume history seems to have been Natalis Rondot, *Rapport sur les objets de parure, de fantaisie et de goût* (Paris: Imprimerie impériale, 1854), 68–72. Rondot cites Fabri, *Diversarum nationum ornatus* (1591), but folding fans also appear in Cesare Vecellio's *Habiti Antichi, et Moderni di tutto il Mondo* (Venice, 1598 [1590]), Jean-Jacques Boissard's earlier *Habitus variarum orbis gentium* (Cologne, 1581), and even earlier in *Imperii ac sacerdotii ornatus* (Cologne, 1578). They do not, however, appear in François Desprez's earlier *Recueil de la diversité des habits qui sont de present en usage dans les pays d'Europe, Asie, Affrique et Isles sauvages* (Paris: Richard Breton, 1562), nor in Ferdinando Bertelli's *Omnium fere gentium nostrae aetatis habitus* (Venice, 1563). For a discussion of early costume histories, see Margaret F. Rosenthal and Ann Rosalind Jones, *The Clothing of the Renaissance World* (New York: Thames & Hudson, 2008), 15–20.

30 "Asie" here likely refers to West rather than East Asia.

31 Rosenthal and Jones, *Clothing of the Renaissance*, 15–16.

32 Vecellio, *Habiti Antichi*, 477. Although not reproduced in the figure, the text comments on the scimitar (*scimitarra*) and poignard (*pugnale*) carried by young Japanese men, and refers the reader to the hall of arms at the Council of Ten in Venice ("et tutte queste cosi si veggono nella sala delle armi del Conseglio de dieci nella Città di Venetta"). The text presumably refers to the two-sword set worn by samurai, comprised of the *uchigatana* and the *wakizashi*. As Wilson notes, despite the discursive fascination with Japanese dress, which led to extensive apperception and simile, few illustrations survive. See Bronwen Wilson, *The World in Venice: Print, the City, and Early Modern Identity* (Toronto: University of Toronto Press, 2005), 210–21.

33 Wilson, *World in Venice*, 210–21. For a detailed study of this visit vis-à-vis the history of cartography, see Giovanni Raneri, "Folding Screens, Cartography, and the Jesuit Mission in Japan, 1580–1614" (PhD diss., University of Manchester, 2015), especially chap. 2.

34 At least ninety publications covered their visit, with forty-eight appearing in the year 1585 alone. *Kokushi daijiten*, digital version (Tokyo: Yoshikawa Kōbunkan, 2010 [1979–1997]), s.v. "Tenshō ken'ō shisetsu."

35 Wilson, *World in Venice*, 220.

36 Ibid., 215.

37  They were advised to travel in European dress, carrying their Japanese dress
    with them for official functions. Ibid.

38  For a thorough treatment of this painting, see Paola Di Rico and Marino
    Vaginò, "'Don Mancio, Nephew of the King of Hizen': Echoes of the
    Japanese Tenshō Mission to Europe in 1585 in the Portrait of Sukemasu
    Itô by Domenico Tintoretto," in *Changing Hearts: Performing Jesuit Emotions
    between Europe, Asia, and the Americas*, ed. Yasmin Haskell and Raphaële Gar-
    rod (Leiden: Brill, 2019), 284–301. An inscription on the painting's back
    makes its subject clear.

39  *La com[m]une accoutre ala polonaise. Ung Capitaine de Japon*, December 1600.
    From the published journal of Olivier van Noort, 1601–2 (and/or 1646).
    Etching, ink on paper, 14.5 x 22.5 cm. Rijksmuseum, Amsterdam, https://
    www.rijksmuseum.nl/en/collection/RP-P-OB-75.407.

40  Period accounts of the Tenshō mission even compared their clothing to
    that of classical Roman costume – a temporal rather than a cultural dis-
    placement. See Wilson, *World in Venice*, 211. Fróis, too, compares Japanese
    women to the Spanish as regards the use of fans.

41  Lippit, "Southern Barbarian," 252.

42  See, for instance, Sofía Sanabrais, "From *Byōbu* to *Biombo*: The Transforma-
    tion of the Japanese Folding Screen in Colonial Mexico," *Art History* 38, no.
    4 (Sept. 2015): 779–91.

43  Her work on the topic has been extensive: Annemarie Jordan, "Exotic Re-
    naissance Accessories: Japanese, Indian, and Sinhalese Fans at the Courts
    of Portugal and Spain," *Apollo* 150 (1999), 25–35; Annemarie Jordan,
    *Retrato de Corte em Portugal: O Legado de António Moro (1552–1572)* (Lisbon:
    Quetzal Editores, 1994), 175–7; Annemarie Jordan Gschwend, "Los Prim-
    eros Abanicos Orientales de los Habsburgos," in *Oriente en Palacio: tesoros
    asiáticos en las colecciones reales españolas*, ed. Alfonso Mola Marina (Madrid:
    Palacio Real de Madrid, 2003), 267–71; Johannes Beltz and Annemarie
    Jordan Gschwend, *Elfenbeine aus Ceylon: Luxusgüter für Katharina von
    Habsburg (1507–1578)* (Zurich: Museum Rietberg, 2010); Annemarie Jor-
    dan Gschwend, "Antoine Trouvéon, un portraitiste de Leonor d'Autriche
    récemment découvert," *Revue de l'art* 159 (2008): 11–20.

44  For more on these activities, see Joanna Woodall, *Anthonis Mor: Art and Au-
    thority* (Zwolle: Waanders, 2007), 213ff.

45  Jordan Gschwend, "Los Primeros Abanicos Orientales," 269.

46  Beltz and Jordan Gschwend, *Elfenbeine aus Ceylon*, 105.

47  Ibid. A similar, posthumous portrait in the Kunsthistorisches Museum in
    Vienna likewise has her holding a folding fan, albeit in a different position.
    Jordan, *Retrato de Corte em Portugal*, 175–6.

48 Beltz and Jordan Gschwend, *Elfenbeine aus Ceylon*, 55 and 105. Following the 1552 visit of Bernardo, a Japanese Jesuit convert who was the first Japanese person to visit Europe, the use of fans further proliferated; see Beltz and Jordan Gschwend, *Elfenbeine aus Ceylon*, 55. See also Karina Corrigan, Jan van Campen, Femke Diercks, and Janet C. Blyberg, eds., *Asia in Amsterdam: The Culture of Luxury in the Golden Age* (Salem, MA: Peabody Essex Museum, 2015), 80.

49 Rondot purported that the French had introduced fan making to Spain. Rondot, *Rapport*, 101n1. Nevertheless, Thomas Coryat (1577–1617), author of *Coryat's Crudities* (1611), asserted that at the turn of the seventeenth century, the French were importing all of their fans from Italy and Spain. Ina Baghdiantz McCabe, *Orientalism in Early Modern France: Eurasian Trade, Exoticism, and the Ancien Régime* (Oxford: Berg, 2008), 252.

50 Jordan, "Exotic Renaissance Accessories," 26.

51 Casal notes that it was Catherine de Medici who introduced "folding-fans based on Sino-Japanese prototypes" to France following her marriage to Henry II in 1533. Casal, "Lore," 113. See also Nakamura, *Nihon no ōgi*; and Parr, "The Fan," 402–3. Indeed, this has long stood as the prevailing theory against which Jordan Gschwend argues. See especially Jordan, "Exotic Renaissance Accessories."

52 On the significance of the term "Indian" in early modern Europe and the pervasive "geographical indeterminacy," see Daniela Bleichmar, "The Cabinet and the World: Non-European Objects in Early Modern European Collections," *Journal of the History of Collections* 33, no. 3 (Nov. 2021): 435–45.

53 Beltz and Jordan Gschwend, *Elfenbeine aus Ceylon*, 54, 105.

54 Jordan Gschwend argues Asian fans were "the most important export article of the sixteenth century" for royal and aristocratic women. Ibid, 54. She notes that already before 1564, Catherine had expressly placed an order for some 178 Ryūkyūan fans. Catherine was in possession of the largest collection of East Asian luxury goods of her day, a situation that may have bearing on the greater gendering of East Asian artefacts in the European imagination. Beltz and Jordan Gschwend, *Elfenbeine aus Ceylon*, 53.

55 Charlotte von Verschuer, *Across the Perilous Sea: Japanese Trade with China and Korea from the Seventh to the Sixteenth Centuries*, trans. Kristen Lee Hunter (Ithaca: East Asia Program, Cornell University, 2006), 160. See also her excellent reading (160–8) of the political manoeuvring that allowed for Japan to exercise a favourable trade balance in East Asia prior to the arrival of the Portuguese and Spanish. Von Verschuer cites (73) the *Huang Chao Leiyuan*, book 60, which contains an anecdote suggesting Japanese fans were luxury

goods available for purchase on the open market in China as early as the late eleventh century.

56  Ibid., 159. For more on the missions, see Yi-T'ung Wang, *Official Relations Between China and Japan, 1368–1549* (Cambridge, MA: Harvard University Press, 1953).

57  The similarity with the situation in the nineteenth century is striking. Folding fans were not valued in China at first, being but odd novelties, but after the Yongle emperor (r. 1402–24) distributed them among his courtiers, they came into vogue throughout elite society. See Wang, *Official Relations,* 90ff.

58  According to the manifest of the 1433 mission, each fan was worth 300 *wen*, making its value equal to that of one *catty* of copper. Ibid.

59  As von Verschuer puts it, the Japanese were "vexing partners." The most egregious episode in this history was the embassy of 1523, now known as the Ningbo Incident. Extraordinary violence erupted when the rival Hosokawa-sponsored and Ōuchi-sponsored embassies landed in close succession. See von Verschuer, *Perilous Sea,* 144. For more on the tribute trade and the Ningbo Incident – especially in relation to piracy – see Peter D. Shapinsky, *Lords of the Sea: Pirates, Violence, and Commerce in Late Medieval Japan* (Ann Arbor, MI: Center for Japanese Studies, The University of Michigan, 2014), 206–18. As Shapinsky notes (21), violence itself was a commodity within this semi-piratic trade structure. For a reading of sixteenth-century trade in East Asia, see von Verschuer, *Perilous Sea,* 140–9.

60  Percival MacIver, *The Fan Book* (London: T.F. Unwin, 1920), 202. Cf. Casal, who argues that the Dutch and English did not actively import Japanese fans, but that Japan exported them "en masse" throughout East and Southeast Asia through its "Red-Seal Ships." Casal, "Lore," 114–5.

61  As evidence of how robust this market was, note the 342 Japanese fans (*abanos*) listed in a 1616 inventory of items left by the priest Manuel Barreto (1563–1620) in Macao – with export and domestic fans clearly distinguished. Carvalho and Castel-Branco, *Luis Frois,* 29.

62  For the grievance, see *The Case of the Fann-Makers Who Have Petitioned the Honorable House of Commons, against the Importation of Fanns from the East-Indies* (N.p., 1695; digitized by the University of Michigan Library). The Worshipful Company of Fan Makers was formally incorporated in 1709 and survives as a charitable trust. For a late-nineteenth-century history of the Company, see William Carew Hazlitt, *The Livery Companies of the City of London: Their Origin, Character, Development, and Social and Political Importance: with Two Coloured Plates and Numerous Illustrations* (London: Swan Sonnenschein, 1892), 478–80.

63 In the mid-nineteenth century it was estimated that eighteen to twenty persons were involved in the creation of a single French fan. Rondot, *Rapport*, 78–81.

64 J.B. da Silva, "Chinese Fans and the Porcelain Trade with the West," *Fans: Bulletin of the Fan Circle International* 19 (Autumn 1981): 21–6, cited in Bennett, *Unfolding Beauty*, 18.

65 For more on the issue of obliquity, see Janet W. Adams, "The Ornamental Background," in Michael Komanecky and Virginia Fabbri Butera, *The Folding Image: Screens by Western Artists of the Nineteenth and Twentieth Centuries* (New Haven: Yale University Art Gallery, 1984), 16.

66 Kazuko Mende, "Distortion in Pictorial Scenes on Japanese Fans," *Journal for Geometry and Graphics* 11 (2007): 93–103.

67 The most prominent example would be the *Senmen Hokekyō*, a ten-volume transcription of the Lotus Sūtra onto fan-shaped codices.

68 For the classic essay on the hypo-semiotic status of the ground, see Meyer Schapiro, "On Some Problems in the Semiotics of Visual Art," *Semiolus: Netherlands Quarterly for the History of Art* 6, no. 1 (1972): 10.

69 He describes the situation as follows: "the design is carried out in exactly the same way as it would have been if the material were always to remain tightly stretched. In use, however, the leaf, of whatever it is composed, is *not* flat, and besides the lines caused by the folds, there is also the play of light and shade which results from the plaits being always slightly contracted. The recognized convention, however, was to treat the decoration as if these lines and the folds were non-existent, and, as a rule, no attempt was made to take the bull by the horns and make them an interesting feature in the decoration, or at least to make them play an important, if subservient, part. The painter ignored them, and they retaliated by breaking up the composition of his best groups, and cutting across delicate painted figures." MacIver, *Fan Book*, 21.

70 The subject itself is noteworthy, as tanning was a profession reserved for outcasts in Japan.

71 Donald F. Lach, *Asia in the Making of Europe, Volume II: A Century of Wonder, Book 3* (Chicago: Chicago University Press, 1977), 446–89.

72 Pomponius Mela, *Cosmographia, sive De situ orbis. – Dionysius Periegetes. De situ orbis*, trans. Priscianus (Venice: Erhard Ratdolt, 1482).

73 Onoda, "Reception," 34.

74 For a discussion of Japan in Ortelius's cartography, see ibid., esp. 38–54. Abraham Ortelius, *Theatrvm orbis terrarvm* (Antwerp: Aegid. Coppenium Diesth, 1570).

75  Ortelius, *Tartaria siue magni chami imperivm*, in *Theatrvm orbis terrarvm*
    (Antwerp: Aegid. Coppenium Diesth, 1570). Codex atlas with hand-
    coloured maps, 43 cm high. Library of Congress, Geography and Map Divi-
    sion, https://www.loc.gov/resource/g3200m.gct00126/?sp=104.
76  Katherine Parker, "A Mind at Work, Urbano Monte's 60-Sheet Manuscript
    World Map" (La Jolla, CA: Barry Lawrence Ruderman Antique Maps, 2017),
    https://s3.amazonaws.com/rumsey3/Monte/Urbano+Monte+Catalog
    .pdf; see also "Largest Early World Map - Monte's 10 ft. Planisphere
    of 1587," https://www.davidrumsey.com/blog/2017/11/26/largest
    -early-world-map-monte-s-10-ft-planisphere-of-1587.
77  Urbano Monte, *Tavola nona, che ha sua superiore la tavola terza. Libro terzo*,
    from a manuscript of a planisphere wall map (approx. 3 m$^2$), 1587. Draw-
    ing, ink and pigments on paper, 40 x 51 cm. David Rumsey Historical Map
    Collection, Stanford University, https://www.davidrumsey.com/blog
    /2017/11/26/largest-early-world-map-monte-s-10-ft-planisphere-of-1587.
78  Parker, "A Mind at Work," 20. See also Marisa di Russo, ed, *Quando il Giap-
    pone scoprì l'Italia*, 60.
79  Parker, "Mind at Work," 20.
80  An extant Japanese fan purportedly once in the possession of Toyotomi Hid-
    eyohi (1537–1598) bears a map of East Asia on its surface; note, however,
    that although it is oriented with north on top, the lines of the fan converge
    at bottom, rather than on top. It is now in the collection of Osaka Castle.
81  Angelo Cattaneo, "The Mutual Emplacement of Japan and Europe During
    the Nanban Century," in Victoria Weston, ed., *Portugal, Jesuits and Japan:
    Spiritual Beliefs and Earthly Goods* (Boston: McMullen Museum of Art, 2013),
    27–35. As Loh stresses, European cartography did not predominate in
    Japan until the nineteenth century. Loh, "Worlds Collide," 58.
82  For more on *nanban* cartographic screens, see two recent dissertations: Ran-
    eri, "Folding Screens;" and Loh, "Worlds Collide."
83  Cattaneo, "Mutual Emplacement," 31. An interesting case study in this re-
    gard would be the landmark map designed by Matteo Ricci (1552–1610)
    in China, the *Complete Map of the Earth and Manifold Nations* (*Kunyu wanguo
    quantu*, 1602). Cited and discussed in Loh, "Worlds Collide," 190–1.
84  Lach, *Asia in the Making of Europe, Volume II: A Century of Wonder, Book 3*,
    463–4.
85  Raneri, "Folding Screens," chap. 2, especially 84–90. Note that the Tenshō
    mission returned with cartographic works, including Ortelius's *Theatrum*.
86  Franziska Ehmcke and Barbara Kaiser, eds., *Ōsaka zu byōbu: ein Stellschirm mit
    Ansichten der Burgstadt Ôsaka in Schloss Eggenberg* (Graz: Schloss Eggenberg,
    Universalmuseum Joanneum, 2010). For an English précis, see Barbara

Kaiser and Paul Schuster, *Schloss Eggenberg: Architecture and Furnishings* (Graz: Schloss Eggenberg, Universalmuseum Joanneum, 2016), 134–41.

87  The average quadrant diameter of 25 cm was comparable to that of fans. See Gerard L'E. Turner, *Scientific Instruments, 1500–1900: An Introduction* (London: Phillip Wilson, 1998), 29–30.

88  "Probably no Asian land was so frequently and thoroughly described in sixteenth-century European reports as Japan." Lach and Van Kley, *Asia in the Making of Europe, Volume III: A Century of Advance, Book Two: South Asia*, 1829.

89  Note, moreover, that paper was the material subtending this implicated interchange.

# chapter three

# From Textile to Text: Cloth, Slavery, and the Archive in the Dutch Atlantic

CARRIE ANDERSON

It is well known that the Dutch West India Company (WIC) played a key role in the inhumane transportation of enslaved people between Africa, South America, and North America. Often overlooked, however, is the fact that enslaved people were forced to travel with an abundance of essential commodities destined for the Dutch colonies and trading posts, including food, tools, and – importantly – textiles. The textiles carried on these ships ranged from coarse to fine, each serving a different purpose along the trans-Atlantic trade routes: blue-and-white loom-patterned textiles were traded for enslaved people on the African coast; European linens were presented as diplomatic gifts to various Indigenous groups in Dutch Brazil; and, of course, a wide range of textiles were made into clothing to be worn by inhabitants of the colonies, including the enslaved people who were forcibly brought there.

Understanding the relationship between the cloth, clothing, and people transported on Company ships is a particularly fraught task because textiles and enslaved human beings were both treated as commodities in WIC documents. In the case of textiles, inventories and cargo lists adhered to the semantic necessities of early modern accounting practices. Thus, textiles were typically grouped according to attributes like colour, pattern, size, or quality, rather than by the social value they may have had for a given consumer group. This method of accounting, in other words, was entirely dependent on the systematic translation of visible material characteristics into descriptive text. The same approach to record keeping was used to document the buying and selling of human beings. Values were assigned according to age, gender, and physical strength, without any concern for a person's internal system of beliefs, sociopolitical ideology, or ancestral past. In short, in Dutch West India Company cargo lists, textiles and enslaved human beings were distinguished only by their relative values, which were calculated according to observable, external qualities. These documents also demonstrate unequivocally that textiles travelled next to – but were not permitted to be worn by – the (often nude) enslaved people with whom they shared contiguous spaces in the hold.

As textiles and human beings moved between the disparate geographies of the early modern Atlantic world, they remained in a purely commodified state. But whereas archival records belie the sociability of people and things, images of clothed bodies reify their interconnectedness. Once absorbed into local sartorial systems, WIC textiles became highly charged social mediators that pointed to inequities within Dutch colonial territories, but also signalled independent systems of meaning operating beyond the purview of Company officials. Images of enslaved people wearing these textiles reveal the multivalent potential of clothing, for these images transform cloths from pure commodities into active social agents. This essay will reconsider the semantic and rhetorical mechanisms that describe the relationship between textiles and enslaved people in the documents and images pertaining to the Dutch Atlantic world. As I will demonstrate, there were both resonances and disparities between these texts and images – disjunctures that reveal the fragmented and uneasy connections between the textiles and enslaved people carried on Company ships.

### From Object to Archive: Textiles in the Dutch Atlantic World

In the Dutch Atlantic, textiles played a critical role in intercultural negotiations, where they were used to facilitate or encourage trade and to build diplomatic alliances. The following example is somewhat typical of how such negotiations proceeded. In 1701 Joan van Sevenhuysen, the Director-General on the Gold Coast from 1696 to 1702, sent WIC employee David van Nyendael (1667–1702) into Asante territory to create an alliance with Asante King Osei Kofi Tutu.[1] Nyendael and his envoy were sent with gifts and "extensive instructions on how to behave," the prescriptiveness of which suggests the importance of this diplomatic endeavour.[2] The gifts to be presented to Osei Tutu and his entourage included velvet and silk textiles, a large gilt mirror, a helmet, sheets of gold leather, and bottles of brandy.[3] After presenting the gifts, Nyendael was instructed to request permission to trade freely and without impediment in the region; he was also told to provide the king and his entourage with a list of the types of products – and their prices – that would be available through WIC merchants, which included *slaaplakens* (bedsheets) and other textiles, mirrors, knives, and beads, among other items.[4] The presentation of textiles not only constituted an important prerequisite to trade, therefore, but was also a critical element of the trade itself. Given the importance of textiles for trade in the Dutch Atlantic – especially on the western coast of Africa – merchants needed to ensure their ships were laden with an abundant supply and variety of this critical commodity.[5]

The textiles imported into Dutch-occupied regions reflected the global reach of the Dutch trading companies, which – over the course of the seventeenth and eighteenth centuries – circulated enormous quantities of textiles throughout the world, including Indian cottons; European woolens, linens, and velvet; and raw silk from Persia, to name only a few. But while the geographical origins of the textiles transported on Dutch ships reflected the breadth of the Republic's mercantile interests, the destinations and the uses of these textiles-in-transit were wholly determined by the local sartorial needs of their consumers in African and American markets. For example, Osnabruck – a coarsely woven linen – was preferred by the so-called Brasilianen, an Indigenous group in Brazil who were essential allies of the Dutch West India Company in their defence against the Portuguese. To maintain this critical alliance, the Dutch had to ensure the Brasilianen were well-stocked with linen, which they presented to them as both gifts and payment for their services in the Dutch militia.[6] Duffel, a coarse woollen European cloth, was preferred by Indigenous traders in New Netherland because it could be wrapped around the body like a garment during the day and used as a blanket at night.[7] *Slaaplakens* (bed sheets), which were reportedly incorporated into various ceremonies and everyday rituals on the west coast of Africa, were shipped in staggering numbers: between 1710 and 1715, for example, 187,476 pieces were sent on WIC ships to various locations on the African coast.[8] In addition, textiles procured in Asia by East India Company (VOC) ships were sent to Europe, repackaged, then loaded on WIC ships to be traded in Africa and the Americas. These included loom-patterned textiles made in India, such as guinea cloth (discussed below), which were especially popular on the western coast of Africa. Chintz also appears on WIC cargo lists, as does the occasional Japanese robe, demonstrating the wide range of textiles that found a market in Africa and the Americas.[9] The WIC also participated in the complex and competitive inter-African textile trading networks, especially between the Benin Kingdom and the Gold Coast, shipping 12,461 pieces of the

Benin cloth called *mouponoqua* to the Gold Coast between 1633 and 1634 and another 16,000 between 1644 and 1646.[10]

In the rich paper trail they have left in the archives, the textiles that were carried on WIC ships are quantified and priced according to their material attributes. This documentation is important because few of the textiles traded in the Dutch Atlantic during the seventeenth and eighteenth centuries survive today, making it hard to identify extant samples of some cloth types, especially those with names that are now obsolete.[11] One of the most valuable types of document when it comes to textiles is called a *factuur*, or invoice, an itemized list of goods describing the contents of a given ship, along with the person or entity who is owed money for the commodities listed. These documents list each textile, often with modifiers that count, describe, and price each type of cloth. Colour was perhaps the most frequent descriptive category used in these documents, with blue, green, red, and white fabrics making fairly frequent appearances.[12] Sometimes textile descriptions were further modified with indications of particular patterns, like striped or checkered.[13] Textiles might also be described by their origin, such as "Haarlem" or "Leiden," modifiers that must have been a clear indication of the cloth's physical properties for merchants at the time. For example, a ship called the *St. Marcus* that was headed towards the west coast of Africa in 1713 carried in its hull (among other items) 909 pieces of *nickanees* (a striped, loom-patterned cloth popular on the western coast), of which 320 pieces are described as "fine, Holland," 364 as "fine, English," and 325 as "coarse, Holland."[14] Though *nickanees* varied in quality, its ubiquitous presence in the WIC archives attests to its importance for African trade.[15] In another example, the textile's origin was used to indicate its authenticity (and thus price), as was the case with the 114 pieces of chintz carried by the WIC ship *Adrichem* in 1714, which were described as *inlandse* (native), presumably to distinguish them from the imitation chintz being produced in the Netherlands and England at the time.[16] Size is also an important metric of value in archival documents. Lengths were typically measured in ells or the more ambiguous "pieces" (the length of each piece would often depend on the textile type).[17] Textile modifiers might also correspond to tactile, material qualities, as when a textile was described as "fine" or "coarse," as seen above, attributes that were dependent on both the textile type and the density of its warp and weft.

Although the WIC archives are rich in basic adjectival textile descriptors, there is still a great deal that gets lost in the translation from object to text. For example, when a given textile is described as "blue," rarely is any indication given of its particular shade. One might also be left wondering what exactly a "striped" textile might have looked like. Were the stripes thin? Thick? Were they evenly spaced or irregular? Unless a swatch book was included in the records – which was not common until later in the eighteenth century – this information is rarely provided (see, for example, fig. 3.1). What is also left unwritten in the documents is any indication of the social significance of each textile type – either before or after it was loaded onto a Dutch ship – a consideration that certainly would have been beyond the scope or purpose of the *factuur*, the primary concern of which was to justify the values of the commodities itemized on its pages. But while a *factuur* would naturally exclude any consideration of a textile's social importance, it also draws attention to the state of latency that such documents prescribe, one in which an object's "social life" is temporarily suspended, trumped by its commodity status.[18]

A category of textile referred to as "guinea cloth" is pertinent here, as it exemplifies the rich web of social meaning that remains largely hidden by the semantic structure of the archives.[19] Guinea cloth was a broad term used to describe a variety of inexpensive loom-patterned, often (but not exclusively) striped or checked blue-and-white cotton textiles that were made in India and transported – via Europe – to the so-called Guinea Coast of Africa, where they were used to purchase enslaved people, among other commodities.[20] Although initially the term "guinea cloth" seems to have been an indication of its ultimate destination, by the eighteenth century it was being transported all over Europe, Asia, and the Americas.[21] In fact, blue-and-white cloths became so popular and so essential to trade that knock-offs were made: the Zeeland Archives in Middelburg houses a 1753 letter from a textile trader that included two types of blue-and-white cloths, one labelled *oostindische* – an indication of its "authentic," Asian provenance – and one labelled *nagemaakte*, or counterfeit.[22] The National Archives in The Hague also has a 1788 swatch book that features a number of loom-patterned blue-and-white cloths with characteristics similar to guinea cloth (fig. 3.1).[23]

For early modern Europeans, the association of blue-and-white cloth with people from the African continent was pervasive in both travel literature and art, representing a type of social categorization whereby textiles and geography were closely intertwined. An early seventeenth-century visitor to Senegal, for example, writes about seeing people wearing cotton robes "full of blue stripes, like feather bed tykes" – perhaps a pattern similar to the one represented on the bed in the background of Esaias Boursse's (1631–1672) painting *Interior with Woman Cooking*

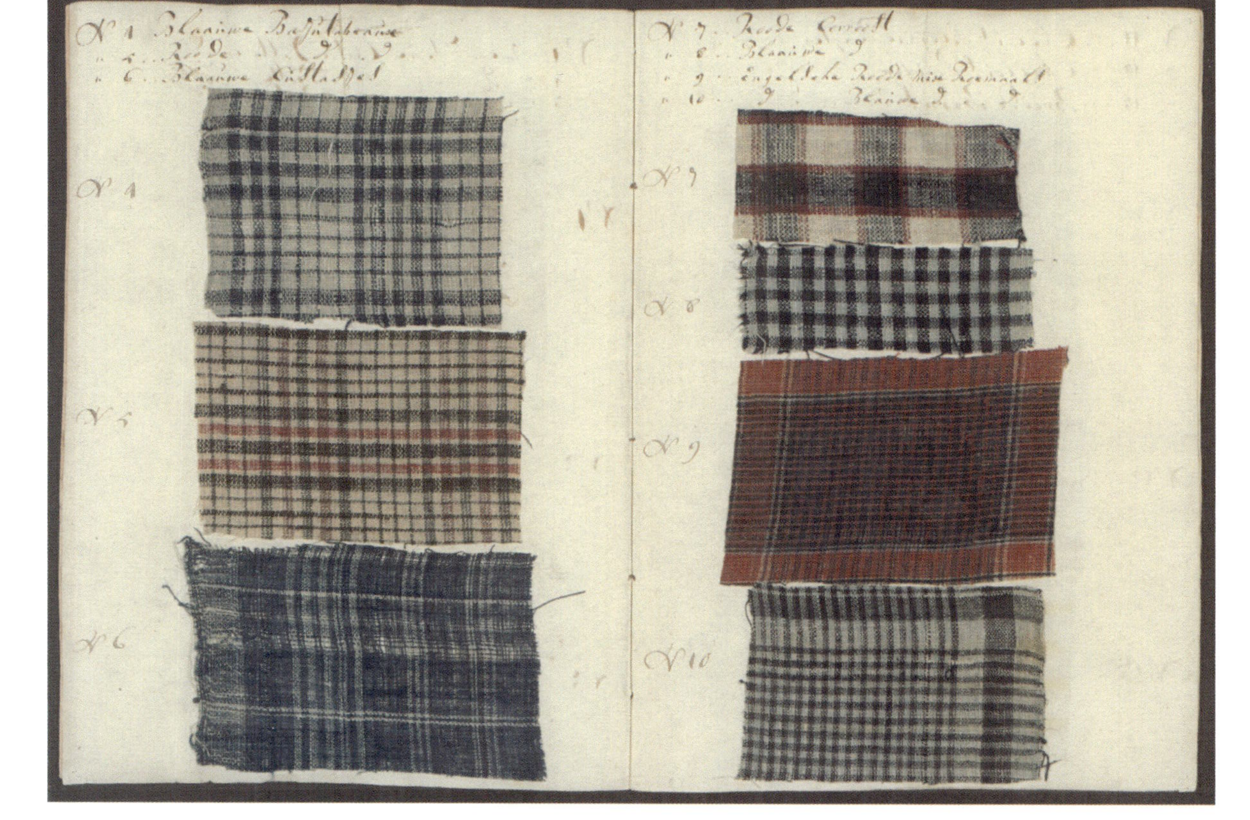

Figure 3.1. Fabric samples from the *Vrouwe Maria Geertruida*, 1788. Nationaal Archief, West India Company Archive, inv. no. 179

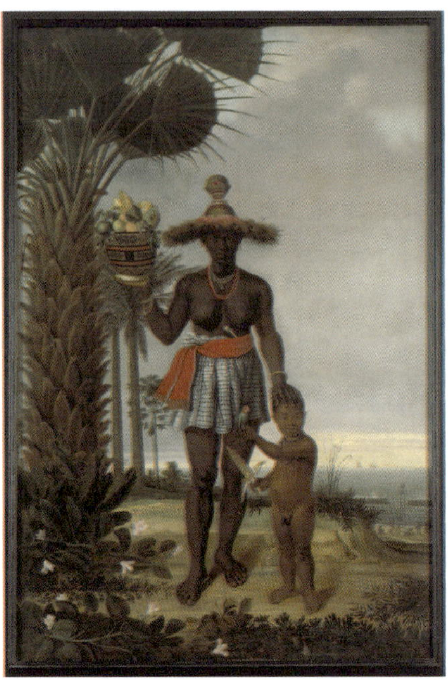

Figure 3.2. Albert Eckhout, *African Woman and Child,* 1641. Oil on canvas, 282 x 189 cm. Courtesy of National Museum of Denmark, Ethnographic Collections, Copenhagen

in the Wallace Collection.[24] Olfert Dapper (1636–1689), on the other hand, although he had certainly never been to Africa himself, nevertheless describes a blue-and-white cloth that was woven in Benin, and other visitors describe similar cloths.[25] Images of Dutch Brazil reinforce this association between blue-and-white cloth and Africa by the frequency with which enslaved Africans are depicted wearing blue-and-white striped garments. Albert Eckhout (1610–1655), the court painter to Governor-General Johan Maurits, painted a series of eight near-life-sized figures depicting people living in Brazil in relation to European notions of civility. Eckhout's *African Woman,* one of the paintings in this series, wears a blue-and-white striped skirt made of cloth with a pattern similar to ones in the swatch book in the National Archives (compare figs. 3.1 and 3.2).[26] The drawings of Zacharias Wagener (1614–1688), an amateur artist and WIC employee living in Brazil at the same time as

Eckhout, also show enslaved men and women dressed in blue-and-white cloth in a number of instances.[27]

As social mediators, however, textiles are nothing if not multivalent, and there is no reason why scholars should prioritize this Eurocentric reading of blue-and-white textiles. In a brilliant demonstration of this phenomenon, Cécile Fromont has shown how the Kongo elite "re-invented notions and expressions of prestige in the new Atlantic context" through the acquisition of foreign objects and textiles – especially blue-and-white textiles acquired through foreign trade.[28] As evidence, Fromont turns to a series of oil sketches by Eckhout, which picture five members of a Kongo embassy that visited Johan Maurits in Recife, Brazil.[29] One of these sketches carefully records a Kongo ambassador wearing a *zimpu* (hat/cap) decorated with shells; a foreign-made, dark wool mantle over his shoulders; and a red sash, animal pelt, and strip of imported blue-and-white fabric around his waist.[30] As Fromont demonstrates, the blue-and-white textile that comprises part of the regalia around the ambassador's waist resonated symbolically within this broader Atlantic context, for it could "signify access to foreign trade and links to European trade routes," but – significantly – it also worked in the service of local sartorial systems, which could "herald new notions of power."[31] Textiles, then, can shift easily between commodified and social states, positions that are contingent upon the rhetorical, iconographical, and cultural frameworks that bind them. In the sections that follow, I will continue to explore the ways in which archival, visual, and social modes of textile presentation in the Dutch Atlantic world resonated with one another, creating and reinforcing local systems of meaning.

**From Body to Archive: Describing Enslaved People in the WIC Archives**

As is well known, the Dutch West India Company played a significant role in the Atlantic slave trade.[32] Although the Dutch position on slavery may have been somewhat ambivalent at the beginning of the seventeenth century, this position changed dramatically once the WIC definitively wrestled the northeastern region of Brazil from the Portuguese in 1630. WIC officers and stakeholders were eager to profit from the sugar plantations established there by the Portuguese, but unable – or unwilling – to partake in the arduous and dangerous task of sugar cane harvesting and refinement. Under the leadership of governor-general Johan Maurits (1604–1679), however, the WIC soon became an active participant in the slave trade.[33] After taking control of the Portuguese fort at Elmina in 1637, the WIC fostered connections with local rulers along the coast from modern-day Ghana to Angola, ensuring that a steady supply of enslaved people was sent to the colonies in the Americas until the Company dissolved in 1740.[34] The WIC continued to keep meticulous records of all the commodities loaded onto its ships, which now included enslaved people. And, just as textiles were transformed into commodities when they became a part of the West India Company's financial records, so too were the hundreds of thousands of people who were purchased, inventoried, and transported from the west coast of Africa to the Americas.

When Dutch ships arrived on the West African coast, their first stop was often the fort at Elmina, where they would unload supplies. From there ships might stop at a number of other ports along the coast to trade for enslaved people and other sought-after commodities before heading across the Atlantic towards one of a number of ports in Brazil, Suriname, or Curaçao. The route and cargo of the ship *Leeuwinne* is representative of a typical journey: when the *Leeuwinne* arrived in Elmina, it carried in its hold a number of textiles – such as *kannekyns* (woven cloths produced in India for Asian and African markets) and *salempores* (cotton cloth, also made in India, varying widely in quality) – as well as other commodities like iron rods and red coral, which were popular trade items.[35] These commodities were delivered to Arend Jacobzoon Monfort, the Director-General at Elmina from 18 July 1639 to 6 January 1641. The ship then left Elmina, stopping in Ardra and then Calabar – trading for enslaved people along the way – before crossing the Atlantic, where 260 enslaved people would disembark in Pernambuco on 8 March 1641. In letters written by Jacobzoon and Dirck Geerlofsen, who was stationed in Ardra, the two men report the number of enslaved people transported on the *Leeuwinne*: 65 from Elmina, 150 from Ardra, and finally 101 from Calabar, of which 53 were men and 48 women, all between the ages of 20 and 30.[36] The archival modifiers assigned to this ship full of enslaved human beings are limited to age, gender, and port (not place) of origin. No attempts were made at recoding the names of the people being enslaved. The callous brevity of these descriptions – briefer even than those modifiers assigned to textiles – reveals how little these WIC officers cared about the lives and identities of the people they enslaved.

This descriptive brevity can perhaps be further contextualized as a consequence of the structure of the archival documents. As discussed above, the modifiers given to particular commodities in the documents were in large part a way of justifying their assigned value. In the case of textiles, this value may be obvious because of their material make-up (silk, for example), but more often modifiers such as "blue," "striped," "coarse" or "fine," for instance, would be an indicator of their market appeal (in the case of blue or striped) or their material refinement (coarse or fine). The semantic structures of the documents, in this case, are based on agreed-upon and fixed conditions of value that were expected to hold true for the duration of the sea voyage. In other words, value could be assigned at the point of departure for a textile because it was assumed that value would remain more or less constant for the duration of the journey, not accounting for unanticipated fluctuations in sale price, product appeal, or catastrophic losses at sea. For enslaved people, their "quality" was a reflection of their labour potential. This labour potential could not be assigned prior to their departure, since the inhumane conditions of the middle passage could result in severe illness, permanent disability, or death. For this reason, the widespread WIC practice of assigning value to commodities at the point of embarkation could not be maintained in the case of the slave trade, for value could only be determined by physical examination upon arrival at their intended port – after enduring the extreme hardships of the middle passage. Indeed, 51 enslaved people died on the *Leeuwinne* during the middle passage, giving the journey a mortality rate of 16 per cent.[37]

This commodification of human life is perhaps best understood in a drawing by Zacharias Wagener (1614–1668), part of a personal, unpublished account that documents the four-year period he spent in Dutch Brazil as a WIC employee and steward for Johan Maurits. This book, now housed in Dresden, includes 109 illustrations of life in the Dutch colony, including the flora, fauna, and people who lived there, some of which appear to be based on works by Albert Eckhout. The most interesting drawings in the book, however, are Wagener's own original conceptions, which include the drawing, "Pernambuco slave market" (fig. 3.3).

On the adjacent page, Wagener writes: "these poor people, half dead from hunger and thirst, are taken one by one, as if pigs or sheep leaving the pen, to be counted better; Portuguese and Dutch traders examine them in front and behind, if they are young or old, [if] they have scurvy, French disease or any other serious illness."[38] This description of the brutality of human trafficking is amplified by a detail in the middle ground, left of centre, which depicts a European man dressed in brown breeches, a doublet, and hat reaching out with his right hand to physically inspect the "quality" of the man who is being considered for

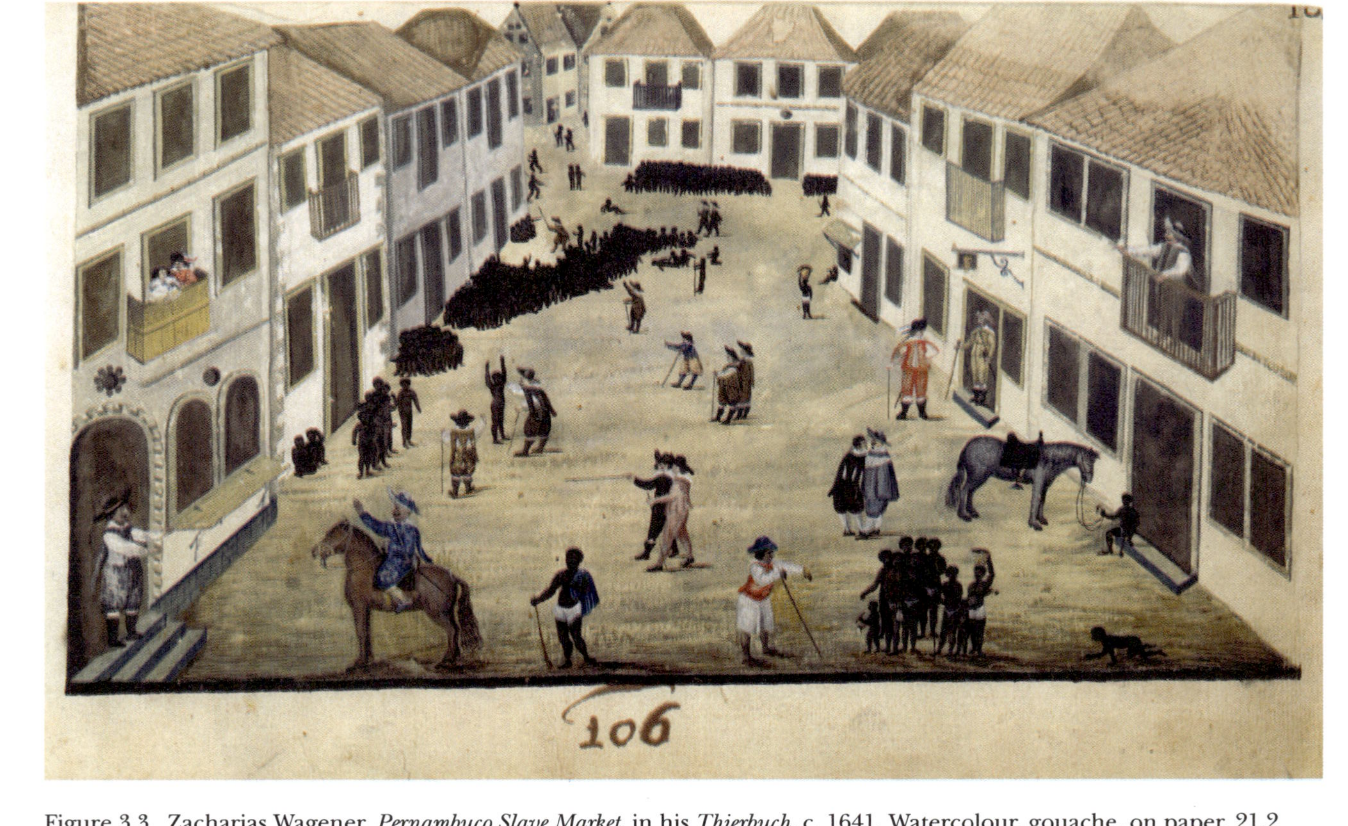

Figure 3.3. Zacharias Wagener, *Pernambuco Slave Market*, in his *Thierbuch*, c. 1641. Watercolour, gouache, on paper, 21.2 x 33.5 cm. Inv. Ca 226 a, leaf 106. Kupferstich-Kabinett, Dresden. Photo Credit: bpk Bildagentur/Dresden, Kupferstich-Kabinett/Herbert Boswank/Art Resource, NY

purchase. Of the many appalling scenes pictured in this drawing, this detail is perhaps the most heinous because it reduces human value to an external, observable condition – physical strength – thereby creating an equivalency between material objects and human life. But whereas the quality of a textile might be assessed through the close examination of the fabric's material composition, or the density of its warp and weft, the quality of a human life is here being assessed by the corporeal, organic make-up of muscle tissue.

Wagener's drawing is traditionally dated to 1641, although it is unclear if it pictures a particular "slave market" at which he was present or if it is an amalgamation of a number of such "markets." Sadly, in 1641 there would have been ample opportunity for Wagener to witness such events: in that year alone, five different ships carrying a total of 1,143 enslaved people were brought to Pernambuco from the African coast, although their final destinations are not always clear.[39] In fact, the *Leeuwinne*, discussed above, was one of the ships that arrived in Pernambuco in 1641, docking on 8 March. By 22 March 1641 – a short two weeks later – a *factuur* was written up documenting the sale of the *Leeuwinne*'s human cargo (fig. 3.4).[40]

In this *factuur*, any indication of origin or age has been removed, although gender is still recorded. The selling price is also recorded – calculated per person, although there is no explicit mention of how this per person price was determined. Instead of being grouped according to their port of origin – which, however rough, at least connected each person to some kind of geographical identity on paper – they are now grouped only by the name of the enslaver who purchased them.

In the extensive and meticulous records of the WIC, this change in the information recorded is merely a shift in document type: the *Leeuwinne*'s 1641 *factuur* is not a list of available commodities, as were the letters from Jacobsen and Geerlofsen; it is instead a list of commodities sold and money owed. But while this shift in document type may have simply been a matter of secretarial formality for WIC administrators, the regrouping of enslaved people as the anonymous possessions of named buyers clearly held significance far beyond the document's semantic structure and is indicative of widespread attitudes towards slavery. This semantic structure is also echoed, for example, in Wagener's drawing, which pictures African men and women huddled in groups overseen by a European enslaver, their identities indistinguishable beyond their association with the person who purchased them. Wagener's written comments suggest that he was appalled by the inhumane treatment of enslaved people

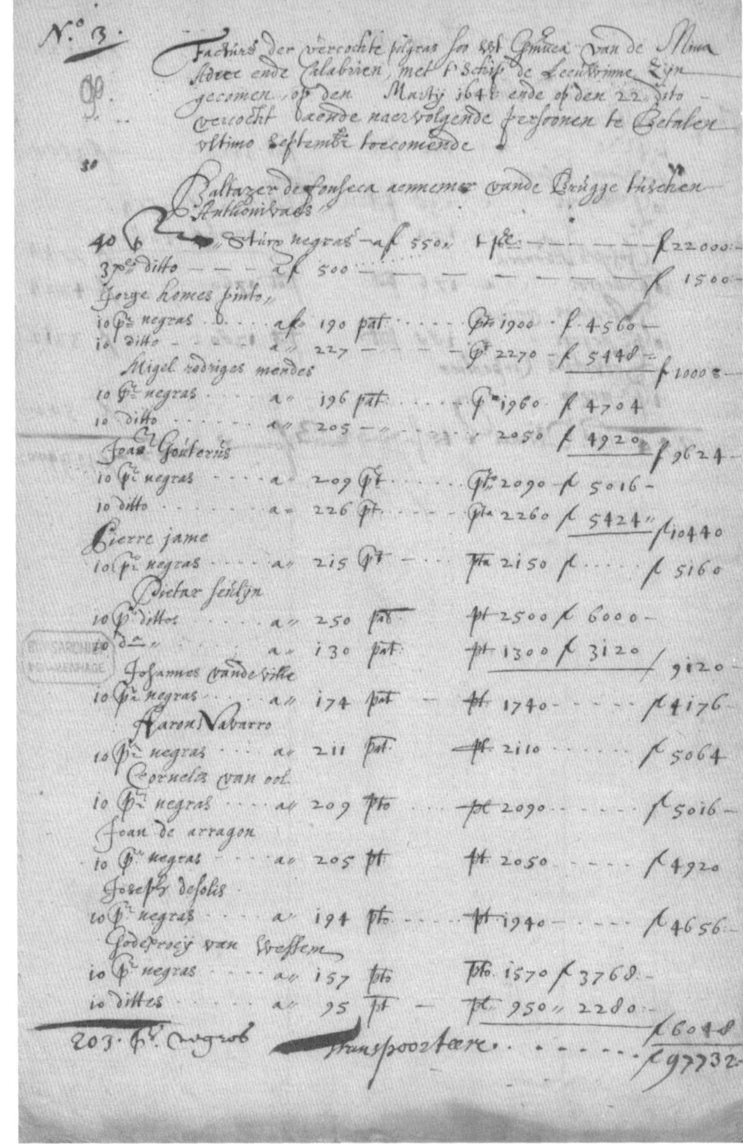

Figure 3.4. Invoice documenting the sale of enslaved people brought to Pernambuco on the WIC ship *Leeuwinne*, 22 March 1641. Nationaal Archief, West India Company Archive, inv. no. 56, doc. 90, page 1 of 2

brought to the Dutch colony. His drawing seems to confirm this, as it offers a scathing critique of the colony's enslavers by conforming to the organizational parameters of the *factuur*, which strips enslaved people of their identities and transforms them into commodities. The drawing, in other words, effectively pictures the cruelties of the slave trade by mirroring the semantic structure of the *factuur*.

Despite these semantic similarities, the reason Wagener's drawing is so striking is because it makes visible that which is absent from the *factuur*. Ann Laura Stoler has urged us to "distinguish between what was 'unwritten' because it could go without saying and 'everyone knew it,' and what was unwritten because it could not yet be articulated, and what was unwritten because it could not be said."[41] Using this model as a framework for understanding archival absence, it becomes clear what is not explicitly stated in the *Leeuwinne*'s 1641 *factuur*, but is pictured in Wagener's drawing: that the price of an enslaved person was determined by the observable, physical properties of the human body, like age, health, and physical strength. Yet, to borrow from Stoler's paradigm, this pricing system is "unwritten" not because it "could not yet be articulated" or because it "could not be said." On the contrary, enslavers frequently remarked that the physical health of the people they enslaved was a key determinate in price, as did for example Mathias Beck (d. 1668), vice-director of the WIC in Curaçao from 1655 to 1668, who wrote, in a 1660 letter sent from Curaçao, "I have received from Cabo Verde with the ship Den Gidion only 28 slaves, old and young, as per receipt issued to the skipper. Their condition and age make them almost worthless." Beck continues on, assuring the Council that the next shipment would be "healthy" and "would fetch a better price in proportion."[42] To our modern eyes, Wagener's horrific drawing makes visible what was left unsaid (but what was plainly understood) in the *factuur*.

**Contiguous Cloth: Textiles and the Slave Trade in New Netherland**

In the first two sections of this essay, I have demonstrated how the practice of assigning value to commodities was predicated upon external, observable variables that were easily translated into text. In documents related to Dutch Brazil, it becomes clear that this practice of assigning commodity values was applied to both human and non-human commodities, between which little distinction was made. By looking at archival documents alongside images from the period, such as Wagener's drawing of a slave market, we can see the resonances between image and text, but also the disparities – those aspects that were left unstated or were not pictured. In what follows I will shift my attention from Brazil to New Netherland, where – although on a lesser scale – enslaved people and other commodities procured by Dutch merchants were shipped from Curaçao, the Dutch colony that served as a central hub of the slave trade for both Dutch and Spanish colonies in the Americas. Although dependence on the labour of enslaved people was not as widespread in New Netherland as it was in Brazil – owing to the fact that the economy of the North American colony was in large part built around the acquisition of pelts rather than the labour-intensive harvesting of sugar or tobacco – there was nevertheless a persistent effort to bring enslaved people to the Dutch colony.[43] In the section that follows I will examine a group of documents that arrived in New Netherland in 1661 on the ship *Nieuw Nederlantse Indiaen*, a ship that carried both enslaved people and textiles in its hold.

As on the African and Brazilian coasts, textiles were an essential part of mercantile life in New Netherland, where they were necessary for survival in the colder temperatures, but also critical for merchants wanting to do business with Indigenous traders in the region, who desired a woollen cloth called duffel – in addition to beads made from shells, called wampum – in exchange for the beaver pelts sought by the settlers.[44] According to WIC secretary Isaack Rasière (1595–after 1654), who arrived in New Netherland in 1626, Indigenous traders valued duffel as a textile that could be used as clothing during the day and a blanket at night. It was with seeming frustration, then, that Rasière wrote to the Amsterdam Chamber of the WIC to complain about his perennially short supply of duffel cloth, which – he pressed – must be sent to him post haste, but only in the proper colours. Dark blues and grays were preferred, he wrote, whereas reds were refused by Indigenous hunters because the bright colour was a hindrance to hunting – a situation that was also undesirable to Dutch traders, who relied on indigenous hunters for beaver pelts.[45] Rasière's frustration becomes evident in his claim that, without the proper cloth, indigenous traders would retort, "Why should we go hunting? Half the time you have no cloth" – an ultimatum that makes clear the perceived importance of duffel for the acquisition of beaver pelts.

But while access to duffel cloth facilitated successful local trade, cloth and clothing were also essential for protecting colonists from the harsh North American winters. Archival documents indicate that large pieces of uncut cloth in a limited range of colours were sent to New Netherland to be made into clothing by tailors living in the Dutch colony.[46] Probate inventories also suggest that those who could afford it had more colourful sewn garments and other personal adornments sent from Europe, although this was rare.[47] More often clothing in the Dutch colony was somewhat drab – largely browns, blacks and, less often, blues – and eminently practical. Nevertheless, proper clothing was not just a concern for European colonists. Colonial administrators also recognized the need to clothe the enslaved people they forcibly shipped from the warmer climates of Curaçao to the much colder climes of New Netherland. For example, in 1659 Matthias Beck, vice-director of the WIC in Curaçao, wrote to Pieter Stuyvesant (1612–1672), the director-general of New Netherland between 1647 and 1664. Stuyvesant had previously requested that Beck send him "some fifteen or sixteen" slaves. Beck writes back, "They would have been able to come over now, but because we lack *groff* [coarse/heavy] cloth here with which to clothe them, we were afraid that they would not be able to survive during the winter." He continues by promising he will send slaves (and presumably the "coarse cloth" as well) in the spring and requests that Stuyvesant let him know in the meantime if he "will require any more ... and what ages and quantity your honour desires sent."[48]

About two years later, Beck seems to have made good on his promise to send both enslaved people and coarse fabric to Stuyvesant in New Netherland. An inventory carried on the *Nieuw Nederlantse Indiaen*, a ship captained by Dirck Jansen van Oldenburgh that left Curaçao for New Netherland on 21 July 1661, lists a number of documents carried on the ship: two letters (items 1 and 4, now lost), two receipts and an account (items 2, 6, and 7), a bond for an enslaved woman (item 3), and a manifest of the cloth loaded on the ship (item 5).[49] The receipt listed as item 2 is for 40 "healthy" enslaved people – fifteen men, fourteen women, six boys, and five girls – sent by Matthias Beck and intended for Pieter Stuyvesant.[50] Item 5 on this inventory of documents – the cloth manifest – also survives and its contents are telling: the first item listed is one chest containing 40 pieces of *pijlaken*, a coarse white woollen cloth (fig. 3.5).[51] This striking, exact correspondence between the number of *pijlaken* in chest 35 and the number of enslaved people on the ship was surely no coincidence.[52] These are most certainly the cloths that Beck had been unable to send when he wrote to Stuyvesant in August of 1659, but that now – two years later – he is at last able to provide.

The emotionless, secretarial precision of the inventory of documents juxtaposes human bodies and the cloth meant to protect them, each relegated to the status of itemized commodity. This callous form of accounting – justified, or so it seems, by the semantic structures of the

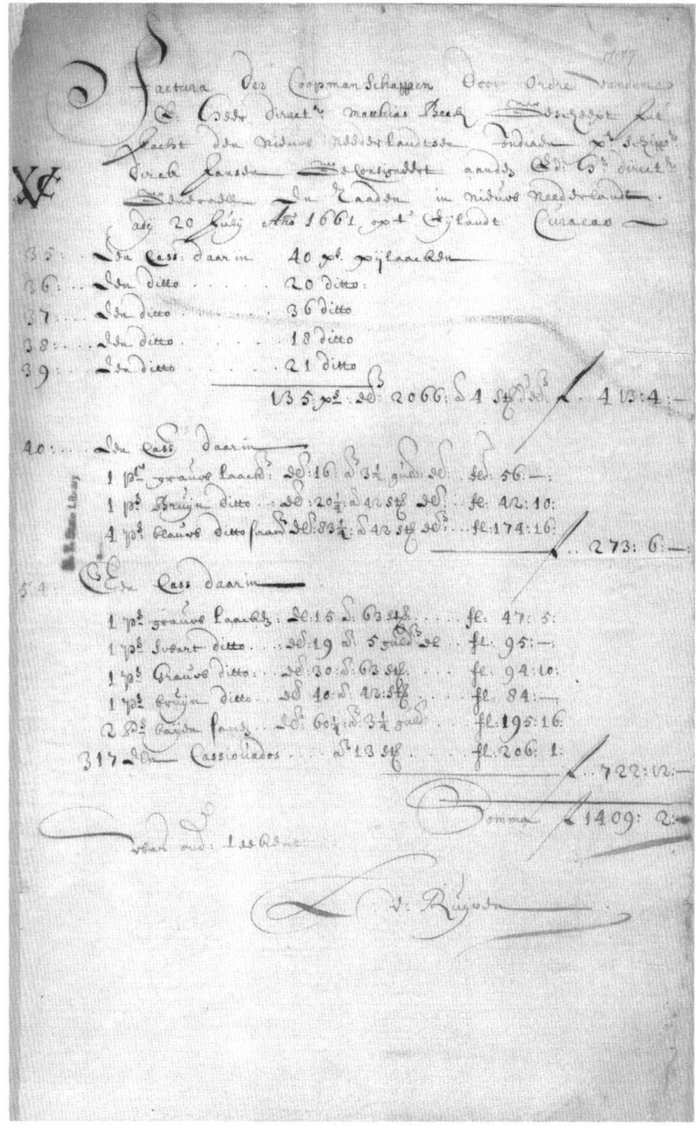

Figure 3.5.  Invoice of sundry cases of cloth shipped from Curaçao to New Netherland with bill of lading, 20 July 1661. New York State Archives. New York (Colony). Council. Curaçao records, 1640–65. Series A1883–78. Volume 17, document 77

document – treats all commodities equally. But the harsh contiguousness of this inventory of documents was not relegated to a page in an account book. Company ships regularly carried enslaved people and supplies – including cloth and food provisions – in discrete sections of WIC ships during transportation.[53] Cloth or clothing – even if intended to be worn by the enslaved people carried on the ship if/once they reached the destination – would be withheld from them until it was purchased by their future enslavers. In fact, most enslaved people were purposefully stripped of their clothing before they boarded Company ships, a practice attested to by many contemporary witnesses. For instance, Willem Bosman, WIC employee and author of *Nauwkeurige beschrijving van de Goud- Tand- en Slavekust* (*An accurate description of the Guinean Gold, Ivory and Slave Coast*), reported that before enslaved people were forced to board the European ships that would take them across the Atlantic "their masters [would] strip them of all they have on their backs; so that they come aboard stark naked, as well women as men."[54] The stripping of clothing, Robert DuPlessis has argued, was a "symbolic measure" intended to signal their new status as enslaved people before they crossed the Atlantic, a visual signifier that would be reinforced by the way in which their nudity subjugated them to their enslavers.[55] We can return to Zacharias Wagener's contemporary visual account to confirm this: throughout his "Pernambuco Slave Market," groups of recently transported Africans huddle together – naked, sick, and dying – as they wait to be inspected and purchased (fig. 3.3). Although Wagener's text does not explicitly mention their nudity, the image leaves little room for interpretation – despite the fact that Wagener has clothed a few people in the foreground, a concession I suspect was motivated more by issues of decorum than documentation.

The separation of enslaved Africans from the cloth that is so persistent in the cargo lists is echoed loudly in Wagener's drawing, where a visual distinction is made between European colonizers and the people they were enslaving: whereas the European men pictured here are distinguished by their different types of dress – different colours or styles of breeches, capes, hats, and boots – the nameless, enslaved Africans in this outdoor space become homogenized by their nearly uniform nudity. Not only are they stripped of their clothing, but they are denied the identities that are signified through clothing. Returning to the inventory of documents and the cloth manifest from the *Nieuw Nederlantse Indiaen,* we are reminded that not only were the 40 enslaved people on this ship separated from the 40 pieces of *pijlaken* that were likely earmarked for them, but that this "coarse cloth" was also separated from the cloth that was intended for the residents of New Netherland. In contrast to the plain white *pijlaken* in chests 35–9, for example, chests 40 and 54 comprise a broader range of colours, including grey, brown, blue, and black. The textiles in chests 40 and 54 are also considerably more expensive. Whereas *pijlaken* are uniformly listed at 4 *stuivers* per ell, which is very inexpensive, the average price per ell of the textiles in chests 40 and 54 is about 55 *stuivers* per ell – reaching as high as 5 *guilders* per ell. Thus, it was both the cost of the cloths as well as their appearance that created and reinforced social and cultural differences in the minds of enslavers, creating hierarchies that existed in the colonies, including New Amsterdam, as well as in the documents.

Robert DuPlessis has shown that enslaved people have consistently been the subject of a number of sumptuary practices aimed at visually differentiating them from free people and that "incomplete corporeal concealment" was a means of signalling their lower status in colonial society.[56] In the Americas the cloth designated for enslaved people was relatively consistent over time – usually inexpensive coarse woollens or linens. These fabrics, typically supplied by the enslaver, would be made into two garments: a loose-fitting jacket, and breeches or a skirt.[57] Just as the stripping of clothing enacted a "symbolic measure" before an enslaved person was forced across the Atlantic, so too was their "re-dressing" a symbolic act meant to underline their status as enslaved.[58] Thus, it was both the materiality of the garments and the act of "re-dressing" that created difference for European enslavers. Wagener's drawing of a "slave market" again serves to illustrate this practice: in the foreground, a lone figure follows behind a European man wearing a blue garment with a white collar, topped by a white hat with a blue ribbon, and riding a brown horse. Dressed only in a loincloth, the man who follows behind this elegantly dressed figure drapes a length of blue-and-white striped fabric over his shoulder – a piece of cloth that was presumably acquired by the man on the horse in order to dress the enslaved man he has just purchased (fig. 3.6).

Though they were kept separate in their journey across the Atlantic, this enslaved man and this piece of cloth – both commodities in the eyes of the West India Company – are brought together in Wagener's drawing. That both this man and this blue-and-white cloth were purchased at this "market" offers a brutal reminder of the fraught entanglements between the products of human creation – textiles – and the gross cruelty of human practices – the Atlantic slave trade.

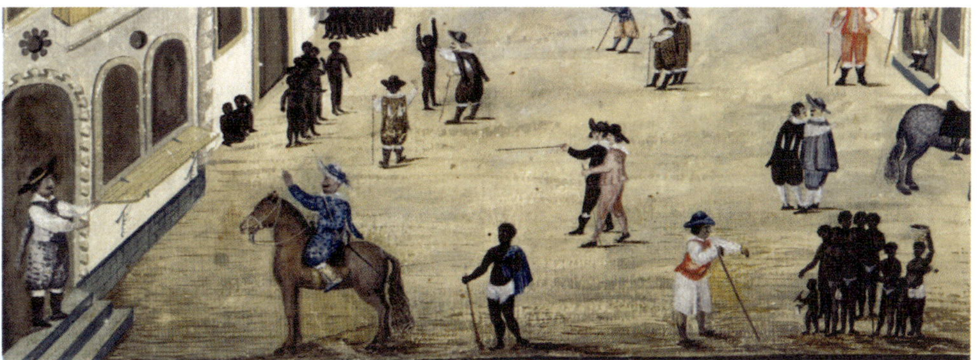

Figure 3.6. Zacharias Wagener, *Pernambuco Slave Market* (fig. 3.3)

## Conclusion

One of the aims of this essay has been to draw attention to the ways in which the semantic structures of WIC archival documents were closely entangled with the rhetorical conventions of images representing enslaved Africans living in the Dutch colonies. Stoler has argued that colonial governing systems were "prolific producers of social categories" and that "colonial archival documents serve less as stories for a colonial history than as active, generative substances with histories, as documents with itineraries of their own."[59] Along the same lines, I have demonstrated in this essay that WIC administrators were likewise "prolific producers" of commodity categories, the itineraries of which both reflected and contributed to broader social paradigms. In the case of textiles, this commodification disassociated textiles from the social practices they mediated. But in the context of the Atlantic slave trade, the act of identifying a human being as a commodity in the archival record had dire consequences, for it reinforced and generated enormous asymmetries of power while matter-of-factly justifying the atrocities of the slave trade on economic grounds.

The commodity categories that were cultivated in the West India Company's documentation were repeated and reasserted in visual media, often manifesting in the "incomplete corporeal concealment" so often seen in images of enslaved people living in the Dutch colonies. Although I have focused largely on Wagener's "Pernambuco slave market" in this essay, this type of sartorial signalling is ubiquitous in images of the Dutch colonies, including many of Frans Post's landscape paintings and drawings, Eckhout's *African Woman*, and Dirck Valkenburg's *Ritual Slave Party on Sugar Plantation in Surinam* (1706–8), to name only a few. As these images suggest, in the regions of the Dutch Atlantic where slavery was legal – Brazil, New Netherland, Curaçao, Suriname – enslaved people are shown, almost without exception, as partially clothed in contrast to their fully dressed European counterparts. For the European audiences for whom these images were intended, these sartorial impositions stand in marked contrast to the images of free Black people living in the Netherlands – where slavery was illegal – whose bodies were fully covered in clothing that corresponded to their (low) economic status, rather than their Blackness – however linked these two categories may have been.[60] This disparity of dress reinforced a system that justified the legality of slavery in the Dutch colonies, while simultaneously denying the gross inequities suffered by Black people living in the Dutch Republic in the early modern period. As I hope to have shown, these images were part of a larger systemic practice, the semantic and rhetorical conventions of which implicitly and explicitly justified the administrative authority and governing ideology of those in power.

## NOTES

1  On this mission, see Henk den Heijer, "David van Nyendael: the first European Envoy to the Court of Ashanti," in *Merchants, Missionaries & Migrants. 300 Years of Dutch-Ghanian Relations*, ed. W.M.J. Van Kessel (Amsterdam: KIT Publishers, 2002), 41–9; A. van Dantzig, compiler and trans., *The Dutch and the Guinea Coast, 1674–1742. A Collection of Documents from the General State Archive at the Hague* (Accra: GAAS, 1978), esp. 74–80. Van Nyendael was the first of thirteen Dutch envoys to visit the Asantehene court, who also sent its own envoys to the fort at Elmina. M.R. Doormont, "An Overview of Dutch Relations on the Gold Coast in light of David van Nyendael's Mission to Ashanti in 1701–02," in Van Kessel, *Merchants, Missionaries & Migrants*, 20.

2  Dantzig, 75. In another example, a WIC officer describes in a 1733 journal entry a ceremonial meeting that took place between the author and the King of Dahomey in the latter's palace. The king arrived at the meeting wearing fine European clothing, changing multiple times throughout the interaction into other European garments, all of which were likely

presented to him as gifts from European merchants. For a description of the encounter, see Dantzig, 296–7. See also Colleen Kriger, *Cloth in West African History* (Lanham: AltaMira Press, 2006), 35.

3 Dantzig, 79–80.

4 Ibid., 76–7.

5 Henk den Heijer, *Goud, ivoor en slaven. Scheepvaart en handel van de Tweede Westindische Compagnie op Afrika, 1674–1740* (Zutphen: Walburg, 1997), 114. Den Heijer estimates that textiles made up 50.6 per cent of the value of the commodities imported to Africa on Dutch ships between 1700 and 1724.

6 For more on WIC gifts of linen to the Brasilianen, see Carrie Anderson, "Mapping Colonial Interdependencies: European linen and Brasilianen Identity," *Artl@s Bulletin* 7, no. 2 (2018): 56–70.

7 Jaap Jacobs, *The Colony of New Netherland. A Dutch Settlement in Seventeenth-Century America* (Ithaca, NY: Cornell University Press, 2009), 137. This information is according to WIC employee Isaac de Raière; see discussion below.

8 Stanley B. Alpern, "What Africans got for their Slaves: A Master List of European Trade Goods," *History in Africa* 22 (1995): 11.

9 See, for example, National Archives, The Hague (NA) 1.05.01.02, inv. no. 1295, for a 1714 cargo list that includes two Japanese robes ("Japonese rokken") and 250 pieces of chintz.

10 F.C. Ryder, *Benin and the Europeans, 1485–1897* (London: Longmans, 1969), 93. According to Ryder, the English, who were posted in Arbo and Ughoton along with the Dutch – trading outposts outside of, but regulated by, Benin – purchased Benin textiles in even larger quantities. On the pre-existing inter-African trade routes with which Europeans became involved, see also Kwame Yeboa Daaku, *Trade and Politics on the Gold Coast, 1600–1720* (Oxford: Clarendon Press, 1970), 3, 6–7, 24, 39–40.

11 This scholarly problem provided the impetus for the digital project, "Visualizing Textile Circulation in the Dutch Global Market, 1602–1795," co-led by Carrie Anderson and Marsely Kehoe (http://dutchtextiletrade.org).

12 The following observations are drawn from the *factuurs* of the ships sailing between the Netherlands and the African coast between 1710 and 1715, which are housed in the National Archives in The Hague (NA 1.05.01.02, inv. nos. 1291 through 1296).

13 It is worth noting, of course, that colour preferences varied widely according to local markets. The brightly coloured textiles that were popular on the African coast would not have passed muster in the North American colony of New Netherland, where more subdued colours like brown and grey were preferred by Indigenous hunters, as will be discussed below.

14  NA 1.05.01.02, inv. no. 1294: "fine holl," "fyne Engelse," and "grove holl." The *St. Marcus* left from Texel on 1 January 1713, and stopped in Whydah on the African Coast before leaving for Curaçao. For more information on this ship's journey from Whydah to Curaçao, see also the slave voyages database (slavevoyages.org). Definitions of *nickanees* cloth vary, but most agree that it was a type of cloth that was critical for success in the slave trade.

15  For contemporary definitions of *nickanees*, see Alpern, "What Africans Got for Their Slaves," 7; John Irwin and P.R. Schwartz, *Studies in Indo-European Textile History* (Ahmedabad India: Calico Museum of Textile, 1966), 69; K.N. Chaudhuri, *The Trading World of Asia and the East India Company, 1660–1760* (Cambridge, UK: Cambridge University Press, 1978), 501. Interestingly, although many scholars identify *nickanees* as a textile produced in Gujarat, this example suggests that imitations were also made in Europe.

16  On the imitation of Asian textiles in Europe, see Melinda Watt, "'Whims and Fancies.' Europeans Respond to Textiles from the East," in *Interwoven Globe: The Worldwide Textile Trade, 1500–1800*, ed. Amelia Peck (New York: Yale University Press, 2013), 82–103.

17  The length of an ell varies somewhat but is approximately 69 cm, or 27 inches.

18  Arjun Appadurai, *The Social Life of Things: Commodities in Cultural Perspective* (Cambridge, UK: Cambridge University Press, 1986).

19  In the archival records, guinea cloths are typically listed as "guinees" or "guinea-stoff."

20  See Kriger, *Cloth in West African History*; see also Kriger, "'Guinea Cloth': Production and Consumption of Cotton Textiles in West Africa before and during the Atlantic Slave Trade," in *Spinning World: A Global History of Cotton Textiles, 1200–1850*, ed. Giorgio Riello and Prasannan Parthasarathi (Delhi: Primus Books, 2012), 105–26.

21  Irwin and Schwartz, *Studies in Indo-European Textile History*, 65. Liza Oliver has shown how guinea cloth also came to be fashionable in elite European markets in the late seventeenth and eighteenth centuries in her fascinating study, *Art, Trade, and Imperialism in Early Modern French India* (Amsterdam: Amsterdam University Press, 2019), 74–91. Guinea cloths are also listed in many cargo lists of Dutch WIC ships headed to Africa. See, for example, NA 1.05.01.02, inv. no. 1293. To complicate matters further, there are many other textiles that have been categorized by modern scholars as a *type* of guinea cloth, making it difficult to know how to differentiate between them.

22  Zeeland archives, Middelburgsche Commercie Compagnie (MCC) archive, inv. no. 70.7. Thank you to Jun Nakamura for bringing this example to my

attention. For additional information, including samples of the textiles aboard the *Unity*, an MCC slave ship, see https://eenigheid.slavenhandelmcc .nl/trajecten-van-de-reis-en/afrika-en/samenstelling-cargazoen/textiel -slavenhandel/?lang=en.

23 NA 1.05.01.02, inv. no. 179.

24 Quoted in P.J.P. Whitehead and M. Boseman, *A portrait of Dutch 17th century Brazil: Animals, plants, and people by the artists of Johan Maurits of Nassau* (Amsterdam: North-Holland, 1989), 74. Original quotation from S. Purchas, *Purchas his Pilgrims* [...] (London, 1625). A "tyck" or "tike" is a mattress case, often made of blue-striped linen. Thank you to Marsely Kehoe for bringing the Boursse painting to my attention: https://wallacelive.wallace collection.org/eMP/eMuseumPlus?service=ExternalInterface&module =collection&objectId=65100&viewType=detailView.

25 Ryder, 93–4. Olfert Dapper's *Naukeurige Beschrijvinge der Africaensche Gewester* (*Accurate Description of the Regions of Africa*) (1668), which is based on the texts of earlier authors – especially Pieter de Marees – is an important source for Benin, but one that should be treated cautiously. On Dapper, see Adam Jones, "Decompiling Dapper: A Preliminary Search for Evidence," *History in Africa* 17 (1990): 171–209; and Elizabeth Sutton, *Early Modern Dutch Prints of Africa* (Routledge, 2017), 115–7.

26 Rebecca Brienen has convincingly argued that Eckhout's *African Woman* represents an enslaved woman in Brazil, whereas his *African Man* pictures a slave trader from the Gold Coast. Brienen, *Visions of Savage Paradise: Albert Eckhout, Court Painter in Colonial Dutch Brazil* (Amsterdam: Amsterdam University Press, 2006), 133–54.

27 In addition to his sketches after Eckhout's *African Man* and *African Woman*, Wagener also pictures blue-and-white-striped garments in at least three other drawings from his *Thierbuch*.

28 Cécile Fromont, *The Art of Conversion. Christian Visual Culture in the Kingdom of Kongo* (Chapel Hill: University of North Carolina Press, 2014), chap. 3.

29 These oil sketches are from the *Libri Picturati* in the Jagiellonian Library, Krakow, A 34, fols. 1, 3, 5, 9, 11.

30 Fromont, 116–21. *Libri Picturati* 34, fol. 3r.

31 Fromont, 136.

32 On the Dutch involvement in the slave trade, see, most recently, *Slavery: The Story of João, Wally, Oopjen, Paulus, Van Bengalen, Surapati, Sapali, Tula, Dirk, Lohkay*, ed. E. Sint Nicolaas and V. Smeulders (Amsterdam: Atlas Contact, 2021). See also Johannes Postma, *The Dutch in the Atlantic Slave Trade 1600–1815* (Cambridge, UK: Cambridge University Press, 1990); Charles Boxer, *The Dutch in Brazil, 1624–1654* (Oxford: Oxford University Press, 1957).

33  On Johan Maurits and his critical role in initiating Dutch participation
    in the slave trade see, most recently, Elmer Kolfin, "Black in the Art of
    Rembrandt's Time," in *Black in Rembrandt's Time* (Amsterdam: WBOOKS
    Zwolle/Museum Het Rembrandthuis, 2020), 12–37. See also see L. van der
    Vinde, ed., *Shifting Image: In search of Johan Maurits* (The Hague: Maurit-
    shuis; Zwolle: Waanders, 2019); and Carolina Monteiro and Erik Odegard,
    "Slavery at the Court of the 'Humanist Prince.' Reexamining Johan Maurits
    van Nassau-Siegen and his Role in Slavery, Slave Trade and Slave-smuggling
    in Dutch Brazil," *Journal of Early American History* 10, no. 1 (2020): 3–32.

34  There were two iterations of the Dutch West India Company: the first com-
    pany lasted from 1621 to 1674, the second from 1674 to 1740.

35  Although definitions for these two types of cloth vary widely according to
    contemporary secondary sources, their repeated presence in WIC cargo
    lists headed to the African coast suggests their perceived importance for
    trade there.

36  NA 1.05.01.01, inv. no. 56, doc. 134.

37  This statistic is from the slavevoyages.org database.

38  Transcribed and translated in C. Ferrao and J.P. Soares, eds., *Dutch Brazil,
    The "Thierbuch" and "Autobiography" of Zacharias Wagener*, vol. 2, trans. D.H.
    Treece and R. Trewinnard (Rio de Janeiro: Editora Index, 1997), 195.

39  These statistics are based on the slavevoyages.org database. The names of
    the five ships (all Dutch) are followed parenthetically by the number of
    enslaved people who arrived in Pernambuco: *Wapen van Delft* (315), the
    *Zwarte Arend* (238), *Amersfoort* (249), *Leeuwinne* (265), and *Orpheus* (76).
    These numbers indicate the enslaved people who *arrived* in Pernambuco in
    1641; 252 people died on the middle passage, which is a collective mortality
    rate of 22 per cent.

40  NA 1.05.01.01, inv. no. 56, doc. 90.

41  Ann Laura Stoler, *Along the Archival Grain* (Princeton: Princeton University
    Press, 2009), 3.

42  New York State Archives, Curaçao records, 1640–65. Series A1883–78.
    Vol. 17, doc. 57.

43  On New Netherland and slavery, see Jaap Jacobs, *The Colony of New Nether-
    land. A Dutch Settlement in Seventeenth-Century America* (Ithaca, NY: Cornell
    University Press, 2009), especially 55–6 and 202–6. Jacobs estimates that by
    1664 enslaved people made up between 6 to 8 per cent of the population
    in the colony at large, with New Amsterdam having a higher percentage,
    around 10 to 17 per cent. Jacobs, 55.

44  On "Dutch-Indian" trade in New Netherland, see Jacobs, especially chap. 4.

45  Letter from Isaack Rasière to the Amsterdam Chamber of the West India
    Company, 23 September 1626. Document F in *Documents related to New*

*Netherlands 1624–1626 in the Henry E. Huntington Library*, trans. and ed. A.J.F Van Laer (San Marino, CA: The Henry E. Huntington Library and Art Gallery, 1924), 224–31.

46 New York State Archives, Curaçao records, 1640–65. Series A1883–78. Vol. 17, doc. 77.

47 For probate inventories, see Jacobs, 219–20.

48 New York State Archives, Curaçao records, 1640–65. Vol. 17, doc. 41.

49 New York State Archives. Curaçao records, 1640–65. Series A1883–78. Vol. 17, doc. 71.

50 This receipt remains: New York State Archives. Curaçao records, 1640–65. Series A1883–78. Vol. 17, doc. 73.

51 New York State Archives. Curaçao records, 1640–65. Vol. 17, doc. 77. Since enslavers were required to clothe the people they enslaved, these 40 pieces of *pijlaken* were probably offered to Stuyvesant for purchase. The additional *pijlaken* (in chests 36–39) would likely have been made available to other enslavers, who might have needed to replace old or worn garments.

52 On the Cape Colony – where winters could be cold – *pijlaken* were typically used to construct the outer fabric for doublets made specifically for enslaved people, so it comes as no surprise to see it imported into New Netherland as well. Miki Sugiura, "Garments in Circulation. The Economies of Slave Clothing in the Eighteenth-Century Dutch Cape Colony," in *Dressing Global Bodies. The Political Power of Dress in World History*, ed. Beverly Lemire and Giorgio Riello (London: Routledge, 2020), 115.

53 For a 3D reconstruction of the Middelburgsche Commercie Compagnie slave ship, the *Unity*, see the online "Slave Trader" exhibition developed by the Zeeland Archives: https://www.zeeuwsarchief.nl/en/agenda/slave-trader/. This reconstruction shows how enslaved people and other provisions were held in different compartments on the ship.

54 Willem Bosman, *A New and Accurate Description of the Coast of Guinea. Divided into the Gold, The Slave, and The Ivory Coasts* (London: Printed for J. Knapton, et al., 1705), 364a. Bosman was a WIC employee, working his way up to the position of Chief Factor by 1698. For more biographical information on Bosman, see Sutton, *Early Modern Dutch Prints of Africa*, especially chap. 7, which deals with Bosman and other authors who borrowed from Pieter de Marees's earlier text, *Beschryvinghe ende Historische verhael van het Gout Koninkrijk van Gunea anders de Gout-cust de Mina genaemt … (Descriptions and historical account of the Gold Kingdom of Guinea, otherwise known as the Gold Coast of Mina …)* (1602). On the nudity of enslaved people on the Middle Passage – from accounts of both enslaved African and European eyewitnesses – see Jermone Handler, "The Middle Passage and the Material Culture of Captive Africans," *Slavery and Abolition* 30, no. 1

(2009): esp. 2–4. On occasion, it seems that some enslaved people were provided scant covering for the Middle Passage. Ryder, *Benin and the Europeans*, 37, 64.

55  Robert DuPlessis, *The Material Atlantic: Clothing, Commerce, and Colonization in the Atlantic World, 1650–1800* (Cambridge, UK: Cambridge University Press, 2016), 130.

56  Robert DuPlessis, "Sartorial Sorting in the Colonial Caribbean and North America," in *The Right to Dress. Sumptuary Laws in a Global Perspective, c. 1200–1800*, ed. Giorgio Riello and Ulinka Rublack (Cambridge, UK: Cambridge University Press, 2019), 365; see also DuPlessis, *The Material Atlantic*, 130–5.

57  DuPlessis, *The Material Atlantic*, 130–40. Sartorial practice varied only slightly over time and geography: that of the Dutch East India Company's Cape colony, for example, was slightly modified due to change in climate, consisting of both winter and summer garments, but the basic idea remained consistent. Ibid., 145–6.

58  Ibid., 128–35.

59  Stoler, *Along the Archival Grain*, 1.

60  See the recent Rembrandthuis catalogue and exhibition *Black in Rembrandt's Time* (Amsterdam: WBOOKS Zwolle/Museum Het Rembrandthuis, 2020).

# chapter four

# Drawing Worlds: Bodies and Smoke in the Courtly Ballet *Il Tabacco* (1650)

ELISA ANTONIETTA DANIELE

On 1 March 1650, the last day of carnival, at the court of the Duchy of Savoy in Turin, northern Italy, a ballet entitled *Il Tabacco* (*Tobacco*) was staged for the delight of Christine Marie of France, sister to Louis XIII and regent of the Duchy.[1] We know of this ephemeral performance thanks to the commemorative volume produced after the event by Ducal secretary and court calligrapher Giovanni Tommaso Borgonio: in ink and watercolour with silver or gold accents, the drawings in this album take the viewer on a journey tracing tobacco's movement across the world. Imaginary figures from the Americas to the Middle East are depicted gracefully preparing and consuming tobacco according to diverse geographical customs.[2]

This event was part of a series of spectacles staged at the Savoy court over the course of several years. Attesting to the importance of these performances is a large body of textual and visual documentation compiled in fourteen volumes. These are manuscript albums that Borgonio put together after the events; they are incisive representations designed to commemorate each performance in all its scenic elements, including sets, dancers, costumes, choreography, and lyrics. The albums allow us to observe that, even though Turin – unlike other prominent centres where this type of event was staged – was not engaged in any colonial activities, four of the ballets featured a strikingly large number of foreign characters, from the Arctic (*La Primavera Trionfante dell'Inverno*, 1657), the Arabian Peninsula (*La Fenice Rinovata*, 1644), the Indonesian archipelago (*L'Unione per la peregrina Margherita Reale e Celeste*, 1660), and the Americas where *Il Tabacco* was set.[3] While many previous studies have described these costumed extra-European peoples in ways that underline their stereotypical and imaginative exoticism, in this chapter I look closely at the objects and ornamental details included in the depictions of these figures in order to assess the specific cross-cultural influences they convey.[4] I view these elements as interstices that open onto a vision of new worlds, trade routes, and goods. They attest to changing historical currents and, as in the case of tobacco, a new economic flow.

Before delving into the Borgonio album, it is worth briefly addressing the wider phenomenon of which this ballet is an example. Indeed, performances involving parades of national personifications were a ubiquitous feature of *ballets à entrées* in many European courts in the first half of the seventeenth century.[5] The aim of the *Ballet des Nations* genre, staged in an especially impressive way at the French court of Louis XIII, was to assert specific geopolitical orders by celebrating global – or, at least, what was considered global – diversity.[6] These performances, staged for the enjoyment of an audience of aristocrats and ambassadors, were acted out by nobles of the court and sometimes even the sovereigns themselves. The structure was always more or less the same: there was an opening prologue followed by various appearances, each one composed of a group of singing figures representing people from different geographical areas indistinctly designated as "nations."[7] The costumed performers embodied what were perceived as national, ethnic, or racial features and characteristics in a way that would have been easily recognizable to the audience through the symbolism of their clothing, ornaments, skin colour, or distinctive ways of moving and gesturing. Jesuit scholar and theorist of images Claude-François Ménestrier, for instance, writes in his treatise *Des ballets anciens et modernes selon les règles du théâtre* that this form of spectacle should speak to the eyes through images that use costuming to clearly convey the identity of the character on stage: the Turks have their peculiar "vest et le turban" (vest and turban), the Moors "la couleur noire" (the colour black), and the Amerindians "leurs habits de plumes" (their feather garments).[8] Rather than the often all but non-existent plot, these foreign characters were the true focal point of these ballets.

This aspect is confirmed and even accentuated by the drawings in Borgonio's albums. Here, individual floating dancers appear in the middle of a blank page in a way that invites the viewer's gaze to linger on the figure's presence, bodily appearance, and costume, so as "to extract some ultimate meaning from it and it alone."[9] Each of the characters is represented frozen in a different dance move, but they all "come alive" when the pages of the album are turned rapidly in the manner of a flipbook. Indeed, the empty space around the figures and their location on the page, the same for every character, makes it so that their movements shift gradually from one page to the next, giving album viewers the illusion of watching a dance.

Christine of France made the courtly *ballet à entrée* formula popular in the Duchy in an effort to model her courtly life in Turin after those of the great European dynasties, and especially that of her brother Louis. She entrusted her favourite, Count Philip d'Agliè, with organizing all of the ballets recorded by Borgonio (together with many others for which there is no visual documentation, totalling approximately twenty-six performances between 1627 and 1667).[10] These events – ballets, as well as tournaments and even unusual banquet-balls – were conceived, set to music, and choreographed by Philip d'Agliè to celebrate and legitimize Christine's political and diplomatic choices during a troubled period in which the Duchy served as the unwilling battleground for clashing French and Spanish powers.[11] The historical expediency that inspired the creation of *Il Tabacco* was an event from three years earlier in which Christine issued a decree regulating the cultivation and marketing of tobacco, setting up a form of government monopoly.[12] The spectacle celebrated this legislation, asserting the Duchy's worthiness to participate in the expanding web of a global community of consumption.

The ballet was composed of three acts. It began with a prologue introducing the land where the product was grown and from which, the text in the album tells us, "through trade, it is passed on to all the nations of the world." This land is described as a small island located near the "New Andalusia, so-called Venezuela, discovered by Alonso d'Ovieda," and is depicted in the only fixed backdrop of the entire show (fig. 4.1).[13] The audience was thus called on to use its imagination to project the story and dances staged in the foreground space of the performance onto this speck of land portrayed in the distance. After the prologue, four pairs of figures representing the "American nations" appeared on stage in four separate *entrées* to introduce the product of tobacco as it was processed and consumed in its place of origin. These characters were followed by four other pairs of figures representing countries from the Old World that imported and used tobacco in various ways and for various purposes. Finally, as was common practice in this type of spectacle, all the figures took to the stage together in the final grand ballet.

For page after page, Borgonio's album presents the dancers performing the various *entrées*. The sheets with figures are interspersed with sheets presenting the ballet's libretto, with texts that include descriptions as well as spoken parts (fig. 4.2). Two different calligraphic styles are used

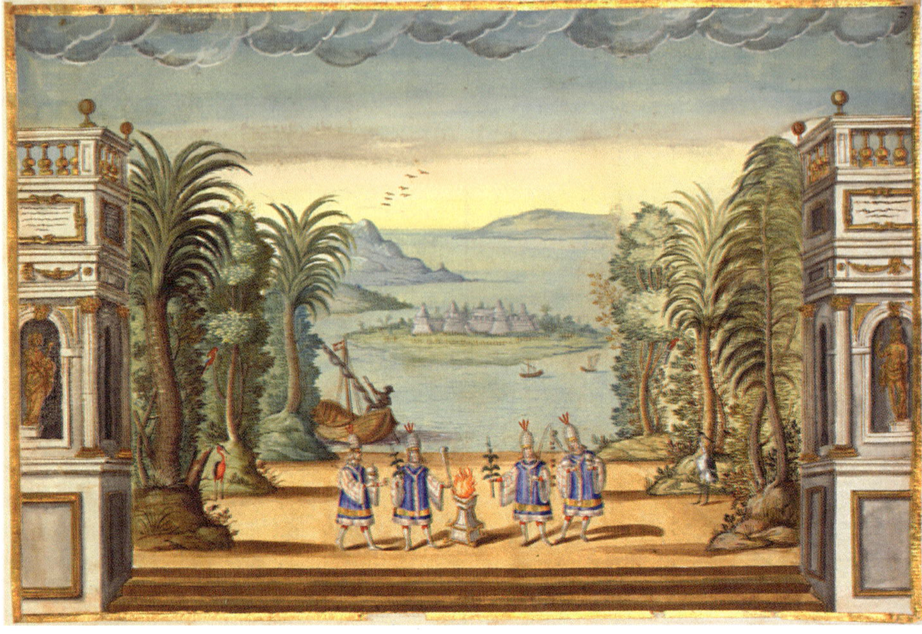

Figure 4.1.  Giovanni Tommaso Borgonio, *Il Tabacco*, n.d. [second half of
the seventeenth century], fol. 3r. Pencil and gouache on paper, 57 x 41 cm.
Ministero della Cultura, Biblioteca Nazionale Universitaria di Torino

to distinguish these, the first in lowercase and the second in cursive.[14]
In addition to the written word, these in-between pages feature ink lines
twining to form elaborate ornaments that not only frame the titles or
paragraphs of text, but also encroach on the figures. These ornaments
include winged cherubs, centaurs, satyrs, two-tailed sirens, and Bacchus-
and Minerva-like characters cavorting across the pages. Borgonio's play-
ful rendering transforms these bodies into immaterial silhouettes made
up of rhythmic curlicues. Moreover, these ornamental figures – which
have nothing to do with the main body of the ballet – provide the sole
allusion to classical iconography in a spectacle that is unusually devoid
of references of this kind. These calligraphic sheets do evoke the ballet's main theme, however, in the slender pipes that appear nearly every-
where, poking out from among the festoons or grasped in the hands of
the mythological figures. Some of these characters, such as the cherubs,

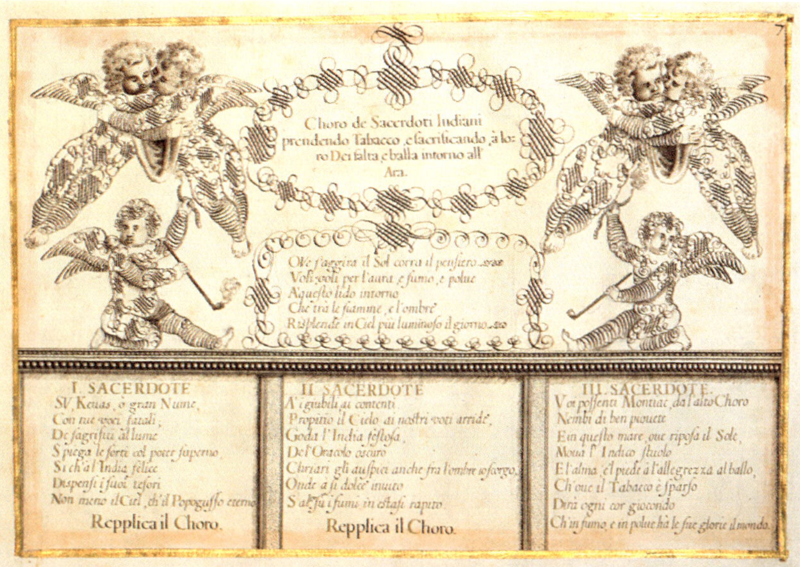

Figure 4.2. Giovanni Tommaso Borgonio, *Il Tabacco*, n.d., fol. 7r. Pencil and gouache on paper, 57 x 41 cm, Ministero della Cultura, Biblioteca Nazionale Universitaria di Torino

puff greedily on the pipes while others wield them with comical inability, holding them aloft as if they were spears or writing nibs.

The prologue appears on the first sheet of the album after the title page. It is preceded by a short introductory paragraph presenting the subject of the ballet in poetic verse, which states that the many virtues of this little spectacle, namely the wit of its theme and skill of its performers, were extracted like gold in a process akin to alchemy: "Comic ballet which, pulled from the forge of thoughts, like an Alchemy of Ideas, extracts gold from powders and vapours like the virtue that is performed in a thousand ways by His Royal Highness and his Knights."[15] The author then lists some of the names for the tobacco plant as it is known "In the contours of that Climate," namely *Petun, Pascielt, Senochis, Goobba,* and *Perebesenuc.*" These names represent an arbitrary and confused nomenclature. In reality, only the first two refer to varieties of *Nicotiana tabacum* or *Nicotiana rustica,* the two main plant species that produce tobacco; the others derive from misinterpretations or mistaken associations with tobacco borrowed from early travel reports and botanical treatises.[16] *Gooba*, for example, might be a misspelling of *cohoba*, the Spanish name for a narcotic snuff that Ramon Pane, a Catalan friar who accompanied Columbus on his second expedition to America in 1493, reported being used in religious ceremonies to induce a state of trance.[17] *Perebesenuc*, according to Fernández de Oviedo, was a plant employed by Hispaniola natives as a vulnerary for healing wounds.[18] Both *cohoba* and *perebesenuc* were mistakenly identified with tobacco in late-sixteenth-century medical and botanical treatises, thus attributing to tobacco the narcotic power of the former and the curative properties of the latter.[19]

Similar misinterpretations also appeared in the very first scene of the ballet, which showed four priests lighting a fire atop an altar to make a sacrifice to their gods. In the drawing, the two central priests hold branches of *Nicotiana tabacum*, identifiable by their pinkish flowers, while in their other hands they hold up a golden vase and long pipe (fig. 4.3). As is their custom, the text explains, the priests took up handfuls of tobacco powder from the vases and threw it into the flames to achieve ecstasy and turn themselves into oracles. This divinatory act was termed *Popogusso*, a name that was likely extrapolated from the *True Report of the New Found Land of Virginia* by Thomas Harriot only to be stripped of its original meaning – namely that of an endlessly fiery place in the afterlife – and transposed here to instead label an obscure form of sorcery.[20] The prologue of the ballet thus emphatically endowed tobacco with otherworldly powers, forging a connection between the substance and a form of intoxication leading to divination. In so doing, it built on a common trope that had been familiar to European audiences since the previous century, when reports and treatises fostered an association between tobacco and witchcraft.[21]

As noted, the prologue refers to an "Alchemy of Ideas," claiming that the ballet itself was an inventive process that "extracts gold from powders and vapours." Intriguingly, this alchemical procedure is similar to the sacred and transformative experience of smoking tobacco. Through this metaphor, the narrator created a unified image in which alchemical arts, poetic-artistic processes, and tobacco smoking are merged by virtue of their common ability to re-shape and transform their basic elements into something more potent. The purpose of this intricate and subtle rhetorical construction was not only to literally embellish the narrative; it also served to shift the focus from the religious "inspiration" or intoxication depicted in the first scene to the more harmless realm of poetic inspiration, thus showcasing a use of the potentially dangerous ecstatic

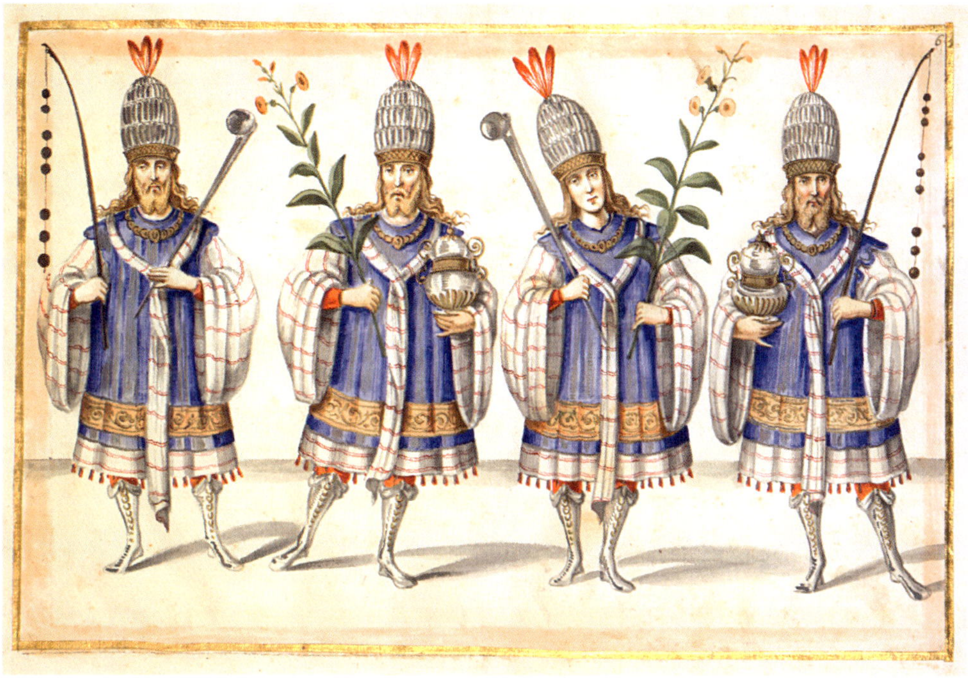

Figure 4.3.  Giovanni Tommaso Borgonio, *Il Tabacco*, n.d., fol. 6r. Pencil and gouache on paper, 57 x 41 cm. Ministero della Cultura, Biblioteca Nazionale Universitaria di Torino

powers of tobacco more appropriate for the spectacle's European audience. Notably, this is not the only text to frame tobacco as a fruitful ally for poets and their creative work: by the time the ballet was staged, this association was a fully developed literary topos.[22]

All the names cited in the prologue, whether historical figures or words associated with various nomenclatures for the plant, appear with the very same errors of transcription or interpretation in another text, which I believe was probably d'Agliè's source for creating the performance.[23] The text in question, *Regole della sanità* (*Rules for Health*), was published in Turin in 1618 and written by Ugo Benzi, a doctor and philosopher from Siena. It features commentary by Giovanni Ludovico Bertaldi, who served as physician to Christine's father-in-law Charles Emmanuel I. This text is a collection of rules for improving one's health through anything that could be inhaled or consumed, and it includes a chapter devoted entirely to tobacco. In the opening of this chapter, the text states that "in every part of the world there is something for its own use, something that from nature is denied to other countries. ... And thus it is that tobacco, which nature made to grow only in the Americas, was freed to spread throughout the world thanks wholly to the labours of man." The authors hold a largely negative view of this spread, however, as they consider tobacco harmful not only to the bodies of those who consume it, but also to the economies of the countries that import it. They conclude: "We see that it is not useful for maintaining health, [it] is harmful to politics, [and] to household economies ... emptying the coffers of money, which ends up in the hands of hostile Pagans."[24] Such negative assessments were not echoed in the ballet, however, which instead opted for celebrating the merits of the plant, as we are going to see shortly. The change in approach between the spectacle and the earlier treatise might indicate a crucial historical shift in the appreciation of the product. Indeed, the Duchy and many other European states in this period were beginning to regulate domestic tobacco crops or pass taxes allowing them to take economic advantage of the new imported commodity. Thus, while tobacco might still have been harmful to the human body, it was no longer considered harmful to the political body.[25]

In the ballet, the celebration of tobacco as a consumer good is most evident in the first act. The first pair of figures to appear on stage after the priests' exit were two Amerindians (fig. 4.4). Unlike the figures in the prologue, in the album drawing these characters – labelled "Tapuia" and "Paracussa" – are entirely detached from any form of landscape or environment, with only the shadows at their feet anchoring them to the ground so that they do not float in a completely undefined space. At first glance, they are characterized by the conventional repertoire of iconographic elements that had been associated with allegorical representations of the Americas since the sixteenth century, namely bows and arrows, tattooed bare torsos, and feathered headgear.[26] What sets this scene apart, however, is the inclusion of brown oblong objects that are held aloft by the two figures, intruding with an unusual degree of realism into an otherwise conventionally allegorical spectacle. These objects are coiled ropes of tobacco. The image thus demonstrates familiarity with a particular way of processing the leaves of the plant, in which they are twined together to form thick lanyards in preparation for export.[27] According to the text, the dancers in the ballet appeared to twist these ropes between them as they moved across the stage, twirling so that their

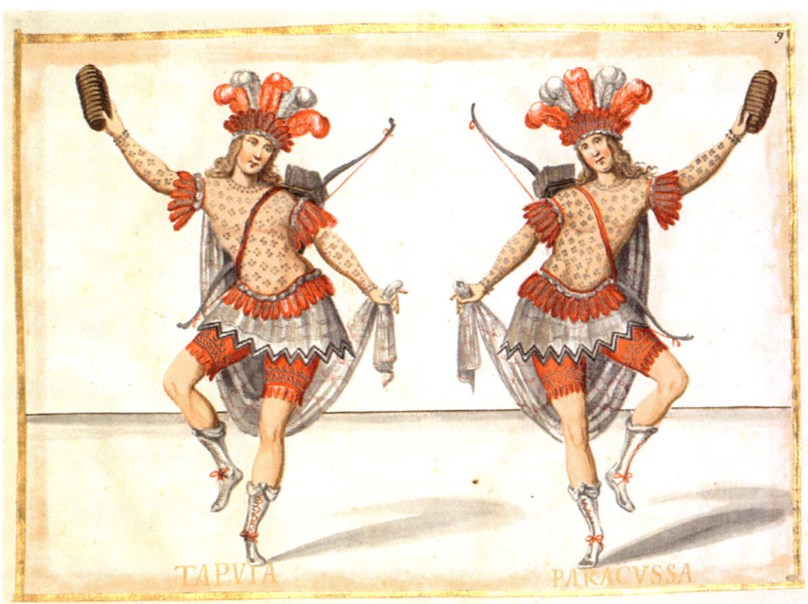



Figure 4.4. Giovanni Tommaso Borgonio, *Il Tabacco*, n.d., fol. 9. Pencil and gouache on paper, 57 x 41 cm. Ministero della Cultura, Biblioteca Nazionale Universitaria di Torino

movements replicated the act of coiling the tobacco cords. The result was a sort of symbiosis between the preparation of the product and the movements and gestures of the dancers' bodies.

This type of choreographic movement was repeated, albeit less blatantly, by all of the figures that followed. The next couple to appear on stage pulverized tobacco in gold mortars, a gesture accompanied by rhythmic foot-stamping. The third pair of figures drew pinches of tobacco powder, intended to be inhaled, from small vases filled with chestnuts, walnuts and shells, interspersing – the text explains – this repeated gesture with sneezes (fig. 4.5). The last pair used serpentine movements to mimic the wafting of smoke while the product itself was consumed by dancers inhaling smoke from a pair of two-foot-long pipes, lit by the smouldering wicks they held in their hands.[28] All of these details were derived from various travel reports: for example, the sneezing characters refer to the custom of snorting tobacco snuff as described, to cite one

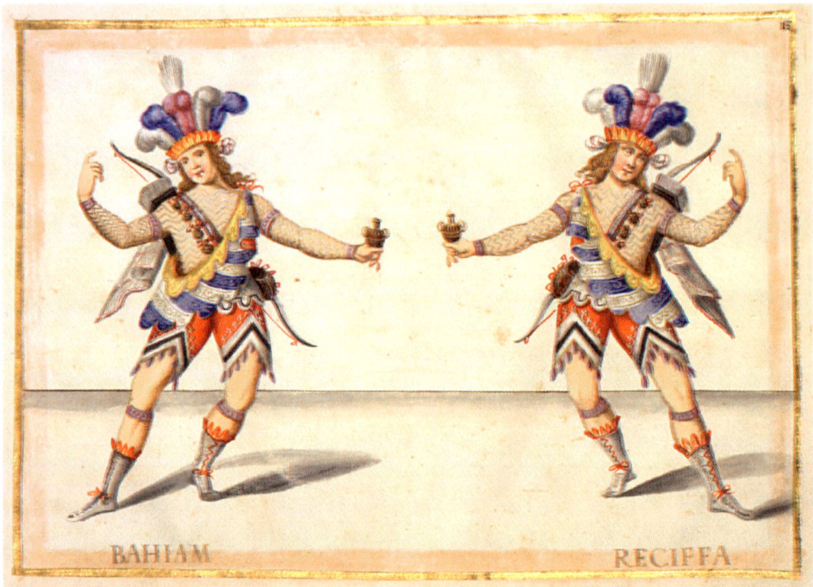


Figure 4.5. Giovanni Tommaso Borgonio, *Il Tabacco*, n.d., fol. 13r. Pencil and gouache on paper, 57 x 41 cm. Ministero della Cultura, Biblioteca Nazionale Universitaria di Torino

of the earliest sources, by Oviedo in *Historia general de las Indias*. As for tobacco crushed in mortars, an early reference appears in José Acosta's *Historia natural y moral de las Indias*. And one of the first references to plaited tobacco is found in the 1586 Latin version of Jean de Léry's account of his voyage to Brazil.[29]

The small jars of snuff carried by the third-to-last pair invoked an object and practice that had garnered particular attention. For instance, snuff-takers were featured in an Italian mock-heroic poem by Francesco Zucchi entitled *La Tabaccheide. Scherzo estivo sopra il Tabacco*. This is one of the earliest known publications that outlines the various materials used to make snuff boxes – clay, lupine, bone, crystal, gold, ivory, or other materials – besides providing a curiously lengthy digression into the various types of noses, more or less ample, suited to consuming it. Zucchi also devises a mythologic history of the origin of the tobacco plant and the way "it was dispersed throughout the world," stating that "it is good

for every devil and is taken in many different forms."[30] We do not know
if this text served as direct inspiration for our ballet, but it does indicate
widespread interest in the origins, uses, and accoutrements of tobacco
consumption.

To give an idea of the dancers' distinctive movements, choreographed
to convey the act of processing or consuming tobacco (rope pirouette/
twisting, foot pestle/mortar pestle, serpentine/smoking movements),
the drawings depict each pair frozen in a different pose. These poses
not only suggest the dancers' specific movements (see the first pair's
position, for instance (fig. 4.4), with one outstretched leg, pointed toe
resting on the ground, and the other leg, bent at the knee, held up to
suggest a pirouette), but they are also presented as a continuation, each
one leading to the next so as to evoke the movement of flipping through
the pages. The details of the costuming are likewise instrumental in aug-
menting the idea of choreographed movements. All the dancers' bare
torsos were covered in a shimmering silk fabric called *ormesino*, probably
chosen for its ability to mimic naked skin.[31] In the drawings, what appear
to be tattoos on the bodies of the dancers were actually small arabesques
of glowing silver and gold thread woven into this fabric, which was embroidered with pearls or multicoloured gems. These glimmering lines
create complex patterns on the dancers' bodies: geometric forms are
juxtaposed with serpentine shapes on the skirts, while plant-inspired ornaments are paired with segments. For the viewer perusing the album,
these detailed linear embellishments create a sense of movement, an
impression of incessant vibration within the silhouettes of the figures
that is accentuated by the blankness of the empty pages around them.

The following four pairs of figures to appear in the ballet performed
the spread of tobacco throughout the Old World, here comprised of
Europe, the Islamic world, and northern Africa.[32] This second act showcased the reasons why people used tobacco, illustrating how it had been
adopted for various uses in different parts of the world after initially pen-
etrating the international market. All of the figures appeared on stage
holding in one hand a short silver or gold pipe – a tool that had taken
a firm hold on smokers in Western Europe from early on – while bran-
dishing in their other hand an object exemplifying the ways tobacco was
used. The group included two Turks, dressed in fine silver-cloth tunics
with long sleeves, who claimed to consume tobacco to spur themselves on
in battle (in fact, their props in the drawing are swords). The source of
inspiration in this case was probably a travel report as well. For instance,
in his *Relation of a Iourney*, published in London in 1615, George Sandys

gives a brief account of smoking in Constantinople that includes a detail that is very similar to the custom represented in our ballet. Indeed, he reports that the Turkish habit of taking opium as well as tobacco is able to "expelleth all feare," making users particularly courageous.[33] The following two Moors explained, in song – as stated by the text of the ballet – that they use tobacco both as a poison for anointing their dart tips and as a counter-poison to heal wounds inflicted by the same deadly darts ("Make and weld at the same time harsh wounds / the darts dyed with Petun's fire)."[34] The last two couples instead use tobacco to affect the mind: the Spaniards to improve their mood, and the Poles, the last pair of dancers, to clear the brain of the lingering stupor of alcohol.[35] Their dances, briefly described in the text, were intended to convey the idea of the changes caused by tobacco consumption. Both the couples thus had to switch repeatedly and suddenly between different types of movements: the Spaniards between slower, "melancholy" movements, and high-spirited dancing, while the Poles, alternating sips of wine from a silvery flask with puffs from a pipe, interspersed more measured and controlled movements with "unconventional" dancing.

While the Spaniards may initially seem more rational than the drunken Poles, they were actually the couple most targeted for satire; as such they provided an opportunity to poke fun at Spain, the country Christine had been at war with the decade before.[36] The two characters appeared on stage accompanied by the sound of castanets and wrapped in the fumes wafting from their pipes, thus adding real smoke – the text explains – to the metaphorical smoke of their haughtiness and decadent pomp. Their outfits of stockings, jackets, short cloaks, and full breeches gathered at the waist and knees may have been drawn from Cesare Vecellio's costume book, with the addition of ridiculously voluminous flowered bows on their shoes and fluffy feathers on their hats.[37] Their physical description also subtly pointed out their shortcomings. According to the album, which adopts a medical lexicon, the two Spaniards have "hot" blood ("adusti nel sangue") and a "melancholic" appearance ("malenconici nel sembiante"). It is worth highlighting that, while "melancholic" referred specifically to one of the four temperaments of humourism (sanguine, choleric, melancholic, and phlegmatic), "hot" was the main quality associated with the blood of choleric people. Indeed, this laconic yet pointed description can be framed within what Mary Floyd-Wilson terms "geohumoralism," namely the thinking that projected the four-part humoural typology onto geographical areas in order to articulate ethnic differences.[38] Scholars such as Jean Bodin at the end of the sixteenth century and Pierre Charron shortly afterward classified peoples in the south as melancholic, peoples in the north as phlegmatic, and those inhabiting the middle zones as choleric or sanguine depending on the latitude.[39] By saying that the Spaniards have "hot blood," the text attributes a choleric temperament to the Spanish, and the people in this grouping – those inhabiting the middle zones that Jean Bodin, for instance, believed to include Spain – were usually described in humoural theory as arrogant, passionate, aggressive, and volatile, exactly as the two Spaniards are presented in our ballet. However, the text adds that they have a melancholic appearance in keeping with the peoples of the south. This likewise fits within a geohumouralist framework: Spain's geographical position at the southern edge of the middle zone meant that its residents could take on traits similar to those of the populations inhabiting both the middle and the southern parts of the globe. Pierre Charron expressed this idea when writing that the temperament of peoples inhabiting the middle areas is also affected by that of the "region to which they are the nearest neighbours."[40] Humouralism thus provided a useful framework for injecting further satirical content; these few words offer us the opportunity to see how the characters' ethnic and national differences were conveyed in the ballet not only through sartorial choices but also through the adjectives used to describe the figures, presumably as they made their entrances on stage.

While national characteristics were emphasized throughout, also of note is the specific gendering of all the figures. In other similar ballets that Philip d'Agliè created for Christine, female characters prevailed and were variously involved in buying and selling the commodities presented in each show. For example, *Il Gridelino* and *L'Unione per la peregrina Margherita Reale e Celeste*, staged at the Savoy court three and ten years later respectively, offer viewers a bustling procession of female manufacturers and merchants of gemstones and fabrics.[41] In *Il Tabacco*, by contrast, all of the characters were male. A likely reason for this gendering is that smoking was considered a uniquely male habit (albeit obviously only in theory). Moreover, it was perceived as a practice with the dangerous potential to make women act in inappropriately masculine ways. This belief was clearly expressed, for instance, by a German broadsheet dated 1652 that depicts a woman eagerly smoking along with two men seated around a table. The caption comments: "The woman who smokes believes herself to be man's equal and therefore apes him …. Soon they [the women] will wear trousers."[42] Offering up ranks of all-male personages, unlike other spectacles revolving around different commodities,

*Il Tabacco* chose not to challenge this assumption. As we will shortly see, the potential (and virtual) re-gendering power of tobacco is not the only dangerously transformative ability attributed to the act of smoking that is emphasized in the performance.

What is markedly emphasized in the ballet is tobacco's circulation across geographies and peoples. To better express the idea of its pervasive and contagion-like spread in poetic verse, tobacco was addressed not only as a commodity – a new good from the New World – but also as a deity – a new god from the New World, eager to dethrone old gods and idols. As one of the priests proclaimed at the beginning of the ballet: "All the world must worship it, / and with lively affection / pouring fumes in the altar of Bacchus / all the world makes up a new Idol of Tobacco."[43] The representation of tobacco as a new deity, often clashing with the ancient god of wine Bacchus, was taken up in a variety of poems and carnivalesque productions in the decades before our ballet. For instance, in the antimasque preceding the *Masque of Flowers* in London in 1614, a contest was staged between the Virginian tobacco god Kawasha and the satyr Silenus, a companion of Bacchus.[44] During the diatribe, Kawasha boasted that "More incense hath been burn'd / At great Kawasha's foot / Than to Silen and Bacchus both, / And take in Jove to boot" before listing the many virtues and uses of the sacred plant."[45] To give another example, *The Smoaking Age, or The man in the mist with the life and death of Tobacco* by Richard Brathwaite inserts tobacco into a fictional scenario that indicates how the wide-ranging spread of this new fashion was destined to rapidly evolve into consolidated custom.[46] The beginning of this text casts tobacco in a mythological origin story whereby the plant appears as the illegitimate son of Bacchus and Proserpine and, therefore, the "brave Bastard" of Pluto, Proserpine's husband. Upon Pluto's request, Jupiter transforms his unwelcome bastard into a plant and exiles him to earth. There, tobacco is condemned to travel "through the noses" of the European countries, such as France and, most of all, England.[47] Brathwaite's text, however, illustrates the trajectory and effects of tobacco not only in the macrocosm of an interconnected world but also in the microcosm of a permeable self. Indeed, throughout the text, tobacco is represented and personified as a wanderer with the very dangerous power of unleashing a progressive corruption of the bodies of smokers, a corruption that begins on the inside and spreads to mark the outside as well.[48]

A significant visual representation of this concept is provided by the frontispiece to the text, engraved by William Marshall (fig. 4.6). The image shows three English men smoking heavily inside a tobacco shop.

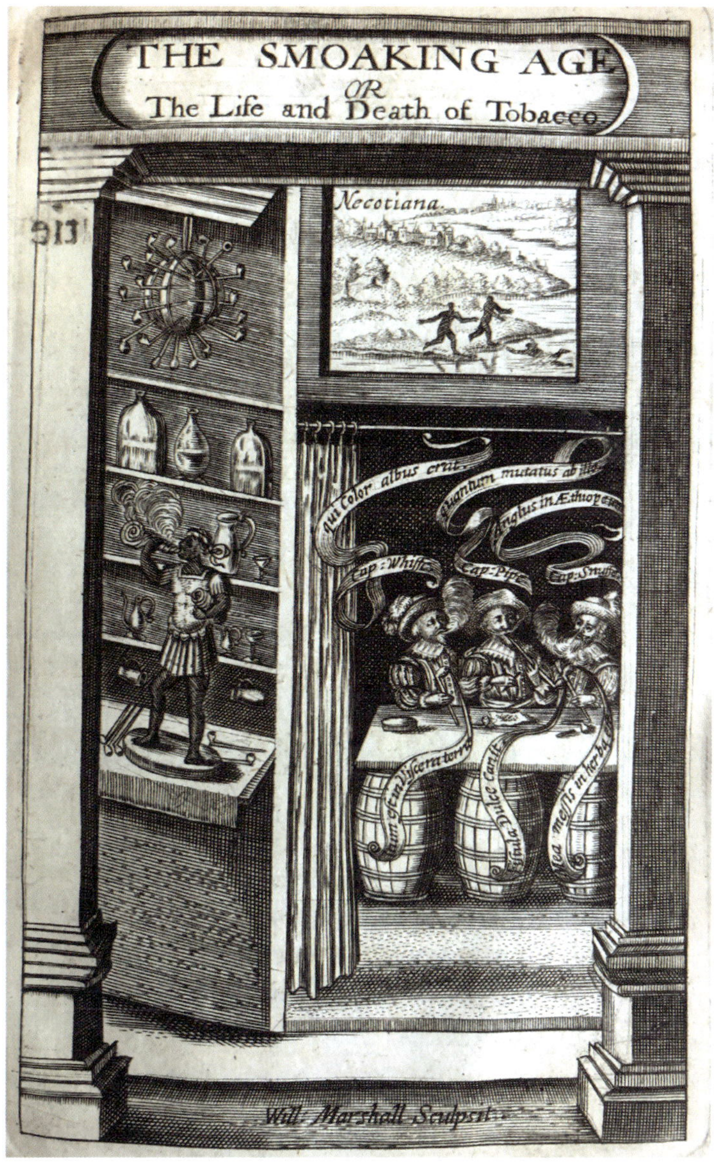


Figure 4.6. William Marshall, *The Smoaking Age*, in Richard Brathwaite, *A Solemne Ioviall Disputation* (London: E. Griffin 1617). Engraving. The William Andrews Clark Memorial Library, University of California, Los Angeles

The sinuous motion of the dense swirls of smoke issuing from their mouths and noses is reiterated by the wavy scrolls surrounding their heads. These read: "How much changed from white are these Englishmen transformed into Ethiopians."[49] On the left side of the image, the statuette of a Black African man smoking is juxtaposed to this scene. This frontispiece, as Kristen Brookes observes, played on the common colonial fear that the English colonizers, with their proclivity for consuming exotic goods and imitating exotic habits, could in turn find their cultural and national identity contaminated by the peoples they had colonized. Such virtual contamination was often rendered, as in the frontispiece, through the idea of a visible change in skin colour.[50] The image employs diverse strategies to suggest this transformation. In addition to the scroll words and the juxtaposition of the Black African statue with the three Englishmen, closer examination reveals an intensification of the hatching lines around the outer edges of the faces, seemingly suggesting a progressive darkening of the skin, which might seek to visually convey the idea of contamination. According to the perspective suggested here, tobacco smoke was thus the medium through which the foreigner – a category conceptualized here as being as capacious as it was indistinct – penetrated the domestic bodies of Englishmen. Exactly as with the concerns surrounding the potential re-gendering of tobacco smoke outlined above, this contamination anxiety revolved around a conception of the self as extremely porous and vulnerable.[51]

This image is a particular and striking visual depiction that encapsulates a very broad pan-European debate. This debate over tobacco's relative dangerousness was particularly lively in Jacobean England, where it gave rise to countless anti-tobacconists texts. Indeed, King James I himself took a strong stand against tobacco in his 1604 *Counterblaste,* belittling it as one of those "toys and trifles" that New World natives seemed foolishly to prefer over gold and precious stones. He stated that "there cannot be a more hurtfull, corruption in a Countrey" than the "vile use of taking Tobacco" and "It is the King's part (as the proper Phisician of his Politicke-body)" to purge the country of this disease.[52] He accused smokers of slavishly imitating a foreign novelty and tobacco traders of impoverishing the nation through their commerce. Indeed, given that tobacco was purchased from Spanish merchants at the time James was writing, smoking also meant enriching the coffers of one of England's rivals in the colonial enterprise. From this point of view, tobacco was foreign twice over and therefore constituted a two-fold threat to both individual health and national wealth.

This last argument resonates with the Turin medical treatise *Rules for Health* (1618) and its largely negative view of tobacco, a product not made from native plants that "grow in the gardens of our house" and, therefore, considered as harmful to the human body as it is to household economies.[53] While, as noted above, the ballet *Il Tabacco* probably drew many elements from this text, the spectacle is nevertheless distinctive in relation to its source and to similar literature. By stating that "Gold has no value ... / without the dark coal of tobacco," the ballet's libretto was clearly making a very different assertion from, for instance, James I's statements.[54] To help explain this discrepancy, I turn in conclusion to the argument developed by anthropologist Fernando Ortiz in his text *Cuban Counterpoint: Tobacco and Sugar*. Ortiz examines the history of tobacco's introduction in Europe and argues that the new plant was not "completely grafted on the trunk" of European culture until a wholly new use was found for it, namely "that of serving as a great source of tax revenue to satisfy the monetary needs of government." What had been a sacred social institution among the Indians became an economic institution on the other side of the Atlantic. In other words, tobacco came to constitute what Ortiz identifies as "a characteristic phenomenon of a complete transculturation."[55] This transculturation clearly came through in the course of the ballet's three acts. In the prologue, tobacco was presented – albeit very coarsely, in a portrayal brimming with misunderstandings and pure invention – as a herb whose transformative powers granted prophetic visions to Indian priests and poetic visions to the author of the ballet. In the dance by the first set of figures, the main protagonist was actually the plant, in all its processes and phases of production. In the next act, by contrast, tobacco appeared in the form of smoke, a product being consumed. As the performance unfolded, therefore, tobacco shifted from a sacred, inspiring product to a commodity engendering a widespread set of cultural habits. What Ortiz terms "the new economic, commercial, and tax-yielding significance" that tobacco was acquiring in Europe at the time the ballet was staged was the specific motivation driving this celebration of tobacco as a lucrative product to be purchased and consumed for personal pleasure.[56] In conclusion, the ballet succinctly performed the power of a novel commodity, previously described as a trivial toy-like trifle, and its capacity to generate new commercial networks. Intriguingly, the same economic flows generated by tobacco's mobility across geographies could be likened to the wafting of smoke, by virtue of their shared pervasiveness and ever-changing character. This comparison is visually suggested in the ballet by the dancers' choreographed movements. Indeed, the sequences of repeated gestures that we have seen embroiling all the figures were the perfect metaphors for evoking the dynamics of an economic-social system, here in its budding stage, that depended on the potential of commodities to cross boundaries and move in unpredictable and contagious ways.

## NOTES

1 Christine had officially been regent of the Duchy from the 1637 death of her husband, Vittorio Amedeo, until her son's majority in 1648. However, she unofficially retained power until her death in 1663.

2 Borgonio is usually identified as the author of the pen-and-ink texts in the albums, the calligraphic ornamentation, and the pencil and gouache drawings, with contributions by others as well. The ballets he documented, even years after the event, were all staged from 1640 to 1681; Mercedes Viale Ferrero, *Feste delle Madame Reali di Savoia* (Turin: Istituto Bancario San Paolo, 1965); Franca Varallo, "Il Laberinto de Groppi," in *Le dessin et les arts du spectacle*, ed. Cordélia Hattori (Paris: AEC, 2019) 109–24. The album is located in the National Library of Turin (call number Q V 59).

3 *Spring Triumphant over Winter; The Phoenix Renewed; The Union for the Royal and Celestial Pilgrim Margeritha.* National Library of Turin, respectively: Q V 55; Q V 63; Q V 53.

4 Margaret M. McGowan, *L'Art du Ballet de Cour en France, 1581–1643* (Paris: CNRS, 1963), 115; Ferrero, *Feste delle Madame Reali*, table X; Marie-Françoise Christout, *Le ballet de cour au XVIIe siècle* (Genève: Picard, 1987) 113–51; Bernadette Majorana, "L'immaginario universale," in *Milano, l'Ambrosiana e la conoscenza dei nuovi mondi*, ed. Michela Catto and Gianvittorio Signorotto (Rome: Bulzoni, 2015), 417.

5 Each act of this kind of ballet consisted of a number separate entries by dancers onto the stage. A representative overview of previous literature on this efflorescence includes Christout, *Le ballet de cour*; Helen Watanabe-O'Kelly and J.R. Mulryne, eds., *Europa Triumphans: Court and Civic Festivals in Early Modern Europe*, vol. 1 (Aldershot: Ashgate, 2004) 3–75; Margaret M. McGowan, *Dance in the Renaissance: European Fashion, French Obsession* (New Haven: Yale University Press, 2008). Mark Franko's study *Dance as Text: Ideologies of the Baroque Body* (Cambridge, UK: Cambridge University Press, 1993), is focused specifically on dance

and the language of choreography as instrumental to the significance of court ballet. The phenomenon in Turin is addressed by, among others, Ferrero, *Feste delle Madame Reali*; Margaret M. McGowan, "Les fêtes de cour en Savoie," *Revue d'histoire du théâtre* 3 (1970): 214–15; Clelia Arnaldi di Balme and Franca Varallo, eds., *Madame Reali: cultura e potere da Parigi a Torino* (Genoa: Sagep, 2019); and Majorana, "L'immaginario universale," 399–435. Only Christout and Majorana focus on the issue of extra-European peoples on stage.

6 James H. Hyde, "The Four Parts of the World as Represented in Old-Time Pageants and Ballets, Part I," *Apollo* 4 (1926): 232–8; and "Part II," *Apollo* 5 (1927): 19–27; Ellen R. Welch, "Performing France in the Seventeenth-Century Ballets des nations," *Journal for Early Modern Cultural Studies* 13, no. 2 (Spring 2013): 3–23; Maria-Claude Canova-Green, "Dance and Ritual: the 'Ballet des nations' at the Court of Louis XIII," *Renaissance Studies* 9, no. 4 (1995): 395–403.

7 Ellen R. Welch, *A Theater of Diplomacy* (Philadelphia: University of Pennsylvania Press, 2017), 62.

8 Claude-François Ménestrier, *Des ballets anciens et modernes selon les règles du théâtre* [*Ancient and Modern Ballets According to the Rules of the Theatre*] (Paris: René Guignard, 1682), 143.

9 Franko, *Dance as Text*, 104.

10 Menestrier, *Des ballets anciens et modernes*, 56.

11 Ferrero, *Feste delle Madame Reali*, 9–10.

12 Christine's decree, dated 20 September 1647, regulated the cultivation of tobacco crops and levied a *gabella* (government tax) on the industry and on the marketing of tobacco as a product; see Felice Amato Duboin, "Della gabella del tabacco," in *Raccolta per ordine di materie delle leggi, cioè editti, patenti [...] emanate negli stati di terraferma sino all'8 dicembre 1798 dai sovrani della real Casa di Savoja*, vol. 11 (Turin: Tipografia Baricco e Arnaldi, 1847–1868); Giovanni Cappellari della Colomba, *Le imposte di confine, i monopoli governativi e i dazi di consumo in Italia* (Florence: Stamperia Reale, 1896), 229; *Direzione generale delle privative. Cenni storico statistici sul monopolio del tabacco in Italia* (Rome: Tipografia nazionale G. Bertero, 1900), 8; Antonio Ceci, "Il monopolio del tabacco in Italia. Ascesa e declino di una industria di Stato," *Historia et ius* 8 (2015): 4.

13 From the prologue: "Ove bagna il vasto Oceano pacifico l'India occidentale nella nuova Andalusia meridionale detta Venezuele, scoperta da Alonso d'Ovieda siede L'Isola del Tabacco così chiamata, perché tal pianta abbondante, e perfetta alligni in quel Terreno" (fol. 2r).

14  Ferrero, *Feste delle Madame Reali*, 39–43; Varallo, "Il Laberinto de Groppi,"
    116–18.
15  "Balletto ridicolo il quale cavato dalla fucina dei pensieri, quasi Alchimia
    delle Idee, tra le polveri, & i fumi n'estrae l'oro della virtù esercitata in
    mille modi da S. A. R. e da suoi Cavalieri" (fol. 2r). "His Royal Highness"
    refers to Christine's son, for whom she was regent, and who appeared as
    dancer in the Turks' scene. "Fumi" appears in Borgonio's album, but in
    the text online by Lorenzo Girodo (Turin 2002) it has been transcribed as
    "fiumi".
16  "Nei contorni di quel Clima" (fol. 2r). One of the first times "petun"
    appears is in *Les singularitez de la France Antarctique* (Antwerp: Cristopher
    Plantin, 1558) by the Franciscan friar André Thevet; see Jerome E. Brooks,
    ed., *Tobacco: Its History Illustrated by the Books, Manuscripts and Engravings in
    the Library of George Arents, Jr*, 5 vols (New York: The Rosenbach Company,
    1937–1952), 1:217–20, 252–9. See also Beverly Lemire, *Global Trade and the
    Transformation of Consumer Cultures: The Material World Remade, c. 1500–1820*
    (Cambridge, UK: Cambridge University Press, 2018), 197. As for "pascielt,"
    this might be a mistaken spelling of *picietl*: see Brooks, *Tobacco*, 1:528–32,
    and Marcy Norton, *Sacred Gifts, Profane Pleasures: A History of Tobacco and
    Chocolate in the Atlantic World* (Ithaca: Cornell University Press, 2008), 20. I
    did not find any source or reference to "senochis" indicating what it might
    be or stand for.
17  *De orbe novo decades*, incorporated in Peter Martyr's *Opera*, published in
    Alcalá de Henares (Arnaldo Guillen, 1516); Brooks, *Tobacco*, 1:193–9.
18  Fernández de Oviedo, in his *Historia general de las Indias* (Seville: Juam
    Cromberger, 1535), does not state that tobacco and *perebecenuc* are the same
    thing; he only refers to the latter as a wild-growing plant that the natives use
    medicinally. It is a later botanical treatise, specifically a text written by the
    Spanish physician Nicolás Monardes and translated into Latin by Charles
    de l'Escluse, *De simplicibus medicamentis* (Antwerp: Cristopher Plantin,
    1574), that states that, according to Oviedo, *perebecenuc* is the local name for
    tobacco on the island of Hispaniola and that it was employed by the natives
    as a powerful vulnerary; Brooks, *Tobacco*, 1:207 for Oviedo, 260 for l'Escluse.
    See also Daniela Bleichmar, "Books, Bodies, and Fields: Sixteenth-Century
    Transatlantic Encounters with New World *Materia Medica*," in *Colonial
    Botany: Science, Commerce, and Politics in the Early Modern World*, ed. Londa
    Schiebinger and Claudia Swan (Philadelphia: University of Pennsylvania
    Press, 2005), 83–99; Norton, *Sacred Gifts, Profane Pleasures*, 107–21.
19  *Cohoba*, according to Fernando Columbus (Brooks, *Tobacco*, 1:244), Pane,
    and Oviedo, among others, is a powder employed to induce a state of

trance. However, none of these commentators states that this powder is actually derived from the tobacco plant. By the end of the sixteenth century the term was nonetheless accepted in Europe as a native Haitian word for tobacco. Jean de Léry, for example, uses it in his *Historia navigationis in Brasiliam* (Geneva: Eustace Vignon, 1586), the Latin translation of *Histoire d'un voyage*; Brooks, *Tobacco*, 1:292–4.

20 Harriot reports that, for the natives of the coastal area of North Carolina, *popogusso* is "a great pitte or hole" juxtaposed to a place of "perpetual blisse and happinesse"; see Tobias Döring, *Performances of Mourning in Shakespearean Theatre and Early Modern Culture* (New York: Palgrave Macmillan, 2006), 96. The prologue of the ballet also named the specific gods invoked in this ritual, Montiac and Keuuas. These names presumably derived from a distortion of "Mantoac" and "Kewasowok," gods who also appear in Harriot's account: the first name refers to the set of divinities making up the coastal Algonquian pantheon, the second to the human-shaped idols of these gods placed by the natives in their temples.

21 Sabine Schülting, "Tobacco—Sacred and Profane" in *Performances of the Sacred in Late Medieval and Early Modern England*, ed. Susanne Rupp and Tobias Döring (Amsterdam: Rodopi, 2005), 189–203. Its first ritualistic use is documented by Jean de Léry in his 1578 account *Histoire d'un Voyage* (La Rochelle: Antoine Chuppin, 1578); Brooks, *Tobacco*, 1:280–3. Ritualistic and ceremonial usages of tobacco are also reported by Thomas Harriot and by Francisco López de Gómara in his *Historia general de las Indias* (Zaragoza: Agustín Millan, 1553); Norton, *Sacred Gifts, Profane Pleasures*, 60.

22 See, for instance, John Beaumont, *Metamorphosis of Tobacco* (London: Felix Kingston for John Flasket, 1602).

23 Ugo Benzi, *Regole della sanità e natura de' cibi arricchite di vaghe annotazioni e di copiosi discorsi naturali e morali dal sig. Ludovico Bertaldi* (Turin: Heredi di Gio. Domenico Tarino, 1618), 877. There are multiple historical figures connected by the two texts through the importation and distribution of tobacco in Europe, including Walter Ralegh ("Ralergh" in Benzi's text, "Ralic" in the text of the ballet), Jean Nicot (identified as "Nicotio" in both texts), and Richard Grenville ("Grenfeldio," "Grenfeld"). The names drawn from Thomas Harriot also appear.

24 "Perché noi vediamo che non è utile per conservar la sanità, dannoso per la politica, all'economia di casa … evacuando le borse de danari, quali van[n] o nelle mani de' Pagani inimici"; Benzi, *Regole della sanità*, 866, 884–5.

25 Brooks, *Tobacco*, 1:36 and passim; Bleichmar, "Books, Bodies, and Field"; Norton, *Sacred Gifts, Profane Pleasures*.

26  Borgonio's Amerindians appear as a conflation of different Indigenous identities, in this case Andean (the headdress and robe worn by "Indian" priests) and Floridian (the cloak hung diagonally across the chest, for instance) as they are outlined by Vecellio; see Cesare Vecellio, *Habiti antichi et moderni di tutto il mondo di nuovo accresciuti di molte figure* (Venice: G. B. Sessa, 1598), 494–9.

27  See, for instance, Niccolò Gavelli, *Storia distinta e curiosa del tabacco concernente la sua scoperta, la introduzione in Europa, e la maniera di coltivarlo, conservarlo e prepararlo ec. per servirsene* (Ferrara: F. Altieri per il Giglio, 1758), 11–12, 65–7. This processing method is described, for example, in Richard Brathwaite, *Barnabees Journall* (London: John Haviland, 1638), and on its title page tobacco is depicted in this peculiar shape.

28  The earliest known representation of an Indian smoking a pipe appears in an image by Jacques Le Moyne illustrating native methods of healing the sick in Florida, included in his *Brevis narration eorum quae in Florida* (Frankfurt: Ioanis Wecheli, 1591).

29  For Oviedo (*General History of the Indies*) and Léry, see Brooks, *Tobacco*, 1:207 and 1:292–4; José Acosta, in his *Historia natural y moral de las Indias* [*Natural and Moral History of the Indies*] (Seville: Juan de León, 1590), describes tobacco being pounded in mortars along with scorpions, spiders, salamanders, and vipers burnt alive before the altar and thus reduced to ashes, to make a filthy unction; Brooks, *Tobacco*, 1:310.

30  Francesco Zucchi, *La Tabaccheide. Scherzo estivo sopra il Tabacco* [*The Tobacconist. Summer Scherzo on Tobacco*] (Ascoli: Maffio Salvioni, 1636), quoted in Brooks, *Tobacco*, 2:218–20.

31  This material was named after the port of Hormuz from which it originally hailed. In the period when this ballet was performed, however, *ormesino* was being produced on the Italian peninsula, mainly in Genoa, Milan, and Venice; Edoardo Demo, *Mercanti di Terraferma: uomini, merci, e capitali nell'Europa del Cinquecento* (Milan: Angeli, 2012); Giovanna Tonelli, *Affari e lussuosa sobrietà: traffici e stili di vita dei negozianti milanesi nel XVII secolo* (Milan: Angeli, 2012).

32  For these images, see Internet Culturale: http://www.internetculturale .it/jmms/iccuviewer/iccu.jsp?id=oai%3Awww.internetculturale.sbn .it%2FTeca%3A20%3ANT0000%3ABNU_q_V_59

33  George Sandys, *Relation of a Iourney* (London: R. Cotes, 1652), 52.

34  Fol. 20r. While we have some reports about the practice of packing tobacco into poisoned arrow wounds in Mexico to promote healing, the European accounts that mention the introduction of tobacco to the western coast of the African continent only reference the pipes employed by the inhabitants.

See, for instance, Richard Jobson, *The Golden Trade, or a discovery of the River Gambra* (Nicholas Okes: London, 1623), 122; see also Lemire, *Global Trade*, 204. As for the texts describing the practice of healing wounds caused by poisoned arrows in Mexico, see Oviedo, *Historia general*; Nicolás Monardes, *Segunda parte del libro des las cosas…de nuestras Indias* (Alonso Escrivano: Seville 1571); and Francisco Hernández, *Quatros libros de la naturaleza, y virtudes de las plantas* (D.L. Daualos: Mexico, 1615), in Brooks, *Tobacco*, 1:208, 248, 530 respectively. In this regard see also Girolamo Benzoni, *Historia del mondo nuovo* (F. Rampazetto: Venice, 1565), fol. 55r.

35  On the popularity of wine in Poland (and its related economic and financial consequences), see the observations of Giovanni Botero, a Jesuit scholar who served at the Savoy court of Christine's father-in-law, in his *Relazioni Universali* (Venice: G. Angelieri, 1599), 2:40–1. Regarding the belief that tobacco was able to make a drunk man sober, see Sander L. Gilman and Zhou Xun, eds., *Smoke: A Global History of Smoking* (London: Reaktion, 2004), 41; Brooks, *Tobacco*, 1:334–5.

36  On the death of Christine's husband Amedeo, the widow's regency was disputed between the pro-French factions who supported her – albeit at the cost of threatening her autonomy – and opposing pro-Spanish factions led by Christine's brothers-in-law, who sought to depose her; Ferrero, *Feste delle Madame Reali*, 12–20 and table XI.

37  Vecellio, *Habiti antichi et moderni*, 253–4; see also, for the Poles, 346–7.

38  Mary Floyd-Wilson, *English Ethnicity and Race in Early Modern Drama* (Cambridge, UK: Cambridge University Press, 2003), 36–9; Craig Rustici, "Tobacco, Union, and the Indianized English," in *Indography: Writing the Indian in Early Modern England*, ed. Jonathan Gil Harris (New York: Palgrave Macmillan, 2012), 124.

39  As observed by Floyd-Wilson, "despite Europe's contact with the New World, the classification of people and nations during this period still conformed to the ancient tripartite divisions of climatic regions – northern, southern, and temperate zones"; Floyd-Wilson, *English Ethnicity*, 2.

40  Ibid. Pierre Charron, *Of Wisdome* (London: E. Blount & W. Aspley, 1612), 164.

41  *Il Gridelino* [*Gridelin*] (1653), album at the National Library of Turin, Q V 71; *L'Unione* (1660), Q V 53.

42  *Lobspruch des edlen hochberühmten Krauts Petum oder Tabak, von dessen Ankunft und garloblichen Gebrauch bey manchen teutschen Helden* [*Laudation of the Noble and Well-Known Herb Petun, or Tobacco, Pertaining to Its Origin, Its Highly Praiseworthy Use by Many German Heroes*] (Nuremberg: Paul Fürst, 1652). The

caption reads: "Ich glaub fürwahr / es soll nit lang anstehen / so werden sie auch gar in hosen gehen." See image at https://digitalcollections.nypl .org/items/0d86e960-52b8-0134-f5d0-00505686a51c (see vignette "G"). On women smoking in sixteenth-century treatises, see Brooks, *Tobacco*, 1:282, 218, 324, and passim.

43  "Tutto il mondo l'adori [i.e. the tobacco plant], / e con acceso affetto / spargendo fumi ne l'altar di Bacco / faccia un Idolo nuovo del Tabacco" (fol. 4r).

44  *The Maske of Flowers* (London: printed by N.O. for Robert Wilson, 1614); see E.A.J. Honigmann, ed., "The Masque of Flowers," in *A Book of Masques: In Honour of Allardyce Nicoll* (London: Cambridge University Press, 1967), 151–2; Joan Pong Linton, *The Romance of the New World* (Cambridge, UK: Cambridge University Press, 1998), 125–6.

45  Honigmann, "The Masque of Flowers," 165; Amy L. Tigner, *Literature and the Renaissance Garden from Elizabeth I to Charles II* (New York: Routledge, 2016), 181–2.

46  The text is included in *A Solemne Ioviall Disputation, Theoreticke and Practicke, briefly shadowing the law of drinking* (Oenozps [i.e.y] thopolis: At the Signe of Red-eyes [i.e. London: E. Griffin], 1617).

47  Brathwaite, *Barnabees Journall*, 143–50.

48  Jeffrey Knapp, "Elizabethan Tobacco," *Representations* 21 (1988): 26–66.

49  "Qui color albus erat / quantum mutatus ab illo / Anglus in Aethiopeum." See Kristen G. Brookes, "Inhaling the Alien: Race and Tobacco in Early Modern England," in *Global Traffic: Discourses and Practices of Trade in English Literature and Culture from 1550–1700*, ed. Barbara Sebek and Stephen Deng (New York: Palgrave Macmillan, 2008), 157–78; Rustici, "Tobacco, Union, and the Indianized English," 117–31. Both of these scholars address a crucial issue raised by this image, namely the conceptual association not only between Amerindians and tobacco, and therefore between the product and the land where it was originally grown, but also between African peoples and tobacco. This latter association can be seen in not only the scrolls, but also the small statue of a black African man caught in the act of smoking tobacco located on the left-hand side. While small pipes are scattered at his feet, he is smoking what seem to be dried, rolled-up *nicotiana* leaves. With his left hand he is embracing a huge roll of tobacco in ropes. See also Schülting, "Tobacco – Sacred and Profane," 190.

50  Brookes, *Tobacco*, 2:157–9, 168.

51  Linton, *The Romance of the New World*, 118.

52  James I, *A Counterblaste to Tobacco* (London: R. Barker, 1604); see "To the Reader" and 1–2, 12. See also Penny McCarthy, "*It was not tobacco, stupified my braine*. The Tobacco Controversy of 1602," *The Modern Language Review* 110, no. 3 (July 2015): 631–48.

53  Benzi, *Regole della sanità*, 827.

54  "Oro non vale ... / senza il fosco carbonchio del Tabacco" (fol. 4r).

55  Fernando Ortiz, *Cuban Counterpoint: Tobacco and Sugar*, trans. Harriet de Onís (Durham: Duke University Press, 1995), 216–20.

56  Ortiz, *Cuban Counterpoint*, 192.

# chapter five

# From Hot Reverence to Cold Sweat: Christian Art and Ambivalence in Early Modern Japan

BENJAMIN SCHMIDT

### Francis's and Inoue's Pictures

The sixteenth and seventeenth centuries witnessed a remarkable renaissance for Christian art, which flourished, propagated, and circulated in all sorts of interesting quarters of the world. From the Far Eastern reaches of these early modern global circulations come two instructive anecdotes. In August 1549, the Jesuit missionary Francis Xavier landed on the southwestern tip of Japan, in Kagoshima on the island of Kyushu, bearing with him a cache of pictures.[1] Soon after his arrival, Francis managed to gain an audience with the daimyo (lord) of Satsuma, Shimazu Takahisa (1514–1571), whom he hoped to convert to Christianity; and to this task the legendary Apostle of the Indies brought said pictures, which he believed would sway the ruler. On the eastern-most precipice of his known world, Francis trusted in the efficacy of Christian art. When the "duke" (as the Jesuits referred to the daimyo) saw the European-made paintings, he was reportedly entranced and "very contented"; he "kneeled down before [a] picture of the dead Christ and Our Lady, and adored it with reverence, showing much delight" – or so the Jesuits believed. A few days later, Takahisa asked on behalf of his elderly mother, who had been particularly charmed by the artwork, for copies of these unusual *namban* (foreign) images – they likely would have been painted in oil on canvas, with illusionistic shadow and linear perspective. The daimyo's request proved tricky, however, "since we could not find materials in that place" to produce the art, the Jesuits reported.[2] Takahisa and his mother remained intrigued, all the same, by Christian art, if not, as it turns out, by Christianity, which they would soon prohibit in their lands.[3]

Jump ahead a century, and Christian art still intrigued the Japanese, possibly even more so, yet its affective qualities had significantly shifted, invoked and adopted in radically different ways. By the mid-seventeenth century, with the Tokugawa *bakufu* (shogunate) firmly in place, antipathy towards Christianity had demonstrably hardened – yet Christian *art* still had a place in Japanese society, its efficacy seemingly intact. While it may possibly have been "adored" by and brought "contentment" to some – there remained a community of *Kakure Kirishitan* (clandestine Christians) who worshipped sub rosa – Christian imagery was, by this time, more regularly deployed by the governing regime as an instrument of control. It was used, first, to expose the Christian faithful – perceived to be a fifth column of resistance – and, second, to account for the Japanese population; for it was enlisted as part of a perverse form of inquisition-cum-census, a way simultaneously to extract practitioners of Christianity, now strictly banned, and to tally the population. In the ceremony of *e-fumi*, the Japanese were asked to tread on Christian art – to stomp on images of the Virgin, the Pietà, the Crucifixion, et cetera – in order to demonstrate their indifference to Christian iconography and thus their allegiance to the Tokugawa shogunate (fig. 5.1). In the instruction manual for this ordeal, drafted by the grand inquisitor and powerful Tokugawa bureaucrat Inoue Masashige, we learn of the enduring efficacy of Christian art in Japan:

Old wives and women when made to tread upon the image of Deus [Jesus] get agitated and red in the face. They cast off their headdress; their breath comes in rough gasps; and sweat pours from them. And, according to the individual [informant], there are reportedly women who venerate the *fumi-e* [that is, Christian art], but in a way to remain unobserved.[4]

Over the course of a century, then, conditions have shifted from "contented ... reverence" to "agitated ... sweat," from the initial delight expressed by those originally introduced to Renaissance Christian art to the visceral anxiety faced by those subjected to the cunning form of coerced iconoclasm that was *e-fumi*. In all cases, it is clear that Christian art flowed to Japan, and it is just as clear – even as forms of its consumption altered dramatically – that it worked.[5]

Christian art turned out to be enormously popular in early modern Japan and evidently effective, as well. Tens, if not hundreds, of thousands of works of Christian art circulated in Japan over a period spanning the mid-sixteenth to the early eighteenth century: visual sources of various

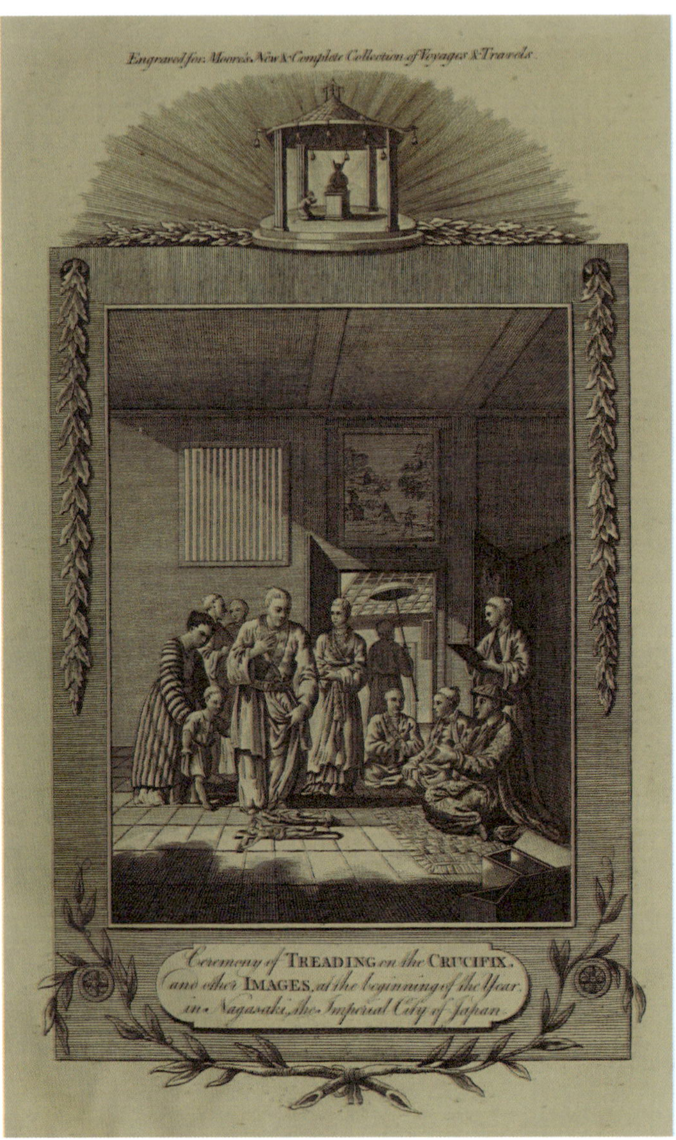


Figure 5.1. *Ceremony of Treading on the Crucifix, and other Images, at the beginning of the Year, in Nagasaki, the Imperial City of Japan*, in John Hamilton Moore, *A New and Complete Collection of Voyages and Travels* (London, 1780). Engraving, 17 x 28 cm. Wellcome Collection, London

materials and genres that conveyed Christian themes, typically in forms that originated in (or replicated those of) European ateliers.[6] Yet this surge of art did not necessarily flow in the same direction, let alone in the same stream. The works of Christian art that landed in Japan derived from different sources and functioned in sometimes drastically different ways. They were, moreover, deployed dissimilarly and experienced by distinct audiences in varying – and often unexpected – forms. Christian art flowed to Japan originally on the ships of Catholic missionaries, above all the Jesuits, who hoped to enlist prints, paintings, and plaquettes on behalf of "the greatest enterprise," as Alessandro Valignano (1539–1606), the Visitor of Missions in the Indies, described the epic project of converting the Japanese archipelago to Christianity.[7] Yet images of "the dead Christ and our Lady" (which would presumably have been a *Pietà* or *Lamentation*) appealed, as well, to many who were neither Christian nor inclined to convert. More generally, early modern Japan had an obsessive interest in "obtaining images" (as Timon Screech has described it), and Christian art was readily assimilated into a broader stream of visual fare.[8] It was admired by the military daimyos as well as other sophisticates at court, and it is no wonder that many of those who were "made to tread upon the image of Deus" would, at a minimum, have resented being crudely imposed upon to step on much-esteemed works of art. Meanwhile, the militantly devoted, for altogether different reasons, would have more than resented the *bakufu*'s demand to desecrate Christian images. They would have endured, surely with great anguish, what amounted to a wrenching and coerced performance of apostasy.

The forms of Christian art used for *e-fumi* had their origins, of course, in Europe, and those Europeans who visited, evangelized in, and trafficked with Japan over this period might also be described as image-obsessed. There was, broadly speaking, a vast expansion of image making in early modern Europe, a period that embraces not only the Renaissance (for lack of a better word), but also the Reformation, when image making and images per se became central to a continent-wide struggle over power and faith. The Jesuits certainly believed in the power of images, in some ways even more so than established Catholic practice. They subscribed to Ciceronian methods of rhetoric, which counselled using visual art "to delight, teach, and move" the viewer ("delectare, docere, et movere").[9] More vitally, images helped the Jesuits reach across language barriers in their global mission of conversion.[10] Meanwhile, on the other side of the Reformation divide and its fiery debates over images stood Calvinist reformers who, by contrast, condemned religious imagery as

potentially idolatrous and called for its removal from places of worship –
often by forcible, even violent means, as occurred spectacularly in the
iconoclastic outbreaks in the Low Countries. Indeed, both iconophilic
Jesuits *and* iconoclastic Calvinists believed fiercely in the power of images
and harboured intense feelings about the efficacy of visual fare.[11] And
this belief would suggest that not only did the "old wives and women"
of Japan sweat this matter but so, too, did the young European men in
Japan – Jesuit missionaries – and sober European merchants in Japan –
by the mid seventeenth century, exclusively the Dutch – who also found
themselves facing the distressing prospect of performing *e-fumi*.

It would be tempting to say that, their shared anxiety over Christian
art notwithstanding, much was lost in translation: that Europeans and
Japanese were sweating over different matters. Yet that would be not
only clichéd – a simplistic and impoverished understanding of global
exchange – but also wrong insofar as it underestimates the sophisticated
estimation by the early modern Japanese of Christian art, its multiple
functions, and its fluid meanings. In fact, the Japanese well appreciated
the power of Christian icons, no less the aesthetic novelty of Western-style
religious painting. The Tokugawa shogun grasped the utility of Christian
images and the benefit of controlling them just as well as his European
counterparts did: his inquisitors implemented in his territories a cunning variation of the princely principle of the Peace of Augsburg, *cuius
regio, eius religio* (whose realm, his religion). The shogun's bureaucrats
happened also to *collect* Christian art, indeed none more so than the *omet-
suke* (grand inquisitor) Inoue Chikugo no kami Masashige (1585–1661),
who ordered numerous prints and paintings from Europe (via Dutch
merchants), several of which inevitably featured Christian subject matter. Inoue and the other Tokugawa elite who collected Christian art did
so not so much to empathize with their victims' anguish or to catalogue
their tools of torture as to appreciate a fresh form of visual expression
and much-coveted cultural commodity. They enjoyed it.[12]

Or, rather, they could enjoy it, they could exploit it, they could collect
it, they could manipulate it, they could desecrate it, and they could sometimes, even if surreptitiously, venerate it. (Inoue, as it happens, was very
likely himself a Christian and remained so well into the seventeenth century.)[13] The many and sundry consumers of Christian art in early modern
Japan, not unlike their contemporaries in early modern Europe, experienced Christian visual materials in multiple registers, and this should
discourage any singular or simplistic set of suppositions about their an-
tagonism towards Europe or the directional flow of cultural influence in

the first age of globalism. The Japanese engaged with Christian art – just as did those Europeans who trafficked with them, above all the Jesuits and Dutch – with profound ambivalence. Shifting modes of engagement with Christian art indicate the shifting meanings and purposes of Christian art. This fluidity suggests, furthermore, different ways to narrate the global story of art, of "objects in motion," and of cultural engagement in the early modern world.[14]

The history of Christian art in Japan and, more particularly, of its role in the ceremony of *e-fumi* offers an exceptionally rich narrative of global things and their mediated meanings: of Christian art's production and importation into global spaces; of its myriad manners of reception and entanglement; of its role as a sacred artefact, no less a visual novelty; of its purpose, most basically, as a form of "memento religio"; of its function, most unsettlingly, as an instrument of torment; and so on. *E-fumi* serves as a crucible of sorts where all of these implications can be observed under conditions of intense pressure: where Japanese believers and inquisitors, European missionaries and merchants, multi-national artists and craftsmen, all converged – if sometimes reluctantly – to work out the significance of the object at hand. It is a history of entanglement, to be sure, yet also of ambivalence: the fluid meanings of *fumi-e* are hard to pin down. The ultimate history of *fumi-e* and of Christian art in early modern Japan presents not so much a case of European versus Japanese modes of reception as a set of intersecting narratives, which do not always follow the paths traditionally charted for them. These narrative paths illustrate histories of early modern art and its global mobility, of cultural flow and transformation, and, above all, of a shared faith among Europeans and Japanese in the efficacy of images – of Christian art's insistent visual power.[15]

### Demand and Supply

Christian art arrived in Japan in 1549 on the same ship that bore the Jesuit missionary Francis Xavier (1506–1552) to what was then understood to be the furthest limits of Europe's *oecumene*.[16] Francis's ship reached the southern tip of Kyushu a mere half-dozen years after Portuguese traders first docked there – the first Europeans to reach the remote archipelago – and only nine years after the foundation of the Society of Jesus. Artworks made the journey with Francis, since the Jesuits believed fiercely in the power of images, which they used as a matter of course in their missionary projects – in Europe and, still more so, overseas. Ignatius of Loyola (1491–1556) had always intended to produce his *Spiritual Exercises* with illustrations, which he imagined would allow the unlettered to access his work. And while this project never came to pass in Ignatius's lifetime, Jerome Nadal (1507–1580) later organized the production of the *Evangelicae historiae imagines* (*Illustrations of the Gospel Stories*) in much the same spirit: to elucidate Christian stories and concepts in a simple and accessible visual form.[17] (Nadal's *Imagines* in fact reached China.)[18] This same strategy guided Francis's missionary efforts. Before Japan, Francis preached in India, where he was known to rely on visual cues: paintings depicting standard Catholic iconography, which could be held or hung before a crowd as a rhetorical aid; simple, inexpensive prints meant for distribution among the faithful; or perhaps more durable plaquettes cast of bronze, which could be passed around in more intimate gatherings. In André Reinso's (c. 1590–after 1641) influential series of oil paintings representing the life of the future saint, multiple panels show Francis engaging with images. In *Saint Francis Preaching in Goa* (fig. 5.2), for example, two small paintings within the composition occupy the space behind the evangelizer – it is a meta-painting, as it were, which depicts paintings within a painting – offering a vivid demonstration of Francis's strategy of deploying art in, and thus conveying pictures to, the Indies.[19]

In Japan, too, Christian images imported by European missionaries played a significant role, although not always in the manner the Jesuits had bargained for. They served as religious icons, of course. Francis, who believed in the miraculous properties of icons, presented them as such to potential converts, as the case of Shimazu Takahisa well illustrates.[20] Yet Christian artworks also functioned as exemplars of an exotic visual tradition, which would have appealed to picture-loving Japanese elites on several levels. They were valued – as Takahisa's example also demonstrates – for their novelty and their material-cum-visual qualities. The layers of thick and richly pigmented oil paint; the illusion of depth produced by shadow and perspective; the form of the human body as shown in the all-but-nude representations of Christ (for example, in a *Crucifixion*): all of this would have captivated Japanese connoisseurs of art. And it was likely for these reasons – novelty, aesthetics, distinctiveness – that these intriguing images served so well as diplomatic gifts. Christian art fit seamlessly into the elaborate Japanese tradition of courtly exchange and ritual munificence. Moreover, for their association with innovative things and devices lately imported from Europe – muskets, above all, which radically altered the landscape of Japanese warfare in this period – Christian art also appealed to those daimyos interested in affiliating themselves with European styles and material technologies. For multiple reasons,

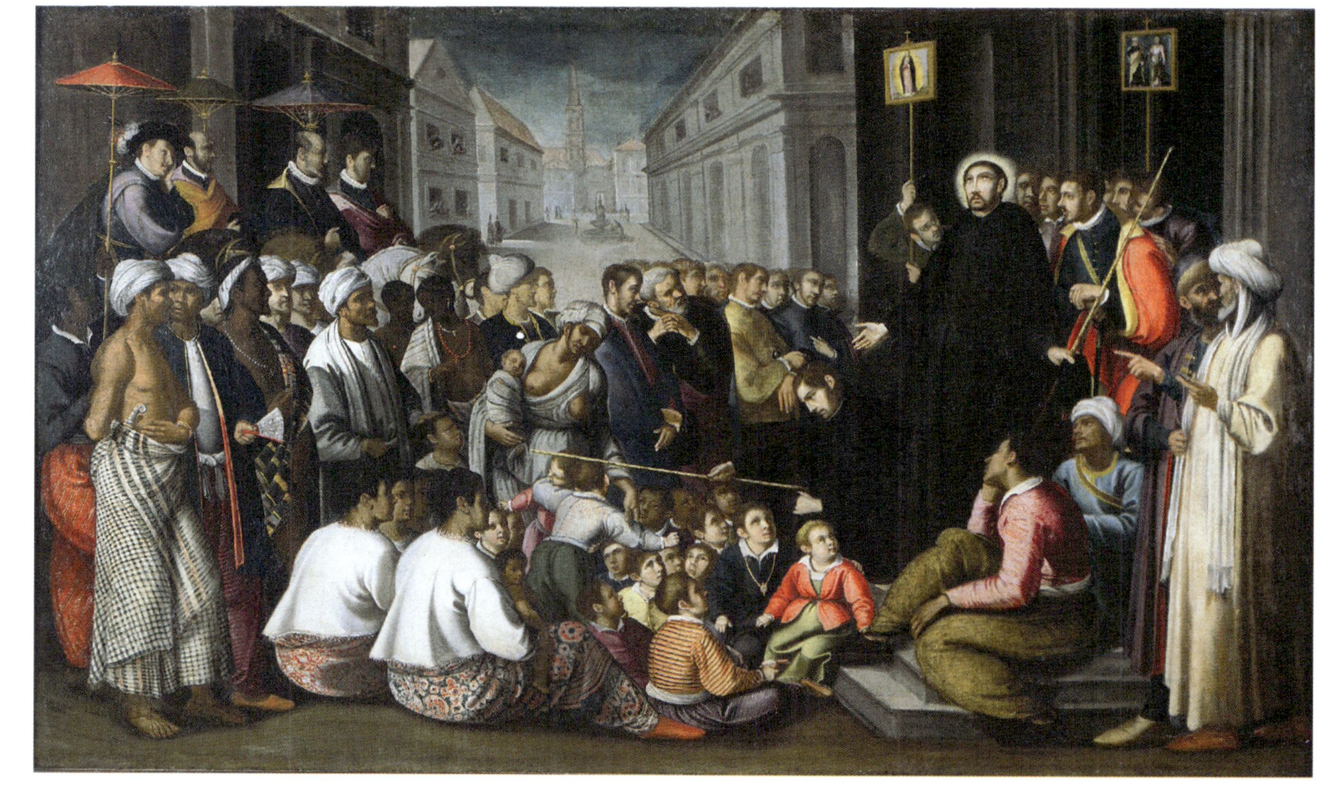

Figure 5.2. André Reinoso, *St. Francis Preaching in Goa*, 1619. Oil on canvas, 165 x 104 cm. Igreja de São Roque, Lisbon

then, Christian art in its European form became a highly popular and sought-after commodity in later sixteenth- and early seventeenth-century Japan. It was used by the missionaries as a mechanism of conversion; it was admired by the daimyos and tendered as courtly gifts; and, as a fashion associated with *namban-jin* (foreigners "from the south"), it was assimilated by various warring factions of Japan, as were European firearms, as a signifier of innovation, progress, and change.[21]

These several sources of demand notwithstanding, the most strenuous pleas for Christian art issued from the growing number of Japanese Christians. Indeed, the rising tide of Christian converts – by the late sixteenth century, estimated at some two hundred and fifty thousand – and the rising demand, otherwise, for Christian art fed a steady stream of Jesuit requests for images from Europe.[22] Meanwhile, the Japanese market for images coincided and competed with a broader surge of interest – in some instances, perhaps even a vogue – for European-style painting, as elites in Ming China, Mughal India, Safavid Persia, and the Ottoman empire all shared in the wider fascination with Christian art. Demand, in short, superseded supply. Portuguese merchants endeavoured to import what they could – prints and paintings done in the Flemish style current in Lisbon or, more likely, mass-produced in Flanders for the export market.[23] And Japanese court artists were known to make copies of certain works admired by the daimyos; this was a pattern, as well, in other courts across Asia. There would also have been shipments from Chinese and Indian workshops, where non-Christian artists produced Christian art for the global market (a growing problem from the perspective of the Portuguese crown, which issued multiple edicts demanding that "infidels" and "gentiles" cease to make "any paintings or sculptures of images of God").[24] Yet petitions persisted. Father Luís Fróis (1532–1597), a Portuguese missionary and resident at the court of the great warlord and collector Oda Nobunaga (1534–1582), sent a letter in 1566 asking "for blessed rosaries, relics … veronicas, [above all] images" to meet the demand. Another pressing request in 1577 for "images of Christ our Lord or of our Lady or of saints" in whatever form possible – prints, paintings, plaquettes – testifies to the robust Japanese market for and the insistent interest in Christian art.[25] Yet there was still not enough. Thus, in 1583 the Jesuits, on instruction from Alessandro Valignano, took the extraordinary step of setting up a *seminário de pintura*: an on-site school of painting geared to train artists to make images and thereby slake the thirst for Christian art in Japan.

The *seminário*, which ran for thirty impressively productive years, was exceptional in certain ways, yet it also fit neatly and more broadly into the context of late sixteenth-century Christian art.[26] It was the quintessential picture-making machine in the quintessential age of Christian-picture making. Under the direction of the multi-talented Neapolitan Giovanni Niccolò (1560–1626), the *seminário* functioned, first, as a roving arts academy, which trained painters, sculptors, and engravers in multiple workshops; and, second, from 1600, by which time it had settled in Nagasaki and come into its own, as "the largest mission art academy ever founded in Asia."[27] Its ambitiously outfitted ateliers included local Japanese artists as well as Chinese and European ones, who "executed oil paintings on copper, wood panel, and probably canvas, in addition to watercolour and ink paintings on paper." They also manufactured bronze plaquettes and other forms of sculpture, which, as was the case with the paintings, were produced "on a vast scale."[28] A printing press was soon introduced, and a workshop organized for copper-plate engraving. Models for *seminário* artists included a few European paintings that made it to Japan, yet above all prints, which derived, like the paintings, primarily from the Antwerp school of Counter-Reformation iconography. And here it is worth pointing out that the *seminário*'s work coincided almost exactly with another major, Jesuit-driven, visual project, Jerome Nadal's aforementioned *Evangelicae historiae imagines*, published in 1593 – a series of didactic prints issued by a similarly-organized hive of artistic energy based in Antwerp, which was likewise an image-making machine in these years.[29] Antwerp had been, of course, infamously the site of image *un*making only a few years earlier: the *Beeldenstorm*, or Iconoclasm, of 1566, for which the defacing of Antwerp's Onze-Lieve-Vrouwekathedraal by crowds of Calvinists counts as the iconic event. Less well known is the *Stille*, or quiet, *Beeldenstorm* of 1581, when the briefly installed Calvinist city council of Antwerp ordered the purging of all religious images (which, in this instance, were mostly sold rather than destroyed). In any event, the city fell to Habsburg troops just a few years later (1585), at which point a massive image-*making* project commenced in order to refurbish the city's churches and to re-educate its citizens with simple devotional prints – images not unlike the Christian art produced across the globe on the island of Kyushu.[30]

### *Fumi-e* as Christian Art: Traumatic Beauty

The *seminário de pintura* flourished into the early seventeenth century, after which shifts in the political winds in Japan led to shifts in the production and function of Christian art in Japan. With the rise, around the turn of the century, of the Tokugawa *bakufu* – which consolidated power and passed legislation that banned, first, evangelization and, next, the evangelizers, twenty-six of whom were horrifically martyred in 1597 – came the fall of the missionaries and the shuttering of the *seminário*. Production ceased in 1614. In the years that followed, a series of spectacular executions drove Japanese Christians underground and drove all of the remaining Jesuits (along with other Catholic missionaries) out of the country. It was also in this period that the shogun restricted Iberian traders – they would soon be outlawed altogether – and granted the Dutch a commercial toehold in their stead. The former – the mostly Portuguese merchants, along with the Catholic missionaries who typically accompanied them – were perceived to be too close to the Jesuits and too ostentatiously Christian. Meanwhile, the latter – the Dutch heirs of the Calvinist iconoclasts – were considered more palatable both as trading partners and when it came to religious practice.[31] This moment also marks the beginning of the Tokugawa policy of *sakoku* (鎖国: "locked country"), when the *bakufu* closed the archipelago to all foreigners, exclusive of the small enclaves of Dutch and Chinese merchants stationed in Nagasaki. More generally, Tokugawa officials cracked down on anything that smacked of "foreignness," particularly Christianity. This was even more harshly the case following the Shimabara rebellion of 1637–8, an uprising waged literally and figuratively under the banner of the Cross (the rebellion was sparked by punitive tax burdens as well as anti-Christian edicts; the battle flag borne by the rebel army bore an image of the sacramental chalice and a cross beneath the words "Louvado Seja o Santíssimo Sacramento" ["Praised be the Most Holy Sacrament"]).[32] Henceforth, for more or less the next two centuries, all expressions and material evidence of the Christian faith attracted intense government scrutiny. Christian artefacts were deemed intolerably subversive.

As for Christian art, it did not so much go underground (although in some cases it did) as become repurposed *on* the ground: as *fumi-e*. Sculptural *fumi-e* are a most peculiar form of "Christian" art (fig. 5.3). Modestly-sized, low-to-medium relief plaquettes, typically cast in bronze or brass and bearing simple Counter-Reformation iconography, *fumi-e* were enlisted by the Japanese regime chiefly for the performance of *e-fumi*. Literally "stepping-on pictures," *fumi-e* (踏み絵) are the material icons, thus technically objects of Christian art, while *e-fumi* (絵踏み) refers to the performative act of iconoclasm. The latter took the form of an extraordinary enactment of apostasy, typically done on an annual basis, as choreographed by the Tokugawa *bakufu*: stomping on

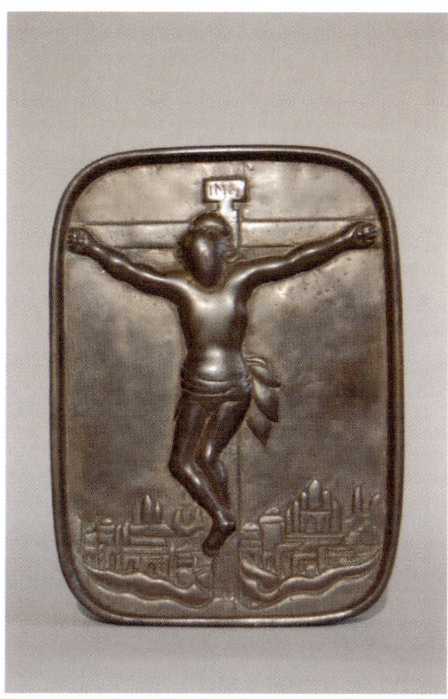

Figure 5.3. Hagiwara Yosuke, *Crucifixion*, 1670. Bronze (brass?), 18.3 x 14 x 3.5 cm. WTAC Gallery, New York

objects of Christian art.[33] Yet *fumi-e* were surely idiosyncratic art objects, which could gesture far beyond iconoclasm. In the absence of a more robust supply of Christian artefacts – which, by the second decade of the seventeenth century, could no longer be manufactured by the Jesuit art school in Nagasaki nor be imported into Japan by Portuguese merchants – *fumi-e* came to embody Christian art during an era of visceral anti-Christianity. This paradoxical character reflects, in turn, the ambivalent role Christian art had always played in Japan – and, for that matter, could play in other contexts, as was the case in the Netherlands during its own drama of iconoclasm. *Fumi-e* served ingeniously – albeit perversely – as a bureaucratic device of control for the *bakufu*; while they also circulated as bona fide Christian icons – if discreetly and, likewise, perversely – to those who remained faithful to the suppressed religion. Meanwhile, *fumi-e* attracted the attention, as well, of those who had developed, for altogether different purposes, an interest in European visual forms – Inoue Masashige, for example, and the other Tokugawa courtiers who continued to order Western art throughout this period via the Dutch East India Company.[34] In these various ways, then, *fumi-e* qua material artefacts bore multiple rich, fascinating, sometimes conflicting, and ultimately ambivalent meanings.

There are, in truth, many intriguing, no less disquieting, things about *fumi-e* and their histories – about the perversity of the performance of apostasy that they compelled (introduced, inter alia, in the late 1620s); about the agonizing ordeal endured by hundreds of thousands of Japanese Christians made to desecrate objects of sacred resonance; about the ingenious manipulation by the Tokugawa regime of Christian icons and iconophilia; about the bizarre incongruity borne by those craftsmen who sculpted art objects for the sake of their degradation (the inescapable material outcome of the process); about the poignant predicament faced by employees of the Dutch East India Company (often overlooked in these histories) who were ineluctably ensnared in the drama of *e-fumi* (and were, incidentally, not quite "Dutch" insofar as their ranks comprised a range of northern Europeans who staffed the company's ships and factories, including Catholics and Lutherans who would not easily have abided the prospect of iconoclasm).[35] Yet perhaps the most compelling angle spotlights the *fumi-e* itself: an art object made and manipulated to be distressed and desecrated. It is a category of "thing," moreover, that presents an especially vivid narrative of early modern global flow.[36]

As art object and visual genre, *fumi-e* can be difficult to pin down. Technically speaking, *fumi-e* could assume various material forms, the only requirement being the images they bore – the religious icons that would be subject to a ritualized form of iconomachy. The very earliest samples would have comprised printed – that is, paper – images; there is archival evidence for such, including several contemporary literary allusions, yet no identifiable artefacts (which would have been stomped, presumably, into oblivion).[37] These "picture" *fumi-e* would have invariably originated in European ateliers: devotional prints imported by the Jesuits and, by the early seventeenth century, comparably-styled prints produced by the on-site engravers of the *seminário de pintura*. The more durable plaquettes that replaced these fragile prints derived initially from the stock of Jesuit imports – once again, from European ateliers (fig. 5.4) – and, later, from the *seminário*'s workshops, which had been outfitted to cast sculpture. Yet in subsequent years, as older bronze sculptures became worn and ineffective, and with the Jesuit-schooled artists

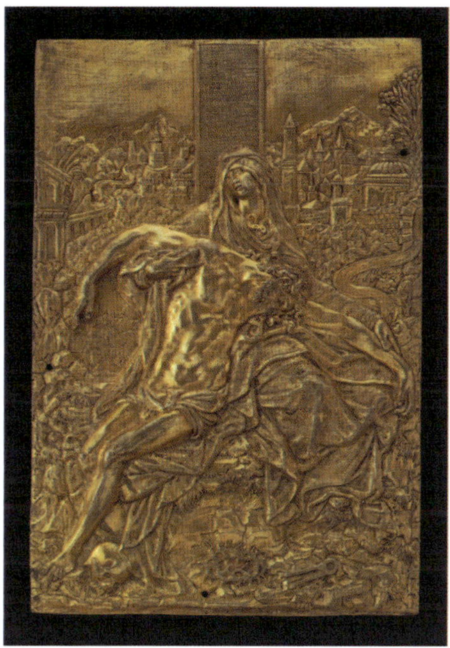

Figure 5.4. Jacob Cornelis Cobaert [attrib., after Guglielmo della Porta], *Pietà*, 1580. Gilt bronze relief, 18.5 x 12.8 cm. National Gallery of Art, Washington, D.C.

banned and expelled, new plaquettes were cast by Japanese foundries, as commissioned by Tokugawa officials; and this produced a new inventory of *fumi-e* and, consequently, a new style of Christian art (fig. 5.5). In all instances, whether pressed on paper or cast in metal, whether made in Europe or modelled in Japan, the iconography of *fumi-e* flowed consistently from the Counter-Reformation hub that was Antwerp: via objects that came directly from Flanders, on board Portuguese carracks; via objects produced by local, European-managed workshops, modelled on the prevalent Flemish style favoured by the Jesuits; or via objects made in autonomous Japanese foundries, inevitably fashioned after the extant, Flemish-designed imagery on hand.

The shift from artefacts created by or under the auspices of European artists to ones crafted independently in Japan marks a subtle shift in materiality, and this material modification tracks, as well, certain stylistic

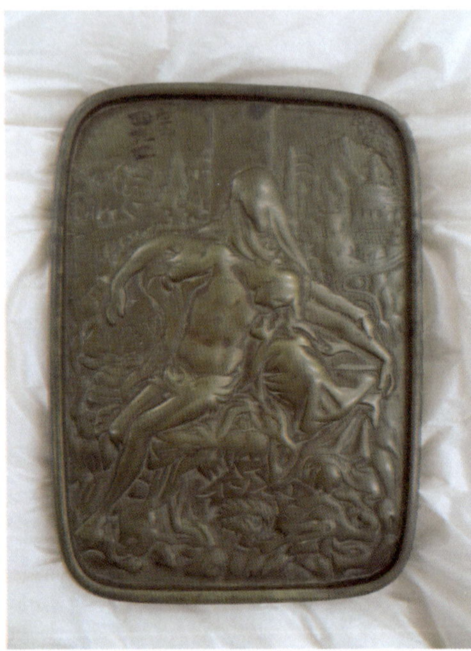

Figure 5.5. *Pietà* [seventeenth century]. Brass (?), 18.8 x 13.8 x 2.3 cm. Tokyo National Museum, Tokyo

shifts in the production of *fumi-e*. The typical casting material used in seventeenth-century Japanese metallurgy falls under the rubric of *sentoku* (宣徳), a kind of brass that takes its name from the Chinese reign mark *xuande* (rendered in Japanese as *sentoku*) found on certain imported Chinese vessels of this period.[38] It is often translated as "Chinese bronze," sometimes identified as *karakane*, and in all cases constitutes a type of *irogane*, or Japanese "coloured metals" (色金), so-called for their pattern of patination. Whatever its name, it is an alloy that blends copper, zinc, tin, and lead to form a material that falls somewhere between bronze, which was the preferred metal of Renaissance European sculpture (naturally darker than *sentoku*, which colours yellow to brown), and brass, which is more typical of East Asian metallurgy of this period.[39] Some *fumi-e* are plainly made of bronze, more than likely cast in European workshops, while others are made using *sentoku*, devised in Japan. The former can

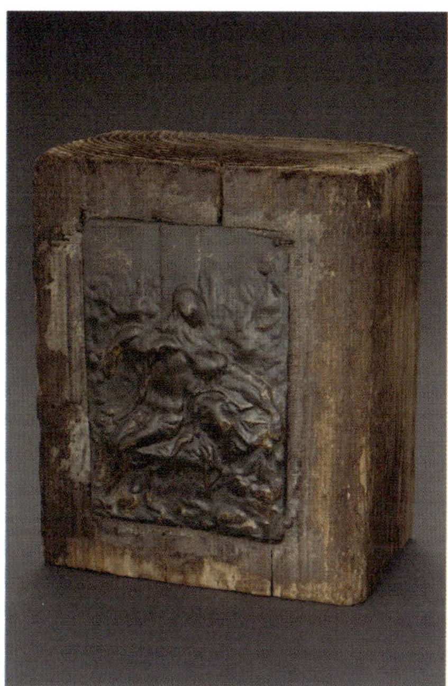

Figure 5.6. *Pietà* [seventeenth century]. Bronze relief medallion mounted in wood (keyaki?) with nails, 21 x 7.7 x 10.6 cm. Asian Civilisations Museum, Singapore

take the form either of basic plaquettes or bronze sculpture encased in wooden frames or mounts, typically of *keyaki* (*Zelkova serrata*, also known as Japanese elm); in this case they form *ita-e*, or wood-pictures (fig. 5.6). The latter – fabricated of brass-like *sentoku* – are not only lighter-coloured than the bronze examples; they also show unmistakable signs, stylistic no less than material, of Japanese production (see figs. 5.3 and 5.5).

Whether produced in bronze or brass, of *sentoku* or *keyaki*, surviving *fumi-e* are few and far between. Only a limited number have been ar-chived, and, even for these, material details and provenance are sparsely documented. Most of the known ones are collected in the Tokyo National Museum, which possesses twenty-nine, and these have been virtually the only ones cited in the scholarly literature (a striking case of agnotology – to adopt a term from philosophers of science for a kind of purposeful ignorance – since far more examples turn up in smaller museums and galleries).[40] About the objects that can be firmly identified, a few general points can be made. First, the subject matter and iconography of those *fumi-e* catalogued by the Tokyo National Museum are notably consistent, no matter their size, shape, or material. They replicate five recurring designs, all of which rank among the most pervasive motifs of early modern Catholic iconography, especially the sort emanating from Antwerp and Rome: the *Pietà*, with the tools of Christ's torment and crucifixion scattered in the foreground, and the background offering a cityscape of Jerusalem in schematic form; *Ecce Homo* (sometime referred to as "Christ as a Man of Sorrows"), with a crown of thorns, rope, and staff as Christ's accoutrements; a variant of the Virgin and Child known as the *Madonna of the Rosary*, which shows Mary clasping the Christ child as she hands a rosary to Saint Dominic (this scene is sometimes itself surrounded by a rosary); the *Madonna Immaculata*, which places Mary within a mandorla and standing on a moon, following recent Catholic Reformation iconography; and, lastly, the *Crucifixion*, staged before a stylized skyline of Jerusalem, sculpted in this instance somewhat more roughly than the version in the *Pietà*.[41]

A second point, which follows logically from the first, pertains to the repetition of these iconographies across the range of identified *fumi-e*. Although their configurations could vary – sometimes cast in oval format, sometimes rectangular; sometimes including greater detail, sometimes less – designs were repeated over multiple runs. They were codified, as it were – set pieces, streamlined for workshop replication – such that there are several examples of the *Crucifixion*, *Pietà*, *Ecce Homo*, and so on. The relatively simplified design of *fumi-e*, especially in their later, Japanese-produced formulations, would have offered benefits in terms of iconographic efficacy and workshop efficiency: they were easy to identify and easy to make.[42] Indeed, while there are mild variations among the designs of a theme, there are also series of *fumi-e* that show striking similarities, all but identical in terms of their detail and artistic work. And this leads to a further point: *fumi-e* were sometimes produced in quantity, with certain distinguished Japanese foundries issuing multiple copies of a single design. The Hagiwara atelier, for example, inscribed one known variant of a *Crucifixion fumi-e* "nijū no uchi ni" ("of twenty, number two" [廿、内二]), indicating a serial process of production (fig. 5.7).

When mild variations of motif or format do exist, these differences can be revealing. Subtle distinctions can sometimes be extracted from a plaquette's design: a cluster of figures off to the side of two variations of

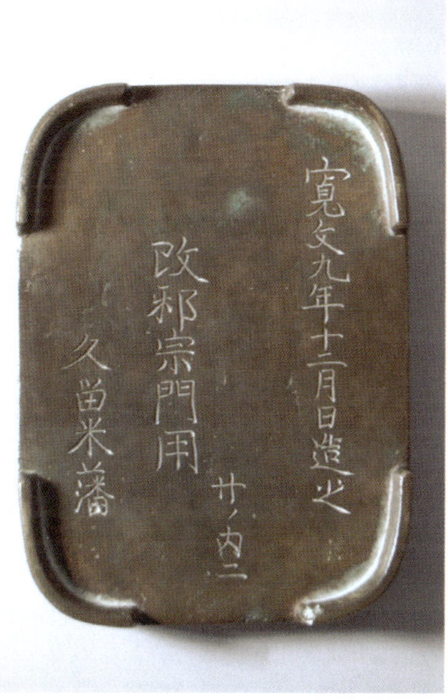


Figure 5.7. Hagiwara Yosuke, *Crucifixion* (*fumi-e*, rear view), 1670. Bronze (brass?), 18.3 x 14 x 3.5 cm. WTAC Gallery, New York

the *Madonna of the Rosary fumi-e,* arranged with ever-so-slight discrepancies, indicate separate castings.[43] Yet more tangibly evident are the variations in the materiality and framing among different *fumi-e,* and these elucidate modes of production as well as consumption. Sculptural *fumi-e* were fabricated in either bronze or brass, the former a typically European technique, the latter more prevalent in Asian metallurgy; and it is easy to note differences between designs in the respective materials. Bronze plaquettes replicate designs and forms common in early modern European art; they can be readily matched with European prototypes (cf. figs. 5.4 and 5.6). Plaquettes made in *sentoku* (brass), by contrast, are stylistically more schematic: the details have been simplified, the landscapes abridged, and the perspective flattened (cf. figs. 5.4 and 5.5; see also 5.3).[44] More to the point, the bronze plaquettes tend to be cast in smaller formats – these are the ones encased in Japanese boards (*ita-e*) – and the wood frame brings them to a size that matches the brass *fumi-e*. The mounted *ita-e* are logically European-forged sculptures repurposed in Japan: Baroque sacred art refabricated by Tokugawa bureaucrats (see fig. 5.6). Meanwhile, the brass *fumi-e* invariably include feet to support their distinctively rounded corners (see fig. 5.7). This combination yields similarly designed motifs delivered in dissimilarly shaped formats, in both cases producing a sculptural object that can rest stably in a horizontal position – for example, on the ground. And this raises another related aspect of *fumi-e*: whatever their material and design, *fumi-e* are generally uniform in size, even when the bronze plaquettes are mounted in wooden frames. The frames effectively bring the smaller plaquettes to a standard size, which corresponds to that of the brass *fumi-e*, of circa 20–24 by 14–18 centimetres. And here it may be worth noting that these dimensions match almost precisely the size of an average early modern Japanese foot. Material conditions, in short, render the sturdy, steady, sculpted icon a perfect target for stomping.[45]

This last point brings up a perhaps obvious, yet absolutely fundamental feature of all *fumi-e*, whatever their design, their size, or their material. They all share a more or less similar state of repair. Or rather of *disrepair*, since all documented *fumi-e* are unfailingly tarnished, worn down, and rubbed smooth, their figures literally effaced from repeated, intense use. And this dulled material condition suggests an interesting paradox. While *fumi-e* qua art objects show signs of meticulous, exquisite craftsmanship, *fumi-e* as instruments of government bureaucracy demonstrate evidence of enduring, distressing use. They exhibit, somewhat incongruously, what the critic Makoto Fujimura has described as a sort of "traumatic" beauty.[46]

### *Fumi-e* and the Ambivalence of Christian Art

*Fumi-e* are richly fascinating things, and they suggest myriad ways to think about global art and its mobilities, also material flows and their transformations, in the early modern world. In *fumi-e*, we have an object of religious conversion, for that is the original purpose of the bronze plaquettes borne by Catholic missionaries to the East to facilitate their project of evangelization in Japan. In *fumi-e*, we have an object of apostasy, that original conversionary purpose having been inverted by the shrewd counsellors of the shogun, who well understood the affective role of art and iconophilia to early modern Christians. In *fumi-e*, we have an object of blunt authoritarian control for the centralizing Tokugawa regime; yet in *fumi-e* we also have an object of visual and aesthetic value, esteemed by certain upper-ranking Tokugawa courtiers (like Inoue Masashige), who demonstrated a keen appreciation of innovative, exotic art. In *fumi-e*, most critically, we have an object of broad, abject torture: for Japanese Christians, forced to desecrate a religious icon; for Catholic missionaries lingering in Japan (despite the *bakufu*'s edicts of expulsion); and, not least, for Dutch East India Company factors stationed in Japan, who were not always Dutch (but rather part of an international company of employees) and, if Dutch, not always Calvinist and, even when Calvinist, not always happy, it turns out, to engage in rituals of iconoclasm.[47] Finally, in *fumi-e* we have an object of art – a meticulously designed, skilfully crafted, elegantly executed work of sculpture, possessing all the affective power and subtle complexities of Christian art.

That genre – "Christian art" – presents something of a paradox, particularly when viewed in the context of early modern Japan. *Fumi-e* functioned, in many ways, as crude instruments of administrative control, yet they also retained, for those Christians obliged to step on them, the ineffable quality and enduring force of a Christian icon.[48] Several *fumi-e* began their lives in an altogether different visual and cultural tradition – as bronze plaquettes cast in Flanders, or perhaps Italy, to be shipped with Catholic missionaries to the Indies. Others derived from Japanese foundries, commissioned by shogunal officials who wished to obtain works of religious art, albeit for the purpose of their desecration. The genre of Christian art, that is to say, bore multiple layers of conflicting meaning for those early moderns who engaged with it, in Japan and elsewhere – this goes for the lord of Takahisa's mother and the old wives "made to tread upon the image of Deus," no less than for the visually adept Jesuits proselytizing in all corners of the globe and the iconoclastic Calvinists rampaging in the Low Countries. *Fumi-e* concentrated these contradictions in a singular thing, the material object and the sacred image alike bearing richly ambivalent messages. Highlighting their status as works of art underscores not only the global meanings and transcultural flows of *fumi-e*, but also the ways these meanings and flows could shift across time, space, and interpretive regimes.

The latter is critical. For while all *fumi-e* share certain generic qualities and obtain their operative value by replication – their standardization, stipulation, and circulation of a prescriptive set of images – they ultimately functioned, as most Christian art does, as singular works of art. And, while they only infrequently possess reliable artistic attribution, *fumi-e* do on occasion include instances of specific inscription, which indicate an individual artist, a place of production, and a date of creation. One such example bears the markings of the master forger Hagiwara Yoshisuke, who carved his signature into his work in late January or February 1670: "Kanbun kyūnen jūnigatsu hi kore o tsukuru" ("made on a day in the twelfth month of the ninth year of Kanbun" [寛文九年十二月日造之]) (see fig. 5.7).[49] There is not much known about Yoshisuke (or Yosuke), yet archival traces in Kyushu and a curious narrative tradition describe a sculptor bearing a similar name, Hagiwara Yusa, who, upon making an exceptionally exquisite *fumi-e*, was reportedly brought before the magistrates of Nagasaki to account for the very beauty of his creation.[50] The authorities had apparently found Yusa's *fumi-e* so compelling, so persuasive, and so inherently lovely, that they decreed it genuine "art" and a work of sacred sculpture – not an *inversion* of a Christian icon, but a bona fide icon of affective beauty, thus worthy of worship, a thing possessing what Walter Benjamin might have called the "aura" of art. Yusa admitted his responsibility and offered to step on his creation to show his indifference to it, likewise his lack of Christian faith. He even offered to destroy his art, along with all other *fumi-e* in his workshop – yet to no avail. Ultimately, the authorities found his protests less convincing than the object itself, and the artist lost his head accordingly. Grisly though it may have been, Yusa's execution made a certain amount of sense in the context of early modern Japan, where one could be invested in Christian art, though not Christianity per se; where Christian icons could bear meaning – indeed, multiple meanings – even for those who had no truck with Christianity. This is the inexorable lesson of *fumi-e*, and the sculptor lost his head over this seeming paradox: his art – the ambivalent art of *fumi-e* – was deemed too compelling. In all events, while his head was lost, Yusa's *fumi-e* may well have survived, although it is not clear what the authorities ultimately did with a thing of such manifest beauty, urgent meaning, and apparent power over life and death.

#### ACKNOWLEDGMENTS

I am very grateful to Angela Vanhaelen and Bronwen Wilson for their editorial guidance and for organizing the volume; to David Spafford and Isabel Schmidt for their help with Japanese-language queries; to Dieuwke Eijer and John Schloss for permission to reproduce images of the *fumi-e* in their collection (and for their wonderful gallery); and to Louise Townsend for her expert editing.

## NOTES

1  Scholarship is not entirely settled on how many paintings Francis (and his assisting Japanese convert, Yajiro, sometimes recorded as Anjiro, later baptized as Paulo) brought with him to Kagoshima. There were certainly two, described roughly as a *Madonna* and a *Madonna and Child*: see *The Letters and Instructions of Francis Xavier*, trans. M. Joseph Costelloe (St. Louis, MO: Institute of Jesuit Sources, 1992), 306; and cf. Grace A.H. Vlam, "The Portrait of S. Francis Xavier in Kobe," *Zeitschrift für Kunstgeschichte* 42 (1979): 48–60. Gauvin Bailey specifies that one of the paintings was an *Annunciation*: Gauvin Alexander Bailey, *Art on the Jesuit Missions in Asia and Latin America, 1542–1773* (Toronto: University of Toronto Press, 1999), 60; see also Clement Onn, "Christianity in Japan, 1549–1639," in *Christianity in Asia: Sacred Art and Visual Splendour*, ed. Alan Chong (Singapore: Asian Civilisations Museum and Honolulu: University of Hawai'i Press, 2016), 173.

2  Juan Ruiz-de-Medina, ed., *Documentos del Japon, 1547–1557*, Monumenta Historica Societatis Jesu 137, Monumenta Missionum Societatis Jesu 52, Monumenta Historica Japoniae 2 (Rome: Instituto Histórico de la Compañía de Jesús, 1990), 2:156–7, cited, also in the original Spanish, in Alexandra Curvelo, "Copy to Convert: Jesuit Missionary Artistic Practice in Japan," in *The Culture of Copying in Japan: Critical and Historical Perspectives*, ed. Rupert Cox (London: Routledge, 2008), 114–15. "Quando Paulo [aka Yajiro, the Japanese convert assisting Francis] fue a hablar con el duque, el qual estava cinco leguas de Cangoxima, llevó consigo una imagen de nuestra Señora muy devota que traíamos con nostros. Y holgó a maravilla el duque quando la vido, y se puso de rodillas delante de la imágen de Christo nuestro Señor y de nuestra Señora, y la adoró con mucho acatamiento y reverencia, y mandó a todos los que con él estaban que hiziesen lo mismo. Y después mostráronla a la madre del duque, la qual se espantó en verla, mostrando mucho plazer. [¶] Después que tornó Paulo a Congoxima donde nós estábamos, dahí a pocos días mandó la madre de duque un hidalgo para dar orden cómo se pudiese hazer otra imagen como aquella. Por no aver materiales en la tierra se dexó de hazer."

3  The daimyo would place a prohibition on baptism within a year or so (c. 1550): see George Elison, *Deus Destroyed: The Image of Christianity in Early Modern Japan* (Cambridge, MA: Harvard University Press, 1973), 34.

4  Elison, *Deus Destroyed*, 204 (mildly edited for clarity), which includes an extensive extract from the so-called *Kirishito-ki* (Records of Christians), which is the title given to Inoue's manual for "inquisition."

5   It is also clear, in both cases, that gender informs these events and,
    more generally, that early modern Japanese consumers of Christian art
    comprised – naturally, yet perhaps also particularly – women. This was
    surely not the case *in toto*, yet these anecdotes from the archives do offer an
    intimation that Japanese women especially engaged with this novel form of
    art right from the get-go.

6   Estimates of Christian-themed artworks in early modern Japan vary, yet they
    suggest a quantity that would easily have exceeded fifty thousand pieces (in-
    cluding both art imported by the Portuguese and works produced domes-
    tically), which is the number of devotional images requested by the Jesuit
    missionary Luís Fróis already in 1584 to meet demand. For an overview of
    the Jesuit mission in Japan, with particular attention to its art program, see
    Bailey, *Art on the Jesuit Missions*, 60–81 (noting the "extraordinary volume"
    and "grand scale" of production of Christian images in Japan [71], as well
    as Fróis's 1584 request [66]).

7   J.F. Moran, *The Japanese and the Jesuits: Alessandro Valignano in Sixteenth-
    Century Japan* (London: Routledge, 1993).

8   Timon Screech, *Obtaining Images: Art, Production, and Display in Edo Japan*
    (Honolulu: University of Hawai'i Press, 2012); cf. also Morgan Pitelka, *Spec-
    tacular Accumulation: Material Culture, Tokugawa Ieyasu, and Samurai Sociability*
    (Honolulu: University of Hawai'i Press, 2015).

9   The Ciceronian method is explicated in *De Oratore*, 27.115 (Loeb edition,
    280–1); on Francis's adaptation of it, see René B. Javellana, "The Invention
    of an Icon: From Francisco Xavier of Navarre to San Francisco, Patron of
    Missions and Apostle to the Indies," in *Portugal, Jesuits, and Japan: Spiritual
    Beliefs and Earthly Goods*, ed. Victoria Weston (Chestnut Hill, MA: McMullen
    Museum of Art, 2013), 20.

10  The Jesuit strategy was epitomized in Jerome Nadal's *Evangelicae historiae
    imagines* (*Illustrations of the Gospel Stories*) (1593), taken up below; see also
    the discussion of Jesuit evangelization and its reliance on the visual image
    in Javellana, "Invention of an Icon," 20.

11  See the arguments in this regard in Joseph Koerner, "The Icon as Icono-
    clash," in *Iconoclash: Beyond the Image Wars in Science, Religion and Art*, ed.
    Bruno Latour and Peter Weibel (Cambridge, MA: MIT Press, 2002), 14–37;
    and, more broadly, Koerner, *The Reformation of the Image* (Chicago: Univer-
    sity of Chicago Press, 2003).

12  Timon Screech, "A 17th-Century Japanese Minister's Acquisition of West-
    ern Pictures: Inoue Masashige (1585–1661) and His European Objects," in
    *Transforming Knowledge Orders: Museums, Collections and Exhibitions*, ed. Lar-
    issa Förster, Morphomata 16 (Paderborn: Fink Verlag, 2014), 72–106. Inoue

ordered images mostly in broad, generic terms – in one case, anatomical pictures, in another, "animals." In a few instances, however, he made specific requests: for example, for a Jacob Cats emblem book – this would have been the *Spiegel van den ouden ende nieuwen tijdt* (1632), with engravings by Adriaen van de Venne – and a perspective box of the type popularized by Samuel van Hoogstraten. While not quite the Baroque Catholic art favoured by the Jesuits and later banned by the shogun, these Dutch-imported visual materials would have included Christian themes, all the same. In the case of Cats, the engravings in the *Spiegel* bore numerous images of the hand of God reaching down from the heavens or otherwise intervening in human affairs – namely, Protestant forms of domestic art. Meanwhile, perspective boxes typically included images of domestic interiors, where paintings typically hung – for example, a salon or sitting room decorated with religious art. See, for an approximate example, Pieter Janssens Elinga's contemporaneous *Perspective Box with Interior* (c. 1660–80; Museum Bredius, The Hague), which includes interior paintings of Jesus and Mary Magdalen in the garden ("noli me tangere") and a *Samaritan Woman at the Well.*

13  Evidence suggests that Inoue remained Christian until circa 1625 (age 40), when his most powerful patron, Iemitsu, became shogun, at which point the need to remove impediments to promotion (i.e., Christian practices) became more pressing. See Ton Vermeulen et al., eds., *The Deshima Dagregisters: Their Original Tables of Contents* (Leiden: Leiden Centre for the History of European Expansion, 1986–2010), 12:147; as well as the discussions in Screech, "A 17th-Century Japanese Minister," 73; and Elison, *Deus Destroyed,* 192.

14  Cf. Daniela Bleichmar and Meredith Martin, eds., *Objects in Motion in the Early Modern World* (Oxford: Wiley-Blackwell, 2016); and the classic account of Arjun Appadurai, ed., *The Social Life of Things: Commodities in Cultural Perspective* (Cambridge, UK: Cambridge University Press, 1986).

15  "Christian art" is used here and throughout this essay broadly to describe figurative art, of all media, that depicts or invokes Christian subject matter, themes, and motifs. The literature on early modern (as opposed to late ancient) "Christian art" as a stand-alone genre is surprisingly meagre and generally more allusive than precise. The topic does come up (although is rarely theorized) in discussions of Christian evangelization and Christian art objects in early modern Asia (less so America). See, for example, Alan Chong, "Christian Art in Asia," in Chong, *Christianity in Asia,* 9–13; and Pedro Moura Carvalho, "What Makes Asian Art Christian?" in ibid., 14–19.

16 On the history of Christianity in early modern Japan, see Ikuo Higashib-
   aba, *Christianity in Early Modern Japan: Kirishitan Belief and Practice* (Leiden:
   Brill, 2001); Elison, *Deus Destroyed* (focused mostly on the early years and
   persecution); and C.R. Boxer's classic study, *The Christian Century in Japan,
   1549–1650* (Berkeley: University of California Press, 1951). On the Jesuit
   mission more particularly, see M. Antoni J. Üçerler, "The Jesuit Enterprise
   in Sixteenth- and Seventeenth-Century Japan," in *The Cambridge Companion
   to the Jesuits,* ed. Thomas Worcester (Cambridge, UK: Cambridge University
   Press, 2008), 153–68.

17 Jerónimo Nadal, *Evangelicae historiae imagines: ex ordine evangeliorum,
   quae toto anno in missae sacrificio recitantur, in ordinem temporis vitae Christi
   digestae* (Antwerp: [Martinus Nutius II], 1593). Nadal's work appeared
   posthumously and was republished in 1594 and 1595 in amplified volumes. These editions had the effect of circulating widely what became,
   arguably, the most instrumental text and images of the Jesuit evangelical
   enterprise.

18 Bailey, *Art on the Jesuit Missions*, 93, 98, and passim.

19 André Reinoso, *St. Francis Preaching in Goa* (1619), oil on canvas, 165 x
   104 cm, Igreja de Sáo Roque, Lisbon. One of the interior paintings clearly
   shows the Virgin Mary within a mandorla, a standard Counter Reformation
   motif; the other appears to show two saints. On Francis and the visual, see
   Rose Marie San Juan, *Vertiginous Mirrors: The Animation of the Visual Image
   and Early Modern Travel* (Manchester: Manchester University Press, 2011),
   86–124; and Javellana, "The Invention of an Icon."

20 Francis's belief in the "miraculous properties" of images is noted in Bailey,
   *Art on the Jesuit Missions*, 60; see also San Juan, *Vertiginous Mirrors.*

21 Inês Carvalho Matos, "Namban Labyrinth," *Bulletin of Portuguese and Japanese
   Studies*, series 2, 1 (2015): 77–108.

22 The number of Christians in early modern Japan is not fully clear. It is,
   moreover, not fully debated among historians so much as it is asserted,
   based largely on missionary estimates from the early seventeenth century
   that have been codified by scholarship of the mid-twentieth century and
   later. Boxer offers the most thorough review of the evidence, acknowledging that it derives chiefly from the Jesuits, who would have had reason to
   exaggerate their success. That granted, he considers the estimate of 300,000
   converts offered by Padre Valentim de Carvalho in 1614 (the year of the
   Jesuit's expulsion) "reliable" and also cites approvingly another documented estimate from that year of 250,000 (*Christian Century*, 320–1). Bailey
   adopts Boxer's upper limit of 300,000 without further critical comment: *Art
   on the Jesuit Missions*, 53.

23 On the Flemish export market, particularly overseas, see Neil De Marchi and Hans J. Van Miegroet, "The Antwerp-Mechelen Production and Export Complex," in *In His Milieu: Essays on Netherlandish Art in Memory of John Michael Montias*, ed. Amy Golahny, Mia M. Mochizuki, and Lisa Vergara (Amsterdam: University of Amsterdam Press, 2007), 133–47. On Japanese imports, more particularly, see Bailey, *Art on the Jesuit Missions*, 60; and Javellana "Invention of an Icon," 20–1.

24 The edicts are extracted from the "Provisões a favor da Cristandade" (Historical Archives of Goa, ms. 7693, sig. 22; translation in Pedro Moura Carvalho, "What Makes Asian Art Christian?" 14) and reflect the widespread anxieties of the Lisbon authorities. On the impressive output of Christian art, nonetheless, from Indian and Chinese workshops (above all, those of Goa and Macau), see Jay A. Levenson, ed., *Encompassing the Globe: Portugal and the World in the 16th and 17th Centuries*, with contributions by Jack Turner and Diogo Ramada Curto (Washington, DC: Arthur M. Sackler Gallery, Smithsonian Institution Press, 2007); and, on the mass production of Christian ivories, more particularly, Gauvin Alexander Bailey, Jean Michel Massing, and Nuno Vassallo e Silva, *Ivories in the Portuguese Empire = Marfins No Imperio Portuguese* (Lisbon: Scribe, 2013).

25 Fróis is quoted in Pedro Moura Carvalho, "The Circulation of European and Asian Works of Art in Japan, circa 1600," in Weston, *Portugal, Jesuits, and Japan*, 40. See also Yoshimoto Okamoto, *The Namban Art of Japan*, trans. Ronald K. Jones (New York: Weatherhill and Tokyo: Heibonsha, 1972), and n. 6 above.

26 On the *seminário*, which remained active in Japan from 1583 to 1614 (after which it shuttered, many of its artists relocating to Macau), see Bailey, *Art on the Jesuit Missions*, 66–72; Onn, "Christianity in Japan"; and Curvelo, "Copy to Convert." On the Jesuits' visual program in Japan, more generally, see Noriko Kotani, "Studies in Jesuit Art in Japan" (PhD diss., Princeton University, 2010). Note that the Jesuits, of course, also deployed and produced images for their evangelical mission in the Americas.

27 Bailey, *Art on the Jesuit Missions*, 66.

28 Ibid., 68.

29 Nadal's *Evangelicae historiae imagines*, published after his death in 1580, was completed by the Flemish engravers Marten de Vos and Hieronymus and Anton Wierix II (with help from the Roman artist Bernardino Passeri), and the Antwerp publishers Christophe Plantin and Martinus Nutius II. Its immense popularity over the coming decades coincided almost precisely with the busiest years of the Jesuit *seminário de pintura* in Japan, which was heavily influenced by its engravings.

30  On the historic shift in the city's art production – and this historic moment
    in the history of Antwerp's art – see Koenraad Jonckheere, *Antwerp Art after
    Iconoclasm: Experiments in Decorum, 1566–1585* (New Haven, CT: Yale Univer-
    sity Press, 2013).

31  On the experience and expulsion of the missionaries (whose ranks in-
    cluded Dominicans and Franciscans, as well), see Elison, *Deus Destroyed*;
    and Neil S. Fujita *Japan's Encounter with Christianity: The Catholic Mission in
    Pre-Modern Japan* (New York: Paulist Press, 1991). On the commercial shift
    from Portuguese to Dutch trading partners, see Boxer, *Christian Century*;
    and Adam Clulow, *The Company and the Shogun: The Dutch Encounter with
    Tokugawa Japan* (New York: Columbia University Press, 2014). And on the
    Dutch in Japan and their complicated relationship with the shogunate, see
    (along with Clulow) Jan de Hond and Menno Fitski, *A Narrow Bridge: Japan
    and the Netherlands from 1600* (Amsterdam: Rijksmuseum and Nijmegen:
    Vantilt, 2016).

32  The Shimabara Rebellion (and the Banner of Amakusa Shiro, which is
    currently held in the Amakusa Christian Museum, just off the Shimabara
    Peninsula) is discussed in Geoffrey C. Gunn, *World Trade Systems of the East
    and West: Nagasaki and the Asian Bullion Trade Networks* (Leiden: Brill, 2017),
    chap. 5, "The Shimabara Rebellion (1637–38) Revisited," 122–42; and
    Elison, *Deus Destroyed*, 217–21. The persecution of Christians in Japan is
    surveyed in Stephen Turnbull, *The Kakure Kirishitan of Japan: A Study of Their
    Development, Beliefs and Rituals to the Present Day* (Surrey, UK: Curzon [Japan
    Library], 1998).

33  *Fumi-e* – which have received scant scholarly attention, until recently, out-
    side of Japan – are taken up in Bailey, *Art on the Jesuit Missions* (esp. chap.
    3, "'The Greatest Enterprise': The Jesuit Mission to Japan, 1549–1622");
    Thomas DaCosta Kaufmann, "Interpreting Cultural Transfer and the Con-
    sequences of Markets and Exchange: Reconsidering Fumi-e," in *Artistic and
    Cultural Exchanges Between Europe and Asia, 1400–1900: Rethinking Markets,
    Workshops and Collections*, ed. Michael North (Farnham: Ashgate, 2010),
    135–61; and Kristi Beth Jamrisko, "Empiricism and Exchange: Dutch-
    Japanese Relations Through Material Culture, 1600–1750" (MA thesis,
    University of Maryland, 2015). Jamrisko, in particular, does an excellent job
    of gathering and synthesizing the older scholarship; hers, furthermore, is
    the only English contribution that engages directly with the Japanese schol-
    arly literature.

34  Screech, "A 17th-Century Japanese Minister."

35  Jan de Vries and Ad van der Woude, *The First Modern Economy: Success,
    Failure, and Perseverance of the Dutch Economy, 1500–1815* (Cambridge, UK:

Cambridge University Press, 1997), 642–7, where it is estimated that, from the 1660s, more than half of VOC employees were non-Dutch. See also Roelof van Gelder, *Het Oost-Indisch Avontuur: Duitsers in Dienst van de VOC (1600–1800)* (Nijmegen: Uitgeverij SUN, 1997).

36 The allusion here is to "thing theory" and the critical work of Bill Brown et al.; see Brown, ed., *Things* (Chicago: University of Chicago Press, 2004); Brown's agenda-setting essays, "Thing Theory," *Critical Inquiry* 28 (Autumn 2001): 1–22, and "Objects, Others, and Us (The Refabrication of Things)," *Critical Inquiry* 36 (Winter 2010): 183–217; and, on "things" and their global flow, Jennifer L. Roberts, "Things: Material Turn, Transnational Turn," *American Art* 31, no. 2 (Summer 2017): 64–9.

37 See, for example, the textual description and engraved depiction in Arnoldus Montanus, *Gedenkwaerdige gesantschappen der Oost-Indische Maetschappy in 't Vereenigde Nederland, aen de Kaisaren van Japan* (Amsterdam: Jacob van Meurs, 1669), 294–5.

38 The name goes back to a Ming-era minting die found on imported Chinese vessels from c. 1426–35. A contemporaneous Tokugawa example can be found inscribed on the reverse of an Edo-era *tsuba* (the hand guard between the blade and hilt of Japanese swords and other bladed weapons) in the collection of the British Museum, which categorizes the metal of fabrication as "sentoku": https://www.britishmuseum.org/collection/object/A_OA-3319. Cf. also Markus Sesko, *Encyclopedia of Japanese Swords* (Morrisville, NC: Lulu, 2014), 385.

39 European bronze of this period – roughly the fifteenth through eighteenth centuries – was an alloy of copper and tin, although other elements might be added in small amounts, while European brass of the period comprised copper and zinc. Japanese brass of the same period would be more likely to contain small measures of tin and lead, as well.

40 For a representative reference to the *fumi-e* collected by the Tokyo National Museum (TNM) as, putatively, the only known examples, see Thomas DaCosta Kaufmann, *Toward a Geography of Art* (Chicago: University of Chicago Press, 2004): "the only items to be identified with reasonable surety as *fumi-e* are those now in the Tokyo National Museum" (313). On agnotology – in this case, the stubborn resistance of the scholarly literature to accept the broader archive of *fumi-e*, scattered across global collections – see Robert N. Proctor and Londa Schiebinger, ed., *Agnotology: The Making and Unmaking of Ignorance* (Stanford: Stanford University Press, 2008).

41 The TNM's collection of *fumi-e* are catalogued in the *Illustrated Catalogue of Tokyo National Museum Kirisitan* [*sic*] *Objects: Christian Relics in Japan*

*16th–19th Century* (Tokyo: Tokyo National Museum, 2001). Note that "Christ as a Man of Sorrows" (or *Misericordia*) is the term used when wounds of the Crucifixion are visible, which may be the case in some of the Ecce Homo *fumi-e*, even if the material wear makes this detail difficult to discern. The staff in this depiction is meant to mock Jesus as "king of the Jews."

42 Jamrisko notes the irony of this design strategy: "In the European case, simplification [of image and iconography] was designed to facilitate Counter-Reformation devotion; in Japan, it facilitated a ritual [*e-fumi*] that was devotion's very opposite" ("Empiricism and Exchange," 75).

43 Differences in the foreground scene and in the marginal figures of two variations of the *Madonna of the Rosary* indicate a different cast used (or a cast reconfigured) for the *fumi-e* catalogued by the TNM as C719 and C725. See *Illustrated Catalogue*, 31–2.

44 Kaufmann, *Toward a Geography of Art*, 331–3. It is worth noting, however, that the impression of "flattening" – of a lack of depth and perspective – would be enhanced by the sheer repeated use of the *sentoku*-forged *fumi-e*, which would have been particularly and perceptibly flattened by incessant wear.

45 There are obvious challenges to gauging premodern foot size, as the data are elusive and invariably incomplete. Roughly speaking, however, foot size can be calculated from height, and the latter can be extracted from various dependable material sources. The data for historical height reliably show a 10 per cent increase from the close of the Tokugawa era to the present. The average height for Japanese of the late twentieth century (170.8 cm/male and 158.3 cm/female) thus indicates the average height of Japanese in the Edo period (155.3 cm/male and 143.8 cm/female); see Max Roser, Cameron Appel, and Hannah Ritchie, "Human Height" (2013; rev. 2019), Our World in Data, https://ourworldindata.org/human-height, (accessed 28 April 2020). Height to foot size correlation is 6.5:1, which means that premodern foot sizes in Tokugawa Japan would have been c. 23.9 cm for men and 22.1 cm for women; see Pradeep K. Pawar and Abhilasha Dadhich, "Study of correlation between human height and foot length in residents of Mumbai," *International Journal of Biological & Medical Research* 3, no 3 (2012): 2232–5.

46 Makoto Fujimura, *Silence and Beauty: Hidden Faith Born of Suffering*, foreword by Philip Yancey (Downers Grove, IL: IVP Books, 2016), 103–6.

47 On the delicate situation of the employees of the Dutch East India Company and their controversial role in *e-fumi*, see Siegfried Huigen, "'Dit bedryf van onze Natie': François Valentyn over het abjecte gedrag van de Nederlanders in Japan," *Tijdschrift voor Nederlandse Taal- en Letterkunde* 127

(2011): 343–70; and Benjamin Schmidt, "La pesanteur des icônes: Les objets d'apostasie au Japon et leurs itinéraires à l'époque modern," in *Objets Nomades: Circulations matérielles, appropriations et formation des identités à l'ère de la première mondialisation, XVIe-XVIIIe siècles*, ed. Ariane Fennetaux, Anne-Marie Miller Blaise, and Nancy Oddo, Global Matters 1 (Turnhout: Brepols, 2020), 114–30. The irony of Dutch Calvinists engaged in *e-fumi* – ritualized iconoclasm – is explored in Mia Mochizuki, "Deciphering the Dutch in Deshima," in *Boundaries and Their Meanings in the History of the Netherlands*, ed. Benjamin Kaplan, Marybeth Carlson, and Laura Cruz (Leiden: Brill, 2009), 63–94, where the author assumes, incorrectly, the Calvinist composition of the VOC.

48 David Freedberg, *The Power of Images: Studies in the History and Theory of Response* (Chicago: University of Chicago Press, 1991).

49 Kanbun 9 is often rendered as 1669, but the actual date here corresponds to a day between 22 January and 19 February 1670. The inscription adds: "Jashūmon aratame yō / Kurume-han" (改邪宗門久甾米藩): "For use in investigating evil sects, Kurume domain." "Jashūmon" refers generally and primarily to Japanese Kirishitan, although it means more literally "evil sects," and it was used also to refer to a particular sub-sect of Nichiren-shū, the Lotus sect, known as "fuju fuse." Within this context, however, it clearly refers to those who practice Christianity.

50 Nagayo Yoshirō, *The Bronze Christ*, trans. Kenzoh Yada and Henry P. Ward (New York: Taplinger, 1959), narrates the events, also affirming the basic facts of Yusa's story (see "Author's Note," 8). On Nagayo's well-regarded work and its engagement with Christianity, see Massimiliano Tomasi, *The Dilemma of Faith in Modern Japanese Literature: Metaphors of Christianity* (London: Routledge, 2018), 179–85.

# chapter six

# Eggs, Cheese, and (Francis) Bacon

HELEN SMITH

This is an essay about the role of dairy in the creation of the world. Or, rather, it is an essay about the part eggs and cheese played in imagining how the world came into being, how it was held together, how life was created, and how it perpetuated itself. It shows how multitudinous worlds were generated from foodstuffs that were, and remain, at once ordinary and remarkable. Though I have been unable to resist the lure of a title that triangulates eggs and cheese with one of their most energetic students, the philosopher and statesman Francis Bacon, this essay takes in a wide range of texts, images, and artefacts to show how thought-provoking breakfast could be when the mysteries of creation were understood to be encapsulated within the shell of an egg or the rind of a cheese.

A key thinker, to whom I return throughout the chapter, is Margaret Cavendish. Cavendish repeatedly, and wittily, brings the processes of worldmaking down to earth. Her vigorous and frequently satirical challenges to natural philosophical tradition and contemporary experiment help to bring the possibilities and limits of worldmaking into view. Cavendish's characteristic willingness to entertain multiple hypotheses is key to my argument about the kinds of worldmaking that inhere in the act of imagining and reframing the making of the world. Her interventions respond energetically to the early modern "explosion of images, descriptions, measurements, hypotheses, and debates about the nature of the world."[1] Cavendish's presence is also important to this essay's acknowledgement of women's work and the diverse ways in which gendered labour shaped and defined the central cosmological projects of early modern natural philosophy. While Cavendish places herself decisively on the side of the philosophers, albeit within a network of female correspondents, I also take seriously other women's hands-on experience of generation and creation as acts of worldmaking, possessed of a compelling imaginative force.

Eggs and cheese, and their representations in visual art, were enmeshed in networks of international exploration and trade. Eggs in particular neatly illustrate Paula Findlen's persuasive observation that "the single most important new development in the history of early modern things concerns the geography of objects and its implications for seeing the history of material culture as an essential component of global history."[2] Drawing on the work of Findlen and others, I recognize the world-wide ubiquity of the egg, as well as noting cheese's status as a marker of civilization in ancient ethnography. But I also show the extraordinary degree to which these everyday comestibles provided food for thought, allowing early modern natural philosophers to unspool not global histories but the history of the globe: the generative metamorphoses of chaotic matter and shaping form.[3] By tucking into eggs and cheese, this chapter aims, in part, to rethink the relationship between material things and matter itself. Jonathan Goldberg has influentially argued for a reorientation of the "material turn," which "in studying material objects, has largely ignored the theoretical question of materiality."[4] Eggs and cheese trouble the category of material culture: they are the products of natural processes, but they are thoroughly intertwined with cultivation and husbandry; they are graspable (and edible) things that open up some of this period's extraordinary attempts to understand the world as an instance of the flows of matter.

The uses of eggs and cheese to articulate the most fundamental questions of worldmaking – where did the world come from, and how is life reproduced? – reveal the utility of analogy as a natural philosophical mode. Terming analogy "the most imaginative, fictionalizing figure of rhetoric," Claire Preston argues that "early-modern science was often analogical, that its insights and expression had the structure of a rhetorical figure."[5] The figurative, imaginative worlds of early modern natural philosophy are fully on display in this essay, which zooms in on the twinned terms of "similizing" and "similitude," arguing that these constitute acts of recognizing and acknowledging, rather than creating, similarity. Natural philosophical comparison, I argue, is not simply an exercise in identifying likeness, but a discovery and articulation of structural and material sympathies: a kinship between the things compared, including, for the purposes of this essay, specific continuities between eggs or cheese and the fecund, created world. The shapes and operations of matter constituted the most pressing questions of early modern philosophy; this chapter explores how the substance and transformations of the world were illuminated on the page, in the dairy, and in the worldmaking projects observed and set in train within those sites.[6]

### "The Reason why we begin with a Henns egge"

In the second of her *Philosophical Letters* (1664), Margaret Cavendish addresses with lacerating scorn the question of whether all animals are generated from eggs: "it is said, that the first Woman was made of a mans ribb; but whether that ribb was an egg, I cannot tell."[7] Cavendish notes that her unnamed addressee has been reading the physician William Harvey's *Anatomical Exercitations Concerning the Generation of Living Creatures* (1653) and been left bubbling with questions. It is little wonder that Cavendish's correspondent was intrigued – in Harvey's account, eggs are wonderful things. An egg, he reflects, "is the *Terminus à quo*, the Point or Original from which all the *Cocks* and *Hennes* in the world do arise and spring: and it is also the *Terminus ad quem*, the Aim and End proposed by nature, to which they direct themselves all their life long. ... The *Egge* is at were [*sic*] the Period of this Eternity; for it is hard to say, Whether the *Egge* be made for the *Chickens* sake, or the *Chicken* for the *Eggs*."[8]

The riddle of priority – in other words, which came first, the chicken or the egg? – goes back a long way. As John Beaumont summarized it towards the end of the seventeenth century, "*Plutarch* tells us, it was the Opinion of *Orpheus* and *Pythagoras*, that the Egg was the principle and ordinary source of Generation; and that *Orpheus* held the Egg not only more ancient than the Hen, but to have the Seniority of all things in the World."[9] Cavendish, however, has little patience for this ancient conundrum: she grumbles that the "common question, whether the Egg was before the Chick, or the Chick before the Egg, ... is but a thred-bare argument, which proves nothing, for there is no such thing as First in Eternity" (Pp2v). Dismissing this question, Cavendish forecloses debates surrounding the creation and existence of prime matter: did God create both matter and world in a single utterance, or did some kind of primal stuff exist even before the omnipotent maker? Harvey, in contrast, promises to "copiously handle" the timeless puzzle of which came first as part of his extensive treatise on the nature and processes of animal reproduction. Even before he addresses the question of priority directly, he answers it in two ways, first establishing the hen's egg as the observational site through which he will address all of animal generation (the egg not just as progenitor of the hen, but as the foundation of scientific enquiry), and secondly, in the lines cited above, establishing the egg as both elliptical and infinite, the origin and *telos* of every creature.

Eggs are good to think with. Encased within an eggshell is the mystery of life: its spark, quickening, and metamorphoses. Eggs are, as Harvey notes, drawing on the work of the Italian anatomist Fabricius ab Acquapendente (1533–1619), remarkable objects, both agent and matter, "*the Instrument, and all other things, whatsoever are necessary requisites to* Generation" (K6r). Part of their miracle is nature's ability to confine everything required to build a chick inside an egg's fragile shell. Harvey, like Acquapendente and Aldrovandi before him, made minute, repeated observations of eggs, slicing them open one after another at different points in the germinal process.[10] This method had also been proposed by Francis Bacon, who, in his manuscript *History and Inquiry Concerning Animate and Inanimate,* calls for a rigorous, empirical investigation into eggs and their propagation.[11] Bacon speculates upon and observes eggs at various moments throughout his extensive writings. He argues, for instance, against Bernardino Telesio's hypothesis as to how animals are moulded into shape inside the womb, objecting "that similar shaping goes on in egg shells where no such corrugations or inequalities exist."[12] Bacon, who memorably described his relationship to Aristotle as that of "a good house-hen, which without any strangeness will sit upon pheasants' eggs," repeatedly observes and comments upon eggs' mundane transformations.[13] He notes especially that "Fire makes eggs contract and, as far as their whites are concerned, changes them from transparent to milky white" and that "even if a shelled egg be thrown into good strong spirit of wine it is poached and goes white."[14] Bacon was alert to eggs' manifold uses in medicine and especially household cures, advising those who were, like him, squeamish about the prospect of cutting open pigeons and placing them still warm on the soles of the feet in the event of severe illness, to instead use "things similar to the substance of the human body," including milk, butter, and egg yolks.[15] And his writings suggest some familiarity with domestic husbandry, pointing out that "Eggs ... are sometimes hatched by the fire's heat, which thus exactly mimics animal heat."[16] Bacon's statement hovers between anecdote, observation, and hearsay: he does not claim to have seen chicks hatch in front of the fire himself, nor does he report it as something he has read or been told. Instead, he proposes the surprise emergence of a hearth-side chick as common knowledge, an observable phenomenon that helps to explain the operations of heat.

More broadly, throughout this period, eggs were fascinating objects. They were a staple of *Wunderkammer*, or cabinets of curiosity, testaments to the copious wonders of the world. Figure 6.1 shows a cassowary egg, recovered from the wreck of the Dutch East India Company pinnace yacht *Witte Leeuw*, sunk in a battle with two Portuguese carracks off St. Helena in 1613.[17] Bacon would have welcomed this well-preserved egg as an object of study. "I have heard it claimed as a proven fact," he remarks, "that an egg which had lain for a long time at the bottom of a moat was found evidently to have turned into stone, with the colours and distinctions of the yolk, white and shell still remaining, save that the shell was broken here and there and it glittered with little encrustations."[18] This reported egg is wonderful in its preservation, transformed into something jewel-like and distinctly precious. John Tradescant's "collection of rarities," which became part of the founding collection of the Ashmolean Museum, included not only a cassowary or emu egg and eggs from crocodiles, ostriches, and soland geese (gannets) but also "Divers sorts of Egges from *Turkie*: one given for a Dragons egge" and "Easter Egges of the Patriarchs of *Jerusalem*."[19] Eggs range from the foreign to the mythological, taking in the religious relic and the souvenir: the Catholic Patriarch of Jerusalem still gives out eggs, emblems of the resurrection, at Easter. As Findlen notes, "the early modern period was repeatedly defined and redefined by episodes in which different societies became familiar with each other's things." Attention to the geography of objects, their transportation, and their redefinition allows us to understand "the history of material culture as an essential component of global history."[20] As part of this quasi-ethnographic and wholly acquisitive mode, eggs – a coherent category, but remarkable in their variety, especially of size – offered one way to comprehend the early modern world's proliferating contact zones.[21]

Cavendish hints at the relatively commonplace (though still elite) nature of eggish exotica by the mid-seventeenth century, dismissing the Cartesian idea that "that which moves the whole body, is as a Point, or some such thing in a little kernel or *Glandula* of the Brain, as an Ostrich-egge is hung up to the roof of a Chamber" (Ccc1r).[22] Though she does not say so explicitly, Cavendish's casual employment of this comparison suggests that the dangling ostrich egg had itself become relatively unremarkable, a decorative feature of any curious household. Even humble hen's eggs had a place within the culture of wonder and artifice. In his *Phænomena universi* (*Phenomena of the Universe*), Bacon recounts a courtly game in which eggs are sucked empty and filled with perfumed water before

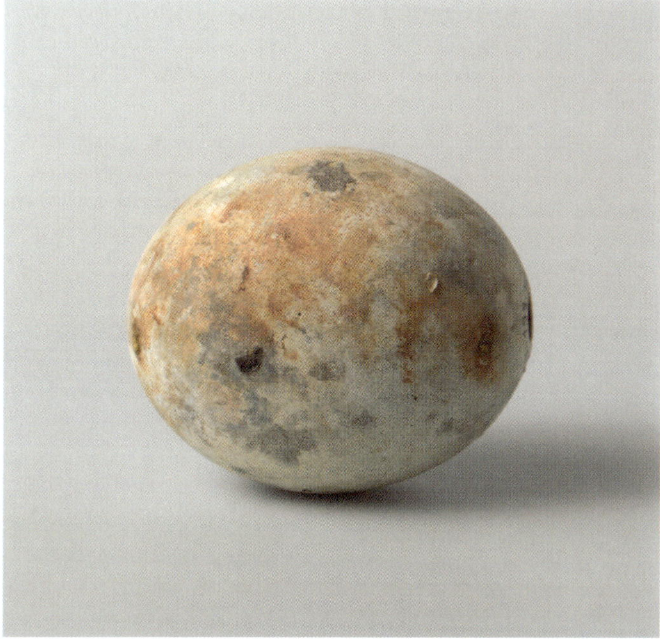

Figure 6.1. Cassowary egg from the wreck of the Dutch East India ship *Witte Leeuw*, before 1613. Rijksmuseum, Amsterdam, NG-1977–192-W.
© Rijksmuseum, Amsterdam

being "thrown in play and broken to imbue the air with a sweet fragrance."[23] This olfactory bait-and-switch, presumably designed to surprise an unwitting target, plays with the egg's inherent mystery: its satisfying impermeability, and the hard-to-explain transformations possible within its shell. In these contexts, eggs exemplify both of the apparently incompatible collecting impulses described by Lorraine Daston and Katharine Park: they are part of a medieval tradition within which *Wunderkammer* and individual objects were "repositories of wealth and of magical and symbolic power," especially when richly mounted or decorated (as eggs often were); and they were also objects of interest within an early modern frame which embraced cabinets and their contents as "microcosms [and] sites of study."[24] Eggs were, as we will see, understood quite literally as microcosmic – highly condensed renderings of the world.

Harvey's eggs are not Cavendish's only target in the *Philosophical Letters*. She moves on to lampoon an aspect of Peripatetic philosophy, declaring, with robust humour, "Nay, why may not the whole World be likened unto an Egg? Which if so, the two Poles are the two ends of the Egg; and for the Elements, the Yolk is the Fire, the White, the Water; the Film, the Air; and the Shell it self will very well serve for the Earth" (Qqqq2v). Though Cavendish presents this possibility as both fantastical and ridiculous, eggs were widely used as figures for or types of the world, thanks not only to their encapsulation of the mysteries of germination but also to their striking concentric structure. In John Rastell's *A New Interlude and a Mery of the Nature of the .iiij. Elements* (c. 1520), an ambitious attempt to present natural philosophical knowledge in the form of a morality play, a personified Nature describes the elemental composition of the world, in which "ponderous and heuy" earth is at the centre, wrapped about with water. The hotter, lighter elements, fire and air, "compasse them euery where obycularly / As the whyte a boute the yolke of an egg doth lye."[25] The well-known but always remarkable internal organization of the egg – "the colours and distinctions of the yolk, white and shell," in Bacon's terms – becomes a means to conceive of the shape and structure of the earth. This is a different mode of worldmaking: it is not the variety of eggs that encapsulates the copiousness of the natural world, as in a *Wunderkammer*, but the specific mysteries of any given egg that allow for the imagining and articulation of the structures of the world and the universe.

The analogy between world and egg was summarized again in 1533 by Thomas Paynell, in his translation of Ulrich von Hutten's treatise on syphilis, *De morbo Gallico*: "there is in an egge a certayne shewe of the worlde, bothe because it is made of the foure elementes, and agayne bycause it is gathered rounde in sphere fascion, And hath a lifely power."[26] Constituted of the four elements, or rather representing the elements in its concentric layers, an egg "shows" or represents the world. This is a view that Hutten and others attribute to Alexander of Aphrodisias, writing in the late second and early third century CE. In his popular *Haven of Health* (1636), Thomas Cogan reflected,

> *Alexander Aphrodissaeus* hath a pretty saying of an egge. *Orbis vniversi quem inundum vocamus, speciem in ovo dixeris demonstrari: nam & exquatuor constat elementis, & in spherae facium conglobatur, & vitalem potentiam obtivet.* The shell hee likeneth in qualities to the earth, that is cold and dry: the white, to the water that is cold and moyste the fome or froth of the white to the ayre, that is hot and moyst: the yolk to the fire, that is hot and dry. So he maketh the egge as it were [microcosmos], a little world.[27]

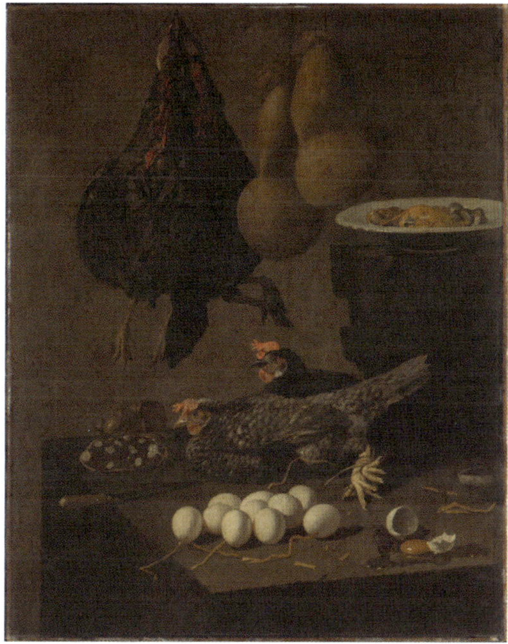

Figure 6.2. Giovanni Battista Recco, *Still Life with Chickens and Eggs*, 1640–60. Oil on canvas, 108 x 87 cm. Rijksmuseum, Amsterdam, SK-A-3884. © Rijksmuseum, Amsterdam

In a marginal note, Cogan glosses his quotation from Book III of Alexander's *Problemata* (now considered of doubtful attribution) with a phrase that recurs in his own volume's closing index, "An egge resembleth the whole world." The term "resembleth" had a stronger force than it does today, denoting features and properties in common – a material kinship rather than a passing likeness.[28]

The analogical tradition described here adds a striking resonance to Giovanni Battista Recco's detailed and morbid *Still Life with Chicken and Eggs* (c. 1640–60), in which live chickens, their legs bound, sit uneasily below their slaughtered fellows, next to the point of a knife and a sliced black pudding (fig. 6.2).[29] A clutch of eggs are gathered at the front of this scene of implicit culinary violence, perhaps a further nod to mortality, given the sterile fate of most harvested eggs.[30] Close to the viewer lies a broken egg. This image serves, in part, as a reminder of the artist's materials and the proximity between the objects of the kitchen and those of the studio. "You should always temper your colours with egg yolk," the artist Cennino Cennini (c. 1360–before 1427) instructed, "and temper it well, always as much of the yolk as of the colours you temper with it."[31] Within the larger context traced here, this egg takes on further significance, encapsulating the elemental complexity and fragility of the world.[32] Julie Hochstrasser notes that "still-life painting brings the world of things to center stage"; Recco's painting suggests that still lives also had the ability to reflect upon the mysteries of the world *in* things, bringing out the extraordinary mysteries of generation and world creation inherent in the most everyday of foodstuffs.[33]

Cavendish quickly finds the limits of the longstanding analogy between egg and world, at least in one of its incarnations, noting that if the shell were properly to be equated with earth it would need to be at the egg's centre rather than its periphery: "But then it must first be broken, and pounded into one lump or solid mass, and so swim or sink into the midst of the liquid parts" (Qqqq2v). Cavendish does not address Harvey's alternative take on this tradition, in which he compared not the shell but the yolk with the earth: "as in the greater world, the earth is deposited in the Center the Air and the Water being round about it, so also the yolk, as the more earthy part, is incircled by the two whites, whereof the one is grosser, the other finer" (E6v). As a triumphant exercise in *reductio ad absurdum*, Cavendish crowns her observations by remarking, "Or it might be said, that the Chaos was an Egg, and the Universe, the Chicken" (Qqqqq2v). As absurd as it seems in Cavendish's rendering, this opinion too (the chaotic egg, rather than the universal chicken) had a long heritage: Sanskrit scriptures offer the earliest versions of the cosmic egg, or Brahmanda. The egg was also a powerful alchemical symbol. Pamela H. Smith describes one illustration in the gorgeously illuminated *Splendor Solis* (*The Brightness of the Sun*), a version of an alchemical text attributed to Salomon Trismosi that dates from around 1582. In it, a Hermaphrodite holds an egg in one hand, and the cosmos, symbolized by the four elements, in the other. "The egg," notes Smith, "symbolises the beginning of all things, out of which the entire universe develops."[34]

Early moderns invoked the Greek Orphic tradition in accounts of the chaotic egg. In Aristophanes' telling,

> in the boundless bosom of Erebus did black-winged Night at the very start bring forth a wind egg, from which as the seasons revolved came forth Eros the seductive, like to swift whirlwinds, his back aglitter with wings of gold.

And mating by night with winged Chaos in broad Tartarus, he hatched our own race and first brought it up to daylight.[35]

This tradition was readily Christianized. Alexander Ross, for instance, asked his readers, "when they write that *Zephyrus* begot *Cupid* of an egge; what can it else mean, but that the spirit of God did manifest his love, in drawing out of the informed and confused egge of the *Chaos*, all the creatures?"[36] *Purchas his Pilgrimage* (1626) goes so far as to make a direct comparison between the creator and a chicken, arguing that the Bible called the originary Chaos "waters" not because of any inherent dampness but because "of that want of stability, whereby it could not abide together, but as the Spirit of GOD moued vpon these waters, to sustaine them; and as the Hen sitteth on her egges to cherish and quicken."[37]

Bacon drew on the story of Cupid's hatching as part of his extended interpretation of the ancient matter theory he read as embedded in creation myths. In *On Principles and Origins*, he explains:

> they relate that this Love was the most ancient of all the gods and therefore older than all things except Chaos, which they claim to be coeval with him. Further, Love is presented quite without a parent. But he himself by his intercourse with Chaos begat both the gods and all things. Nevertheless, some people report that he came from an egg laid by Night. He is given various attributes, such as that he is always an infant, blind, naked, winged and a bowman. But his principal and peculiar power is effective in uniting bodies; and the keys of ether, land and sea were also entrusted to him.[38]

This story, for Bacon, contains the essence of Democritean philosophy, setting out "with a parable's brevity *the doctrine concerning the principles of things and the origins of the world.*"[39] Chaos represents the raw congregation of matter while Cupid stands for matter's power, nature, and capacity for movement. Night symbolises the obscurity of the origins of things, territory that must, for Bacon, remain opaque to even the most ambitious enquirer, and can only be known through negative principles and exclusions. At the heart of these myths are truths about physical reality: from the careful stripping away of possibilities and hypotheses "something is affirmed and established, and an egg hatched, as it were after an appropriate period of incubation."[40] The egg, or rather the chick, becomes knowledge, patiently nurtured by the broody natural philosopher.

We have come a long way from Harvey's detailed observations of the particularities of chicken embryos at each developmental stage. And yet

Harvey's breathless account of the egg as possessed of generative mystery and material potential chimes in striking ways with traditions in which a humble egg could provoke thinkers to grapple with and comprehend the structures of the universe. Why did this everyday foodstuff possess such extraordinary imaginative potential, both as an object of empirical enquiry and as a pattern for cosmic mysteries? A major part of eggs' appeal as tools for practical exploration was precisely their ubiquity. As Harvey notes, "since *Egges* are a cheap merchandize, and are at hand at all times, and in all places; it is an easie matter to observe out of them, which are the first evident, and distinct ground-works of *Generation;* what progress nature makes in *formation,* and with what wonderfull providence shee governes the whole worke" (B1v). Eggs are "at hand," easy to access, worlds in miniature that are generative because they are commonplace.

Cavendish's dismissive yoking together of Harvey's observations and the eggy analogies of classical and alchemical matter theory is part of her larger suspicion of "similizing" (*Philosophical Letters*, Qqqqq2v). "Some studious Men," she concludes, "by long study upon one part of the body, conceive and believe that all other parts are like that one part; like as those that have gazed long upon the Sun, all they see for a time, are Suns to them." Aiming equally at natural philosophical tradition and at Harvey's empirical observations, Cavendish cautions against seeking analogy or similitude instead of embracing constant and surprising variety. Bacon, in contrast, defended the use of simile, writing in *The Wisdom of the Ancients* that storytelling of one kind or another "leads the vnderstanding of man by an easie and gentle passage through all nouell and abstruse inuentions, which any way differ from common receiued opinions."[41] His classical precursors, he argued, used "Fables, aenigmaes, parables, and similies of all sortes ... to teach and lay open, not to hide and conceale knowledge" (A10r). Similitude, for Bacon, remained valuable: "he that would illuminate mens minds anew in any old matter, and that not with disprofit and harshnesse, must absolutely take the same course, and vse the help of similies." Comparisons between egg and world, and between the generativity of eggs and the fecundity of Chaos, demonstrate that analogy was not simply a didactic mode but a fertile technique that rooted ambitious speculation in observable specifics.

Despite her distrust of "similizing," Cavendish herself uses eggs as a point of comparison elsewhere in her letters, clarifying that when she writes about the purity of rational matter "I do not mean that it is thin like a rare egg but that it is subtil and active" (Ooooooo2v). Hen's eggs come briefly into view as eminently available and at the same time wonderful,

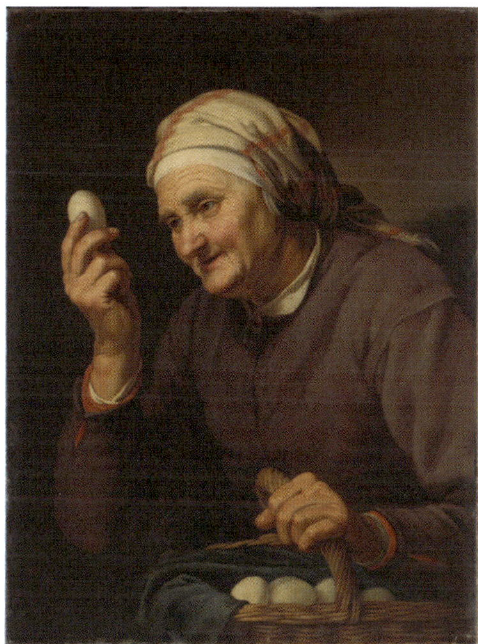

Figure 6.3. Hendrick Bloemaert, *Old Woman Selling Eggs*, 1632. Oil on canvas, 76.5 x 58 cm. Rijksmuseum, Amsterdam, SK-L-4215. © Rijksmuseum, Amsterdam

marked out in this instance by the delicacy of a fine shell.[42] Cavendish's casual analogy marks the moment at which the unobserved becomes re-markable; once handled, the egg stops being "at hand" as a mundane thing and becomes an object of thought, something "rare." Distinguish-ing between hawking and hen-care, Marcy Norton contrasts the fierce "beingness" attributed to a hawk with the deadening categorizations im-posed by avian husbandry, "organized around chickens as things (edible flesh, useful feathers) and as producers of things (eggs)."[43] The modes of thinking I have described above, however, emphasize how tentative the "thingness" of the egg was – how potent it was as potential being on both a micro- and a macrocosmic scale.

Hendrick Bloemaert's 1632 *Old Woman Selling Eggs* (fig. 6.3), which shows an elderly woman resting her arm on her basket and holding up an example of her wares, reminds us that egg sellers were frequently women. The contrast between the woman's wrinkled skin and the smooth shell is striking, forging a contrast between decrepit age and generative potential. The discrepancy becomes still more evident when the painting is opposed to the take on the same theme by Hendrick's father Abraham Bloemaert, in which a young female vendor offers up for scrutiny an egg whose curves mimic the generous rotundity of her cleavage.[44] In the light of the egg-based philosophies I have explored thus far, I wonder how fitting the title of Bloemaert the younger's painting really is. Is the woman selling eggs or scrutinising them? Rather than seeing the sitter as the object of our vision, we are, I propose, invited to join our gaze to hers and consider the mysteries, both reproductive and cosmic, of the egg. A scene of commercial life is equally a thought-provoking meditation on the composition and substance of the world.

### "Is cheese rational?"

A slim manuscript, dating from the middle of the seventeenth century, and now held at Chetham's Library, Manchester, offers its readers "A similtud to Contemplat y<sup>e</sup> Generation of Eternall nature."[45] Given the ambitions inherent in this title, it is something of a surprise to encounter a recipe for making cheese. But this is dairy with a twist: each step in the process of caseiculture is rendered analogous to the generation of life from chaotic matter. In ways that are both like and unlike the eggish speculations of the first half of this chapter, cheese turns out to feed far-reaching speculation about the creation of the world, the formation of meaningful substance from incoherent stuff, and the generation of life. Thinking with cheese is another act of imaginative world making rooted in a familiar, fascinating foodstuff. Like chicken husbandry and egg selling, cheese making was a gendered process, a life-sustaining practice that was largely, though not exclusively, the province of women. Moving in and out of the detail offered by the compelling anonymous manuscript housed at Chetham's, the closing half of this essay describes how widespread the connection between cheese making and world making turns out to be, and how the observation and consumption of cheese also opened up questions of generation and the kindling of life. And it returns to the question of analogy or "similizing" as itself a mode of world making, forcefully present from the second word of the manuscript's title.

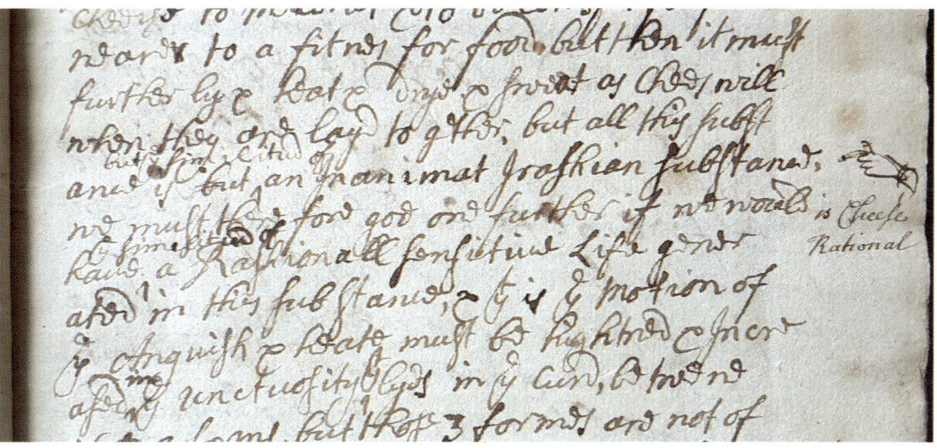

Figure 6.4. Detail from Chetham's Library MS MunA374, fol. 2r. Reproduced by kind permission of Chetham's Library, Manchester

The Chetham's manuscript begins with a set of directions on how to transform milk into a "more solid & palpable substance." The writer goes on to detail how to achieve, in the shape of a ripening cheese, a model of "Inanimat Irashion[al] substance" (2r): lifeless, thoughtless matter. But the writer's ambitions do not end there; the manuscript continues, describing how the cheese-marker can produce "[/\y^e similitud of] a Rashionall sensitiue Life." As is apparent in figure 6.4, the phrase 'y^e similitud of" is a second thought or clarification, inserted above the line of text. Where the overarching title is clear that this is an exercise in analogy, the text of the manuscript seems less sure, twice forgetting and then inserting the fact that this is not an experiment in generation but a comparison with it. In contrast with Bacon's clarity about the distinction between useful tales and physical truths, this manuscript suggests that similitude entails a blurring of distinctions. As with the idea of "resemblance," the cheese-making progress repeatedly moves from being *like* the act of world making to being coterminous with it, before being hauled back to the realm of comparison by an interlinear insertion. This quirk of the manuscript points to the uneasy status of this experiment-cum-analogy: at what point does an exercise in culinary comparison become an enterprise in world making?

At this stage, a different hand appears in the margin, posing a sceptical question: "is Cheese Rational"? The questioner returns on the following leaf. Where the author, having subjected the curds to massive pressure, explains that "no sooner doe y$^e$ fire Inkindle it self in y$^e$ unctuosity of y$^e$ curd & chese, but it generats pure flame & Light, y$^e$ Pure flame is y$^e$ perfection of y$^e$ fire, & is [/\a similitud of] y$^e$ true sensible feeling life" (2v), the margin demands, "who can see it. is Cheese animate & do we Eat it Alive"? To which we might answer, "that depends on the cheese."

The "similitud" and its interlocutor are rooted in two different intellectual traditions: on the first page, the writer of the Chetham's manuscript suggests that the milk which is about to be violently forced into life corresponds "to what I B in his Arora| calls y$^e$ first water." This is a reference to the writings of Jakob Boehme, whose theosophist philosophy, first translated into English in 1656, mingled theology, alchemy, and Paracelsian medicine, creating a supple, though often obscure, vision of a vital world infused with the spirit of God.[46] Our anonymous experimenter embraced Boehme's characteristic fusing of natural philosophy and mystical religion, repeatedly invoking an "Abissal deity," a reference to Boehme's vision of the primal Chaos, which he describes as an "Abyssal or bottomlesse Eternity ... the *Select* place of the glory of God."[47] This is the vision stirred up by the gelatinous and separating milk manifested in the early stages of cheese manufacture. The marginal questioner, in contrast, seems more conventional. Their queries correspond to the psychology of Aristotle and his followers, for whom the soul was comprised of three parts: the vegetative, concerned with growth, nutrition, and reproduction; the animal, crucial to locomotion and perception; and the rational or intellective soul, which belongs only to humans.[48] So what might look like a build-up to us – is cheese rational? is it alive? – is in some sense a descent down the Aristotelian hierarchy, from the ability to reason to the lesser capacity for movement and sensation.

While striking, the Chetham's manuscript is far from unique in its emphasis on the vitality of cheese. Cheese's liveliness lurks, perhaps surprisingly, in the static formations of still-life painting. As Kathryn Murphy notes, stacks of cheese feature prominently in early seventeenth-century Dutch *ontbijtjes*, or breakfast pieces, still lives that depict a relatively modest table, often in a strikingly stark, contrast-laden style.[49] Murphy argues that these painted cheeses manifest an "interest in the concealed sources of animation": the changes and subtle metamorphoses of cheese as it dries and cracks, discolours and hardens, or comes alive with mould or worms. Painted cheeses, argues Murphy, are "sites of latent animation, liable to spontaneous generation, the potential habitat of millions." The teeming vibrancy of cheese, as well as its cosmological significance, is memorably articulated in Carlo Ginzburg's influential 1976 study, *The Cheese and the Worms*, which charts the distinctive cosmogony of the miller Domenico Scandella, also known as Menocchio. Describing the creation, Menocchio explained to the agents of the Inquisition that "in my opinion, all was chaos, that is earth, air, water, and fire were mixed together; and of that bulk a mass formed – just as cheese is made out of milk – and worms appeared in it, and these were the angels."[50] Cheese-making is an instance of the creation of the world. But Menocchio notably goes a step further by observing the presence of maggots in cheese, and incorporating this too into his world view, prompting questions of generation and reproduction that resonate with those prompted by Harvey's eggs.

The coincidence of the Chetham's manuscript, separated from Menocchio by roughly a century, as well as by confessions, languages, and around a thousand miles, suggests that Menocchio's maggot-ridden creation story is less idiosyncratic than has been assumed. As Murphy notes, the maggots in cheese (like many insects that appeared to generate spontaneously from dirt or other organic matter) were a subject of intense natural philosophical speculation. In *The Description of a New World, Called the Blazing-World*, a fantastical companion piece to her 1668 *Philosophical Opinions*, Cavendish imagines a debate between the Empress (a thinly-veiled quasi-autobiographical fantasy) and her philosophers (bird-men and bear-men) about whether some animals are wholly lacking in blood, including "Nits, Snails, and Maggots, as well as those that are generated out of Cheese."[51] Debating the nature of reproduction, the Empress's philosophers place insects in the category of offspring who do not resemble their origins, "as for example, Maggots bred out of Cheese, and several others generated out of Earth, Water, and the like." Cheese, in this schema, is the maggots' parent, albeit one that has little resemblance to the life it brings forth.

The debate continues with the Empress arguing that maggots and cheese are remarkably similar: neither contains blood and they have "almost the same taste" (a reference to the occasional practice of eating the maggots along with the cheese). "This proves nothing," answer her philosophers, "for Maggots have a visible, local, progressive motion, which Cheese hath not." The debate here, like that encapsulated in the Chetham's manuscript's marginal notes, concerns cheese's animate status: maggots can move, cheese is notoriously stationary. Somewhat tenuously, the Empress responds, "That when all the Cheese was turned into Maggots, it might be said to have local, progressive motion. They answered, That when the Cheese by its own figurative motions was changed into Maggots, it was no more Cheese" (F3r). Defeated, the Empress confesses weakly "that she observed Nature was infinitely various in her works," returning us perhaps to Cavendish's declared preference for variety over resemblance. As bathetic as this conclusion is, it drives home the extent to which the apparently spontaneous generation of worms from cheese prompted speculation as to the nature of generation and the creation of life from matter.

In his *History and Inquiry Concerning Animate and Inanimate*, Bacon had also turned his attention to "animals generated from putrefaction," reflecting that "practically nothing is familiar to us except the formation of bees and perhaps of worms generated (as the Dutch ones usually are) from cheese."[52] Once again, familiarity is the basis of observation. In the *Sylva sylvarum* Bacon speculates on an "excellent experiment" to see if worms grow better on an alcoholic diet: "For the *Inducing* of *Putrefaction* ... Try it also with *Holland-Cheese*, hauing *Wine* put into it, whether [it] will breed *Mites* sooner, or greater?."[53] And in *The Advancement of Learning*, Bacon invokes a biblical passage that may underpin both Menocchio's testimony and the Chetham's manuscript in thinking about cheese making as an act of gathering and creation, not of the world but of man: the archetypal microcosm. Waxing lyrical about the scientific lessons available to diligent Bible readers, Bacon remarks, "So likewise in that excellent Booke of *Iob*, if it be reuolued with diligence, it will be found pregnant, and swelling with naturall Philosophie; as for example, Cosmographie, and the roundnesse of the world."[54] In this distinctly rotund and gendered phrasing, the generative subject matter of the Book of Job parallels and reinforces the fecund shape of the globe. Bacon works through a list of biblical verses that he reads as commenting directly upon natural philosophical topics, including the crucial subject, "Matter of generation," which he glosses with the words "*Annon sicut lac mulsisti me, & sicut caseum coagulasti me, &c.*" Taken from Job 10:10, these lines translate as "Have you not poured me out like milk, curdled me like cheese?" In Job, cheese making is divine: God pours out the milk of humankind and acts as the rennet, the agent that turns the milk and divides it into curds and whey. These lines echo in Helkiah Crooke's description of the immature human body in his *Mikrokosmographia*: "In Infancy and Child-hood all the spermatical parts are exceeding soft, and the bones like curdled or gathered butter, and coagulated or sammed cheese."[55] Aristotle too compares the action of semen in generation to that of rennet in cheesemaking.[56] The human body is a world in miniature, a cheese brought to full, rational life.

The ability to make cheese was used as a marker of Britain's own journey from uncultivated to cultured, a world making operation in and of itself.[57] In his *Theatrum orbis terrarum* (*Theatre of the World*), Ortelius reports that Ovid described Britons in mixed terms, using as evidence of their "rude and barbarous" character the fact "that although they haue great store of milke, yet they know not how to make cheese."[58] That was certainly not the case by the seventeenth century. How, though, did the Chetham's manuscript's author know so much about cheese making unless they had done the stirring and squeezing themselves? As with Bacon's invocation of fire-hatched eggs, caught between experience, observation, and hearsay, the Chetham's manuscript invokes and relies upon curiously displaced forms of knowledge. How far is it based on observation, and how far on report? Do these directions derive from printed or manuscript guides to cheese production? Available printed instructions included Bartholomew Dowe's *Dairie Booke for Good Huswiues*, published together with a translation of Torquato Tasso's *The Housholders Philosophie* in 1588, and Richard Surflet's 1616 translation of John Liébault, *Maison Rustique, or The Countrey Farme*.[59] Or does the similitude emerge from an attentive observation of the realities of the dairy? Twice, in passing, the Chetham's manuscript's author makes reference to another agent: "in order to make cheise y$^e$ maid takes her hand & breakes y$^e$ curd all to peses. her hand moueth backwards & forward" (1r), and "when this is done y$^e$ curd is by y$^e$ maid put in to a Cloath & squesed yt y$^e$ whay may be seperated from y$^e$ curd" (1v). As noted above, cheese making, like egg selling, was work generally associated with women. In Cavendish's play *Youths Glory, and Deaths Banquet*, for instance, a group of snooty scholars consider what girls should be taught, given the evident unsuitability of natural philosophy. Their advice is that girls should learn the skills of "high huswifry ... as milking Kyne, as making Cheese, Churning Butter, and raising past."[60] These are the skills made briefly visible in the Chetham's manuscript's passing references to the work of the dairymaid.

At one level, the dairymaid's appearances mark the eruption of the mundane into this otherwise mystical manuscript, reminding us of the degree to which natural philosophy was informed by the observation of domestic practices and the interrogation of familiar experiences.[61] At the same time, they ask us to consider the dairymaid as an agent of knowledge creation: an empirical and conceptual worker, moving between embodied responses and abstract thought.[62] Wendy Wall has influentially described how recipes, nodal points "for attracting consumers to join an increasingly complicated global commerce system," both expressed and inculcated the complex skills of kitchen workers, who exercised and circulated "modes of thought that now appear to us to rest at the intersection of physiology, gastronomy, decorum, knowledge production and labor." The end result is a "striking fusion of mental and manual activities," taking place in the kitchen, the stillhouse, and other domestic locations.[63]

Wall's focus is on some of the more elaborate creations of the kitchen, including sugar confections, culinary tricks (bacon and eggs crafted from marzipan!), and modes of marking and inscribing, whether through quills and paper or pastry and pies. The Chetham's manuscript, and the wide-reaching scope of cheese-based natural philosophical speculation more generally, suggest the degree to which the mundane processes of cheese making, as well as brewing, baking, and other acts of material transformation, encouraged readers and workers to contemplate extraordinary mysteries, including their own status as made beings and the formation of the world. Where Cavendish devalues women's traditional skills (it is clear her imagined philosophers are wrong to steer women away from the delights of scientific speculation), the dairymaid appears as a potent kinaesthetic agent in the Chetham's manuscript. Her hand moving "backwards & forward" through the curdling milk surely invokes Genesis 1:2: "And the earth was without form, and void; and darkness was upon the face of the deep: and the Spirit of God moved upon the face of the waters" (*KJV*), while her actions in breaking and squeezing the curds bring Job 10:10 to mind. For the Chetham's author, the dairymaid is a maker of worlds.

The dairymaid's presence in this quirky essay in philosophical "similizing" lends force to the waspish grumbling of Sir Walter Ralegh who, in the prefatory materials to his *History of the World*, reflects, "The Cheese-wife knoweth it as well as the Philosopher, that sowre Rennet doth coagulate her milke into a curd."[64] Ralegh's observation is part of a critique of what he sees as Aristotelian obscurity, and serves as a preface to his account of debates about the creation of the world and the pre-existence (or otherwise) of its constitutive matter. It is scarcely a full-throated acclamation of the cheese-wife's philosophical potential: Ralegh insists that our understanding of natural causes and effects is the product of time "and not reason ... experience, without Art." His point is not that dairy workers *can* explain the transformations they catalyze, but that philosophers, unwilling to trust the ineffable will of an omnipotent God, *cannot*: "there is nothing to be found in vulgar Philosophie, to satisfie this and many other like vulgar questions." Nonetheless, Ralegh's preface suggests that the dairymaid knows through practice something that the philosopher has learned painfully through art. She is at least as well-attuned to the mysteries of the world, and possibly far more acute in not reaching after the excesses of philosophical speculation, immersing herself instead in the particulars of matter and its conversions.

### "Prest Curds, New Laid Eggs, Season'd Bacon"

In her *Orations of Divers Sorts* (1662), Cavendish includes a peasant speech-maker who praises rural life. He celebrates simplicity and humility, asking "Can there be a more Delicious Sweet than Honey? More Wholesome Food than warm Milk, Fresh Butter, Prest Curds, New Laid Eggs, Season'd Bacon, Savory Bread, Cooling Sallets, and Moist Fruits?"[65] In the closing oration of the book, in contrast, an imagined student lectures his fellows, complaining about the excesses of matter theory, and the extent to which scholars attempt "to make the Matter of the Universe to be Nothing, as that it is made of Nothing, and shall return to Nothing; the Worst of all is, that they Dispute so Elevating, as to make all Divinity like as a Logistical Egg, which is Nothing" (Rr4r). The "Logistical Egg" is an egg created through the excesses of reason – a philosophical speculation rather than a material fact. This chapter, in contrast, has attempted to navigate the relationship between the materiality of eggs and pressed curds as commonplace foodstuffs and the extraordinary natural philosophical speculation devoted both to the physical questions of egg and cheese production and reproduction and to the ambitious "similizing" that the everyday – but never unremarkable – transformations of eggs and cheese brought within reach. It has, in other words, attempted to tease out connections between the mundane egg and the Mundane Egg: the former the everyday stuff of yard and table, the latter the cosmic mystery of the creation of the world. Whether they engaged in the global trade in curious eggs or looked to the generative worlds made visible in eggs' distinctive structures and the metamorphoses of cheese, early modern philosophers turned to "Wholesome Food" to illuminate and speculate upon how the world was made. In doing so, they engaged in influential, worldmaking fantasies, grounded in the generative worlds of the early modern coop and dairy, the egg seller and the cheese wife.

## NOTES

1　Ayesha Ramachandran, *The Worldmakers: Global Imagining in Early Modern Europe* (Chicago: University of Chicago Press, 2015), 5.

2　Paula Findlen, "Early Modern Things: Objects in Motion, 1500–1800," in *Early Modern Things: Objects and Their Histories, 1500–1800,* ed. Paula Findlen (Abingdon: Routledge, 2013), 15.

3　On the category of the "everyday" and its utility for the study of objects, see Patricia Fumerton and Simon Hunt, eds., *Renaissance Culture and the Everyday* (Philadelphia: University of Pennsylvania Press, 1998); Tara Hamling and Catherine Richardson, eds, *Everyday Objects: Medieval and Early Modern Material Culture and Its Meanings* (Farnham: Ashgate, 2010).

4　Jonathan Goldberg, *The Seeds of Things: Theorizing Sexuality and Materiality in Renaissance Representations* (New York: Fordham University Press, 2009), 2. For a stimulating study that addresses theories of materiality in relation to the early modern period, see Jonathan Gil Harris, *Untimely Matter in the Time of Shakespeare* (Philadelphia: University of Pennsylvania Press, 2011).

5　Claire Preston, *The Poetics of Scientific Investigation in Seventeenth-Century England* (Oxford: Oxford University Press, 2015), 5.

6　On literary and philosophical approaches to the problem of matter, see John Rogers, *The Matter of Revolution: Science, Poetry, and Politics in the Age of Milton* (Ithaca: Cornell University Press, 1998); Kurt Smith, *Matter Matters: Metaphysics and Methodology in the Early Modern Period* (Oxford: Oxford University Press, 2010).

7　Margaret Cavendish, *Philosophical Letters, or, Modest Reflections Upon Some Opinions in Natural Philosophy* (London, 1664), Qqqq2r.

8　William Harvey, *Anatomical Exercitations Concerning the Generation of Living Creatures to Which are Added Particular Discourses of Births and of Conceptions, &c* (London, 1653), K5r.

9　John Beaumont, *Considerations on a Book, Entituled the Theory of the Earth, Publisht Some Years Since by the Dr. Burnet* (London, 1693), X2v. Beaumont was responding to Thomas Burnet's *Telluris theoria sacra, or Sacred Theory of the Earth,* first published in Latin in 1681 and translated into English in 1684, which drew upon classical precursors to argue for an ovoid earth.

10　Ulisse Aldrovandi (1522–1605) "was the first biologist since Aristotle to open the eggs of hens regularly during their incubation period, and to describe in detail the appearances which he found there"; Joseph Needham, *A History of Embryology,* 2nd ed., rev. (Cambridge, UK: Cambridge University Press, 1959), 100. Fabricius ab Acquapendente's (c. 1533–1619) influential *De formatione ovi et pulli* (published in 1621) contains the first

printed illustrations showing the development of the chick. See *The Embry-
ological Treatises of Hieronymus Fabricius of Aquapendente. The Formation of the
Egg and of the Chick* [*De formatione ovi et pulli*]. *The Formed Foetus* [*De formato
foetu*], *A Facsimile Edition with an Introduction, a Translation and a Commentary*,
ed. H.B. Adelmann, 2 vols. (Ithaca: Cornell University Press, 1942). For the
later history of embryology and illustration, see Nick Hopwood, *Haeckel's
Embryos: Images, Evolution and Fraud* (Chicago: University of Chicago
Press, 2015).

11 "We should likewise observe in eggs what daily developments may take
place right up to the hatching of the bird," writes Bacon ("Videndum
similiter in ouis qualis sit diurnus processus vsque ad exclusionem auis"),
*The Oxford Francis Bacon*, vol. 13, *The Instauratio magna: Last Writings*, ed.
Graham Rees (Oxford University Press, 2000), 234.

12 "Debuerat autem notare similem efformationem in Testis Ouorum, vbi non
sunt rugæ aut inæqualitas." *The Oxford Francis Bacon*, vol. 11, *The Instauratio
magna, Part II: Novum organum*, ed. Graham Rees and Maria Wakely (Oxford
University Press, 2003), 436.

13 "Master Francis Bacon of the colours of good and evil, to the Lord
Mountjoye," Harley MS 6797, fol. 53r-v, cited by Alan Stewart, introduction
to "Promus of Formularies and Elegancies," *The Oxford Francis Bacon*, vol. 1,
*Early Writings 1584–1596* (Oxford University Press, 2012), 520. Bacon's *bon
mot* is intended to suggest his ability to hatch productive enquiry from the
underdeveloped eggs of his predecessor.

14 "Ova contrahuntur ab Igne, & quatenus ad Albumen ipsorum, colorem mu-
tant à claro in candidum." Francis Bacon, *History of Dense and Rare (Rawley's version)*, in *The Oxford Francis Bacon*, 13:134. Bacon notes this phenomenon again
in *The History of Life and Death*: "Quin etiam si *Ovum* testa exutum injiciatur
in *spiritum* vini *bonum & fortem*, elixatur, & fit candidum; similiter & *offa panis* in-
jecta in ipsum devenit quasi tosta"; "Why even if a shelled egg be thrown into
good strong spirit of wine it is poached and goes white; and in the same way a
hunk of bread thrown into the spirit almost becomes toast" (13:137).

15 "Post *Sanguinem* igitur *Recentem, similia Substantiæ Corporis Humani*,
sunt *Alimentosa; Carnes* pinguiores, *Bouinæ, Suillæ, Ceruinæ; Ostrea* inter
*Pisces; Lac, Butyrum; Vitella Ouorum; Pollen Tritici; Vinum Dulce*, aut *Sacchara-
tum*, aut *Mulsum*." Francis Bacon, *The History of the Winds*, in *The Oxford Francis Bacon*, Vol. 12, *The Instauratio magna Part III: Historia naturalis et Historia
vitæ*, ed. Graham Rees and Maria Wakely (Oxford University Press, 2007),
323. Much more about the use of eggs and cheese in household medicine
can be found in *The Workes of that Famous Chirurgion Ambrose Parey* (London,
1665). A short list of "medicinal meats" includes "Horns Heoves. Hairs.

Feathers. Shels. Sculls. Scales. Sweats. Skins. Fats. Flesh. Blood. Entraile. Urine. Bones. Extreme parts. Hearts. Liver. Lungs Brain. Womb Secundine. Testicles. Pizzle. Bleader Sperm. Tail. Ceats of the Ventricle. Exspirations. Bristles. Silk. Webs. Tears. Spittle Heny. Wax. Egge. Milk. Butter. Cheese. Marrow Rennet" (Qqq1v).

16  "Etiam Oua aliquandò excluduntur per Calorem Ignis; id quod prorsùs imitatur Calorem Animalem." *The Oxford Francis Bacon*, 11:315.

17  Cassowary egg from the wreck of the Dutch East India ship *Witte Leeuw*, Rijksmuseum NG-1977–192-W.

18  "Accepi rem fidei probatæ, de *Ovo*, quod diu jacuerat in fundo *Aquæ*, quæ circuibat ædes; quod inventum versum erat manifesto in *Lapidem*, manentibus coloribus & distinctionibus *vi*telli, *albuminis*, *testæ*: sed Testa erat fracta hic, illic, & splendescebat in crustulis." *History of Dense and Rare*, in *The Oxford Francis Bacon*, 13:149.

19  John Tradescant, the younger, *Musæum Tradescantianum: or, A collection of rarities* (London, 1656), B1r.

20  Findlen, "Early Modern Things," 8; 15.

21  Mary Louise Pratt uses the idea of "contact zones" to describe the sites where "cultures meet, clash and grapple with each other, often in contexts of highly asymmetrical relations of power, such as colonialism, slavery, or their aftermaths as they are lived out in many parts of the world today." *Imperial Eyes: Travel Writing and Transculturation*, 2nd ed. (New York: Routledge, 2008), 8.

22  Ostrich eggs were remarkable primarily for their size and hardness but also because of the ostrich's mode of propagation: "She laieth egges as other foules do, but she neglecteth to brood her egges, the which egges be raken in grauel, and only be brought forth by heat & nourishing of the dust." Stephen Batman, *Batman vppon Bartholome his booke De propreitatibus rerum* (London, 1582), Ii7v.

23  "Nos idem cum ovo vitreo experti sumus, & aquam receptam circa octavam partem conteni reperimus; tantum scilicet aër per exsuctionem erat extensus." Francis Bacon, *Phænomena universi*, in *The Oxford Francis Bacon*, Vol. 6, *Philosophical Studies c.1611–c.1619*, ed. Graham Rees (Oxford University Press, 1996), 44. In this text, Bacon cites "the same egg raw and cooked" as an example relating to "the history of the variation of weights in individual substances" (33).

24  Lorraine Daston and Katharine Park, *Wonders and the Order of Nature, 1150–1750* (New York: Zone Books, 2001), 68. Daston and Park note in passing the popularity of eggs within medieval collections, including the eleven "griffin eggs" contained in the shrine of Saint Cuthbert at Durham (69).

25 John Rastell, *A New Iuterlude [sic] and a Mery of the Nature of the iii. Elements Declarynge Many Proper Points of Philosophy Naturall* (London, 1520), B6v. The interlude is edited as *The Four Elements*, ed. R. Coleman, foreword Brooke Crutchley (Cambridge, UK: University Printing House, 1971).

26 Ulrich von Hutten, *De morbo Gallico*, trans. Thomas Paynell (London, 1633), K2v.

27 Thomas Cogan, *The Haven of Health* (London, 1636), Y4r.

28 *OED*, third edition, March 2020, s.v. "resemble," v.1, def. 1.a.

29 Giovanni Battista Recco, *Still Life with Chickens and Eggs* (c. 1640–60), Rijksmuseum SK-A-3884.

30 On culinary violence, see Wendy Wall, *Staging Domesticity: Household Work and English Identity in Early Modern Drama* (Cambridge, UK: Cambridge University Press, 2002), chap. 6.

31 "che ti conviene temperare i tuoi colori sempre con rossume d'uovo, e ben temperati: sempre tanto rossume quanto il colore che temperi." Cennino Cennini, *Il libro dell'arte*, ed. Renzo Simi (Lanciano: R. Carabba, 1913), 100. On the intimate, embodied relationships between artists and their materials, see Pamela H. Smith, *The Body of the Artisan: Art and Experience in the Scientific Revolution* (Chicago: University of Chicago Press, 2004).

32 Julie Hochstrasser notes the art historical narrative that sees the "rich symbolic allusions" attached to objects within medieval and Renaissance painting as being stripped away at the turn of the seventeenth century, and asks "how much of this sort of symbolic reference lingered on in the emerging genre of still life?" ("Stil-Staende Dingen: Picturing Objects in the Dutch Golden Age," in Findlen, *Early Modern Things*, 107). She argues that these paintings teeter on the "significatory brink" (120) between detailed descriptive renderings and a rich allusive heritage.

33 Hochstrasser, "Stil-Staende Dingen," 105.

34 Smith, *The Body of the Artisan*, 132.

35 Aristophanes, *Birds*, in *Birds. Lysistrata. Women at the Thesmophoria*, ed. and trans. Jeffrey Henderson, Loeb Classical Library 179 (Cambridge, MA: Harvard University Press, 2000), 117. A "wind egg" is an unimpregnated or imperfect egg, sterile.

36 Alexander Ross, *Mel Heliconium, or, Poeticall Honey Gathered out of the Weeds of Parnassus* (London, 1642), H3r.

37 *Purchas his Pilgrimage. Or Relations of the World and the Religions Obserued in all Ages and Places Discouered* (London, 1626), B3v.

38 "Narrant itaque Amorem illum omnium Deorum fuisse antiquissimum, atque adeo omnium rerum, excepto chao, quod ei coævum perhibetur. Atque Amor iste prorsus sine parente introducitur. Ipse autem cum

chao mistus, & Deos & res universas progenuit. A nonnullis tamen ovo
prognatus incubante nocte traditus est. Ejus vero attributa ponuntur di-
versa, ut sit infans perpetuus, cæcus, nudus, alatus, Sagittarius. Vis autem
ejus præcipua, & propria, ad corpora unienda valet: etiam claves Æth-
eris, Maris, & Terræ ei deferebantur." Francis Bacon, *On Principles and Origins* in *The Oxford Francis Bacon*, Vol. 6, *Philosophical Studies c. 1611-c.1619*,
ed. Graham Rees (Oxford: Oxford University Press, 1996), 197.

39  "Fabula ista cum sequenti de Cœlo, brevi parabolæ complexu proponere
videtur *Doctrinam de Principiis rerum & Mundi Originibus.*" Ibid.

40  "ea scilicet ut post debitas exclusiones & negationes, aliquid affirmetur, &
constituatur, & ut Ovum quasi à tempestiva & matura incubatione excluda-
tur." Ibid., 203.

41  Francis Bacon, *The Wisedome of the Ancients* (London, 1619), A9v.

42  In *The Worlds Olio*, Cavendish describes phlegmy coughs as rising "like the
Scum of a Pot on the Fire, or like Whites of Eggs that are put into any hot
Liquor" (London, 1655), Cc4r.

43  Marcy Norton, "Going to the Birds: Animals as Things and Beings in Early
Modern Modernity," in Findlen, *Early Modern Things*, 53.

44  Warm thanks to Bronwen Wilson for introducing me to Abraham Bloe-
mart's take on this iconographic tradition.

45  Chetham's Library MS MunA374, fol. 1r. The manuscript and marginalia
are described at https://library.chethams.com/blog/is-cheese-rational/.

46  For recent work on Boehme, see Roland Bach, "Jacob Boehme," in *Protestants and Mysticism in Reformation Europe*, ed. Ronald K. Rittgers and Vincent
Evener (Leiden: Brill, 2019), 265–86.

47  Jacob Boehme, *Aurora, that is, the Day-Spring, […] that is, the Root or Mother of
Philosophie, Astrologie, & Theologie from the True Ground*, trans. John Sparrow
(London, 1656), P4v-Q1r.

48  On the tripartite soul, see Katharine Park and Eckhard Kessler, "Psychology: The Concept of Psychology," Park, "The Organic Soul," and Kessler,
"The Intellective Soul," in *The Cambridge History of Renaissance Philosophy*,
ed. Charles B. Schmitt et al., (Cambridge, UK: Cambridge University Press,
1988), 453–63; 464–84; 485–534.

49  Kathryn Murphy, "More to Cheese than Meets the Eye?," *Apollo: The International Art Magazine*, 11 March 2017, https://www.apollo-magazine.com
/cheese-meets-eye-dutch-still-life/. The Netherlands' mercantile ambitions
are fully present in these images, which frequently depict the delicate
blue-and-white China dishes that had newly arrived in Europe as part
of what Findlen calls "the Dutch cornucopia of global things" (Findlen,
"Early Modern Things," 12). See also Timothy Brook, "Something New," in

Findlen, *Early Modern Things*, 369–74. For more on China's influence and reception, see Eugenia Zuroski Jenkins, *A Taste for China: English Subjectivity and the Prehistory of Orientalism* (New York: Oxford University Press, 2013); Benjamin Schmidt, *Inventing Exoticism: Geography, Globalism, and Europe's Early Modern World* (Philadelphia: University of Pennsylvania Press, 2015).

50  Cited in Carlo Ginzburg, *The Cheese and the Worms: The Cosmos of a Sixteenth-Century Miller* (first published 1976; Baltimore: Johns Hopkins University Press, 1992), 5–6.

51  Margaret Cavendish, *The Description of a New World, Called the Blazing World* (London, 1668), F1v.

52  "nobis fere nihil innotescat nisi efformatio apium & fortasse vermiculorum (vt Batauj solent) ex caseo." *History and Inquiry Concerning Animate and Inanimate*, in *The Oxford Francis Bacon*, 13:231. In the *Novum organum*, Bacon refers to "cheese and flesh, which when putrefied turn into animalcules" ("ipsa quæ putrefacta soluuntur in animalcula, vt Caro, Caseus"); *The Oxford Francis Bacon*, 11:241.

53  Francis Bacon, *Sylva sylvarum: or A Natural Historie* (London, 1627), HH2r.

54  Francis Bacon, *The Advancement of Learning*, in *The Oxford Francis Bacon*, Vol. 4, *The Advancement of Learning*, ed. Michael Kiernan (Oxford: Oxford University Press, 2000), 35. On the potent connections between theology and natural philosophy, see especially Peter Harrison, *The Bible, Protestantism, and the Rise of Natural Science* (Cambridge, UK: Cambridge University Press, 1998); and Kevin Killeen and Peter Forshaw, eds., *The Word and the World: Biblical Exegesis and Early Modern Science* (London: Palgrave Macmillan, 2007).

55  Helkiah Crooke, *Mikrokosmographia a Description of the Body of Man* (London, 1615), F4r.

56  *De generatione animalium*, Bk. II, 739b, 22–31. See Sandra Ott, "Aristotle among the Basques: the "Cheese Analogy" of Conception," *Man*, n.s., 14 (1979), 699–711.

57  On how ideas of "barbarity" were used to distinguish England from its own racialized past, see Ian Smith, *Race and Rhetoric in the Renaissance: Barbarian Errors* (New York: Palgrave Macmillan, 2009).

58  Abraham Ortelius, *Theatrum orbis terrarum*, trans. W.B. [William Bedwell?] (London, 1606 [1608?]), ixv.

59  On household manuals, see especially Wall, *Staging Domesticity*, chap. 1.

60  Margaret Cavendish, *Plays Written by the Thrice Noble, Illustrious and Excellent Princess, the Lady Marchioness of Newcastle* (London, 1662), Lll1v.

61  On the domestic settings of early modern natural philosophy, see Alix Cooper, "Homes and Households," in *The Cambridge History of Science*, Vol. 3,

*Early Modern Science*, ed. Katherine Park and Lorraine Daston (Cambridge, UK: Cambridge University Press, 2008), 224–37; Michelle di Meo, "'Such a Sister Became Such a Brother': Lady Ranelagh's Influence on Robert Boyle," *Intellectual History Review* 25, no. 1 (2015): 21–36; Simon Werrett, *Thrifty Science: Making the Most of Materials in the History of Experiment* (Chicago: Chicago University Press, 2019).

62 Pamela H. Smith, Amy R.W. Meyers, and Harold J. Cook, eds, *Ways of Making and Knowing: The Material Culture of Empirical Knowledge* (Chicago: University of Chicago Press, 2017) demonstrates how artisan knowledge-making paralleled processes of scientific or natural philosophical experimentation and observation.

63 Wendy Wall, *Recipes for Thought: Knowledge and Taste in the Early Modern Kitchen* (Philadelphia: University of Pennsylvania Press, 2015), 1; 2; 3. See also the blog posts and resources collected at The Making and Knowing Project (https://www.makingandknowing.org) and The Recipes Project (https://recipes.hypotheses.org).

64 Sir Walter Ralegh, *The History of the World in Five Books* (London, 1621), B6r.

65 Margaret Cavendish, *Orations of Divers Sorts Accommodated to Divers Places* (London, 1662), Kk1v-Kk2r.

# PART II

# IN-BETWEEN SPACES

# chapter seven

# The Production of Imprecision: Reframing Non-European Objects in Early Modern European Collections

## DANIELA BLEICHMAR

### The World in a Room

Early modern European *Wunderkammern* had global aspirations. Cabinets were often conceived, arranged, and encountered as miniature universes, microcosms that brought inside a room or a building selected samples of objects that in their abundance, rarity, variety, diversity, and wondrousness allowed the collector and the visitor to imagine themselves as experiencing the entire world, at reduced scale.[1] The cabinet might not hold a sample of every single thing that there was out there in the world, but it could include enough things, of enough kinds, from enough places, to give a sense of what lay out there. Cabinets could provide the impression and fulfil the fantasy of having access to almost everything. London gardeners John Tradescant the Elder (c. 1570s–1638) and the Younger (1608–1662) signalled their ambitions to be modern-day Noahs when they chose to call their celebrated cabinet "The Ark." A poem celebrated the collection as holding "what is rare, in land, in seas, in air ... a world of wonders in one closet shut."[2]

Such worldly ambitions are evident in manuscript and printed inventories of early modern collections, as well as in the catalogues that flourished as a published genre in the seventeenth century. Inventories and catalogues alike frequently demonstrate a keen interest in non-European things and highlight objects' foreign origins. This is also the case with accounts penned by collectors and visitors to cabinets. In 1599, the twenty-five-year-old Swiss physician Thomas Platter (1574–1628) visited one of the earliest collections in London, the cabinet of Walter Cope (d. 1614). He described it as "an apartment, stuffed with queer foreign objects in every corner" – rarity, foreignness, and abundance impressed him above all. Platter noted that, although there were "other people in London interested in curios," Cope's collection was "superior to them all for strange objects, because of the Indian voyage he carried out with such zeal."[3] Thus, for Platter, "foreign" and "strange" referred above all to things originating outside Europe. Of the fifty entries that he recorded as particularly noteworthy, half of them involved objects with non-European provenance. According to Platter, they had come to London from Africa, India, the Indies, China, Java, Arabia, Virginia, and Turkey.

Platter was not alone in his attention to objects originating beyond Europe and in his relating them to travel, actual or imaginary. In 1634, the English merchant Peter Mundy visited the Tradescants' Ark while on home leave from the East India company. He wrote the first recorded account of that collection and singled out in particular the fact that it contained all sorts of objects "of sundry nations [and] countries," while the adjoining garden presented "diverse outlandish herbs and flowers, whereof some that I had not seen elsewhere but in India" as well as "toys ... from other parts." Mundy concluded that, at the Ark, "a man might in one day behold and collect into one place more curiosities than he should see if he spent all his life in travel." He was one to know: at the time of his visit, Mundy had already voyaged to Istanbul and India; he would later return to India and also travel to China and Japan. Other visitors who left accounts of their experiences at the Ark also made a point of highlighting the foreign origin of the objects they had admired, regardless of whether they approached the collection with specialized interests in natural history or from a more general perspective.[4]

This idea was repeatedly stated by collectors and visitors to cabinets throughout Europe, in the late sixteenth and throughout the seventeenth centuries. Visitors to the collection of French physician Pierre Borel (1620–1671), located in the town of Castres, were greeted by a lengthy Latin inscription inviting them to "behold a world in the home ... it is a microcosm or Compendium of all rare things." The statement, reproduced in the 1649 published catalogue of the collection, described Borel's cabinet as a gathering of "rare things" and singled out in particular the presence of "exotic" objects from America and Africa.[5] A contemporary account of the famous collection assembled in Copenhagen by Ole Worm (1588–1654) claimed that many notable visitors "ask to see the museum on account of its great fame and what it relates from foreign lands."[6] The cabinet's published catalogue, *Museum Wormianum* (Leiden, 1655), includes objects described as coming from Mexico, Turkey, Persia, China, Japan, Malabar, and Ethiopia, among other non-European locations. This was the case as well with the collections belonging to other scholars, physicians, naturalists, and pharmacists, among them Ulisse Aldrovandi (1527–1605), Antonio Giganti (1535–1598), and Ferdinando Cospi (1606–1686) in Bologna; Manfredo Settala (1600–1680) in Milan; and the Dutch physician Bernhard Paludanus (1550–1633).[7] It was likewise the case for the collections put together by learned societies and institutions, including those of the Jesuit *Collegio* in Rome, assembled by Athanasius Kircher (1602–1680), and London's Royal Society (founded 1660).[8] And it was no different for collections belonging to members of royal, noble, or elite families, such as the noteworthy Habsburg collections in various locations in Spain, Prague, Graz, and Ambras Castle near Innsbruck; the cabinet of the Bavarian court in Munich; the royal collections of the kings of France and Denmark; or the collections of the Medici in Florence.[9] In short, every major European collection of the sixteenth and seventeenth centuries included foreign objects procured through travel or trade. Collectors and visitors envisioned cabinets as repositories of things from around the globe that provided the opportunity to encounter the world at large without having to leave Europe.[10]

## Worldmaking and Knowledge Production in the Cabinet

Given that early modern Europeans conceived of cabinets as containing "the world," what do collections from the period tell us about how exactly those who assembled, owned, and visited them imagined and understood the world at large? What meanings did items from around the globe take on in early modern European collections? What vision of the world did cabinets create, exactly? This essay investigates these questions by contrasting the global ambitions expressed by early modern collectors and visitors to collections with the concrete ways in which they addressed the foreignness of non-European objects. My observations come from manuscript and published inventories and catalogues from the sixteenth and seventeenth centuries, and draw on pioneering work by scholars who have variously examined individual collections and collectors, the presence of items from specific regions of the world across multiple collections, or inventories as a genre. By connecting multiple individual case studies, I consider the overall pattern of early modern European attitudes to non-European objects and cultures as expressed through collections. What emerges from this analysis is an intriguing juxtaposition between the specificity, particularity, and precision of the individual, material object in the collection and the vagueness, generality, and mutable imprecision of the geographical and cultural interpretations produced by those objects when accumulated into assemblages.

In the sixteenth and seventeenth centuries, the idea of the cabinet as a place to gather the entire world was more than a metaphor. Rather, it reflected a novel awareness of the vastness and diversity of the globe as well as the intense attention paid to the many objects arriving in Europe through imperial, colonial, missionary, and commercial networks. The notion that collections could and should include items from around the world, along with the capacity to procure them, both emerged from and depended on European global expansion. Collectors aspired to possess the entire world in miniature while European monarchs, armies, settlers, merchants, and trading companies carried out the project at the level of global geopolitics. Foreign objects often aroused interest above all due to their novelty, rarity, materials, and associations with wonder and the marvellous.[11] Collecting, depicting, and imagining other places and other peoples around the globe served to define both the other and the self: as Benjamin Schmidt has shown, the process of inventing the exotic global also invented its counterpart, the non-exotic European.[12]

Cabinets were thus more than repositories for world-gathering: they were crucial sites for worldmaking. "Worldmaking" refers to the active, self-aware creation of new models, theories, interpretations, or depictions of the world – a project that, as Ayesha Ramachandran has shown, consumed scholars and artists, and theorists and practitioners, throughout the sixteenth and seventeenth centuries. According to Ramachandran, worldmaking became "the central intellectual task of the late Renaissance," affecting "all aspects of early modern life and thought."[13] Ramachandran has studied worldmaking in the work of prominent innovators who primarily created worlds on paper, in the pages of books. In this essay, I turn to the cabinet as a privileged site for early modern worldmaking. Collecting entailed the purposeful acquisition, assembly, display, and narration of objects – including books and other works on paper – to compose a model and a vision of the things and peoples of the world near and far, modern and ancient. Collectors created composite wholes, articulating new understandings of both the assemblage and the individual parts. This relationship between parts and whole is central to early modern worldmaking. According to Ramachandran, worldmaking arose out of "a need to synthesize new global experiences into a structure that would bind individual fragments into a collective unity. To comprehend the world thus required deft oscillation between local details and global frameworks and a re-configuration of the particular against the universal. It was a task of metaphysical, and not just practical, dimensions."[14] In the cabinet, the rare, foreign object went from global to local, domesticated through possession and interpretation.

In examining what visions of the globe early modern cabinets helped to craft, I am particularly interested in the complex relationship between worldmaking and the production of knowledge. Scholars of *Wunderkammern* have analysed the many ways in which cabinets functioned for collectors and visitors: as indexes of princely power through ideas of *representatio*; as materializations of social relationships and networks; as sites for accumulation related to ideas of luxury as taste-making; as links between cultures of curiosity and commerce; as places for the production of knowledge.[15] This last idea has been particularly powerful for historians of science, and historians of knowledge more broadly, whose research since the mid-1990s has dismantled an earlier view of early modern cabinets as assemblages of oddities jumbled together in carnivalesque disarray without rhyme or reason – "a room of wonder, not of inquiry."[16] Instead, scholars have demonstrated the specific ways in which early collections functioned as places for study, research, and learning: sites where owning led to knowing.[17] The early modern cabinet, particularly when composed by a learned man such as Worm or Aldrovandi, has been interpreted as a privileged "locus for intellectual pursuits" and an "instrument of learning;" a "new and very practical kind of collection" whose goal was "to stimulate new learning and expand useful knowledge."[18] From this perspective, the early modern cabinet is envisioned as a research institution, a site to collect and investigate materials with the express purpose of producing new knowledge.

This idea of the collection as a sort of laboratory originated with early modern scholars themselves, some of whom proposed that cabinets could function as a kind of research centre or laboratory. The earliest known treatise on collecting, Samuel Quiccheberg's *Inscriptiones vel titule theatri amplissimi* (Munich, 1565), explicitly states this aspiration in its title page, which reads in full:

*Inscriptions; or, Titles of the most ample theater*

That houses exemplary objects and exceptional images of the entire world, so that one could also rightly call it a:

Repository of artificial and marvelous things, and of every rare treasure, precious object, construction, and picture. It is recommended that these things be brought together here in the theater so that by their frequent viewing and handling one might quickly, easily, and confidently be able to acquire a unique knowledge and admirable understanding of things.[19]

According to Quiccheberg, the cabinet was – or could be – a theatre where the collector and the visitor would come to know the world by observing and manipulating its things, "quickly, easily, and confidently."

These ambitious aspirations, I suggest, might have been an idealized goal rather than the norm, and apply to some objects but not to all. For many collectors and collections, the connection between owning the world in a room and gaining knowledge about either the things in the room or the world outside it was far from the quick and easy process Quiccheberg promised. The relationship between possession and knowledge might have been more sharply defined for the natural history and anatomical collections that learned men and women used expressly for research purposes than for many other types of items in those same cabinets, or for other kinds of collections and collectors. In particular, it is unclear whether the enormous interest in human-crafted objects of extra-European provenance that we see so frequently stated by early modern collectors and visitors led in fact to the production of knowledge about these objects themselves, the places where those objects originated, or the people who created them.

### Where and What Is the World? Practices of Geographical Indeterminacy in the Cabinet

Manuscript and published accounts suggest that understandings of the geographical and cultural origins and meanings of objects in early modern European collections were commonly based on vague, imprecise, and elastic criteria. Many foreign objects were described as inscrutable, escaping the possibility of knowledge production: a commentator would describe an item and then shrug their shoulders, concluding that nobody really knew what it meant, but maybe someday someone would. Other times, objects would be addressed through interpretive manoeuvres that yielded ambiguous and inconclusive information. To be clear, my point is not that cabinets aimed for precise knowledge but failed to produce it – that they were, so to speak, bad labs, with bad results. Rather, I suggest that geographical indeterminacy was both a specialized methodology and its end result, flinging non-European objects through a sort of interpretive pinball machine that kept them in constant motion, never settled, never fully knowable.

Sources reveal at least four practices of geographical indeterminacy for the interpretation of non-European objects in early modern European collections: (1) the use of unclear geographical markers, which are at times void of any clear or specific geographical meaning; (2) constant misattribution; (3) the instability and remarkable mutability of the geographical descriptors used to qualify objects; and (4) the frequent lack of information regarding geographical and cultural origin. Thus, while many early modern European cabinets held objects from around the world, in many if not most cases the responses to foreign objects led to a particular way of understanding non-European places, things, and peoples that Schmidt has characterized as "exotic geography": the invention of an undifferentiated, composite, and non-specific exotic other, imagined in juxtaposition to the related invention of a unified and non-exotic pan-European self.[20]

The first practice of geographical indeterminacy in early modern cabinets concerns the use of vague, broad categories that lump together objects from multiple regions and cultures and often do not seem to refer to specific parts of the world. The most notorious case is the idea of "the Indies." The word "India" originated in ancient Sanskrit to refer to the geographical area around the river Indus and entered European languages through ancient Greek. The term grew elastic over time. In the fourteenth century, Marco Polo used it to refer not only to the South Asian subcontinent but also to parts of East Asia and Africa. In 1492 Columbus, believing he had reached the islands of Japan, referred to the inhabitants he met as "Indians." The category continued to stretch over the course of the sixteenth and seventeenth centuries with European voyages and global expansion, coming to encompass a huge swath of the planet including South Asia, Southeast Asia, East Asia, Indonesia and other Pacific Islands, the American continent, and the Caribbean.[21] Over time, the word became commonly used to refer not to any specific geographical location but rather "allusively for a region or place yielding great wealth or to which profitable voyages may be made."[22]

Collectors and visitors to cabinets constantly described objects as "Indian" and "from the Indies" – as was the case with Platter, mentioned above. Variants of that category may be the most frequent attribute used to describe non-European objects in early modern collections. The quandary that the category poses is not that it demarcated a very capacious area of the world, aggregating places and cultures that we today see as distinct; rather, the issue is that the "Indies" could signify almost anywhere that was considered rare, different, and distant. Often, the "Indies" did not mean somewhere in particular but, rather, a sweeping "out there." The category possessed such tremendous elasticity that it could mean almost anything. As Jessica Keating and Lia Markey have documented, German and Italian inventories of the period attached variants of the adjective "Indian" to objects that originated in the Americas, India, Africa, China, Japan, and the Levant. The term accompanied entries in these inventories that itemized such disparate objects as Mexican feather works, Indian mother-of-pearl chests, African weapons, Hebrew manuscripts, Mughal miniatures, and Chinese porcelain. This was also the case with Spanish inventories, as Kate Holohan has shown, as well as with collections elsewhere in Europe. This attribution was not made because collectors mistakenly believed that all these objects came from India, or from America, or from any one region, however narrowly or broadly conceived. Careful analyses of variations in wording – such as "from India," "from the Indies," "Indian," "alla indiana" – suggest that these different descriptors were used so irregularly that it is impossible to generalize or to draw any correlation, weak or strong, between specific forms and precise geographical regions. An inventory might use variants to describe a single type of object from the same region, as well as objects that we today consider extremely distinct in their material qualities as well as cultural and geographical provenance. As Christine Göttler has noted, the designation often seems to have mapped "moral rather than geographical landscapes."[23] In effect, the term "Indian" served to group a vast range of objects into a single category that ultimately served to convey, above all, foreignness.[24]

Other terms that might at first glance suggest geographical or cultural specificity, such as "Moorish," "Turkish," or "Chinese," in fact regularly operated comparably to the category "Indian." They were applied liberally and with great flexibility to describe non-European objects, sometimes suggesting a concrete geographical or cultural origin; sometimes a much broader, vague, or indeterminate origin; and sometimes attributes related to foreignness and exoticism in general.[25] Mexican objects were regularly characterized in inventories as "Moorish," as is the case with a 1561 inventory of the "jewels from the Indies" ("joyas de las Yndias") belonging to Charles V that describes two Mexican feather works as "Moorish hats;" feather objects in the 1575 inventory of a *Kunstkammer* in Tettnang, Germany; a Mexican wooden sculpture in a 1590 inventory of the Vienna cabinet; and a feather coat, perhaps also Mexican, listed in the 1596 inventory of the collection at Ambras Castle.[26] The Aztec ruler Moctezuma II was described in 1577 as a "Moorish king."[27] Spanish royal inventories similarly used the phrase "from China" variously to describe objects from that region, objects from elsewhere in East Asia, and objects from the Spanish Americas.[28] As a result, many entries are almost impossible to interpret with any level of certainty.

A work by the composer and musical theorist Michael Praetorius (1571–1621) exemplifies the interplay between specificity and indeterminacy that characterizes early modern approaches to non-European objects. Praetorius wrote an erudite and expansive treatise on music, the *Syntagma musicum* (Wolfenbüttel, 1614–1620). An appendix to the second of three volumes presents a "Theatre of Instruments" (*Theatrum Instrumentorum,* Wolfenbüttel, 1619), a paper museum consisting of forty-two plates of woodcuts that accurately illustrate nearly two hundred instruments known in Europe at that time, grouped in families and depicted to scale. The images and captions make fine distinctions among multiple European instruments of a given kind – lutes, flutes, clavichords, and so on. At the bottom of many of the plates, the image of a scale measure underscores the precision of the plates by providing a guide to the relative size of each instrument. Three of the plates depict twenty-seven non-European instruments (see figs. 7.1 and 7.2). Unlike their European counterparts, these instruments are not organized according to type: what defines the class is foreignness. Many of the figures are believed to illustrate individual specimens held in European collections at the time, and at least a few are derived from woodcuts that appeared in earlier publications. The content and layout of the page are not different from those used for European instruments, with individual items distributed across the page, numbered, and accompanied by a scale measure. This insistence on precision is countered by the confusion of geographical descriptors applied to the instruments. Six of the nine instruments on plate 29 (fig. 7.1) are characterized as "American" (*Americanisch*), among them a Javanese gong, *kempuls,* and *bonang* (labelled 6) as well as two drums (8 and 9), the latter of which is a *ntumpani* from Ghana. The following plate (fig. 7.2) depicts a "small Turkish drum" that may in fact be Turkish (1), two "Muscovite" drums that are from the Guinea Coast (2) and perhaps Morocco (3), an "Indian" horn that is an Afro-Portuguese ivory oliphant (4), a double-bell "made from iron and played like our kettle drums," without geographical referent but of African origin (5), and an "Indian" drum (7) that is, in effect,

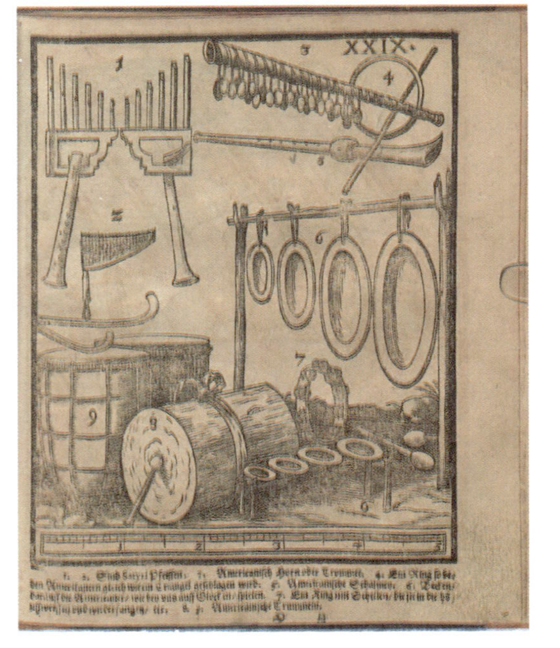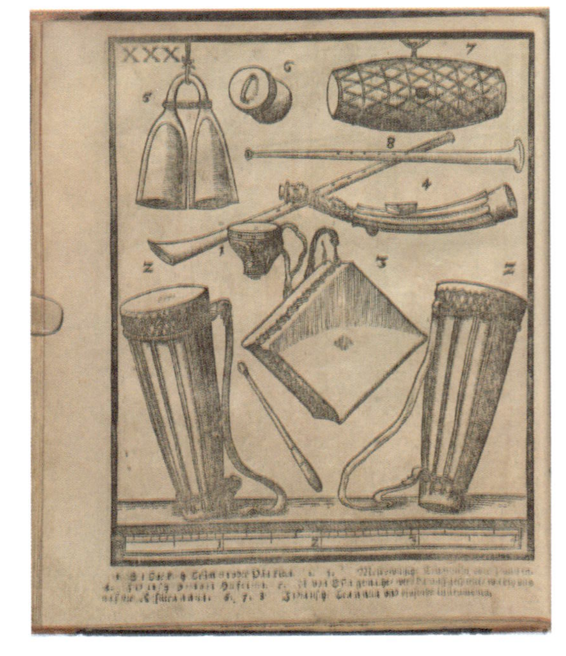

Figures 7.1. and 7.2.  Woodcuts illustrating non-European musical instruments, with measurement scale and identifying captions, in Michael Praetorius, *Theatrum instrumentorum* (Wolffenbüttel, 1619), plates XXIX and XXX. 4 Mus.th. 1249-2,2. Bayerische Staatsbibliothek, Munich

an Indian *mrdangam*.[29] Many elements in the publication attest to the author's and artist's expertise and dedication to accuracy and precision, so this geographical confusion is not a result of carelessness or indifference. The woodcut images throughout the publication are regarded by musicologists as extremely trustworthy – one of the "Muscovite" drums is rendered so clearly that a contemporary scholar has been able to equate it with an African instrument in the Tradescants' collection, held today at the Ashmolean Museum at Oxford.[30] Thus, in a publication characterized by expertise, authority, and precision, the most volatile element appears to be the geographical origin of non-European instruments. One of the more puzzling elements is that, at least in some cases, the captions for figures taken from earlier books provide a different geographical origin than the one given in the source publication: the Javanese gamelan presented here as "American," for instance, appears to be based on an engraving published two decades earlier in a well-known account of the first Dutch expedition to the East Indies, which unmistakably located the instrument in Java.[31]

At times, early modern sources used not one but two imprecise geographical categories to refer to a single object, producing even greater ambiguity. This happened not infrequently with objects that for Europeans combined ideas related to "China" and "the Indies," connected by historical sources in ways that are far from obvious to present-day readers. Thus, a writing desk (*escribanía*) appears in an inventory of Philip II's possessions as "from China, black and painted on the outside with many figures of Indians." The entry might refer to a Chinese object whose decoration the writer for some reason perceived as related to the Americas; or to an American item created in imitation of a Chinese technique or style (something that happened regularly with ceramics and woodwork in the seventeenth century); or to an American object entirely unrelated to China that, for some reason, a European viewer associated with that region.[32] The connection of the categories "Indian" and "Chinese" also appears in the 1649 inventory of Pierre Borel's collection, which lists a "fruit of the Indies" decorated with "signs, and letters or figures ... that resemble Chinese characters."[33] Platter likewise associated "Indian" and "Chinese" in his account of his 1599 visit to Cope's cabinet. The third entry in the list of fifty items that he found noteworthy registers "beautiful Indian plumes, ornaments and clothes from China."[34] The indeterminacy in this case applies not only to the two geographical markers but also to the entire phrase. The entry might suggest that Cope exhibited Native American and Chinese artefacts together or next to each other;

that he showcased them nearby; or that he exhibited them separately but in Platter's mind they were connected enough to merit writing them down in the same sentence. It is also unclear whether Platter considered "India" and "China" to be related, proximate, or even overlapping geographical regions – it is far from obvious, in short, what Platter might have meant by "Indian" and "China." Cross-checking Platter's text with other accounts, inventories, and catalogues does not resolve the uncertainty, given the many different, incompatible, or even contradictory manners of characterizing objects. The writings penned by visitors describing what they had seen in a cabinet often reveal that the manner in which collectors displayed their possessions, the stories they might have told about those objects, and the ways in which the visitors themselves perceived them often made connections that stimulated such geographical promiscuity. As Holohan concludes in her study of Spanish Habsburg royal inventories, the descriptors "Indian" and "Chinese" in these documents represent "two sides of the same coin: strange and foreign, indubitably desirable, but essentially inscrutable."[35]

Other geographical descriptors that a modern reader might be tempted to imagine as more precisely and narrowly defined often turn out to be equally imprecise. Spanish royal inventories often used the descriptor "Peru" in the indeterminate and fluid way in which they applied "the Indies." A single group of objects could be described in one inventory as coming "from Peru" and in another as originating in "the Indies," and vice versa. It is particularly striking that many of the objects listed in the various inventories of Charles V's collections as "Peruvian" were in reality the gifts that Hernán Cortés had sent the emperor from Mexico.[36] The failure to register these particular items as Mexican is noteworthy given that they were some of the most celebrated and discussed American objects in the imperial collections – it is one thing to mislabel a little-known or undervalued object, but quite another to do so with a renowned centrepiece.[37] To make matters even more complicated, while many objects described as "Peruvian" came from other parts of the world, at times the adjective was applied to items that did in fact originate in the region.

A second practice of geographical indeterminacy concerns misattribution, which was ubiquitous and constant. Even when geographical terms were used to refer to concrete regions rather than to connote general ideas of foreignness or exoticism, they were frequently used unreliably. Examples are legion and have been meticulously traced, almost always in relation to the provenance of specific items in the collections of modern

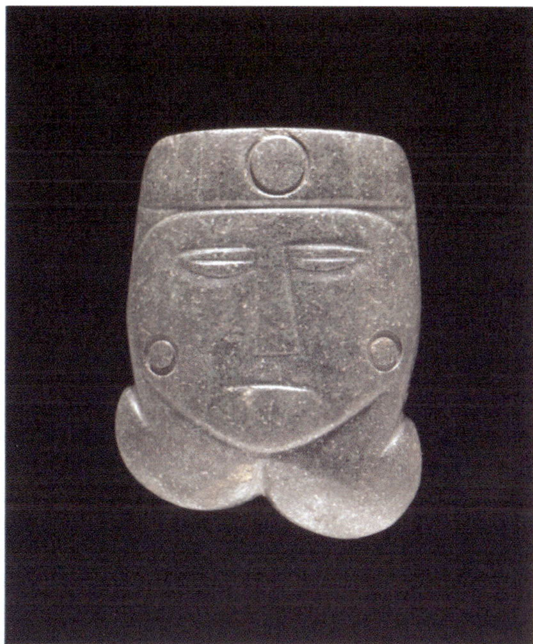

Figure 7.3. Mexican stone pendant/figurine identified in Hans Sloane's collection as an "Egyptian head of the sun." Am, SLAntiq.518. The British Museum, London.  © The Trustees of the British Museum

ethnographic museums. Thus, a Brazilian feather cape held in Brussels was described at one point as having belonged to the Mexica ruler Moctezuma.[38] The manuscript inventory of Hans Sloane's London cabinet – the founding collection for the British Museum when it was established in 1753 – lists a Mexican stone figurine from the Mixteca-Puebla region as an "Egyptian head of the sun" (fig. 7.3).[39] Taíno *zemis* from the Caribbean were described as African and Mexican, while a Javanese *kris* was in turn misidentified as a *zemi*, and an object from Florida registered as a "Mexican idol."[40] A 1674 inventory of the Danish Royal *Kunstkammer* described a Japanese bronze mirror as Chinese.[41] An early colonial Mexican obsidian mirror in the Vienna *Schatzkammer* was also listed as Chinese. Six Brazilian bows held in Copenhagen were described in 1689 as Japanese or East Indian.[42] This phenomenon continued into the nineteenth and twentieth centuries, with collection records registering, to give just one example, American objects as originating variously in Tahiti, New Zealand, China, and Madagascar.[43]

African objects were almost universally misallocated. Through a series of systematic and comprehensive studies, Ezio Bassani has been able to identify at least 818 African objects held in early modern European collections. Very often, however, sources recorded them as originating elsewhere: documents describe a Yoruba ivory bracelet as East Indian, and a Kongo basket in Worm's collection as a "Brazilian hat."[44] An Akan sword in the Copenhagen Royal Kunstkammer appeared in the 1674 catalogue as a "sword from the East Indies."[45] The most commonly held African objects in sixteenth- and seventeenth-century *Wunderkammern*, Afro-Portuguese ivories (such as the oliphant depicted by Praetorius in 1619, see fig. 7.2, no. 4), frequently garnered the descriptors of "Indian," "Oriental" or, more frequently, "Turkish."[46] Although records did at times describe objects as having been crafted in "Africa" or "Guinea," it is extremely unclear what the latter term meant for those who used it.[47]

A third practice of geographical indeterminacy concerns the instability and remarkable mutability of the descriptors used to qualify objects. All too frequently, an object's purported origin fluctuated from document to document, with elements in a description changing or disappearing without apparent reason. Thus a group of objects in Charles V's collection appears in inventories from 1545 and 1556 as coming "from the Indies from the island of Peru," but in a third inventory produced in 1561 as coming "from the Indies," losing the Peruvian connection.[48] The 1545 inventory also lists "seventy-five pieces of copper money from the Indies, having holes through the middle," which in the 1561 inventory became "seventy-five copper medals of ancient money."[49] The items simultaneously shed the American attribution and gained a historical one, with spatial distance giving way to temporal distance. Without explanation, they mutated from exotica into antiquities.

An object's stated point of origin could change drastically over time, without documents providing any information about the reasons for that transformation. An item described as an "Indian boat of leather" in a 1621 inventory, likely a kayak, became a "leathern Japanese little ship" in a 1737 inventory. Documents cataloguing Worm's collection characterize a wooden pipe now understood to be of Iroquois provenance as "Brazilian" in 1655, a "West Indian tobacco pipe called 'Calicot'" in 1673, and "East Indian" in 1690 – over a span of forty-five years, a single object in a single collection gained and lost associations with South America, the West Indies, South Asia, and the East Indies. Had the pipe itself not survived in Copenhagen, it would be nearly impossible to ascertain its identity.[50] And this is not a rare case resulting from a particularly disorganized collection or unreliable set of documents; indeed, it seems to have been commonplace. A rather similar situation arises, for instance, with the cabinet that the Spanish collector Vincencio Juan de Lastanosa (1607–1681) assembled in his native town of Huesca, in the province of Aragon. Four separate textual accounts of the collection, produced between c. 1640 and 1662, describe a single object variously as an "ivory horn," "an ivory horn ... from a Japanese King" carved "with a caiman head that grabs with its mouth the head of a king," and "an ivory horn" carved with "the head of a crowned Indian. It belonged to an Indian king." While the object's location is now unknown, an unsigned drawing produced c. 1635 depicts what is unmistakably an Afro-Portuguese ivory oliphant.[51]

Lest a sceptical reader imagine that only relatively obscure objects transmogrified in this manner, it is not difficult to find examples among some of the most remarkable and best-known non-European objects in European collections of the period. A spectacular Aztec headdress made with the long and vibrant green tail feathers of the quetzal, with details in gold and other bird feathers, was first held in the cabinet at Ambras Castle and later transferred to the collection in Vienna (fig. 7.4). It first appears in inventories as "Moorish" (*mörisch*, in 1596 and 1613) but changed without apparent reason to "Indian" (*indianisch*, between 1621 and 1822). After seeing it in Ambras in 1629, the learned author Martin Zeiller described it in a publication as having belonged to the "King of Cuba." The headdress became "Mexican" only in 1855. At some point it acquired a prestigious historical association and began to be known as "Moctezuma's Headdress," an attribution that remains popular and that has lent the object enormous significance in discussions of Mexican cultural heritage.[52] Another striking and rare Aztec object in the same collection, a feathered shield (*chimalli*) with an animal figure, is one of only four such shields that have survived to this day from the thousands thought to have existed at the time of the Spanish invasion of Mesoamerica (fig. 7.5). The shield appeared consistently in manuscript lists of 1596, 1613, 1621, 1663, 1730, 1788, and 1818, but its geographical and cultural origin changed over time. No provenance at all was attributed until 1788, when it suddenly and mysteriously is described as "Chinese."

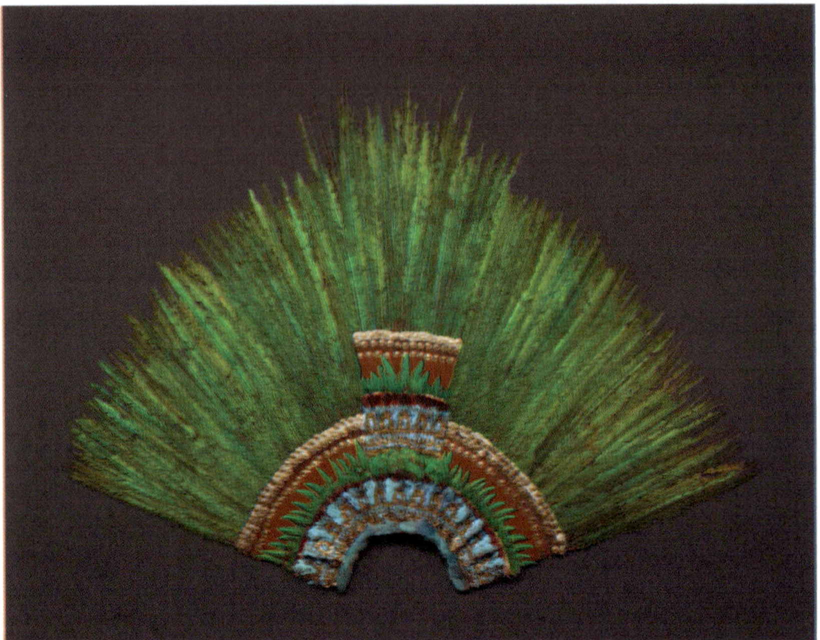

Figure 7.4.  Quetzal feathered headdress, Mexico, early sixteenth century.
Feathers of the quetzal, cotinga, roseate spoonbill, squirrel cuckoo, and
kingfisher; wood, fibres, paper, cotton, leather, gold, brass, and pigment. Inv.
no. 10402, Ambras collection. KHM-Museumsverband, Weltmuseum, Vienna

That origin changed to "Indian" in 1818 and then to "ancient Mexican"
in 1882. Its central figure also garnered changing monikers over time,
described as a "dragon" between 1596 and 1818 and becoming a "monster" in 1882, when it was first recognized as Mexican.[53] Scholars later
identified the figure as an *ahuizotl*, an Aztec mythological water animal,
but have most recently proposed it is actually a coyote, an animal associated with a warrior group.[54]

The remarkable instability and mutability of geographical markers for
objects in early modern collections does not necessarily imply indifference or carelessness on the part of collectors, visitors, and writers. As
already noted, they all prized foreign and rare objects, making sure to
procure, display, view, and comment on them. In fact, in at least some

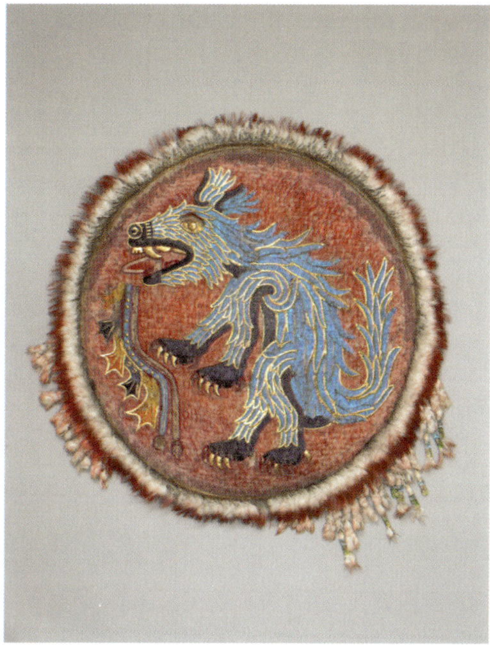

Figure 7.5. Feather shield with coyote, Mexico, before 1521. Feathers, gold plate, cane, and leather. Inv. no. 43380, Ambras collection. KHM-Museumsverband, Weltmuseum, Vienna

cases, the changing geographical attribution that an object received over time signals the interest it garnered. For instance, the rare pre-Hispanic Mixtec manuscript that the Bolognese collector Cospi received in December 1665 as a Christmas gift from Count Valerio Zani (d. 1696), now known as the *Codex Cospi*, figures in the 1667 catalogue of the collection as a "book ... from India."[55] Ten years later, a second edition of the catalogue modified the entry to a "Mexican book."[56] Yet another revision appears materially inscribed on the hard-board binding that covers the manuscript itself. A legend documenting Zani's gift to Cospi initially characterized the work as a "book from China" but was at some point corrected to "book from Mexico," leaving a palimpsest of the earlier attribution faintly visible under the new one.[57] The changing attributions attest both to the geographical instability that the manuscript experienced in seventeenth-century Italy and to the interest it awoke and attention it received, as no corrections would have been needed had the object gone unnoticed.

The great degree of uncertainty and imprecision surrounding the geographical or cultural origin of objects was not invisible to early modern observers. Indeed, some inventories use phrases that highlight the difficulty of epistemic precision regarding those elements while also indicating which aspects could be ascertained with greater confidence. Spanish Habsburg royal inventories often tempered descriptions with qualifiers such as "that they say" (*que dicen*).[58] One document, for example, lists "A large green stone, *that they say* is plasma of emerald, that came from New Spain and served as an idol, with a face on the end, *that they say* is good for the side (of the body), wrapped in green taffeta; that weights two *marcos*, one *onza*, and one *ochava*: valued at twelve *ducados*." The entry combines great precision regarding the exact weight and monetary value of the piece – elements that had been measured and calculated in Europe and could be expressed with certainty – with imprecision concerning information from the Americas, which could only be stated as hearsay and supposition.[59]

A fourth practice of indeterminacy regards the very absence of information concerning the geographical and cultural origin of non-European objects in early modern European collections. Very often, inventories and catalogues did not address where an item came from, even though that origin would have been obvious, remarkable, and valued at the time. For example, the very first shipment of Mesoamerican objects that Hernán Cortés sent Charles V from Mexico in 1519, which included the valuable items he had received from the Aztec emperor Moctezuma, contained sixteen shields adorned with stonework. In Europe, these shields awoke admiration for their brilliant blue turquoise mosaics and intricate craftsmanship, as well as their rarity, novelty, and exotic appeal. Charles presented some to his closest relatives, giving six in 1523 to Archduchess Margaretha of Austria, his aunt and former guardian, and another one the following year to his brother Ferdinand. The latter's son, Ferdinand II, owned a Mexica turquoise mosaic shield in his large and well-known cabinet at Ambras Castle in Innsbruck (an object that still survives, in rather damaged condition, fig. 7.6). It is uncertain whether this was the same shield that his father had received from Charles or was another one from Cortés's first shipment from Mexico, but it is clear that it formed part of that group of Mexican objects as it appears in a drawing created by the German artist Hans Burgkmair the Elder (1473–1531)

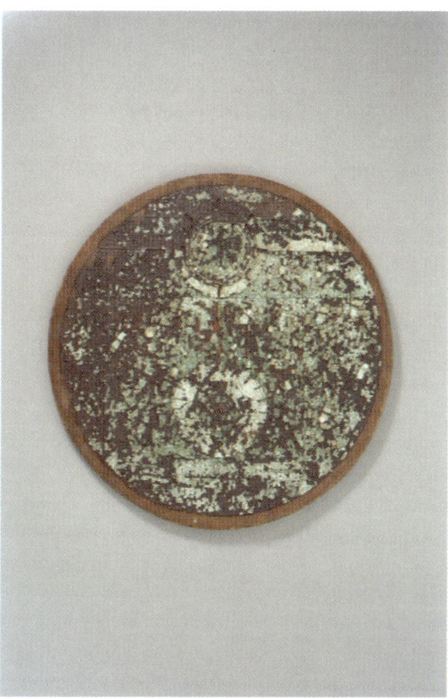

Figure 7.6. Ceremonial or dance shield, Mexico, before 1521. Wood, turquoise, green stone, and resin. Inv. no. 43379, Ambras collection. KHM-Museumsverband, Weltmuseum, Vienna

in the 1520s (fig. 7.7).[60] Despite the shield's rarity, interest, illustrious history, and prestigious provenance, its entry in the 1596 inventory of the Ambras collection merely registers "a mosaic with little stones in it." There is no indication whatsoever of the connection to Mexico, Moctezuma, Cortés, or Charles V. The inventories of 1613 and 1621 repeated that description; the 1663 inventory modified it only to add that the object was "perfectly round." In 1730, a new inventory described "A round mosaic edged with leather, therein figures made of little stones." The shield disappeared altogether from the inventories of 1788 and 1818. No provenance was ever suggested until the inventory of 1882, which for the very first time recorded the shield as "Mexican." Until that point, the various inventories had focused exclusively on the material qualities of the object but not connected them to its geographical or cultural origin, or

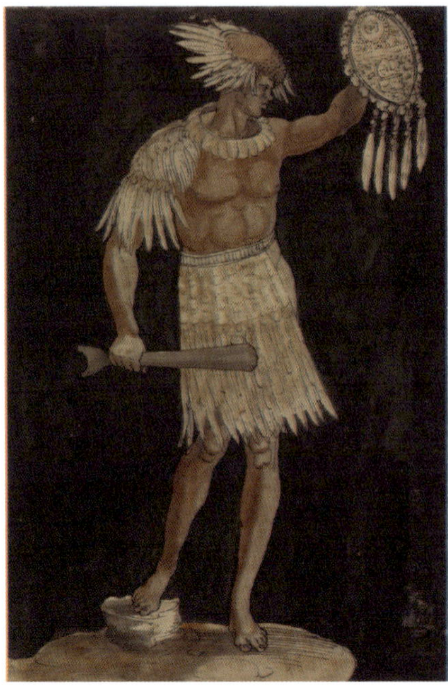

Figure 7.7.  Hans Burgkmair the Elder, drawing of a black youth, standing, dressed in American feather skirt, cape, and headdress, and holding a club and shield, 1520s. Pen and black ink, with brown, black and grey wash, 23.5 x 16 cm. Sl, 5218.128. The British Museum, London. © The Trustees of the British Museum

its history. It was only in 1891 that the shield was recognized as an Aztec object, when the American scholar Zelia Nuttal first identified it as such roughly 370 years after the object arrived in Europe.[61]

Such archival silences obscure the presence of non-European objects in early modern European cabinets and make it even more difficult to assess how owners and viewers at the time used these objects to generate ideas about their expanding world. Archival silences and absences have also caused a loss of information about the histories of the precious few objects that remain today from cultures and regions severely affected by European expansion. When the British Museum tallied its collection of Mexican mosaics in 1822, sixteen of the twenty-two had no documented history whatsoever.[62]

These practices of indeterminacy make it extremely difficult, when not altogether impossible, to draw solid conclusions about geographical and cultural origins from sixteenth- and seventeenth-century inventories. The issue is not that inventories and catalogues were hopelessly ill-informed or negligent, or that people at the time did not care about acquiring accurate information about the objects they owned, viewed, wrote about, or read about. My point is not whether collectors or those who composed inventories got the facts about particular objects right or wrong, but rather to highlight that sources demonstrate that attention to record-keeping and interest in foreign objects did not always result in the production of knowledge about the objects or the regions or cultures they came from. This was not due to lack of interest. The fact that inventories regularly list as many descriptive elements about an object as possible and make a point of recording presumed geographical or cultural origin indicates that such information mattered to people at the time. The objective was to possess, view, and register foreignness rather than to gain knowledge about foreign objects, places, or peoples. The fact that they used unspecific terms and that entries frequently changed without improving accuracy indicates a level of comfort with inexact, imprecise, and unstable information, particularly regarding non-European items.

## Conclusion

The high level of fuzziness surrounding foreign objects in early modern European collections often presents a striking contrast to the much greater precision applied to local objects, many times in the very same manuscript or publication. The catalogue of Borel's collection, for example, appeared as the last of four sections in a single publication. The first part of the treatise presents an extremely knowledgeable and detailed account of the "antiquities, rarities, plants, minerals, and other significant things of the town and county of Castres" and its surroundings, including notes on local history, historical figures, and buildings. The second part travels outward from the town to address a broader geographical area, listing the Roman inscriptions and antiquities in the regions of Languedoc (where Castres was located) and neighbouring Provence. The third part widens the geographical scope once again, addressing the "main curiosity cabinets, and other remarkable things that can be seen in the major cities of Europe," organized alphabetically city by city, and enumerating within each city all the cabinets, listed by owner. The reader thus moves from the town to the region to the rest of Europe, just as travellers from Castres might have done as they set out on a voyage. Finally, the fourth part returns to Castres to catalogue the contents of Borel's cabinet, which is at once the most circumscribed repository – when compared to city, region, continent – and the most capacious one – in that it is advertised as a "world."[63] The information in this section is both the most detailed, in listing the exact contents of a single collection, and the most imprecise, when it comes to foreign objects. The publication thus operates in nested spheres that move outwards, from the city, to the region, to other locales across Europe. While the ambitions are presented as global, to possess the entire world, the viewpoint and expertise turn out to be extremely local – what Richard Kagan has described as a "communicentric" perspective.[64]

The generalized imprecision of geographical and cultural attributes in cabinets is in stark contrast with the precision and specificity (actual or desired) that characterize other practices of European worldmaking at the time, as well as other products of European global exploration. European cartographers attempted to pin down in their maps foreign places whose specific location, contours, and characteristics mattered enormously to commercial, imperial, and missionary projects (fig. 7.8).

Maps depicted the globe via a precise, fixed, evenly distributed, and stable grid; cabinets presented a global geography that was imprecise, mutable, clumpy, and unstable. These two forms of worldmaking were indeed interrelated: one centrifugal, the other centripetal. As Europeans spread around the globe, establishing settler colonies, commercial bases, and missionary outposts, they produced two complementary visions of the world. One, associated with cartographic space, was predicated on the production of knowledge about a world envisioned as a stable, fixed entity that could be reached, settled, claimed, and known. The other, associated with the collection, was predicated on the absorption, recontextualization, and repurposing of things from far away that could be brought home and domesticated: a larger world that was non-linear, non-gridded, and constantly mutating. Worldmaking entailed imagining and inventing as well as discovery, keeping things uncertain as well as achieving precision. In a time when the puzzle of the world was being put in place, piece by piece, cabinets allowed not only for worldmaking but also for world re-making. The pieces could be reordered to create a vision of the whole that juxtaposed the precision of some places with the imprecision of others, and at times might combine precise and imprecise elements of a single place. Cartographic space imagined a single and unique location for Mexico, Peru, or China; collection space

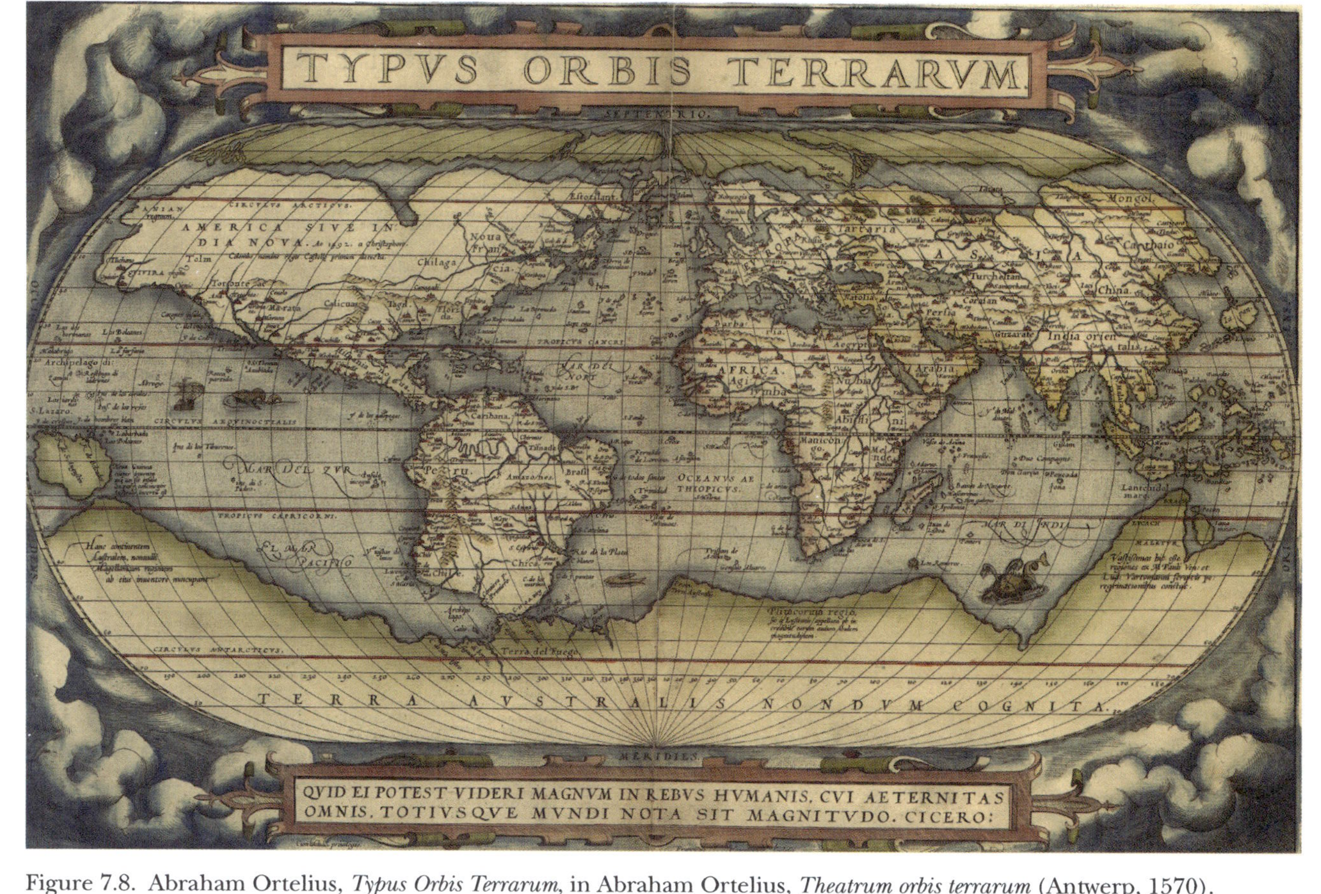


Figure 7.8.  Abraham Ortelius, *Typus Orbis Terrarum*, in Abraham Ortelius, *Theatrum orbis terrarum* (Antwerp, 1570). Engraving with watercolour (hand colouring). The Library of Congress, Geography and Map Division, G1006.T5 1570b

insisted on the interchangeability and recombinable nature of these regions and their objects.

## ACKNOWLEDGMENTS

My thanks to Bronwen Wilson and Angela Vanhaelen for their helpful feedback on this piece at various stages and for their patience, and to the colleagues who have provided comments on this research. This article is a revised and expanded version of "The Cabinet and the World: Non-European Objects in Early Modern European Collections," *The Journal of the History of Collections* 3, no. 3 (November 2021): 435–45.

## NOTES

1 Joy Kenseth, "'A World of Wonders in One Closet Shut,'" in *The Age of the Marvelous*, ed. Joy Kenseth (Hanover, NH: Hood Museum of Art, Dartmouth College, 1991), 81–101. From the abundant literature on *Wunderkammern* in general, see especially Oliver Impey and Arthur MacGregor, eds., *The Origins of Museums: The Cabinet of Curiosities in Sixteenth and Seventeenth-Century Europe* (Oxford: Oxford University Press, 1985); Krzysztof Pomian, *Collectors and Curiosities: Paris and Venice 1500–1800* (Cambridge, UK: Polity Press, 1990); Joy Kenseth, ed., *The Age of the Marvelous* (Hanover, NH: Hood Museum of Art, Dartmouth College, 1991); Paula Findlen, *Possessing Nature: Museums, Collecting, and Scientific Culture in Early Modern Italy* (Berkeley: University of California Press, 1994). On wonders, see Lorraine Daston and Katharine Park, *Wonders and the Order of Nature, 1150–1750* (New York: Zone Books, 1998).

2 Quoted in Arthur MacGregor, "The Tradescants: Gardeners and Botanists," in *Tradescant's Rarities: Essays on the Foundation of the Ashmolean Museum, 1683, with a Catalogue of the Surviving Early Collections*, ed. Arthur MacGregor (Oxford: Clarendon Press, 1983), 15.

3 Thomas Platter, *Thomas Platter's Travels In England 1599*, trans. Clare Williams (London: Jonathan Cape, 1937), 171–3. See also Arthur MacGregor, "The Cabinet of Curiosities in Seventeenth-Century Britain," in Impey and MacGregor, *The Origins of Museums*, 148.

4 Arthur MacGregor, "The Tradescants as Collectors of Rarities," in MacGregor, *Tradescant's Rarities*, 20–2, Mundy quote on 20–1 (I have modernized the spelling).

5  Pierre Borel, "Catalogue des choses rares qui sont dans le cabinet [...]," in *Les antiquitez, raretez, plantes, mineraux, & autres choses considerables [...]* (Castres, 1649), book 2, 132. As translated and quoted in Kenseth, "'A World of Wonders in One Closet Shut,'" 86.

6  Quoted in Arthur MacGregor, "Collectors and Collections of Rarities in the Sixteenth and Seventeenth Centuries," in MacGregor, *Tradescant's Rarities*, 80.

7  On the Italian collections, see especially Findlen, *Possessing Nature*; Laura Laurencich Minelli, ed., *Bologna e il Mondo Nuovo* (Bologna: Grafis, 1992); Laura Laurencich-Minelli, "A New Glance at Bologna's Sixteenth- and Seventeenth-Century Museums and Their Mexican Items," in *Turquoise in Mexico and North America: Science, Conservation, Culture and Collections*, ed. John C.H. King et al. (London: Archetype Publications and the British Museum, 2012), 165–72; Antonio Aimi, Vincenzo De Michele, and Alessandro Morandotti, *Septalianvm Mvsævm: una collezione scientifica nella Milano del Seicento* (Florence: Giunti Marzocco, 1984); Antonio Aimi, "The Exotica of the Settala Museum and Other Northern Italian Collections," in King, *Turquoise in Mexico and North America*, 155–64. On the Northern collections, see Daniel Margócsy, *Commercial Visions: Science, Trade, and Visual Culture in the Dutch Golden Age* (Chicago: University of Chicago Press, 2014); Valdimar Tr. Hafstein, "Bodies of Knowledge: Ole Worm & Collecting in Late Renaissance Scandinavia," *Ethnologia Europaea, Journal of European Ethnology* 33, no. 1 (2003): 5–20.

8  Eugenio Lo Sardo, ed., *Athanasius Kircher: Il Museo Del Mondo* (Rome: De Luca, 2001), esp. Aldo Mastroianni, "Kircher e l'Oriente nel Museo del Collegio Romano," 65–78; Paula Findlen, *Athanasius Kircher: The Last Man Who Knew Everything* (New York: Routledge, 2004).

9  Among the extensive literature, see: On Habsburg Spanish collections, Kate Elizabeth Holohan, "Collecting the New World at the Spanish Habsburg Court, 1519–1700" (PhD diss., New York University, 2015); Cinta Krahe, *Chinese Porcelain in Habsburg Spain* (Madrid: Centro de Estudios Europa Hispanica, 2016). On Habsburg Central European collections, the many publications by Christian Feest, especially Christian F. Feest, "Mexico and South America in the European Wunderkammer," in Impey and MacGregor, *The Origins of Museums*, 237–44; Christian F. Feest, "Zemes Idolum Diabolicum. Surprise and Success in Ethnographic Kunstkammer Research," *Archiv für Völkerkunde* 40 (1986): 181–98; Christian F. Feest, "Vienna's Mexican Treasures: Aztec, Mixtec, and Tarascan Works from 16th Century Austrian Collections," *Archiv für Völkerkunde* 44 (1990): 1–65; Christian F. Feest, "North America in the European Wunderkammer Before 1750. With a

Preliminary Checklist," *Archiv für Völkerkunde* 46 (1992): 61–109; Christian F.
Feest, "European Collecting of American Indian Artefacts and Art," *Journal
of the History of Collections* 5, no. 1 (1993): 1–11. On the Medici collections,
Lia Markey, *Imagining the Americas in Medici Florence* (University Park, PA:
Pennsylvania State University Press, 2016). Many of the manuscript invento-
ries have been published and are cited in these works.

10  On foreign objects in early modern European collections see, in addition
to works already cited, the following essays in Impey and MacGregor, *The
Origins of Museums*: Ezio Bassani and Malcolm McLeod, "African Material in
Early Collections," 245–50, Julian Raby, "Exotica from Islam," 251-258, John
Ayers, "The Early China Trade," 259–66, Oliver Impey, "Japan: Trade and
Collecting in Seventeenth-Century Europe," 267–73, and Robert Skelton,
"Indian Art and Artefacts in Early European Collecting," pp. 274-280; see
also Anthony Alan Shelton, "Cabinets of Transgression: Renaissance Collec-
tions and the Incorporation of the New World," in *The Cultures of Collecting*,
ed. John Elsner and Roger Cardinal (Cambridge, MA: Harvard University
Press, 1994), 177–203; Isabel Yaya, "Wonders of America: The Curiosity
Cabinet as a Site of Representation and Knowledge," *Journal of the History of
Collections* 20, no. 2 (2008): 173–88; Ezio Bassani, *African Art and Artefacts in
European Collections: 1400–1800* (London: British Museum Press, 2000); Elke
Bujok, *Neue Welten in europäischen Sammlungen: Africana und Americana in
Kunstkammern bis 1670* (Berlin: Reimer, 2004). More generally, see Daniela
Bleichmar and Meredith Martin, eds., *Objects in Motion in the Early Modern
World* (Chichester: John Wiley & Sons, 2016); Daniela Bleichmar and Peter
C. Mancall, eds., *Collecting across Cultures: Material Exchanges in the Early At-
lantic World* (Philadelphia: University of Pennsylvania Press, 2011).

11  Adriana Turpin, "The New World Collections of Duke Cosimo I de' Medici
and Their Role in the Creation of a Kunst- and Wunderkammer in the
Palazzo Vecchio," in *Curiosity and Wonder from the Renaissance to the Enlight-
enment*, ed. R.J.W. Evans and Alexander Marr (Aldershot: Ashgate, 2006),
63–85; Yaya, "Wonders of America"; Elke Bujok, "Ethnographica in Early
Modern Kunstkammern and Their Perception," *Journal of the History of
Collections* 21, no. 1 (May 1, 2009): 17–32. On wonders and marvels in this
period, see Stephen Greenblatt, *Marvelous Possessions: The Wonder of the
New World* (Chicago: University of Chicago Press, 1991); Daston and Park,
*Wonders and the Order of Nature*; Pamela H. Smith and Paula Findlen, eds.,
*Merchants & Marvels: Commerce, Science and Art in Early Modern Europe* (New
York, NY: Routledge, 2002).

12  Benjamin Schmidt, *Inventing Exoticism: Geography, Globalism, and Europe's
Early Modern World* (Philadelphia: University of Pennsylvania Press, 2015),

14–15. Schmidt terms this approach "exotic geography" and dates it to c. 1660s–1730s; however, it seems to be present at least a century earlier in cabinets and their associated documents. On the importance of "New World" objects and peoples for redefining the "Old World," see Anthony Pagden, *European Encounters with the New World: From Renaissance to Romanticism* (New Haven: Yale University Press, 1993); Peter Mason, *Infelicities: Representations of the Exotic* (Baltimore: Johns Hopkins University Press, 1998); Peter Mason, *Deconstructing America: Representations of the Other* (New York: Routledge, 1990); Peter Mason, "From Presentation to Representation: Americana in Europe," *Journal of the History of Collections* 6, no. 1 (1994): 1–20.

13 Ayesha Ramachandran, *The Worldmakers: Global Imagining in Early Modern Europe* (Chicago: University of Chicago Press, 2015), 6.

14 Ramachandran, *The Worldmakers*, 7.

15 See for instance Thomas DaCosta Kaufmann, "Remarks on the Collections of Rudolf II: The Kunstkammer as a Form of *Representatio*," *Art Journal* 38, no. 1 (Autumn 1978): 27; José Miguel Morán and Fernando Checa Cremades, *El coleccionismo en España: de la cámara de maravillas a la galería de pinturas* (Madrid: Cátedra, 1985); Pomian, *Collectors and Curiosities*.

16 Steven Mullaney, "Strange Things, Gross Terms, Curious Customs: The Rehearsal of Cultures in the Late Renaissance," *Representations* 3 (1983): 42.

17 See for instance Findlen, *Possessing Nature*; Margócsy, *Commercial Visions*; Juan Pimentel, *The Rhinoceros and the Megatherium: An Essay in Natural History* (Cambridge, MA: Harvard University Press, 2017); James Delbourgo, *Collecting the World: Hans Sloane and the Origins of the British Museum* (Cambridge, MA: Harvard University Press, 2017).

18 These quotes in Kenseth, "'A World of Wonders in One Closet Shut,'" 84–5; Mark A. Meadow, introduction to *The First Treatise on Museums: Samuel Quiccheberg's Inscriptiones, 1565*, by Samuel Quiccheberg, ed. and trans. Mark A. Meadow and Bruce Robertson (Los Angeles: Getty Research Institute, 2013), 2, 6. Comparable statements are frequent throughout the secondary literature.

19 As translated in Quiccheberg, *The First Treatise on Museums*, 61.

20 Schmidt, *Inventing Exoticism*.

21 Jessica Keating and Lia Markey, "'Indian' Objects in Medici and Austrian-Habsburg Inventories: A Case-Study of the Sixteenth-Century Term," *Journal of the History of Collections* 23, no. 2 (November 2011): 286–8; Nicolás Wey Gómez, *The Tropics of Empire: Why Columbus Sailed South to the Indies* (Cambridge, MA: MIT Press, 2008), especially 159–228 on the pre-Columbian tradition and 293–392 on geo-climactic understandings of

"the Indies" as the tropics; Elizabeth Horodowich and Alexander Nagel, "Amerasia: European Reflections of an Emergent World, 1492–ca. 1700," *Journal of Early Modern History* 23, no. 2–3 (2019): 257–95. See also Rudolf Wittkower, "Marvels of the East. A Study in the History of Monsters," *Journal of the Warburg and Courtauld Institutes* 5 (1942): 159–97; E.F. Tuttle, "Borrowing versus Semantic Shift: New World Nomenclature in European Languages," in *First Images of America: The Impact of the New World on the Old*, ed. Fredi Chiappelli, Michael J. B Allen, and Robert Louis Benson, 2 vols. (Berkeley: University of California Press, 1976), 2:595–611.

22  The *Oxford English Dictionary*, as cited in Keating and Markey, "'Indian' Objects," 286.

23  Christine Göttler, "Extraordinary Things: 'Idols from India' and the Visual Discernment of Space and Time, circa 1600," in *The Nomadic Object: The Challenge of World for Early Modern Religious Art*, ed. Christine Göttler and Mia Mochizuki (Leiden: Brill, 2017), 41.

24  Keating and Markey, "'Indian' Objects"; Holohan, "Collecting the New World," 15, 19; Alessandra Russo, "Cortés's Objects and the Idea of New Spain Inventories as Spatial Narratives," *Journal of the History of Collections* 23, no. 2 (1 November 2011): 229–52.

25  Bassani, *African Art*, 23 (no. 59); Bujok, "Ethnographica in Early Modern Kunstkammern and Their Perception," 19; Feest, "Mexico and South America," 240; Feest, "Zemes Idolum Diabolicum," 183; Christian F. Feest, "The Collecting of American Indian Artifacts in Europe, 1493–1750," in *America in European Consciousness, 1493–1750*, ed. Karen Ordahl Kupperman (Chapel Hill: University of North Carolina Press, 1995), 335; Christian Feest, "Mexican Turquoise Mosaics in Vienna," in King, *Turquoise in Mexico*, 114; Keating and Markey, "'Indian' Objects," 284, 289.

26  Feest, 12; Feest, "Zemes Idolum Diabolicum," 183; Feest, "Mexico and South America," 238.

27  Feest, "Vienna's Mexican Treasures," 13.

28  Holohan, "Collecting the New World," 131.

29  Jeremy Montagu, *Timpani and Percussion* (New Haven and London: Yale University Press, 2002), 55–7; Andreas Meyer, "In Sound Similar to the Harps: Early Descriptions of African Musical Instruments," in *Instruments in Art and Science: On the Architectonics of Cultural Boundaries in the 17th Century*, ed. Helmar Schramm, Ludger Schwarte, and Jan Lazardzig (Berlin: Walter de Gruyter, 2014), 270–3. Quotation as translated in Meyer. The African instruments are noted in Bassani, *African Art*, xxxi.

30  Montagu, *Timpani and Percussion*, 56. The "Muscovite" drum appears as "a drum from *Ginny*" in the Ashmolean's 1656 catalogue; John Tradescant,

*Musæum Tradescantianum: Or, A Collection of Rarities* (London, 1656), 45. It was first identified in K.P. Wachsmann, "A Drum from Seventeeth Century Africa," *The Galpin Society Journal* 23 (1970): 97–103.

31 Montagu, *Timpani and Percussion*, 56; Willem Lodewijckz, *D'eerste Boeck. Historie van Indien [...]* (Amsterdam, 1598).

32 Holohan, "Collecting the New World," 163–4, quote on 164.

33 Borel, "Catalogue", book 2, 140–1.

34 Platter, *Thomas Platter's Travels In England 1599*, 171.

35 Holohan, "Collecting the New World," 163–4.

36 In fact, no Spanish or Austrian Habsburg inventory from 1661 to the mid-eighteenth century used the label "Mexico," as noted in Feest, "Collecting of American Indian Artifacts," 340.

37 Holohan, "Collecting the New World," 74, 76, 80–1, 90–7, 136–7.

38 The cape was likely collected in the sixteenth or seventeenth century but not inventoried until 1781. Shelton, "Cabinets of Transgression," 192–3.

39 Shelton, 203; H.J. Braunholtz, *Sir Hans Sloane and Ethnography* (London: British Museum, 1970), 31 (plate 22).

40 Feest, "Zemes Idolum Diabolicum," 190. On the *kris*, see also Christine Göttler, "The Place of the Exotic in Early Seventeenth-Century Antwerp," in *Looking East: Ruben's Encounter with Asia*, ed. Stephanie Schrader (Los Angeles: The J. Paul Getty Museum, 2013), 89–107; Christine Göttler, "'Indian Daggers with Idols' in the Early Modern *Constcamer*. Collecting, Picturing, and Imagining 'Exotic' Weaponry in the Netherlands and Beyond," in *Netherlandish Art in Its Global Context*, ed. Eric Jorink, Frits Scholten, and Thijs Weststeijn, Netherlands Yearbook for History of Art 66 (Leiden: Brill, 2016), 80–109; Göttler, "Extraordinary Things."

41 Bente Gundestrup, "The Danish Royal *Kunstkammer* and the Indian chamber," in *Exotica: Portugals Entdeckungen im Spiegel fürstlicher Kunst- und Wunderkammern der Renaissance. Die Beiträge des am 19. und 20. Mai 2000 vom Kunsthistorischen Museum Wien veranstalteten Symposiums*, ed. Helmut Trnek and Sabine Haag (Mainz: Von Zabern, 2001), 166.

42 Feest, "Mexico and South America," 240; Feest, "Vienna's Mexican Treasures," 5.

43 Feest, "Collecting of American Indian Artifacts," 335.

44 Bassani, *African Art*, xv. See also Ezio Bassani and Malcolm McLeod, "African Material in Early Collections."

45 Bassani, *African Art*, xxxiv.

46 Bassani, *African Art*, xxviii.

47 Bassani, *African Art*, xv.

48 Holohan, "Collecting the New World," 19.

49  Holohan, 74; Fernando Checa Cremades, *Los Inventarios de Carlos V y La Fa-milia Imperial*, 3 vols. (Madrid: Fernando Villaverde, 2010), 1:221, 320.

50  Feest, "North America in the European Wunderkammer," 92, 94; Feest, "Collecting of American Indian Artifacts," 335. The pipe is in the collection of the Natural History Museum, Copenhagen, no. E.Dc16, and illustrated in an published essay by Christian Feest, "An Early Nineteenth Century East-ern Ojibwa Wooden Effigy Pipe," fig. 6, available at https://www.academia .edu/39673713/An_Early_Nineteenth_Century_Eastern_Ojibwa_Wooden _Effigy_Pipe.

51  Daniela Bleichmar, "Seeing the World in a Room: Looking at Exotica in Early Modern Collections," in *Collecting across Cultures: Material Exchanges in the Early Atlantic World*, ed. Daniela Bleichmar and Peter C. Mancall (Philadelphia: University of Pennsylvania Press, 2011), 15–30.

52  Feest, "Vienna's Mexican Treasures," 11. Feest provides the reference to Martin Zeiller, *Itinerarium Germaniae novae antiquae* (Strassburg, 1632), 356. For recent studies of the headdress, see Christian F. Feest and Lilia Rivero Weber, "Shared Heritage: The Ancient Mexican Feather Head-dress in Vienna," in *Der altmexikanische Federkopfschmuck / El penacho del México antiguo*, ed. Sabine Haag (Vienna: Museum für Völkerunde; Mexico City: CONACULTA, 2012), 1397–1401; A. G. Karydas et al., "Handheld XRF Analysis of the Old Mexican Feather Headdress in the Weltmuseum Vienna," *X-Ray Spectrometry* 43, no. 3 (2014): 138–45.

53  Feest, "Vienna's Mexican Treasures," 16.

54  Recent accounts of the shield include Eduardo Matos Moctezuma and Felipe R. Solís Olguín, eds., *Aztecs* (London: Royal Academy of Arts, 2002), 350–1, 475 (cat. 299); Manuel Aguilar-Moreno, *Handbook to Life in the Aztec World* (New York: Facts on File, 2006), 211–12; Laura Filloy Nadal and María Olvido Moreno Guzmán, "Precious Feathers and Fancy Fifteenth-Century Feathered Shields," in *Rethinking the Aztec Economy*, ed. Deborah L. Nichols, Frances Berdan, and Michael E. Smith (Tucson: University of Arizona Press, 2017), 156–94.

55  Laura Laurencich-Minelli and Michael D. Coe, "Codex Cospi," in *Circa 1492: Art in the Age of Exploration*, ed. Jay A. Levenson (Washington: National Gallery of Art; New Haven: Yale University Press, 1991), 545. Citing Lorenzo Legati, *Breve descrizione del museo [...] Cospi* (Bologna, 1667).

56  "Libro messicano"; Lorenzo Legati, *Museo Cospiano* (Bologna, 1677), book 3, 191.

57  "Libro della China" became "Libro del Messico," as can be seen on the cover.

58  Holohan, "Collecting the New World," 138.

59  My emphasis. "Una piedra grande verde, que dicen ser plasma de esmeralda, que vino de la Nueva España y servía de ídolo, con un rostro al cabo, que dicen es buena para la hijada, envuelta en un tafetán verde; que pesa dos marcos, una onza y una ochava: tasada en doce ducados," as translated in Holohan, 145. The original Spanish appears in J. Sánchez Cantón, *Inventarios reales. Bienes muebles que pertenecieron a Felipe II*, 10 vols. (Madrid: Real Academia de la Historia, 1956), 1:274.

60  Feest, "Mexican Turquoise Mosaics," 107. Feest finds it unlikely that Ferdinand II's Ambras shield, depicted by Burgkmair and now in Vienna, is the same one presented to his father in 1524 as proposed by Karl Anton Nowotny, *Mexikanische Kostbarkeiten aus Kunstkammern der Renaissance im Museum für Volkerkunde Wien und in der Nationalbibliothek, Wien* (Vienna: Museum für Volkerkunde, 1960), 38–9.

61  My account is drawn from Feest, "Mexican Turquoise Mosaics," 104. The Vienna shield and one at the British Museum are the only two surviving Aztec turquoise mosaic shields from those taken to Europe in the sixteenth century; all other extant examples come from twentieth-century archaeological findings. Feest, 108–10.

62  Feest, "Mexican Turquoise Mosaics," 103. The British Museum today holds nine Mexican turquoise mosaic objects, but all acquired 1860–94.

63  Borel, "Catalogue," quotes on title page and 124.

64  Richard Kagan, *Urban Images of the Hispanic World, 1493–1793* (New Haven: Yale University Press, 2000), 16–17, 107–50.

# chapter eight

# *Le Jeu du monde*: Games, Maps, and World Conquest in Early Modern France

TING CHANG

This essay examines a group of interrelated board games and maps produced in France in the seventeenth and eighteenth centuries that invited particular forms of engagement. Handling these copperplate engravings enabled a virtual experience of travel through spaces in the world. I focus on the ways in which both their overt and implicit content encouraged French expansion into remote, foreign territories. If the proliferation of educational toys in France in the 1640s has been attributed to the tender age of the child king Louis XIV, a greater impetus came from vast historical processes such as Western competition to chart and dominate the globe, and the corresponding growth of European missionary activities and trade routes.[1] Games, I propose, were creative forms of making and also unmaking the world.[2]

Antoine-Maxime Monsaldy's engraving of 1797, *Le Triomphe des armées françaises* (*The Triumph of the French Armies*), appearing at the chronological end of my study, offers a provocative introduction (fig. 8.1).[3] The print celebrates the Revolutionary Wars when France not only defeated internal enemies but also extended its borders into Flanders, the Netherlands, the Rhine region, and Italy. In this commemorative image Monsaldy shuns the familiar rhetoric of conquest – absent are the battle scenes, captured enemies, or war booty – and shows instead four men handling maps in peculiar ways. We might well ask why they hold up maps that stand on the ground and rise stiffly above their heads, severed along arbitrary contours in some areas, and in others perforated with voids like missing pieces of a puzzle. Why, we might further ask, does one man stand in the space between two maps?

Monsaldy's print sums up what educational games in geography aimed to achieve: by encouraging learning about nations and peoples through

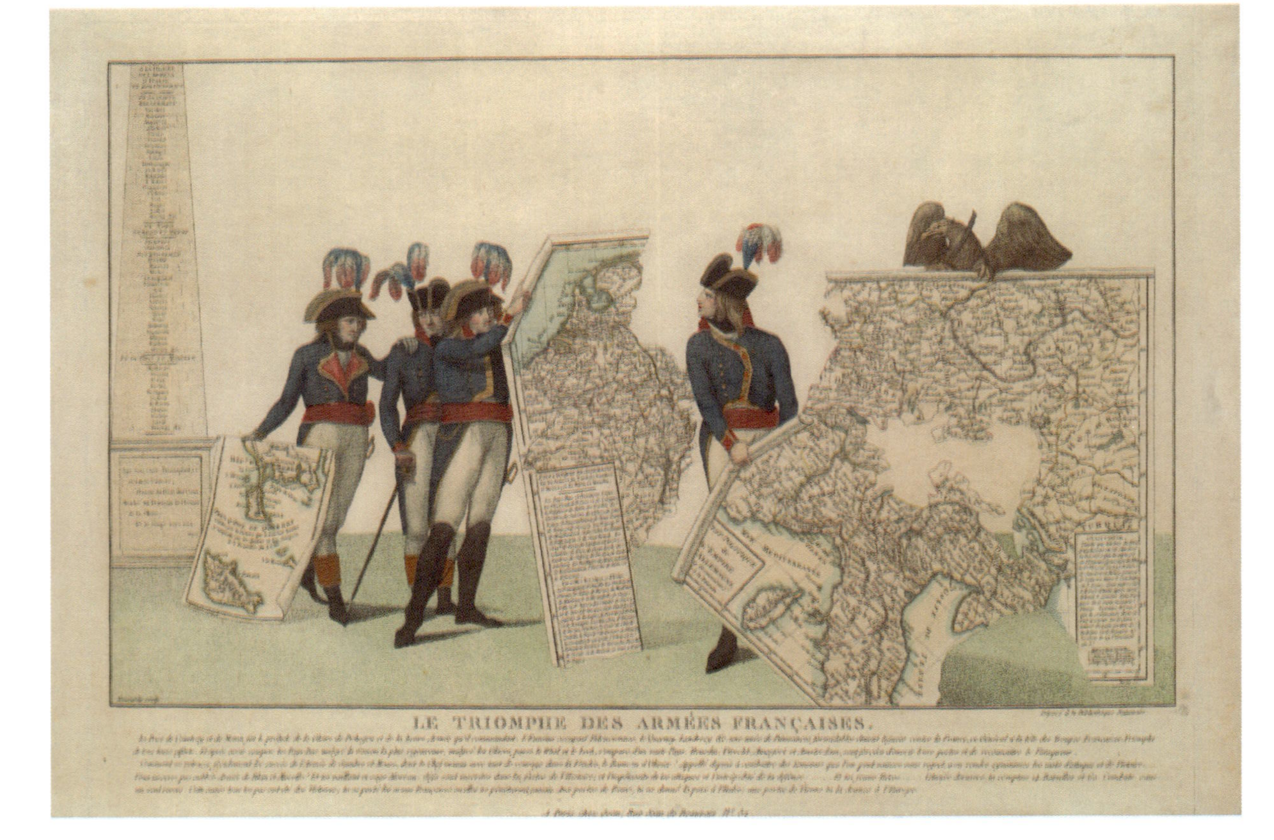


Figure 8.1.  Antoine Maxime Monsaldy, *Le Triomphe des armées françaises* (Paris, 1797). Engraving on paper, 45 x 35 cm. P980009. The Getty Research Institute, Los Angeles

multisensory engagement, they incited pupil-players to interpose themselves physically in the world. The effect was most acute in my first object of analysis, *Le Jeu du monde* (*The Game of the World*), a board game invented in the early 1640s that compelled movements back and forth on the world map. Related games by others include *Le Jeu de la géographie* (*The Game of Geography*), a set of playing cards designed in 1644, and *Le Jeu de la guerre* (*The Game of War*), a board game created later in the seventeenth century. Each game enabled players to learn certain kinds of knowledge.

### *Le Jeu du monde*

Pierre Duval (1619–1683) was the first to combine maps and board games. He trained as a mapmaker with his uncle, Nicolas Sanson (1600–1667), a military engineer and pre-eminent cartographer in seventeenth-century France.[4] Both were *géographes de cabinet* who relied on texts and existing maps, rather than their own measurements and surveys in the field, to produce their maps.[5] Duval created the board game *Le Jeu du monde* in the early 1640s by adapting the highly popular game of the goose, or *jeu de l'oie*, from the Italian *gioco dell'oca*. The earliest recorded mention of the *gioco dell'oca* dates to the fifteenth century, and the oldest dated example to survive was printed in Rome in 1598 (fig. 8.2).[6] Goose games proliferated across Europe after Francesco de' Medici (1574–1587) sent one to King Philip II of Spain, where they took hold and spread.[7]

A minimum of two and a maximum of six participants played the spiral race game with two dice and individual markers that they moved back and forth on the game board. In its original form, the favourable spaces on the board that allowed a player to jump forward were denoted by a goose, hence the term "goose game." There were also unfavourable spaces, or hazards on the track, where players variously had to pay a rival or pay the pool, move back a certain number of spaces, lose one to two turns, stop advancing until replaced by another player landing on the same spot, or start again. The first to arrive at the end of the race, typically space 63, won the game and the pool of money.[8]

*Le Jeu du monde* was a betting game designed for adults, who had to agree to the value of the stake at the outset. Duval stipulated that "players will agree the amount, a *denier*, a *sol*, a *teston*, or a *pistole* if one wishes, that each will put in the little world in the middle of the gameboard" before starting the match.[9] However, in general goose games could be enjoyed by players of all ages competing to win counters or tokens of no

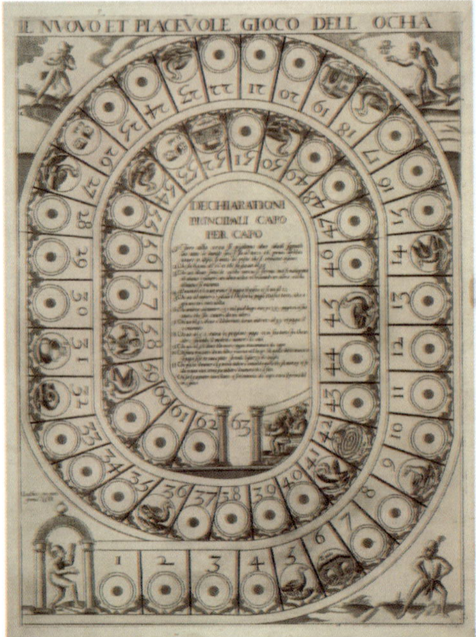

Figure 8.2. Lucchino Gargano, *Il Nuovo et Piacevole Gioco dell Ocha,* 1598. Engraving on paper, 50.7 x 37.8 cm. Image ID: 00017738001. The British Museum, London. © The Trustees of the British Museum

monetary value.[10] The fact that it was a throw of the dice in combination with the rules of the game, and not a competitor's skill or strategy, that determined the moves, made it amenable to all ages. Evidence of children playing goose games emerged in the late eighteenth century when young participants could wager nuts, sweets, biscuits, and small images or figurines instead of coins.[11] A modified goose game dating to the Second Empire (1852–70) began with the explicit statement that "several children can play this game" ("plusieurs enfants peuvent prendre part à ce jeu"), and they could use pictures, toy soldiers, fruit, or "any other stake" ("ou tout autre enjeu").[12]

The earliest use of a spiral race game for didactic purposes occurred in France in the seventeenth century.[13] Duval was the first to exploit the popularity of goose games for the purpose of teaching geography. He inserted sixty-three small maps on the track of *Le Jeu du monde,* printed on a sheet of paper measuring 64.8 by 44.8 centimetres (fig. 8.3).[14] Duval conspicuously departed from such cartographic norms as the representation of a spherical earth drawn on a flat plane, as in Gerardus Mercator's world map of 1569, to put a sequence of discs containing vignette maps on a single line coiling in a counter-clockwise direction towards the centre. Inset maps of the four continents anchor the corners of the rectangular engraving. Europe occupies the top left, next to the "Explanation of the figure" ("Explication de la figure"), a paragraph that explains the representation ("la figure") on the board. A map of Africa occupies the top right corner of the sheet next to the text, "The Order of Play" ("Ordre du jeu"), that sets out the initial steps of play. A map of Asia is placed in the lower right corner, and America, on the bottom left, is adjacent to the rules of the game, the "Rules of the Game" ("Loix du jeu").

Duval's invention both accomplished and undermined his goal: in his effort to teach world geography he also unmade the world. He sent his players through space in a topsy-turvy manner that flouted the geometrical organization of maps. Reading the texts, "Explication de la figure," "Ordre du jeu," and "Loix du jeu," from the top left of the game board in a clockwise direction, players would arrive at the lower left corner where they began the game. A putto points to the first space on the board to direct players to the world's poles, indicating visually the statement in the "Explication de la figure" that "the first circle marks the polar world" ("Le Monde Polaire est representé dans le premier Cercle"). But to begin, one immediately had to reverse direction to embark on a counter-clockwise loop. The game then obliged players to proceed in a zigzag fashion, with unavoidable movements back and forth. The classic game of the goose had a favourable space at number 6 – a bridge that propelled the player to space 12 – followed by hazards: at 19, an inn where one lost two turns; at 31, a well where one had to wait until another arrived to exchange places; and at 42, a maze that sent one back a few spaces. One might land in prison at 52, which had the same penalty as the well, or one could meet death at 58, which returned the hapless player to the beginning. Competitors traded places whenever two landed on the same spot, the incumbent moving to the later arrival's previous position. The first player to arrive at 63, the final space, won the game. Overthrows of the dice that exceeded 63 were counted backwards, and if that resulted in landing on 58, death, one had to start again. It was chance rather than skill or strategy that determined the outcome.

Duval employed the format of the goose game, but *Le Jeu du monde* differed from the classic distribution of favourable and unfavourable

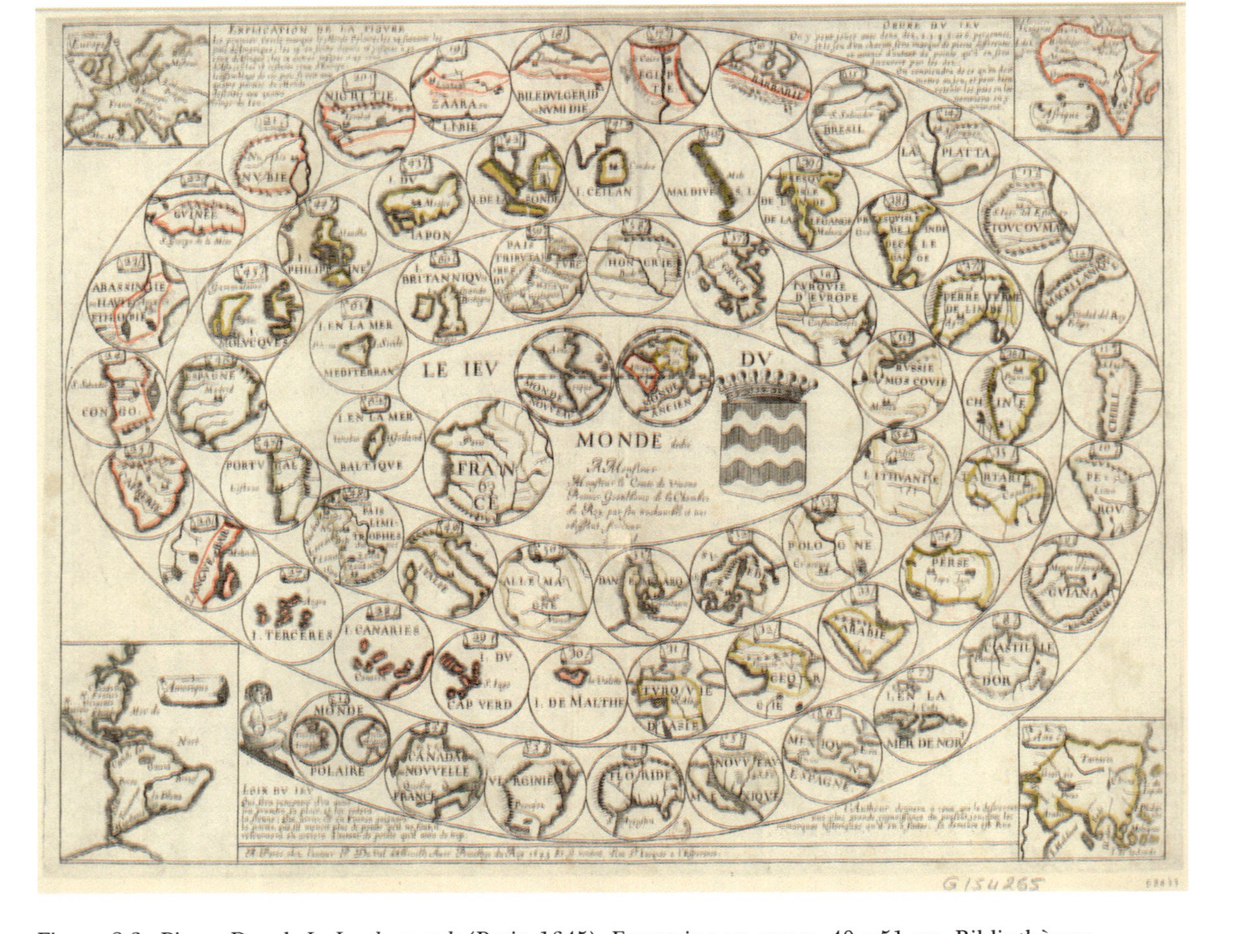

Figure 8.3. Pierre Duval, *Le Jeu du monde* (Paris, 1645). Engraving on paper, 40 x 51 cm. Bibliothèque nationale de France, Paris, https://gallica.bnf.fr/ark:/12148/btv1b8404114p

spaces. He wrote on the game board that "to remember the countries one should name them on arrival." The goose game's operational logic, the erratic movements imposed by the dice, afforded players many chances to pronounce and repeat such names. It is noted in the lower right corner of the board that "the author will supply to those who desire a greater knowledge of the present game with historical observations that he made."[15] These additional historical observations, in a separate text, were detailed rules of play that also conveyed dominant views of the world's nations.[16]

Duval wrote that landing on space 3, Virginia, where English settlers began the Jamestown colony in January 1607, instantly advanced the player to space 60, Great Britain, where "the ladies are held in high esteem" ("où les Dames sont beaucoup considerées"). In contrast, a player landing on 5, New Mexico, not only had to pay but also had to "stay among the savages until someone else charitably takes your place" ("y demeurera parmy les Sauuages, jusques a ce que quelqu'un le délire charitablement en prenant sa place"). Viewers today might infer from the relatively basic level of information and the pointing putto that the game was for children, but Duval's references to immorality, harems of women, and wife beating in the rules were far more likely addressing adults. A player landing in Asia could linger in Egypt, 17, to indulge freely in its pleasures, he wrote, or keep moving to avoid "leading a licentious life with the natives" (mener une vie si licentieuse que les habitans"). In Persia, 34, the player had no choice but to frequent the alluring ladies at court, take pleasant strolls in the city of Siras, and lose two turns as the others continued to roll the dice. In effect, Duval mapped Orientalist clichés of Eastern sensuality and immobility onto the rules of the game. Landing on China, 36, was most objectionable for one had to pay a penalty calculated at twice the throw of the dice because "the Chinese forbade entry to their kingdom" ("les Chinois ne luy permettant pas l'entrée de leur Royaume").

Europe, too, had unfavourable spaces, including the worst one, death (meaning, start again) at 52. However, the hazards indicated geo-political relations instead of stereotypes about nations and peoples. The threat for the French from their rivalry with Spain was a recurring theme: those who landed in Spain, 46, were obliged to go to the West Indies and regress by disembarking at Havana, 7, in addition to paying an exit fee to quit the Spanish empire. Arriving in Germany, 51, brought a halt to collect taxes from all those who passed through the Sound, the strait that marked the Swedish border. One met death in Sweden, 52 (rather than 58): the unlucky player was shipwrecked on the coast and was then blown by high winds to the polar world to begin anew. These hazards reflected territorial possessions and facts of physical geography rather than national depravity. However, moral character was also at play, weakening at the eastern limit of Europe. In Muscovy, 55, married men were said to show love for their wives by beating them. In Transylvania, 59, one had to pay to avoid captivity in the Turkish harem at Constantinople. The first to survive all the hazards of travel and land in France, 63, won "the game and all that is assembled in this little world" ("gagnera la partie, & tout ce qui se trouuera dans le Petit Monde").

Duval's rules evidently conveyed the beliefs of his culture and time. More importantly, to learn the names of foreign nations in this goose game, to know of their existence and their interrelationships in the world, was to take a first step in their potential, imaginable conquest. The game's very design conjured that possibility. After the polar worlds in the lower left corner, the first map on the spiral was, tellingly, "Canada Nouvelle France" (Canada New France), and the final, winning space was France. The player thus travelled through a world that began and ended in France while encountering regions of French interest along the way.

Off the game board, "La France Antarctique," in eastern Brazil, competed with Spanish, Portuguese, and Dutch claims on the South American continent in the seventeenth century. Pierre de Vaulx produced a map of the *La France Antarctique* in 1613; some decades later Duval, too, made a map titled *La France Antarctique autrement Le Rio Janeiro* based on the voyages of Villegagnon and Jean de Léry in 1557 and 1558. Duval also drew on the travelogues of Ribaut, Laudonier, and Gourgues in the 1560s to produce his map of *La Floride Françoise*.[17] These and other examples of his cartographic work showed Duval's alertness to French colonial and commercial interests.

One could play the map of *Le Jeu du monde*, moving one's marker on the track. Through the engagement of eyes, ears, minds, and fingers the players were physically situated in the world. Naomi Lebens has recently noted the language of travel in Duval's instructions.[18] The mapmaker used an embodied language to begin every rule in the same way: "Qui ira en Virginie, cotté 3, ... Qui ira en France cotté 63 gagnera la partie," or "One who goes to Virginia, space 3, ... One who goes to France, space 63, wins the game." *Le Jeu du monde* induced the sensations of speaking and hearing the words "qui ira" as players "went" to sixty-three different places on the globe. They waited if they lost one or two turns as others advanced according to the rules, or moved backward along the spiral for having landed on a penalty space. The game created in this way a multisensory experience of acting out a virtual journey. The motions of casting dice, sliding the marker with fingers forwards and backwards across the smooth surface of the paper game board, paying out and taking in money while reading the rules aloud, or pronouncing place names and/or listening to the words spoken by others engaged the participant's sight, touch, hearing, and speech. These small gestures were acts of in-corporation, of bringing Duval's rules and their ideological content into the body. The rivals cognitively and somatically experienced a delay, a leap forward, a move backward, a windfall in the game. By mobilizing their eyes, minds, and fingers, players were located in the world and moved virtually through nations.

One of the most significant ways in which Duval broke with European cartographic convention lies in the order of continents on his racetrack. Geography manuals and atlases regularly presented Europe before Asia, Africa, and America, as the mapmaker well knew. He reversed the sequence to begin with "Canada Nouvelle France" in the Americas before introducing Africa and Asia. He set Europe after the other continents on the spiral in order to put France in the space of victory on the board. He further scrambled the presentation of countries within each continent. The last country in the Americas on the spiral was Brazil (15). Duval then introduced Africa, beginning on the Barbary Coast (16). Next, he inexplicably moved east to Egypt (17), turned sharply west to the country in North Africa situated south of Mount Atlas, called "Biledulgerid ou Numidie" (ancient Numidia) (18), then southwest to "Zaara [Sahara Desert] ou Libie" (19), "Nigritie" (Nigritia or Negroland, south of the Sahara and north of the Gold Coast of West Africa) (20), moved east again to "Nubie" (Nubia, the desert in Egypt) (21), veered west to "Guinée" (Guinea) (22), eastward again to "Abassinie" (Abyssinia or the Ethiopian Empire) (23), and so on in this fashion. His itinerary through all four regions took similarly haphazard jumps. The arbitrary crisscrossing produced a reordering, and in a sense an un-ordering, of the world. *Le Jeu du monde* taught players to make the world through ludic learning, yet his design unmade it by freeing countries and continents from the European world order as given in geography manuals and atlases.

Duval dedicated his game to Gabriel de Rochechouart de Mortemart, comte de Vivonne (1600–1675), a member of one of the oldest noble families in France after the Bourbons. The Rochechouart coat of arms occupied the centre of the game board next to the map of the old world and above Duval's polite dedication as "his very humble and obedient servant." The comte de Vivonne, a childhood friend of Louis XIII, had accompanied the king on several military expeditions; in 1630 he was named *Premier Gentilhomme de la Chambre du Roi* (First Gentleman of the Royal Bedchamber). In 1669, the comte de Vivonne was appointed governor of Paris. His son, Louis-Victor (1636–1688), future duc de Vivonne, a mere child when Duval designed his game, would in turn secure key victories in Flanders and Italy for Louis XIV, the next monarch. Later, the duc de Vivonne was also named *Premier Gentilhomme de la Chambre du Roi* as a reward for his military feats. He became viceroy of Sicily and *Maréchal de France* (Marshal of France).

By dedicating his invention to the ruling elite, Duval sought patronage for his work as a young mapmaker.[19] Since his uncle Nicolas Sanson, from whom he learned his métier, was royal tutor in geography to Louis XIII and Louis XIV, it is likely that Duval's game found its way into the young Dauphin's lessons.[20] Evidence exists in text and image of generations of royalty, nobles, training cadets, officers, and soldiers playing goose games. Jean Héroard, physician to the young Louis XIII, meticulously noted instances of the latter enjoying goose games in 1612.[21] Chardin exhibited a painting at the Salon of 1743, subsequently engraved by Pierre-Louis Surugue in 1745, of aristocratic children throwing dice on a goose game. Bonaparte declared it his favourite pastime during the Italian campaign in 1797, as recorded in a detailed account.[22] A self-referential example from the First Empire represented soldiers and officers playing a goose game in the lower right corner of the game board of *Le Nouveau jeu militaire dédié aux Héros de l'Empire Français* (*The New Military Game Dedicated to the Heroes of the First Empire*) of 1808.[23]

The countries on Duval's goose game, spun loose from the established order, unrolled like a yo-yo, or like the globe held in the putto's right hand that could be thrown and returned, as if a ball. The map-based game reconfigured the map of the world. The inventor had already transformed the rectangle of sheet maps and the circle of terrestrial globes into an oval. That he went even further is all the more significant in an age when much effort was being made to explore and chart unfamiliar regions with increasing accuracy. In 1533, the Dutch mathematician Gemma Frisius developed a method of triangulation that enabled the positioning of distant places for mapmaking.[24] New techniques and expeditions in the following centuries by rival powers produced knowledge in world geography incrementally and continuously. Duval's game, too, was a redrawing of the map.

*Le Jeu du monde* is important for changing the spatial imaginary of the seventeenth century, turning the world into a terrain of learning and competition. Duval did so repeatedly, translating different maps into a total of eight goose games and sets of playing cards, in every instance rupturing the assumed link between spatial reality and cartographic representation. The spiral track of *Le Jeu du monde* doubled as a platform for social interaction and performance. Duval furnished a script rich in ideological content and mechanisms to engage the player's cognitive, physical, and imaginative skills, rendering the game an opportunity for vicarious travel and, by extension, potential conquest. His map-based goose game, mediated by engraving on paper and markers as avatars, enabled players to enact a mental journey with their touch, sight, speech, and hearing.

### *Le Jeu de la géographie*

In 1644, Jean Desmarets de Saint Sorlin (1595–1676), a member of the Académie française, prolific playwright, and holder of high offices such as *Contrôleur général de l'Extraordinaire des guerres* (*Comptroller General of the Extraordinary of Wars*) devised playing cards for young Louis XIV to learn history and geography. He produced four sets: *Le Jeu des rois de France* (*The Game of the Kings of France*), *Le Jeu des reynes renommées* (*The Game of Renowned Queens*), *Le Jeu des fables* (*The Game of Fables*), and finally *Le Jeu de la géographie* (*The Game of Geography*).[25] The last, a deck of fifty-two cards with short texts by Desmarets and illustrations by the Florentine engraver Stefano Della Bella (1610–1664), is central to our enquiry.[26] Like Duval and others at the time, Desmarets organized the world into four main parts – Europe, Asia, Africa, and America – each explained in thirteen cards. It was only after the death of both Desmarets and Della Bella that the artist's etched plates went to the publisher Florent Le Comte, who in 1698 added the letters R (*Roi*, King), D (*Dame*, Lady) and VA (*Valet*, Jack) to the face cards, and suit marks of hearts, spades, diamonds, and clubs to all the cards, in the third edition.[27] Manuals on card games such as *Le jeu du piquet* (*The Game of Piquet*), the first of its kind in France, brought out by the Parisian bookseller Charles Hulpeau in 1632, and the uninterrupted growth of the genre indicate the popularity of card-playing as a social activity.[28] It was likely, as Lebens has proposed, that the inclusion of suit marks made Le Comte's edition appealing to adults as well as children.[29]

Paris Amanda Spies-Gans remarks that no one has deduced how *Le Jeu de la géographie* might have been used for card games, hence it was more plausibly an educational tool "disguised, or mediated by the imitated form of a common early modern pastime."[30] However, a letterpress sheet accompanying the third state of *Le Jeu de la géographie*, in 1644, clearly indicates that the cards are to be used for card games, and it identifies particular ones.[31] The text lists colours that distinguish parts of the world: yellow or gold for Europe, *colombin* (red-purple) for Asia, green for America, and black to identify the skin of figures in Africa. Each region is represented by a female figure; they are the king cards. The document further explains that within every region a country personified by an attacking figure on horseback and a flying Glory is equivalent to a queen card. Four unaccompanied bellicose riders are jacks. All others are pip cards numbered one to ten.[32]

The text on *Le Jeu de la géographie* states that "when one plays Hoc, France and Spain are the Hoc, like the queen of spades and the jack of diamonds," and refers to *Le Jeu des reynes renommées* by Desmarets for detailed instructions.[33] The corresponding sheet in the game to teach Louis XIV history through the great queens explains the use of four colours "that relate to the four symbols, heart, diamond, spade, and club; and in each colour there are cards from an ace to the equivalent of a king." Arranging the cards by colour and number lets one play "all kinds of games" including Hoc, for which the rules are given.[34] By association, *Le Jeu de la géographie* has equal versatility for gameplay.

This text of 1644 not only clarifies how to use *Le Jeu de la géographie* as a deck of playing cards for games but, more importantly, shows official attitudes to ludic education. Valentin Conrart (1603–1676), royal secretary in charge of issuing royal privileges from the 1630s to 1650s, signed the document. Writing in the name of young Louis XIV, Conrart lauded Desmarets for the invention of "a pleasant and easy way for us to sample a king's most noble and compulsory learning without making us brave the difficulties experienced in the ordinary way of teaching it to other men."[35] Desmarets gained permission to engrave his work in wood or copper, burin or etching, with or without colour, and in any size and format, and to print, sell, and distribute his cards, exempt from the ordinary taxes on cards and dice and any taxes in the future.[36]

Conrart's text is most significant for revealing an official embrace of education through play. On the death of Louis XIII, in 1643, the *roi-enfant* (child king) "inherited a realm awash in political and geographic flux," as Spies-Gans notes.[37] The child's education was all the more urgent.[38] Conrart's language indexed his awareness of the performativity of learning: he praised Desmarets on the king's behalf "de nous faire agreablement exercer en la connoissance de l'Histoire, & des Sciences conuenables aux personnes de notre naissance & de nostre rang."[39] His choice of the verb *exercer* is crucial. Variously translatable as to practise, to apply, or to work with, in "to *practise* enjoyably knowledge in history and those subjects appropriate to persons of our birth and rank," Conrart showed that royal advisors valued learning through an agreeable, embodied engagement at this historical juncture.

Each card in *Le Jeu de la géographie* measures 8.7 by 5.3 centimetres, containing a short text by Desmarets and an illustration. It is not possible in this essay to discuss Della Bella's imagery at length except to note his use of enthroned, seated, standing, and galloping female figures to represent countries and parts of the world. Europe, according to Desmarets, was "the smallest [continent] but ranks first in the world for its fertility, and for its valour, civility, science, renown and the multitude of its peoples, and as the seat of Christendom. She is situated towards the north, in the cold and temperate zones."[40] Africa was the second part of the world, "situated in the south, in the burnt zone. The regions are sterile and sparsely populated, except near the coasts and in a few other places. The people are black or brown."[41] In this manner *Le Jeu de la géographie* conveyed information on geography like Duval's *Le Jeu du monde* goose game, but without maps. As Spies-Gans has argued, the aim was to teach young Louis XIV about the diversity of nations and the place of France among them.[42] Desmarets promoted a Eurocentric and Francocentric world order, one that encouraged exploration and conquest. America, "the fourth part of the world, discovered 150 years ago, was otherwise called the West Indies or the new world."[43] Peru was the queen card, "the richest province of the world for her stores of gold and silver," followed as jack by Mexico "or New Spain, the most beautiful province of America."[44] The author implicitly compared Spain's gains from conquering Peru and Mexico in the early sixteenth century to Nouvelle France, a vast territory in Canada "covered in trees and poorly cultivated."[45] In an understated way, Desmarets encouraged Louis XIV and all potential players to develop New France more profitably.

Although the gestures involved in playing cards were different from those required for Duval's board game, the sensations of reading aloud and hearing the lessons embedded as play were common to both games. *Le Jeu de la géographie* condensed world geography into a deck of cards, thereby allowing players to pick up and put down countries, mix and cut regions of the world, win or lose territories and even entire continents in a single hand, and then repeat and vary the process. Playing card games was indeed an exercise of knowledge and power – in Conrart's words, "a pleasant and easy way for us to sample a king's most noble and compulsory learning."[46] Thus, whether employing *Le Jeu de la géographie* as individual cards containing short, beautifully illustrated passages to be learned, or using it in a more complex way for card games, the player assimilated with eyes and fingers, through repeated gestures, a system of values and the French hierarchy of nations. Through play one inhabited and incorporated the ideological content of games. Both games intensified the imperial gaze with touch.

## Games, Maps, Globes

In the 1660s Jean-Baptiste Colbert aligned cartography and national administration in an effort to modernize the French state. He invited the leading cartographer and astronomer of Europe, Giovanni Dominico Cassini, to direct the Paris Observatory and lead the project to produce an accurate map of France. In 1682, after years of surveying, measuring, and calculating with new techniques, the members of the Académie Royale des Sciences delivered their historic manuscript map.[47] Louis XIV was shocked to learn that the great scientific project divested him of more land than any war had gained: France now occupied only 25,386 instead of the 31,659 square leagues on older maps.[48] The discrepancy of some 6,000 square leagues (approximately 54,000 square miles) was roughly equal in size to Florida.[49]

A few years later, in 1688, the renowned globe maker and cartographer Vincenzo Coronelli (1650–1718) produced his map, *Le Royaume de France Avec Ses Acquisitions Divisé en Gouvernemens de Provinces*, which also listed the king's territorial conquests (fig. 8.4). Louis XIV reportedly gained 2,447 square leagues, thereby enlarging his domain by one-tenth. However, France measured 22,859 square leagues according to Coronelli, even less than the landmark map of 1682. Improved cartographic technologies unmade the world as it had been known. Notwithstanding their methodological rigour, the changes in borders and the expansion and reduction of surface areas seem arbitrary at times, as if in a game.

The two realms of cartography and play merged in the cartouche above the table of annexed lands on Coronelli's map. Designed by Nicolas Guérard (c.1648–1719), the engraver, publisher and merchant of prints and maps whose name appears just below the date, the cartouche presents the title in an egg-shaped oval.[50] The fortified cities then under French control are positioned without apparent geographical or

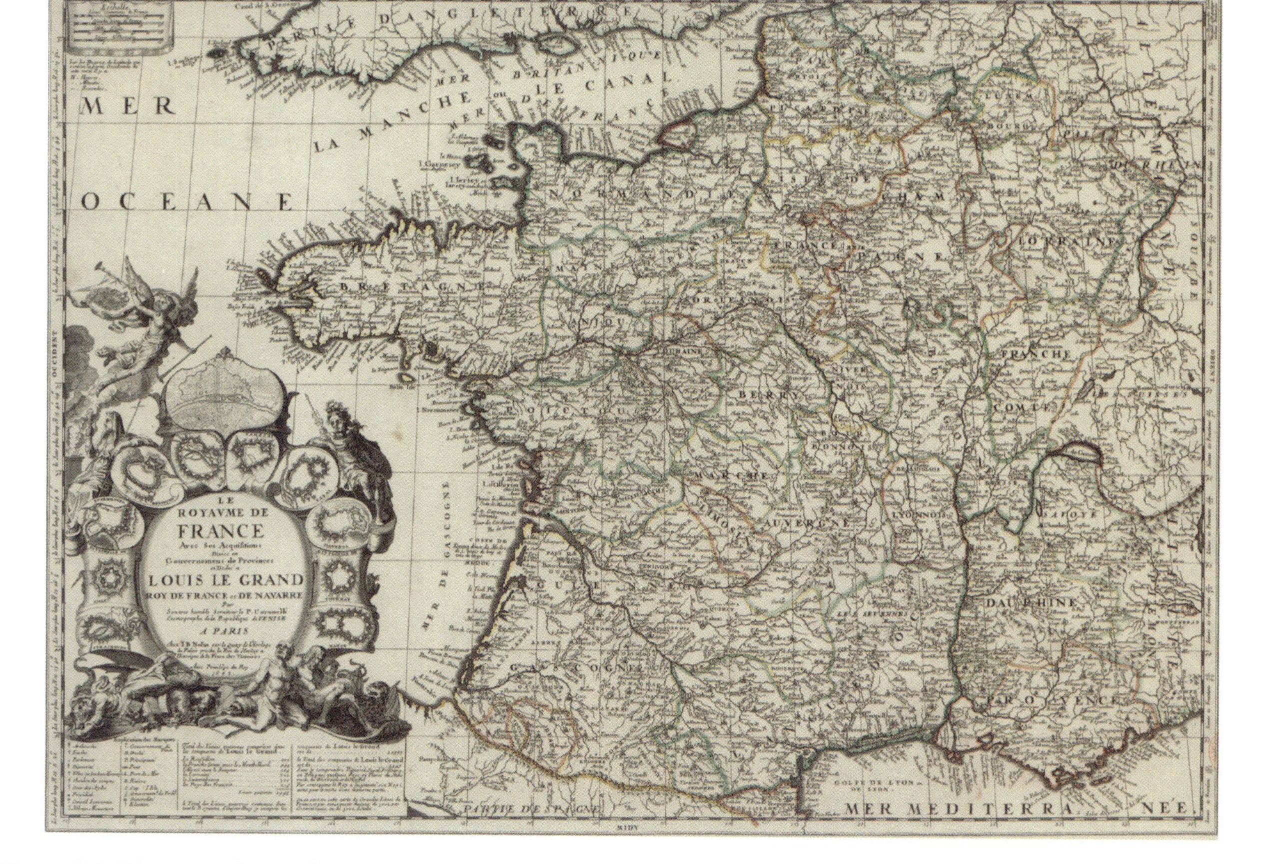

Figure 8.4. Vincenzo Coronelli, *Le Royaume de France Avec Ses Acquisitions Divisé en Gouvernemens de Provinces* (Paris: J-B Nolin, 1688). Engraving by Guerard. Engraving on Paper, 60.7 x 45 cm. Bibliothèque nationale de France, Paris, https://gallica.bnf.fr/ark:/12148/btv1b8492908k

directional logic. A map of Paris sits above Donquerque (Dunkirk) and Cambray, given a higher position and a larger form than all the others. Putting fortifications around the oval recalls the spaces on the track of a goose game, many of which, like the Italian game printed by Lucchino Gargano (fig. 8.2), were set on the vertical axis. The winning spot by analogy is the largest area in the middle, identified by title as *The Kingdom of France with its Acquisitions Divided into Government by Province and Dedicated to Louis the Great, King of France and of Navarre.*[51]

Guérard made winged Glory the highest figure on the top half of the cartouche. Below her are the allegorical figures of Religion and War leaning respectively against Besançon on the left, and Casal (Cassel in Flanders), recently taken by France, on the right. Floating alone in the air, Glory sounds her trumpet, from which the Bourbon standard hangs. France triumphs over the traditional symbolic enemies, crushed at the lower edge of the cartouche. Still further below, in the bottom left corner of the map, are the conquered territories. The inventory of annexed lands, when viewed together with the cartouche-cum-goose game, now reads like a list of the king's winnings: "Total of square leagues included in the conquests of Louis the Great: Roussillon, 200; the France Comté with Montbelliard, 448," and on it goes like a game of *Monopoly* until the total of 2,447 square leagues is reached.[52]

Forty-three years (or roughly two generations) had elapsed between the first map-based goose game, Duval's *Le Jeu du monde*, and Coronelli's map of 1688. The different modes of representation now intermingled in Coronelli's cartouche; the border between games and maps has become permeable. Fingers that moved markers from one spot to another on the oval track could slide across a map's surface to find particular locations, tracing the lines of routes and rivers and, on occasion, following the movement of armies as they changed the borders of France through war.

In 1650, Duval gained the title of *géographe du roi* (royal geographer). The fact that the rules of *Le Jeu du monde* were reprinted in a compilation of game rules, *La Maison des jeux académiques*, first published in 1654, and then repeatedly in the second half of the seventeenth century, points to the durability of the first map-based goose game.[53] Among the eight more games designed by Duval was a set of playing cards, *Les Tables de Géographie réduites en un Jeu de Cartes*, in 1669, later dedicated to "Monseigneur le Dauphin" (1661–1711), eldest son of Louis XIV.[54] Like Desmaret's inaugural pack, Duval's version contained key facts about countries, such as the names of their sovereigns and their major cities, but also included the locations of various regions in the world. The mapmaker provided more information for the heir to the throne to learn in *Les Tables de Géographie réduites en un Jeu de Cartes*. Duval's cards most likely inspired an English version, *Geographical Cards*, made and sold for Henry Brome in London in 1675.[55] Theory followed practice in 1671 when the Jansenist theologian and moralist Pierre Nicole (1625–1695) wrote in the *Traitté de l'éducation d'un prince* (*Treatise on the Education of a Prince*) that children should be taught geography "not strictly with maps but also through entertaining exercises."[56] In 1725, the publisher Vouillemont reprinted another of Duval's goose games, *Le Jeu de France* of 1659, for more sales among the dominant class.

## Ludic Princely Education

Games and toys featured in the education of future monarchs. Like Louis XIV, who began his military training early in life, his son, Monseigneur le Dauphin, played with toy swords, pistols, a toy army in silver and lead, and even a little drum garnished with diamonds that cost its donor 100,000 *livres*.[57] The Dauphin was taken in childhood on his father's campaigns and on a tour of fortifications in the north of France before the age of ten.[58] So vital was his military education that Louis XIV reserved the task for himself; in 1678, the king added a section titled *Mémoires militaires pour l'instruction du Dauphin* (*Military Memoirs for the Education of the Dauphin*) to his official memoirs in progress.[59] He also appointed experts in mathematics, ballistics, and fortification, namely, Sauveur, Blondel, Puységur, and Vauban, to teach the royal princes. To that end each produced technical treatises between 1680 and 1700.[60]

Blondel wrote *L'Art de jeter des bombes* (*The Art of Throwing Bombs*) and *Nouvelle manière de fortifier les places* (*New Fortification Methods*) in 1673 to educate Monseigneur le Dauphin, then about twelve.[61] During this surge of technical writing, Gilles Jodelet de La Boissière, the Engineer in Ordinary to the King (*ingénieur ordinaire du roi*) designed a board game for the Dauphin's younger brother, the duc de Berry. The game's long title described the content: *Le Jeu de la guerre ou tout ce qui s'observe dans les Marches et campements des armées dans les batailles, combats, sièges et autres actions militaires, et exactement représenté avec les définitions et les explications de chaque chose en particulier* (*The Game of War, or all that occurs in the marches and encampments of armies in battle, combat, siege and other military operations, and accurately depicted with definitions and explanations of every specific manoeuvre*).[62] In 1698, La Boissière made a second version for the duc de

Bourgogne (1682–1712), son of Monseigneur le Dauphin, and grandson of Louis XIV (fig. 8.5).[63] This time it was the game's vendor, Jean Mariette (1660–1742), engraver and publisher, who showed his understanding of the seriousness of play as a form of pedagogy for royals. He wrote in his dedication to the adolescent prince:

> All of France is aware that you have little taste for games, and that you have no time to spend on even the most amusing recreations for a prince of your age except when required by duty or decorum. I have been careful to submit none other than a game of war, which assembles in images what is already the subject of your most serious contemplation. Through this study you advance daily in the aptitude of heroes; and at the first chance to exploit your vast knowledge you will turn the most difficult undertaking into mere play.[64]

The protocol of sycophancy aside, Mariette noted the unrelenting education of a future monarch.[65] To play a board game was also to train for war. Mariette made this practice unequivocal in his dedication on another game by La Boissière, *Le Jeu des fortifications* (*The Game of Fortifications*). Like *Le Jeu de la guerre* it was equally a combination spiral race game and card game. Addressing "the illustrious youth" studying at the Military College of Louis le Grand, Mariette wrote: "if the study of the sciences are the object of your attention today, the art of war will shortly follow; and whatever affection you now have for the Muses, you will soon be obliged by your noble blood and your great courage to join the side the Mars. I do not fear disturbing any of your ordinary exercises by offering you a game that contains the first elements of military science for your amusement. I merely follow the light of those who raise and guide you with such wisdom and success."[66]

La Boissière offered two forms of engagement with *Le Jeu de la guerre*. One could use it as a board game with dice and markers. It is a goose game like Duval's *Jeu du monde*, but the layout of rectangles here countermanded the swirling movement, and the frontal presentation allowed only one position from which to read the board. The engineer did not fully reconcile the different design requirements of education and play. The second option was to have the plate glued on pasteboard and cut into fifty-two cards.[67] Each showed a definition of a precise military term, explained the action in plain language, and gave an illustration. The card on "Escalade" noted that it "is a sudden attack effected with ladders to gain control of a wall, a rampart or another form of fortification."[68]

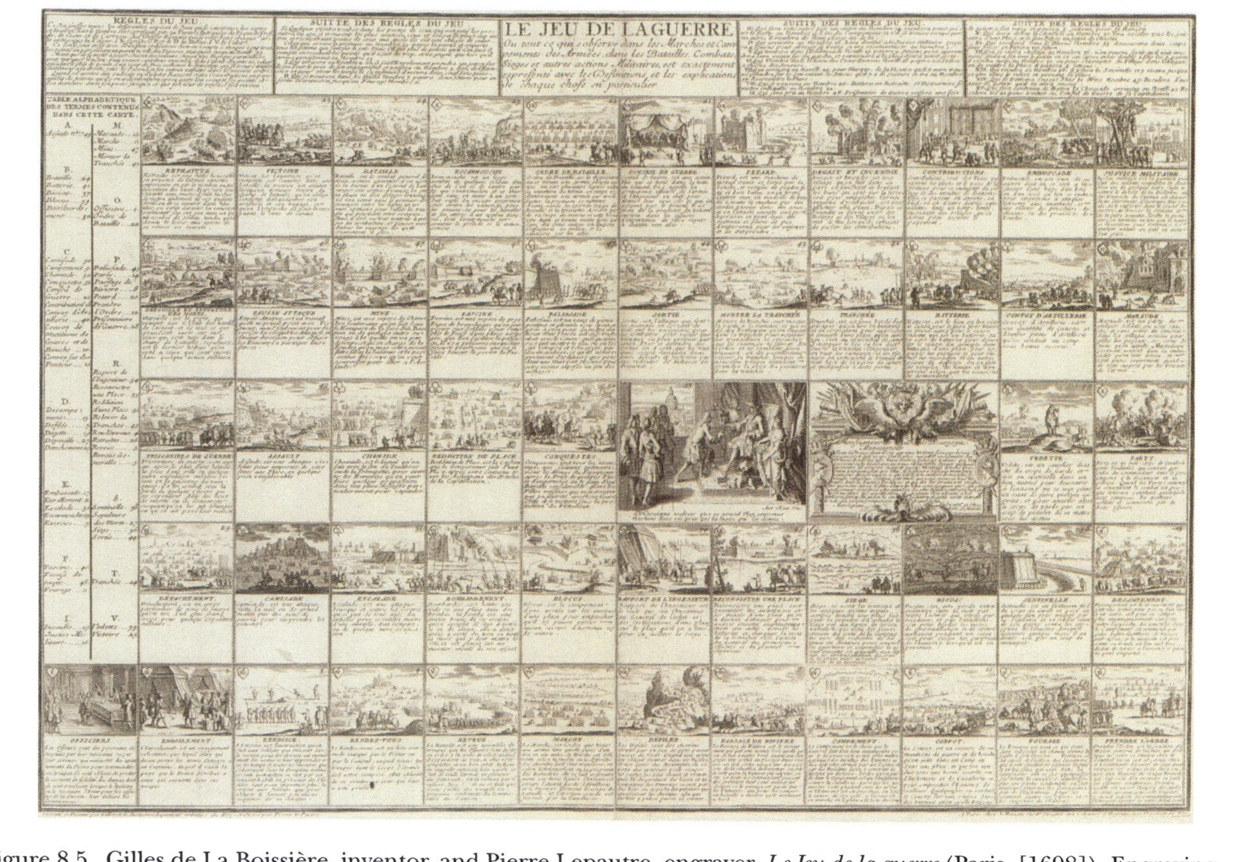

Figure 8.5. Gilles de La Boissière, inventor, and Pierre Lepautre, engraver, *Le Jeu de la guerre* (Paris, [1698]). Engraving on paper, 51.5 x 72.5 cm. Bibliothèque nationale de France, Paris, https://gallica.bnf.fr/ark:/12148/btv1b105285617

"To bombard is to strike a city or a site with bombs; the bomb is a large hollow ball of iron filled with gunpowder and nails. It has two handles beside a hole containing the fuse that must be lit by fire and is placed on a mortar mounted on a gun-carriage."[69] These much-simplified lessons drew on contemporary texts such as *Les Travaux de Mars ou 'L'art de la guerre* of 1671, among others.[70] The game also inculcated a moral code of combat in the most violent scenes on the board: marauding soldiers who looted neighbouring villages often died in an ambush, or met severe punishments when caught by their superiors, according to the text, whereas despoiling the dead in battle was only to take "the profit that was their due."[71] Burial was the last honour owed to those who died in action.

In contrast to *Le Jeu du monde*, which offered vignette maps and a single, gesticulating putto but no figure with whom a player could identity on the board, *Le Jeu de la guerre* prominently displayed the scene of victory and honour to which all competitors aspired. The winning space, 53, stood near the centre of the board, next to Mariette's dedication. The climactic scene of Louis XIV rewarding the winner was based on a painting by Antoine Dieu, indicated by "Ant. Dieu Inv." in the lower right corner.[72] Five elegantly dressed men on the left observe as the winner steps forward to receive a baton from the king, flanked by Justice and Fortune. As the culmination of the game, the image offers a self-reflexive summary: the men in shadow on the left are those who lost the competition, while the victor alone advances into the light. The true goal of all players in *Le Jeu de la guerre* is affirmed by the inscription below: "the heroic character crowned by the king cherishes in these rewards only the hand that bestows them."[73] Words and image work in harmony in this, the largest and most important of scenes, which is conspicuously filled with hands. This aspect is visible on the left, where the observer points with his index finger to the award ceremony, and continues with the victor extending his right hand to accept the baton offered by the king, below the hand of Justice holding her scales. Both the picture and the inscription thus highlight the part of the body that is vital in playing the board game, and eventually in battle.

The message was unambiguous: one trained to fight for territory and wealth in the service of the absolute monarch. In keeping with this idea, a large window shown behind the men on the left opened on to the Église Saint-Louis des Invalides in Paris, the church for war veterans completed by the architect Jules Hardouin Mansart in 1679. It is of further significance that the scene of triumph linked together games, wars, and lives as experienced by men such as the comte and the duc de Vivonne, a father and son rewarded for their victories by another dynastic pair, Louis XIII and Louis XIV respectively.

Bourbon succession was of utmost importance. Louis, duc de Bourgogne (1682–1712) to whom the game was dedicated in 1698, was the eldest son of Monseigneur le Dauphin, eldest son of Louis XIV. The young prince could identify with the victor in the depicted ceremony, and also, by succession, with the king, who is depicted as a youthful monarch to facilitate the prince's identification with him.

On the death of Monseigneur, in 1711, the duc de Bourgogne became dauphin until his own death a year later, in 1712. A pair of engravings by Nicolas Bonnart, first published in the final years of the seventeenth century, depicts Louis XIV looking on with approval at the image on the other side of the album, *Le Royal Jeu des fortifications* (*The Royal Game of Fortifications*, fig. 8.6).[74] The latter depicts the duc de Bourgogne at play with his brothers Philippe, duc d'Anjou (1683–1746) and future King Philip V of Spain, and Charles, duc de Berry (1686–1714). The "royal jeu des fortifications," comparable to obstacle billiards, required players to send balls through the gate of a miniature fortress placed on the billiard table. The balls re-emerged or rebounded, eventually stopping against the wall of a fortification.[75] The link between the two engravings is made clear by the final sentence below the monarch: "He governs his States with great tranquillity having married his only son Monseigneur le Dauphin with the Princess of Bavaria, who rendered him grandfather of the duc de Bourgogne, the duc d'Anjou and the duc de Berry."[76] The king's concern for the military education of his heirs makes the pairing entirely sound. More germane to our study is the resonance between the inscription below the young royals and Mariette's dedication in *Le Jeu de la guerre*: "these three princes playing this game of war / presage for us that one day by their extraordinary deeds / they will show all the lands on Earth / that they are the worthy sons of king Louis."[77] In other words, war games would coach the princes to victory on real battlefields. Artefacts, texts, and images reinforce each other in this symbolic economy to promote ludic pedagogy at the highest level in France.

All the engraved board games above were disseminated through sale to the upper echelons of French society in the seventeenth and eighteenth centuries.[78] The invention of puzzles made of sheet maps mounted on wood board and cut into pieces offered another learning aid to privileged pupils. Also called "dissected maps," they were most likely first made at home by parents, tutors, and governesses long before their commercial debut.[79] Jeanne-Marie Le Prince de Beaumont, a Frenchwoman living

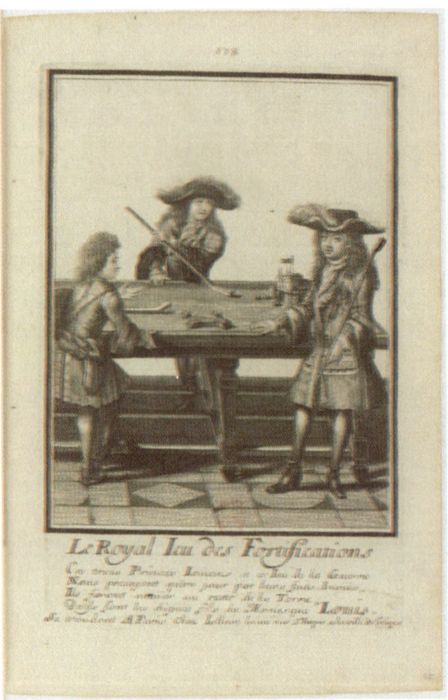


Figure 8.6. *Recueil de modes*, vol. 7, 1750, plates 64, 65 ([Paris], 1750). Engraving on paper, 36.5 x 25 cm. Bibliothèque nationale de France, Paris, https://gallica.bnf.fr/ark:/12148/btv1b105296308, views 70, 71

in London between 1748 and 1762, advertised her use of "les cartes de géographe en bois" to teach aristocratic girls at her school on Henrietta Street, Cavendish Square.[80] Through Madame de Beaumont, the Royal Governess to the heirs of George III, Lady Charlotte Finch (1725–1813), commissioned sixteen dissected maps for her young charges in 1764 or 1765.[81] A decade later map puzzles were available for sale beyond the royal family in England.[82]

The first French map puzzles appeared within twenty years of Madame de Beaumont's advertisement.[83] Guillaume Delisle, *Premier géographe du Roi* and member of the Académie Royale des Sciences, published the *Carte d'Europe dressée pour l'Usage du Roy sur les Itinéraires anciens et modernes et sur les Routiers de mer assujetis aux observations astronomiques* in 1724.[84] His son-in-law, Philippe Buache, republished the map "augmented with new knowledge in geography ... in 1760 and 1769." Delisle's associates and descendants sold maps alongside globes, spheres, and a variety of teaching aids such as puzzle-maps ("cartes découpées & collées sur bois pour faciliter aux enfans l'étude de la Géographie,") blank maps ("cartes muettes"), and unmarked globes useful in testing or challenging pupils.[85]

Delisle's *Carte d'Europe*, engraved on paper then mounted on wood and cut into forty-six pieces, formed puzzles that measure approximately 63 by 50 centimetres when assembled. The puzzle is now inoperable because the pieces are kept in individual plastic sleeves.[86] However, Delisle's *Carte de France* "dissected map" offers a rare opportunity to incorporate handling, learning and play to my historical enquiry (fig. 8.7).[87] As with most puzzles, the fifty-four surviving pieces vary in shape, size, and weight. The borders containing straight edges are the easiest to assemble. Completing the rest requires a combination of knowledge in geography, the visual recognition of contours, and a basic dexterity to fit the pieces together. In brief, the puzzle obliges the user to activate a particular knowledge and a visual tactility. Each of my successive attempts to complete the puzzle took less time, indicating its efficacy as a teaching aide: the "dissected map" engaged my cognitive and sensory skills and indeed facilitated my study of geography.

The puzzle-map of France of 1776 returns us to Monsaldy's *Le Triomphe des armées françaises* with which we began (fig. 8.1). Katie Hornstein considers Monsaldy's print a form of visual participation by proxy for civilians during the Revolutionary and Napoleonic Wars in her recent monograph, *Picturing War in France, 1792–1856*.[88] On the engraving's far left is General Lazare Hoche, who routed an attack by émigré Royalists and their British allies on the Quiberon peninsula in Brittany in 1795. Next to Hoche stands Jean-Charles Pichegru, general-in-chief of the Army of the Sambre and Meuse, the only figure without a cartographic accessory. Pichegru is partly obscured by Jean-Victor Moreau, commander of the Army of the Rhine and Moselle, who lifts a portion of a giant map of France and the newly conquered areas of Flanders, the Netherlands, and the Rhine. Northeast of the Rhine the map is blank except for grid lines.

Napoleon Bonaparte stands alone in contrapposto on the right half of the engraving, physically separated from his colleagues but connected through his powerful gaze across the section of map raised by Moreau. Bonaparte and an eagle on the far right display the rest of the oversize map of Europe; he looks leftward in the image as he reaches across his body to grip in his right hand a map of the French Alps and the neighbouring lands to the east. Hornstein observes that "The European continent has been literally taken apart; the process of military conquest

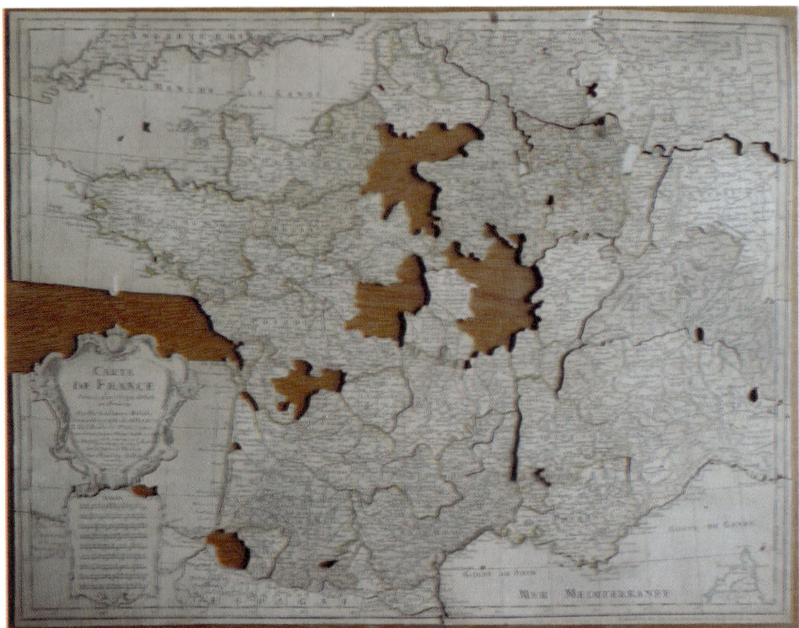

Figure 8.7.  Guillaume Delisle, *Carte de France dressée pour l'Usage du Roy, en Avril 1721. Par Feu Guillaume Delisle, Premier Géographe de Sa Majesté. De l'Académie R[ ]le des Sciences. Et augmentée en 1764 par Philippe Buache, son Gendre [...], Revue en 1775.* Engraving on paper on wood, 64 x 50 cm. Bibliothèque nationale de France. Photograph by Frédérique Desbuissons

is reduced to a nearly effortless tearing of paper, obscuring the violent struggle required to wage war."[89] In her interpretation, the print articulates not only French ambition but also anxiety about the borders constantly redrawn in these turbulent years of war.[90]

For my enquiry, Monsaldy encapsulates what educational games and toys aimed to achieve. Like a number of the objects above, it is a hybrid form that contains a map, with all its military values, and a celebration of war. The obelisk on the extreme left of the print bears the inscription "A la Gloire des Armées d'Italie et des généraux" ("To the glory of the Armies of Italy and the generals"), immediately followed by the names of "Buonaparte" and Kellermann at the top of the list. The rolled edge of the map in Bonaparte's hand somewhat obscures the title "L'Etat Politique de l'Empire d'Allemagne, 29 Germinal An 5e" ("The Political

State of the German Empire, 29 Germinal Year 5"), as the general breaks through the cartographic space. Indeed, his uniformed torso occupies the area where the contiguous land mass of France and Germany should be. The engraving functions as a theatre of war in a double sense. The four generals show, through their maps, the sites of their various victories. The writing within and below the image further identifies locations and personnel. Monsaldy's composition also presents the generals as actors on a shallow stage with a *repoussoir* obelisk anchoring the left side. They manoeuvre their maps like stage sets. Their roughly equal height with the map emphasizes the ease with which they can intervene in a controllable, compact landscape. The generals are shown to act in a theatre of war while the miniaturized maps introduce a dimension of play. As the publisher Jean Mariette had written fawningly a century before to the duc de Bourgogne, future Dauphin, in dedicating *Le Jeu de la guerre* of 1698, "through this study you advance daily in the aptitude of heroes; and at the first chance to exploit your vast knowledge you will turn the most difficult undertaking into mere play."

In a second proof prior to the inclusion of "Monsaldy sculp." Bonaparte's body, having intervened in space, is connected to the map to his left by three horizontal lines of latitude that cut into the contour of his chin, upper arm, and hip.[91] Thus, while taking apart the map of Europe he is also the central figure who puts it back together with his very body, linking western France with Europe to the east. Those who learned geography with "dissected maps" or puzzles rehearsed making and unmaking terrains.

Considering the above objects together, it is as if the players of the cartouche goose game on Coronelli's map of 1688, having been released from the rigidity of normative cartography by Duval's *Le Jeu du monde* and Desmarets's *Le Jeu de la géographie*, and learned to build and also besiege fortifications, among other military manoeuvres, through La Boissière's *Le Jeu de la guerre*, leapt across the symbolic chasm with their minds and fingers to land on Coronelli's map of France. They trained to use their bodies to interfere physically with space, whether playing with cards and board games or assembling a map puzzle. Through play they intruded corporeally and imaginatively in space. Like Bonaparte, players stood in the place of maps; they stood in the spaces between maps. They emulated Monsaldy's generals to disorder and unmake boundaries by shuffling cards and moving markers on a spiral. Players created worlds.

The mobilization of the body built into toys and games, whether at the minute scale of hands and fingers or more dynamically running to capture a flag or a fort, is a new area of enquiry in French studies. In British historiography, James A. Mangan was among the first to examine the role of sports and games in forming an imperial subjectivity among the educated elite.[92] The remark attributed to the Duke of Wellington, commander-in-chief of the British and allied armies, that the battle of Waterloo was won on the playing fields of Eton has been rejected as apocryphal. However, "the games played on the fields of Eton (and elsewhere) may not have determined the outcomes of particular battles or wars but the ethos behind them was enormously significant in shaping the moral economy of the Victorian Age."[93] After Mangan a new generation of scholars have analysed the ideological and functional aspects of play. Most recently Megan A. Norcia examines the formative role of parlour games, home theatricals, and map puzzles in shaping the imperial consciousness of young children in nineteenth-century Britain.[94]

French historians now explore similar terrain in the footsteps of British colleagues who investigated "the links connecting bodily discipline and human value systems."[95] As Nicolas Bancel and Daniel Denis write in a recent article, the Scout movement taught French boys to build camps outdoors and play games such as "Capture the Fort" that proved to be forms of physical conditioning and latent preparation for colonial administration. They assert that of all French colonial administrators active after 1945, 63 per cent had participated in a Scout movement in their youth in the 1930s.[96] More details are necessary, and the causal relationships will need to be handled with nuance, but the material culture of ludic pedagogy is demonstrably rich and compelling.

The objects I examined in this essay were precursors to modern war games in the multiple ways in which they interpellated and trained imperial subjects. Even the simplest examples were designed with the view that their players would move from winning at cards and board games to conquests on a much bigger scale. Playing games created the world.

## ACKNOWLEDGMENTS

My deepest thanks go to the Leverhulme Trust for a Leverhulme Research Fellowship in 2018–19 that made possible the travel and research behind this essay. I also thank Bronwen Wilson and Angela Vanhaelen, first for inviting me to the "Making Worlds" conference at the Clark Library in Los Angeles, and then for their astute comments on my essay. My gratitude further goes to David Bindman, Lucy Bradnock, Venanzio Capretta,

Frédérique Desbuissons, Ulysse Desbuissons, Marc Gotlieb, Catherine Hofman, Cristina Ion, Katharina Lorenz, Geoffroy Phelippot, Lara Pucci, Roger Rouse, Adrian Seville, Abigail Solomon-Godeau, Richard Taws, Greg Thomas, Richard Wrigley, colleagues in the women and non-binary writing group in the School of Cultures, Languages and Area Studies, and the Centre for Advanced Studies at the University of Nottingham for the different ways in which they contributed to my completion of this essay.

**NOTES**

1 Jill Shefrin, *Such Constant Affectionate Care: Lady Charlotte Finch, Royal Governess and the Children of George III* (Los Angeles: The Cotsen Occasional Papers, 2003), 79, remarks that Louis XIV spurred an industry of educational games in France when he inherited the throne at the age of four.

2 My focus and argument are different from recent media studies such as Mark J.P. Wolf, *Building Imaginary Worlds: The Theory and History of Subcreation* (New York: Routledge, 2012).

3 Antoine-Maxime Monsaldy, *Le Triomphe des armées françaises* (Paris, 1797). The Getty Research Institute, Los Angeles (P980009).

4 On Pierre Duval, see Mireille Pastoureau, *Les Atlas français, XVIe-XVIIe siècles: Répertoire bibliographique et étude* (Paris: Bibliothèque nationale de France, Département des cartes et plans, 1984), 135–7. Also Adrian Seville, "The Geographical Jeux de l'Oie of Europe," *Belgeo. Revue belge de géographie* 3–4 (2008), http://doi.org/10.4000/belgeo.11907.

5 Christine Marie Petto, *When France was King of Cartography: The Patronage and Production of Maps in Early Modern France* (Lanham, MD: Lexington Books, 2007), 148.

6 For the most recent and comprehensive study see Adrian Seville, *The Cultural Legacy of the Royal Game of the Goose* (Amsterdam: Amsterdam University Press, 2019). See 23 for the earliest printed reference to the goose game, in Italy in 1463. Jill Shefrin, *The Dartons: Publishers of Educational Aides, Pastimes & Juvenile Ephemera 1787–1876, A Bibliographic Checklist* (Los Angeles: Cotsen Occasional Press, 2009), 52, notes the earliest English edition recorded in the Stationers' Register dates to 16 June 1597, by the printer John Wolfe, but asserts that the goose game must have arrived in England earlier because of the marriage between Philip II of Spain and Queen Mary I in 1554.

7 Seville, "The Geographical Jeux de l'Oie of Europe."

8 On the numerological significance of 63, see Seville, *The Cultural Legacy of the Royal Game of the Goose*, 28–9.

 9  See Duval, "Nouvelle Explication de ieu du monde," plate 13 in the atlas
    of maps titled *Cartes de géographie les plus nouvelles et les plus fidèles, avecque
    leurs divisions régulières, qui marquent les bornes des États, selon les derniers traités
    de paix* (Paris, 1688), in which he wrote: "On conuiendra de ce qu'on doit
    mettre au Jeu, d'un denier, d'un sol, d'un teston ou d'une pistole, si on
    veut, que chacun mettra dedans le petit Monde au milieu du Jeu." Duval
    repeated the instruction in *Le Jeu des princes souverains de l'Europe* [*The Game
    of the Sovereign Princes of Europe*] (Paris, 1662).
10  Seville, *The Cultural Legacy of the Royal Game of the Goose*, 13.
11  Seville, "The Shows and Sights of Georgian London: A Board Game Tour
    of the Metropolis," lecture at the Society of Antiquaries of London, Burl-
    ington House, London, 7 May 2019, and Seville, private communication to
    author, 5 February 2020.
12  *Jeu de l'État-major français* published by Pellerin & Cie, undated. See https://
    gallica.bnf.fr/ark:/12148/btv1b53027219f for a digitized image.
13  Henri-René d'Allemagne, *Le Noble jeu de l'oie en France de 1640 à 1850*, iden-
    tified the first educational goose game as *Jeu chronologique utile pour apprendre
    la suites des siècles et ce qui est arrivé de plus remarquable et chascun*, published by
    Pierre Mariette and G. Le Juge, and dated it to 1638. Seville, *The Cultural
    Legacy of the Royal Game of the Goose*, 49–50, has questioned that date.
14  Pierre Duval, *Le Jeu du Monde dédié à Monsieur, Monsieur le Comte de Vivone,
    premier gentilhome de chambre du Roy par son très humble et très obéissant serviteur
    Duval.* (Paris, 1645). See also the digitized version, https://gallica.bnf.fr
    /ark:/12148/btv1b8404114p.
15  Duval, *Le Jeu du monde*: "L'Autheur donnera a ceux qui le desireront une
    plus grande connoissance du present jeu, avec les remarques historiques
    qu'il en a faites." See also Seville, *The Cultural Legacy of the Royal Game of the
    Goose*, 46–8, 81–2 on Duval's game.
16  Duval, "Nouvelle Explication de ieu du monde."
17  See Pierre Duval, *Diverses cartes et tables pour la geographie ancienne pour la chro-
    nologie et les itineraires et voyages modernes* (Paris, 1665), plates 63 and 64.
18  Naomi Lebens, "Prints in Play: Printed Games and the Fashioning of Social
    Roles in Early Modern Europe" (PhD diss., Courtauld Institute, 2016), 123.
19  Geoffroy Phelippot, "Naissance de la géographie ludique au XVIIe
    siècle. Les jeux pédagogiques de Pierre Duval" (MA thesis, Université
    Paris-Sorbonne, 2016), 83, notes that Duval dedicated his next game, *Le Jeu
    de France* of 1659, to Guillaume de Lamoignon (1617–1677), marquis de
    Basville.
20  Catherine Hofmann, chief curator of the Département des Cartes et Plans,
    Bibliothèque nationale de France, in conversation, 3 April 2019.

21 Michel Manson, *Jouets de toujours* (Paris: Fayard, 2001), 102. See also Seville, *The Cultural Legacy of the Royal Game of the Goose*, 75.

22 Antoine Vincent Arnault, *Souvenirs d'un sexagénaire* (Paris: Duféy, 1833), 3:330–1.

23 *Le Nouveau jeu militaire dédié aux Héros de l'Empire Français* (Paris: Jean Marchand d'Estampes, 1808), https://gallica.bnf.fr/ark:/12148/btv1b6941017j.

24 *History of the World in Maps: The Rise and Fall of Empires, Countries and Cities* (Glasgow: Times Books, 2015), 109.

25 See Orest Ranum, "Jeux de cartes et instruction du prince," in *Les Jeux à la Renaissance, Actes du XXIIIe colloque international d'études humanités*, ed. Philippe Ariès and Jean-Claude Margolin (Paris: J. Vrin, 1982), 553–61, and more recently, Paris Amanda Spies-Gans, "A Princely Education through Print: Stefano della Bella's 1644 *Jeux de Cartes* Etched for Louis XIV," *Getty Research Journal* 9 (2017): 1–22. On Desmarets de Saint Sorlin's life and career, see Hugh Gaston Hall, *Richelieu's Desmarets and the Century of Louis XIV* (Oxford: Clarendon Press, 1990).

26 Jean Desmarets de Saint-Sorlin and Stefano Della Bella, *Le Jeu de la géographie* (Paris, 1644). The BnF has digitized the third state, in colour and without suit marks. See https://gallica.bnf.fr/ark:/12148/btv1b105222579 for the full set.

27 Alexandre de Vesme, *Stefano Della Bella: catalogue raisonné* (1906), reprinted with introduction and additions by Phyllis Dearborn Massar (New York: Collectors Editions, 1971) 1:105: Florent le Comte published the games under the title *Jeux historiques des Rois de France, Reine renommées, Géographie et Métamorphose, par feu Mr. J. Desmarets ..., gravez par Do.* [*sic*] *La Bella* in 1698.

28 *Le Jeu du picquet* (Paris, 1632).

29 Lebens, "Prints in Play," 86.

30 Spies-Gans, "A Princely Education through Print," 1.

31 See Desmarets and della Bella, *Le Jeu de la géographie*, "Jev de cartes de la géographie," https://gallica.bnf.fr/ark:/12148/btv1b105222579/f105.item.

32 Ibid.: "Les quatre parties sont comme les quatre Rois d'vn Ieu ordinaire. Les Royaumes dont la Figure est à cheual en façon d'vne personne qui attaque, & qui a vne Renommée qui vole après elle, valent autant que les Reynes. Les Figures qui sont à cheual en façon d'vne personne qui est sur la deffensiue, & qui n'est acccompagnée d'aucune autre Figure, valent autant que les Valets des autres Ieux. Les autres Cartes valent selon le chiffre qui est marqué en chacune."

33 Ibid.: "Quand on jouë au Hoc, France & Espagne sont les Hoc du Ieu, comme la Dame de pique, & le Valet de carreau, outre les quatre parties du Monde qui sont comme les Rois. Si on veut joüer le Hoc au Ieu de la

Geographie comme à celuy des Reynes Renommées, à cause qu'il est fort diuertissant par les Cartes qui payent au Ieu, & font comme vne poule pour celuy qui fait le dernier Hoc; on prend les mesmes Cartes que les Reynes Renommées; A sçauoir les trois, qui payent vn au Ieu quand on les jouë, les six qui payent deux, & les huict qui payent trois; lesquelles Cartes ne peuuent estre Hoc; & on suit en cela les regles du Ieu des Reynes Renommées."

34  Desmarets and Della Bella, *Le Jeu des reynes renommées* (Paris, 1644), "Le ieu de cartes des reynes renommées," https://gallica.bnf.fr/ark:/12148 /btv1b105222450/f103.item: "quatre couleurs ... qui se rapportent aux quatre peintures, cœur, carreau, pique & trefle; & de chacune couleur il y a depuis l'as jusqu'à celle qui vaut autant que le Roy; & ainsi en se separant son Ieu par chaque couleur, & mettant les jaunes ensembles, les grises ensembles, & ainsi des autres, & en les rengeant selon les chiffres, on peut joüer à toutes sortes de Ieux."

35  Desmarets and Della Bella, *Le Jeu de la géographie*, "Jev de cartes de la géographie," https://gallica.bnf.fr/ark:/12148/btv1b105222579/f105.item: "Jean Desmarets, nous a fait remonstrer que le zele qu'il a pour nostre service, luy ayant fait penser à quelque moyen agreable & facile, de nous faire gouster les sciences les plus nobles & les plus necessaire aux Rois, sans nous faire éprouver les difficultez qui se rencontrent dans la manière ordinaire de les enseigner aux autres hommes."

36  Ibid. It was further noted that Desmarets transferred his privilege to the printer and bookseller Henry Le Gras to sell the games at the price of 30 *sols* per deck of cards, or 40 *sols* for a coloured set ("jeux enluminez").

37  Spies-Gans, "A Princely Education through Print," 10.

38  Pascale Mormiche, *Devenir prince. L'école du pouvoir en France* (Paris: CNRS Éditions, 2015), especially 51–8.

39  Desmarets and Della Bella, *Le Jeu de la géographie*, "Jev de cartes de la géographie," https://gallica.bnf.fr/ark:/12148/btv1b105222579/f105.item.

40  Desmarets and Della Bella, *Le Jeu de la géographie*, "Europe": "La moindre mais la premiere partie du monde, pour sa fertilité, et la valeur, ciuilité, science, renommée et multitude de ses peuples, et pour estre le siege de la Chrestienté. Elle est située vers le Septentrion, sous la zone froide et la temperée," https://gallica.bnf.fr/ark:/12148/btv1b105222579/f1.item.

41  Desmarets and Della Bella, *Le Jeu de la géographie*, "Afrique": "Située vers le midy, sous la zone brulée. Ses pays sont steriles et peu habitez, exceptés vers les costes et en quelques lieux. Ses peuples sont noirs ou bazanez," https:// gallica.bnf.fr/ark:/12148/btv1b105222579/f3.item.

42  Spies-Gans, "A Princely Education through Print," especially 6–10.

43  Desmarets and Della Bella, *Le Jeu de la géographie*, "Amerique": "Quatrièsme partie du monde, découverte depuis 150 ans, autrement dicte, les Indes

Occidentales, ou le nouveau monde," https://gallica.bnf.fr/ark:/12148
/btv1b105222579/f7.item.

44  Desmarets and Della Bella, *Le Jeu de la géographie,* "Peru": "La plus riche
province du monde pour l'or et l'argent qu'elle porte," https://gallica.bnf.
fr/ark:/12148/btv1b105222579/f15.item; "Mexique, Ou nouuelle Espagne,
la plus belle province de l'Amerique," https://gallica.bnf.fr/ark:/12148
/btv1b105222579/f23.item.

45  Desmarets and Della Bella, *Le Jeu de la géographie,* "Nouvelle France": "Paÿs
couuert d'arbres, et mal cultiué," https://gallica.bnf.fr/ark:/12148
/btv1b105222579/f101.item.

46  Desmarets and Della Bella, *Le Jeu de la géographie,* "Jev de cartes de la géographie": "ayant fait pensé à quelque moyen agreable & facile, de nous faire
gouster les sciences les plus nobles & les plus necessaires aux Rois," https://
gallica.bnf.fr/ark:/12148/btv1b105222579/f105.item.

47  Petto, *When France was King of Cartography,* 6–7.

48  Ibid., 7.

49  Ibid.

50  On Nicolas Guérard, "graveur, éditeur et marchand d'estampes et de cartes
géographiques; graveur ordinaire du Roi," see https://catalogue.bnf.fr
/ark:/12148/cb15325218m.

51  Vincenzo Coronelli, *Le Royaume de France Avec Ses Acquisitions Divisé en
Gouvernemens de Provinces et dedié à Louis le Grand, Roy de France et de Navarre*
(Paris: J.B. Nolin, 1688), https://gallica.bnf.fr/ark:/12148/btv1b8492908k.

52  Ibid. The original legend in French: "Total des Lieües comprises dans les
conquestes de Louis le Grand. Le Roussillon, 200; la France Comté avec le
Montbelliard, 447."

53  La Marinière, *La Maison academique: contenant un recueil general de tous les
jeux divertissans pour se rejouyr agreablement dans les bonnes compagnies par le
sieur D.L.M.* (Paris: chez Robert de Nain et Marin Leché, 1654). The author
"D.L.M." or Sieur de La Marinière was earlier confused with Jean Pinson de
La Martinière, a high court judge. My thanks to Adrian Seville and Thierry
Depaulis for information on La Marinière. The rules for Duval's *Le Jeu du
monde* appeared in *La Maison academique,* 1654, pages 189–94, and reap-
peared in the 1659, 1665, 1666, 1668, and 1674 editions.

54  Pierre Duval, *Les Tables de Géographie réduites en un Jeu de Cartes* (Paris, 1669),
https://gallica.bnf.fr/ark:/12148/btv1b10525454r.

55  *Geographical Cards made and Sold for Henry Brome at Ye Gun in St. Pauls
Church-Yard. London 1676* (London: Printed for Henry Brome, 1675). The
UCLA Clark Memorial Library has an identical set of 52 *Engraved English
geographical playing cards* (record ID 3719102).

56  Pierre Nicole, *Traitté de l'éducation d'un prince, avec quelques autres traittez sur diverses matières morales* (Paris: Veuve Charles Savreux, 1671), cited by Rabecq-Maillard, 21.

57  Pascale Mormiche, "Eduquer le Dauphin: *exempla*, image du père, éducation exemplaire?" *Bulletin du Centre de recherche du château de Versailles* (2014), http://doi/org/10.4000/crcv.12368.

58  Ibid., paragraph 46.

59  Louis XIV, *Mémoires de Louis XIV, écrits par lui-même, composés pour le Grand Dauphin, son fils, et adressés à ce prince: suivis de plusieurs fragmens de mémoires militaires, de l'instruction donnée à Philippe V, de dix-sept lettres adresées à ce monarque sur le gouvernmenent de ses États, et de diverses autres pièces inédites* (Nîmes: Lacour-Ollé, 2009).

60  Mormiche, *Devenir prince*, 375.

61  Ibid., 578n66.

62  Ève Netchine, ed., *Jeux de Princes, Jeux de vilains* (Paris: Bibliothèque nationale de France, 2009), 93.

63  Gilles Jodelet de La Boissière, *Le Jeu de la guerre* (Paris, [1698]), https://gallica.bnf.fr/ark:/12148/btv1b105285617. Pierre Lepautre (1652?–1716), the leading engraver in France, made the copperplate. See Philippa Plock and Adrian Seville, "The Rothschild Collection of Printed Board Games at Waddesdon Manor," in *Of Boards and Men: Board Games Investigated. Proceedings of the XIIIth Board Game Studies Colloquium (14–17 April 2010)*, ed. Thierry Depaulis (n.l., n.d), 108, who identify *Le Jeu de la guerre* as a companion piece to La Boissière's *Le Jeu des fortifications*, c. 1700. The first game treats attack and the second treats defence in war. Also Seville, *The Cultural Legacy of the Royal Game of the Goose*, 60–2.

64  Jean Mariette, dedication in *Le Jeu de la guerre*, 1698: "Toute la France sçait assez que tous les Jeux sont peu de vostre goust; et que ce qui fait le plus agreable amusement des Princes de vostre age, vous devient à charge à moins que la necessité ou la bienseance ne vous obligent d'y donner quelques moments. Je n'aurois eu garde aussy, Monseigneur, de vous presenter tout autre Jeu que celuy de la Guerre, ou vous trouverez reuni sous diverses images ce qui fait deja la matiere de vos plus serieuses reflexions. C'est par cette etude que vous avancez tous les jours dans la Science des Heros; et que dès les premieres occasions que vous aurez de faire éclater les hautes connaissances que vous en avez, vous ne vous ferez plus qu'un Jeu des plus difficiles entreprises."

65  Mormiche, *Devenir prince*, 187, noted that the young princes were constantly occupied by learning activities and duties, to the extent that even during mealtimes they had to listen to literary texts read aloud to them.

66 Mariette, dedication in *Le Jeu des fortifications,* "si l'étude des Sciences fait aujourd'huy toutte vôtre application, celle de la Guerre luy succedera dans peu de temps, et quelque attache que vous ayez maintenant pour les Muses, la Noblesse de vôtre sang jointe a la Grandeur de vôtre courage obligera bientost plusieurs de uous à se ranger du costé de Mars. Ie ne crains pas même de troubler aucun de vos exercices ordinaires en uous offrant pour matière de vos divertissements un Ieu qui contient les premiers elements de l'Art Militaire. Je ne fais que suiure les lumieres de ceux qui uous eleuent et qui uous conduisent auec tant de sagesse et de succés." I thank Adrian Seville for pointing out this parallel example. For an uncoloured engraving of 1763, published by Jean-Baptiste de Poilly, see https://gallica. bnf.fr/ark:/12148/btv1b10528568c. Adrian Seville's private collection includes a coloured engraving published earlier by Jean Mariette.

67 Seville, *The Cultural Legacy of the Royal Game of the Goose,* 62, notes that it would have been tiresome to cut out the engraved plate and prepare the cards. Jesuit writer Claude-François Ménestrier, *Bibliothèque curieuse et instructive de divers ouvrages anciens et modernes de literature et des arts* (Trevoux: E. Ganeau, 1704), 2:197, earlier complained that games that combined a spiral race game and a set of cards were too cluttered.

68 La Boissière, *Le Jeu de la guerre,* 1698, "Escalade est une attaque brusque et contre les formes qui se fait de jour avec des eschelles pour se rendre maître d'une muraille, d'un rampart, ou de quelque autre fortification."

69 Ibid., space 32, "Bombardement": "Bombarder, c'est battre une ville ou une place avec des bombes, la bombe est une grosse boule de fer creuse, qu'on remplit de feux d'artifice et de cloux: elle a deux anses a costé du trou ou tient la fusée qui y doit mettre le feu, et est placée sur un mortier monté de son affust."

70 Alain Manesson-Mallet, a mathematician and engineer who specialized in fortifications, wrote *Les Travaux de Mars ou l'art de la guerre,* 1671.

71 La Boissière, *Le Jeu de la guerre,* 1698, "Depouïlle est le profit qui revient aux soldats des hardes d'argent, et de tout ce que pouvoient avoir sur eux, ceux qui sont tués dans le champ de battaille."

72 *Le Jeu de la guerre,* 1698, space 53.

73 *Le Jeu de la guerre,* 1698, space 53, "L'heroique valeur que ce grand Roy couronne n'estime dans ces prix que la main qui les donne."

74 *Recueil de modes,* vol. 7 ([Paris], 1750), plates 64 and 65 (https://gallica.bnf .fr/ark:/12148/btv1b105296308, views 70, 71). The engravings were originally published by Jollain l'aîné, who also published some of Duval's maps.

75 René d'Allemagne, *Sports et jeux d'adresse* (Paris: Hachette, 1903), 266. I thank Adrian Seville for pointing me to this reference.

76  *Recueil de modes*, vol. 7, "Louis XIV": "Il gouverne ses Estats avecque grande tranquillité ayant marié son fils unique Monseigneur le Dauphin avec la Princesse Electorale de Baviere qui la fait grand pere dez Enfans le Duc de Bourgogne, le Duc d'Anjou, et le Duc de Berry," https://gallica.bnf.fr/ark:/12148/btv1b105296308/f70.item.zoom.

77  *Recueil de modes*, vol. 7, "Le Royal Ieu des fortifications": "Ces trois princes joüant a ce jeu de la guerre / Nous présagent qu'un jour par leurs faits inoüis, / Ils feront avoüer au reste de la Terre / Qu'ils sont les dignes fils du monarque Louis," https://gallica.bnf.fr/ark:/12148/btv1b105296308/f71.item.zoom.

78  Seville, *The Cultural Legacy of the Royal Game of the Goose*, 39, notes that in the second half of the eighteenth century a high-quality engraved and hand-coloured goose game printed in Paris cost 16 to 18 *livres*. George D. Sussman, *Selling Mothers' Milk: The Wet-Nursing Business in France 1715–1914* (Urbana: University of Illinois Press, 1982), 58–9, notes that in 1756 a lackey earned 10 *livres* a month. In late eighteenth-century Paris a journeyman artisan earned 20 to 25 *livres* a month.

79  Jill Shefrin, "Games, Cartographic," in *The History of Cartography* volume 4, *Cartography in the European Enlightenment*, ed., Matthew H. Edney and Mary Sponberg Pedley (Chicago and London: University of Chicago Press, 2019), 427.

80  Shefrin, *Such Constant Affectionate Care*, 5–6, notes an undated advertisement (c.1755–60) by Mme de Beaumont: "Les demoiselles qui ne viendront que le jour payeront une guinée d'entrée et une demi-guinée pour les cartes de géographie en bois."

81  Shefrin, *Such Constant Affectionate Care*, 7, 93, states that eight of the dissected maps were printed from plates for the first edition of Jean Palairet, *Atlas méthodique composé pour l'usage de son altesse sérénissime monseigneur le prince d'Orange et de Nassau, Stadhouder des Sept Provinces-Unies, etc. etc. etc.* (London, 1755).

82  Shefrin, *Such Constant Affectionate Care*, 80. The English printers and booksellers John Spilsbury, Thomas Jefferys and his successor William Faden, Robert Sayer, and Carington Bowles sold games and puzzles based on maps by cartographers and map engravers Thomas Kitchin, John Rocque, Emanuel Bowen, and John Gibson.

83  This is contrary to Shefrin's claim that commercially produced geographical games took a century to migrate from England to France. Shefrin, *Such Constant Affectionate Care*, 80.

84  Guillaume Delisle, *Carte d'Europe dressée pour l'Usage du Roy sur les Itinéraires anciens et modernes et sur les Routiers de mer assujetis aux observations*

astronomiques [*Map of Europe drawn for the King on ancient and modern routes and on sea routes based on astronomical observations*] (Paris, 1724). See Petto, *When France was King of Cartography*, 6–7.

85  "Maps cut and glued on wood to facilitate children's study of geography," listed in *Catalogue des cartes et ouvrages géographiques de MM. de L'Isle et Buache, … de celles de M. Jaillot, … qui composent le fonds géographique du sieur Dezauche* (Paris: Dezauche, n.d.); *Catalogue des cartes et ouvrages géographiques de Guillaume Delisle et Philppe Buache, Premiers Géographes de l'Académie des Sciences; de ceux des sieurs Dezauche, Jaillot et autres auteurs, lesquels composent le fonds géographique du Sr Dezauche* (Paris: Dezauche, 1793), 30; *Catalogue des cartes et ouvrages géographiques de Guillaume Delisle et Philipe Buache, de ceux de J.C. Deauche, Jaillot, Chauchard et autres auteurs, lesquels composent le fonds géographique de J.C. Dezauche, … ainsi que le Catalogue général des cartes de la Marine de l'Empire* (Paris: Dezauche, 1806).

86  Guillaume Delisle, *Carte d'Europe dressée pour l'Usage du Roy sur les Itinéraires anciens et modernes et sur les Routiers de mer assujetis aux observations astronomiques. Augmentée des Nouv[el]les connoiss[an]ces Géographiques par Phil. Buache, gendre de l'auteur, janvier 1760 et 1769* (Paris, 1769). See *Jeux de Princes, Jeux de vilains*, 92, for a photograph of the puzzle of Europe reconstructed. The pieces for France, Poland, and Russia are missing.

87  Guillaume Delisle, *Carte de France dressée pour l'Usage du Roy, en Avril 1721. Par Feu Guillaume Delisle, Premier Géographe de Sa Majesté. De l'Académie R[ ]le des Sciences. Et augmentée en 1764 par Philippe Buache, son Gendre [...], Revue en 1775* (Paris, [1775]). My thanks to Frédérique Desbuissons for the photograph and Ulysse Da Silva for transmitting it to me.

88  Katie Hornstein, *Picturing War in France, 1792–1856* (New Haven and London: Yale University Press, 2017), 10. The engraving measures 45 x 35 cm.

89  Hornstein, *Picturing War in France*, 9.

90  Hornstein, *Picturing War in France*, 10.

91  Monsaldy, *Le Triomphe des armées françaises* (Paris: chez Jean, rue Jean de Beauvais, 1797). The BnF catalogue entry describes it as "Seconde épreuve de la planche Hennin n° 12344. Celle-ci est avant le nom de Monsaldy." The engraving can be viewed here: https://gallica.bnf.fr/ark:/12148/btv1b8412715t.

92  James A. Mangan, *The Game Ethic and Imperialism: Aspects of the Diffusion of an Ideal* (London: Frank Cass, 1985; 2nd rev. ed., 1998).

93  Michael Budd, "Book Reviews," *Culture, Sport, Society* 2, no. 1 (2007): 127.

94  Megan A. Norcia, "Playing Empire: Children's Parlor Games, Home Theatricals, and Improvisational Play," *Children's Literature Association Quarterly* 29,

no. 4 (Winter 2004): 294–314; *X Marks the Spot: Women Writers Map the Empire for British Children, 1790–1895* (Athens: Ohio University Press, 2010); *Gaming Empire in Children's British Board Games, 1836–1860* (London: Routledge, 2019).

95 Michael Budd, *The Sculpture Machine: Physical Culture and Body Politics in the Age of Empire* (New York: New York University Press, 1997). Allen Guttmann, *Games and Empires: Modern Sports and Cultural Imperialism* (New York: Columbia University Press, 1994).

96 Nicolas Bancel and Daniel Denis, "Becoming 'Homo Imperialis' (1910–1940)," in *Colonial Culture in France since the Revolution*, ed. Pascal Blanchard et al. (Indiana University Press, 2013), 282.

# chapter nine

# The World Contained in an Imperial Ottoman Album

EMINE FETVACİ

In this essay, I focus on an imperial album put together by the courtier and album maker Kalender Pasha (d. 1616) for the Ottoman sultan Ahmed I (r. 1603–17) because its eclectic contents seem to embody the very notion of imagined worlds. In it are calligraphies, imperial portraits, pages from historical accounts, narrative scenes, and individual depictions of types of people from different geographies – from India to Western Europe – and representing various professions. The enumerated materials come from the Ottoman imperial studio, the urban art market in Istanbul, and from artistic centres as diverse as Isfahan, Qazvin, Baghdad, Karbala, and Central Asia. In addition, a number of prints created in Antwerp, Rome, Paris, and Poland were once part of this album, but they have since been removed.[1] The title of the album, *Album of the World Emperor Sultan Ahmed Khan*,[2] prominently inscribed on the first folio, claims world dominion for Sultan Ahmed I, and raises the possibility that the contents suggest at least symbolic control over the vast territories whose people and artistic styles and products are represented in the album. Moreover, the salon-like gatherings in which albums were viewed, discussed below, allowed for participants to intellectually wander through literary and earthly realms, providing the perfect context for imagining different worlds.

These wanderings, however, were far from haphazard, as is made evident both by the organizational logic of the album, which depends on comparative viewing, and by the seven-page preface written by Kalender.[3] The *Album of the World Emperor* was meant to reflect the world under Ahmed's dominion – a world that extended far beyond the actual borders of the Ottoman Empire. Western Europe and Iran, not surprisingly given the longstanding artistic and political relationships between the

Ottomans and these neighbours east and west, are parts of this imagined
territory. Perhaps somewhat surprisingly for modern viewers, the album
also contains evidence of an artistic and political competition with the
Mughal Empire of India. Ottoman-Mughal artistic, diplomatic, or commercial links have not been studied by historians in a systematic fashion.[4]
And yet visual and verbal evidence from the album, examined in the
following pages, suggests that there were plenty of contacts between the
courtly and artistic communities of these two early modern empires and
that the Ottomans, at least, were aware of not only political but also artistic developments at the Mughal court.

The *Album of the World Emperor* not only showcases Indian figures and
artworks that copy Mughal Indian examples, but it also displays conceptual links to Mughal art that suggest a deep knowledge of Mughal
album-making practices. The Mughal court in India produced multiple
albums in the early seventeenth century that contained similar categories of objects to what we find in the *Album of the World Emperor*. The
organization of the contents also points to a common logic of presentation that enhances the meanings of the artworks. The title of the album,
to be discussed in more detail below, was surely a subtle challenge to
Mughal claims of world domination, which were crystallizing at around
this time. Both the Indian figures and these conceptual parallels, which
would have been evident to the refined viewers of this album, amplify
Ahmed I's claims to aesthetic discernment, collecting abilities, and political power. In what follows, I will first discuss the album's context of viewing and audience in order to explain how the album creates imagined
worlds, and then examine how the competitive relationship between the
Ottomans and the Mughals as represented in the *Album of the World Emperor* enriches the world imagined through the album and contributes to
its message of power.

### Creating Imagined Worlds through the Album

In the seven-page preface that accompanies the *Album of the World Emperor*,
Kalender invites the album's viewers, the educated and refined courtiers
around Ahmed I, to carefully examine the relationships between the artworks on each page and suggests that their careful contemplation will
lead the viewer to greater wisdom and pleasure, with emphasis placed
on connoisseurship and on learning by viewing examples.[5] The preface
clearly shows that the album was meant to evoke thoughts and ideas
beyond what could be seen on the folio, and encourage the viewer to

imagine and learn. In these first pages, Kalender follows what had become a traditional order of preface topics: praise of God, his creation, and the Prophet Muhammad, praise of the four Sunni caliphs, praise of the sultan Ahmed I, and finally, a brief description of the contents and the reason for compiling the album. His explanation of the contents and his rationale for organization leaves no doubt that the album was prepared with careful planning.

Such careful planning is evident when we examine individual folios. On folio 24b (fig. 9.1), for example, Kalender brings together a Frankish (generic Western European) type in the lower right corner with a figure in contemporary Safavid Iranian elite costume facing him. They are identifiable by their clothes, especially by the black hat of the Frankish figure and the oversized turban of the Safavid youth. The two figures seem to be engaged in a conversation across the frame that divides them: the Safavid youth in red coquettishly holds on to his ermine-lined blue cloak and tilts his head forward as if he is listening to the Frankish figure, who is gesturing with his hands in conversation. The third figure to their left (identifiable as Circassian from his costume) is reading from a long-format poetic book. He may be considered the representation of the rival (*rakib*) who is present in the background story to many Ottoman lyric poems.[6] The dervish figure on the far left is drawing our attention to this trio, not only with his finger pointing at them, but also with the bands of his clothes blowing in an imaginary wind towards them. Another conversation, this time between a merchant or shopkeeper and a young *çelebi*, a gentleman, takes place in the upper row of figures, directly above the first couple just discussed. To their left is an archer from the Ottoman military. A Persian lyric poem written on an oblong sheet of paper constitutes the uppermost section of the folio. This poetic page is just the kind and size that would have been in a poetry book like the one held by the Circassian rival in the bottom row, providing the viewer with a suggestion as to how the single figure images could come together in a romantic narrative.[7] The viewers of the album could gaze over this page, imagining the implied relationships between the individuals pictured here and even, probably, conjuring the urban bazaar setting to which the poetry on the folio alludes. The relationships between the disparate figures of various backgrounds, loosely suggested through their placement with respect to each other and on the same folio as a love poem, would be animated by the viewers of the album. The sultan and his companions could thus imagine a world populated by the figures on the folio, and wander through it in their imagination.

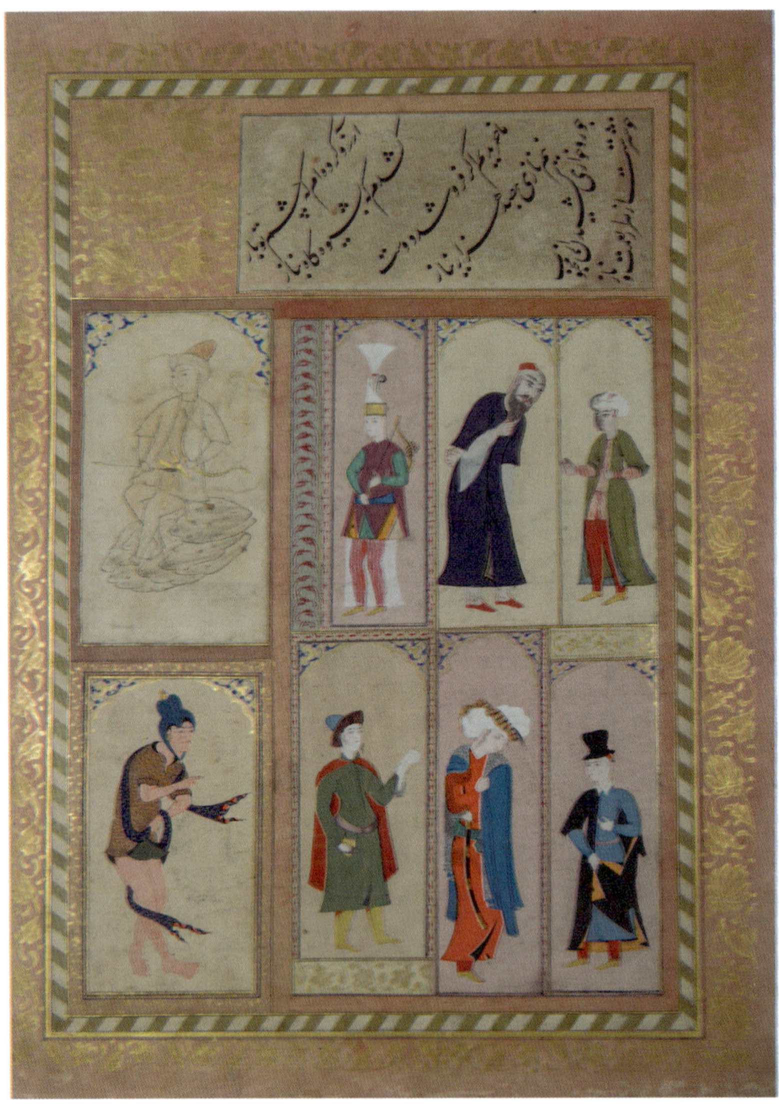

Figure 9.1.  Kalender, *Album of the World Emperor*, Istanbul, 1614–16, fol. 24b.
Ink, gold, and opaque watercolour on paper, 47.5 x 33.5 cm. Album folio.
B 408. Topkapı Sarayı Müzesi Kütüphanesi, Istanbul. Photograph by Hadiye
Cangökçe. By permission of Milli Saraylar İdaresi Başkanlığı, the Presidency of
the Republic of Turkey

Kalender, renowned for his skills in paper joinery, created a unified artwork out of the disparate elements that make up folio 24b.[8] He brought together depictions of different types, but presented them within a collage by selecting, arranging, affixing, and illuminating the various elements of the composition. The seams between the different pieces of paper are highlighted by the nestled frames and borders he created for them. Delicate arch-like frames turn each figure into a figurine in an architectural niche; floral frames embedded within colour-block patterns dazzle the eye and emphasize the varied origins of the collected artworks at the same time as they unite them into a single composition. The varied origins are also made evident through the different colours of the papers on which the figures are depicted. This emphatic eclecticism is united by the consistent aesthetic provided by Kalender's frames and margins. The visual tactics we see in figure 9.1 are applied throughout the album, creating a kaleidoscope of styles and genres that nonetheless hold together and encourage the viewer to interpret or derive lessons from the album, to think of it as a united although multivalent artwork.

As important as Kalender's intentions and visual tactics are, the context in which albums were viewed, and the audience, were also essential for activating the messages of any given folio or album. Albums were usually enjoyed in literary gatherings called *majālis* (sing., *majlis*), where they served as centrepieces around which intellectual exchanges would take place.[9] The physical arrangement of the folios, which points to different ways of moving through the album, invites collective engagement. Participants in a *majlis* might gather around an album and view it from different directions. Albums could be opened at random; viewers were free to move in different directions.[10] They would undoubtedly have conversations about what they were looking at and discuss the visual characteristics of the images, the qualities of the calligraphy, and the merits of the poetry contained on the folios. They would compare materials on different pages, discuss their relationships to each other, and comment on the choices made by the album compiler. Comparisons would almost certainly be made to works of art that were not in front of them, such as other books, paintings, and albums, either in the collections of those present, or renowned examples known to all. This comparing was not confined to the visual realm: many album materials refer to a shared literary consciousness and only make sense with reference to texts outside the album.[11] Albums, like the poetry of the period, demand an intertextual reading, based on shared knowledge of tropes, literary and visual models, and the cultural lore that surrounds them, in order to make sense.[12] As such, they presuppose the existence of a mental world beyond the covers of the album, shared to a significant extent by the elite men of various professions (officials, merchants, scholars, courtiers, poets) who would participate in these literary gatherings. The cumulative effect of an album allows for multiple interpretations to result from divergent experiences of the object. The competitive references to India in the *Album of the World Emperor* would have been activated in such a viewing context, and would no doubt be amplified through the conversations around the object.

### The World in the Album

The *Album of the World Emperor* is, among other things, a microcosm of the world that Kalender's patron Sultan Ahmed I claimed for himself; it references not only the actual territory of Ottoman lands, but also the rest of the world as imagined from Istanbul. The social and ethnic varieties of the Ottoman world are represented through types common to costume books compiled and sold in the bazaar, often for visitors. Types such as janissaries, ascetics, shopkeepers, gentlemen, loose women, and housewives can be found both in this album and in contemporary costume books[13] But the album does not stop at the empire's borders: Persians, Georgians, and Circassians are also represented, as are various types from Mughal India and parts of Europe. The costumes of these figures mark them as being from various locales – Circassia, for example, or Shiraz, or Isfahan, or India. They clearly represent variety through their costumes, identifiable through comparison to contemporary costume albums made mostly for Europeans.[14]

The album opens unto a world beyond the Ottoman empire not only through the foreign peoples represented in it, but also through artworks from different cultural and geographical contexts, in different styles and media. The European prints, the Safavid paintings and drawings, and the calligraphies from Iran all function in this way. The artworks linked with India are included in the album precisely to enhance the global variety represented therein. Since the European and Iranian materials are better known and studied, I will simply introduce them here briefly, and focus in the rest of this essay on the more subtle competition with Mughal India that the album reveals.

Iran is certainly the neighbour that is most present in the album, due to its proximity and rival political status, but also as a result of the shared legacies of Ottoman and Safavid artistic production. Both visual traditions built on the same artistic past: fifteenth-century Timurid and Turkman art was admired and collected in both contexts, and the Timurid court served as an idealized model of artistic production and courtly patronage for both Safavid and Ottoman elites and intellectuals.[15] Images of Safavid types, or paintings based on Safavid Persian originals, were not perceived as exotic in the Ottoman context. They were considered a part of the Ottoman visual world, both due to constant diplomatic and military contact between the two empires, and due to the artists, artworks, and trade goods moving between Istanbul and the Safavid cities of Isfahan, Tabriz, and Shiraz.[16] Compilations of urban types such as in figure 9.1 find parallels in Safavid art of the early seventeenth century. At the same time as this album was being produced, similar albums were also made in large numbers in the Safavid context.[17] Safavid artists were keen to represent single figure types, presumably urban figures one could see on the streets of Isfahan, in the many single-page paintings and drawings that survive from this period (fig. 9.2).[18] Such types are also to be found painted on the walls of palaces and even market areas in Isfahan.[19] Thus both Iranian artworks, and Iranian approaches to art making, are represented here.

European costume books present other visual parallels and potential sources of inspiration, especially for the comparative placement of different sartorial types.[20] In addition to affinities with European (or made for European consumption) costume books, the album also contains printed European artworks of mythological and religious subject matter. Even if not as numerous as Iranian materials, the Western European artworks in the album stand out because of the different techniques and materials used. The folios on which these printed images are accommodated have been unified with Kalender's touch just as the other folios of the album: they have been organized with similar compositions to the other folios, and have been framed and illuminated in the same ways, with the same range of motifs and colours (fig. 9.3). The Ottomans' trade and diplomatic connections with Western Europe, as well as the presence of local Christian communities, explains the presence of these materials in the album.[21] The period in which the *Album of the World Emperor* was created was an exceptionally active period in Ottoman-Western European relations. Against the background of the Ottoman-Habsburg wars of 1593–1606, trading capitulations for the French and the English were renewed in 1604 and 1606. In 1610, the sultan began to allow the Dutch to trade under their own flag in Syria and, after 1612, out

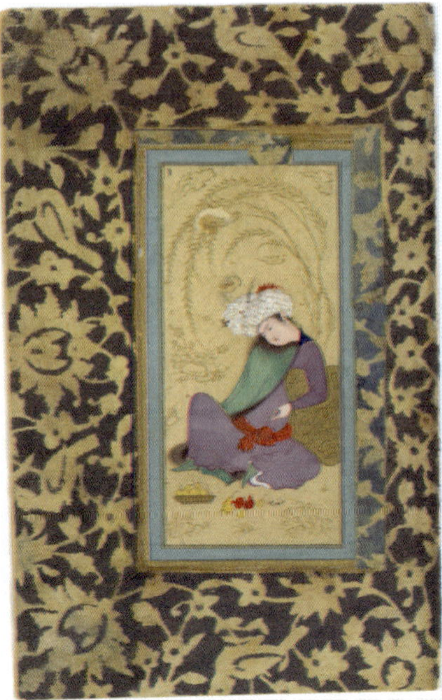

Figure 9.2. Aqa Riza, *Man in a Fur-Lined Coat*, Isfahan, ca. 1600. Ink, gold, and opaque watercolour on paper, 13.6 x 6.4 cm. Rogers Fund 1955 (55.121.39). The Metropolitan Museum of Art, New York

of Istanbul too.[22] All these diplomatic events meant that numerous envoys and their retinues were active in Istanbul. The vivid presence of Europeans on Istanbul streets, and awaiting meetings with the sultan and his courtiers and agents, makes itself felt on the folios of the album, both through the European artworks and through the images of European types. In the context of the lively diplomatic and mercantile engagements with Western Europe, the European artworks in the album allowed the sultan to lay claim to a more global empire and demonstrate his power over his rivals.

Through content, format, and genre, the *Album of the World Emperor* gestures to a world beyond the Ottoman court. However, it does so while being firmly anchored in the concerns of its maker, patron, and intended elite audiences, to whom these materials would have signalled

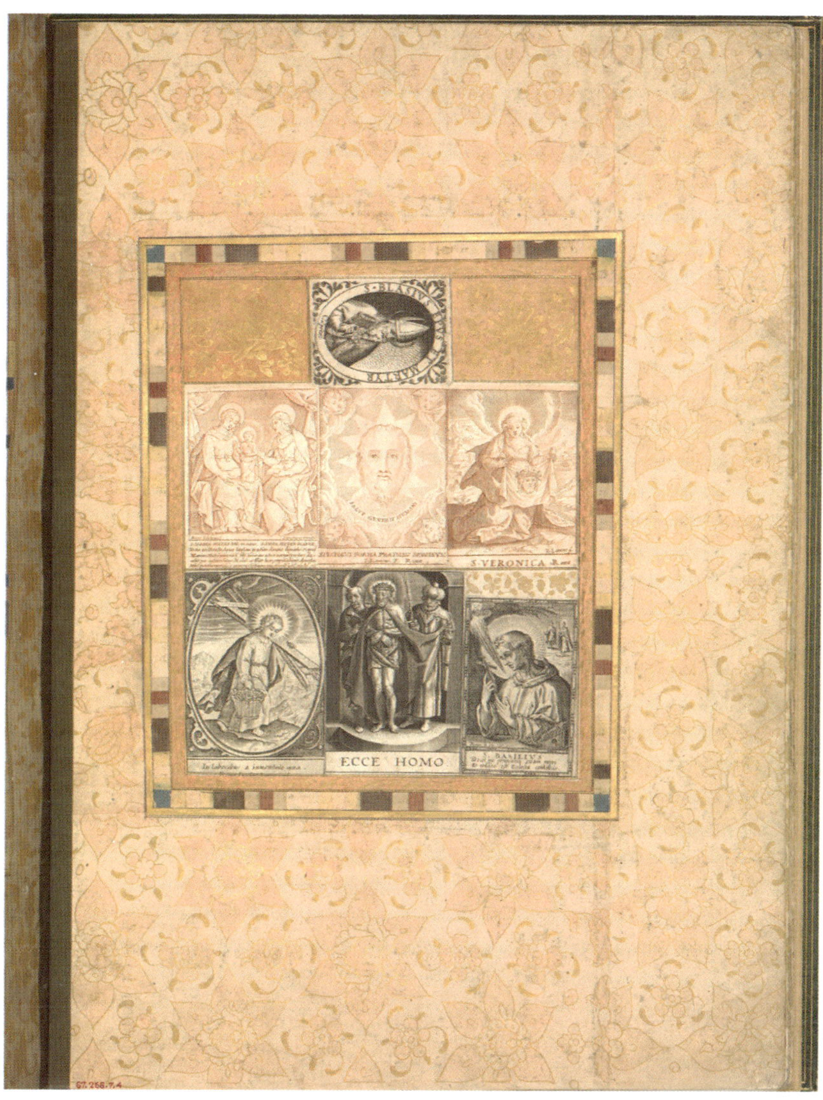

Figure 9.3. Jacobus Laurus, Thomas de Leu, et al., *Seven Devotional Scenes*, Rome and Paris, ca. 1600. Ink, gold, and opaque watercolour on paper, 45.4 x 32.1 cm. Folio from the "Bellini Album." Louis V. Bell Fund, 1967 (67.266.7.4r). The Metropolitan Museum of Art, New York

worldly ambitions as well as proof of connoisseurship, collecting abilities, and aesthetic discernment. Significantly enhancing this message of discernment and collecting powers are the hitherto unexamined materials pointing to the Mughal empire. It is to these that I now turn.

## Indian Images in the Album of the World Emperor

Our knowledge of Ottoman-Mughal interaction is minimal compared to the vast amount of ink that has been spilled over Ottoman-Safavid conflicts, the presence of Persians in Ottoman employ, and Ottoman interest in Safavid art.[23] Similarly, the Safavid-Mughal fights over Qandahar, the importance of Safavid émigré artists to the development of Mughal art, and the Mughal collection of Persian art have also been well studied.[24] Although a thorough archival study of Ottoman-Mughal relationships still needs to be conducted, the material evidence shows that the two were well informed about each other. There were political and economic reasons for this familiarity as well as artistic ones. The Ottomans and Mughals competed over control of the Indian Ocean in the sixteenth century, as we know from Giancarlo Casale's work. One of the important issues of contention was which empire had the right to protect Hajj routes, and how these routes were protected. Geographically, the Arabian peninsula (which was under Ottoman suzerainty) – the object of the Hajj – was accessible both from the heart of the Ottoman Empire and through the Indian Ocean, an important arena of competition.[25] Mughal embassies arrived at the Ottoman court from time to time, and Ottoman ones were dispatched to Delhi.[26] In the eighteenth century we have plenty of evidence of Indian goods, especially cotton textiles, flooding the Ottoman market.[27] And in the realm of the arts of the book, the Khoda Bakhsh Library in Patna contains an illustrated imperial Ottoman history recording the Hotin campaign of Mehmed III that has the seal of the Mughal princess Jahanara on it.[28] Multiple eighteenth-century Ottoman albums with Indian materials are currently in the Topkapı Library.[29]

The India-related materials in the *Album of the World Emperor* show that there were seventeenth-century contacts as well. I begin my analysis of the album's references to India through three images that offer the most concrete and explicit evidence of Ottoman courtly perceptions of India at the time. The three images in question also help explain the role India played in the world view presented by the album – first and foremost, these images attested to the wide reach of Ahmed I's power.

Folio 16b (fig. 9.4) contains the most obviously India-inspired image in the album, that of an Asian elephant with two mahouts (elephant care-takers/riders) on its back. The mahouts are dressed in Mughal garb, the turbans on their heads accord with contemporaneous Mughal headwear, and their outer garments, which are fastened with a high cross-over in the front, are Mughal rather than Ottoman or Safavid costumes. The distinctive yellow worn by the figure on the back of the elephant is also related to the colour known as Indian yellow used in Mughal painting.[30] What is this Indian elephant doing in the sultan's album? Its primary function is to point to India, and to the sultan's ability to procure artworks from this distant land that could form the basis for images in the album. The significance of the elephant goes beyond attesting to the foreignness of the artwork, however: it also encompasses the symbolism of the animal itself.

The symbolism of the elephant is evident in how it came to Istanbul. During the sixteenth century, a small number of elephants were gifted to the Ottoman court, starting with the elephant sent to Selim I in 1512 by the Mamluk ruler of Egypt and Syria, Qansuh al Ghawri, who in turn had received two of these magnificent beasts from India as a gift.[31] All of the elephants in Istanbul were from India.[32] Mahouts usually accompanied these elephants throughout their journey, and remained with them for at least some time, so the two men pictured here might have been a familiar sight to viewers in Istanbul.[33]

How the elephants were used and treated in Istanbul also explains their meaning in the album. In the Ottoman context, similarly to how exotic animals functioned in other early modern European courts, elephants were mainly displayed as symbols of wealth and global reach, but were not actually used for battle, transport, or sport as they were in India.[34] They were kept in Istanbul, among other animals seen rarely in the Ottoman heartlands, at a menagerie near the Topkapı palace, which held one of the "largest and most diverse" animal collections in the early modern world.[35] Thomas T. Allsen refers to exotic animals in Eurasian royal collections as "valuable political capital because they documented a ruler's reach, his contacts with distant, storied lands, and his ability to attract gifts and goods from far-off princes."[36] Ottomans and Western Europeans alike were dependent on the Indian Ocean trade to procure these rarely seen animals.[37]

The animals in Istanbul were perceived as impressive displays of imperial power by foreign visitors, an important audience for trade and diplomacy. In 1531, the Habsburg envoys to the Ottoman court were impressed with the sight of two elephants (and some horses) in the first

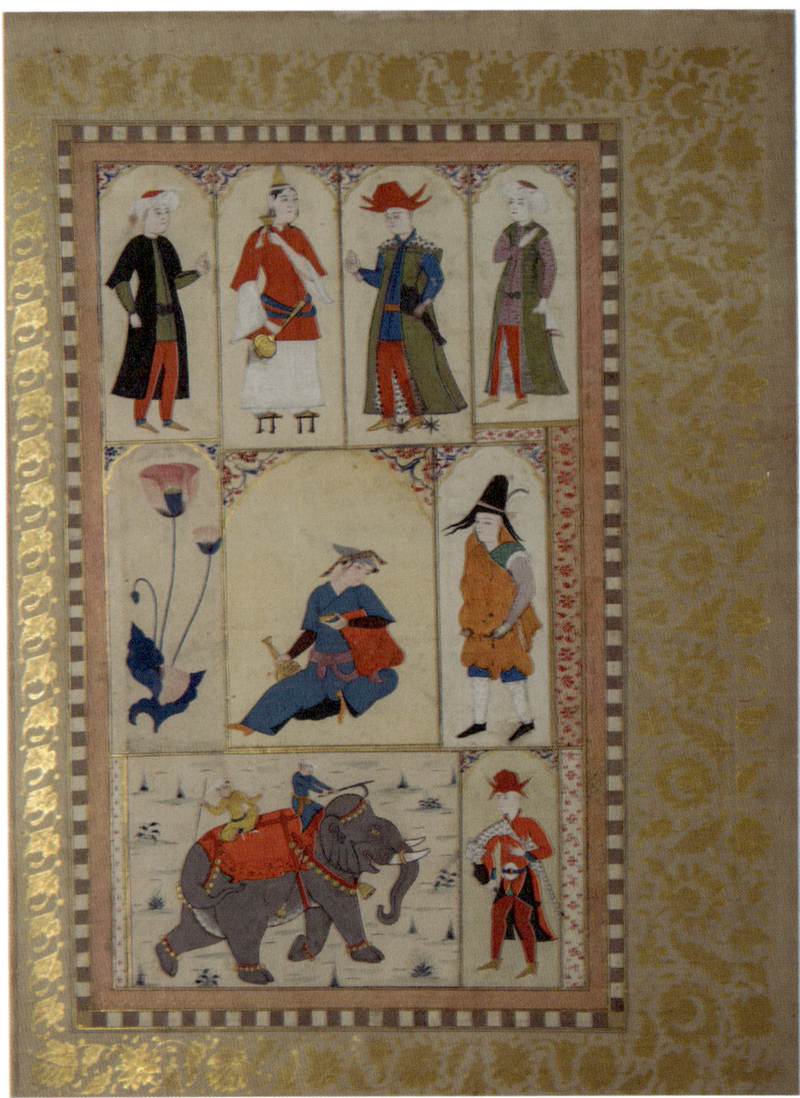

Figure 9.4. Kalender, *Album of the World Emperor*, Istanbul, 1614–16, fol. 16b. Ink, gold, and opaque watercolour on paper, 47.5 x 33.5 cm. Album folio, B 408. Topkapı Sarayı Müzesi Kütüphanesi, Istanbul. Photograph by Hadiye Cangökçe. By permission of Milli Saraylar İdaresi Başkanlığı, the Presidency of the Republic of Turkey

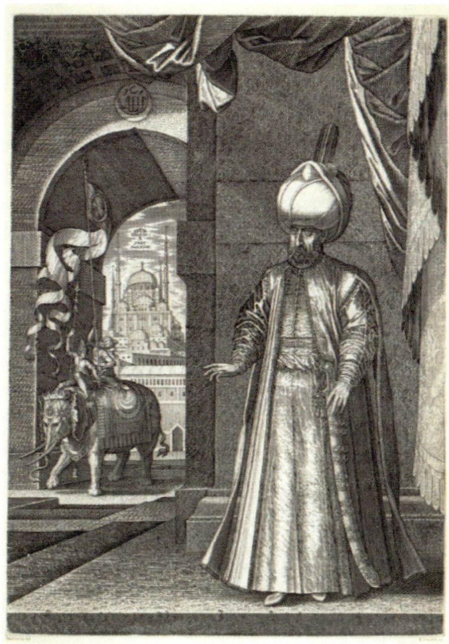

Figure 9.5. Melchior Lorichs, *Sultan Süleyman with the Süleymaniye Complex Seen from an Arched Portal of the Old Palace*, 1559. Engraving, ink on paper, 43.4 x 31.3 cm. 1848, 1125.24. The British Museum, London. © The Trustees of the British Museum

courtyard of the Topkapı. The Habsburg envoy to Sultan Süleyman's court, Ogier Ghislain de Busbecq, too, writes enthusiastically about a dancing elephant he saw in the palace a few decades later: "When this Elephant was bid to dance, he did so caper or quaver with his whole Body, and interchangeably move his Feet, that he seem'd to represent a kind of Jig; and as for playing at Ball, he very prettily took up the Ball in his Trunk, and sent it packing therewith, as we do with the Palm of the Hand."[38]

The efficacy of these animals in conveying imperial splendour is evident in the portrait of Sultan Suleyman by the artist who accompanied Busbecq to Istanbul, Melchior Lorichs (fig. 9.5).[39] This 1559 engraving shows an aged Süleyman on the right-hand side of the composition, with an elephant riding through a monumental archway (possibly representing the first gate of the Topkapı Palace) at the centre, through which one can see Suleyman's imperial mosque, completed just a few years earlier. While it makes perfect sense for the mosque carrying the sultan's name to be a part of his portrait, the inclusion of the elephant appears at first glance to be incongruous with the image of an Ottoman ruler in Istanbul, since elephants were not native to this geography. When we consider these animals as part of "conspicuous courtly splendour," as Hedda Reindl-Kiel interprets them, however, the inclusion of the elephant makes more sense. The elephants at the Topkapı fulfilled their intended role of impressing visitors to the court with the Ottoman ruler's ability to procure such exotic fauna. Moreover, as Alan Mikhail makes clear, when it came to the procurement and appreciation of "charismatic megafauna," Western European and Ottoman monarchs and viewers were in a similar situation; thus, Lorichs and his audience would know exactly what the elephant signified.

Exotic animals were perceived as signs of imperial splendour by Ottoman audiences as well. This perception is made evident in a painting from the *Book of Kings of Sultan Selim* (*Şehnāme-i Selīm Ḫān*, Istanbul, c. 1571–81) depicting the display in Istanbul of a hippopotamus head sent from Egypt (fol. 59b) and a rhinoceros sent from Ethiopia (fol. 152a, fig. 9.6). In both images, there are members of the public viewing the animals in wonder.[40] The mere inclusion of these displays in a manuscript that explicitly eulogizes the Ottoman ruler as a world conqueror through military victories in far-flung places like the Persian Gulf, Tunisia, Moldavia, Ethiopia, Cyprus, and Yemen suggests that these animals were understood by Ottoman audiences, historians, and artists to contribute to the image of world power. The illustration cycle of the *Book of Kings of Sultan Selim* is devoted almost exclusively to these military victories (avoiding any mention of the 1571 Ottoman defeat at Lepanto). The few exceptions, such as the two images of exotic animals in Istanbul, enhance the image of worldly dominion. The depiction of African and Indian exotic animals, first in the *Book of Kings of Sultan Selim*, and later in the *Album of the World Emperor*, clearly is intended to contribute to this image of worldly power and to the idea that the Ottoman ruler had command over great resources.

In addition to clarifying the role of the elephant in the *Album of the World Emperor*, considering the *Book of Kings of Sultan Selim* elucidates one other point: the authorship of the elephant image. Comparing the awkward depiction of the rhino in figure 6 with the relatively elegant image

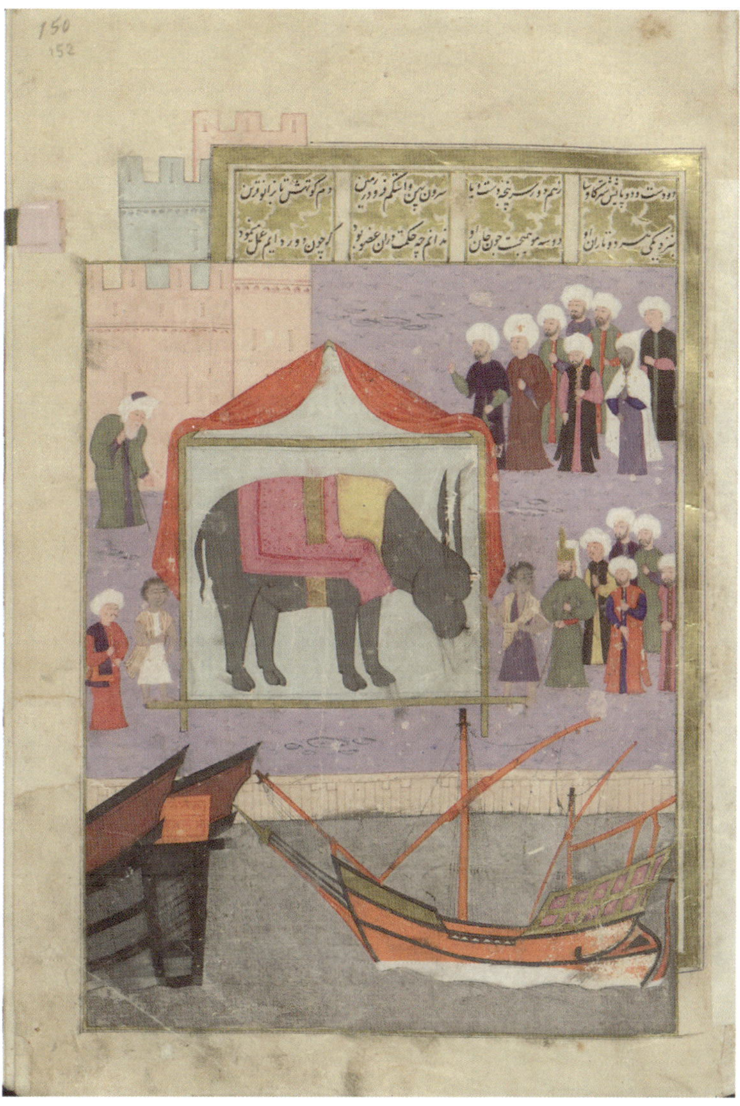

Figure 9.6.  The display of the rhinoceros sent as a gift by the Ethiopian ruler, *Şehnāme-i Selīm Ḫān*, Istanbul, 1571–81, fol. 152a. Ink, gold, and opaque watercolour on paper, 23.6 x 34.3 cm. A. 3595. Topkapı Sarayı Müzesi Kütüphanesi, Istanbul. By permission of Milli Saraylar İdaresi Başkanlığı, the Presidency of the Republic of Turkey

of the elephant in figure 9.4 points to a difference in the artists' ability to capture the image of an animal that cannot simply be attributed to style. Horses in the same manuscript, for example, are illustrated with much more grace, which shows that the issue is one of a lack of familiarity both with exotic animals and with the practice or tradition of depicting such foreign beasts. The elephant image in figure 9.4 is most likely not an original Ottoman composition: it probably copies a Mughal painting, which would render it even more "authentic" as a reference to India, helping to capture the exotic between the covers of the album. Given the prevalence of elephant imagery in Mughal painting, and the ease with which works on paper travelled between Islamic courts in the early modern period, this derivation is quite likely.[41]

The Indian elephant is not the only exotic animal in Sultan Ahmed's worldly, albeit two-dimensional, collection. The album also includes images of lions in captivity or being hunted. One of the lions appears in a narrative scene, calm as a statue at the court of the Ottomans' ancestors on folio 8a, another is being handled by an animal tamer who also sports a monkey, on folio 11a. The latter image has been incorporated into a composition consisting of other such single-figure studies, and suggests a courtly gathering around Selim I, pictured in the upper part of the folio. Thus, this lion is at the court of an Ottoman ruler – one who is known to have received an elephant from Qansuh al Gawri. Lion hunts appear on the folio facing the elephant, and finally, two lion studies are juxtaposed with an Uzbek warrior on folio 21a, along with a lyric poem.[42] What an actual elephant (or lion) on the streets of Istanbul or in the palace courtyard did for the image of earlier sultans, the images of these exotic animals were now supposed to do for Ahmed, in this microcosm of a world presented between the covers of his album.

Ahmed did have access to actual exotic animals, as the British diplomat Thomas Gainsford, who was in Istanbul in 1607, attests: "Under the [palace's] walls are stables for seahorses called Hippopotami, which is a monstrous beast taken in Nilus, Elephants, Tygres, and Dolphines: sometimes they have Crocadiles and Rhinoceros: within are Roebuckes, white Partridges, and Turtles, the bird of Arabia, and many beasts and fowles of Affrica and India."[43] Yet, despite the global access or power suggested by this royal menagerie, the Ottoman state seems to have lost influence over Indian Ocean trade at the end of the sixteenth century. Precisely because Ahmed could not actually boast the same kind of control over the Indian Ocean that his predecessors could, the album, like his actual menagerie, was meant to project certain ambitions, however unrealizable.

While the routes taken by the elephant and other exotic animals were determined by diplomatic contacts and added to the awe and splendour they were supposed to evoke, the route likely taken by the image of the elephant is indicative of the strength of trade networks and the presence of an active art market in the early seventeenth century. Indeed, despite loss of Ottoman control over some routes, many individual Ottomans, including officials in Yemen, Egypt, Eritrea, and Jiddah, were increasingly involved in and were significantly enriched by the Indian Ocean trade networks.[44] In fact, various concessions for Ottoman merchants were sought at Akbar's court in 1602, suggesting an acceptance of Mughal power over much of this trade.[45] The increasing circulation of artworks across imperial borders and class lines, coupled with the growing success of individual Ottoman merchants in the Indian Ocean trade, suggests that the elephant image might have originated in the art market rather than being produced exclusively for a courtly context. This origin is also in keeping with some of the other images in the album. The single figures that accord with the costume albums made for European consumption might also have been acquired in the art market. The same is true of the Safavid figures.[46] The image of the elephant therefore also points to the shaping of courtly tastes by urban predilections, a possibility evoked by the rest of the album. Individual images that might on their own simply refer to an urban context, or in a non-imperial collection might point to cosmopolitanism, come together in this case to signal larger political aspirations.

It is difficult to chart the exact trajectory of Mughal images arriving at the Ottoman court in the late sixteenth or early seventeenth centuries. Mughal paintings, especially portraits, circulated in Europe, especially from the 1640s–50s onwards, but the *Album of the World Emperor* was compiled in 1610–12. There is little evidence of Mughal paintings circulating in Europe in the first quarter of the seventeenth century.[47] If the Ottoman artists of the images in the *Album of the World Emperor* saw any Mughal paintings or albums, in other words, they would have come from the east, rather than the west. The images might have made their way to Istanbul from Safavid lands, or through the hands of Ottoman merchants doing business with Mughal India. Their presence here underlines the continuing centrality of trade routes across the Indian ocean and overland, as well as the increasing importance of the art market and the constant circulation of artists and artworks in early modern Eurasia.

How the image functions in the folio provides yet another clue as to what it was supposed to mean in the broader context of the album.

The urban and the foreign mix seamlessly on the folio with the elephant, which demonstrates an important visual strategy Kalender uses throughout the album, that of juxtaposing individual artworks in ways that suggest a narrative scene without actually creating such a narrative.[48] Included on the top left and right corners are two young men, probably from the newly formed class of "city boys" who appeared in large numbers in Istanbul as a result of massive urban migrations linked with unrest in the countryside in the early seventeenth century.[49] Also in the top row is a wine-serving woman in bath slippers who faces a figure that appears to be a falconer, a member of the large palace/military retinue. This top row could easily be read along romantic lines, in keeping with the poetry of the period. At the centre of the page is a Safavid youth, seated coquettishly and enjoying a cup of wine, following a typical way of depicting the beloved inspired by the lyric poetry of the period.[50] To his right is a *derviş* type, a wandering ascetic belonging to one of the antinomian Sufi orders. At the bottom right, facing the Indian elephant, is another hunter, perhaps with the skin of the leopard or cheetah he has hunted. This last figure, as Ottoman as he is in the depiction of his style and costume, might also be a reference to Mughal practices of hunting. Cheetahs were not so common in Ottoman paintings, but Mughal imperial histories are filled with images of cheetah hunts where the big cats were used to hunt other animals. At any rate, this too is an exotic animal that points to lands beyond the Ottoman empire. The page as a whole, then, signals broad horizons.

There are two other "Indian" images in the album other than the elephant. Folio 23b includes a painting that is difficult to place (fig. 9.7). The background is reminiscent of Mughal paintings inspired by European prints, and might indeed be from India. The use of atmospheric perspective and the situating of a diminutive castle in a landscape in the far distance are techniques seen more often in Mughal works responding to European prints than in any Ottoman materials.[51] The image depicts an outdoor meeting between three men, two of whom are elderly. They might represent Sufi figures based on their costumes: they are both wearing very humble cloaks, one has a red-and-white turban, and the other's loosely wound white turban is flowing down his back in a manner reminiscent of images of wise old men in Mughal and Safavid drawings and paintings from the period. The composition, too, showing a small group in a landscape setting, find parallels in Mughal and Safavid artwork from the period depicting yogis and Sufis. The painting is juxtaposed with the images of two beautiful youths. Based on the style of

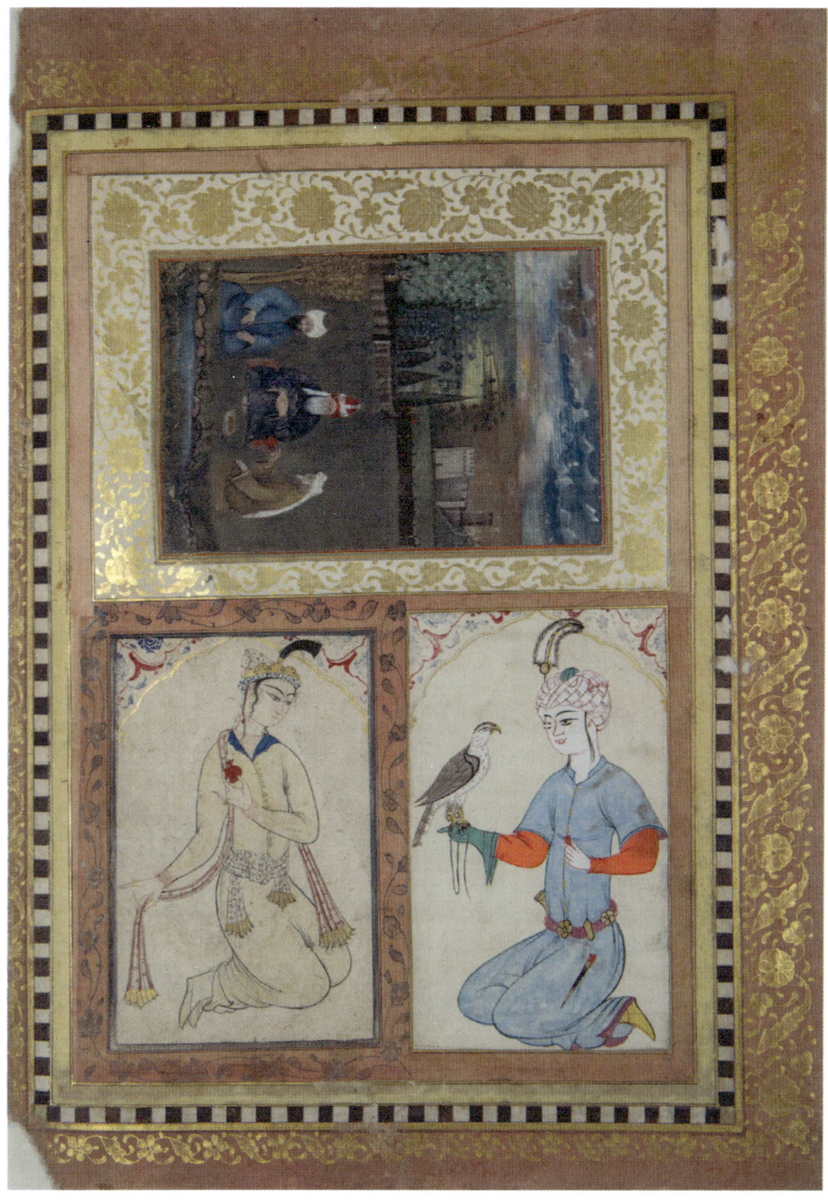

Figure 9.7. Kalender, *Album of the World Emperor*, Istanbul, 1614–16, fol. 23b. Ink, gold, and opaque watercolour on paper, 47.5 x 33.5 cm. Album folio, B 408. Topkapı Sarayı Müzesi Kütüphanesi, Istanbul. Photograph by Hadiye Cangökçe. By permission of Milli Saraylar İdaresi Başkanlığı, the Presidency of the Republic of Turkey

their costumes, their accoutrements such as the tiara worn by the figure
on the left or the belt and pen knife worn by the figure on the right, and
their poses, these are both Safavid types of the late sixteenth century.
While the flurry of lines delineating the figure on the left seem to accord
with Safavid drawings of the period, the figure on the right is drawn with
a more solid line, possibly, though not necessarily, an Ottoman copy of
a Safavid original. These two figures too are in a meeting of sorts, com-
municating with each other across the frames separating them as they
appear to gaze at each other.

And finally, folio 26a (fig. 9.8) presents yet another Indian type – as
can be deciphered from his clothes – depicted probably by Ottoman
artists. Seated in the lower right corner of the folio, this figure holds
a long-form poetic book (*safina*), a chap book of sorts, and appears in
conversation with the much smaller Ottoman female figure gesturing
towards him from the other side of the frame separating them. They
are accompanied by other studies of single figures from various regions,
though mostly Ottoman, in the upper portion of the folio.

The role of the Indian (or Indian-inspired) images on folios 23b and
26a (figs. 9.7 and 9.8) is similar to that of the elephant in that they too
represent foreign types, expanding the reach of the empire. They also
point to a certain kind of wealth or plenty by representing variety and
help to show the empire under the control of the "World Emperor" to
be a rich and varied place. They are not as significant as the elephant
in evoking exotic sources, but point to a certain cosmopolitan artistic
landscape in which artworks from diverse contexts were available and
appreciated. Their message, however, is one that builds up as one examines the entirety of the album. The networked globe evoked by the
album through its multiple types also raises the possibility of dominating
that globe. The elephant and the other Indian figures clearly enhance
the multiplicities of the album and underline the global aspirations of
Ahmed I, and his image as a world ruler as claimed for him by the title
of the album.

### Conceptual Links between the *Album of the World Emperor* and Contemporary Mughal Albums

The elephant and the Indian types in the album enhance Ahmed I's
claim to global dominance, but they also make a more specific message
possible – a competitive response to the Mughal emperor Jahangir and
his claims of world domination. This message becomes clearer when

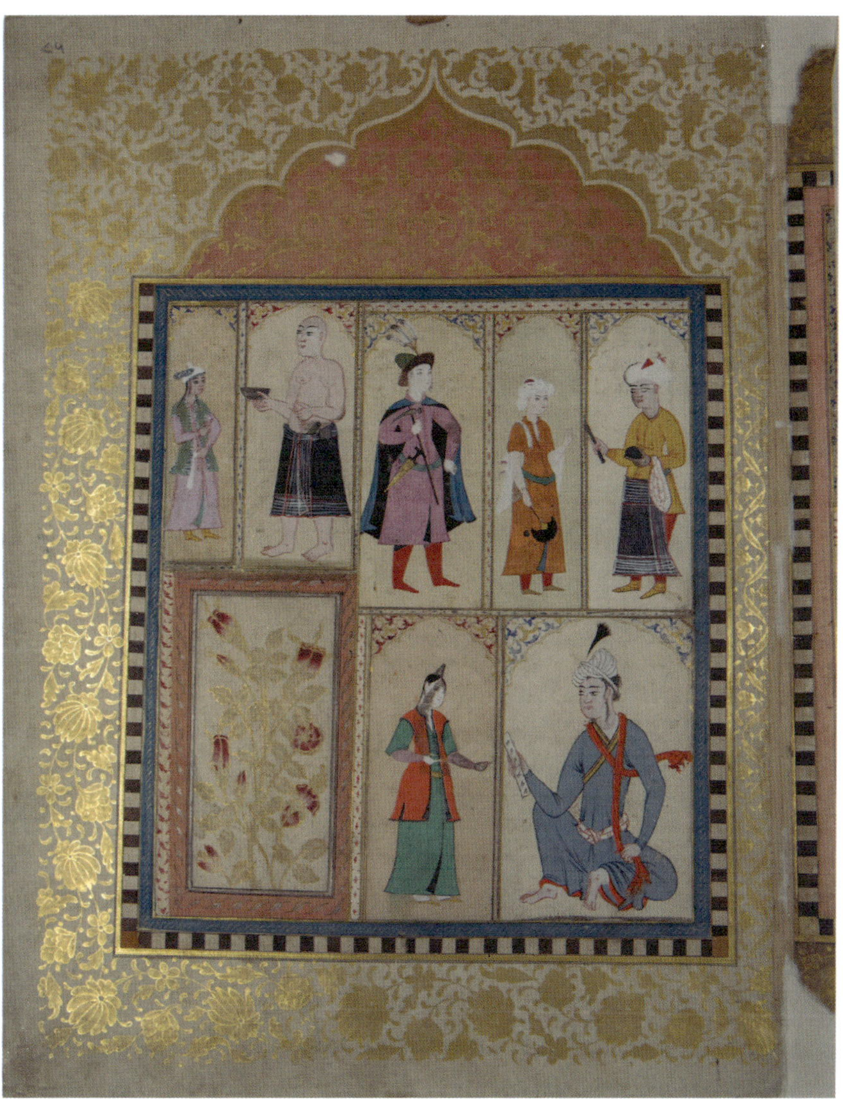

Figure 9.8.  Kalender, *Album of the World Emperor*, Istanbul, 1614–16, fol. 26a.
Ink, gold, and opaque watercolour on paper, 47.5 x 33.5 cm. Album folio,
B 408. Topkapı Sarayı Müzesi Kütüphanesi, Istanbul. Photograph by Hadiye
Cangökçe. By permission of Milli Saraylar İdaresi Başkanlığı, the Presidency of
the Republic of Turkey

we examine other parallels between this album and Mughal examples. While a certain amount of overlap between Ottoman and Mughal albums is to be expected due to the album genre's genesis at the Timurid court and the Timurid heritage of both Ottoman and Mughal artistic traditions, it is important to note that the parallels I identify here are of a more specific nature and do not pertain to other Ottoman albums. Important conceptual links suggested by the album's title, the classes of materials in it, and the way European prints are incorporated suggests more than superficial familiarity with Mughal albums and their bold claims of world domination.

During the first quarter of the seventeenth century, the Mughal emperor Jahangir ("world seizer," r. 1605–28) and his courtiers were actively engaged in a visual and historiographical propaganda campaign in which they presented Jahangir as the ruler of the world.[52] This included individual paintings that famously show him standing atop the globe, as well as albums that make the same visual argument across multiple folios in a more sustained manner.[53] Jahangir had come to the throne two years after Ahmed's own accession, choosing the regnal title of Jahangir over his given name of Salim (Selim), which was shared with two former Ottoman rulers (Selim I, r. 1512–20; Selim II, r. 1566–74).[54]

The very title of the *Album of the World Emperor* (*Muraqqa-i Padishah-i Jahan*) is rather unusual in the Ottoman context. The title of *padishah-i jahan* was claimed by Jahangir, and not common in Ottoman titulature. Contemporaneous Ottoman documents usually refer to the Ottoman ruler as Sultan Ahmed Khan, and list his genealogy as a legitimating source. Sultan and khan are the preferred titles, rather than padishah, which stands out as an unusual choice.[55] On another folio of the *Album of the World Emperor*, Ahmed refers to himself as the Imam of the Muslims, another very unusual title for an Ottoman ruler, and a competitive reference to Safavid titulature.[56] Similarly, the title *padishah-i jahan* is most likely deliberately making claims to challenge Ahmed's Muslim competitors to the east, the Mughal rulers. It is also significant that both Ahmed and Jahangir cultivated an apocalyptic, millennial imperial image that depended upon being precisely the ruler of a world at peace and also representing the Mahdi, the Redeemer, who is expected to usher in the End Times.[57]

One of the ways in which Jahangir's albums claimed world domination was through inclusion of multiple classes of materials, in particular the juxtaposition of imperial portraits with depictions of courtiers, and European prints with calligraphy samples.[58] This is also the case in the

*Album of the World Emperor*, and the fact that it is not so in other Ottoman albums of the period makes it significant.

The use of European prints in albums seems to begin at the same time in the Mughal and Ottoman contexts. European prints were circulating in Mughal India as early as 1550, and were available in even larger numbers after the 1580s, when a Jesuit mission was established at Akbar's court.[59] They began to be incorporated into Mughal albums made for Jahangir, around 1600–18, corresponding with the period in which the *Album of the World Emperor* was made.[60] Yael Rice argues that Mughal artists viewed prints as aesthetic counterparts to Mughal paintings, drawings, and calligraphies, and especially considered them as akin to the calligraphic arts due to their emphasis on line.[61] They seem to have held similar aesthetic appeal to the album maker Kalender, who organized the European prints in the *Album of the World Emperor* in the same way as he organized the rest of the album. Prints of similar subject matter are placed together on a page so they can be visually compared with each other, and visual relationships are set up between them as they are on other folios of the album (fig. 9.3).

Kalender seems to have had access to the same kinds of prints as his counterparts in India. Among the print makers represented in both contexts is Thomas De Leu.[62] A portrait of François of Valois made by De Leu was incorporated onto an album folio at the Mughal court, painted over to resemble Mughal imperial portraits and embellished with clouds and cherubs to create an expanded composition, akin to how Kalender treated some of the images in the *Album of the World Emperor*. Rice dates the folio containing the De Leu print to around 1610, precisely the same time period in which the *Album of the World Emperor* was made. However, Kalender did not paint over the European imagery, merely expanding compositions with illumination, so there are also important differences between the way the prints were incorporated.

Another artist common to the *Album of the World Emperor* and Mughal albums is Marten de Vos, especially as rendered through the prints made by the Wierix brothers after De Vos. Friederike Weiss has convincingly argued for the use of Wierix prints as the basis of two separate Mughal compositions showing courtly scenes involving the emperors Jahangir and Babur.[63] While the *Album of the World Emperor* only contains the European prints and not local depictions based on them, these prints were used as the basis for other Ottoman paintings at the court of Ahmed I and earlier.[64] Similarly to the Mughal interest in iconography and composition, Ottoman use of European prints also demonstrates a focus on creating legible compositions; yet unlike the Mughals, the Ottomans were not interested in incorporating the European style of depiction.[65] As with De Leu, the prints by De Vos and Wierix seem to have been used around the same time in Ottoman and Mughal albums.

Like the *Album of the World Emperor*, Mughal albums too were closely connected to their patrons, often representing their social and political ambitions, standing in for their larger collections of art, and demonstrating their refinement as connoisseurs. They contained records of intimate friendships, a trait also shared by albums of the Safavid court, suggesting that this feature might be inherited from Timurid concepts of album making.[66] However, the specifics of how this feature is executed in Mughal albums and in the *Album of the World Emperor* go beyond precedent. Inscriptions in the Mughal Gulshan album, for example, name the patron Jahangir by his princely name of Shah Salim and Padishah Salim as well as his eventual regnal title of Jahangir.[67] Similarly, the *Album of the World Emperor* contains artworks dedicated to the album compiler Kalender and other pieces done by figures at or close to the Ottoman court.[68]

Another parallel lies in the organization of albums: Mughal albums of the early seventeenth century often began with an image of the patron.[69] The *Album of the World Emperor* begins instead with the handwriting of the sultan, followed by imperial portraits of his ancestors. It does include a portrait of Ahmed I, but later in the album. In both cases, the albums are organized with attention to double folios that faced each other. These were given a certain kind of unity, with objects of similar size and proportion placed on facing pages, and margins with related designs surrounding them.[70] The margins of an opening (two facing pages) do not always have the same colour in Jahangir's albums, and neither do they in the *Album of the World Emperor*. Albeit a bit later in date, the Mughal Dara Shikoh album is similarly almost entirely made up of alternating pages of calligraphy and paired portraits, such that every opening either has two examples of calligraphy, or two portraits gazing at each other across the gutter of the book.[71] Similarly, the single figures in the *Album of the World Emperor*, although not quite portraits, do appear to be engaging with each other across margins and gutters, creating smaller yet multiple versions of the pairs in Mughal albums.

In both the Mughal and the Ottoman cases, the portraits and types one finds in albums are closely related to contemporary literary trends. In an article on Indo-Persian *shahrashub* (City Thriller) poetry (odes to cities listing the virtues of a city, often understood as the beautiful people resident therein), Sunil Sharma convincingly shows that Mughal poets were writing city thrillers to praise Mughal cities as places where "the seven climes of the world have come together and people of every country reside." Sharma argues that the variety of professions mentioned by the poets were intended to convey a sense of the dynamic and complex structure of Mughal urban society.[72] Similarly, the single figures in the *Album of the World Emperor* are related to the Ottoman version of this genre, known as *şehrengiz*, which emerged in the early sixteenth century and retained its popularity in the seventeenth century.[73] As with the beauties in the City Thriller poems, the figures in the album are types, rather than fleshed-out individuals. They are visually vague in terms of their individuality, but not in terms of their social status, and are rendered with the same ethos of direct simplicity as the language of the poetry. The local urban types depicted in the album are directly inspired by the poetry of the period, which increasingly described familiar urban types as the beloved rather than other-worldly ideal figures.[74] The end result is an album filled with figures that evoke the multiplicities of the urban context of the Ottoman capital, much like the Mughal albums did. This result is not because of any direct imitation of Mughal albums, but because both Ottoman and Mughal album-making practices were closely embedded in their literary context, and Ottoman and Mughal poets of the early seventeenth century were part of the same Persianate literary sphere.[75]

## Conclusion

The different types of people represented on the folios of the *Album of the World Emperor* signal a variety that metaphorically and summarily points to the various peoples of the world, and the Indian images in the album are an important component of this signalling. Indeed, they concretize the global claims of the album by bringing in the faraway and exotic realm of India into the sultan's microcosmic compilation. Yael Rice writes, "The juxtapositions of these disparate materials in the royal album invited the viewer to recognize stylistic, compositional, material and temporal differences and similarities."[76] I have argued in a recent monograph on the *Album of the World Emperor* that Kalender uses a similar tactic, that of the comparative gaze, to encourage the viewer to move through the album, comparing and contrasting the similar figures and noticing their relationships to each other, enhanced by the repeating figures in different poses or slightly different renderings that invite just such a comparative viewing. Another one of Kalender's tactics was to dazzle the viewer with multiplicity, and by this I mean both the different types of artworks (calligraphies, prints, drawings, paintings; Ottoman, Safavid, European, perhaps Mughal) and different types of people represented in the album. The "world" encapsulated by the *Album of the World Emperor*, stretching from Western Europe to India, encompasses more than simply types of people from different geographies. The multiple styles, materials and media represented here also encompass a different kind of world, one made up of multiple visual traditions. The *Album of the World Emperor*, with the aid of Iranian, Indian, and Western European materials and figures, allowed its patron Ahmed I to style himself as the World Emperor, presenting the world between the covers of an album. That it displays knowledge of Mughal album-making practices and titulature adds to the efficacy of its message while also allowing Ahmed to counter the very same claims being made by his contemporary Jahangir.

## NOTES

1  These Western European prints now constitute part of what is known as the Bellini Album, housed in the Metropolitan Museum of Art in NYC (67.266.7.2r; 67.266.7.2v; 67.266.7.3r; 67.266.7.3v; 67.266.7.4r; 67.266.7.4v; 67.266.7.5r; 67.266.7.5v are the folios with the prints. In addition, 67.266.7.1r; 67.266.7.1v; 67.266.7.8r; and 67.266.7.8v were also extracted from this album, or possibly another one made by Kalender Pasha for Ahmed I).

2  Kalender, *Muraḳḳaʿ-ı Pādişāh-ı Cihān Sulṭān Aḥmed Ḫān* (*Album of the World Emperor Sultan Ahmed Khan*), Topkapı Sarayı Müzesi Kütüphanesi, Istanbul, B 408, fol. 1b. For an overview of the album and a full translation and transcription of its preface, see Serpil Bağcı, "Presenting *Vaṣṣāl* Kalender's Works: The Prefaces of Three Ottoman Albums," *Muqarnas* 30 (2013): 255–313, especially 263–9; and Ahmed Süheyl Ünver, "L'Album d'Ahmed Ier," *Annali dell'Istituto Universitario orientale di Napoli*, n.s., 13 (1963): 127–62. The title is translated by Wheeler Thackston for "Appendix II C: Translation of the Preface to the Ahmed I Album, B 408 (fols. 1b-4b)," in Bağcı, "Presenting Vaṣṣāl Kalender's Works," 305. I examine the album more fully in Emine Fetvacı, *The Album of the World Emperor: Cross-Cultural Collecting and the Art of Album-Making in Seventeenth-Century Istanbul* (Princeton University Press, 2019).

3  I have discussed the organizational logic of the album in the *Album of the World Emperor*, 62–87.

4  A few works that highlight political, commercial, and diplomatic links are
   Giancarlo Casale, *The Ottoman Age of Exploration* (Oxford: Oxford University
   Press, 2010); Salih Özbaran, *Ottoman Expansion Towards the Indian Ocean in
   the Sixteenth Century* (Istanbul: Bilgi University Press, 2009); and Rachel Mil-
   stein, "From South India to the Ottoman Empire: Passages in 16th Century
   Miniature Painting," in *Ninth Congress of Turkish Art* (Ankara: Ministry of
   Culture, 1995), 497–506, who points to the prevalence of Indians in Bagh-
   dadi paintings from the turn of the century. Suraiya Faroqhi's recent publication, *The Ottoman and Mughal Empires: Social History in the Early Modern
   World* (London: I.B. Tauris, 2019) is purely a comparative study that looks
   at structural similarities and differences between the two empires in terms
   of political power, social constitution, and economic production. Stephen
   Frederic Dale, *The Muslim Empires of the Ottomans, Safavids and Mughals*
   (Cambridge, UK: Cambridge University Press, 2010) likewise does not con-
   sider Ottoman-Mughal interactions.
5  Fetvacı, *Album of the World Emperor*, 62–9; Bağcı, "Vassal Kalender," 268;
   Emine Fetvacı, "The Album of Ahmed I," *Ars Orientalis* 42 (2012): 127–38.
6  Walter Andrews and Mehmet Kalpaklı, *The Age of Beloveds: Love and the
   Beloved in Early-Modern Ottoman and European Culture and Society* (Durham,
   NC: Duke University Press, 2005), 109.
7  *Arzu karda-ām ke cheshm-e to bāz*
   *Koshadam gah be shive gah be nāz*
   *Mā kherīdim eger ferushad dust*
   *Nīm nāzī be ṣad hezār niyāz*
   *Jor o khvārī keshiden āz maḥbūb*
   *Hoshter ast āz hezār nimat o nāz*

   Your open eyes, I want that they
   Kill me, sometimes from mannerism, sometimes from coquettishness
   I buy whatever the friend is selling
   Half coquettishly, with a hundred thousand prayers
   Cruelty and wretchedness from the beloved
   Are better than a thousand riches and blandishments
8  The deliberately unified aesthetics of the album become even more obvious
   when we compare the folios of this album with other examples from the
   Ottoman context and beyond. See for example the albums made for Murad
   III and Mehmed III: Aimée Froom, "Adorned like a Rose: The Sultan
   Murad III Album (Austrian National Library Cod. Mixt. 313) and the Per-
   sian Connection," *Artibus Asiae* 66, no. 2 (2006): 137–54 and Banu Mahir,
   "Sultan III. Mehmed İçin Hazırlanmış Bir Albüm: III. Mehmed Albümü,"

in *16. Yüzyıl Osmanlı Kültür ve Sanatı 11–12 Nisan 2001 Sempozyum Bildirileri*, (Istanbul: Sanat Tarihi Derneği, 2004), 169–86.

9   An excellent analysis of the nature of literary gatherings and their role in intellectual and social exchange in the Ottoman empire, especially in its Arab provinces, is provided by Helen Pfeifer, "Encounter After the Conquest: Scholarly Gatherings in 16th-century Ottoman Damascus," *IJMES* 47 (2015): 219–39. See also Samer Ali, *Arabic Literary Salons in the Islamic Middle Ages* (Notre Dame, IN: University of Notre Dame Press, 2010); Dominic P. Brookshaw, "Palaces, Pavilions and Pleasure-Gardens: The Context and Setting of the Medieval Majlis," *Middle Eastern Literatures* 6, no. 2 (2003): 199–223; Maria Subtelny, "Scenes from the Literary Life of Tīmūrid Herāt," in *Logos Islamicos: Studia Islamica in Honorem Georgii Michaelis Wickens*, Papers in Medieval Studies 6, ed. Roger Savory and Dionisius Agius (Toronto: Pontifical Institute of Medieval Studies, 1984): 137–55; Haluk Ipekten, *Divan Edebiyatinda Edebi Muhitler* (Istanbul: Milli Eğitim Bakanlığı, 1996).

10  Some other codex format materials also functioned in this way. Anthologies, for example, which became increasingly popular in the seventeenth century, are a prime example. Some anthologies or miscellanies from the Islamic context are discussed in Hatice Aynur et al., eds., *Mecmûa: Osmanlı Edebiyatının kırkambarı* (Turkuaz: Istanbul, 2012); David J. Roxburgh, "The Aesthetics of Aggregation: Persian Anthologies of the Fifteenth Century," in *Princeton Papers: Interdisciplinary Journal of Middle Eastern Studies* 8 (2001): 119–42; and Kathryn Babayan, *The City as Anthology: Eroticism and Urbanity in Early Modern Isfahan* (Stanford: Stanford University Press, 2021). For European examples, see Bronwen Wilson, "Assembling the Archipelago: *Isolarii* and the Horizons of Early Modern Public Making," in *Making Space Public in Early Modern Europe: Performance, Geography, Privacy*, ed. Angela Vanhaelen and Joseph P. Ward (New York: Routledge, 2013), 101–26.

11  For a detailed discussion, see Fetvacı, *Album of the World Emperor*, 8–11, 76–9.

12  David J. Roxburgh, *The Persian Album 1400–1600: From Dispersal to Collection* (New Haven: Yale University Press, 2005), and David J. Roxburgh, *Prefacing the Image: The Writing of Art History in Sixteenth-Century Iran* (Leiden: Brill, 2001). Hatice Aynur, "Ottoman Literature," in *The Cambridge History of Turkey*, vol. 3, ed. Suraiya Faroqhi (Cambridge, UK: Cambridge University Press, 2006), 502: "to be skilled in versification was part of the identity of a member of the Ottoman elite." Similarly, of Ottoman lyric poetry, Walter G. Andrews, "Literary Art of the Golden Age," in *Süleyman the Second and His Time*, ed. Halil Inalcık and Cemal Kafadar (Istanbul: Isis Press, 1993), 355, writes of "the inescapable and uncompromising intertextuality of this particular poetic tradition, its tendency to base its logic and meaning on

access to a common fund of information unavailable to outsiders." He also describes a "presupposition that the audience of poetry will have an encyclopedic familiarity with the tropes of the tradition and the lore that accompanies them" (356).

13 Eleanor Sims, "Hans Ludwig von Keufstein's Turkish Figures," in *At the Sublime Porte: Ambassadors to the Ottoman Empire (1550–1800)*, ed. Philip Mansel, Eleanor Sims, and Annie Gilet (London: Hazlitt, Gooden & Fox, 1988), 20–40; Ann Rosalind Jones, "Habits, Holdings, Heterologies: Populations in Print in a 1562 Costume Book," in "Meaning and Its Objects: Material Culture in Medieval and Renaissance France," special issue, *Yale French Studies* 110 (2006); Rudolf H. W. Stichel, "Das Bremer Albumn und seine Stellung innerhalb der orientalischen Trachtenbücher," in *Das Kostumbuch des Lambert de Vos*, ed. Hans-Albrecht Koch (Graz: Akademische Druck- u. Verlagsanstalt, 1991), 31–54; Joanne Olian, "Sixteenth Century Costume Books," *Costume* 3 (1977): 20–48; Leslie Meral Schick, "Ottoman Costume Albums in a Cross Cultural Context," in *Tenth International Congress of Turkish Art*, ed. Déroche et al., 626; William Kynan-Wilson, "'Painted by the Turcks Themselves': Reading Peter Mundy's Ottoman Costume Album in Context," in *The Mercantile Effect: Art and Exchange in the Islamicate World during the Seventeenth and Eighteenth Centuries*, ed. Sussan Babaie and Melanie Gibson (London: Gingko Library, 2017), 39–50.

14 I made particular comparisons in my book, *Album of the World Emperor*, especially 69–76, 113–17.

15 Thomas W. Lentz and Glenn Lowry, *Timur and the Princely Vision: Persian Art and Culture in the Fifteenth Century* (Los Angeles: Los Angeles County Museum of Art; Washington, DC: Arthur M. Sackler Gallery, Smithsonian Institution, 1989), 303–27; Gülru Necipoğlu, "From International Timurid to Ottoman: A Change of Taste in Sixteenth-Century Ceramic Tiles," *Muqarnas* 7 (1990): 136–70; Gülru Necipoğlu, "Early-Modern Floral: the Agency of Ornament in Ottoman and Safavid Visual Cultures," in *Histories of Ornament: From Global to Local*, ed. Gülru Necipoğlu and Alina Payne (Princeton, NJ: Princeton University Press, 2016), 132–55.

16 Filiz Çağman and Zeren Tanındı, "Remarks on Some Manuscripts from the Topkapı Palace Treasury in the Context of Ottoman-Safavid Relations," *Muqarnas* 13 (1996): 132–48; Lale Uluç, *Turkman Governors, Shiraz Artisans and Ottoman Collectors: Sixteenth Century Shiraz Manuscripts* (Istanbul: Türkiye Iş Bankası, 2006).

17 Roxburgh, *Persian Album.*

18 Anthony Welch, *Artist for the Shah: Late Sixteenth Century Painting at the Imperial Court of Iran* (New Haven: Yale University Press, 1976); Massumeh

Farhad, "Safavid Single Page Painting 1629–1666" (PhD diss., Harvard University, 1987); Sussan Babaie, Kathryn Babayan, Ina Baghdianz-McCabe, and Massumeh Farhad, *Slaves of the Shah: New Elites of Safavid Iran* (London: IB Tauris, 2004).

19  Sussan Babaie, *Isfahan and its Palaces: Statecraft, Shiʿism, and the Architecture of Conviviality in Early-Modern Iran* (Edinburgh: Edinburgh University Press, 2008); Sussan Babaie, "Frontiers of Visual Taboo: Painted Indecencies in Isfahan," in *Eros and Sexuality in Islamic Art,* ed. Francesca Leoni and Mika Natif (Farnham: Ashgate, 2013), 131–56.

20  Bronwen Wilson, "'Foggie diverse di vestire de'Turchi': Turkish costume illustration and cultural translation," *Journal of Medieval and Early Modern History* 37, no. 1 (2007), 95–138; Jones, "Habits, Holdings, Heterologies"; Olian, "Sixteenth Century Costume Books"; Schick, "Ottoman Costume Albums in a Cross Cultural Context."

21  On Christian communities in Istanbul, see Eric Dursteler, *Venetians in Constantinople: Nation, Identity and Coexistence in the Early Modern Mediterranean* (Baltimore: Johns Hopkins University Press, 2006); Natalie Rothman, "Visualizing a Space of Encounter: Intimacy, Alterity, and Trans-Imperial Perspective in an Ottoman-Venetian Miniature Album," in "Other Places: Ottomans Traveling, Seeing, Writing, Drawing the World. Essays in Honor of Thomas D. Goodrich," part 2, ed. Baki Tezcan and Gottfried Hagen, special issue, *Osmanlı Araştırmaları / Journal of Ottoman Studies* 40 (2012): 39–80; Natalie Rothman, *Brokering Empire: Trans-Imperial Subjects between Venice and Istanbul* (Ithaca: Cornell University Press, 2011); Nirit Ben-Aryeh Debby, "Crusade Propaganda in Word and Image in Early Modern Italy: Niccolò Guidalotto's Panorama of Constantinople (1662)," *Renaissance Quarterly* 67, no. 2 (2014): 503–43.

22  G.R. Bosscha Erdbrink, *At the Threshold of Felicity: Ottoman-Dutch Relations During the Embassy of Cornelis Calkoen at the Sublime Porte 1726–1744* (Ankara: Türk Tarih Kurumu Basımevi, 1975), 4. For a recent art historical analysis of the Dutch side of this relationship, see Claudia Swan, *Rarities of These Lands: Art, Trade and Diplomacy in the Dutch Republic* (Princeton: Princeton University Press, 2021).

23  Sinem Casale, "Iconography of the Gift: Diplomacy and Imperial Self-Fashioning at the Ottoman Court," *The Art Bulletin* 100, no. 1 (2018): 97-123; Bekir Kütükoğlu, *Osmanlı-Iran Siyâsî Münâsebetleri (1578–1612),* 2nd ed. (Istanbul: Istanbul Fetih Cemiyeti, 1993); Cornell H. Fleischer, *Bureaucrat and Intellectual in the Ottoman Empire: The Historian Mustafa Âli* (Princeton: Princeton University Press, 1986), 273–92; Necipoğlu, "Early Modern Floral"; Uluç, *Turkman Governors;* Rhoads Murphey, *Essays on*

*Ottoman Historians and Historiography* (Istanbul: Eren, 2009); and many other sources.

24 Priscilla P. Soucek, "Persian Artists in Mughal India: Influences and Transformations," *Muqarnas* 4 (1987): 166–81; John Seyller, *The Adventures of Hamza: Painting and Storytelling in Mughal India*, with contributions by Wheeler M. Thackston et al. (Washington, DC: Freer Gallery of Art, Arthur M. Sackler Gallery, Smithsonian Institution; Azimuth Editions, London, 2002); Elaine Wright, ed., *Muraqqa': Imperial Mughal Albums from the Chester Beatty Library* (Alexandria, VA: Art Services International, 2008); and many other sources.

25 Casale, *Ottoman Age of Exploration*; Özbaran, *Ottoman Expansion*.

26 Naimur Rahman Farooqi, "Mughal-Ottoman Relations: A Study of Political and Diplomatic Relations between Mughal India and the Ottoman Empire, 1556–1748" (PhD. diss., The University of Wisconsin-Madison, 1986) remains the best source, grounded in primary documents, that discusses these embassies.

27 Halil İnalcık, "The Ottoman Economic Mind and Aspects of the Ottoman Economy," in *Studies of the Economic History of the Middle East*, ed. Michael Cook (Oxford: Oxford University Press, 1970), 207–18, and Suraiya Faroqhi, "Ottoman Cotton Textiles: The Story of a Success That Did Not Last, 1500–1800," in *The Spinning World: A Global History of Cotton Textiles, 1200–1850*, ed. Giorgio Riello and Prasannan Parthasarathi (Oxford: Oxford University Press, 2009).

28 Emine Fetvacı, *Picturing History at the Ottoman Court* (Bloomington, IN: Indiana University Press, 2013), 281–2.

29 Topkapı Palace Museum Library, ms nos. H 2162, H 2137, H 2142, and others.

30 Victoria Finlay, *Color: A Natural History of the Palette* (New York: Random House, 2004), 203–17.

31 Hedda Reindl-Kiel, "Dogs, Elephants, Lions, a Ram and a Rhino on Diplomatic Mission: Animals as Gifts to the Ottoman Court," in *Animals and People in the Ottoman Empire*, ed. Suraiya Faroqhi (Istanbul: Eren, 2010), 279; Alan Mikhail, *The Animal in Ottoman Egypt* (New York: Oxford University Press, 2014), 120.

32 Reindl-Kiel, "Dogs, Elephants, Lions," 280

33 It is interesting to note that a slightly later image in the seventeenth-century Taeschner album containing images made in Istanbul of Istanbul life for European consumers includes the image of an elephant with the same pose (feet placed identically, the tail swaying in exactly the same way) and the same trappings (belled anklets, same-shaped large textile over

its back, straps in the same places, and bells in the same places), but with only one rider, and painted in a more rudimentary style. Might the two images share a model? Or is the Taeschner one possibly based on the *Album of the World Emperor* image? Franz Taeschner, *Alt-Stambuler Hof- und Volksleben, ein türkisches Miniaturenalbum aus dem 17. Jahrhundert* (Hanover: Orient-Buchhandlung H. Lafaire, 1925), plate 27.

34 Mikhail, *The Animal in Ottoman Egypt*, 109–22; Asok Kumar Das, "The Elephant in Mughal Painting," in *Flora and Fauna in Mughal Art*, ed. Som Prekash Verma (Mumbai: Marg Publications, 1999), 36–54.

35 Mikhail, *The Animal in Ottoman Egypt*, 112. See also Metin And, *16. Yüzyılda Istanbul: Kent-Saray-Günlük Yaşam* (Istanbul: Yapı Kredi Yayınları, 2011), 129–32; and Thomas T. Allsen, *The Royal Hunt in Eurasian History* (Philadelphia: University of Pennsylvania Press, 2006), 204.

36 Allsen, *Royal Hunt*, 204.

37 Mikhail, *The Animal in Ottoman Egypt*, 109–14.

38 Mikhail, *The Animal in Ottoman Egypt*, 116.

39 British Museum, 1848, 1125.24.

40 Topkapı Sarayı Müzesi Kütüphanesi, A 3595. For an analysis, see Emine Fetvacı, "The Production of the *Şehnāme-i Selīm Ḫān*," *Muqarnas* 26 (2009): 263–315, and "Others and Other Geographies in the *Şehnāme-i Selīm Ḫān*," *The Journal of Ottoman Studies* 40 (2012): 81–100.

41 For an overview of elephant imagery in Mughal art, see Das, "The Elephant in Mughal Painting."

42 Fetvacı, "Love in the Album of Ahmed I," *Journal of Turkish Studies* 34, no. 2 (Fall 2010): 37–51.

43 Quoted in Mikhail, *The Animal in Ottoman Egypt*, 112–13.

44 Casale, *The Ottoman Age of Exploration*, 182–5.

45 Casale, *The Ottoman Age of Exploration*, 184.

46 For the presence of a lively art market, see Fetvacı, *Album of the World Emperor*, 71–6.

47 Yael Rice, "The Global Aspirations of the Mughal Album," in *Rembrandt and the Inspiration of India*, ed. Stephanie Schrader (Los Angeles: The J. Paul Getty Museum, 2018), 61–77.

48 Fetvacı, *Album of the World Emperor*, 62–9.

49 Marinos Sariyannis, "Mobs, Scamps and Rebels in Seventeenth Century Istanbul." *International Journal of Turkish Studies* 11, no. 1–2 (2005): 1–15.

50 For young men/boys as objects of desire in the Ottoman context, see Andrews and Kalpaklı, *Age of Beloveds*; Selim Kuru, "Sex in the Text"; and Abdulhamit Arvas, "From the Pervert Back to the Beloved: Homosexuality and Ottoman Literary History, 1453–1923," in *The Cambridge History of Gay*

*and Lesbian Literature*, ed. E.L. McCallum and Mikko Tuhkanen (Cambridge, UK: Cambridge University Press, 2014), 145–63.

51 For examples, see those described by Rice, "The Global Aspirations of the Mughal Album," especially figs. 42, 46, and 47.

52 Rice, "Global Aspirations"; Yael Rice, "Jahangir's Dream," *Khamseen: Islamic Art History Online* (16 October 2020); Robert Skelton, "Imperial Symbolism in Mughal Painting," in *Content and Context of Visual Arts in the Islamic World*, ed. by Priscilla Soucek, Carol Bier, and Richard Ettinghausen (University Park, PA: Pennsylvania State University Press, 1988), 177–91; Sumathi Ramaswamy, "Conceit of the Globe in Mughal Visual Practice," *Comparative Studies in Society and History* 49, no. 4 (2007): 751–82; Kavita Singh, *Real Birds in Imagined Gardens: Mughal Painting Between Persia and Europe* (Los Angeles: The Getty Research Institute, 2017), 55–70.

53 Yael Rice, *Agents of Insight: Artists, Books, and Painting in Mughal South Asia* (Seattle: University of Washington Press, forthcoming); Singh, *Real Birds*, 55–70.

54 I am grateful to Giancarlo Casale for this reminder.

55 Rhoads Murphey, *Exploring Ottoman Sovereignty: Tradition, Image and Practice in the Ottoman Imperial Household, 1400–1800* (London: Continuum, 2008), 77–97, carefully points to how the title *sultan* was used only sporadically before 1453. On 97, he writes: "While in the limited context of Safavid-Ottoman relations the Ottomans sometimes invoked their position as the main defenders of the true (that is, Sunni orthodox) religion, it cannot be said that, overall, religious identity or overtly religious epithets played a very important part in Ottoman titulature."

56 Fetvacı, *Album of the World Emperor*, 26.

57 For an explanation of how the claim of Mahdi was made for Ahmed, and the role of this album in that fashioning, see Fetvacı, *Album of the World Emperor*. For Mughal apocalyptic claims, see Azfar Moin, *The Millennial Sovereign: Sacred Kingship and Sainthood in Islam* (New York: Columbia University Press, 2014), and Rice, *Agents of Insight*.

58 For an overview, see Wright, *Muraqqaʿ*.

59 Rice, "Global Aspirations," 62.

60 Elaine Wright, "The Salim Album, c. 1600–1605," 54–67, and Elaine Wright, "The Catalogue," 264–79, both in Wright, ed., *Muraqqaʿ*, discuss the Salim album, which has compositions based on European prints. The Gulshan album appears to be among the earliest containing actual prints, and it dates to c. 1600–18; see Wright, "The Catalogue," 282–7, and Yael Rice, "Lines of Perception: European Prints and the Mughal *Kitābkhāna*," in *Prints in Translation, 1450–1750: Image, Materiality, Space*, ed. Suzanne Karr Schmidt and Edward Wouk (London: Routledge, 2016), 203–24.

61  Yael Rice, "The Brush and the Burin: Mogul Encounters with European Prints," in *Crossing Cultures: Conflict, Migration, and Convergence; The Proceedings of the 32nd International Congress of the History of Art,* ed. Jaynie Anderson (Carlton, Australia: Miegunyah Press–Melbourne University Press, 2009), 305–10; Yael Rice, "Lines of Perception," 203–24.

62  Rice, "Global Aspirations," 66, plate 57.

63  Friederike Weiss, "A Painting from a Jahangirnama and its Compositional Parallels with an Engraving from the Evangelicae Historiae Imagines," in *Arts of Mughal India: Studies in Honor of Robert Skelton,* ed. Rosemary Crill, Susan Stronge, and Andrew Topsfield (London: Victoria and Albert Museum; Ahmedabad: Mapin Publishing, 2004), 119–28.

64  Fetvacı, *Album of the World Emperor,* 140–7.

65  Fetvacı, *Album of the World Emperor,* 146–7.

66  Roxburgh, *Persian Album,* 196–212; Rice, "Global Aspirations," 70, 72; Ebba Koch, "The Mughal Emperor as Solomon, Majnun, and Orpheus, or the Album as a Think Tank for Allegory," *Muqarnas* 27 (2010): 277–311; Milo Cleveland Beach, "The Mughal Painter Abu'l Hasan and Some English Sources for His Style," *Journal of the Walters Art Gallery* 38 (1980): 7–33.

67  Milo Cleveland Beach, "Muraqqaʿ-i Gulshan: The Inscriptions," in *No Tapping Around Philology: A Festschrift in Honor of Wheeler McIntosh Thackston Jr.'s 70ᵗʰ Birthday,* ed. Alireza Korangy and Daniel J. Sheffield (Wiesbaden: Harrassowitz Verlag, 2014), 439–40.

68  Fetvacı, *Album of the World Emperor,* 94.

69  Elaine Wright, "The Salim Album, c. 1600–1605," in Wright, *Muraqqaʿ,* 59.

70  Milo Cleveland Beach, "Jahangir's Album: Some Clarifications," in Crill, Stronge, and Topsfield, *Arts of Mughal India,* 115.

71  J.P. Losty, "Dating the Dara Shukuh Album: the Floral Evidence," in *The Mughal Empire from Jahangir to Shah Jahan,* ed. Ebba Koch in collaboration with Ali Anooshahr (Mumbai: Marg, 2019), 246–87, especially 247.

72  Sunil Sharma, "The City of Beauties in the Indo-Persian Poetic Landscape," *Comparative Studies of South Asia, Africa and the Middle East* 24, no. 2 (2004): 74, 75.

73  Agah Sırrı Levend, *Türk Edebiyatında Şehrengizler ve Şehrengizlerde Istanbul* (Istanbul: Istanbul Fethi Derneği, 1958), 16–17, suggests that Nesihi's *şehrengiz* is the first Ottoman example of the genre, and dates to just before the author's death in 1512. Sunil Sharma, in "The City of Beauties," 73–4, and "'If there is a paradise on Earth, it is Here': Urban Ethnography in Indo-Persian Poetic and Historical Texts," in *Forms of Knowledge in Early Modern Asia: Explorations in the Intellectual history of India and Tibet, 1500–1800,* ed. Sheldon Pollock (Durham, NC: Duke University Press, 2011),

240–56, delineates the reference to the quotidian urban world in Persian lyric poetry written by elite as well as urban poets. Michele Bernardini, "The masnavi-shahrashubs as Town Panegyrics: An International Genre in Islamic Mashriq," in *Narrated Space in the Literature of the Islamic World*, ed. by Roxanne Haag-Higuchi and Christian Szyska (Wiesbaden: Harrassowitz, 2001), 84; he also gives Western examples of town odes from the late sixteenth and seventeenth centuries and suggests this may have been a parallel development.

74  For an overview of Ottoman literature of this period, see Hatice Aynur, "Ottoman Literature," 481–520. For the tendency to focus on this-worldly beloveds, see Selim S. Kuru, "Naming the Beloved in Ottoman Turkish Gazel – the Case of Ishak Çelebi (d. 1537–8)," in *Ghazal as World Literature II: From Literary Genre to a Great Tradition: The Ottoman Gazel in Context*, ed. Angelika Neuwirth, Michael Hess, Judith Pfeiffer, and Börte Sagaster (Wurzbürg: Erlon Verlag Wurzbürg, 2006), 163–73.

75  Nile Green, ed. *The Persianate World: The Frontiers of a Eurasian Lingua Franca* (Oakland: University of California Press, 2014); Selim Kuru, "The Literature of Rum: The Making of a Literary Tradition (1450–1600)," in *The Cambridge History of Turkey*, vol. 2, ed. Suraiya Faroqhi and Kate Fleet (Cambridge, UK: Cambridge University Press, 2013), 548–92; Paul Losensky, *Welcoming Fighānī: Imitation and Poetic Individuality in the Safavid Mughal Ghazal* (Costa Mesa, CA: Mazda Publishers, 1998).

76  Rice, "Global Aspirations," 70.

# chapter ten

# World Building, the Folger Folios, and the University of British Columbia

PATRICIA BADIR

The Rare Books and Special Collections (RBSC) Library of the University of British Columbia (UBC) opened its doors for the first time in 1960. The University's most valuable collections would now be stored in the new wing of the library, named for Walter Koerner, a British Columbia (BC) businessman and philanthropist who made his fortune in the mid-twentieth century in the province's booming forestry industry. Koerner marked the occasion by donating his copy of the Second Folio publication of Shakespeare's plays (1632) to the new special collections room. A special guest was also present: Louis B. Wright, the librarian of the Folger Shakespeare Library in Washington, DC, was there to hand over a set of four Shakespeare Folios, including Folger First Folio 14 (F.1. no. 14, 1623). The volumes would be placed on "indefinite loan" in the fledging collection and, as a measure of the significance of the gift, Wright would the following day receive the University's highest recognition – a doctoral degree *honoris causa*.

This chapter takes a closer look at the Folger loan in order to consider how early modern things – in this case four seventeenth-century books – helped to build modern universities. Bronwen Wilson and Angela Vanhaelen have advocated that "the close study of made things can reveal what grand narratives of globalization sometimes conceal, providing opportunities for a finer-grained analysis of the ambivalent dynamics of early modern worldmaking." This proposition has directed attention, amongst early modernists, towards the movement of materials and artefacts across borders while also taking note of the creative experiments, artistic and otherwise, that both activated and responded to these movements.[1] I want to build upon this idea of "worldmaking" or "mondialization," by shifting from the early modern to the modern and to an example in which "Renaissance" world-building productivity – as it was reconceptualized in the twentieth century – was harnessed in the shaping of academic worlds in North America.[2] The story of the UBC-Folger Folios, I argue, shows how the Shakespearean things we find in university collections resonate with a world-building creativity that qualifies or at least complicates narratives of colonialism and globalization to which the exportation of Shakespeare can often be bound.

If my discussion of the Folio loan shifts this volume's focus away from the early modern to read seventeenth-century objects outside their time, it can do so because the global trajectories of these books were anticipated by their makers. The most valuable of the four books on loan to UBC was, of course, *Mr. William Shakespeare's Comedies, Histories, & Tragedies*, containing thirty-six plays compiled by Shakespeare's colleagues, John Heminge and Henry Condell, and published in 1623 by the stationer Edward Blount and the publishers William and Isaac Jaggard. Ben Jonson was one of the first to acknowledge the publication milestone, famously commending the timeless humanism of Shakespeare's art ("He was not of an age, but for all time!") as materialized in single physical object:

> Thou art a moniment, without a tombe,
> And art aliue still, while thy Booke doth liue,
> And we have wits to read, and praise to giue.[3]

Indeed, from the very beginning, the volume's status as an object associated with Shakespeare's person – or what Adam Hooks has vividly described as his "corpus" or his "remains" – has accompanied our sense of the volume's contribution to literary history.[4]

On the other hand, as Emma Smith has shown, the volume was also, from its very beginnings, a marker of prestige – an indication, on the part of its first owners, "of aspirational self-presentation, interpersonal bonds, and luxury shopping."[5] While the mania for buying and selling First Folios does not really begin until the nineteenth century, we find Heminge and Condell, in the volume's first pages, encouraging their "great variety of readers" not just to "read and censure" the plays but also to "buy" the book, cementing the Folio's commodity status within the early modern publishing economy. Even though the book is not particularly rare – there are 235 known copies, a third of them housed in the Folger Shakespeare Library[6] – they have become, as Smith describes, "things to be read, imposed, gifted, traded, deified: thinged."[7] This kind of rarefication acquired a very specific valence in nineteenth- and early twentieth-century North America as the Folios were purchased by ambitious and well-monied collectors as well as by aspiring public and private library collections. If, as Stephen Greenblatt has famously argued, the collected works became "widely acknowledged as the central literary achievement of English culture" and indeed "a fetish of Western civilization," then the possession of a First Folio was a marker par excellence of the kind of stature and distinction generally reserved for the finest of Old World collections. In this context the Shakespeare Folio functions, as Jyotsna Singh argues, as "a key signifier within colonial discourse, while demarcating the familiar binaries: barbarism and civilization, tradition and modernity."[8]

Thus, the loan of the Folios would have been acknowledged as a significant milestone for an aspirational university library claiming a place as credible research institution in the same league as best universities in the world. The possession of the Folios would lend to UBC the antique lustre of Oxbridge or at least that of the University of Toronto.[9] However, while the UBC-Folger arrangement's entanglement in the discourses of British colonialism is at the centre of my account of the books' journey from DC to BC and back, as I move through this story's archive, I want to be attentive to Hooks, who, in taking on the question of the First Folio as fetish, discourages us from thinking of the book as providing a stable and uncomplicated Shakespeare: "to simply accept a singular version of Shakespeare," he writes, "is to neglect what the Folio excludes, to misunderstand how and why it was produced, and to misjudge what it actually accomplished."[10] While the Folios' stay at UBC is a story of a young Western Canadian institution hoping to enrich its reputation through the acquisition of a particularly significant set of seventeenth-century books, I argue that the tale also brings to light threads of tactical resistance to these narratives, as a hybrid Shakespeare, at once British and American, helps to disclose the critical engagements of the humanities within a growing research institution that was, in 1960, casting its gaze upon the new geo-political order brought into being by the Cold War. The story of the Folios is, in other words, bound to the story of the early days of the culture wars.

We don't know who purchased Folger F.1. no.14 from its publishers in 1623, though we know that they would have been reasonably wealthy. We also don't know how often the book changed hands in the centuries that followed, though again, First Folios acquired greater value as book collecting became a more popular pastime and book auctions arose in response to a new demand for prestige acquisitions.

The worth of First Folios continued to increase into the nineteenth century, at which point books begin to leave England for the US.[11] F.1. no.14 crossed the Atlantic in 1894 when it was purchased for £750, for the collection of Miss Abby E. Pope (neé Hanscom) of Brooklyn, NY, by Ellis & White of London. Pope's library was a significant collection of seven to ten thousand volumes, including the other three Folios. Henry Clay Folger, president of Standard Oil of New York, voracious collector of Shakespeareana, and eventual founder of the Folger Shakespeare Library, attempted to purchase F.1. no.14 just a year after Pope acquired it, but Pope's entire library had, by then, been purchased by Dodd, Mead, & Company.[12] The four Folios were then sold to Robert Hoe (1839–1909) and it was from him (through the agency of J.O. Wright) that Folger purchased F1. no. 14 alone in 1896.[13] The other three volumes that completed the Folger-UBC loan were Second Folio no. 30 (1632); Third Folio no. 19 (1663) and Fourth Folio no. 20 (1685).[14]

The story of the UBC loan begins with Wright's "happy thought of placing sets [of Folios] on permanent loan in important libraries in various parts of the world."[15] The first library to be honoured with such a gift was the University of St. Andrews in Scotland. The second (and last) was the University of British Columbia. Apart from Wright's statement, in his annual report for 1959–60, that "the most spectacular single action of the Library" for that year was "the placing of two sets of our seventeenth-century Folios at St. Andrews University in Scotland and at the University of British Columbia in Canada," nothing about the negotiations that led up to the loan is to be found in either the UBC or the Folger archives.[16]

Documentary evidence pertaining to the loan transaction begins in 1960 with a letter to UBC president N.A.M. MacKenzie, which notes that the Trustees of Amherst College, who were the governors of the Folger Library until 2005, had approved the presentation of the set of Folios to the UBC library "that they may be exhibited in the library; and that they may be consulted by scholars engaged in serious research requiring the use of these original works."[17] Mackenzie's response to the trustees states "how very grateful we are for this most generous gesture" and that "these editions will be a source of great interest to students and faculty and that they will attract scholars from other universities in both Canada and the United States."[18] This account suggests that the Folios' potential for UBC lay in their ability to foster a culture of research in the humanities both within and outside of UBC. Everyone will want to learn from these "original works," the Folger library assumes, though what this "serious research" would entail is more elusive – the books' arrival predates the new editorial scholarship of the later twentieth century as well as the rise of book history and the new materialisms. The Folios happened on UBC while Shakespeareans were reading the myth-infused archetypal criticism of Northrop Frye, the historicism of E.M.W. Tillyard, and the New Criticism of F.R. Leavis. Though scholars would have to wait until 1968 for a complete facsimile of the First Folio, Shakespeare's "original" plays were, by 1960, readily available in hundreds of scholarly and student editions, so it feels safe to wager that, at least on the surface of things, the books' principal appeal to the students and scholars of UBC would come from their enchanting ability to materialize the "origin" of the plays – Shakespeare's mind – within the walls of their new special collections room. If Shakespeare had arrived, well then so had UBC.

The public-facing presentation of the Folios, for which there are extensive records, expresses the intention of the loan in precisely the terms we might expect. For instance, the press release, dated 21 October 1960, twins humanist education with the vestiges of English imperialism:

> The Folger Library had decided to place the four Folios on permanent loan because of its interest in the diffusion of humanistic learning and its desire to place a few of its most significant duplicate volumes where they will serve as a symbol of the Folger Library's concern for learning in the English-speaking world.[19]

In his speech at the opening of the new UBC Library, Wright states that UBC had been selected for the loan because Folger wanted to present the volumes to a "region of the British Commonwealth, where they might be needed, where they would serve as a symbol of the common heritage and mutual interests of the English-speaking peoples," and it was hoped that the books would serve to remind generations of UBC students and faculty of "the Folger Library's concern for the history of British civilization in those centuries that saw the spread of the English-speaking peoples throughout the world."[20] The invocation of the British Commonwealth is not in itself surprising – as Singh and others have noted, Shakespeare was a powerful tool of Empire – and it would take at least another generation of scholarship for Shakespeareans to acknowledge the accumulated mythology that "assumed into existence" (a concept borrowed from Dipesh Chakrabarty) both Shakespeare's Englishness and his universality.[21] Wright's uncritical statement in part reflects what Leah Marcus has articulated as the peculiar fact that "the more Shakespeare's texts became immersed in the project of civilizing conquered peoples, the less he was imagined as even incipiently complicit in the colonial project."[22] Shakespeare was "a symbol of the common heritage and mutual interests of the English-speaking peoples," and this heritage and these interests were part and parcel of European "humanistic learning," in Wright's terms, at its universalizing best. However, what resonates as different here is that the icon of Empire was being handed to a Canadian university not by a British institution but by an American one. Why British Columbia was chosen over Ontario remains unclear. Perhaps "British" Columbia was understood, by Wright and the Folger trustees, to be more hospitable to Shakespeare's legacy. Or perhaps UBC was perceived to be more provincial than the University of Toronto, which had location, history, and reputation on its side. In any case, the loan is a fascinating example of the degree to which Canadian "translations," to borrow another formulation from Chakrabarty, of the mythologies of British imperialism become complicated by their proximity to emerging narratives of American cultural hegemony as colonialism becomes intertwined with the resource-based economies of global capitalism[23]

It was the intention of the Folger Library to leave the Folios "on deposit at the University of British Columbia indefinitely," assuming that they were properly cared for and of enduring use – but the terms of the loan were always conditional. Wright's original letter clearly specified that "if at any time the Folger Library should need these four volumes, or any one of them, it is understood that they can be recalled."[24] And, indeed, twenty-five years later they were. On 22 April 1986, Folger Director Werner Gundersheimer, wrote the following to UBC President K.G. Pedersen:

The Trustees of Amherst College, who administer the Folger Library, have indicated that it is now an appropriate moment to recall the Folios from loan…. We know that the University of British Columbia has watched over the Folios with great care. We hope that the volumes have fulfilled their intended purpose in helping to stimulate interest in Shakespeare studies at the University.[25]

A copy of Wright's letter was enclosed. A month later the new University President, David Strangeway, responded, observing that UBC had been "greatly enriched by [the Folios'] presence" and that "we have, of course, taken very good care of them." The letter concludes by stating that University Librarian, Douglas McInnes, will make arrangements for the books' transport in due course.[26] On 9 October, McInnes, in response to shipping instructions sent from the Folger, writes:

> We will return the volumes promptly, though with great regret. We have enjoyed having them at the University and, frankly, expected to have them available indefinitely. They have been very useful in stimulating interest in Shakespeare studies and we are grateful to the Folger Shakespeare Library for lending them to us.[27]

Gundersheimer's recall letter concludes by noting that "happily" UBC library readers now have access to the Norton Facsimile "and can become acquainted with the textual problems of the First Folio in a way which was not possible twenty-five years ago,"[28] but a facsimile has neither the magic nor the prestige of a Folio, and the UBC librarians were clearly upset. They held onto the books as long as they could, finally returning them sometime in early 1987.[29]

The discussion between the Folger trustees that prompted the recall is just as mysterious as the decision to send them to UBC in the first place. The only evidence in the UBC or the Folger archives of concern of any sort lies back in Wright's annual report for 1959–60, in which he states obliquely: "For a variety of reasons, which I shall explain orally, it would seem desirable to attempt no further loans for the present."[30] Apparently something about the arrangement was, from the onset, problematic.[31] What we do know, however, is that the Folger had a history of moving its most valuable books about. For instance, a substantial portion of the library's Shakespeare collection was, toward the end of the Second World War, sent to Amherst College, where it was stored in a vault until peacetime. And then again in 1950, when DC was perceived to be under threat of Russian nuclear attack, the Folger Trustees returned a number of Folios to Amherst for further safe keeping.[32] The Cold War history of the Folger Folios warrants deeper study than I can undertake here; but some gesture to that history brings to the foreground the competing affective bonds that were being formed around these early modern artefacts in the late 1950s and 60s and in so doing provides useful context for the Folger-UBC exchange.

Wright's correspondence files from this period are an arresting account of nuclear threat from the perspective of a man charged with the protection of America's Shakespeare. "The world situation is getting no better fast," writes Wright to Paul D. Weathers, the Treasurer of Amherst College, in December of 1950, "and we are making such advance plans as we can here against possible crisis." From Wright's perspective, the situation faced by the library in 1950 differed radically from that faced in the 40s. The feeling was that the conflict would go on indefinitely, which meant that relocating the entirety of the library's resources was unfeasible. "The emergency is going to be with us the rest of our lives," concludes Wright, "and a library can't pack up and go out of business because there is danger. We shall simply have to do what European libraries have done for years – gamble on survival."[33]

The Folger archives also include a substantial collection of letters written to rare books librarians at all the major US libraries, enquiring as to their plans for their collections in the face of nuclear war. In every instance, Wright's colleagues respond that there is little or nothing to be done. Libraries are a public resource and they simply cannot close their doors indefinitely. Wright clearly concurred for, in a report on measures to protect Folger resources, he draws attention to the library's reputation for the miserly accumulation of Shakepeareana and the possible financial consequences of long-term sequestration of its materials.

> Because Mr. Folger kept his book in storage during his life-time, he had an unfavorable press throughout the world and was called a 'miser of books.' We have not yet overcome this impression abroad or at home. Because the Folger alone among libraries stored the bulk of its research materials in World War II, it was severely criticized. If we hide away all of our resources again for an indefinite period, the inevitable repercussions will be serious. We cannot overlook the seriousness of abandoning an educational program upon which our tax exemption must be justified.[34]

Folger trustee William Heller agreed with Wright by pointing to the library's humanistic role in a world threated by nuclear annihilation.

> When a collection like the Folger is put into the public domain, tax exempt, its custodians are also responsible for seeing that it is put to the public use. The Folger's responsibility is to promote the study in this country of the historical background of the English-Speaking peoples everywhere. The present is no time to suspend such study anywhere. On the contrary there has

never been a time, I believe when there was better reason for keeping it up
even at some risk. To be sure we are now faced by new and terrible physical
dangers. But you and I will probably never know a time when such dangers
will be entirely absent. [35]

Heller's commitment to the Folger's public in the face of nuclear annihilation is palpable despite his inability to see the colonial violence
shaping the backbone of the "background" he sought to protect. Shakespeare's work, published globally in modern editions, would certainly
have survived even a devastating attack on the Folger, but for Heller and
Wright it was critical to make sure that the antique repositories of genius
lived on, because without them Shakespeare's still-living vitality would
be greatly diminished, at least in America. We see here an illustration of
what David McKitterick calls the "awakening realization" on the part of
librarians "that as private collections become national ones, so responsibilities change and became public," creating a tension between security
and access.[36] In response to this realization, a laborious process of mi-
crofilming unique volumes began at the Folger as duplicate volumes,
including a number of First Folios, were sent box by box to Amherst.[37]
Shakespeare was on the move for the second time in a decade, but this
time some portion of the Folger bounty would be left behind in order
to shore America up as it stood perched on the brink of Armageddon.
Measures were taken to bomb-proof the Folger building so as to protect
the books that remained behind. Wright bought himself a "couple of
cots" for the basement of the Folger "because if things get really bad,
some of us are going to stay here day and night."[38] This state of house
arrest lasted until 1959, when the material sent to Amherst was finally
restored to the new wing of the library.[39]

This story of dispersal and retrieval is relevant here because the 1960
Folger-UBC loan appears to have been part of library's attempt, despite
increasing international tension in the lead-up to the Vietnam war, to
turn a new leaf, to enter a global age of Shakespeare by sharing rather
than sequestering its priceless early modern artefacts. A library report of
1959 recommends that rare books in storage at Amherst be returned after the completion of a new addition to the building that could store, in
logical sequence, "the great collection of editions of Shakespeare." The
same report notes growing international interest in the library ("scholars
from Europe, Asia, and Africa [are] constantly at work in [the] collections") and proposes, for the first time on record, that UBC, Toronto,
and St. Andrews be considered as possible destinations for loans.[40] The

archive surrounding the UBC loan thus unfolds as a network of relationships that positions the Folger as a growing public institution, expanding to serve an increasingly global interest in Shakespeare, while also unbinding itself from the legacy of Cold War geopolitics.

However, the Folger's itinerant Folios would not be so easily unbound. At the ceremony for the UBC graduating class of 1960 – the event which in part brought Wright and his Folios to UBC – University Chancellor Albert E. Grauer invoked the Cold War context:

> Since the Second World War the extent to which the Soviet Union has used higher education as a means of building a modern society and as an instrument in the waging of the cold war has become apparent. A physics laboratory is a more strategic asset than a battleship, and the shock troops are no longer the soldier armed with a rifle but the scientist in his laboratory and the technician in his factory. ... A modern state cannot be built without a sound educational foundation and a modern struggle, especially in developing countries, will be won not so much as on the playing fields of public schools as in the lecture rooms of universities.[41]

Already enmeshed in a Cold War history of their own, when the Folger books arrived at UBC they instantly became associated with the university's militaristic reorientation towards STEM. Grauer's speech identifies graduates as a new affluent class of professionals no longer forced to abandon their education at an early age to tend the fields or fight for King and Country. But this new demographic should probably not, Graver concludes, orient themselves towards the humanities. While he states that "the principles of experiment in science and experience in the humanities" must remain among the universities' priorities, he concludes his speech (rather ironically) with French author André Maurois' statement: "It is easier to produce ten volumes of philosophical writing than to put one principle into practice."[42] As the university entrenched itself on the STEM side of the culture wars, the "experience" of the humanities gave way to the urgency of "practice."[43]

Following his keynote address on 28 October, Wright would participate in a panel discussion on "The Future of Our Universities" chaired by John L. Keyes, the director of the forestry giant MacMillan Bloedel. David Meyers, dean of Applied Science, and C.P. Snow were Wright's co-panelists.[44] Snow, the English novelist and physical chemist, was in the spotlight having just published his 1959 lecture "The Two Cultures," in which he bemoaned the hostility between literary intellectuals on the one side and physical scientists on the other, pointing ominously to the "gulf of mutual incomprehension" between the two that resulted in a "sheer loss to us all." It's not difficult to imagine Snow mediating between the driving forces of technological progress – embodied at UBC in the person of the dean of Applied Science – and the civilizing presence of Shakespeare in Folio form accompanied by its guardian, the librarian of the Folger Library. The solution, Snow argued, was education. "It is obligatory for us ... to look at our education with fresh eyes," he writes. "Isn't it time we began? The danger is, we have been brought up to think as though we had all the time in the world. We have very little time," he concludes, "so little that I dare not guess at it."[45] Snow's sense of the culture war between scientists and literary intellectuals would come under fire almost immediately for its uncritical championing of science, which "had the future in its bones" despite its insensitivity to, and indeed ignorance of, what he called "traditional culture."[46] In fact, Snow's characterization of literary intellectuals as "luddites," relentless in their dissatisfaction with modernity and tenacious in their critique of progress, would put up the backs of literary critics, beginning with F.R. Leavis, for generations to come.[47]

Yet the urgency in Snow's appeal for educational reform – and the role of the humanities within that reform – implicates the Folios directly in the developing understanding of the humanities in general, and English literature in particular, as the part of a University designed to train, but also civilize, Cold War bomb builders.[48] Later that same year UBC President N.A.M. MacKenzie would continue to marshal the authority of the European Renaissance by channelling François Rabelais in his assertion that at moments of great worldmaking, the humanities must form the conscience of progress. "It is imperative," he writes, "that the traditional studies of history, literature, language, philosophy not be neglected. We may well gain the whole world and yet lose that world as well as our own soul, unless those enriching and sustaining studies which explain Man, his actions, his dreams, his yearnings and his aspirations continue to develop harmoniously and coincidentally side by side with the natural and social sciences."[49] If the world could be "gained" by the globalizing forces of science and technology, it would have to be enriched and sustained by the humanities in general and Shakespeare, in the material form of "original" books, in particular. It is difficult to imagine a more succinct articulation of the complicity of four seventeenth-century artefacts in the formation of the neo-liberal university, itself bound to the Cold War logics of capitalism and globalism.

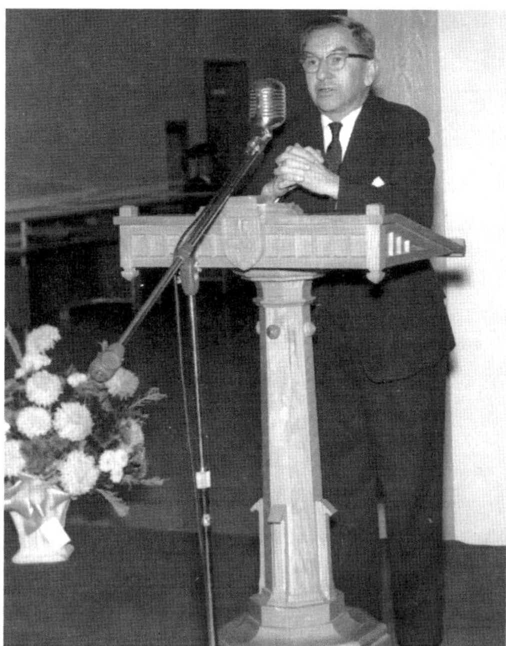

Figure 10.1. *Louis B. Wright Speaking at Opening of Walter Koerner Wing in Main Library*, 1960. 9.5 x 12 cm. UBC 23.1/427–1. University of British Columbia Archives Photograph Collection, Vancouver

On the other hand, Wright – the man who slept in his library through the darkest days of the Cold War – knew well that new worlds could not be built without destroying old ones. For him, the role of Folio volumes – and by extension the humanities – was to remind us of the violence at the core of all world-building initiatives. The librarian's remarks at the opening of RBSC are something of a provocation, I think, and are thus worth citing at length:

The growth of Libraries in the western hemisphere in a little more than a century represents a tremendous dispersal of books from the Old World to the New. This sort of transfer of cultural materials has gone on since the world began. In an earlier time, conquerors brought back jewels, carvings, sculptures, pictures, and manuscripts from the civilized countries that they subjugated. In a later day, the artifacts of civilization followed economic power. Wealthy men became collectors and bought the objects of older civilizations that they admired and wanted.

This passage is best glossed by Ana Maria Fernandez, a recent UBC English student who encountered Wright's speech while working on the provenance of the Koerner Second Folio. She writes that the Folio acquisition "now seems much more of a socio-political move within the world of academia – a symbol of exclusivity, status, and prestige, rather than an instrument of learning made available to all."[50] She is right, of course: the Folger Folios' trajectory from England to the US and then to Canada, as Wright infers, is located within a history of the movement of cultural capital from the Old World to the New World and then on to a new(ish) university. But before Wright makes this point, he first gestures rather presciently to the export of artefacts from "subjugated" nations that he takes pains to describe as "civilized." Wright, perhaps not surprisingly for a librarian, shows a materialist's attention to the circulation of objects in the world and in particular to those objects that moved from colony to colonial power, flagging the destructive power relations undergirding a nascent global capitalism. Wright isn't exactly critical of his books' trajectory, asserting that anyone who might object to the transfer of the jewels of the Empire to the coffers of the profiteers of the New World should "take the trouble to visit the British Museum," where one could admire British custodianship of "treasures from older civilizations." Nevertheless, he understands the Folios' history in terms that Nicholas Thomas would describe as "entangled," a word that now carries with it connotations of both generation and destruction, building and ruin.[51] When Wright begins to describe a subsequent stage of Western expansion and domination, in which a new generation of North American entrepreneurs, men like Henry Clay Folger and Walter Koerner, would leverage the dividends of New World resource extraction to purchase rarefied pre-modern objects that signalled the assurance, the confidence, and the lofty culture of European settlers, he acknowledges that any glory the Old World books bring to UBC is inextricably tied to the exploitation of unceded territories and the genocide that accompanied early modern colonization.

The final stage of Wright's history is inaugurated by the loan of the Shakespeare Folios, which would facilitate the development of a new research collection at a flagship provincial university. "Great as are Harvard, Yale, Columbia and Princeton," Wright opines, "they cannot provide sufficient leadership," thus "one of the most significant educational developments taking place is the advance of the provincial universities to positions of prominence and eventual influence," for "not even the Establishment can subsist indefinitely on the supply of leaders it gets from the older universities."[52] The transfer of institutional authority from America to Canada, Wright asserts, makes a claim for the importance of the humanities at the very beginning of the rise to prominence of the STEM disciplines. Understood in this context, the Folio loan becomes evidence of tactical resilience – a marshalling of cultural capital on behalf of the humanities, already at odds with the mandate of the "new" university.[53] Such an argument lends some currency to University Librarian Neil Harlow's statement that "the placing of the folio recognizes the importance of the University of B.C. in Canadian higher education ... and emphasizes particularly our work in the humanities."[54] When they arrived at their new temporary home, at the edge of a world still considered to be lacking the authority that comes with European history, the Shakespeare Folios had their work cut out for them.

Wilson and Vanhaelen argue that early modern "assemblages" or artefacts "resulting from and contributing to global flows of things" can "set in motion possibilities for imagination and reorientations – for thinking in new ways." They make the point that, during the early modern period, interactions between objects and their handlers "gave rise to often unanticipated and new ways of crafting and understanding an increasingly interconnected world."[55] The point I am making here is that these objects continue to do this kind of work over time, surfacing at critical junctures in history where they subtly shift the nature of our conversations. The fact that the Folios, themselves artefacts of Old World imperialism, would be housed in the newly opened special collections room of a library named for a man whose philanthropy and passion for rare books were made possible by his success in the BC forestry industry locates F.1. no. 14 and its companion volumes where they had been for centuries – at the nexus of colonialism, imperialism, and capitalism. But, as Wilson and Vanhaelen argue, "the close study of made things accordingly can reveal what grand narratives of globalization often attempt to conceal." The Folios ask us to think about "the artistic and material aspects of global interconnectivity" and, in so doing, provide us with an opportunity to see the complexity of UBC's colonial legacy by considering "the differences that accrue to objects and the manifold perspectives that they afford."[56] In other words, as objects fostering connections between institutions and like-minded individuals, it can be argued that the Folios were part of something like resistance or possibly even protest.

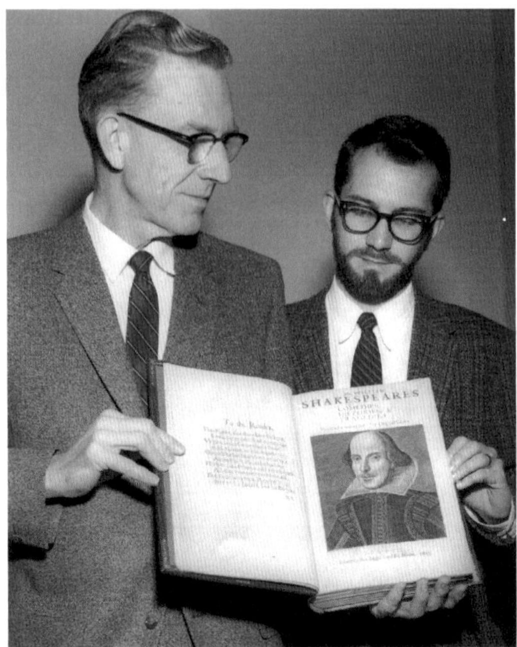

Figure 10.2. *Basil Stuart-Stubbs and Neal Harlow with First Folio of Shakespeare* [P], 1 January 1960. UBC 3.1/720-2. University of British Columbia Archives Photograph Collection, Vancouver

In his first annual report to the University in 1960, the first director of UBC's Rare Books and Special Collections Library, Basil Stuart-Stubbs, begins by proposing that most theories of history are "unreliable and we find that the only universals that can safely be used are the most basic and easy to discern." One of the basic universals, he contends, is "that it is man's nature to collect and protect the records he makes" and it is this "universal desire which accounts for the long history of the library as an institution, and ultimately for the existence of rare book rooms or special collection divisions." Stuart-Stubbs is making the point that McKitterick articulates so succinctly: "libraries manage memory."[57] Stuart-Stubbs is also laying bare the tension between security and protection on the one hand and access on the other that forms the core of a library's responsibilities – the very tension with which Wright also grappled as he sought to strike the right balance between protecting Shakespeare and sharing him with an increasingly global community of visitors and scholars. Stuart-Stubbs proceeds to describe his fledgling collection as dominated by pre-1900 Canadiana and Pacific Coast history, with the remainder of the collection consisting of "a miscellany of books notable for their beauty, rarity or provenance; outstanding in the category are the four Shakespeare folios deposited here by the Folger Library as an act of consecration in October 1960." McKitterick warns us that words like "rare" and "beauty" and "provenance" are never chosen randomly to describe books, and they beg us to question "how our printed inheritance, and hence memory, should be selected, managed, made available, used and preserved."[58] The librarian's report, in this sense, deliberately separates and distinguishes Old World "inheritances" from the acquisitions preserving a more local and recent history. However, while Stuart-Stubbs may not have seen the connection between Canadiana, Pacific Coast history, and Shakespeare, I do. Tracing the Folio's movements from Old World Britain to British Columbia challenges those of us who use this collection – particularly those of us trained as historicists – to think about why it matters that we study Shakespeare at UBC – a provincial university located in a place we still rather strangely refer to as the Pacific Northwest, upon land unceded by the xʷməθkʷəy̓əm (Musqueam) people, in a nation, a province, and city that regularly congratulate themselves on their histories of tolerance and progressive politics.

The Folios' Vancouver-bound journey, and their relationship to this unfolding history, plays out in a larger arena by signalling Canada's complicated geopolitical position, in 1960, between the rock of the British Empire and the hard place of the United States. As Phillip Buckner and R. Douglas Francis have pointed out, we are beyond thinking of Canada's transition from colony to nation in simple, linear terms. Even after the Second World War, the belief (at least in English Canada) in the potency of the British Empire remained strong.[59] On the other hand, the Suez Crisis of 1956 forced Canadians to reassess their nation's role in international affairs as the situation in the Middle East prompted heated debate over the country's relationship with both Britain and the US. Canada emerged from the crisis with a new identity – that of the peacekeeper.[60] This image of Canada as an affable nation largely recognized for its diplomacy may have well have consolidated the Folger's decision to send the Folios to Vancouver. However, Brian D. Palmer's work on Canada in the 1960s has illustrated the degree to which this identity operated as a national myth disguising the increasingly powerful link between Canada and the US. While Canadians may have "cherished the illusion" that, as a middle party, they were "immune from the political and cultural fallout" of the Cold War, Canadian identity, "inasmuch as it was tied to middle-power peacekeeping, was a Cold War project of continental integration dressed in the narcissisms of small difference and dependent on considerations of international trade and the dollars it garnered."[61] Canadian collusion with the political and economic agendas of the US would, as Palmer illustrates, become irrefutable in the later 1960s as Canada became complicit in the US war in Vietnam.

There is yet another side to this account, though – one that makes it all the more important that the Folios came to Vancouver. If the books can be considered Old World travellers crossing the BC border in the company of military industrialists, politicians, diplomats, and trade negotiators, we should also take account of the draft dodgers and military deserters leaving the US to seek asylum in Vancouver.[62] The activism associated with cross-border migration would join forces with fledgling organizations like Greenpeace in order to cement British Columbia's place at the centre of the anti-American, the anti-war, and the environmentalist movements.[63] At UBC there would be considerable resistance to American inroads into Canadian autonomy. The English Department would develop a robust program in Canadian literature, supported by library acquisitions like the volumes of pre-1900 Canadiana and Pacific Coast history that Stuart-Stubbs mentions in his report.[64] Faculty and students would become heavily engaged in disarmament activity – one example of which was the formation of the UBC Nuclear Disarmament Club in November of 1960 under the presidency of Michael Audain (who would go on to found the BC Civil Liberties Union). Top among the club's founding principles was its opposition to the presence of nuclear weapons on Canadian soil.[65] As Shakespeare settled into his new home in RBSC alongside the fire insurance maps of turn-of-the-century Vancouver, student unrest percolated outside the library's doors.

Thinking through an archive that refuses to entirely reveal the story of the Folios allows for the intriguing possibility that the involvement of Shakespearean things in the making of new worlds (and new universities) might be about more than the shifting of fortune and cultural capital between business men, nations, and institutions in a manner entirely consistent with both colonialism and late capitalism. In their emphasis on creativity, Wilson and Vanhaelen have made no attempt to bury the iconoclasm, the environmental destruction, and the genocide that have been historically connected to colonialism and to globalization. "Our emphasis on creativity," they write "takes into account how the process of making worlds is historically connected with the devastation of worlds." But in their attention to the correlative process of "mondialization," they strive to understand interrelated process of "making, unmaking, and re-making worlds."[66] This premise is a useful modulation, I think.

As I wrap this story up it, it occurs to me that little has been said about the thirty-six plays that are to be found within the Shakespeare Folios, eighteen of which would not be known today were it not for their appearance in the 1623 first edition. Shakespeare's "art" (to use Jonson's phrase) seems to have no bearing on this discussion, which reads four early modern books as ciphers for twentieth-century geo-politics and culture wars. And yet, as Brian Cummings trenchantly points out, all modern encounters with these books – including my own – are characterized by "an avowed sense of the power and mystery involved in things as objects."[67] F.1. no. 14 and its companion Folios could not have been written by anybody at any time, and their origins and their authorship haunts our library in ambivalent ways. As mobile artefacts from a world distant from our own, penned by a figure who continues to tower over English literary history, they provide an occasion for us, as located moderns faced with both the human and environmental costs of globalization, to complicate our understanding of the history of our discipline and our university. Shakespeare's journey from the seventeenth century to the twentieth century, and from England to Washington to Vancouver, illustrates the degree to which a four-hundred-year confrontation between materiality and mobility that was a result of the forces of colonialism and capitalism not only built a university but quietly and creatively – in the hands of librarians – enabled a critique of it. Fernandez concludes her reflections on UBC's Folios with this comment:

> Looking out right now from the wings of [the UBC Library], there is certainly no "wilderness of Point Grey" ... I see a fountain and a perfectly manicured lawn. Most poignantly, in opposition to [Wright's] speech given here 68 years ago, I see the newly built Indian Residential School History and Dialogue Centre. Times have certainly changed; however, I cannot help but wonder, how much do we still prize and obsess over artifacts of the "literary and cultural heritage of Great Britain"? As English Literature majors I think this question needs to be asked more often.[68]

The behind-the-scenes dealings of world builders like Wright, Harlow, and Stuart-Stubbs have, I think, helped us get to a point where we can, along with students like Fernandez, ask questions about the heritage we profess and, in the process, reorient our perceptions about the premodern past and its relation to both the present and future of the places in which we live and work.[69]

## NOTES

1  Bronwen Wilson and Angela Vanhaelen, "Introduction" to this volume, 8. See also their introduction to a special issue of the *Journal of Early Modern History*, "Making Worlds: Art, Materiality, and Early Modern Globalization," 23 (2019): 103–20.

2  The notion of "mondialization," or world building, is drawn from Jean-Luc Nancy's work, *The Creation of the World or Globalization*, trans. François Raffoul and David Pettigrew (Albany: State University of New York Press, 2007). Nancy articulates the difference between the English word "globalization," which invokes the notion of an indistinct totality that is in fact a "non-place," and the French word *mondialisation*, which potentially keeps at hand the semantics of the word "world." "By keeping the horizon of a 'world' as a space of possible meaning for the whole of human relations," Nancy understands "mondialization" as more creative heuristic than the indications of "enclosure in the undifferentiated sphere of a unitotality" implied by the term "globalization" (27–8).

3  Ben Jonson, "To the memory of my beloued, The Author Mr. William Shakespeare," in *Mr. William Shakespeare's Comedies, Histories, & Tragedies* (London, 1623), STC 22273, A4-A4v.

4  Adam Hooks, "How Shakespeare's First Folio Became a Star," podcast from the Shakespeare Unlimited podcast series, Folger Shakespeare Library, 6 September 2016, https://www.folger.edu/shakespeare-unlimited /how-first-folio-became-a-star.

5  Emma Smith, *Shakespeare's First Folio: Four Centuries of an Iconic Book* (Oxford: Oxford University Press, 2016), 15.

6  For details on the extant First Folios see Charlton Hinman, *The Printing and Proof-Reading of the First Folio of Shakespeare* (Oxford: Clarendon Press, 1963); Anthony James West, *The Shakespeare First Folio: The History of the Book*, 2 vols. (Oxford: Oxford University Press, 2003); and Eric Rasmussen and Anthony James West, *The Shakespeare First Folios: a Descriptive Catalogue* (Basingstoke, NY: Palgrave Macmillan, 2012). For examples of recent scholarship on the First Folio, see W.W. Greg, *The Shakespeare First Folio: its Bibliographical and Textual History* (Oxford: Clarendon Press, 1955); Emma Smith, ed., *The*

*Cambridge Companion to the First Folio* (Cambridge, UK: Cambridge University Press, 2016); and Emma Smith, *The Making of Shakespeare's First Folio* (Oxford: Bodleian Library, 2015).

7  Stephen Greenblatt, "Martial Law and the Land of Cockaigne," in *Materialist Shakespeare: A History*, ed. Ivo Kamps (London and New York: Verso, 1995), 134; Smith, *The Making of Shakespeare's First Folio*, 120.

8  Jyotsna G. Singh, *Colonial Narratives/Cultural Dialogues: 'Discoveries' of India in the Language of Colonialism* (London: Routledge, 1996), 104.

9  The University of Toronto's Fisher Rare Books Room houses one of only two First Folios currently in Canada. The University's rare books collection is named in honour of Thomas Fisher (1792–1874), who came from Yorkshire to Upper Canada in 1821 to run a grist mill. The Fisher Folio was donated by Fisher's grandson, Sidney Fisher (who was a banker and a collector of Shakespeareana), at the opening of the new library in 1973. The other Canadian Folio was very recently acquired by UBC (see n. 69).

10  Adam G. Hooks, "Afterward: The Folio as Fetish," in *The Cambridge Companion to Shakespeare's First Folio*, ed. Emma Smith (Cambridge, UK: Cambridge University Press, 2016), 185.

11  This First Folio "life cycle" is heavily indebted to Steven K. Galbraith's essay, "Collectors," in *The Cambridge Companion to Shakespeare's First Folio*, ed. Emma Smith (Cambridge, UK: Cambridge University Press, 2016), 146.

12  For more on the life and collections of Henry Folger see Louis B. Wright, *The Folger Library: Two Decades of Growth, an Informal Account* (Charlottesville: University Press of Virginia [for the Folger Shakespeare Library], 1968); Louis B. Wright, ed., *Shakespeare Celebrated: Anniversary Lectures Delivered at the Folger Library* (Ithaca: Cornell University Press [for the Folger Shakespeare Library], 1966); Stephen H. Grant, *Collecting Shakespeare: The Story of Henry and Emily Folger* (Baltimore: Johns Hopkins University Press, 2014).

13  West, *The Shakespeare First Folio: The History of the Book*, 2:160.

14  The Folger Library catalogue notes that Folger F.2 no. 30 belonged to Mrs. George Smith; Folger F.3 no. 19 was formerly owned by Frederick Bulley, and Folger F.4 no. 20 contains a bookplate that reads "Williams's Library Cheltenham" on the fly verso. F.2 no. 30 is cited in A.W. Pollard, *Short-title Catalogue of Books Printed in England, Scotland, & Ireland and of the English Books Printed Abroad, 1475–1640*, 2nd ed. (London: London Bibliographical Society, 1976–91) as 22274a. F.3 no. 20 and F.4 no. 21 are cited in D. G. Wing, *Short-title Catalogue of Books Printed in England, Scotland, Ireland, Wales, and British America, and all of English Books Printed in other Countries, 1641–1700*, 2nd ed. (New York: Index Committee, 1973–1998) as S2914 and S2915 respectively. All three are also cited in W.W. Greg, *Bibliography of*

*English Printed Drama to the Restoration* (London: Oxford University Press for the Bibliographic Society, 1939–1959), 1113–21.

15  George Vernon Akrigg, "U.B.C's First Shakespeare Folio," UBC Librarian Sous Fonds, 261–4, UBC Archives.

16  Louis B. Wright, "Annual Report," 1959–60, Folger Library.

17  Letter from Louis B. Wright to N.A.M. Mackenzie, 4 October 1960, UBC President's Fonds, L-2, UBC Archives. Henry Clay Folger was an alumnus of Amherst College, which became, at Folger's death in 1930, the trustee of his fortune as well as his library.

18  Letter from N.A.M. Mackenzie to Louis B. Wright, 7 October 1960, UBC President's Fonds, L-2.

19  Press Release, 21 October 2016, UBC Librarian Sous Fonds, 71–8.

20  Louis B. Wright, "Libraries and the Diffusion of Learning," *UBC Alumni Chronicle* 14, no. 4 (1960): 18. *The Glasgow Herald*, 9 September 1960.

21  Dipesh Chakrabarty, *Provincializing Europe: Postcolonial Thought and Historical Difference* (Princeton: Princeton University Press, 2000), xiv. See also for example: Anston Bosman, "Shakespeare and Globalization," in *The New Cambridge Companion to Shakespeare*, ed. Margreta De Grazia and Stanley Wells (Cambridge, UK: Cambridge University Press, 2010), 285–302; Thomas Cartelli, *Repositioning Shakespeare: National Formations, Postcolonial Appropriations* (London: Routledge, 1999); Jane Hwang Degenhardt, "The Reformation, Inter-imperial World History, and Marlowe's Doctor Faustus," *PMLA* 130, no. 2 (2015): 402–11; Ania Loomba and Martin Orkin, eds., *Post Colonial Shakespeare* (London: Routledge, 1998); Ania Loomba, *Shakespeare, Race and Colonialism* (Oxford: Oxford University Press, 2002); Neil Rhodes, *Shakespeare and the Origins of English* (Oxford: Oxford University Press, 2004); Mary Louise Pratt, *Imperial Eyes: Travel Writing and Transculturation* (London: Routledge, 1992); Shankar Raman, *Renaissance Literatures and Postcolonial Studies* (Edinburgh: Edinburgh University Press, 2011); Jyotsna G. Singh, ed., *Shakespeare and Postcolonial Theory* (London: The Arden Shakespeare, 2019); Jyotsna G. Singh and Abdulhamit Aravas, "Global Shakespeares, Affective Histories, Cultural Memories," *Shakespeare Survey* 68 (2015): 183–96.

22  Leah S. Marcus, *How Shakespeare Became Colonial: Editorial Tradition and the British Empire* (London: Routledge, 2017), 4.

23  Chakrabarty, *Provincializing Europe*, 17.

24  Letter from Louis B. Wright to N.A.M. Mackenzie, 4 October 1960, UBC President's Fonds, L-2.

25  Letter from Werner Gundersheimer to K.G. Pederson, 22 April 1986, UBC President's Fonds L-2.

26 Letter from David Strangeway to Werner Gundersheimer, 26 May 1986, UBC President's Fonds L-2.

27 Letter from Douglas McInnes to Phillip Knachel, Associate Director of the Folger Library, 9 October 1986, UBC Librarian's Fonds, 160–6.

28 Letter from Werner Gundersheimer to K.G. Pederson, 22 April 1986, UBC President's Fonds L-2.

29 A cranky letter from Anne Yandle, the head of the UBC Special Collection Division, informs Frank Mowery, the conservator at the Folger, that the specially designed shipping crate sent by the Folger was delayed at customs; that UBC will pay the duty charged on said crate; and that the Folger will need to wait until her staff had "enough time to pack" the books as November "is a very busy time of year" (25 November 1986, UBC Librarian's Fonds, 160–6).

30 Director Files of Louis B. Wright, 1960, Folger Library.

31 A set of minutes in the Folger Library archives record that a proposal for the return of the St. Andrews and UBC loans was made with reference to a letter from "Falconer," which neither the archivists at the Folger nor at UBC have been able to track down.

32 Charlton Hinman referred to the dispersal in 1954 in a note announcing his great collation project. "About two years will be required for the collation of the Folger First Folios," he writes, for "as a precaution against possible disaster, only about half of the irreplaceable Folger copies are being kept in the Library in Washington; but the other copies will be brought back for collation as soon as work has been completed on the copies now available." "The Proof-Reading of the First Folio Text of *Romeo and Juliet*," *Studies in Bibliography* 6 (1954): 61.

33 Letters from Louis B. Wright to Paul D. Weathers and Newton McKeon, 4 December and 8 December 1950, Folger Library.

34 Louis B. Wright, "Notes on the Protection of Folger Resources," 3, Folger Library.

35 Letter to Louis B. Wright from Folger Trustee William Haller, 8 December 1951. See also Weathers's letter to Wright on 8 December 1951, Folger Library.

36 David McKitterick, *The Invention of Rare Books: Private Interest and Public Memory, 1600–1840* (Cambridge, UK: Cambridge University Press, 2018), 304.

37 The shipping appears to have begun in May of 1951. Folger correspondence files include many letters reporting the shipping and receiving of volumes.

38 Letter from Wright to Weathers, 15 December 1950, Folger Library.

39 See correspondence between Wright and Newton McKeon, the librarian
at Amherst College, July–September 1954, Folger Library. These letters
include amusing accounts of incomplete inventories and missing boxes.

40 "Report on the Folger Library 1959–60," 1, 3, Folger Library.

41 A.E. Gauer, "The Changing University," *UBC Reports* 6, no. 6
(November–December 1960), 2.

42 The citation is from Maurois's *Un art de vivre* ([1939] Ambler, PA: Spiral
Press, 2007, 45). Maurois is, in fact, citing Goethe and Tolstoy.

43 On the culture wars, see Andrew Hartman, *A War for the Soul of America: A
History of the Culture Wars*, second edition (Chicago: University of Chicago
Press, 2019) and Ira Shor, *Culture Wars: Schools and Society in the Conservative
Restoration* (Chicago: University of Chicago Press, 1992).

44 *UBC Alumni Chronicle*, 14, no. 3 (Autumn 1960), 4.

45 C.P. Snow, *The Two Cultures and the Scientific Revolution* (Cambridge, UK:
Cambridge University Press, 1959), 4–5, 54.

46 Snow, 11.

47 Snow, 23. See F.R. Leavis's 1962 response to Snow's lecture in *The Two Cultures?* (Stefan Collini, ed., Cambridge, UK: Cambridge University Press,
2013), 53–88. See also Stefan Collini, "Leavis v. Snow: the two-cultures
bust-up 50 years on," *The Guardian*, 16 August 2013, https://www
.theguardian.com/books/2013/aug/16/leavis-snow-two-cultures-bust.

48 This line of thinking, despite the trenchant critique by poststructuralism
and postcolonialism, tends to resurface at moments of upheaval and unrest
when it becomes pragmatic to dust off a vintage value claim in response to
the terrifying incivility of the times. See Patricia Badir and Sandra Tomc,
"The New and the Noteworthy and the Making of Civil Society," *English
Studies in Canada* 29, no. 1–2 (2003), 7–16.

49 N.A.M. MacKenzie, "Graduate Training at the University of British Columbia," *The President's Report* (Vancouver: University of British Columbia,
1959–60), 6. The Rabelais citation ("[la] science sans conscience, n'est que
[la] ruine de l'âme") is from *Pantagruel* (Gallimard: Paris, [1973], 137).

50 Wright, "Libraries and the Diffusion of Learning", 17; Ana Maria Fernandez, "'Within the Book and Volume of Thy Brain': A journal on my research
process investigating Shakespeare's Second Folio at UBC's RBSC," 14
March 2018, 4. Cited with permission.

51 Nicholas Thomas, *Entangled Objects: Exchange, Material Culture, and Colonialism in the Pacific* (Cambridge, MA: Harvard University Press, 1991).
For recent discussion of the fascination with and circulation of global
goods in early modern Europe, see for example: Ralph Bauer and Mary
Norton, "Introduction: Entangled Trajectories: Indigenous and European

Histories," *Colonial Latin American Review* 26, no. 1 (2017): 2; Daniela Bleichmar and Peter C. Mancall, *Collecting Across Cultures: Material Exchanges in the Early Atlantic* World (Philadelphia: University of Pennsylvania Press, 2011); Paula Findlen, ed., *Early Modern Things: Objects and their Histories, 1500–1800* (New York: Routledge, 2013); Anne Gerritsen and Giorgio Riello, *The Global Lives of Things: The Material Culture of Connections in the Early Modern World* (New York: Routledge, 2016); Meredith Martin and Daniela Bleichmar, "Introduction: Objects in Motion in the Early Modern World," *Art History* 38, no. 4 (2015): 604–19; Jyotsna Singh, ed., *A Companion to the Global Renaissance: English Literature and Culture in the Era of Expansion* (Chichester: Wiley-Blackwell, 2009); and Barbara Sebek and Stephen Deng, eds., *Global Traffic: Discourses and Practices of Trade in Early Modern Literature and Culture from 1550 to 1700* (London: Palgrave, 2008).

52 Wright, "Libraries and the Diffusion of Learning," 17.

53 On the subject of the tactic, see Michel de Certeau, *The Practice of Everyday Life*, trans. Steven Rendall (Berkeley: University of California Press, 1984), 19.

54 UBC Librarian Sous Fonds, 71–8.

55 Wilson and Valhaelen, "Making Worlds," 108.

56 Wilson and Vanhaelen, "Making Worlds," 113.

57 Basil Stuart-Stubbs, "The University of British Columbia Special Collection Division First Annual Report, Sept. 1960–Aug. 1961," UBC Special Collections Sous-Fonds, 153-13, 1. UBC Archives; McKitterick, *The Invention of Rare Book*, 4.

58 McKitterick, *The Invention of Rare Book*, 17; Stuart-Stubbs, "First Annual Report," Preface.

59 Phillip Buckner and R. Douglas Francis, "Introduction," in *Canada and the British World: Culture, Migration, and Identity*, ed. Phillip Buckner and R. Douglas Francis (Vancouver: University of British Columbia Press, 2006), 8–9.

60 The Suez crisis began on 29 October 1956, with the invasion of Egypt by Israel. On 1 November, Britain and France launched air attacks against Egypt. The UN General Assembly adopted an American resolution calling for a ceasefire. Canada abstained on the resolution rather than vote against it. Canada would subsequently propose the creation of a UN international police force to supervise the ceasefire and to ensure peace in the Middle East. See José Igartua, "'Ready, Aye, Ready' No more? Canada, Britain, and the Suez Crisis in the Canadian Press," in *Canada and the End of Empire*, ed. Phillip Buckner (Vancouver: University of British Columbia Press, 2004), 47–65.

61  Bryan D. Palmer, *Canada's 1960s: The Ironies of Identity in a Rebellious Era*
    (Toronto: University of Toronto Press, 2012), 50–2. In *Cold War Canada: The
    Making of a National Insecurity State* (Toronto: University of Toronto Press,
    2009), 24, Reg Whitaker and Gary Marcuse argue that Cold War Canada
    was essentially conservative:

> Those who wanted to maintain the status quo of capitalism and its unequal class
> structure did well; those who wanted radical, egalitarian change in the structure
> of privilege did poorly. Those who wanted an economy or armament expenditure
> did well; those who wanted disarmament and the diversion of resources towards
> social goals did poorly. Those who preferred a strong state to repress dissent did
> well; those who would have liked greater freedom of expression and openness
> did poorly. Those who wished to see a greater integration of Canada within the
> American Empire did well; those who wished for a greater degree of Canadian
> autonomy and neutrality did poorly.

62  See Joseph Jones, *Happenstance and Misquotation: Canadian Immigration Pol-
    icy 1966–1974, the Arrival of U.S. Vietnam War Resisters, and the Views of Pierre
    Trudeau* (Vancouver: Quarter Sheaf, 2008); John Hagan, *Northern Passage:
    American Vietnam War Resisters in Canada* (Cambridge, MA: Harvard Uni-
    versity Press, 2001); and Jessica Squires, *Building Sanctuary: the Movement to
    Support Vietnam War Resisters in Canada, 1965–1973* (Vancouver: University
    of British Columbia Press, 2013).
63  Richard Cavell reminds us that Canada's Cold War was, for many,
    anti-American. See "Introduction: The Cultural Production of Canada's
    Cold War" in *Love, Hate, and Fear in Canada's Cold War*, ed. Richard Cavell
    (Toronto: University of Toronto Press, 2004), 5. See also Norman Hillmer
    and Adam Chapnick. *Canadas of the Mind: The Making and Unmaking of
    Canadian Nationalisms in the Twentieth Century* (Montreal: McGill-Queen's
    University Press, 2007) and Robert Teigrob, *Warming Up to the Cold War:
    Canada and the United States' Coalition of the Willing, from Hiroshima to Korea*
    (Toronto: University of Toronto Press, 2009).
64  On the history of the English Department at UBC, see Sandra Djwa, *Profess-
    ing English at UBC: The Legacy of Roy Daniells and Garnet Sedgewick* (Vancou-
    ver: Ronsdale Press, 1999).
65  "Atomic Scare Instigates Club," *The Ubyssey*, 24 November 1960. For a discussion
    of Canadian universities and the disarmament movement, see Palmer, 56–8.
66  Wilson and Vanhaelen, "Making Words," 114.
67  Brian Cummings, "Shakespeare's First Folio and the Fetish of the Book,"
    *Cahiers Élizabétains* 93 (2017): 54.

68 Ana Maria Fernandez, 4. For examples of the reorientations Fernandez calls for, see (and this list is far from exhaustive) the work of Dennis Austin Britton, *Becoming Christian: Race Reformation and Early Modern English Romance* (New York: Fordham University Press, 2014); David Sterling Brown, "'Is Black so Base a Hue?': Black Life Matters in Shakespeare's *Titus Andronicus*," and Rebecca Kumare, "'Do you Love me Master: The Erotic Politics of Servitude in *The Tempest* and its Postcolonial Afterlife," in *Early Modern Black Diaspora Studies*, ed. Cassander Smith et al. (New York: Palgrave Macmillan, 2018), 137–55, 175–96; Urvasi Chakravarty, "More Than Kin, Less Than Kind: Similitude, Strangeness, and Early Modern English Homonationalisms," *Shakespeare Quarterly* 67, no. 1 (Spring 2016): 14–29; Ruben Espinoza, "Stranger Shakespeare," *Shakespeare Quarterly* 67, no. 1 (2016): 51–67; Kim Hall, *Things of Darkness* (Ithaca: Cornell University Press, 1996); Jonathan Gil Harris on Shakespeare's presence in India, *Masala Shakespeare: How a Firangi Writer Became Indian* (New Delhi: Aleph, 2018); Graham Holderness, "Arabesque: Shakespeare and Globalisation," in *Global Shakespeares: Video and Performance Archive*, https://globalshakespeares.mit.edu/extra /arabesque/; Carol Mejia La Perle, "'If I might have my will': Aaron's affect and race in *Titus Andronicus*," in *Titus Andronicus: The State of Play*, ed. Farah Karim-Cooper (London: Arden Shakespeare, Bloomsbury Publishing, 2019), 135–56; Noémi Ndiaye, "'Everyone Breeds in His Own Image': Staging the *Aethiopica* across the Channel," *Renaissance Drama* 44, no. 2 (2016): 157–85, and "Aaron's Roots: Spaniards, Englishmen, and Blackamoors in *Titus Andronicus*," *Early Theater* 19, no. 2 (2016): 59–80; and Ayanna Thompson, *Passing Strange: Shakespeare, Race and Contemporary America* (Oxford: Oxford University Press, 2011); as well as the essays collected in vol. 71 of *Shakespeare Survey*, in Nicholas Hudson, ed., *The Cultural History of Race in the Reformation and Enlightenment, 1550–1760*, vol. 4 (London: Bloomsbury Press, 2021), and in Ayanna Thompson, ed., *The Cambridge Companion to Shakespeare and Race* (Cambridge, UK: Cambridge University Press, 2021).

69 These questions and reorientations continue to press upon faculty, librarians, and students at UBC as we now consider the opportunities made possible by the very recent acquisition, in January of 2022, of another First Folio, known as the Cherry-Garrard copy for one of its former owners, the English Antarctic explorer and writer Apsley Cherry-Garrard (1886–1959). The book was formerly owned by a private collector in the United States. UBC purchased it through Christie's New York with funding provided by a consortium of donors from across North America and with the support of the Department of Canadian Heritage. The announcement of the Folio's

move to British Columbia came just as this volume was going to press and thus it serves as a fitting epilogue to my chapter. The current head of RBSC, Katherine Kalsbeek, hails the acquisition in terms that are familiar, describing it as representing "a milestone in terms of our development as both a library and as a university." Her sentiment is shared by UBC president Santa Ono in his statement that "preserving this precious book in the UBC Library makes it accessible for future generations, inspires new knowledge, and furthers our commitment to engage in world-class research in the arts and humanities." For the original press release, see: https://news.ubc .ca/2022/01/12/william-shakespeare-comedies-histories-and-tragedies-ubc/. For media coverage of the acquisition, see: https://www.theglobeandmail .com/arts/books/article-shakespeares-first-folio-acquired-by-ubc-in -once-in-eternity-purchase/ and https://www.cbc.ca/news/canada/british -columbia/shakespeare-first-folio-1.6312592.

# PART III

# OTHER WORLDS

# chapter eleven

# Ascetic Ecology:
# Landscape of a Desert Saint

LYLE MASSEY

Throughout the European Middle Ages, images of Saint Jerome largely reinforced his patristic role as a doctor of the Church and the author of the Latin Vulgate. But in fifteenth-century Italy, depictions of the saint shifted to other aspects of his life, particularly his desert hermitage. Four paintings on this theme were produced by the Venetian painter, Giovanni Bellini, between 1445 and 1505. Bellini's focus on the landscapes in these works has been noted frequently, with special attention paid to how they thematize the saint's humanistic transformation in the Renaissance. However, the paintings also play with Jerome's descriptions of life in the desert, not only in his accounts of his own hermitage (i.e., his retreat to solitary exile), but also in his biography of Christian anchorite Paul of Thebes. That is, they seem to reflect Jerome's complex encounter with the desert setting of his hermitage. This is not to say that Bellini presents us with a topographical portrait of the North African or Middle Eastern desert (because he does not), nor that his celebrated adherence to certain forms of representational naturalism caused him to try and replicate the "true" features of a desert landscape. Rather, in their careful attention to stone, sand, earth, plants, and animals, the four paintings convey the embeddedness of Jerome's body and presence in the desert landscape of his self-imposed exile. Bellini's works strive to show us an imbricated, almost ecological relationship between Jerome and his anchoretic setting, if we rely on nineteenth-century German zoologist Ernst Haeckel's original conception of "oecology" as the embedded relationship of an organism with its animate and inanimate environment.[1]

The paintings also require us to rethink the story of "landscape" itself. The backgrounds in late medieval and early Renaissance paintings of saints have often been interpreted as reflections of those saints' spiritual journeys, filled with iconographical symbols assembled to mark specific aspects in stories of sacrifice and illumination, or of theological exegesis. But it has also been common to treat the backgrounds of these and other Renaissance paintings as *parerga*, a word borrowed in the Renaissance from Pliny the Elder, for whom it describes decorative accessories to the prime content in a work of art.[2] The Renaissance physician and prelate, Paolo Giovio, for instance, uses the term to describe the way backgrounds in the works of Dosso Dossi appeal especially to the eye.[3] Bellini's depictions of Saint Jerome challenge both characterizations, presenting the viewer with a relation of interdependence between saint and ground that not only repositions the landscape from periphery to centre, but also resists certain forms of iconological analysis.[4] He treats Jerome's desert as a self-enclosed system, a world unto itself in which the land absorbs the saint into its determinant features. Bellini's acute attention to finely detailed geologic features (in both a "naturalistic" and an imaginative sense), and his visual focus on the land's textural qualities, invest the pictures with a strong sense of place that moves beyond merely making the landscape a signifier or projection of a spiritual iconography. Instead, the landscapes materialize Jerome's dialectic of transformation. Using terms such as "ecology" and "environment" risks historical anachronism and the imposition of modern subjective constructions on impervious Renaissance or early modern conceptions of land and landscape. But such perspectives on late medieval and early modern cultural studies have the benefit of opening up questions that are often overlooked in the history of art.[5] The following study makes the case that Bellini's paintings require us to see the saint as indelibly connected to and responsive to the material conditions of the desert he describes. That is, he visually imagines Jerome entangled in a psycho-ecological dependence on land that imposes privations, exposure, and renunciation, but also offers salvation, relief, and composure. The paintings show us how Jerome's sojourn was understood in the fifteenth century but also how, and perhaps why, land emerged from the background and increasingly became a subject in its own right.

### Asceticism

Ascetics who chose exile in the arid desert lands of Egypt and Syria were among the most compelling examples of renunciation in the late antique world of nascent Christianity. The desert signified intentional removal from civilization, a place where men and women went to disengage from the world while seeking a soul-amplifying spiritual union with the divine. In patristic accounts of holy hermits and their retreats, the desert signifies the backdrop against which this renunciation is experienced in its most extreme form. Demonic visions, self-mortification, and the subduing of bodily desires are played out in sites noteworthy for withholding succour, comfort, and peace. As many have observed, the desert itself is therefore seldom merely a passive backdrop, and instead often serves as an active catalyst for the hermit's abstinence, torment, and eventual clarity.[6] In fact, in some interpretations of the ascetic experience, the desert is understood to frame disengagement in quasi-ecological terms. It isn't just that the early Christian hermits sought to escape from cities and urban places by finding uninhabited space in some generalized wilderness. Rather, they sought the desert in particular because of its specific lack of water and arable land, as well as its seeming resistance to habitation, accumulation, or settlement. In this, it stood in stark contrast to more hospitable natural environments. For instance, the austere Egyptian desert, where so many fourth-century hermits retreated, contrasted dramatically with the Nile flood plain, notable for its temperate lushness and aqueous fertility. The line that separated these two completely disparate ecologies was a comparatively thin strip of land.[7] The desert thus stood out as the objective negation of the environmental stability and material comforts offered by the river's flood plain.

And yet, while the desert was a site of hardship and solitude, the reality was that hermits frequently formed incipient communities, grouping themselves around water sources, cultivating land, and building shelters. The Egyptian Thebaid, and other places like it, often consisted of loose communitarian gatherings, in which members raised food and exchanged assistance, even as they indulged in lives of self-abnegation.[8] Thus, early Christian writing signalled the desert as at once a symbolic arena of renunciation and a utopian place of salvation, an environment of terrifying loneliness and an oasis of sustenance and spiritual comfort. Judith Adler suggests that as such, the desert constituted a "new, dichotomous moral geography" in the fourth century, one in which the idea of the Christian community was born at the same time as hermitage stood for isolation and stringent, individual, transformative effects.[9]

There is no desert hermit who more clearly gives voice to this moral geography than Saint Jerome. Born in the mid-fourth century in the Roman province of Dalmatia, and converting to Christianity in his twenties, Jerome produced a definitive Latin translation (the Vulgate) of the Hebrew Bible and was revered in ensuing centuries as a doctor of the early church. As a young man wrestling with the tenets of Christianity, Jerome went into a period of self-imposed exile sometime between the years 374 and 377. Sequestering himself in a cave in the desert near Chalcis, between Antioch and Palmyra in what is now modern-day Syria, he engaged in acts of self-mortification (flagellation and fasting) to wrest his body into submission.[10] In his letters, he describes not only his acts of penance during his hermitage, but also his bodily relationship to the land and its effects upon him.

For instance, in a well-known letter to Eustochium, the daughter of his most fervent follower, Paula, Jerome recounts the tortures he suffered:

> Filled with stiff anger against myself, I would make my way alone into the desert; and when I came upon some hollow valley or rough mountain or precipitous cliff, there I would set up my oratory, and make that spot a place of torture for my unhappy flesh.[11]

That this setting was not just any wilderness, but truly desert, is made clear in an earlier reference:

> Oh, how often, when I was living in the desert, in that lonely waste, scorched by the burning sun, which affords to hermits a savage dwelling-place, how often did I fancy myself surrounded by the pleasures of Rome! I used to sit alone; for I was filled with bitterness. My unkempt limbs were covered in shapeless sackcloth; my skin through long neglect had become as rough and black as an Ethiopian's.[12]

Confronting searing sunlight and sunburn, exposure, and rough ground, hiking through valleys and up rocky hillsides, Jerome evokes the specific terrain and climate of the desert. The thin lines between death and survival, desiccation and hydration, exposure and protection point to the mutability and alienation of the desert as place. His description conveys a landscape inscribed with bodily memory but also with transformational effects, signified by his self-description as having become as dark as an "Ethiopian."

Pliny the Elder includes Ethiopians in Book 7 of his *Natural History* among what he calls the monstrous races of men, and attributes their dark skin to their close proximity to the sun.[13] Jerome's statement clearly draws on this late Roman explanation for skin colour. The word Ethiopian was Greek in origin, deriving from *aith* for "burn" or "blaze," and *ops* for "face."[14] Notwithstanding what amounts to environmental causation theory, references to Ethiopians in accounts of the desert saints clearly also carried a racial component. In the language of fourth-century Christian hermits, Ethiopians appeared in diabolical visions as crucibles of beauty and desire, and stood for bodily temptations that needed to be not only resisted but eradicated.[15] This is precisely the role played by an Ethiopian figure in the life of the other canonical desert saint revered in the Renaissance, Anthony. Among the torments he experiences in the desert, a demon of fornication appears as a beautiful Ethiopian boy. As Peter Brown and others have argued, images of Ethiopians in accounts such as the life of Anthony represent an internal force of desire emanating from the hermit, more than an external temptation.[16] The rejection of sexuality was, in fact, a rejection of stability and a pursuit of what Brown calls "social death" in order to attain a new identity.[17] Such racialized allusions were thus less about ascribing features and values to Ethiopians than they were about resisting society's social demands through negation of sexuality. However, blackness was often understood as a metaphorical reflection of darkness in the soul, and much of patristic literature describes awakening as a passage from dark to light, or from black to white. These long-embedded analogies clearly accrued a more evident racial component later, when moral and aesthetic distinctions came to be ascribed more specifically to black skin in later centuries.[18] But Jerome's comment, in contrast, can be understood as pointing to his struggles to reinvent himself. His skin changes colour because he is undergoing both a physical and spiritual transformation in the stark landscape of the Syrian desert. The environment forces Jerome to grapple and come to terms with his bodily experience in the sense that it materially changes his person, making him unrecognizable to himself.[19]

## Jerome's Hermitage in Art

When Jerome's life began to attract renewed interest in the late fourteenth century, representations of the saint also began depicting his desert experience. Giovanni d'Andrea, a Bolognese jurist and professor of canon law who in 1345 authored a widely-read biography of Jerome, the *Hieronymianus*, was responsible for bringing greater attention to Jerome's hermitage.[20] Fascination with Jerome's early life took hold particularly in Tuscany, where newly formed so-called Hieronymite orders found inspiration in his youthful acts of penance. Many early Renaissance representations of Jerome thus show the saint beating himself in the chest

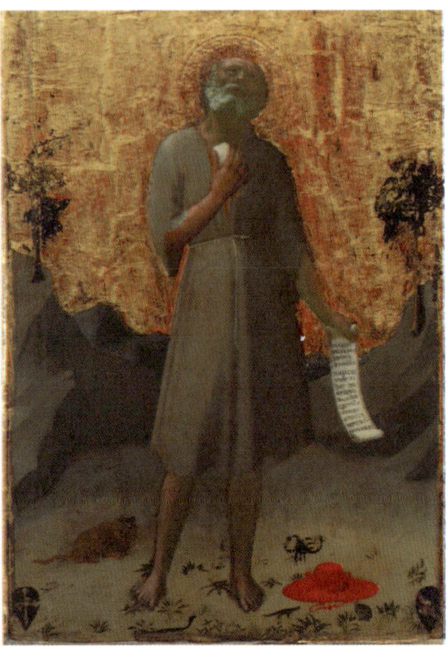

Figure 11.1. Fra Angelico, *The Penitent Saint Jerome*, 1419–20. Tempera on wood panel, 56.5 x 41.2 cm, frame 56.8 x 41.3 x 5.7 cm. Princeton University Art Museum. Bequest of Frank Jewett Mather Jr. y1963–1

with a rock, often in front of a crucifix, in a setting meant to evoke the desert.[21] For instance, an early fifteenth-century version of Jerome engaged in penance in the desert (c. 1420), attributed to Fra Angelico, depicts the saint raising a rock to his chest as he gazes heavenward, while below him a scorpion, lizard, snake, and lion populate the flat, barren land underfoot (fig. 11.1). The scene is illuminated by the sun, the rays of which are evoked through pounded gold. Reduced to an almost hieroglyphic set of signs, the landscape signals its role in testing the saint's resolve. Jerome holds a scroll inscribed with rules from a Tuscan Hieronymite Order: "Subdue your flesh by fasting. A monk should avoid wine as if it were poison. To eat anything cooked is accounted self-indulgence."[22] Here, the ground and sky stand allegorically for privation and penance.

In many ways, this picture reflects a similar approach taken to depictions of St. Anthony.[23] Anthony's life was known through a biography

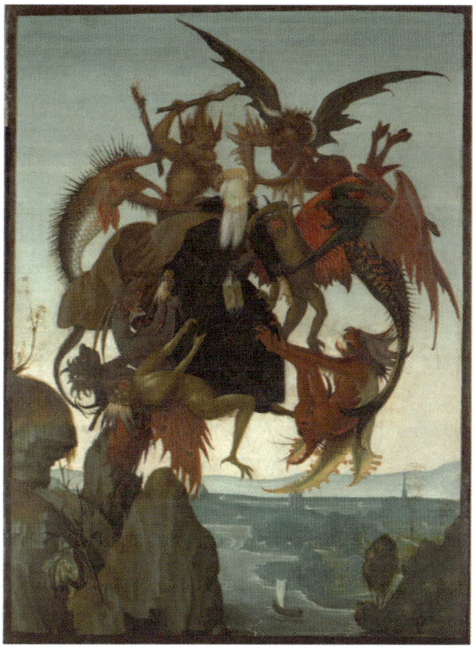

Figure 11.2.  Michelangelo Buonarroti, *The Torment of Saint Anthony*, 1487.
Tempera on panel, 47 x 34.9 cm, frame 68.6 x 56.8 x 5.7 cm. AP 2009.01.
Kimbell Art Museum, Fort Worth, Texas

written by St. Athanasius that describes the ascetic's retreat and temptations in the Egyptian desert. The landscape itself is generally treated
as largely symbolic in Athanasius's account. The desert serves as a
passive ground for the extraordinary bodily torment that Anthony experiences when beset by demons and malign visions. We can see this
in a fifteenth-century painting at the Kimball Museum of Art in Fort
Worth, Texas, by a young Michelangelo, based on a print by Martin
Schongauer (fig. 11.2). Here Anthony levitates, tormented by devils,
above an emblematic landscape that Michelangelo has added (the
print has virtually no landscape). On the left, a group of boulders
represent the desert as a barren, rocky outcrop, while on the right
and into the distance, a river runs through lush, forested countryside
dotted with church steeples and the suggestion of villages. The uninhabited desert stands for Anthony's torment and suffering, while

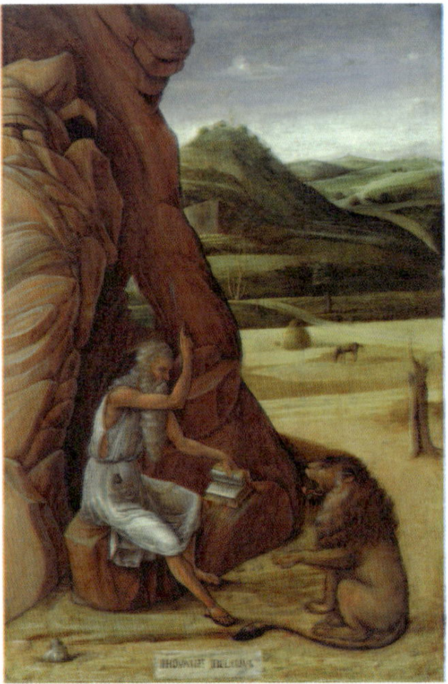

Figure 11.3. Giovanni Bellini, *Saint Jerome in the Wilderness*, c. 1450. Tempera on panel, 44 x 22.9 cm. Photo © Barber Institute of Fine Arts / © The Henry Barber Trust, The Barber Institute of Fine Arts, University of Birmingham / Bridgeman Images

the green landscape represents the world and civilization that he has renounced.

Jerome, however, is seldom depicted beset by devils or hallucinations. His demons are implied as internal, rather than rendered externally, and the desert setting emphasizes the power of the environment to transform him in concert with his own acts of penitence. Perhaps this emphasis on internality is why a more elegiac representation of Jerome began to emerge in the early Renaissance. The *Hieronymianus* was formative for the poet Petrarch and for humanists in the Veneto and Po regions, providing a foundation for a humanist reimagining of Jerome.[24] For instance, a genre of paintings that emerged in Northern Europe as well as Venice focuses on the saint's role as scholar, and bridges the gap between his association with humanistic letters and with more general moral Christian teachings. This genre, which usually depicts Jerome in his study, began to appear more regularly in Italy as well as north of the Alps.[25] One of the best-known Italian versions of these is Antonello da Messina's *Saint Jerome in His Study*, dated to c. 1475, in which the saint labours at a desk in a Renaissance *studiolo*, dressed in a Cardinal's red robes (a late and anachronistic addition to Jerome iconography, as he lived and died before the position of cardinal was invented in the church).[26] At some point, however, the desert hermit was combined with this man of letters, fusing the experience of writing to that of solitude in a way that reinvented Jerome as a humanist saint. It is this image that Bellini exploits and transforms in his paintings.

## Bellini's Saint Jeromes

In all four of Bellini's works, the saint is shown in a complex rocky setting framed by a distant landscape, holding a book and accompanied by a lion and, in some cases, small animals, birds, and lizards. In the earliest of these (c. 1450) (fig. 11.3), now in Birmingham, England, at the Barber Institute of Fine Arts, Bellini shows the saint seated in barren, sand-coloured terrain marked by an elaborate rock formation. In the far distance the hills are green and lush, with some minor signs of habitation: shepherds' huts and fences. The next two paintings, one at the Uffizi (c. 1480–7) (fig. 11.4) and one at the National Gallery in London (c. 1480–5) (fig. 11.5), are very similar and expand on the themes in the earlier painting. In the Uffizi version, the saint is shown with a cross in the foreground, surrounded by a formidable rocky outcrop that seems to hide a cave, while in the distance the green hills now provide a setting for a cityscape. In the London version the cross is gone and the distant landscape has been changed. And in the last version, at the National Gallery in Washington DC (1505) (fig. 11.6), the saint sits with his back to the rock wall, in front of a visible cave entrance. He also faces a carefully articulated well or cistern with clear water from a spring, while the middle ground is now occupied by what appear to be ruins, and across a lagoon a city can be seen in the far distance.

Many interpretations of the landscapes in these pictures have focused on the cities in the background, specifically in the Florence, London, and Washington, DC, versions. These have been alternately identified as evoking heavenly Jerusalem, contrasting the inhospitable desert landscape to the promise of redemption in the distance, or as partially

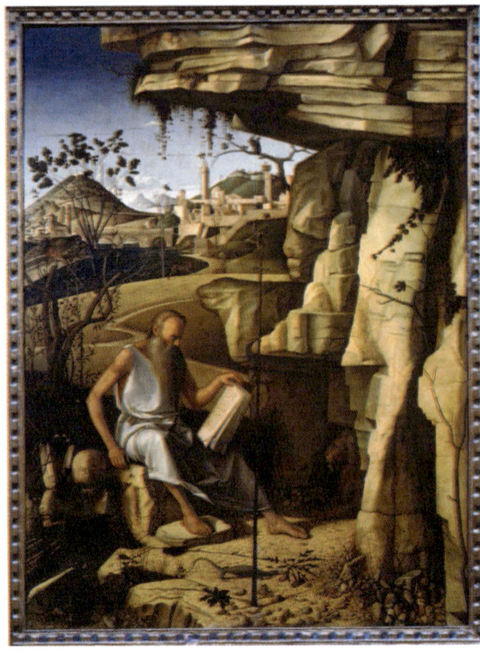

Figure 11.4.  Giovanni Bellini, *Saint Jerome in the Desert*, c. 1480–7. Oil on wood, 151.7 x 113.7 cm. Uffizi, Florence. Alinari Archives / Raffaello Bencini / Art Resource, NY

recognizable depictions of Verona or Ravenna.[27] The other elements of land in these pictures have also mostly been interpreted iconographically. The presence of animals such as rabbits, squirrels, falcons and other birds, lizards, and even some plants is associated with Christological meanings. The rabbits in particular carry seemingly significant symbolism. St. Ambrose, in the *Hexameron* (v. 33), interpreted the changing colour of hares as a symbol of resurrection, essentially providing a Christian framework for Pliny the Elder's assertion (in *Historia naturalis*, viii, 81) that hares change to the colour white in the Alps when they eat snow in the winter. Christiane Wiebel argues that this interpretation might explain why both a brown and a white hare are depicted in the Washington, DC, version: they are, as it were, before and after pictures.[28] In addition, St. Augustine's gloss on Psalm 104 (103), 18, identifies the rock as a symbol of Christ, and hares that naturally dwell in rocks as human

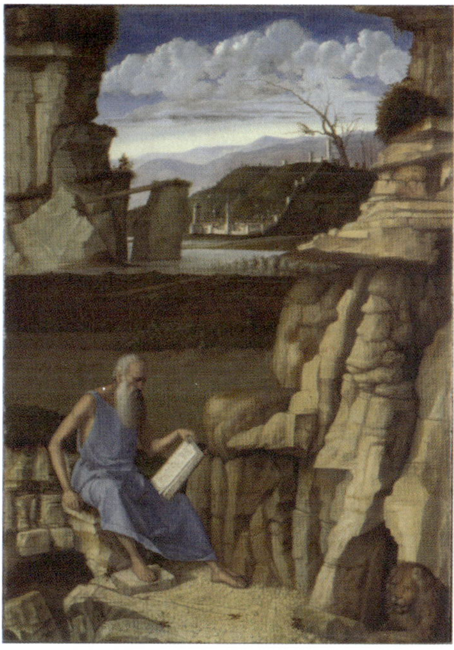

Figure 11.5. Giovanni Bellini, *Saint Jerome Reading in a Landscape*, c. 1480–5. Tempera and oil on wood, 47 x 33.7 cm. © National Gallery, London / Art Resource, NY

souls seeking adjacency to the saviour's holy body.[29] Along these lines, the lizard can be interpreted as a symbol of sin, and the spring as a *fons lucidissimus* or miraculous holy well.[30]

But what is left out of these interpretations is the specificity of the settings themselves. Bellini's paintings combine the scholarly Jerome with the penitent, while emphasizing the beauty of scholarly study as a solitary pursuit. In this, the paintings evoke Petrarch's *De vita solitaria*, written in 1346, in the sense that they evoke solitude as a blessing. That is, the paintings highlight the peaceful qualities of Jerome's hermitage.[31] The setting then is not one of deprivation, but of solace and reflection, and it confers on Jerome the virtues of both Christian ascetic and ancient author. In Hans Belting's view, Bellini's paintings contribute visually to this emerging Renaissance conception of Jerome as a humanist saint by merging the desert penitent with the scholar in the study.[32] Rather

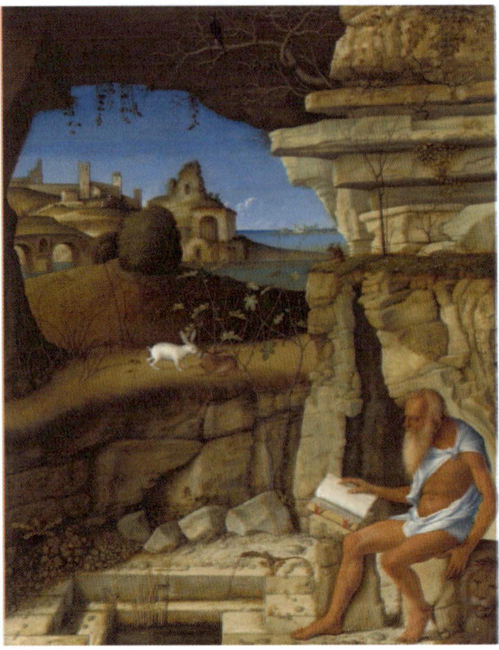

Figure 11.6. Giovanni Bellini, *Saint Jerome Reading*, 1505. Oil on linden panel, 47 x 37.5 cm. Samuel Kress Collection. Courtesy National Gallery of Art, Washington, DC

than associate the saint's escape from the world with a physical place, the saint's retreat is inward – the desert stands for a spiritual journey that invokes the pleasures of meditative solitude, rather than privation.

## The Rocks

The details of Bellini's backgrounds are not fully accounted for, however, in either the iconographical approach or in Belting's more nuanced treatment of the landscape. The most unusual features of Bellini's pictures are the distinctive rock formations that make up the eremitic cave in the foreground. These paintings aren't the first to situate Jerome in a rocky setting. Guarino of Verona owned a painting of Jerome in the desert by Pisanello that was the subject of ekphrastic verse by both Guarino himself and Bartolomeo Facio and may have been among the earliest Renaissance

depictions of the saint in a rock grotto.[33] But all of Bellini's paintings notably foreground massive, rising stone formations, dwarfing the saint himself. In three of the paintings, these grottos are similar to the stone wall in
Bellini's *Saint Francis*, at the Frick Collection in New York City. These similar rock walls have been celebrated for their naturalism and taken as evidence of Bellini's attentiveness to describing nature. That is, they are often
understood as *parerga*, or separate from the content of the works, demonstrating possibly a more general Renaissance interest in geology ascribed
to Bellini. But these rock structures occupy too much of the foreground to
be considered extraneous to the subject or content of the paintings.

The Birmingham painting frames Jerome with a triangular, red, sand-
stone-like structure that would not be out of place in the American southwest (fig. 11.3). Below it a flat, pale, and largely featureless landscape
extends back towards a lush, green mountain range. This landscape resembles a description of the Sahara that the Venetian merchant Alvise
da Ca' da Mosto recalls in his journal recording his travels to Northwest
Africa in 1455 and 1456. Alvise describes the stretch of land between
Cape Cantin and Cape Branco as a "sandy country or desert, called Saara
or Saharra by the natives," that reaches to the ocean with all "dry white
sand, quite low and level, so that no part of it seems higher than any
other."[34] While the expansive flat land in the painting evokes this kind of
eyewitness account, the stone arch is more fanciful and idiosyncratic. It
most likely owes its provenance to notebook drawings by Jacopo Bellini,
Giovanni's father.[35] In both his father's drawings and the Birmingham
Jerome painting, the rock is oriented vertically, swirling upward in patterned folds that present a pleasing and graceful symmetry. In contrast,
Bellini's three later works (figs. 11.4, 11.5, and 11.6) depict rock formations that seem entirely different from the earlier version – they rise in
stacked and jutting horizontal slabs. There is some consensus among art
historians that in these later paintings Bellini was most likely responding
to an encounter with a similar rock formation in a painting or paintings
by Jan van Eyck depicting the *Stigmatization of St. Francis*. A small version
of that painting (fig. 11.7), now in Philadelphia, was, in all likelihood,
brought to Venice in 1471 by a man named Anselm Adornes, an Italian
merchant who lived in Bruges.[36] Embarked on a pilgrimage to the Holy
Land, Adornes made his way through Italy apparently carrying this work,
and it made a strong impression in both Florence and Venice during his
stops in each city. The very character of the rocks – their seemingly ordinary vividness, with visible small fissures, plants and weeds trailing from
cracks, the sheen of moisture on stone faces, the faceted shadows, and

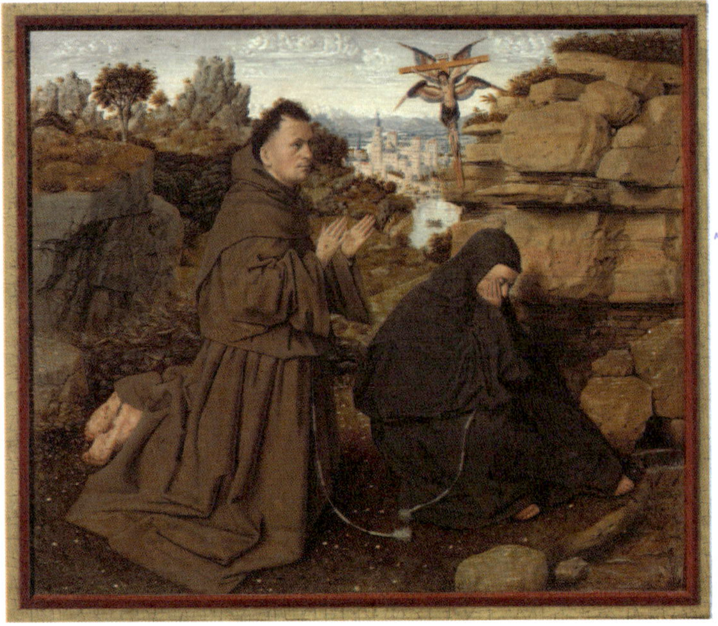

Figure 11.7. Jan van Eyck, Saint Francis of Assisi Receiving the Stigmata, 1430–2. Oil on vellum on panel, 12.7 x 14.6 cm. Philadelphia Museum of Art, Philadelphia

the water of the spring in the lower right corner – stand out as demonstrations of Jan van Eyck's exceptional attention to naturalistic detail.

However, in spite of some similarities, Bellini's approach to the rocks is, in fact, quite different. The stacked geological formations demand attention far and above their putative roles as backdrop, and they stand in excess of both realism and Jerome's iconography.[37] The rock grottos are clearly meant to signify the saint's retreat from civilization, but Bellini's approach also connects the desert's materiality to the experiences of Jerome.

### Paul of Thebe's Desert

Bellini's paintings do not present the desert as a landscape of deprivation or fear, as described in the letter to Eustochium. Instead, his desert is much closer to the landscape surrounding Paul of Thebes, whose life and hermitage Jerome made famous. While his life of Paul of Thebes lingers on aspects of the ascetic's self-deprivation, along with his miracles, Jerome also describes with wonder Paul's hermitage in the desert:

> he fled into the fastness of the mountains, where, awaiting the end of [his brother-in-law's] persecution, he made a virtue of necessity. After careful examination of his surroundings, he found a rocky ridge, at the foot of which there was a cave, its opening shut off by a stone of no great size. Eagerly removing the stone – curiosity is human – he came upon a large chamber open to the sky. The spreading branches of an ancient palm tree protected the vestibule. He discovered, too, a clear spring whose gushing waters were almost immediately swallowed up again by the earth which had given them birth. Throughout the hollowed mountain, there were many smaller chambers in which Paul saw rusty forges and mallets of the kind used in coining money. The place, according to Egyptian accounts, was a secret mint during Anthony's stay with Cleopatra. There in this humble dwelling which he grew to love (just as if God had given it to him), he passed the rest of his life in prayer and solitude. The palm tree supplied his few needs of food and clothing.[38]

The desert setting is not a burdensome test of Paul's resolve. Rather he finds a veritable oasis and refuge in the desert that offers him not only welcome solitude, but also shade, protection, cool fresh water, and food and clothing from the palm tree, as well as particularly specific markers of a past and now moribund civilization.

All four of Bellini's paintings treat the desert similarly not as a site of torment, but of tranquillity and reflection. The painting closest to Jerome's description of Paul of Thebe's life is the Washington, DC, version (fig. 11.6). The pleasure of pure water springing forth in the arid landscape is framed by the curious structure that Bellini depicts in the painting's foreground. Large ashlar blocks are held together with iron ties or clamps to make a kind of cistern or well. Such a construction technique is found in Greek and Roman architecture and, while not widely used in the Italian Renaissance, carried classical associations in the fifteenth century.[39] It is as though the painter wants the viewer to understand the cistern as something quasi-archaeological. Its presence in the painting may have something to do with the Renaissance reception of Jerome. As noted earlier, in the second half of the fifteenth century Jerome's copious knowledge of Roman rhetoric made him a model for learned, Christian humanism.[40] But his personal story also posed a problem. The event that prompted Jerome's hermitage in the desert was a dream he experienced while staying in Antioch. Taking great pleasure in reading Cicero,

Jerome, by his own admission, seems to have been unable to reconcile his love for well-crafted secular rhetoric with the contrasting confusion and poor writing of Christian texts. In his fever of disillusion, he experiences a dream/nightmare. Christ as the Judge appears to him and asks what manner of man he is, and he answers, "Christian," at which point Christ answers, "Not Christian, but Ciceronian." The dream provokes a crisis, and Jerome resolves to move out to the desert and commit himself more fully to Christian texts, while abandoning his beloved Cicero. The story was usually interpreted in the Quattrocento as an admonishment against secular learning. Jerome thus posed a conundrum for humanists because his story at once celebrated and eschewed classical learning, and it often required flexible apologetics to explain why and how his beautiful prose style and love of authors like Cicero could provide a suitable model for Italian Christian humanists.[41]

The Washington, DC, version (fig. 11.6) addresses this conundrum through its novel contrast between the carefully constructed cistern and the rock wall. The cave entrance points to the hermit's renunciation, even as the cistern points to the ancient Roman foundations of Jerome's knowledge and echoes the abandoned Egyptian mint in Jerome's account of Paul. At the same time, its inclusion underlines the pleasure Jerome takes in a solitary and reflective life, meshing Christian connotations – the pool and its crystalline water evoke the cleansing and renewal of baptism – with the succour offered by the desert oasis. Stone in Bellini's painting then offers a symbiosis between the man-made and the natural – the carefully composed blocks of the cistern mirror the rough but geometrically stacked stone around the cave. The visual contrast provokes a rumination on the exchange of learning for Christian enlightenment. The painting uses stone to signify Jerome's transformation from a man seduced by Cicero to a moral arbiter of Christian doctrine.

But the stacked and cracked stone piles in all three later paintings also point to something specific and elemental about stone itself. In his analysis of Bellini's *St. Francis*, David Kim has argued that the painting's vertical wall of stone, with its dramatic cracks, frames Francis's experience as something embedded in or even emerging from the earth itself. The insistence on the rock wall as a full actor in the scene forces a confrontation between the saint's short human life span and the eternal geological time span marked by stone.[42]

Something related seems to activate the rock settings of Bellini's paintings. While the stone appears in one sense to be immovable and eternal, it also transmits a sense of living pulse. It is assembled rhythmically, almost

like masonry, while improbably exhibiting organic elements. Quattrocento geological theories ascribed rock with living, breathing properties.
This ascription is demonstrated, for instance, in Leon Battista Alberti's *De
re aedificatoria*, which conveys an almost biological conception of stone.[43]
In Book 2, Chapter 8, he acknowledges ancient theories of stone formation (largely based on Pliny), such as the idea that stone grows from the
heat of the sun, or from seeds planted by Nature in the earth itself. While
he refrains from exploring these ideas any further, he nevertheless marvels at the discovery that marble has been observed growing in quarries
as though "nourished by time and the earth," and that a stalactite from
Lucania was quite soft while "fresh and still full of its natural juices," and
only became hard when fully dried out.[44] This conception of living stone
was by no means new in the fifteenth century. One of the most powerful
and influential theories of living stone can be found in Albertus Magnus's thirteenth-century *De mineralibus*. In that treatise, Albertus describes
rock as having *virtus formativa*, a term he uses to connote the plastic force
or formative capacity of nature in general.[45] *Virtus formativa* accounts for
the generation of stone as much as it accounts for the generation of animals.[46] In each case it is similar to the way a human artificer imparts form
on his art – the generative force that moulds form emanates from the/a
prime intellect (Albertus draws on Aristotle's notion that every work of
nature, and the very movement of the spheres, are the work of an intelligence).[47] Nowhere is this made more evident than in fossils. Drawing on
the theories of Avicenna, Albertus identifies fossils as the product of *vis
lapidificativa* or the mineralizing power of the earth. He asserts:

> sometimes stones are found that have figures of animals inside and out-
> side. For outside they have an outline, and when they are broken open, the
> shapes of the internal organs are found inside. And Avicenna says that the
> cause of this is that animals, just as they are, are sometimes changed into
> stones, and especially [salty) stones. For he says that just as Earth and Wa-
> ter are material for stones, so animals, too, are material for stones. And in
> places where a petrifying force is exhaling, they change into their elements
> and are attacked by the properties of the qualities [hot, cold, moist, dry]
> which are present in those places, and the elements in the bodies of such
> animals are changed into the dominant element, namely Earth mixed with
> Water; and then the mineralizing power converts [the mixture] into stone.[48]

Thus, animal and mineral matter are transmutable because of the fundamental plastic force that moves all matter.

Bellini's stones project this organic quality through the anthropomorphic and zoomorphic features they contain. Throughout the four paintings, the stone walls surrounding the saint flicker with uncertain but nonetheless visible human and animal faces. For instance, in the Birmingham painting (fig. 11.3), the stone formation envelops the saint with a triangular form, like a cloak. The lion that anchors the bottom right is the same colour as the stone, as if to show that they are of the same substance.[49] At the apex of the stone triangle there is what appears to be a lion's head with an open "jaw" that apes the similarly open mouth of the lion below. Framed between these two lions, one fleshly and one lithic, Jerome is surrounded in a way that insists on his connection to both stone and animal matter.

When Bellini begins to emulate van Eyck's rocky outcrop, the rock walls continue to display face-like images. In the Uffizi version (fig. 11.4), the lion is again mirrored in a feline-like face that emerges from the rock cliff above. In addition, the suggestion of a human face appears in the cave wall behind the lion, imbued with a long "nose" and Easter Island-like monumentality. In the London version (fig. 11.5), the stone lion face has almost disappeared, but there is a vestigial presence, as though it has become a barely perceptible fossil, right next to the face of the actual lion.[50] The larger face in the Uffizi version has begun to fade back into the rock, and now a smaller, chiselled face emerges. The same effects of light illuminate the nose and cheeks of both saint and stone image. In the version in the National Gallery in Washington, DC (fig. 11.6), the anthropomorphic details have disappeared and the chaotic jumble of rock is now instead mitigated by the carefully articulated architecture of the cistern.

These ghostly anthropomorphic and zoological images that emerge from the rock walls are surprising and mysterious. Giacomo Berra suggests that the rock faces represent latent demons, and appear there as symbols of Jerome's temptation.[51] It is certainly true that the vestigial faces would seem to echo Jerome's own sense that the cave he occupied in the desert was sentient and aware of his impure desires: "I feared my cell as though it knew my thoughts."[52] But the faces in Bellini's rocks do not seem threatening or especially demonic. Instead they appear immutable and expressionless, stoically accompanying the saint in his scholarly reflections. The shifting gazes of the stone faces, in some paintings focused on the saint, and in others looking out beyond the picture's frame towards or past the viewer, invite meditation. Their very implacability indicates they are fundamentally united to the rock itself, thematizing the desert's geological permanence. They seem less symbols of desert nightmares than supports for the saint's embeddedness in the land to which he owes his illumination. In Jerome's letters, the desert is conceived as a landscape that is inseparable from the religious transformation he experiences.[53] As silent observers, the faces in the rock testify to Jerome's solitude and ask the viewer to bear witness to the landscape's transformative capacity. The faces indicate the contiguity between Jerome's inner resolution and the landscape's effect on his resolve.

The presence of the lion, both in fleshly form and in the rock wall, alludes even more pointedly to this symbiotic exchange between saint and desert. Jerome's association with a lion comes from a story added to his legend in the *Plerosque nimirum,* one of two anonymously authored ninth-century biographies that established the canon of his life story. In the narrative, Jerome's encounter with the lion doesn't take place during his hermitage in Chalcis, but later at the monastery he established in Bethlehem.[54] The story has deep roots in an Androcles-type folk tale that dates back to at least the first century. Similar stories became associated with a number of early Christian saints, but it was particularly connected to a fifth-century Greek hermit in Palestine named Gerasimus. The confusion caused by the homophone nature of the two saints' names (the Latin form of Jerome's name is Geronimus) probably led to the legend being ascribed to Jerome as early as the seventh century, possibly by mistake.[55] However, the lion story subsequently became indelibly associated with Jerome and was recounted in Jacopo Voragine's thirteenth century *Legenda aurea* (*The Golden Legend*), the most popular medieval source for saints' lives. [56]

A lion appears in most depictions of Jerome from the fourteenth to the fifteenth century.[57] It usually accompanies the saint when he is depicted his study, as well as in the desert.[58] While Jerome is sometimes shown examining the animal's paw, for the most part, when the lion is depicted, it serves as a passive, allegorical symbol. In Bellini's paintings, the lion appears similarly as a conventional symbol of Jerome and serves as his companion in the desert.

It also clear, however, that African lions were associated with a particular dialectic between the wild and civilized in Quattrocento Italy. For instance, Luca Landucci, the Florentine diarist, records a gift Florence received from Sultan Qa'itbay of Egypt, brought to the city by a delegation seeking a trade agreement. The gift included a giraffe, which received the greatest attention because of its exoticism, but also a "domesticated lion" as well as other animals, whose handler could move through the cages unharmed.[59] This intriguing detail of a tame or tamed lion corresponds in interesting ways to the disappointing performance of lions in public spectacles: records indicate that lions all too often failed to demonstrate their assumed wild nature.[60] A similar story about the unexpected behaviour of a lion is told by Giovanni Villani in his account of an event that occurred in Florence in 1259 between a child, Orlanduccio, his mother, and the lion of Calfette. The lion, a gift to the city, escaped his cage and ran rampant in the streets, capturing a small boy. The boy's mother, distraught because this was her only child and her husband had been killed, grabbed the boy from the lion. The boy and his mother then remained unharmed while the lion sat calmly, attacking neither one of them.[61] Villani says that the boy was spared so that he could then go on to rightfully avenge his father's murder, and thus uses the tale to illustrate justified revenge. He then follows the story by praising the Florentines for their humility, moderation, and dedication to each other and their community, thereby making the story about civic virtue.[62] In his view, the lion story reflects the fact that "with their simple life and poverty they [the Florentines] did greater and more virtuous things than are done in our times with more luxuries and riches."[63] There is a sense, then, that the lion's tameness is connected to the asceticism and virtue of the Florentines. Thus the behaviour of the animals was taken to allegorize human morality: by abnegating their wild natures in favour of placidity, they symbolized the self-discipline of humans.

Tameness is a primary affect of the lions in the St. Jerome paintings. As both living animals and rock face imprints, the lions appear to be contiguous with the landscape. At the same time, the lion stands for the wilderness and is at home there. Thus the lion doesn't merely serve as a conventional symbol of the saint. It also represents the mutable ground on which the saint's transformation becomes complete, emblematizing the struggle between the wild and the domesticated that also occurs inside the saint.

The lion's liminal state, somewhere between animal and stone and between wild and tame, is also reflective of the role played by a satyr and a centaur in Jerome's life of Paul of Thebes. In Athanasius's account of nonagenarian Anthony's journey to meet with the even more ancient Paul, he describes Anthony encountering a centaur in the desert. Anthony is horrified by the creature, identifying it as a demonic presence, and wards it off by waving a cross.[64] In Jerome's account of the encounter, however, Anthony, while at first afraid because the beast/man seems threatening, instead soon realizes the centaur is friendly. Through gestures and inchoate grunts, the centaur tells Anthony how to find Paul.[65] The centaur represents both the chaotic and dangerous elements of the wilderness, but also its benign and utopic aspects. In short, it is creature that, like the satyrs and fauns of Greek myth, models what would evolve as the European notion of the Wild Man. As Hayden White has argued, the Wild Man myth holds in balance contradictory views of nature – on the one hand it constitutes a view of man consumed by bestial instincts, and on the other, it embodies a repudiation of both culture and corrupt civilization in favour of a prelapsarian purity; it signifies both base animality, and contrarily, passage to a more essential and pure state of being.[66] Jerome's account instantiates a similar dichotomy. After the centaur departs, Anthony continues on and meets a satyr who, while also part human and part animal, can nevertheless speak and says to Anthony that they share a common Lord. Thus the two human-animal hybrids Anthony meets demonstrate the concept of the Wild Man as spiritually pure. Analogically, they also stand for both Paul and the desert itself. Like the hermit's landscape, the hybrid human/animal offers a dual state of being to the saint: a wildness that is on the one hand threatening (giving in to animal impulses inspired by the Devil) and on the other restorative (offering a path to a purer existence inspired by God). Whereas Athanasius' biography of Anthony focuses on the centaur and satyr as beasts that populate the pantheon of the saint's tormentors, St. Jerome's *Life of Paul of Thebes* recasts the centaur and satyr as benign life forms that are neither fully animal, nor fully human. Instead they are hinges between the desert's brutal effects, and its role in transforming men into saints.

The lion and rock faces index a similar dichotomy in Bellini's paintings. Jerome's lion is tame and placid, a bellwether of the desert's calming force. Here the bestial is negated by the spiritual focus that the landscape brings to Jerome's inward turn. As the lion melds with the stone, and the stone envelopes the saint, the stony faces evoke not torment but the landscape's dual nature. The human is opposed to the non-human, and the animate to the inanimate. Jerome is consumed by the desert around him, absorbed by the rock and stone, becoming an Adam in reverse – no longer made from earth, but returning to it.

## Conclusion

Bellini's paintings are invested with the sense that land is sacred because of its natural qualities and also because it has an irrepressible energy of its own. This potential evokes what John Kirtland Wright called "geopiety," a condition initiated by the sense that a specific topography cloaks hidden powers that determine one's response to it.[67] In anthropomor-phizing the desert, Bellini's paintings posit it as necessary to the saint's reflection and penance, constitutive of the life and thought that rati-fies his existence. In its dualities of threat and solace, the desert is an environment that offers the possibility of metamorphosis. Bellini fore-grounds the power of this particular environment to transform the saint who occupies it, in concert with his own acts of penitence and processes of reflection. The desert is a vital actor in the narrative of Jerome's met-amorphosis, both because it tests his physical limits and because it offers him a mirror for his shelter and solitude. While the desert doesn't need him, he needs the desert – the land is the source of his strength and wit-ness to his transformation. The paintings make visible Jerome's grasp of the spiritual and material "ecology" of hermitage.

## NOTES

1  Haeckel coined the term in 1866. Frank N. Egerton, "History of Ecological Sciences, Part 47: Ernst Haeckel's Ecology," *Bulletin of the Ecological Society of America* 94, no. 3 (July 2013): 222.

2  See Paul Duro, "What is a Parergon?," *Journal of Aesthetics and Art Criticism* 17, no. 1 (Winter, 2019): 23–33.

3  Robert Colby, "Dosso's Early Artistic Reputation and the Origins of Landscape Painting," *Papers of the British School at Rome* 76 (2008): 201–31.

4  This was one of the important insights of a recent exhibition and catalogue at the J. Paul Getty Museum in Los Angeles (10 October 2017–14 January 2018), which focused on the relationship between Bellini's landscapes in general and spirituality. See Davide Gasparotto, ed., *Giovanni Bellini: Land-scapes of Faith in the Renaissance* (Los Angeles: Getty Publications, 2017), exhibition catalogue.

5  See, for instance, Jodi Cranston's reappraisal of the pastoral tradition in the greening of both Venetian painting and urban landscape. Cranston, *Green Worlds of Renaissance Venice* (College Station: Penn State University Press, 2019).

6  Many have written on the role played by the desert in the writing of early Christian saints and in late antique and early medieval conceptions of Chris-tian enlightenment and revelation. See for instance: J.E. Goehring, *Ascetics, Society and the Desert: Studies in Early Egyptian Monasticism* (Harrisburg, PA: Trinity Press International, 1999); Claudia Rapp, "Ascetic Authority," chap. 4 in *Holy Bishops in Late Antiquity: The Nature of Christian Leadership in an Age*

*of Transitions* (Berkeley: University Of California Press, 2005); Belden C. Lane, "Desert Catechesis: The Landscape and Theology of Early Christian Monasticism," *Anglican Theological Review* 75, no. 3 (Summer 1993): 292–315; Susan Power Bratton, "The Original Desert Solitaire: Early Christian Monasticism and Wilderness," *Environmental Ethics* 10 (Spring 1988): 31–53; Michael Uebel, "Medieval Desert Utopia," *Exemplaria* 14, no. 1 (2002): 1–45; Nathalie Roman, "Le desert medieval, expression du merveilleux," *Alif: Journal of Comparative Poetics* 33 (2013): 135–55; Jiri Subrt, "Sic nudus et armatus in Christo solitudinem ingressus est ... (The Motif of Desert in St. Jerome's Legends about the Hermits)," *Listy filolgické/Folia philologica* 123, no. 3/4 (2000): 223–36; and see all the articles in a special issue of *Church History and Religious Culture* titled "The Encroaching Desert: Egyptian Hagiography and the Medieval West," 86, no. 1 (2006).

7   As Peter Brown points out, "The myth of the desert was one of the most abiding creations of late antiquity. It was, above all, a myth of liberating precision. It delimited the towering presence of 'the world,' from which the Christian must be set free, by emphasizing a clear ecological frontier. It identified the process of disengagement from the world with a move from one ecological zone to another, from the settled land of Egypt to the desert. It was a brutally clear boundary, already heavy with immemorial associations." Brown, *The Body and Society: Men, Women, and Sexual Renunciation in Early Christianity* (New York: Columbia University Press, 1988), 216.

8   This is what Athanasius no doubt meant in his *Life of Saint Anthony* when he claimed that monks had made the desert into a city. Athanasius, *Vita Antonii* 14 (PG 26.865B). According to Jacques Le Goff, so many hermits flocked to clustered hermitages that they essentially often ended up building small towns instead of living in solitude. Jacques Le Goff, *The Medieval Imagination*, trans. Arthur Goldhammer (University of Chicago Press, 1988), 50. Referring not to the ancient poem of the same name by Statius, but to the area around Thebes in ancient Egypt to which early Christian hermits retreated, the Thebaid became a subject for reflection and representation in the fifteenth century, particularly in Florence. See Anne Leader, "The Church and Desert Fathers in Early Renaissance Florence: Further Thoughts on a 'New' Thebaid," in *New Studies on Old Masters: Essays in Renaissance Art in Honour of Colin Eisler*, ed. John Garton and Diana Wolfthal (Toronto: Centre for Reformation and Renaissance Studies, 2011), 221–34; Ellen Callmann, "A Quattrocento Jigsaw Puzzle," *Burlington Magazine* 99, no. 650 (May 1957): 149–55; Christian Heck, "The Vision of St. Anthony on a Thebaid Panel at Christ Church, Oxford," *Journal of the Warbuurg and Courtauld Institutes* 59 (1996): 286–94. Thebaids are often depicted as utopian

agrarian landscapes with gardens and plots interspersed with dwellings. However, paintings of Thebaids also sometimes focus on the idea of saintly Dormition, with the landscape serving as a backdrop for dying hermits who will ascend to heaven. Thus the backgrounds are intended less as evocations of the desert than as means to connect the good works and actions of hermits to their salvation. See Alessandra Malquori, "Borrowing Figurative Patterns: The Meaning of the 'Dormition of the Hermit' in Fifteenth-Century Florentine Paintings," in *Transcultural Imaginations of the Sacred*, ed. Margit Kern and Klaus Krüger (Paderborn: Wilhelm Fink, 2019), 163–79.

9 Judith Adler, "Cultivating Wilderness: Environmentalism and Legacies of Early Christian Asceticism," *Comparative Studies in Society and History* 48, no. 1 (January 2006): 17.

10 J.N.D. Kelly, *Jerome: His Life, Writings, and Controversies* (New York: Harper and Rowe, 1975), 46.

11 *Jerome: Select Letters*, trans. F.J. Wright (Cambridge, MA: Loeb Classical Library, 1933), 69.

12 Ibid., 67.

13 See John Block Friedman, *The Monstrous Races in Medieval Art and Thought* (1981; reprint Syracuse, NY: Syracuse University Press, 2000), 15.

14 Beothius, *In Porphyrium commentaria*, 5. Michael Battle, "The Problem of the Aethiop: Identity and Black Identity in the Desert Tradition," *Sewanee Theological Review* 42, no. 4 (Michaelmas 1999): 418n16.

15 To be whitewashed was to be cleansed of desire, as Jerome's characterization of Eustochium's virginity attests. Patricia Cox Miller, "The Blazing Body: Ascetic Desire in Jerome's Letter to Eustochium," *Journal of Early Christian Studies* 1, no. 1 (Spring 1993): 27.

16 Battle, "The Problem of the Aethiop," 424.

17 Peter Brown, *The Making of Late Antiquity* (Cambridge, MA: Harvard University Press), 87.

18 See for instance Joseph Koerner, "The Epiphany of the Black Magus Circa 1500," in *The Image of the Black in Western Art*, Vol. 3, *From the "Age of Discovery" to the Age of Abolition, Part 1: Artists of the Renaissance and Baroque*, ed. David Bindman and Henry Louis Gates. Jr. (Cambridge, MA: Harvard University Press, 2010), 7–92.

19 This is not to diminish the racial components and highly gendered nature of those references, or the solipsism that underlies such expressions of desire. That visions of internal temptation were experienced primarily as figures of women and boys, often described as Ethiopian, clearly demonstrates another, more invidious form of "moral geography" in early Christianity. See Battle, "The Problem of the Aethiop," 420 and Miller, "The Blazing Body,"

27. The discussion of race in the late antique and in early Christianity has recently expanded in important ways. Geraldine Heng, for instance, has argued that Judaisim, Islam, and Christianity have historically employed processes of "race-making" in which "strategic essentialisms are posited and assigned through a variety of practices and pressures, so as to construct a hierarchy of peoples for differential treatment." Geraldine Heng, *The Invention of Race in the European Middle Ages* (Cambridge, UK: Cambridge University Press, 2018), 3. In contrast, in his discussion of representations of Ethiopian eunuchs in Byzantine manuscripts, Roland Betancourt has pointed out that while Western traditions identified and othered "monstrous" races through skin colour in Plinian terms, Byzantine sources tended to take a far more cosmopolitan view of the variation and difference of skin tones and ethnicities present at the court of Constantinople. Roland Betancourt, *Byzantine Intersectionality: Sexuality, Gender & Race in the Middle Ages* (Princeton: Princeton University Press, 2020), 168. Betancourt's study illuminates both the sexual and the racial fluidity of the late antique.

20  John M. McManamon, S.J., "Pier Paolo Vergerio (The Elder) and the Beginnings of the Humanist Cult of St. Jerome," *Catholic Historical Review* 71, no. 3 (July 1985): 365.

21  Images of Saint Jerome in the desert begin to appear slightly before 1400, and proliferated in the first decades of the fifteenth century, especially in Florence. Reverence for Saint Jerome's hermitage was promoted by the Medici family, beginning with Giovanni de Bicci de Medici, friend of the Franciscan Beato Carlo de Montegranelli who founded a hermitage dedicated to St. Jerome in Fiesole around 1360. Giovanni de Bicci's son, Cosimo de Medici, il Vecchio, continued this Medicean interest, not only by commissioning works of art depicting Jerome in the desert, but by collecting Jerome's writings as well as lives of other desert saints. See Amanda Lillie, "Fiesole: Locus amoenus or Penitential Landscape?" *I Tatti Studies in the Italian Renaissance* 11 (2007): 23; and Bernhard Ridderbos, *Saint and Symbol: Images of Saint Jerome in Early Italian Art*, trans. P. de Waard-Dekking (Groningen: Bouma's Boekhuis, 1984), 74–9. The appearance in Tuscany of paintings depicting Jerome in his hermitage around 1400 has been noted by several scholars. See Eugene Rice, *Saint Jerome in the Renaissance* (Baltimore: Johns Hopkins University Press, 1985), and Ridderbos, *Saint and Symbol.* Both Rice and Ridderbos expand on a study first published by Millard Meiss, "Scholarship and Penitence in the Early Renaissance: The Image of St. Jerome," *Pantheon* 32 (1974): 134–40.

22  Rice, *Saint Jerome in the Renaissance,* 76.

23  For a comprehensive account of the many versions and ramifications of biographies of saints and *vitae patrum* in the European Middle Ages, see

Thomas J. Heffernan, *Sacred Biography: Saints and Their Biographers in the Middle Ages* (Oxford: Oxford University Press, 1988). For specifically Italian sources for hagiographies of the saints, see Alessandra Malquori, *Il giardino dell'anima. Ascesi e propaganda nell Tebaidi fiorentini del Quattrocento* (Florence: Centro Di, 2012), 37–52.

24 David Marsh, "Petrarch and Jerome," *Memoirs of the American Academy in Rome* 49 (2004): 85–98. Latin editions of Jerome's *Epistolae*, one of the most important sources for his descriptions of the desert, were published repeatedly all over the Europe in the second half of the fifteenth century, but the *editio princeps* was probably the one printed in Rome in 1468 by a German printer, Sixtus Reissinger. It was followed quickly in the same year by an edition printed in Strasbourg. See Thomas E. Marston, "St. Jerome's Letters and Tracts," *Yale University Library Gazette* 50, no. 4 (April 1976): 219–24.

25 According to Rice, these never achieved quite the popularity of the penitent desert images. He counts 558 that show the penitent Jerome, but only 133 of Jerome in his study. Rice, *Saint Jerome in the Renaissance*, 104.

26 To view this image, see: https://www.nationalgallery.org.uk/paintings /antonello-da-messina-saint-jerome-in-his-study. Jerome was one of four doctors of the church, the others being Gregory, who was a pope, and Ambrose and Augustine, who were bishops. Jerome, however, held neither title. The designation of cardinal did not exist in the Western church until the early sixth century, two centuries after Jerome had died. But because of his perceived lower status than the other doctors of the church, the honorific of cardinal seems to have been added later, in the ninth century, to raise him to a comparable level. In addition, the red robes were also added later, as red was not a prerogative of cardinals until the reign of Pope Paul II (1464–71). Rice, *Saint Jerome in the Renaissance*, 106. See also Grete Ring, "St. Jerome Extracting the Thorn from the Lion's Foot," *Art Bulletin* 27, no. 3 (September 1945): 188–94.

27 See Felton Gibbons, "Giovanni Bellini's Topographical Landscapes," *Studies in Late Medieval and Renaissance Painting in Honor of Millard Meiss*, ed. Irving Lavin and John Plummer (New York: NYU Press, 1977), 174–84; and Augusto Gentili, "Bellini and Landscape," in *The Cambridge Companion to Giovanni Bellini*, ed. Peter Humfrey (Cambridge, UK: Cambridge University Press, 2008), 167–81.

28 See Christiane Wiebel, *Askese und Endlichkeitsdemut in der italienischen Renaissance. Iknologische Studien zum Bild des heiligen Hieronymous* (Weinheim: VCH, Acta Humaniora, 1988), 102–4. See also Pavel Kalina, "Hericiis et leporibus: Giovanni Bellini's St. Jerome in Washington and the Idea of the Hermit's Life in Italy and Central Europe in the Early 16th Century," *Umeni Art* 60,

no. 5 (2012): 351. It seems possible that the hares and their changing colours might allude to Jerome's description of himself as sunburned and dark before emerging from his hermitage enlightened.

29 Hugo Schnell, "Das Massenwerkfenster mit drei Hasen im Kreuzgang des Paderborner Doms," *Mainzer Zeitschrift* 67–8 (1972–3): 169–75.

30 For an extensive excursus on the possible meanings carried by fauna in Saint Jerome paintings, see Herbert Friedmann, *A Bestiary for Saint Jerome: Animal Symbolism in European Religious Art* (Washington, DC: Smithsonian Institution, 1980). Bernhard Ridderbos connects the birds and animals that appear in Antonello da Messina's *Saint Jerome* to the Dominican Thomas of Cantimpré's thirteenth-century *Liber de natura rerum*, which provides examples of animals that can be used to illustrate particular articles of faith. Ridderbos, *Saint and Symbol*, 51.

31 Hans Belting, "St. Jerome in Venice: Giovanni Bellini and the Dream of Solitary Life," *I Tatti Studies in the Italian Renaissance* 17, no. 1 (Spring 2014): 5–33. For more on the value attributed to solitude, see also Christine Göttler, "Realms of Solitude in Late Medieval and Early Modern European Cultures: An Introduction," and Oskar Bätschmann, "Giovanni Bellini's *San Francesco nel deserto*," both in *Solitudo: Spaces, Places, and Times of Solitude in Late Medieval and Early Modern Cultures*, ed. Karl A.E. Enenkel and Christine Göttler (Leiden: Brill, 2018), 1–28 and 293–309 respectively.

32 See Belting, "St. Jerome in Venice," 6.

33 Gasparotto, *Giovanni Bellini*, 58; and Ridderbos, *Saint and Symbol*, 30–1.

34 *The Voyages of Cadamosto and Other Documents on Western Africa in the Second Half of the Fifteenth Century*, trans. and ed. G.R. Crone (London: Hakluyt Society, 1937), vol. 2, chap. 4, section 2.

35 On the basis of Giovanni's use of light, Daniel Wallace Maze argues against the grain that, rather than based on Jacopo Bellini's drawings or even a painting by Jacopo of St. Jerome (in Verona), Giovanni may have instead been responding to Andrea Mantegna's fresco of *The Calling of Saints James and John* in the Overtari Chapel in Padua. See Daniel Maze, *Young Bellini* (New Haven: Yale University Press, 2021), 98.

36 Keith Christiansen, "Bellini and Mantegna," in *The Cambridge Companion to Giovanni Bellini*, ed. Peter Humfrey (Cambridge, UK: Cambridge University Press, 2004), 72; Emanuele Lugli, "Between Form and Representation: The Frick St. Francis," *Art History* 32, no. 1 (February 2009): 33. See also Keith Christiansen, "Giovanni Bellini and the Practice of Devotional Painting," in *Giovanni Bellini and the Art of Devotion*, ed. Ronda Kasl (Indianapolis: Indianapolis Museum of Art, 2004), 39–41; and Katherine Crawford Luber, "Patronage and Pilgrimage: Jan van Eyck, the Adornes Family, and Two

Paintings of 'St. Francis in Portraiture'," *Philadelphia Museum of Art Bulletin* 91, no. 386/7 (Spring 1998): 24–37.

37  David Kim has made a similar observation about Bellini's *St. Francis* at the Frick, arguing that the painting challenges conventional notions of the relationship of figure to ground by inverting the distant landscape, making it dominate the foreground. In so doing, Bellini forces us to confront what the stone wall itself might mean. See Kim, "Stonework and Crack in Giovanni Bellini's *St. Francis in the Wilderness*," in *Steinformen: Materialität, Qualität, Imitation,* ed. Isabella Augart et al. (Berlin: De Gruyter, 2019), 61.

38  St. Jerome, "The First Hermit: St Paul of Thebes," trans. Marie Liguori Ewald, in *Fathers of the Church: Early Christian Biographies,* ed. Roy J. Deferrari (Washington, DC: The Catholic University of America Press, 1952; reprint 1964), 227–8.

39  Nancy Klein, "How Buildings Were Constructed," in *A Companion to Greek Architecture,* ed. Margaret M. Miles (Oxford: Wiley-Blackwell, 2016), 111.

40  Jerome became associated with learned Christian humanism particularly through early fifteenth-century sermons and eulogies by Pier Paolo Vergerio (the elder). See McManamon, "Pier Paolo Vergerio," 353–71. Vergerio is responsible for the Renaissance focus on St. Jerome as an ascetic who "adapted pagan learning (especially rhetoric) in such a way as to enrich the Christian message." Irene Backus, review of *Pierpaolo Vergerio the Elder and Saint Jerome: An Edition and Translation of Sermones pro Sancto Hieronymo,* in *The Catholic Historical Review* 86, no. 3 (July 2000): 504.

41  Rice, *Saint Jerome in the Renaissance,* 84–115.

42  Kim, "Stonework and Crack," 64–7.

43  Jacob Wamberg calls this the "lithic biology" on which the geological speculation of the fifteenth and sixteenth centuries is founded. See Wamberg, "A Stone and Yet Not a Stone: Alchemical Themes in North Italian Quattrocento Landscape Imagery," in *Art and Alchemy,* ed. Jacob Wamberg (Copenhagen: Museum Tusculanum Press, 2006), 51.

44  Leon Battista Alberti, *On the Art of Building in Ten Books,* trans. Joseph Rykwert, Neil Leach, and Robert Tavernor (Cambridge, MA: MIT Press, 1988), 49.

45  Adam Takahashi, "Nature, Formative Power and Intellect in the Natural Philosophy of Albert the Great," *Early Science and Medicine* 13, no. 5 (2008): 456.

46  "For the mineralizing power is a certain power, common to the production of both stones and metals, and of things intermediate between them. And we say in addition that if this is active in forming stones, it becomes a special [power for producing] stones. And because we have no special name for this power, we are obliged to explain by analogies what it is. Let us say, then, that just as in an animal's seed, which is a residue from its food, there comes from the seminal vessels a force capable of forming an animal, which

[actually] forms and produces an animal, and is in the seed in the same way that an artisan is in the artifact that he makes by his art; so in material suitable for stones there is a power that forms and produces stones, and develops the form of this stone or that." Albertus Magnus, *Book of Minerals,* trans. Dorothy Wyckoff (Oxford: Clarendon Press, 1967): 22.

47  Takahashi, "Nature, Formative Power and Intellect," 456–8.

48  Albertus Magnus, *Book of Minerals,* 52. The word "fossil" does not appear until the sixteenth century when Agricola used it in his *De natura fossilium* of 1546, to denote an "inanimate subterranean" body. See Christopher P. Heuer, "Fossils/Force/Earth" in *Leonardo in Dialogue: The Artist Amid His Contemporaries,* ed. Francesca Borgo et al. (Venice: Marsilio, 2019), 323.

49  Bellini's lion is modelled on one of the many lions that appear in a parchment drawing and pattern book once owned by Jacopo Bellini and now in the Louvre. Several of the folios, some from the hand of Jacopo and others not, depict a wide variety of lions in multiple poses, many depicted in great naturalistic detail. All of Giovanni's lions appear to be based on this early set of examples. Conrad Eisler, *The Genius of Jacopo Bellini: The Complete Paintings and Drawings* (New York: Harry N. Abrams, 1989), 79; Gasparotto, *Giovanni Bellini,* 61. The drawing on which Giovanni's Birmingham lion is based, *Seven Lions and Three Stags,* can be found in Jacopo Bellini's sketchbook, fol. 78v, Paris, Musée du Louvre, RF 1475-1556.

50  Across the way, there is also a strange animal-shaped shadow created by the rock hollow shielding a spring to the lower left of the saint. This appears to be in the shape of an ape, and may be intended to comment on the nature of painting itself.

51  Giacomo Berra, "Immagini casuali e natura antropomorfa," *Mitteilungen des Kunsthistorisches Institutes in Florenz* 43, no. 2/3 (1999): 384.

52  Patricia Cox Miller, "Jerome's Centaur: A Hyper-Icon of the Desert," *Journal of Early Christian Studies* 4, no. 2 (1996): 211.

53  Ibid.

54  Jerome does not treat the lion himself, but tells the monks in the monastery to welcome the lion, and wash and treat his wound. And the description makes it clear that the thorn was no longer in the lion's paw when it arrived, and only the wound required attention. David Salter, *Holy and Noble Beast: Encounters with Animals in Medieval Literature* (Bury St Edmunds: St. Edmundsbury Press, 2001), 12; Rice, *Saint Jerome in the Renaissance,* 37.

55  See Rice, *Saint Jerome in the Renaissance,* 44–5, and Malquori, "Borrowing Figurative Patterns," 164.

56  Lions accrued emblematic Christian and moral meanings from the fourth-century Greek *Physiologus* through to late medieval bestiaries, and

were used as exempla in late medieval sermons and encyclopedias such as
Thomas de Cantimpré's *Liber de natura rerum* (1230–45). From the *Physiologus* to the sixteenth century, the behaviour associated with lions under-
went a Christianization, and was analogically linked to moral dogmas: for
instance, a description in the *Physiologus* of lions evading hunters by wiping
clear their own tracks with their tails was taken as a simile for the stealth
God used to evade the devil on earth; or the lion's purported ability to
sleep with its eyes open became linked analogically to Christ's wakeful "dormition" in the tomb before the Resurrection. See Simona Cohen, *Animals
as Disguised Symbols in Renaissance Art* (Leiden: Brill, 2008), 3–4. On the
other hand, as with most animals in the bestiary and exemplum literature,
lions also sometimes carried negative connotations, associated with vices
such as pride (*superbia*). Cohen, *Animals as Disguised Symbols*, 22. As many
have argued, any animal portrayed in Renaissance works of art would have
been understood, by default, to have multiple, layered, intersecting, and
often even contradictory meanings. See Claudia Lazzaro, "Animals as Cultural Signs: A Medici Menagerie in the Grotto at Castello," in *Reframing the
Renaissance: Visual Culture in Europe and Latin America 1450–1650*, ed. Claire
Farago (New Haven: Yale University Press, 1995), 204.

57  Giovanni da Andrea took credit for how Jerome came to be portrayed in
paintings (of which he personally commissioned several), especially for
those images that included a lion. "I have also established the way he should
be painted, namely, sitting in a chair, beside him the hat that cardinals wear
nowadays (that is, the red hat or *galerus ruber*) and at his feet the tame lion;
and I have caused many pictures of this sort to be set up in divers places."
Quoted in Rice, *Saint Jerome in the Renaissance*, 65.

58  Ring, "St. Jerome Extracting the Thorn," 188.

59  "E a di 12 di novenbre 1487, un garzone che governava e lioni, esendo dimes-
ticato co loro, i'modo ch'egli entrava infra loro e toccavagli"; Luca Landucci,
*Diario fiorentino*, ed. I. del Badia (Florence, 1883), 52. Contrary to long-held
beliefs, the giraffe and other animals were probably not gifts to Lorenzo
de' Medici, but instead were presented to the Republic itself. See Angelica
Groom, *Exotic animals in the art and culture of the Medici court* (Leiden: Brill,
2019), 181–90.

60  Gregorio Dati, in his *Istoria di Firenze*, records a cage house that held twenty-four
lions (the cage and lions are also mentioned by Leonardo da Vinci). The animals were used for Roman-style entertainments, or *cacce d'animali*, when Pope
Pius II and Galeazzo Sforza visited Florence in 1459. Piazza della Signoria was
set up as an animal arena into which twenty-six lions were introduced – but it
was anticlimactic as the lions refused to hunt the other animals. Gregorio Dati,

*L'Istoria di Firenze di Gregorio Dati dal 1380 al 1405: illustrata e pubblicata secondo il codice inedito stradiniano, collazionato con altri manoscritte e con la stampa del 1735,* ed. Luigi Pratese (Florence: Bernaro Seeber, 1904), 116. Leonardo da Vinci, in the early 1500s, recorded that in the lion house in Florence "... there are always twenty-five or thirty of them, which breed there." Quoted in Charles Nichols, *Leonardo da Vinci: The Flights of the Mind* (London: Penguin Books, 2007), 163. An enclosure for lions was established in a courtyard near the Piazza della Signoria on what became known as the Via dei Leoni. Groom, *Exotic animals,* 39; Joan Barclay Lloyd, *African Animals in Renaissance Literature and Art* (Oxford: Clarendon Press, 1971), 39–41.

61 "Udendolo la madre che non avea più, e questo fanciullo le rimase in ventre quando il padre gli fu morto, come disperata, con grande pianto scapigliata corse contra il leone, e trassegli il fanciullo tra lle branche; e leone nullo male fece né a la donna né al fanciullo se non ch'egli guatò, e ristettesi." Giovanni Villani, *Nuova Cronica,* ed. Giuseppe Porta (Parma: Pietro Bembo, 1990), 1:363.

62 Glenn Kumhera, *The Benefits of Peace: Private Peacemaking in Late Medieval Italy* (Leiden: Brill, 2017), 176.

63 "loro grossa vita e povertà feciono maggiori e più virtudiose cose, che non sono fatte a' tempi nostri con più morbidezza e con più ricchezza." Villani, *Nuova Cronica,* 1:364.

64 See Laura Fenelli, "From the *Vita Pauli* to the *Legenda Breviarii:* Real and Imaginary Animals as a Guide to the Hermit in the Desert," in *Animals and Otherness in the Middle Ages: Perspectives Across Disciplines,* ed. Francisco de Asís García García, Mónica Ann Walker Vadillo, and María Victoria Chico Picaza (Oxford: Archaeopress, 2013), 37.

65 Ibid., 38.

66 Hayden White, "The Forms of Wildness: Archaeology of an Idea," in *Tropics of Discourse: Essays in Cultural Criticism* (Baltimore: Johns Hopkins University Press, 1978), 168.

67 J.K. Wright, "Notes on Early American Geopiety," in Wright, *Human Nature in Geography* (Cambridge, MA: Harvard University Press, 1966), 235.

# chapter twelve

# The End of All: Worldliness, Piety, and the Social Life of Maps in the Post-Reformation English Household

GAVIN HOLLIS

QUEEN. Ay me! I see the ruin of my house:
The tiger now hath seized the gentle hind;
Insulting tyranny begins to jut
Upon the innocent and aweless throne.
Welcome, destruction, blood, and massacre.
I see, as in a map, the end of all. (*Richard III*, 2.4.50–5)[1]

## Introduction: Maps, Poetics, and the Family of Robert Herrick

The poet Robert Herrick (1591–1674) wrote two poems dedicated to his brothers, Thomas and Nicholas, which describe map-reading practices and their social and spiritual associations in early seventeenth-century England. The attitudes towards map reading in the two poems couldn't be more opposed. "A Country Life: To his Brother Mr. Tho. Herrick" (c. 1613) commends Thomas's "Rurall Sanctuary" and is written in the vein of the pastoral mode, contrasting "The Countries sweet simplicity" with "Vice" that "rules the Most, or All at court."[2] In the middle of the encomium to the bucolic, Herrick describes Thomas's map-reading habits:

thou at home without or tyde or gale
Canst in thy Map securely saile:
Seeing those painted Countries; and so guesse
By those fine Shades, their Substances:
And from thy Compasse taking small advice,
Buy'st Travell at the lowest prise.

Herrick's poem celebrates maps as both educational tools and facilitators of what David McInnis calls "mind-travelling."[3] It also describes his brother's map reading as a form of religious devotion. The passage quoted above is framed by an allusion to Thomas's "daily and devout affaires," which are without "those desp'rate cares, / Th'industrous Merchant has." Thomas "is blest with securest ease," because he can see "these things within thy Map" and can view "them with a more safe survey." To read a map, then, is a pleasurable practice, but it also informs a spiritual life: it is part of Thomas's devotional practice, where he can be both detached from the world and contemplate it; and it leaves him "blest."

Herrick's poem "To his brother Nicolas Herrick" (first printed in 1648) conveys a view of map reading quite at odds with its depiction in his poem to Thomas. It begins as follows:

> What others have with cheapnesse seene, and ease,
> In Varnisht maps; by'th'helpe of Compasses:
> Or reade in Volumes, and those Bookes (with all
> Their large Narrations, *Incanonicall*)
>  Thou hast beheld those seas, and Countries farre;
> And tel'st to us, what once they were, and are.[4]

Nicholas was a merchant adventurer in the Levant, akin therefore to "Th'industrious Merchant" described in "A Country Life." As a result of his "Travails" he can speak about his time in the Holy Land and "Make knowne to us the now [new] *Jerusalem*." The poem contrasts Nicholas's authoritative voice with those who may claim to have "seene" the Holy Land, but have only done so at a remove by mind-travelling with "Varnisht maps." Maps, this poem seems to argue, grant only a superficial vantage. By contrast,

> the man that will but lay his eares, [to Nicholas's accounts]
> As *Inapostate*, to the thing he heares,
> Shall by his hearing quickly come to see
> The truth of Travails lesse in bookes than Thee.

"Inapostate" is Herrick's coinage, by which he seems to denote either someone who has not renounced their faith or someone who once did but then returned to the fold.[5] Its usage to describe someone who is inclined to Nicholas's true account of the Holy Land hints that readers of cheap maps have in effect turned their back on their faith. This sense of map readers as apostatic is amplified in the description of "large narrations,

*Incanonicall*" that have swayed readers along with "Varnisht maps." "In-canonicall" means non-scriptural, but also connotes transgression and a turn away from orthodoxy. To Robert Herrick, who by the time he wrote the poem "To his brother Nicolas Herrick" had taken holy orders (he was a vicar in North Devon between 1627 and the outbreak of the English Civil War), map-reading becomes an almost heretical exercise, a sentiment in stark contrast to that expressed in "A Country Life: To Thomas Herrick," in which map-reading is described as both a form of vicarious travel and as forming part of the household's "daily and devout affaires."[6]

I begin this chapter with Herrick's poems not to adjudicate to which view of maps the poet adhered, but rather because both poems offer insights into map-reading practices in post-Reformation England and their social and religious connotations. The poems do so in three distinct ways. First, they illustrate how contrasting views of map reading were available in the early seventeenth century (even in the work of the same poet). Second, they situate map-reading practices, and the impressions and religious ideologies attached to said practices, in the home – this is explicit in the poem to Thomas, as it is in his "Rurall Sanctuary" that he is able to safely read a map, and implicit in the poem to Nicholas, since map readers are imagined encountering the world at a remove, in contrast to the dedicatee's first-hand experience. Finally, the poems account for a use of maps that derives, in a sense, from their non-use. Map reading in both poems is not practical: it is not for the purposes of wayfaring or navigation, nor is it for the demarcation of property; rather, maps' utility in these poems lies in vicarious pleasures, in divine contemplation, or both.

Expanding on these two poems' insights, this chapter attempts a partial recovery of (to adapt Martin Brückner's formulation) "the social and spiritual life of maps" in post-Reformation England households.[7] It focuses in particular on decorative maps, that is, maps framed by emblematic patterns and figures, some of which are explicitly Christian and others of which are allegorical (including, as I will discuss, personifications of the continents). Spurred by Rayna Kalas's excavation of the cultural valence of "the frame" in early modernity, and her contention that to "frame ... an image, would not have meant to enclose it, but to make, sustain, or advance it," this chapter reads such framing devices on maps as crucial to their design and messaging, and argues that these elements mattered in their domestic deployment.[8] It explores the ways in which these maps, understood in their entirety, frame and all, and not just in terms of their geographical data, appealed to their owner's sense of their own worldliness (as a conduit for "mind-travelling"; as an index of individual or familial global wealth and power) and to their sense of their own piety as people who rejected or purported to reject worldly attachment. It focuses also on the ways in which maps projected and troubled the balancing act of worldliness and piety: as pious objects (by being framed with biblical imagery and paratextual matter); as worldly objects (by representing an abstract of the world or part of it, and also by being framed by pleasing and ornate imagery); and as things whose comprehension is always already out of reach (for their owners, and indeed for historians).

The chapter does so by engaging with three archives. First, it examines varieties of maps (in particular world maps) that were printed in Northern Europe in the sixteenth and seventeenth centuries, focusing in particular on their framing imagery. Second, it draws on probate inventories and wills – drawn from a sample of around two hundred from across Tudor and Stuart England (and one from seventeenth century Bavaria) – so as to aggregate the kinds of maps that were owned by English Protestants and the places where they were kept and displayed within their owners' property; in other words, so as to ask what objects maps were framed by and what they themselves framed. Third, it analyses drama from the period that elucidates the "mapmindedness" or "cartographic imagination" of early modern England.[9] Typically, analyses of maps in early modern English literature have focused on their geo-political, imperialist, and militarized connotations.[10] This chapter contends that the drama of this period also commented on the contemporary vogue for displaying maps in the home or was subtended by such displays. The most conspicuous example, Thomas Middleton's *The Puritan or the Widow of Watling Street* (c. 1606), stages a scene set in what seems like a personal *Kunstkammer* in a gentleman's house in which maps are prominently displayed. Christopher Marlowe's *Tamburlaine the Great* (c. 1587–8) and William Shakespeare's *Richard III* (c. 1593) are the key examples in the penultimate section of the chapter. Both plays engage with the geo-political, imperialist, and militaristic; but both also reckon (albeit quite differently) with the fashion for household display of maps by positing the ways in which it was both a practice of worldmaking and a way of contemplating its unmaking.

### Framing the World: Maps, Worldliness, and Piety

John Dee's oft-quoted description of the ways in which "Some, to beautify their Halls, Parlors, Chambers, Studies, or Libraries ... liketh, loveth, getteth, and useth, Maps, Charts, and Geographicall Globes" is echoed by a number of other commentators from the period.[11] Indeed, so popular was this fashion that it inspired Abraham Ortelius to create the first atlas, *Theatrum Orbis Terrarum* (*Theatre of the World*, 1570), since "broad and large Mappes cannot be opened or spread, that everything may easily and well be seene and discern'd."[12] But Ortelius may have overstated the care with which map readers approached sheet maps. People owned them for the purposes of "Daylie ... delight," according to the Elizabethan mathematician Thomas Blundeville, but he describes a less discerning viewership than Ortelius imagined – people who made rudimentary observations (they "can point to England, France, Germanie, and the East and West Indies") rather than subjecting them to close study.[13]

While Blundeville and Dee's general proposition that maps "delighted" may account for the ownership of maps, the reason for their popularity in the sixteenth and seventeenth centuries is hard to pin down. Perhaps, as Robert Herrick intimates, it was a simple question of their inexpensiveness. For some owners, the choice of maps was likely personal and idiosyncratic. For example, local affinities likely lie behind John English, fellow of St. John's College, Oxford, owning "a mappe of Suffolk" (his home county), or Richard Assheton displaying a "Mapp of Lancaster" in the main parlour of one of his Lancashire homes (Lancaster is the county town of Lancashire).[14] Tessa Watt has argued for the ways in which prints became increasingly popular, including as wall adornments. Anthony Wells-Cole has enumerated the prints from continental Europe that shaped much of the work of artisans overseeing household design and decor in England.[15] As both Watt and Wells-Cole attest, English visual culture was permeated with Christian imagery and sustained aspects of pre-Reformation imagery even in the wake of the so-called "iconoclasm" and "iconophobia" of the English post-Reformation age – an influence that can be found across material culture in cheap prints, in household masonry and carpentry, and, I contend, in printed maps.[16]

The sense from Herrick's "A Country Life," that map reading was both an imaginative and spiritual practice, tallies with both Watt's and Wells-Cole's conclusions about the importance of religious, and specifically biblical, imagery in English visual culture. An overview of examples of printed maps from the period that are framed with biblical imagery or more general pieties makes it possible to draw provisional conclusions about the ways in which the appeal of maps lay not just in delight but also in the provision of moral instruction and encouragement of spiritual contemplation. *The Fool's Cap World*, the oft-reprinted map of the world encased in a jester's hat, is surrounded by various moralizing statements, including "vanitas vanitatum et omnia vanitas" ("vanity of vanities, all is vanity") and "universa vanitas omnis homo" ("every man in his best state is altogether vanity"), famous dicta from Ecclesiastes 1:2 and Psalms 39:5.[17] But *The Fool's Cap World* is not alone among the period's maps in its articulation of this kind of sentiment. Jodocus Hondius's world map, *Novissima ac Exactissima Totius Orbis Terrarum Descriptio Magna* (*A New and Accurate Description of the World*), printed in Amsterdam in 1611, is framed by an image of the Fall at the bottom, in the space between the hemispheres, and the Ascension at the top. A decorative cartouche hovering over North America, and featuring *vanitas* standards such as hourglass and skull, includes an inscription that conflates Isaiah 40:6, "All flesh is grass, and all the goodliness thereof is as the flower of the field," and Romans 6:23, "For the wages of sin is death; but the gift of God is eternal life through Jesus Christ our Lord."[18] Nicolaes van Geelkercken's *Universi Orbis Tabula Deintegro Delineata* (*A Description of the Whole World*, printed one year earlier, also in Amsterdam) is framed by the same imagery, although it lacks the inscription.[19] Both maps frame the world within eschatological time and seem to argue that while life on earth is fleeting – like "grass ... [or] the flower of the field" – the promises of life after death are eternal. Another Hondius map, commonly titled *The Christian Knight Map* (Amsterdam, c. 1596) (fig. 12.1), features a knight (a "Miles Christianus") fending off Mundus (the world), Peccatum (sin), Caro (flesh), and Diabolus (the devil) on its southernmost continent. Hondius's map pivots between a celebration of the world – based as it is on the latest geographical knowledge available – and a caution against too great an attachment to it.[20]

As has been well documented, printed maps were deployed in a number of paintings of the Northern European Renaissance, particularly in representations of domestic settings. Maps were common in *vanitas* art, along with other markers of wealth, time, and decay that were themselves household items repurposed as the stuff of contemplation.[21] The inclusion of maps in this tradition may have been simply fashionable – the presence of maps in a number of "artist-in-studio" paintings seems to comment on their ubiquity in seventeenth-century art – but it could also be attributed to an understanding of maps as informing or being part of household decor that was itself construed as a *vanitas* assemblage of objects, patterns, and stylings.[22] As Tara Hamling argues in regards to the English context, "[e]mbellishing the home was ... a potentially problematic activity for more committed Protestants," since, while "visible expression of wealth was especially important for those seeking social advancement ... the religious and moral values of the Protestant faith

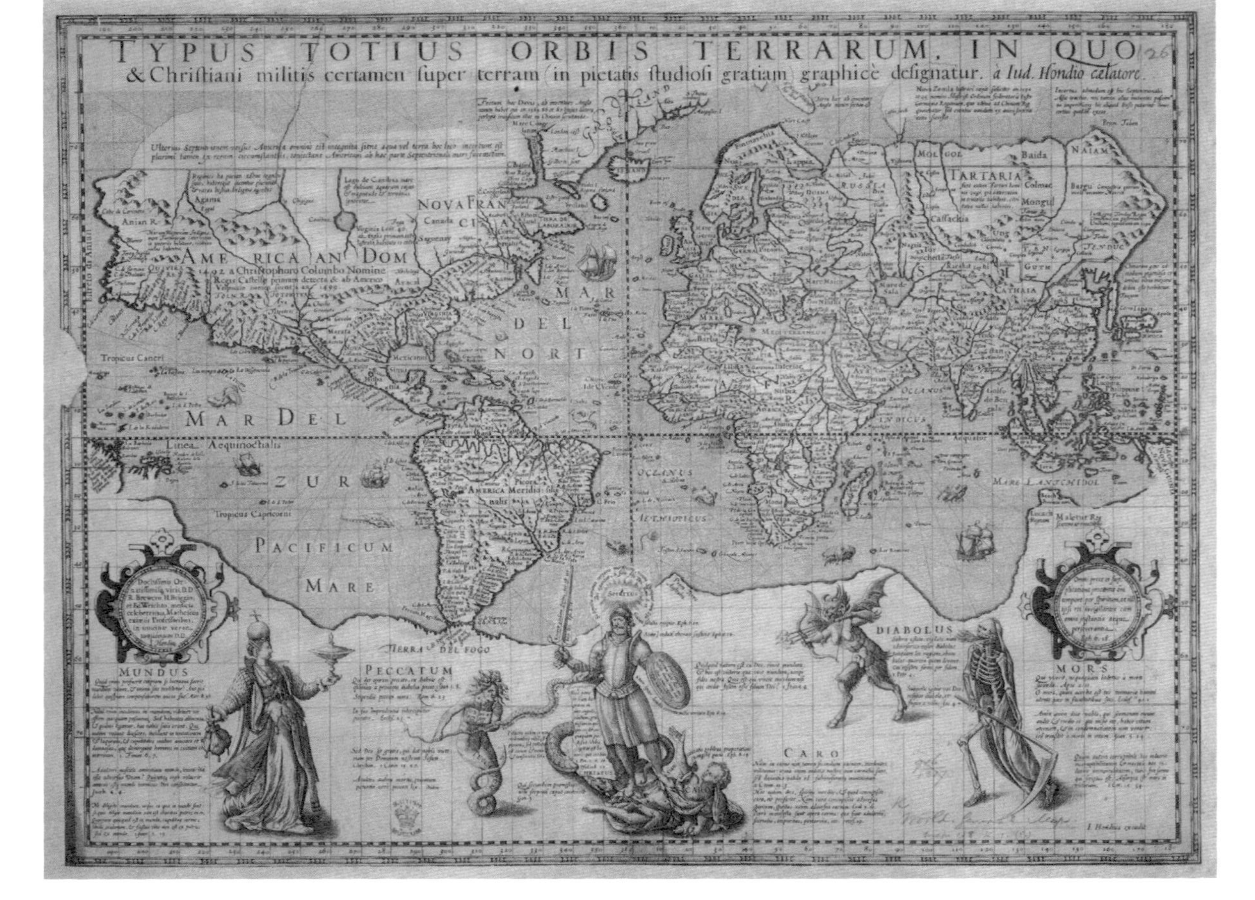

Figure 12.1. Jodocus Hondius, *Typus totius orbis terrarum in quo & Christiani militis certamen super terram, in pietatis studiosi gratiam* (Amsterdam, ca. 1596). Maps.188.k.1.(5). The British Library, London. © The British Library Board

rejected worldly ambition, vanity and luxury and instead demanded a demonstration of humility and modesty." As a result,

> One way to achieve a balance between self-promotion and a show of modesty was through the use of religious imagery as decoration in the home. Interior decoration improved the appearance and status of the building and thus aggrandised the owner, while the depiction of biblical stories indicated that the householder was concerned with spiritual, rather than worldly matters. In this way the decoration of houses with religious imagery served as a badge of social and godly identity to advertise the status and piety of the household.[23]

Hamling's archive comprises a variety of decorative forms that incorporated and wrestled with religious imagery (paintings, tapestries and painted cloths, carpets, wall screens, plaster friezes, wall paintings, stained and painted glass, roof bosses, and woodwork and stonework). It does not include maps, but they too could and should be considered objects that both aggrandized the household and projected a sense of its humility. On the one hand, maps connoted worldly ambition fueled by early modernity's "competitive urge to acquire," as diagnosed by Lisa Jardine and Linda Levy Peck.[24] On the other hand, they were objects intended to foster humility in the face of the divine and reject the vanity of assuming such knowledge for oneself – that is, of adopting God's position looking down on Creation.

As Hamling shows, this balancing act required work. Households are not static – indeed, the term "household" connotes not just the materials within it and its fabricated structure but also the living creatures who pass through it: its inhabitants, its visitors, its infiltrators (human and nonhuman).[25] Households move. Their stuffs have social lives; they are, to borrow from Ian Hodder, not isolated and inert but are entangled with other things.[26] These things can be moved, removed, written on, damaged, and repurposed, and are open to interpretation and appropriation beyond the intentions of their owners (in addition to resisting interpretation and appropriation) by both human and nonhuman forces. A map, displayed with the intention of conveying one's place in the world, or of conveying one's faith, or of conveying one's ability to balance the two, was in and of itself open to entanglement with the things surrounding it. To follow Bill Brown's distinction between objects and things, maps as objects might disclose particular meanings, while as things they exceed interpretation, even as they recede into multiple competing interpretations. The map as conveyer of worldliness tempered with piety, then, was always in process, always being renegotiated, and at some level (to quote Brown) "beyond the grid of intelligibility."[27]

## Maps, Worldliness, and Piety in the Dimpfel Family Collection

The display of maps within the home to project a sense of a household's balance of worldliness and piety can be seen in figure 12.2, as can the difficulty of maintaining this balance. The painting, by local painter and engraver Joseph Arnold, is a depiction of a room in the home of the Dimpfel family of Regensburg, Bavaria, c. 1668, that is filled with many of the family's possessions (or what the viewer is supposed to assume are their possessions).[28] Many items are personal to the life story of the family. The Dimpfel family was a prominent economic and political force in the region, and had made its fortune in mining and the iron trade. The painting depicts a suit of armour and a mounted cannon in the right foreground and five mounted cannons in front of a table on the left hand side. It supplements these nods to the family business with a portrait of a Roman soldier and a painting of a military fort on the right hand wall. Other objects, the kinds of things one might find in a royal or aristocratic cabinet of curiosities, seem to celebrate the wealth and status of the family: decorated seashells, blue-and-white plate-ware, timepieces, compasses, a stuffed armadillo, a horse-shaped ewer, coral, seven large paintings and two smaller canvases, an overflowing bookcase, several statues (at least five of which appear to be gold or gold-plated), and globes and a map (likely a world map). Others promote a sense of the family's religious conviction. There are three versions of the crucifixion: one is a painting mounted on the left-hand wall, while the other two are statues, one a small one on the left hand table and the other a larger one in the middle of the room. There is a Bible open on the table in the middle. The room also contains two skulls – one on the right hand table, and a smaller one perched atop a black plinth on the left hand table.

The painting, then, depicts a *Wunderkammer* of natural, artificial, and hybrid objects. But it tempers its sense of the family's worldliness with displays intended to highlight their piety. It is, as it were, a *vanitas*. And the globes and maps play a crucial role in the mise en scène, particularly in terms of the two vantage points embedded within the painting – the chair and the lectern. The chair has its back to the terrestrial globe and the world map on the right hand table. Hence the room, or the painting of the room, asks viewers to imagine sitting with their back to worldly things and instead holding the divine (represented by three crucifixes and the celestial globes) in their gaze. With the celestial globe hanging from the ceiling, the chair also seems situated under the weight of the heavens. The lectern, by contrast, faces the world – it is directly opposite the terrestrial globe. On it is placed what is most likely a Bible. Were viewers to stand there, they would be opposite the worldly goods that the positioning of the chair seems to reject. Yet this view is mediated by scripture and by the crucifix that stands next to the lectern. The painting, then, invites viewers into the painting; but it also asks them to visualize the Dimpfel family comfortable within their own domestic memento mori. Viewers can imagine them enjoying their wealth; they can also imagine them ruminating on the perils of worldliness, sitting and contemplating the divine without the clutter of the world, and standing up to see the world through the prism of religious faith.

The objects in Arnold's painting are meticulously staged – as Elizabeth Honig notes, even to the extent that the collection imports paintings that look like "those produced by the Middelburg masters," which likely "functioned to 'fill in' the Dimpfel collection." [29] But the painting's careful balancing act between piety and worldliness is undermined, if only ever so slightly, by the world map that is half rolled up and hanging down the side of the right hand table. All of the other objects in the room appear to be fixed on walls or carefully placed on tables. The map, which appears to be a double-hemisphere world map with the eastern hemisphere visible, is positioned precariously. Would it take much for the map to roll off the table? It's a small detail, but given the apparent coherence of the arrangement throughout the rest of the painting, it is worth noting that the only movement hinted at (outside of the painting's encouragement for viewers to imagine their own movement in the room and to visualize the presence of the household) is of something associated with physical motion and that engendered imaginary travel. What might it mean for the potential movement of this particular object – a map – to be downward? If the map does fall, does that mean that the family's worldly aspirations go with it? Or that their worldly aspirations will inevitably yield to their spiritual ones? Given the map tilts down eastward, and given the hostilities between the Habsburg Monarchy and the Ottoman Empire and the recent culmination of the Fourth Austro-Turkish War in 1664 (a military operation that would have been good for the family business), the dangling map might be understood as an allusion to an ongoing Holy War. Perhaps then the hanging map symbolizes the Ottoman Empire, whose fate hung in the balance (especially as the map is close to the armour and weaponry manufactured through the family's trade). But the dangling map might also allude to fears that the Christian world was in danger of being of being pulled down by the Ottoman threat. More locally, it might suggest that the Dimpfel family's world could get pulled down because of their own attachment to what they had accumulated thanks to the wealth generated by their trade. That is, even in their contribution to the defeat of Islam, this family is in danger of venerating the material object, as their Islamic enemy was reputed to do by European Christians.

Any and all of these interpretations are available in this detail in the painting. My purpose here in enumerating them is not to pick one, but rather to point to the ways in which the world map unsettles the balance of the room. The map, that is, calls attention to the difficulty, and maybe even impossibility, of balancing the accumulation of wealth with the attestation of faith through objects. Of course, this uncertainty in and of itself could be said to be a function of the arrangement, which it could be said knowingly unstitches its own neatness so as to project (again) the family's (and/or the artist's) facility with the *vanitas* form, raising the otherwise somewhat clichéd protestations of a balanced life to a new level of sophistication. Or it may be a product of what Brown calls "the thingness of objects" – in this case maps – which foreclose a certainty of meaning – in this case, a certainty that the Dimpfel family had, and ever could have, perfectly balanced their self-projection as a worldly-pious household.[30]

## Maps and Households in Post-Reformation England

There is no image from post-Reformation England depicting map ownership equivalent to the Dimpfel collection painting. There are, however, numerous examples of household records from the period that detail the presence and placement of maps. My research of inventories and wills from various counties in England accounts for nearly two hundred instances of map ownership in the sixteenth and seventeenth centuries.[31] There are a number of examples of households where maps or globes were placed next to religious imagery.[32] On the walls of the Great Chamber of Lumley Castle, the Durham home of John, Lord Lumley, and on the walls of the Long Gallery at the Greenwich home of Henry Howard, Earl of Northumberland, maps and globes were displayed next to Old and New Testament scenes in a variety of media, according to the inventories recorded at their deaths in 1609 and 1614 respectively.[33] Isabella Rood or Rud's goods included a depiction of "The just judgment at

Sallomon, wyth the Quenes Majesties armes" (medium unknown), along with "iii mappes" and "One olde mappe," according to an inventory of her property at Plawsworth, County Durham, dated 1582.[34] The will of Crystofer Smyth, also from County Durham, dated 1603, lists "a mapp [either some kind of geographical image or a simply a picture] of the Prodigall sonne, in a fraime," and "two little framed mappes" on display in the hall.[35] The inventory of George Hocken of Totnes, Devon (also 1603), lists "Fower greate mapps with frames of the fower partes of the world ... One greate mappe of the genealogy of the Byble ... Hoodes Spheares in Coulors ... [and] Fower other littell mapps."[36] Protestant households, then, arranged maps alongside overt religious depictions in tapestries, in hangings, and in imagery in the form of "maps."[37]

Useful as it is, there is a limit to what can be done with the evidence drawn from probate inventories and wills.[38] Much of the documentation concerning maps is cursory, limited in detail, and reflects ownership very close to or at the point of death, which, given that maps were fragile, means that the records may not reflect ownership over the course of a lifetime. Analyses from these sources about what owners did with their maps – in particular where they located them and what they were placed next to – are necessarily tentative, both in terms of quantitative data (maps were almost certainly more widespread than the available documentation allows) and in terms of qualitative data (the records do not tell us why they might have been arranged in a particular order, nor even do they tell us much about the content of the maps themselves). While an inventory reveals, for example, that the Cambridgeshire home of Edward Raven (d. 1558), fellow of St. John's College, Cambridge, was adorned with maps both geographical ("of Fraunce," "of grece," and "the whole world") and biblically-themed ("a mappe of palestina" and "of perigrinatio pauli"), it does not answer why both kinds of maps jostled for space on his walls, at least not on its own.[39]

Yet even if sixteenth- and seventeenth-century written records afford us only a partial view of map ownership, they can be supplemented by other archives. We can look to the archives that Tara Hamling and Anthony Wells-Cole have examined – namely the other, more durable, forms of household decor woven in tapestry or carved in wood and stone. Wells-Cole has demonstrated the ways in which English design features were indebted to ornamental prints that originated from continental Europe – many from the Netherlands.[40] As James Welu and Elizabeth A. Sutton have argued, many of the same print sources (by prominent Dutch engravers like Cornelis and Jacob Floris, Cornelis Bos, Vreedman de Vries,

Maarten de Vos, and Adrien Collaert) influenced mapmakers too.[41] For example, figures from a print of *Miles Christianus* by Hieronymus Wierix, after Maarten de Vos, frame Hondius's *Christian Knight Map*, discussed earlier in this chapter (figure 12.1). The configuration of elements is slightly different on the map. Mundus, Diabolus, and Death are further away from the knight on the map, and all of the figures are positioned at the far reaches of the world – beyond the borders of the known world, in its mythical southern hinterland – rather than occupying an abstract plain. Otherwise, the personifications look identical. The same Miles Christianus image – complete with the various vices he is fighting off – finds its way onto a stone frieze above the fireplace in the Great Hall of Ampney Park, the Gloucestershire estate of John Pleydell, a lawyer and Member of Parliament (fig. 12.3). Whether the stonemason who carved the frieze was inspired by the print or the map is unclear, although the arrangement of the figures more closely resembles the print. But this example serves to remind us of the influence of print culture as arguably the key medium of visual culture in Northern Europe, and in a more localized context it helps explain the appeal of early modern maps, which featured many elements similar to those popular in other visual forms, including in far more costly ones. Not every household could afford an elaborate overmantel, but they might be able to afford a print of the *Christian Knight Map* to decorate their wall.

There are further overlaps between ornamental elements and maps as part of household decor: representations of globes, compasses, astrolabes, and personifications of geography can be found woven into homes, whether in their structural composition or in their movables (for example in furniture and textiles). Here I focus on personifications of the continents, which can be found both on maps and in household decorative art, to suggest ways in which maps and the iconographies that framed them were entangled with other inscriptions of religious and economic life in English homes. In the visual representations, the continents are usually female and are clothed and bedecked with attributes and objects that white Europeans associated with that part of the world. As Heather A. Hughes contends, the publication of Ortelius's *Theatrum Orbis Terrarum* (*Theatre of the World*) in 1570 was the first time that these personifications were committed to print as a set, even though Ortelius pieced them together from earlier sources (both prints and decorative arches built for civic procession).[42] The first atlas' famous title page, with personifications of the continents positioned hierarchically in front of a building façade, influenced Netherlandish print collections that

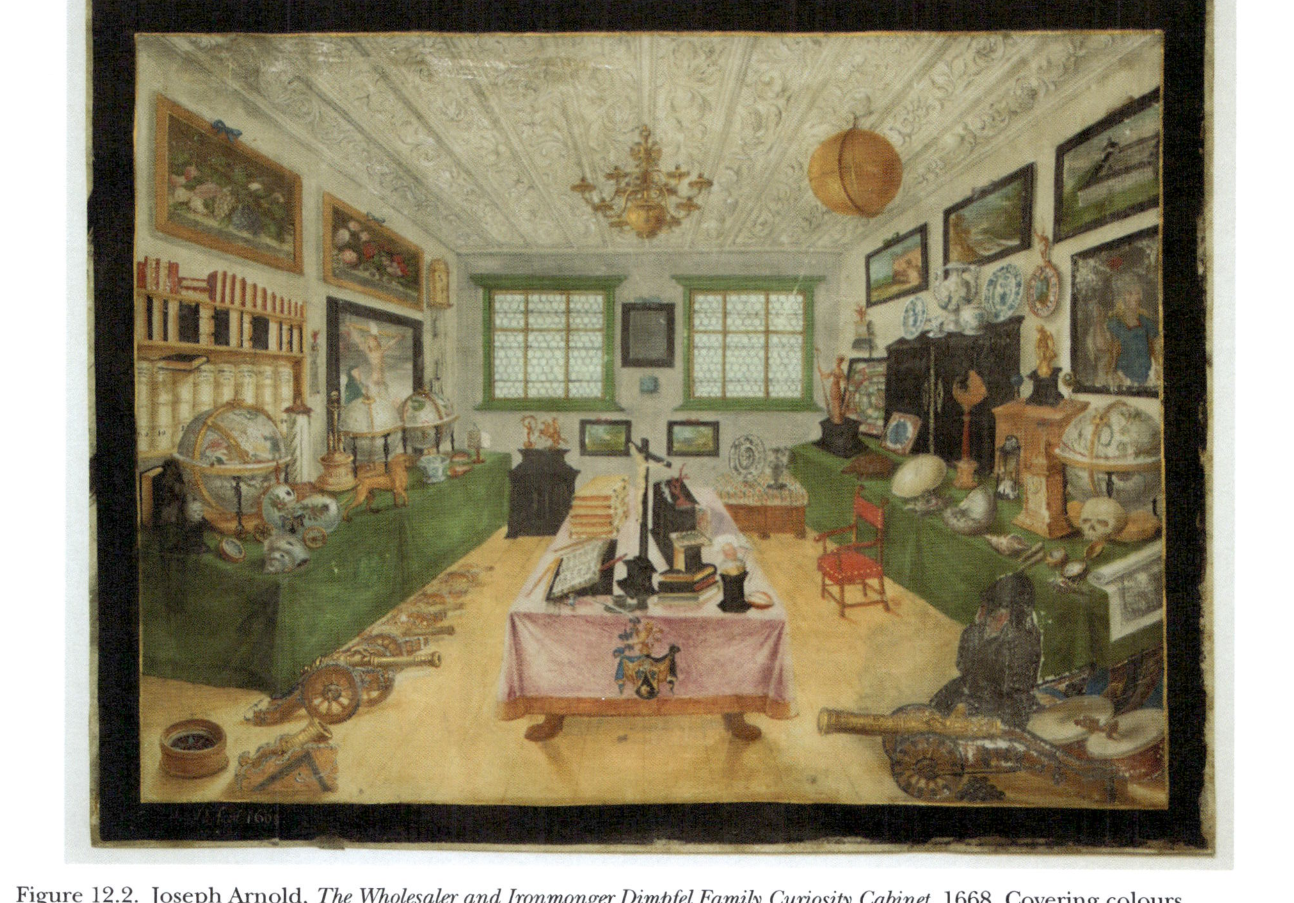

Figure 12.2. Joseph Arnold, *The Wholesaler and Ironmonger Dimpfel Family Curiosity Cabinet*, 1668. Covering colours heightened with punched gold on parchment, 14 x 19.1 cm. Inv. Br: 1952.2611. Museum Ulm, Ulm. © Museum Ulm

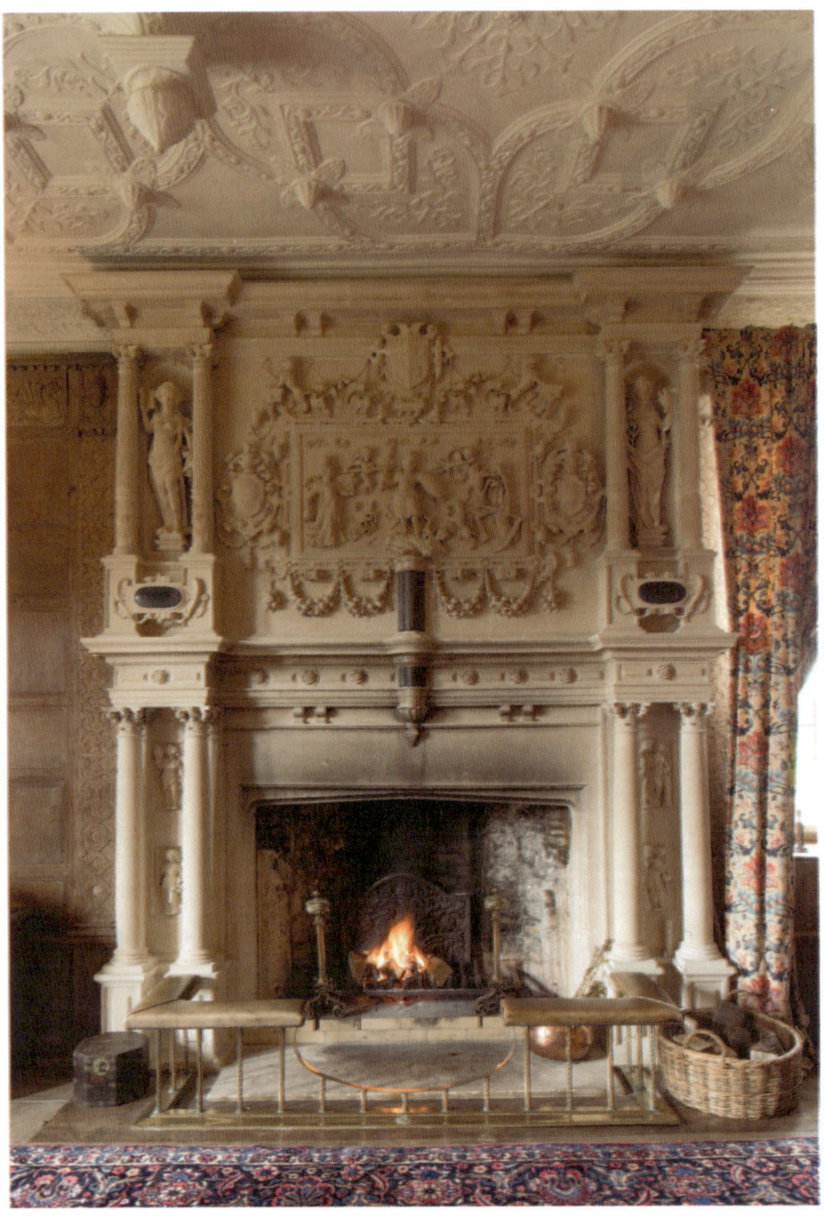

Figure 12.3.  Overmantel, Ampney Park, Gloucestershire, UK, early seventeenth century. Photograph courtesy of the owners of Ampney Park and reproduced with their permission

subsequently circulated in England and in turn influenced designs in a variety of media.[43] These personifications also feature in the marginal decorations of a number of world maps from the period. The frame of Petrus Plancius's *Orbis Terrarum* world map (printed in Amsterdam in 1594) features female personifications of Europa, Asia, Africa, Mexicana, and Peruana, which are positioned along with objects associated with them.[44] Claes Janszoon Visscher's world map, *Nova Totius Terrarum Orbis Geographica Ac Hydrographica Tabula* (*A New Geographical and Hydrographical Map of the Whole World*), printed in Amsterdam in 1639 and much reprinted, features female personifications of the four continents (America by this point having subsumed Mexico and Peru), which are placed in vignettes in each corner.[45]

The continents were quite literally carved into the fabric of English homes. Figure 12.4 shows two personifications of the four continents as part of a frieze in one of the bedrooms at Burton Agnes Hall, Yorkshire, the property of Sir Henry Griffiths. Burton Agnes is famous for its elaborate stone and woodwork carvings, in particular for the decorations in its largest room, the Great Hall, which depict Old and New Testament figures (apostles, patriarchs, evangelists), angels, and virtues alongside carved figures of men and women in contemporary dress and fashions (fig. 12.5). As Tara Hamling writes, "The sculptures stare down ... and serve as overseers to monitor the behaviour of the occupants of the room."[46] Sir Henry's Protestantism is also on display in the Red Room, which has a fireplace decorated with a wooden carving of the Dance of Death, whose skeletal figure tramples on worldly vices, including representations of the Roman Catholic Church. The ornamentation in these more public spaces of the house display the family's Protestant virtues to their visitors and serve to memorialize the household while at the same time instructing it in ordered self-management.[47]

The continents in the bedroom, however, seem to function more equivocally. As can be seen in figure 12.4, America is depicted with breast exposed, wearing some form of headdress, and is framed by leafy plants. Europe carries branches abundant with grapes and leaves in her right hand and some kind of scroll in the left, likely indicating her literacy (the depictions of Asia and Africa are not featured here, but they are also conventional).[48] The continents may have been intended to project the confident, worldly attributes of Burton Agnes Hall's owner. Sir Henry had been among the first figures to be knighted by James I following his accession in 1604, was a member of the Council of the North, and served as high sherriff of Yorkshire. Yet if these personifications of the

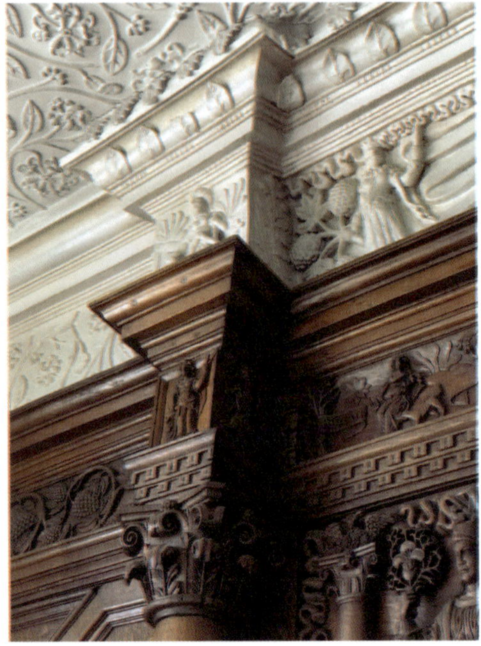

Figure 12.4.  Detail from The Queen's Bedroom, Burton Agnes Hall, Yorkshire, UK, early seventeenth century. Photograph courtesy of the Burton Agnes Hall Trust. © Burton Agnes Hall Trust

four continents are designed to convey the family's ascendancy, they are placed in one of its more private spaces – the so-called "Queen's Bedroom," belonging to Elizabeth "Eleanor" Throckmorton, Sir Henry's wife. While the continents may signal the global ambition of Eleanor too (the Throckmortons were a prominent Elizabethan family with ties to the transoceanic trading companies), they seem also to partake of an ambivalence that is here particularly charged by the fact that this is a woman's bedchamber (indeed, there may be a visual pun between continents and continence). The personifications seem to form part of the room's antithetical ornamentation. The room is also decorated with columns featuring personifications of the feminine virtues and two pediments featuring paradigms of chastity, Judith and St. Barbara. These desirable virtues and celebrated figures are offset, however, by three small carved figures representing vices. The virtues are countered, at least in part, by the continents

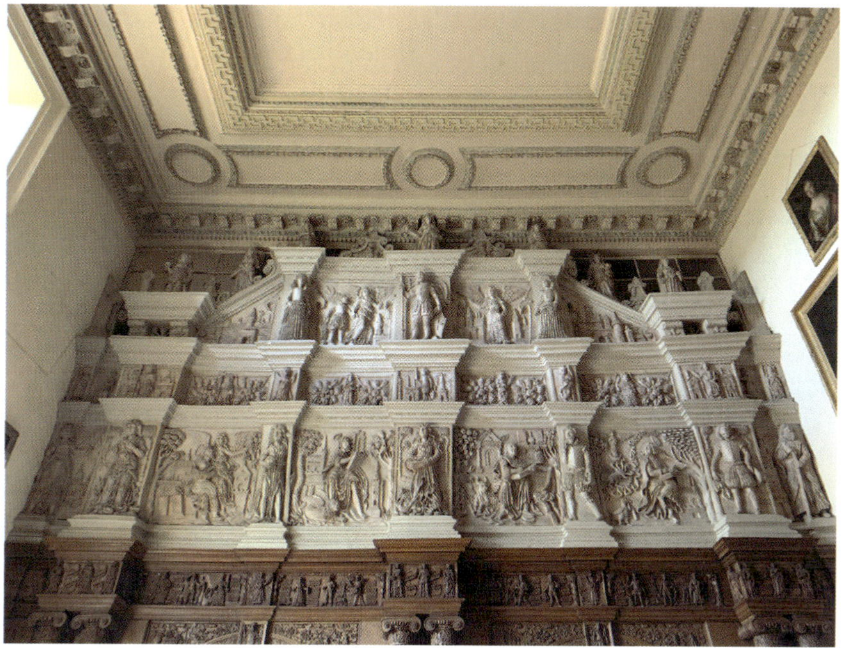

Figure 12.5. The Great Room, Burton Agnes Hall, Yorkshire, UK, early seventeenth century. Photograph courtesy of the Burton Agnes Hall Trust. © Burton Agnes Hall Trust

as well: either the personifications of the continents index a worldly outlook, and celebrate European superiority; or they index an attachment to the world that Eleanor must temper through meditating on the virtues, lest she fall into incontinent vice.[49] If the Great Hall and the Red Room at Burton Agnes Hall display idealized virtues and show the family's awareness of the transience of their good fortune in the face of death, the iconography of the bedchamber may be more unevenly poised.

### Maps on Stage: The Household in Thomas Middleton's *The Puritan*

This chapter's closing sections move out of the home and into the theatre, to explore the ways in which dramatists imagined the domestic display of maps. I say "out of the home" but, as Mimi Yiu has argued, both the early modern household and the early modern playhouse worked through complex paradigms of spatiality in analogous ways. As she contends, architecture, which developed in the second half of the sixteenth century and became established as a discipline in early modern England through "The Great Rebuilding," addressed "not only the physical need for shelter, but also the social and psychic impact of building."[50] Developing Henry S. Turner's excavation of the word "plot" in the development of the spatial arts in sixteenth-century England (including in the theatre), Yiu argues that the playhouse was a "parallel arena of plotting" to the home.[51] Early modern drama was driven by "a desire to examine interior spaces, both physical and psychic"; in its frequent dramatization of home life, "theatre supplied the perfect, self-reflexive crucible for making sense of a home."[52] This capacity can be seen across a swathe of the drama of the time, where households became not only the backdrop against which the action took place but constituted the very substance of the dramatic action itself.[53]

If home and theatre are parallel spaces, what then of the place of maps in the home within the dramatic corpus? This section looks at perhaps the most representative example of map use in early modern drama: Thomas Middleton's *The Puritan or the Widow of Watling Street* (1606), performed by the Boy's Company of St. Paul's. The play, like many in the city comedy genre, satirizes Puritan characters whose displays of piety are undermined by their ambition and their material attachments.[54] It is set in the city of London, close to St. Paul's itself, and stages the sanctimonious household of the titular widow, members of which repeatedly profess pious sentiments. Pieboard, an impoverished and cynical scholar, decides that he will unravel their pretensions, and to do so he takes up the guise of a fortune teller who has "travelled all the world over ... and been in the seven and twenty provinces" (3.2.77–9).[55] The fortune teller seems to have a loose grasp of Protestant theology (and of European geography – the Netherlands had seventeen, not twenty seven, provinces), but despite the manifold red flags his conduct throws up he easily reveals that the Widow's family's commitment to the Puritan cause is shaky to say the least. The Widow's brother Sir Godfrey is obsessed with finery; her son Edmund fritters away his inheritance; her daughters Moll and Frances are intent on marrying up and revel in pomp; her late husband was a swindler who used his religious commitment as a cover story; and the Widow herself marries again to a deep-pocketed knight. With Pieboard's prompting, the members of the household show themselves to be just as money-grabbing as every other Londoner, despite their protestations to the contrary.

While the Widow's household is the main focus, halfway through the play the scene shifts to the London home of an unnamed gentleman. The home boasts "a fine gallery" of "maps, and pictures, and devices, and things" which are organized "neatly, delicately" (3.4.29–34); that is, it includes a room not dissimilar to the one in the Dimpfel family home in Regensburg as painted by Joseph Arnold. Pieboard (who by this point in the play has removed his fortune teller disguise) describes the house as "wholesomely plotted" (18). His companions in the scene are more circumspect: sergeants, who have accompanied Pieboard as he looks to collect money to pay off a debt (and avoid imprisonment), agree that it is "an exceeding fine house" (18). But they disapprove of the maps in the gentleman's collection.

Part of their dislike stems from doubts about maps' efficacy. In a bid to "find the Counter in the Poultry" (one of London's debtors prisons), they turn over a map of the city, only to find it blank: "'Sfoot, here's nothing, all's bare" (106–10). They conclude that maps would be far more useful for policing the city "if we could see men peep out of door in 'em" (115–16). The joke here is at least in part at their expense – they swim in the same shallows as Dogberry and Verges of Shakespeare's *Much Ado About Nothing* – but their distaste for maps revolves around sentiments that extend beyond this being just a belittling, class-based dig. As Andrew Gordon argues, their "inability to comprehend the conceptual apparatus of these two-dimensional representations ... is more than the conventional mockery of constabulary dullness." It points to "what a map *cannot* do" – namely it "does not record, and cannot keep pace with, its inhabitants" (inhabitants that include Pieboard, who escapes the sergeants' clutches through the backdoor of the gentleman's house while they are contemplating the map).[56] To extend Gordon's point, I would argue that the sergeants' suspicion is subtended by a fear that maps have paradoxical, even profane, properties. In their opinion, maps are "too busy" – that is, there is too much information on them, ranging from geographical data to ornamentation. They are also empty, "full of circles," which resemble those used by magicians for "conjurations" (103–4). The sergeants' complaint, that maps "[falsely] say the world's in one of them," points to their understanding of a map's emptiness as a visual sign (104–5). For them, a map does not present the world, there is nothing behind or "a'tha'backside" (109–10): maps are useless, "pretty painted things" (102–3) that signify "nothing" (110). This may seem like dialogue underscoring the sergeants' simple-mindedness. But as is evident in Robert Herrick's poem "To his brother Nicolas Herrick," such sentiments about the heretical possibilities embedded in "Varnisht maps" straddled class lines.

For the sergeants, the gentleman's household's pious leanings are questionable, and the maps are evidence of this. For Pieboard, the interior decor encourages scholars' contemplation, "to walk and study and make verses" (30–1). In his opinion the whole house has been "wholesomely plotted." That the word "plot," a synonym for map (frequently used for a ground plan), is used seems pointed: maps form part of the way in which this home has been designed to be wholesome.[57] There is a further pun in the use of the word "plot," which can also refer to the physical plot, the chart that summarized and visualized a play's action and was posted backstage at the theatre.[58] Pieboard's pretence for seeking out the gentleman is that he has "a device for a masque" (65) to deliver to him in exchange for money that will pay off his debt. While there is no such arrangement – Pieboard and the gentleman have never met before – the gentleman is an able improviser and immediately plays along with Pieboard's "device," namely to use the "device for a masque" as a cover story so that he can escape the clutches of the law and continue his mission to unravel the Widow's family's hypocrisies.

In this scene, then, maps are associated with household performance. A map can seem to form part of a wholesome design, it can seem to convey a worldly outlook, and it can carry the whiff of apostasy. It is also a "device" – a theatrical construct whose meaning is both malleable and also, ultimately, empty. The same word is used to describe the masque that Pieboard is pretending to have devised for the gentlemen and to describe the ruse for escaping with the gentleman's assistance, and it is also another word for a map. In *The Puritan*, then, the gentleman's maps function as markers of the tricky balance between worldliness and piety; and they also operate to promote a sense of a household able to perform both at once – that is, of a household that is sufficiently flexible so that maps become a device of unmoored and interchangeable meaning. Maps, in *The Puritan*, are inherently performative, even as, or perhaps because, an exact decoding of their meaning recedes from view.

**Maps on Stage: The Household in *Richard III* and *Tamburlaine the Great***

*The Puritan* is the most conspicuous example of the display of maps in the household in early modern drama. In this section, I suggest that the tension that Middleton explores between maps being part of a "wholesome" household design and being evidence of a lack of piety subtends other map scenes, even those that at first glance seem less obviously to revolve around the home. My two examples are Christopher Marlowe's two-part play *Tamburlaine the Great* and William Shakespeare's *Richard III*.

Tamburlaine is one of the most famous literary users of maps. Towards the end of *Part 1* he declares to his wife that he will

> confute the blind geographers
> That make a triple region of the world, [i.e. Europe, Africa, and Asia]
> Excluding regions that I mean to trace,
> And with this pen reduce them to a map,
> Calling them provinces, cities, and towns
> After my name and thine, Zenocrate. (4.4.73–8)[59]

Tamburlaine conjures a map so as to announce his intention to both exceed the limitations of medieval geography and remap the world in his (and his wife Zenocrate's) image. Acquisitive and rapacious, Tamburlaine's evocation of world maps (their limits, their possibilities) might strike us as a more typical example of the "mapmindedness" or "cartographic imagination" of early modern English cultural production. Tamburlaine's logic, it has been argued, was symptomatic of a period when maps were instrumental in the geometrization of early modern warfare and in the standardization of land measurement, and became key technologies of European imperial expansion.[60]

An analogous, if less poetically charged and more practical, example of the use of maps as an instrument of war occurs in *Richard III*. Towards the end of the play both the title character and his challenger and eventual successor, the Earl of Richmond and future Henry VII, call for "ink and paper" to "draw the form and model of our battle" (5.3.23–4). Here characters draw maps to determine how best to "part in just proportion our small power" (26).[61] Earlier in the play, however, a quite different sensibility towards maps is staged, one that emerges in a setting far removed from the field of battle, and one that, while lyrical, is quite different to Tamburlaine's. In act two, scene four, Queen Elizabeth, the wife of the late King Edward IV, is informed of the imprisonment and pending execution of her brother and her son at the hands of her brother-in-law, Richard. She issues the following lament, the epigraph to this chapter, which I repeat here:

> Ay me! I see the ruin of my house:
> The tiger now hath seized the gentle hind;
> Insulting tyranny begins to jut
> Upon the innocent and aweless throne.
> Welcome, destruction, blood, and massacre.
> I see, as in a map, the end of all. (2.4.50–5)

Unlike Tamburlaine's, or indeed other, contemporary evocations of maps in dramatic literature, there is no land being conquered, no territory delineated. Shakespeare's *King Lear* begins with a scene in which the titular king uses a map to divide his kingdom between his daughters. In Shakespeare's *Henry IV, Part 1*, Harry Hotspur uses a map to divide England between himself and his fellow rebels. By contrast, Elizabeth's is a map of loss, not the acquisition of "provinces, cities, and towns" (to quote *Tamburlaine*), of a family's end rather than dispersal of property to its "issues ...perpetual" and "hereditary ever" (to quote *King Lear* [1.1.66–7, 79]), of a world's end rather than its division ("Into three limits very equally," to quote *Henry IV, Part 1* [3.1.71]).[62]

Elizabeth's speech also evokes a scene of domestic map reading. The household subtends the syntactic and affective logic of her speech. The top-and-tailing of the speech parallels two scenes of imagined seeing: in the deaths of her kin she sees the fall of the "house" of York; in the "destruction, blood, and massacre" that this fall invites, she sees "the end of all." If the first seeing happens in a realm of metaphor (she does not literally "see the ruin of [her] house"), the second becomes momentarily grounded in some kind of common space of vision – a site of seeing "as in a map, the end of all." She "sees," but through the dependent clause, she opens up that experience to the characters with whom she is on the stage and, by extension, to the audience who attend the play. That common experience of map viewing, and the scaling up and down within these lines that build from "house" to "all," imagines a shared viewing space – "see[ing] as in a map" the finite limits of mortality and possessions – which is not only about a "house," that is, a familial, intergenerational structure of elite kinship, but is also situated within a house, that is, a fabricated structure in which resides a family that may or may not aspire to the status of a "house." Seeing a map, that is, takes place at home, even as that map might presage the destruction of those who populate it – "the end of all."

Queen Elizabeth's lines from *Richard III* help us flesh out possible sensations of what it felt like to look at a map, or how that feeling might be imagined: how a map might not only allow one, like Tamburlaine, to imagine conquests far afield, but also invite one to contemplate mortality and transience closer to, or indeed within, the home. Her lines may also give us a different perspective on *Tamburlaine*'s mapmindedness, in particular the final scene of *Part 2* when Tamburlaine, having dismissed the limitations of cartography, comes to face to face with a map and his own

limits. In the closing scene of *Part 2* – the scene that stages his death –
Tamburlaine calls for a map:

> Give me a map, then let me see how much
> Is left for me to conquer all the world,
> That these my boys may finish all my wants. (5.4.123–5)

Map to hand, he enumerates the waste he has laid, re-mapping his way
through the world. In this moment the map functions instrumentally, as
Tamburlaine uses it to plan his sons' future military campaigns after he's
gone. Then, mid-speech, the function of the map shifts. It becomes an
object of contemplation, as it reminds Tamburlaine, his sons, and the
audience of his mortality:

> Look here, my boys. See what a world of ground
> Lies westward from the midst of Cancer's line
> Unto the rising this earthly globe,
> Whereas the sun, declining from our sight,
> Begins the day with our antipodes. (145–9)

If Tamburlaine's map evocation in *Part 1* characterizes the violence of
imperial imagining, the realization that he has not conquered beyond
the medieval inheritance that he dismissed earlier – all that "lies west-
ward" – leads him to a point of retreat.

This map moment is bound up in the tension of worldliness and piety.
At the point of death, Tamburlaine blasphemously rails against God's
cruelty ("In vain I strive and rail against those powers" [120]) in taking
him from the thing he loves the most – the world, which he has considered his to name and pass on. Tamburlaine has cut a thrust through
Asia and Europe through both plays that bear his name. He has been
"the scourge of God" (248), that is, God's instrument of war. But he
has also been "the scourge of God," that is, an agent of unholy destruction wreaked upon God's creation, the world, over which he has claimed
far-reaching possession. As the play's final scene makes clear, though, it
is death, not Tamburlaine, who is "The Monarch of the Earth" (216).
At the last Tamburlaine turns to a map as both statement of possession
and index of loss, thus turning the stage into an emblem that seems,
at some level, to warn against a hubristic attachment to the world. In
its last scene, then, *Tamburlaine* stages a map-infused memento mori
tableau, with Amyras, Tamburlaine's older son, offering an apocalyptic

inscription that anticipates Elizabeth's mapmindedness in *Richard III*: "Meet, heaven and earth, and here let all things end" (249).

This moment of producing and commenting on a map is also a moment specifically about a household. Indeed, much of *Tamburlaine, Part 2* concerns the world that Tamburlaine will leave behind. In many ways the play is about Tamburlaine's orientation towards, and eventual detachment from, worldly things. But the bequeathal of worldly goods to his children is fraught, as the play also questions whether they will live up to the Tamburlainian promise of continued violent territorial accumulation – whether they can "finish all [his] wants." Memorably, one of the play's scenes involves Tamburlaine's execution of another son, Calyphas, for cowardice because he deems him unable to live up to his inheritance: Calyphas has "such a soul, / Created of the massy dregs of earth" (4.1.120–1); he is unfit to inherit it. In the play's last scene, the surviving two sons are gifted what their father has claimed, and Tamburlaine points to the map in the process of setting down their inheritance: "*Here,* lovely boys, what death forbids my life, / *That* let your lives command in spite of death" (159–60, emphasis added). However, even though they are better suited to following in their father's footsteps than Calyphas (as Tamburlaine proclaims, "I die, / And live in all your seeds immortally" [173–4]), the pair still fall short. Amyras himself acknowledges that he inherits his father's "anguish and his burning agony" (209) rather than his military prowess and abundant charisma. The memento mori map scene that closes *Tamburlaine* is about Tamburlaine's personal or corporeal limits; but it is also about the household that surrounds him and survives him – a household that flanks the stage emblem in the person of his sons, and which will begin to dissolve in the absence of its patriarch.

## Conclusion: Interpreting the Social Life of Maps in Post-Reformation England

In his study of cartography in America between the Revolutionary War and the Civil War, Martin Brückner proposes that thinking through the "social life of maps ... allows us to comprehend more fully the expressed faith in the usability of maps as a prominent and pervasive medium that shaped the lives of the American people to its core."[63] In Brückner's account, maps became affordable and increasingly ubiquitous in schoolhouses and in homes in the eighteenth and the nineteenth centuries, and became formative of an emerging American national consciousness – a formation that was occurring in domestic spaces as much as in statehouses and in Congress. I turn to Brückner in closing, in part, because his concept of maps having a "social life" can be usefully applied to post-Reformation England, as I hope to have shown. Maps in the period I have been discussing shaped English social life and themselves had social lives. Their placement on walls next to other objects points to their symbolic potential, even as the various archives analysed in this essay frequently point to the instability of that meaning and the propensity of maps to exceed the meaning placed on them.

In contrast to the maps and culture that Brückner traces, the social life of maps in post-Reformation English households was entangled in protestations of mortality. Like so many objects from the *vanitas* tradition, maps allure but also remind the viewer of human limits. Even without clear evidence from the visual archive, post-Reformation cultural production provides us with plenty of examples where poets, playwrights, painters, and artisans drew on the ambiguous potential of maps in the English household. Map makers themselves played with *vanitas* imagery, anticipating its deployment in *vanitas* paintings. And both the placement of maps in households alongside objects featuring biblical imagery, and the integration of map iconography with other forms of memento mori iconography in household design, point to the ways in which maps might have functioned to profess both the worldliness and the piety of the household in which they were enmeshed. That this balance was not always stable is evident in the detail of the drooping (dropping?) map on the right hand table of Joseph Arnold's painting of the Dimpfel collection, in the Vices and Continents of the Queen's Bedroom at Burton Agnes Hall, in the depictions of map reading in the drama of Thomas Middleton, Christopher Marlowe, and William Shakespeare – and in the Robert Herrick poems with which this chapter began. Maps both are and are not objects that form part of early modern "devout" practice; maps both are and are not objects that invite apostasy. Maps are objects, which invite looking through to determine cultural meaning; and things, which foreclose the possibility of complete comprehension – both for early moderns and, frequently, for us.

### NOTES

1  William Shakespeare, *Richard III*, ed. James R. Siemon (London: Bloomsbury for The Arden Shakespeare Third Series, 2009).
2  Robert Herrick, "Mr Hericks Country life" (1613), lines 77–82, in *The Complete Poetry of Robert Herrick*, vol. 2, ed. Tom Cain and Ruth Connolly (Oxford: Oxford University Press, 2013), 33–9.

3  "Mind-travelling readers and playgoers sought a simulation of the travel experience, irrespective of whether they were likely to voyage anywhere physically." David McInnis, *Mind-Travelling and Voyage Drama in Early Modern England* (London: Palgrave MacMillan, 2013), 2.

4  Herrick, "To his brother Nicolas Herrick," *The Complete Poetry of Robert Herrick*, vol. 1, ed. Tom Cain and Ruth Connolly (Oxford: Oxford University Press, 2013), 314.

5  The *Oxford English Dictionary* definition of "Inapostate" has only this poem as an example. *Oxford English Dictionary*, 2nd ed. (Oxford: Oxford University Press, 1989), s.v. "Inapostate."

6  On Herrick's faith, and the ways in which his poetics mingled Protestant conviction with celebrating the rituals of rural life (typically rejected by Puritans), see Leah S. Marcus, *The Politics of Mirth: Jonson, Herrick, Milton, Marvell, and the Defense of Old Holiday Pastimes* (Chicago: University of Chicago Press, 1989), especially chap. 5, "Churchmen among the Maypoles: Herrick and *The Hesperides*," 140–68.

7  Martin Brückner, *The Social Life of Maps in America, 1750–1860* (Chapel Hill: University of North Carolina Press, 2018). Brückner's fourfold methodology for recovering the social life of maps – which considers maps' context and situation, their materiality, records of their possession and use, and how (quoting Arjun Appadurai, 13) "their meanings are inscribed in their forms, their uses, their trajectories" – has informed my own approach to maps in post-Reformation England.

8  Rayna Kalas, *Frame, Glass, Verse: The Technology of Poetic Invention in the English Renaissance* (Ithaca: Cornell University Press, 2007), 27.

9  The term "mapmindedness" – "a revolution in cartographic understanding" – comes from P.D.A. Harvey, *Maps in Tudor England* (Chicago: University of Chicago Press, 1993), 17. The term "cartographic imagination" is D.K. Smith's, from *The Cartographic Imagination in Early Modern England: Re-Writing the World in Marlowe, Spenser, Raleigh, and Marvell* (Aldershot: Ashgate, 2008).

10  See Chris Barrett, *Early Modern English Literature and the Poetics of Cartographic Anxiety* (Oxford: Oxford University Press, 2018).

11  John Dee, "His Mathematical Preface," in Euclid, *The Elements of Geometrie*, trans. Henry Billingsley (London: John Daye, 1570), aiiii.

12  Abraham Ortelius, "... to the courteous reader," in *Theatrum Orbis Terrarum: Theatre of the Whole World*, trans. John Norton (London: John Norton, 1606).

13  Thomas Blundeville, "To the Reader," in *A Briefe Description of Vniversal Mappes and Cardes: And of Their Vse: And Also the Vse of Ptholemey his Tables* (London: for Thomas Cadman, 1589).

14 William C. Costin, "The Inventory of John English, B.C.L., Fellow of St. John's College," *Oxoniensia* 11 and 12 (1948/9): 106; Owen Ashmore, "Household Inventories of the Lancashire Gentry, 1550–1700," *Transactions of the Historic Society of Lancashire and Cheshire*, 110 (1958): 73, 80, 82.

15 Tessa Watt, *Cheap Print and Popular Piety, 1550–1640* (Cambridge, UK: Cambridge University Press, 1993); Anthony Wells-Cole, *Art and Decoration in Elizabethan and Jacobean England: The Influence of Continental Prints, 1558–1625* (New Haven: Yale University Press, 1997).

16 Patrick Collinson argued that Protestant iconoclasm gave way, around 1580, to iconophobia, a "total repudiation of all images" that dominated English cultural life for a generation. The argument has been challenged by many, including Tessa Watt, for its basing of iconophobia on a minority of Protestant reformers and for its limited concept of "the picture." Patrick Collinson, *The Birthpangs of Protestant England: Religious and Cultural Change in the Sixteenth and Seventeenth Centuries* (London: MacMillan, 1988), 117; Watt, *Cheap Print*, especially chap. 4, "Idols in the Frontispiece," 131–77.

17 A digital copy of the *Fool's Cap World* can be accessed in the Royal Maritime Museum's online collection: https://collections.rmg.co.uk/collections/objects/206385.html. The translations from the Latin are taken from *The Bible: The Authorized King James*, ed. Robert Carroll and Stephen Prickett (Oxford: Oxford University Press, 2008).

18 The original map is no longer extant, but the cartouche is visible in facsimile. See *The Map of the World by Jodocus Hondius 1611*, ed. Edward Luther Stevenson and Joseph Fischer (New York: the American Geographical Society and the Hispanic Society of America, 1907). The original quotations on the map are in Latin; the translations are taken from *The Bible: The Authorized King James*. See James A. Welu, *Vermeer and Cartography* (PhD diss., Boston University, 1977), 98–113, especially 100.

19 A digital copy of van Geelkercken's map can be accessed in the online collection of the Maritime Museum of Rotterdam: https://www.maritiemdigitaal.nl/index.cfm?event=search.getdetail&id=100128839.

20 Maps were also incorporated into Bibles (in particular Protestant Bibles), and many of these were copies of larger maps (for example, Lorcan Cranach the Elder's woodcut map of the Exodus from Egypt, variations of which appear in a number of European Bibles printed in the 1520s). See Catherine Delano-Smith and Elizabeth Ingram, *Maps in Bibles 1500–1600: An Illustrated Catalogue* (Geneva: Librairie Droz, 1991).

21 See Welu, *Vermeer and Cartography*; Svetlana Alpers, *The Art of Describing: Dutch Art of the Seventeenth Century* (Chicago: Chicago University Press, 1983), especially chap. 4, "The Mapping Impulse in Dutch Art," 119–68;

Bärbel Hedinger, *Karten in Bildern: Zur Ikonographie der Wandkarte in holländischen Interieurgemälden des siebzehnten Jahrhunderts* (Hildesheim: Olms, 1986); Richard Helgerson, *Adulterous Alliances: Home, Stage, and History in Early Modern European Drama and Painting* (Chicago: Chicago University Press, 2000), especially chap. 4, "Soldiers and Enigmatic Girls," 79–120.

22  For an example of an "artist in studio" painting featuring a map, see Jan Miese Molenaer's *The Painter's Workshop* (1631). A copy can be found in the digital database of the Staatliche Museen zu Berlin: http://www.smb-digital. de/eMuseumPlus?service=ExternalInterface&module=collection&objectId =869657&viewType=detailView.

23  Tara Hamling, *Decorating the 'Godly' Household: Religious Art in Post-Reformation Household* (New Haven: Yale University Press, 2011), 88, 90–1.

24  Lisa Jardine, *Worldly Goods: A New History of the Renaissance* (New York: W.W. Norton, 1995), 12; Linda Levy Peck, *Consuming Splendor: Society and Culture in Seventeenth-Century England* (Cambridge, UK: Cambridge University Press, 2005).

25  On the various meanings of the term "household" – as both a container of "stuff" and composed of "stuff" – see Natasha Korda, *Shakespeare's Domestic Economies: Gender and Property in Early Modern England* (Philadelphia: University of Pennsylvania Press, 2002), especially "Introduction," 1–14.

26  See Arjun Appadurai, "Introduction: Commodities and the Politics of Value," in *The Social Life of Things: Commodities in Cultural Perspective*, ed. Arjun Appadurai (Cambridge, UK: Cambridge University Press, 1986), 3–63; Ian Hodder, *Entangled: An Archaeology of the Relationships between Humans and Things* (London: Blackwell-Wiley, 2012).

27  Bill Brown, "Thing Theory," *Critical Inquiry* 28, no. 1 (2001): 5. Brown summarizes his distinction as follows: "We look through objects because there are codes by which our interpretive attention makes them meaningful, because there is a discourse of objectivity that allows us to use them as facts. A *thing*, in contrast, can hardly function as a window. We begin to confront the thingness of objects when they stop working for us." Brown, "Thing Theory," 4.

28  Aside from an engraving housed at The Germanic National Museum in Frankfurt (entitled *Sessio Solennis SRJ Suevici Circuli Ulmae habita de anno 1669*), there do not seem to be any other records of Arnold's work. His father, Jonas Arnold or Arnoul, was also a painter and engraver: among his surviving works there are allegorical paintings (for example his *Allegory of Arithmetic* 1651, private collection) and representations of civic culture (for example *Brautzug in Ulmer Münster*, 1659, housed at the Ulm Museum) – interests which he seems to have shared with his son. See the entry on Jonas

Arnold in *Bryan's Dictionary of Painters and Engravers*, revised edition (London: George Bell and Sons, 1903), 54.

29 Elizabeth Alice Honig, "Making Sense of Things: On the Motives of Dutch Still Life," *Res: Anthropology and Aesthetics* 34 (1998): 182.

30 Brown, "Thing Theory," 4.

31 These records have been assembled from the archives of English Public Records offices – both regional and the UK National Archives – and local historical society publications from the counties of Derbyshire, Gloucestershire, Lincolnshire, Devonshire, Lancashire, Cheshire, Durham, Northumberland, Yorkshire, Cambridgeshire, Sussex, London, and Bristol. I have also relied on the archival reconstruction of private libraries conducted by Elisabeth Leedham-Greene and the reconstruction work of Catherine Delano-Smith on map ownership in sixteenth-century Cambridge. See *Private Libraries in Renaissance England: A Collection and Catalogue of Tudor and Early Stuart Book-Lists*, edited by Elisabeth Leedham-Greene, 4 vols. (Binghamton, NY: Medieval and Renaissance Texts and Studies, 1992); Catherine Delano-Smith, "Map Ownership in Sixteenth-Century Cambridge: The Evidence of Probate Inventories," *Imago Mundi* 47 (1995): 67–93.

32 Of the two hundred map-owners, thirty-five placed religious objects next to the maps or globes (just under 20 per cent). There does not seem to be a regional pattern, as examples are found in the north, west, and south of England.

33 Mary F.S. Hervey, "A Lumley Inventory of 1609," *The Volume of the Walpole Society* 6 (1917–1918): 42; Evelyn Philip Shirley, "An Inventory of the Effects of Henry Howard, K.G., Earl of Northampton [1614]," *Archaeologia* 42 (1870): 357–8.

34 Reprinted in *Wills and Inventories from the Registry at Durham, Part 2*, ed. William Greenwell (Edinburgh: Blackwood and Sons, for the Surtees Society, 1860), 65.

35 Reprinted in *The Injunctions and Other Ecclesiastical Proceedings of Richard Barnes, Bishop of Durham, from 1576–1587*, ed. James Raine (Edinburgh: Blackwood and Sons, for the Surtees Society, 1850), cxliii.

36 Reprinted in *Devon Inventories of the Sixteenth and Seventeenth Centuries*, ed. Margaret Cash (Torquay: The Devonshire Press, 1966), 18–19. The spheres are likely globes made by the English mathematician Thomas Hood.

37 As this brief summary indicates, map owners tended to be of elite status – not necessarily aristocracy or gentry, but still people of some means. This finding may be a product of how relying on probate inventories and wills skews the historical record, as it tended to be people of means whose estates were settled in this manner. Beyond a few records of sailors, there is little evidence about lower or even middling sort map ownership, although given the relative inexpensiveness of maps in contrast to other kinds of

decoration it is possible that some in these groups owned maps as well. This seems to have been the case elsewhere in Europe: see Genevieve Carlton, *Worldly Consumers: The Demand for Maps in Renaissance Italy* (Chicago: University of Chicago Press, 2015); and Elizabeth A. Sutton, *Capitalism and Cartography in the Dutch Golden Age* (Chicago: University of Chicago Press, 2015), especially chap. 2, "Amsterdam Society and Maps," 21–42.

38 My focus here is on map ownership, but I am influenced by Lena Cowen Orlin's caution that inventories are far from disinterested documents. See Orlin, "Fictions of the Early Modern English Probate Inventory," in *The Culture of Capital: Property, Cities, and Knowledge in Early Modern England*, ed. Henry S. Turner (New York and London: Routledge, 2002), 52–84.

39 See Delano-Smith, "Map Ownership," 83.

40 Wells-Cole, *Art and Decoration.*

41 James Welu, "The Sources and Development of Cartographic Ornamentation in the Netherlands," in *Art and Cartography: Six Historical Essays*, ed. David Woodward (Chicago: University of Chicago Press, 1987), 147–73; Sutton, *Capitalism and Cartography.*

42 On the spread of prints of the four continents from the Netherlands to England, see Heather A. Hughes, "The Four Continents in Seventeenth-Century Embroidery and the Making of English Femininity," in *Personification: Embodying Meaning and Emotion*, ed. Walter S. Melion and Bart Ramakers (Leiden: Brill, 2016), 716–49, especially 720–6.

43 A copy of the title page of *Theatrum Orbis Terrarum* can be found in the online collection of the Norman B. Leventhal Map and Education Center at the Boston Public Library: https://collections.leventhalmap.org/search /commonwealth:q524n383g.

44 A copy of the Plancius World Map can be found in the online holdings of the Barry Lawrence Ruderman Map Collection of Stanford University: https://exhibits.stanford.edu/ruderman/catalog/fb595jz5474.

45 See Alex Zukas, "Class, Imperial Space, and Allegorical Figures of the Continents on Early-Modern World Maps," *Environment, Space, Place* 10, no. 2 (Fall 2018): 29–62; and Surekha Davies, *Renaissance Ethnography and the Invention of the Human: New Worlds, Maps and Monsters* (Cambridge, UK: Cambridge University Press, 2016). A copy of the 1652 version of the Visscher map can be found in the online holdings of the Ruderman Collection: https://exhibits.stanford.edu/ruderman/catalog/mc815wh4425.

46 Tara Hamling, "Guides to Godliness: from Print to Plaster," in *Printed Images in Early Modern Britain: Essays in Interpretation*, ed. Michael Hunter (Burlington: Ashgate, 2010), 73.

47 See Wells-Cole, *Art and Decoration*, 180–1, and Hamling, *Decorating*, 127.

48 See Wells-Cole, *Art and Decoration*, 188. The Plancius and Visscher maps and the Ortelius title page associate similar accoutrements with the continents.

49 See Hamling, *Decorating*, 166.

50 Mimi Yiu, *Architectural Involutions: Writing, Staging, and Building Space c. 1435–1650* (Evanston: Northwestern University Press, 2015), 3. See also Julie Sanders, *The Cultural Geography of Early Modern Geography, 1620–1650* (Cambridge, UK: Cambridge University Press, 2011), especially chap. 3, "'Hospitable Fabrics': thinking through the early modern household," 101–32; and Hamling, *Decorating*. W.G. Hoskins coined the phrase "The Great Rebuilding" in "The Rebuilding of Rural England, 1570–1640," *Past and Present* 4, no. 1 (1953): 44–59.

51 Henry S. Turner, *The English Renaissance Stage: Geometry, Poetics, and the Practical Spatial Arts 1580–1630* (Oxford: Oxford University Press, 2006); Yiu, *Architectural Involutions*, 3.

52 Yiu, *Architectural Involutions*, 3, 11.

53 On the prevalence of domestic themes, even in dramatic genres not usually classified as domestic, see Emma Whipday, *Shakespeare's Domestic Tragedies: Violence in the Early Modern Home* (Cambridge, UK: Cambridge University Press, 2019).

54 On city comedy's various stagings of Puritan characters, and on *The Puritan Widow*, see Brian Walsh, *Unsettled Toleration: Religious Difference on the Shakespearean Stage* (Oxford: Oxford University Press, 2016), especially chap. 2, "Happy (Enough) Endings: Puritans and Everyday Ecumenicity in Early Modern City Comedy," 39–85.

55 Thomas Middleton, *The Puritan Widow; or The Puritan; or, the Widow of Watling Street*, edited by Donna B. Hamilton, in *Thomas Middleton: Collected Works*, ed. Gary Taylor and John Lavignino (Oxford: Oxford University Press, 2007), 509–42.

56 Andrew Gordon, "*The Puritan Widow* and the Spatial Arts of Middleton's Urban Drama," in *Thomas Middleton in Context*, ed. Suzanne Gossett (Cambridge, UK: Cambridge University Press, 2011), 38–9.

57 The Oxford English Dictionary offers "Originally: a ground plan, a map; a nautical chart" as definition II.3.b of "plot," and links it to a definition of "plat": "A plan, a diagram, a design, esp. a ground plan of a building or of an area of land; a map, a chart" (II.2). Oxford English Dictionary, 3rd ed. (Oxford: Oxford University Press, 2006), s.v. "Plot." See also Turner, *English Renaissance Stage*, especially "Introduction," 1–40.

58 See Tiffany Stern, *Documents of Performance in Early Modern England* (Cambridge, UK: Cambridge University Press, 2009), especially chap. 7, "Back-Stage Plots," 201–31.

59 Christopher Marlowe, *Tamburlaine the Great: Part One and Part Two*, ed. Mathew R. Martin (Toronto: Broadview, 2014).

60 On Tamburlaine, maps, and power, see Stephen Greenblatt, *Renaissance Self-Fashioning: From More to Shakespeare* (Chicago: Chicago University Press, 1980, repr. 2003), especially chap. 5, "Marlowe and the Will to Absolute Play," 193–221; Richard Wilson, "Visible Bullets: Tamburlaine the Great and Ivan the Terrible," *English Literary History* 62, no. 1 (1995): 47–68; Crystal Bartolovich, "Putting *Tamburlaine* on a (Cognitive) Map," *Renaissance Drama* 28 (1997): 29–72; Bernhard Klein, "*Tamburlaine* and the Heritage of Medieval Cartography," *Reading the Medieval in Early Modern England*, ed. Gordon McMullan and David Matthews (Cambridge, UK: Cambridge University Press, 2007), 143–58.

61 These lines are Richmond's. Richard's equivalent lines are at line 49 of the same scene.

62 William Shakespeare, *King Lear*, ed. R.A. Foakes (London: Bloomsbury, 1997); William Shakespeare, *Henry IV Part 1*, ed. David Scott Kastan (London: Bloomsbury, 2002).

63 Brückner, *Social Life*, 3.

# Enlightenment Cosmology: A Medialogical Interpretation

J.B. SHANK

In his blockbuster bestseller *Astrophysics for People in a Hurry*, Neil deGrasse Tyson begins with a chapter titled "The Greatest Story Ever Told." An opening epigram from Lucretius's *De rerum natura* (*On the Nature of Things*) accentuates his mythopoetic trope, and the first sentence speaks scripturally in announcing: "In the beginning, nearly fourteen billion years ago, all the space and all the matter and all the energy of the known world was contained in a volume one trillionth the size of the period that ends this sentence."[1] The precise quantification of Tyson's point (in both senses of the word) sets the pattern for what follows, namely a brilliantly accessible prose account of that foundational assemblage of quantitative data, empirical facts, and analytical theorizing that is called by practitioners of modern scientific astrophysics "the Big Bang Theory."

Tyson's work overall is anything but an exercise in twenty-first century cosmological poesis, yet with its artful literary framing the book nevertheless gestures towards the way that fictional, as in man-made, worldmaking and ancient narrative poesis remains entangled with modern scientific theorizing about the origins of the universe. No discernible friction is created by Tyson's mythopoetic opening and the rigorously scientific exposition of contemporary cosmology that follows in its wake, and the result points to what Nasser Zakaria describes as the persistent unity of science with mythic storytelling in the twenty-first century, each an essential part of the ongoing writing of the epic of scientific modernity.[2]

Any account of the origins of the cosmos, no matter how modern and scientific, must also be a mythopoetic account, because to explain the origins of all things and to create our imaginative understanding of such beginnings is to do one thing in two related and inseparably entangled ways.

Stated simply, such explanations only work if the origins are captured both scientifically and imaginatively, and Tyson's double-signifying point illustrates the idea perfectly in its union of the quantitative measure of the point's size with its visual referent to the marked dot inked on the printed page. Understanding our cosmological world scientifically and making that understanding visible and comprehensible in the imagination are always two aspects of one fundamentally inseparable human cognitive enterprise. And if this duality is true for a contemporary physicist like Tyson, it was no less a feature of cosmology at that moment in history when a few modernizing *novatores*, or forward-looking innovators, began to try to distil a narrowly and exclusively scientific understanding of the universe from the older Western tradition that combined scientific cosmological enquiry with the ancient mythopoetic tradition of cosmological storytelling.

Modern historians seeking the fledgling beginnings of this explicitly modern, because narrowly scientific and aspirationally anti-imaginative, science of cosmology often arrive at their intended destination in the archive of European science in the eighteenth century. This archive is often labelled "the Enlightenment." This essay is focused on that archive, and the nature of the "Enlightenment cosmology" found within it. Modernist voices seemingly speaking the language of our current cosmological science are certainly to be found in this archive, but alongside them are the voices of others, like the Savilian Professor of Astronomy at Oxford and fellow of the Royal Society of London John Keill, who disparaged the ostensible modernizer René Descartes in 1698 as "the first world-maker this Century produced." "World-maker" was a pejorative term for Keill, and he was mocking Descartes' claim that he "could solve all the phenomena of nature by his principles of matter and motion [alone]." Worthy of further derision was the idea that "God at the beginning had created only a certain quality of matter and motion, and from thence ... by the necessary laws of Mechanism without any extraordinary concurrence of the Divine Power, the world and all that therein might have been produced."[3]

The Cartesian cosmology that Keill is condemning is very close, at least in its basic materialist foundations, to the one that Tyson narrates in his book, yet Keill was standing with none other than Sir Isaac Newton in condemning Descartes for his removal of the providential creator and his divine management of the world from the story of the world's beginnings. This example illustrates how the archive of the Enlightenment is composed of Cartesian voices, Newtonian voices, and many others who argued with both of them, and the nature of the Enlightenment found in this archive is also complex, marking neither a moment of decisive rupture where a new modernity broke clearly with the past, nor a time when new knowledge initiated a great modernizing leap forward. Enlightenment in my usage will mark a site of convergence between the call of the ancients and the promise of a new and progressive future. It will also be understood as a time when impulses towards conservation and innovation negotiated for authority with one another on an even plane, as they always do, without the second being perceived as always implicitly advantageous over the first.

My use of the category "Enlightenment" will especially refuse the idea that the eighteenth century was an intense time of anti-Christian secularization, a refusal already evident in Keill's statements. While new naturalist impulses in cosmological thinking were certainly present – witness the worldmaking of Descartes – they co-existed in a fully integrated way with the authority of Holy Scripture and the mythopoetic creation stories of the ancients. The Enlightenment also appeared a century before the authoritative establishment of professional disciplinary astrophysics as we know it today, and while we can retrospectively perceive in eighteenth-century cosmological storytelling the germs of what astrophysics would later become for people like Tyson, this essay will emphasize instead all the ways that these new beginnings emerged alongside and often in thrall to the influences and assumptions of older patterns of understanding.

Overall, Enlightenment will generally stand in this essay as a marker of European thought in the middle of an eighteenth century conceived as an ordinary moment in the ever-flowing stream of disinterested historical time. Yet in one respect I will emphasize the way that Enlightenment was a significantly novel and transformative moment, namely a time when general changes in the material character of books and print media were creating new possibilities for intellectual innovation. Régis Debray has coined the term "medialogy" to describe the study of human thought in terms of the attendant media structures that allow for its composition, communication, and dissemination. In *God: An Itinerary*, he offers a model of a medialogical interpretation by looking at the changing nature of world religion through an enquiry into the different mediations of divine representation and religious discourse as found in the material environments for writing and communication in which these notions of God and his message were fostered.[4]

This essay is not a medialogical study in that rigorous respect, but it shares a kindred spirit in wanting to treat the changing character of

Enlightenment cosmology in terms of its innovative mediation within new kinds of books and print imagery, and the new cosmological knowers and knowledge makers that this media-cultural moment engendered. In this medialogical mode, the essay will look at European cosmological worldmaking around 1750 in light of the new regimes of book-centred knowledge work, practices that include writing, publishing, graphic design, and image making. The ancient quest to glean the word of God from holy writ will also be followed into the eighteenth century by examining the new media possibilities made available for scriptural exegesis in large, sumptuously illustrated books, along with the medialogical transformations of Biblical hermeneutics they made possible. Enlightenment cosmology from this perspective reveals again the entanglement present in all cosmological knowing between scientific understanding, narrative poesis, and imaginative worldmaking. By returning to the medialogical particularities of Enlightenment cosmology in the context of this volume overall, the goal is to offer one case illustrative of how cosmological science in the eighteenth century was a fusion of ancient and modern understandings, as well as a union of rational scientific explanation with imaginative poesis.

## Enlightenment Cosmology in Modern Retrospect

Contemporary historians seeking to find the first glimpse of a cosmological science that would appear recognizable, at least in primitive form, to practitioners of the secular, scientific discipline of astrophysics today often look back to two works published in close tandem with one another in the 1750s.[5] Thomas Wright of Durham's *An Original Theory or New Hypothesis of the Universe*, published in London 1750, was the first, and it was followed by Immanuel Kant's *Universal Natural History and Theory of the Heavens*, published in Königsberg and Leipzig in 1755 with a full acknowledgment of Durham's previously published arguments.[6] What makes these works familiar to contemporary scientists is their naturalist and secular approach. Both Durham and Kant present the universe as a natural entity with no attachments to any particular god or scriptural story explaining its divine character. Like cosmologists today, and without Hubble's science of the red shift to confirm their hunches, each also broke with Aristotle by defining the cosmos as a creation in time that began at a single moment and evolved from an early primitive state into its current form. Neither explored this final eventuality, but each also left open the possibility of an end times when the cosmological beginning would reach its natural terminus. In this respect secular, naturalist Western cosmology, both then and now, has never really broken free from the sacred Christian plot of universal time, with its wondrous beginning, middle years, and apocalyptic end. Durham and Kant nevertheless represent something of a break in their apparent detachment from any scriptural authority and their failure to deploy, at least assertively, a Christian theological frame in their cosmological worldmaking. Also absent is the explicit character or agency of God, an absence that heightens the perception that theirs were fully naturalist cosmologies that treated the universe as a physical reality defined only by matter and motion and governed only by natural scientific laws and principles.

A path that is most cleanly viewed in retrospect is thus seen to be charted after 1750, leading from Durham and Kant to the epochal if apocryphal statement made in 1800 by Pierre-Simon Laplace to Napoleon Bonaparte that he had no need for the hypothesis of God to explain his naturalist system of the cosmos.[7] Durham and Kant do offer a newly assertive scientific naturalism, and their thinking was prepared in part by Christian Huygens's posthumous *Kosmotheoros*, which was published in Latin in 1698, and in English (1698), Dutch (1699), French (1702), and German (1703) translations before the work was commissioned by the young Tsar Peter the Great in 1717 to be rendered into Russian as an official publication of his new Imperial Russian Royal Academy of Science.[8] Like Durham and Kant, Huygens offered a natural scientific account of the universe free of any scriptural referent or Christian frame, so much so in fact that Tsar Peter's intended Russian publisher balked at the idea, calling the work a "Satanic perfidy."[9] Writing in justification of his position, Huygens declared that "it is evident that God had no design to make a particular enumeration in the Holy Scriptures of all the Works of his Creation."[10] A fully natural history of the universe need not have direct scriptural support to be legitimate, Huygens thus reasoned, and this stance also justified his speculations in *Kosmotheoros* about the imagined creatures living on the different planets in our solar system, each with a size calculated mathematically to conform with the relative size of the planet they inhabited in comparison with the size of human beings as found on our medium-sized Earth.

Voltaire's Saturnine giants, who descend to earth to visit with the seemingly Lilliputian members of the French royal scientific expedition to Lapland in his satirical story *Micromégas*, are one of many examples of the influence of Huygens's theorizing on Enlightenment cosmological thinking.[11] Both Huygens and Voltaire were also drawing on a centuries-old tradition of combining contemporary scientific understanding of the cosmos with imaginative storytelling. Lucian's *Verae Historiae* (*True History*), which Voltaire knew well, offered a second-century CE account of a trip to the moon and the other planets and stars.[12] With its combination of ancient Roman cosmology and imaginative storytelling, it was in line with the explosion of new fantasies of interstellar travel that appeared in the immediate wake of the disruptions to European cosmological thinking caused by the appearance of the "new stars" (or supernova in our parlance) of 1572 and 1604–5, and the provocations of Galileo's work with his telescope in 1610–11. Among these works were Johannes Kepler's *Somnium* (*The Dream*), written before Galileo had pointed his telescope towards the sky;[13] the Leuven theologian Libertus Fromondus's *Saturnine Supper, Variations on the Dream of Celestial Travel*, first published in 1616 and then again posthumously in 1665, with its allusions to Giordano Bruno's scandalous philosophical dinner *La Cena delle ceneri*;[14] Cyrano de Bergerac's 1657 *Other World, or the States and Empires of the Moon*;[15] the English contributions of John Wilkins, a founding fellow of the Royal Society of London, in his *The Discovery of a World in the Moon* and *A Discourse upon a New Planet* in 1640,[16] and of Margaret Cavendish, Duchess of Newcastle, in her 1666 *Discovery of a New World, Called the Blazing World*;[17] and finally, the contribution of Bernard le Bovier de Fontenelle, Secretary of the Académie Royale des Sciences for over forty years and the immediate precursor to Huygens and Voltaire, whose wildly popular *Conversations on the Plurality of Inhabited Worlds*, first published in 1686 and then re-issued in dozens of editions in many languages over the next century, was a European bestseller.[18] In each of these texts, we see the seventeenth-century European entanglement of science with imaginary worldmaking that continually sits at the heart of Western cosmological thinking.

Because of the apparent absence of speculative hypothesizing or fantastical storytelling in the work of Durham and Kant, and because of their apparent break with any explicit Christian or scriptural framing for their work, modern historians recognize in these works a kindred modern scientific attitude, one that seems to point towards our explicitly secular, naturalistic, and, at least in aspiration, wholly positivistic and speculation-free cosmological science. Following Paul Hazard, it is further possible to trace an interpretive line, one that is only undeviating when viewed in retrospect, that connects Huygens's work around 1700 with Durham and Kant's at mid-century and the science of Laplace around 1800.[19] Treating this as the naturalizing arc of scientific change during this period, another interpretive arc is often connected with it that joins the 1719 publication of the scandalous clandestine tract *Les Trois imposteurs* (*The Three Impostors*), with its claim that Moses, Jesus, and Mohammed were fraudulent deceits created by priests to dupe the credulous masses,[20] to Thomas Paine's 1794 *Age of Reason*,[21] which argues that revealed religion is an imaginative fiction only supported by the ignorant. Hazard held that the years 1680–1720 witnessed this naturalizing and secularizing revolution, and that it launched in turn the eighteenth-century Enlightenment as a direct outcome of a "crisis of the European mind" c. 1700, which is to say a great battle between Old Regime religiosity and sacrality and modern scientific naturalism and secularism. Framed this way, Durham and Kant fit neatly as early Enlighteners developing at mid-century the new foundations of a wholly new naturalist and secular cosmological science.[22]

Yet, as Martin Mulsow has shown in meticulous detail, our understanding of *Les Trois imposteurs* as a scandalous freethinking attack on the legitimacy of revealed religion is very different from what historical research shows to be the actual intention of the authors who wrote this tract. They were a group of unabashedly Christian philologists and biblical scholars who in composing this text were having some academic fun with their scholarly colleagues.[23] The publication of the prank, and its circulation in settings governed by standards other than gentlemanly scholarly notions of propriety and judiciousness, certainly led to unintended outcomes, and it is not wrong to see in the print publication of *Les Trois imposteurs* an early sign of the growing force of libertine freethinking and radically anti-Christian sentiment across Europe. And yet Mulsow's scholarship also shows us the distortions that arise when we paint the Enlightenment with a broad brush as a movement directed against the authority of traditional religion, including, and especially, authoritative claims that the Bible offers a divine and sacred account of the formation of the world and its peoples.

Kant, for example, still manifests an attachment to the authority of Christian scripture as a revelatory truth in his mid-century naturalist cosmological theorizing. A good example is his speculation, admittedly offered with a certain whimsy that speaks to a changing spirit, that the Earth may once have had a planetary ring like those found around Saturn, and that its primeval collapse onto the earth may offer a natural physical explanation for the biblical story of the universal flood. Kant further saw evidence in the Bible that possibly supported his theory. The Bible says that God created a rainbow after the flood as a sign to remind his creatures of "the everlasting covenant between God and all living creatures of every kind on the earth."[24] God's choice of this of all possible mementos, Kant suggests with no hesitation about the truth of the biblical story, might be explained, he reasoned, by naturally connecting the rainbow with the planetary rings that were once visible in the sky before their collapse triggered the planetary inundation. "The similarity of the shape of this memorial sign with the event it signified," Kant speculates, "could commend [my] hypothesis to those who are devoted to the dominant tendency of bringing the miracles of revelation into the same system as the ordinary laws of nature."[25] In this passage, Kant does not wholly dismiss the use of the Bible as a legitimate authority in the scientific study of planetary history, and even if his overall naturalistic break with the cosmological storytelling of Genesis is clear and decisive, his refence to a "dominant tendency" among scholars to keep scripture and science together, and his engagement, however whimsical, with the possibility of a biblical confirmation of natural science, points to a deeper complexity that needs to be explored.

### Enlightenment Cosmology as Mosaic Physics

To whom was Kant referring when he noted "the dominant tendency" in the 1750s of connecting "the miracles of revelation" with "ordinary laws of nature?" Had he been speaking a century earlier, a ready suggestion would be the "Mosaic and Christian philosophers," which is what the pioneering historian of philosophy Johann Jakob Brucker called them in his five-volume *Historia, Critical History of Philosophy* published in Leipzig in 1742–4.[26] Ann Blair has done the most systematic study of the "Mosaical philosophy" tradition in European thought, and she sees it as a European phenomenon of the early seventeenth century, especially strong in central Europe, that was in decline by 1700.[27] Yet Brucker recognized this group within his taxonomy of recent philosophical groups of note, and while the phenomenon has never been studied in detail, so-called Mosaic philosophers, which is to say natural philosophers who worked to synthesize empirical science and natural philosophy with the revelation of Holy Scripture, remained authoritative members of the European scientific community well into the eighteenth century.[28] Kant may have had Enlightenment Mosaic philosophers in mind when he referred to those who bring "the miracles of revelation into the same system as the ordinary laws of nature," and if these were the cosmologists to whom Kant was referring, then it is worth noting that, in his estimation at least, theirs was "the dominant tendency" in 1755.

Can we uncover who Kant may have had in mind? No precise reference is discernible, but if one had to hazard a guess, a good bet might be the monumental work of the Swiss naturalist and fellow of the Royal Society of London Johann Jakob Scheuchzer (1672–1733), which was published in Ulm and Augsburg in 1731–5 when Kant was a student and less than a decade before he began his career as a professor of philosophy at the University of Königsberg in 1741. Together with the engraver Johann Andreas Pfeffel (1674–1748), who was listed as an author of the book on its title page, Scheuchzer published a large-sized, four-volume work in German and Latin editions that was called *Kupfer-Bibel,* or in translation *Copper Bible, in which the Physica sacra or sacred natural science of the natural things occurring in the Holy Scriptures is clearly explained and proven.*[29] The book is arguably the most systematic and comprehensive Mosaic physics ever produced, and it was certainly among the most lavish. For as its title *Copper Bible* articulated clearly, the treatise was built upon the foundation of over 750 large copper-plate engravings spread out over more than two thousand folio pages. The book was reviewed in several leading learned periodicals, which is where Kant had learned of Durham's work as well, so the odds of Kant knowing about the publication are high.[30]

*Kupfer-Bibel* was both a major treatise in eighteenth-century cosmological science and a blockbuster Enlightenment print phenomenon, a dimension that was further accentuated by its appearance in a French translation in 1732 that was presented in an even more sumptuous eight-volume format published by the Amsterdam printers Pierre Schenk and Pierre Mortier. Under its French title *Physique sacrée, ou Histoire-naturelle de la Bible* (*Sacred physics, or the natural history of the Bible*), Scheuchzer and Pfeffel's work was reviewed and discussed in the Francophone learned journals, organs of learned discourse that by the 1730s were the closest thing Europe had to a professional scientific literature.[31]

To follow Scheuchzer and Pfeffel through their resplendent treatise is to see how Mosaic physics in the 1730s was not the arcane and specialized exercise of divines and devout university professors seeking to hold together two seemingly opposed intellectual currents. It was, rather, a mainstream project of modern natural philosophy that seamlessly joined science with the Christian religion because, as Augustine had made clear over a millennium earlier, the Book of Nature and Holy Scripture can never contradict one another. It is also to see how Enlightenment print culture, especially the new possibilities created by metal-plate engraving and etching together with the increased sophistication, both material and financial, of commercial book making, provided savants and

Enlightenment readers alike with a new media space laden with intellectual opportunities for sophisticated knowledge work. Here in one source is the intersection of Enlightenment science in all of its strands with the medialogical possibilities created for it by the new currents in eighteenth-century book making and print imagery. These were essential co-determinants, or so this chapter argues, in the creation of Enlightenment cosmology.

Especially powerful were the new capacities to meld text with images, and Pfeffel's spectacular engraving manifests this potency in the way that his images convey the intellectual content of the treatise with a pictorial evocation that saves thousands of unneeded pages of text. Yet the sumptuous images did not make Scheuchzer's writing obsolete even if they did shape its presentation as something far different than a textual explanation that is merely assisted and supported by accompanying illustrations. The text-image dynamic present in large deluxe books of this sort, which began to pour out of Dutch bookshops in ever-greater numbers after 1650, needs to be studied in more detail. But for the purposes of this discussion, the key point to stress is that visual artists and textual authors each had an important role to play, and in many cases each was an author in his own right (or her own right since the active presence of female engravers and widow-owners of print shops in these operations is palpable if still too little studied). Never in this cultural space was the visual artist a mere illustrator of the author's text, and many artists at this time began to theorize a new conception of the illustrated book that argued for placing the primacy of authorship with the image maker rather than the writer of text.[32] Between Pfeffel and Scheuchzer in this project further stood the holy word of God and the truths of the natural world as revealed by science and scripture. Their treatise overall is best understood as a multi-media scientific synthesis of all of these sources of knowledge, one that merged texts of various kinds together with a wide array of visual presentations in the creation of a unified cosmological science.

To illustrate, let us leaf through the first few pages of *Physique sacré* to get a sense of how Enlightenment cosmology as Mosaic physics was pursued. Remembering that eighteenth-century books were typically sold as printed pages that were then taken elsewhere to be bound, and that editions in libraries today often vary accordingly in their composition, I will use the copy found today in the Bibliothèque nationale de France (BnF) since it is available in an open access digital presentation via Gallica.fr.[33] The photographs published in this chapter, by contrast, come from the edition found in the Newberry Library in Chicago, and to illustrate the point, while its images and substantive text seem identical to those found in the BnF edition, it contains none of the prefatory material or portraits found in that edition.

The BnF edition begins with an elaborate allegorical frontispiece facing a title page that lists Scheuchzer as the principal author while also noting Pfeffel's contribution in a slightly smaller font. A full-page portrait of Scheuchzer is then offered, where he is shown holding a book while pointing towards natural specimens sitting atop a pedestal containing Latin inscriptions of his many titles (fellow of the Royal Society of London; member of the Imperial Academy Leopoldina-Carolina and the Prussian Academy). A brief introductory "Preface" is then offered, without illustration, explaining the project of the book.[34] A "Catalogue" in two columns of all the authors and works cited in the treatise then appears, with contributions ranging from Guillaume Ader to Jean (John) Woodward, Thomas Wollaston, and Jean-Jacques Zimmermann. Aristotle is not cited, but Apion, the Hellenistic Egyptian philosopher and commentator on Homer, is. Both Eusebius and Saint Jerome drew upon Apion's account of the six days of creation, and Scheuchzer and Pfeffel also found the source insightful. Plato is not cited, but other ancient pagans are, along with antique Christians like Gregory of Nyssa and Origen, and the antique Jewish philosopher Philo of Alexandria. Modern authors dominate the list, and while some are well-known (the Jesuit Athanasius Kircher; the Oxford professor of natural philosophy John Keill, who we heard above; and the naturalist John Ray, to give three examples) most are obscure to twenty-first century readers. Neither Galileo Galilei, René Descartes, Johannes Kepler, nor Isaac Newton appear on the list, whereas the well-known radical materialist John Toland does, but for his work as a scholar of Judaica, not his libertine tracts like *Pantheisticon*.[35]

Having invited readers into the treatise with this accounting of its textual infrastructure, the book continues with a full-page portrait of Pfeffel depicted with his fingers grasping a page inscribed "PHYSICA SACRA JOHANNIS IACOBI SCHEVCHZERI." This image is presented as if his hands were possessing the textual book and its project. A Neo-Latin verse inscription below the image, written by his son, who is also listed as one the artist collaborators on the project, reinforces the message, saying (in my literal and not particularly poetic translation): "Print handiwork, that ornament of the engraver, Pfeffelius, / who is known to carve from an effigy the appearance of things. / Whose gifts of mind / are exemplary of the hand around the world, / and are celebrated and shown for you in the Holy Bible."[36] After the celebration of the master, Pfeffel, a list of three "able artists" who worked "under his direction" in the production of the work is offered. These include Jean Melchior Fueslin, who did "les desseins" for all the images (the word in French means both drawings and design), Jean-Daniel Preissler, who did "the ornaments" for the plates and the frontispiece, and Tobie Laub who did the portraits of "the author" (the word is left singular in the text even though two portraits appear). The portrait engravings themselves are signed George de Marées, "pinxit," that is, "painted," and Johann Georg Mintz is named as "sculp.," or the artist who actually carved the image into the plate. Was Laub a book-making artist of some sort? The evidence is unclear. Also noted by name are over a dozen other artists who also contributed to the project, including Pfeffel's son and also Scheuchzer's son David. Catherine Hecklin, the wife of the Augsburg artist Jerome Sterling, who also contributed, is also listed. The printers of the *Kupfer-Bibel* in Augsburg (Steinberg) and Ulm (Wagner) are further recognized, giving them credit for the inscriptions found on the plates.[37] It is extremely rare to see the full artistic team behind books like this so fully acknowledged and made visible, even though we know that collaborations like this were the norm in the production of richly-made illustrated books. We can also assume that the variations in font size and the degree of elaboration in the presentation reflect status hierarchies that were certainly present, even if discerning them precisely from these sources is not easily done.

Having concluded the prefatory material in this way, the treatise itself begins on the next page, marked by a shift to a new sequence of non-Roman pagination. This is where the Newberry Library edition begins. An image labelled "Tab. I" serves as the bridge: an elaborate double-page representation of the cosmos as shown here in figure 13.1.

In its summarizing caption in both Latin and German – a sign that the plates were not translated into French in the same way that the text was – the image opens the rest of the book with a dynamic depiction of the created universe, the focus of the eight-volume treatise. In its multiple registers, ranging from the Hebrew tetragrammaton at the top of the plate to the pagan zodiac framing the circular edge of the celestial spheres, the image unifies into one super-folio visual presentation a range of different cosmological claims. These include naturalist representations of the heavens as material realms composed of clouds and light, rendered with chiaroscuro to show their physical corporeality, and instrumental and schematic representations like armillary spheres figuring the celestial mechanism. Various kinds of pictorial, symbolic, and quantitative diagrams, each vaguely standardized by a rudimentary

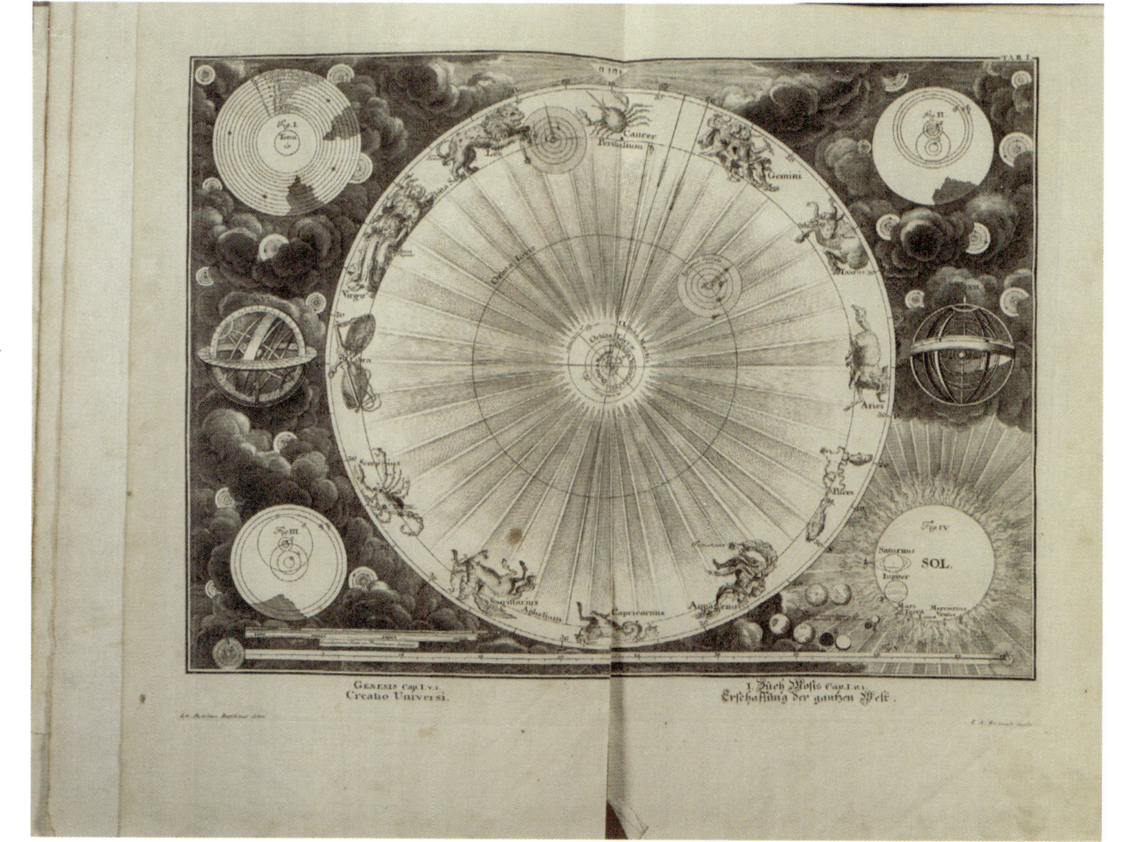

Figure 13.1. *Genesis Cap. I.v.i / Creatio Universi*, tab. I, in Jean-Jacques Scheuchzer and Jean-André Pfeffel, *Physique sacrée, ou Histoire-naturelle de la Bible* (Amsterdam: Pierre Schenk and Pierre Mortier, 1732). Engraving. Courtesy of the Newberry Library, Chicago

scaling rule at the bottom, are also added. The image further introduces the different kinds of cosmological analysis present in the book as a whole through references to material forms and physical processes. Mathematical astronomy and celestial mechanics are present, as are astrology and other interpretive frames, along with Holy Scripture in both the tetragrammaton at the top and the reference to Genesis 1 at the bottom in several different languages. Overall sacred physics is further joined with the latest astronomical science by offering precise heliocentric diagrams of our planetary system, a representation that Galileo would have had no problem accepting, alongside the traditional geocentric representations adhered to by the Roman Inquisition.

With this introduction in place, the book then turns to its core content, which is the presentation of a comprehensive natural and sacred account of the empyrean macrocosm and its terrestrial life worlds through 750 separate and numbered "planches," as they are called. The word *planches* suggests plates, and a full-page visual plate is at the centre of every *planche*. These are identified as "tab.," or *tableau*, numbered with Roman numerals and beginning with the opening tab. I, just discussed. In the German edition, "planches" and "tableaux" were conflated into *Tafeln*, which could be translated as "tables." Whatever the nomenclature, the label was not referencing the image alone, but an assemblage of text, including on some occasions tables of quantitative data and mathematical diagrams, together with the full-page printed copper-plate engraving. The French term *planches* is perhaps drawn from cartographic science, especially as it is found in similar large-scale multi-media atlases and print books. In cartographic tomes, *planches*, or assemblages of text, quantitative data, schematic diagrams, and imagery of various sorts are used in an integrated way to map the world scientifically.[38] The numbered *planches* as they appear in *Physique sacrée* could be accurately called "chapters" in English since each operates as a unit to advance an overall argument and narrative. Yet each is also an illustrated chapter, with text and image working together on several registers in each. In this sense, the word is akin to the French word *figure*, which was another term used in this period for printed text-image ensembles like these.[39] In *Physique sacrée*, it is the interaction of the full page image on one side of the open codex – remember that this is a super-folio-sized book – together with the accompanying textual matter – narrative, analytical explanation, quantitative theorization, and more – that determines the user's reading/ viewing. Building understanding through a dynamic interplay of multi-dimensional imagery and text, the assemblage combines textual and visual signs and representations into cosmological explanation.

To see how this method of natural knowledge making worked in practice, consider the very first *planche* in volume 1, devoted to the primordial beginnings of the universe (fig. 13.2).

*Planche* I is unlike the others that follow in presenting a two-image assemblage, with the opening tab. I embellished with a much smaller allegorical image atop the text containing the interpretive analysis of both images. The biblical passage in question is the very first line of Genesis – "In the beginning, God created the heavens and the earth," to use the King James Version – and while subsequent *planches* will open with a large full-page engraved image standing alongside the text on its other page, the small image atop the text in this case works to add an allegorical iconographic analysis that is not present in all the subsequent *planches*. At a certain level, it also adds another frame for the textual material by giving an iconographic overview of the divine creation as a story of the passage from "Alpha to Omega." Tab. I, by contrast, offers an overview of the creation considered as an accomplished fact, as does the precise biblical passage cited, which announces the same without noting anything about Omega, or the subsequent end times asserted by Christian theology. From this perspective, this second, smaller image is shaping the theological science presented in important ways, and the text draws on both in its presentation.

*Planche* II, and all those after, will avoid this initial two-image assemblage, and with this departure overtly iconographical and allegorical imagery of any kind will also by and large disappear as the rest of the treatise unfolds. The overall authoritative explanatory project of the treatise will also begin with this second *planche*, namely its comprehensive accounting of the sacred unfolding of our universe as the story is found in each of God's sacred revelations: nature and the Holy Scripture of the Bible. *Planche* II also initiates what will become the routine manner of presentation and argument throughout the subsequent thousand pages. The 750 numbered *planches* each open with a full-page framed *tableau*. A precise biblical passage is cited, echoed in the inscription on the engraving on the facing plate. A textual analysis then follows, usually running to a few pages. It adds commentary, explanation, and annotated references to relevant sources, along with tables of quantitative data and occasionally mathematical diagrams that add further detail to the presentation. A symbolic cartouche under the text indicates when a particular *planche* has been completed, and when we turn the page we encounter another full-page framed *tableau* with another biblical citation under it, facing across the spine a textual commentary that adds to the analysis. In this

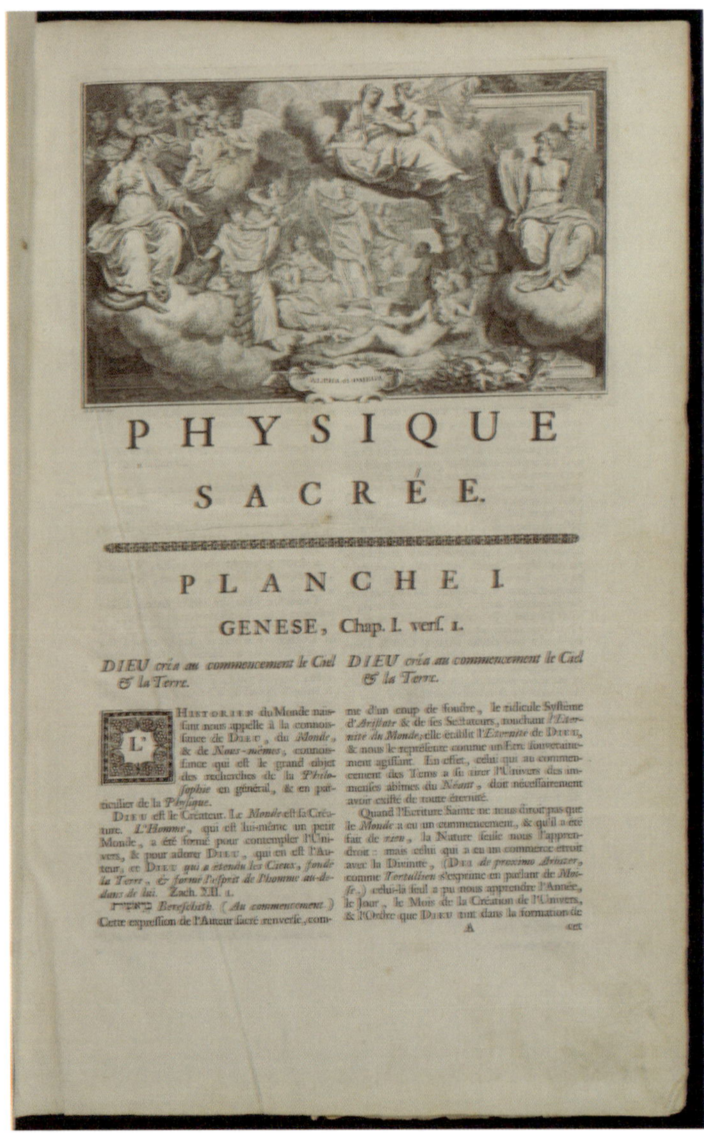

Figure 13.2. *Alpha et Omega, planche* I, 1, in Jean-Jacques Scheuchzer and Jean-André Pfeffel, *Physique sacrée, ou Histoire-naturelle de la Bible* (Amsterdam: Pierre Schenk and Pierre Mortier, 1732). Engraving. Courtesy of the Newberry Library, Chicago

way, each subsequent *planche* proceeds just as every other one has before in revealing through a complex interplay of textual and visual representation the nature/science/sacrality of the cosmos.

Viewed in its entirety as an Enlightenment treatise, what Scheuchzer and Pfeffel offer is an exquisitely produced, multi-media, and scientifically up-to-date natural and scriptural account of the origins of the cosmos as presented through a combination of large, lavish images and textual explanations replete with empirical evidence, source criticism, and scientific arguments, along with diagrams, tabular data, and other printed materials. Together, each part works to advance the project overall, and treated as an ensemble – and this is what makes it Enlightenment cosmology – the treatise never hesitates to show the inseparable unity of Holy Scripture with modern science.

Viewed less historically, one might be tempted to call this "creation science *avant la lettre*," but it is crucial to stress the difference between Enlightenment Mosaic physics of this sort and our seemingly contemporary version of it.[40] Whereas modern creation science uses empirical natural science to defend the scientific veracity of scriptural claims while seeking to show how the Bible can and should be read as a fully scientific text, Mosaic philosophers perceived no contest whatsoever between scripture and science, and felt no need to defend the veracity of Holy Scripture, which stood for them as an unquestioned authority equal too if parallel with the authority of natural explanation.

In *planche* I above, for example, the scriptural line asserting a cosmological beginning where a creator God brought our universe into existence at an initiating instant is supported by a scientific explanation drawn from sacred and profane universal histories and the relatively new textual, quantitative, and astronomical science of chronology. Each part buttresses the scriptural idea of a singular creation as the origin of planetary history, and in this way, *Physique sacrée* works to show the deep harmony between natural and scriptural understandings, not the supreme authority of one versus the other. Also emphasized is the way that the Bible is more fully illuminated through the natural harmonies with it evident in scientific accounts of the natural world. In this sense too, the Mosaic philosopher is different from the creation scientist in recognizing the complexity of the Bible as a text, and the difficulty of its accurate interpretation. Pfeffel and Scheuchzer certainly adhere strictly to the scriptural word, yet in their harmonization of it with natural science they raise no worries about the incompatibility of holy writ with natural explanation. Fully aware of, and comfortable with, the hermeneutical

complexity of the Bible and the complex science of its accurate interpretation, they likewise do not worry about biblical literalism in their
work. As Mosaic philosophers, they use empirical science and philosophical reasoning to make arguments about accurate biblical interpretation
while at the same time using complex scriptural interpretations to clar-
ify and understand the complexities presented by nature. In this sense,
theirs is at once a cosmological science and a Christian theology, not an
effort to re-attach religion to science or to reground science in Christian
scriptural authority as if they were two separate things.

The nature of their enterprise is further illustrated in *planche* II, which
launches the explanatory project of grounding creation in both scripture and natural science, conceived as two equal sources of authority.

The full-page framed image tab. II opens the assemblage (fig. 13.3),
which is focused overall on the very complicated second verse of Genesis 1. The text of *Planche* II begins on the facing page, starting with two
different French translations of Genesis 1:2, along with a summarizing
title of the *planche* at the top: "the work of the first day." The engraved
image here follows in the book's Roman numeral sequence, while the
textual pages follow a separate numeration with Arabic numerals. This
book-making separation between the plates as one series of numbered
pages and the text as another is important, given that binding was not
done by the booksellers but by the owners after they had acquired their
purchase as a stack of loose printed pages from the printer. By separating
the textual pages of each *planche* from the plates, it became possible for
owners to create a separate volume of the images if they so desired, or
a continuous book of text that was free of accompanying images if that
was preferred. This potential is documented in the Newberry Library's
edition of what its catalogue describes as a copy of the Latin edition
of *Kupfer-Bibel*.[41] The actual text is a three-volume bound collection of
Pfeffel's images with the label "Sainte Bible" embossed on the spine.
A wholly different frontispiece is added as the first page, and after that
most, if not all, of Pfeffel's images appear as plates pasted into pages, following the original order of the original publication but without any of
Scheuchzer's or the publisher's added text. I have not seen any copies of
the French translation, *Physique sacrée*, either in libraries or online, that
present the book's contents in this bifurcated way. But I have seen other
large-sized, lavishly illustrated books of this sort that are bound in this
way, so the possibility of finding one certainly exists. We should keep this
instability in mind as we interpret texts like this, not least because of the
potential disconnect evident in these sources between the commercial,

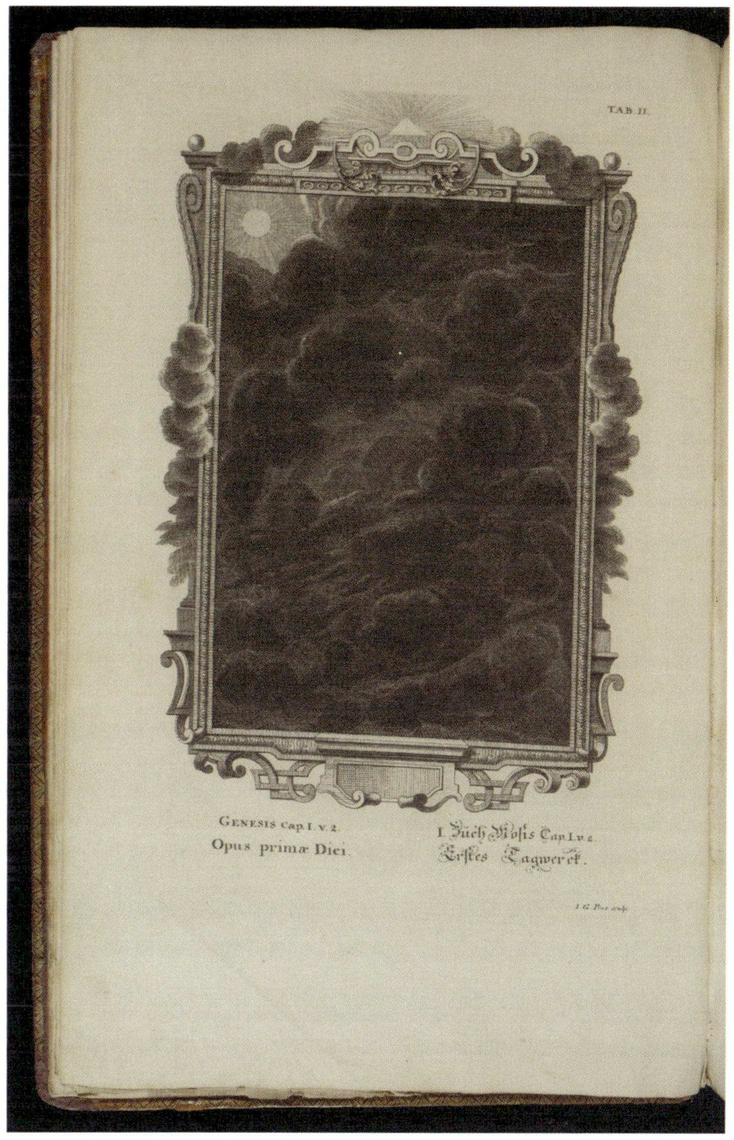


Figure 13.3.  *Opus primae diei*, tab. II, in Jean-Jacques Scheuchzer and Jean-André Pfeffel, *Physique sacrée, ou Histoire-naturelle de la Bible* (Amsterdam: Pierre Schenk and Pierre Mortier, 1732). Engraving. Courtesy of the Newberry Library, Chicago

artistic, and scientific agendas driving their production and publication, which were never one and the same.

Returning to the coherent *Planche* II as found in the BnF edition, what is typical of it with respect to all the subsequent *planches* in *Physique sacrée* is the elaborate full-page framed image to the left, with captions referencing the textual content at issue as elaborated in the separate pages of text that begin on the right. Also representative of the work as a whole is the ornamental framing of the image, and its suggestion of a defined space of depiction isolating the image from the blank page, along with a specifically designated space outside it. Were these frames designed to create a gallery effect, apparent if one were to assemble all the images together into one volume free of their textual accompaniment? The Newberry Library edition of *Kupfer-Bibel* suggests such a reading. Ornaments and other pictorial imagery are also used in this and every other image to establish, but also to undermine, the boundary between the pictorial space inside the frame, which is often a site of naturalist physical illusionism, and the white space on the printed page outside it.

In the case of tab. II (fig. 13.3), the radiating illuminated triangle at the top and outside the frame, redolent with the Christian symbolism of the trinitarian God situated at the heart of the divine light, also offers a symbolic resonance with the naturally rendered radiant sun breaking free of the clouds inside the image in the frame. The naturalistically rendered clouds that curl around the frame from outside it work from the other direction to disrupt the frame as a boundary separating natural from symbolic space. Theologically, these complexities also work to situate God both outside nature, in the immaterial reason of his *logos* and providence, and in nature in the immanence of his divine spirit – traditionally represented as light – in the creation itself. Both aspects of the image therefore provoke an urge to interpret the interplay between the natural events seemingly happening inside the frame and their spiritual, divine aspects beyond it.

Throughout *Physique sacrée*, the visual play of the images within the decorative frames, and the separate spaces they both delimit and struggle to maintain, interact to sustain a complex interpretive dynamic that also operates with the different pictorial registers present, ranging from naturalism, to symbolic iconography, to ornament. Adding further complexity is the continual interplay of these multifaceted images with their textual accompaniments, and given the interpretive difficulties of Genesis 1:2, *planche* II offers a particularly rich example of the complex interpretive dynamics that result.

In *planche* II, the text alongside the image (fig. 13.3) works to negotiate the place of God in nature, or more precisely in his creation, a
negotiation analogous to the pictorial interplay between naturalism and
symbolism in the accompanying *tableau*. Precise physico-theological biblical interpretation is at the heart of the issue. To begin, consider the
verse in Genesis 1 that anchors this *planche* and the one immediately
before it and after it:

1  In the beginning God created the heaven and the earth.
2  And the earth was without form, and void; and darkness was upon
   the face of the deep. And the Spirit of God moved upon the face of
   the waters.
3  And God said, Let there be light: and there was light.
4  And God saw the light, that it was good: and God divided the light
   from the darkness.
5  And God called the light Day, and the darkness he called Night. And
   the evening and the morning were the first day.[42]

Although titled "The work of the first day" ("L'Ouvrage du Prémier
jour"), *planche* II deals only with the second verse, collecting it together
with the large opening *tableau* of the entire creation that focused only on
Genesis 1:1. *Planches* III and IV follow, completing the assessment of the
first day by focusing on verses 3–5. The citations from Genesis are also
offered in each *planche* in two different French vernacular translations
of the Hebrew text. The translation are identical in stating verse 1:1 as
"DIEU créa au commencement le Ciel & la Terre" ("GOD created in
the beginning the Heavens & the Earth") (the typography is rendered
exactly here, with Dieu in all caps); with verse 1:2, however, two different
renditions are offered.[43] I have not been able to determine the sources
of these translations, and no citation is offered in the text. But it is worth
noting that an available and authoritative French translation, that of Jean
(Giovanni) Diodati published in John Calvin's Geneva in 1644, rendered
verse 1:1 in a way more in line with the King James translation, as "Au
commencement, Dieu créa le ciel et la terre" ("In the beginning, God
created the heavens and the earth").[44] The vast majority of French translations I have looked at do the same, and while there is no other evidence
supporting the idea that the authors of *Physique sacrée* where actively engaging in re-translation, the choices made here are certainly significant.
Verse 1:2, which is the exclusive focus of *planche* II, is especially interesting from this perspective. Diodati translates it as "Et

la terre était une chose deserte et vide: et les ténèbres estayent sur la surface de l'abîme, et l'esprit de Dieu se mouvait sur la face des eaux" ("And the Earth was a desolate and empty thing: and the clouds were on the surface of the abyss, and the spirit of God moved over the face of the waters").[45] One of the translations used in *Physique sacrée* changes the earth from "deserte et vide" ("desolate and empty") to "stérile et vuide" ("sterile and empty"), while the other speaks of "la terre sans forme et vuide" ("the earth without form and empty"), a translation that matches the sense of the King James English.[46] Likewise, while each of the translations offered agrees with Diodati in describing clouds (*ténebres*) being present upon the surface of the abyss (*l'abîme*), Diodati speaks of the spirit of God (*l'esprit de Dieu*) moving (*se mouvait*) over the face of the waters, while one of the translations offered in *Physique sacrée* breaks from this formulation by speaking of the spirit of the Lord (*l'esprit du Seigneur*) being carried over or upon the waters (*étoit porté sur les Eaux*). Similar differences exist in the translations offered of Genesis 1:3–5 in *planche* III as well.

Not all of these differences are significant, but given the complexity of verses 1 and 2, and especially their relation to one other as the opening action of divine creation, the differences in those precise verses are in fact very significant. At issue in each is the fundamental Christian doctrine of the relation of God to his creation, and the orthodoxy which holds that any collapse of one into the other constitutes an extreme heresy. Spinoza's God-Nature monism, which was in scandalous circulation throughout Europe by the 1680s, acquired its status as a spectre of philosophical monstrosity precisely because of its assertive claims for an immanent God, present as a universal rationality inherent in the natural world and not as an immaterial creator distinct from it.[47] Forms of Spinoza's argument are present in ancient pagan philosophy, including those strands of it that followed Jesus and his teachings into what came to be called Gnosticism. To secure the orthodox Christian doctrine that laid the foundations for the Christian church, a clear separation had to be secured between God the father and creator, who brought his only son into the world as its redeemer, and the material world that God created, a world separate and distinct from him except in those moments when the divine incarnation of Jesus walked the earth.

The orthodox interpretation of Holy Scripture was shaped by this theological imperative, and among the ways that the separation of God from creation was accomplished was through a Christianizing interpretation of Genesis 1 that made it match, and thus prefigure, John's gospel. In the King James version, the Gospel of John begins:

1  In the beginning was the Word, and the Word was with God, and the
   Word was God.
2  The same was in the beginning with God.[48]


The original Greek word translated here as "beginning" is *arche*, a term
that suggests commencement or beginning. But the same word also conveys the idea of a primitive origin or foundation. In his Latin Vulgate,
Jerome captured this double sense by translating the opening lines of
Genesis as "in principio creavit Deus caelum et terram," as opposed to,
say, "in itium creavit Deus." Had he used *in itium,* a clear sense of creation as an initiation in time would have been suggested, but by translating *arche* as *in principio* in his Latin translation of the Gospel of John, he
was suggesting a structure of divine foundations present at the source of
all things. By further translating the Greek word *logos* as "verbum," rather
than "ratio," which suggests rationality or reason – think about words
like "logic," or the suffix "ology" from *ologoi* – Jerome further situated
John's divine reason (*logos*) of God (*Theos/ Deus*) squarely in the divine
word (*logos/verbum*) of Genesis.[49]

The simplest way for a vernacular translator to maintain the orthodoxy of this theological tradition is to offer a translation that begins
with a statement like "In the beginning," as the King James version
does for both Genesis and John. "Au commencement," as it appears
in the French translations, follows the same model. Scheuchzer's
choice to avoid this temporizing clause and just announce that "God
created at the beginning the heavens and the earth" ("Dieu créa au
commencement le Ciel et la Terre") leads to possible theological/
cosmological problems, especially when one moves to verse 2, which
seems to either continue or complete the first verse. The use of "and"
in the King James translation to start verse 2 is one way to manage the
transition by creating a narrative continuation, and the French often
mimics that with "et." But the French word "Or," as is found here, suggests a different transition in its suggestion of "yet" rather than "and."
Others simply use a period to create two sentences without a transition
between them.

However it is set up, verse 2 still poses problems because the Earth created in verse 1 is stated to be present already in verse 2, together with a
void. It also seems to exist as a mass or body that is "without form" in the
King James version, matched in one of the French translations offered
in *Physique sacrée* as "sans forme," but different in the other as "stérile."
Neither follow Diodati, who calls the earth in verse 2 "a desolate thing"

("une chose deserte"). No matter how the verse is translated, the clear suggestion is that the creation is not necessarily a complete generation of the world *ex nihilo*, but a creation of the earth and the heavens through a transformation of matter (earth, along with the waters and clouds in the void and the abyss) that are already present with God "in the beginning."

Returning to the play across the frame of the image in *planche* II (fig. 13.3), additional hermeneutic meaning is gleaned by reading the image as a pictorial interpretation of this and its adjacent scriptural passages. Moving from tab. I (fig. 13.1) to II (fig. 13.3), we move from the completed creation announced in verse 1 to the divine work that brought this about, starting with the first day. Focusing on verse 2, the image gives us a turbulent mass of dark clouds filling the space inside the frame, and a seeming escape outside of it via the curling clouds around its edges. Clearly outside the frame is the radiating triangle with its trinitarian symbolic resonances, but just inside the frame below the triangle the clouds are shown to be parted, revealing a radiant sun. On the one hand, the sun betrays the literal reading of the scripture, since only in verses 3–5 does light and morning as opposed to night arrive. In verse 2, we have the earth in whatever character it is in, the clouds, the abyss, and the waters over which God moves. Yet if God is the *logos* of John's Gospel, then that *logos* is present, symbolically, in the radiant triangle outside the frame. It is also present in the sun's light, which read in this way is a symbol of the divine light present as the guiding spirit of God in the material substance of creation, and not the naturalistic representation of actual material sunlight that it appears to be. The textual commentary sends a similar message, describing the material present as a "Chaos that has still not been achieved" ("un Cahos, qui n'estoit point encore achevée"), a confused mass ("une masse confuse") that awaits the ordering work of the divine architect.[50]

This presentation certainly separates the divinity of the creator from the material nature of his creation, but in the references offered in the text to ancient and modern natural philosophers who are said to agree with this interpretation of verse 2, further problems persist. The reason why creation *ex nihilo* has traditionally been claimed as the foundation for Christian orthodoxy is because of the way it clarifies beyond dispute the strict separation between God the eternal creator and his material creation, which he originated entirely through his own omnipotence. Treating creation instead as an act of material transformation undertaken by a divine, rational, and providential spirit present, as *Physique sacrée* suggests, alongside and within primordial matter is to blur that distinction, and even to suggest something like a Spinozistic collapse of it altogether. Given the danger of this doctrinal confusion, Christian iconography has established a tradition that clearly avoids it by representing the creator God anthropomorphically as a bearded and robed old man, and the world of his creation as a distinct body, usually a sphere, that God manipulates in producing the cosmos. Suggesting that the cosmos begins as an unformed chaos awaiting God's ordering rationality is certainly possible within this framework; but in the clear and inviolable distinction between the anthropomorphic creator God and the discrete results of his material creation, the traditional iconography works to keep orthodox Christian doctrine secure.

**Situating Enlightenment Cosmology in Its Historical Context**

Whether it is in Michelangelo's classically muscular creator swirling through the heavens on the ceiling of the Roman Catholic Pope's personal chapel in Rome or Lucas Cranach's frontispiece for Martin Luther's vernacular German Bible, with its image of a royally robed and bearded God gazing upon his creation, with saving hands raised and radiating light streaming behind him, we see the way that a particular iconographic arrangement for visualizing God as attendant to but fully separate from his creation served as a visual counterpart of, and pictorial guarantee for, the orthodox understanding of the Christian doctrine of cosmological creation. The inviolable distinction between God and his creation is indeed a tenet as fundamental to Roman Catholic doctrine as it is to Lutheranism, as well as many other Protestant sects (although not all). With the explosion after 1550 of printed vernacular Bibles in many languages, many with extensive illustrations, the convention of visualizing the creation story in Genesis 1 via an anthropomorphic God situated within or adjacent to a naturalistic representation of his created world became a print orthodoxy just as secure as its corresponding doctrinal orthodoxy. It is almost impossible to find an illustrated Bible from this period that does not deploy an anthropomorphic God in this manner in its illustrations, and from this perspective the presentation in *Physique sacrée* represents an innovation, one that may suggest heterodox intentions.

From what sources were Pfeffel and Scheuchzer drawing in creating their cosmological presentation? Staying with the hypothesis that they were wilfully heterodox in their intentions, one might to turn to Spinozism, which some historians have made a modernizing juggernaut pushing all of Europe towards materialist understandings of natural theology. Some Spinozists situated God as an imminent rationality found within the material word, while others, speaking in more orthodox Christian terms, spoke of a divine spirit present in the creation that animates the laws of nature by guiding the order and regularity we find in nature. Einstein's famous statement that his own cosmology supported Spinoza's God-nature unity, if it supported any notion of God at all, is an apt illustration here.

There are certainly close similarities between the natural theology of the creation offered in *Physique sacrée* and the principles of Spinoza's natural philosophy. But Spinoza is also the author of the *Tractatus theologico-politicus*, a book that systematically works to deauthorize the value and status of Holy Scripture. Pfeffel and Scheuchzer, by contrast, are assertive Mosaic physicists who are certainly offering a cosmological account of creation that conforms fully with the latest natural philosophy, but one that also, *and with equal importance*, conforms with the claims of divine revelation and holy writ: in short, cosmological science in line with the Word of God as divine *logos*, but also with the *verbum* of God as found in sacred scripture. Spinozist materialist pantheism was also far less original to him and his late seventeenth-century acolytes than modern historians are inclined to suggest. In his *Critical History of Mani and Manicheanism*, also published at Amsterdam in the same years as *Physique sacrée*, Isaac de Beausobre sought the origin of the Christian notion of creation *ex nihilo* by returning to the early Christian debates between Church Fathers and heterodox Christians with ties to Platonism, Gnosticism, Zoroastrianism, and the wider ancient "oriental philosophy," as it was called at the time.[51] Pfeffel and Scheuczher included citations from literature like this in their commentaries, and from this perspective, which was Beausobre's as well, Spinoza was less a radical modernizer than "an archaizing philosopher returned from Pre-Christian antiquity," one who was reviving the ancient monism underlying everything from Kabbala and Gnosticism to antique Platonism and Stoicism.[52]

These eclectic intersections of critical biblical studies and Christian theology with natural philosophy and science fit well with the work of Pfeffel and Scheuczher, and if one wanted to trace a genealogy for their work back into the seventeenth century, a direct ancestor might be the work of Robert Fludd (1574–1637). Fludd's intricate and lavishly illustrated super-folio-sized Latin treatise on natural philosophy, *Utriusque Cosmi, Maioris scilicet et Minoris, metaphysica, physica, atque technica Historia* (1618–21), is one of the great masterpieces of early modern alchemical

Neoplatonism, and in English the title could read *The metaphysical, physical, and technical history of the two worlds, namely the greater and the lesser.* Yet when the London printer Humphrey Mosley decided to publish a posthumous synopsis of Fludd's work in 1659, he chose the English title *Mosaicall philosophy grounded upon the essentiall truth, or eternal sapience.* This title worked in the public mind to secure the existence of a scientific program called by the name "Mosaical philosophy," with Fludd at its centre.[53] The publisher of Fludd's own Latin synopsis of his text, which appeared after his death in 1638, had used the category in the title of his publication, and Moseley followed that lead in his further-abridged English translation of this work in 1659. In doing so, these London printers were positioning Fludd's work alongside the founders of Mosaic philosophy program, figures like the Bohemian scholar Johan Amos Commenius (1592–1670), irrespective of Fludd's own relationship to the label.[54]

Commenius sits at the heart of the Mosaic physics circle that has been studied in detail by Ann Blair. Echoed in English by Mosley two decades later, Fludd's adoption of the term worked to expand the character and reach of Mosaic philosophy while maintaining the core mission of the program. Later thinkers thereafter had a label to embrace in their work, or one to react against, and in this way, a new kind of Enlightenment Mosaic physics was made possible after 1640, an intellectual stream that found one later eddy in the spectacular volumes of Scheuchzer and Pfeffel published in Amsterdam in the 1730s.

Fludd's work helped to establish the ideal of the Enlightenment Mosaic philosopher and the paradigm within which authors like Pfeffel and Scheuchzer operated in other ways, too. Although not called Mosaic philosophy until later, Fludd's multimedia manner of synthesizing Christian revelation with natural philosophy in *Utriusque Cosmi, Maioris scilicet et Minoris, metaphysica* (1617–21) was one source of influence. Produced at the De Bry bookshop in Oppenheim with the help of the brilliant etcher and engraver Matthäus Merian, who was also an important contributor to the De Bry edition of Michael Maier's influential *Atalanta fugiens* (*Atalanta Fleeing*) published in the same years, the print media aspects of Fludd's work were seminal in preparing a space for the Enlightenment cosmology of *Physique sacrée* a century later.[55]

Fludd's status as perhaps the first publicly declared "Mosaic philosopher," at least in print, was one influence, and his particular conception of Christian biblical natural philosophy was another. But the medialogical connections between Fludd's published work and *Physique sacrée* may have been the most important connection. Following Brucker, who classified Fludd as a "theosophist" and not a "Mosaic and Christian philosopher," Blair does not consider Fludd to be a Mosaic philosopher as she understands the term.[56] It is certainly true that his Neoplatonic Paracelsian natural philosophy was not conceived as a literal verse-by-verse harmonization of scripture with science in the manner of Commenius, the iconic Mosaic philosopher for Blair, or in the manner of *Physique sacrée*. Yet there are good reasons to place Fludd within the Mosaic physics tradition, and even better reasons to situate his lavishly illustrated treatises in natural philosophy, produced with state-of-the-art print media techniques, as one point of origin for the new imaginative and creative Enlightenment cosmological science of Pfeffel and Scheuchzer. This is especially true considering its demand to be understood simultaneously in terms of its innovative textual claims and its imagination-provoking print-medialogical visual argumentation.

To see this genealogy, let us follow Brucker and Blair in considering Fludd to be a "theosophist" rather than a "Mosaic and Christian philosopher." The key difference is that Fludd's magnum opus, *Utriusque Cosmi, Maioris scilicet et Minoris*, and his posthumous *Philosophia mosaica* as well, did not adopt the literal scriptural frame that Pfeffel and Scheuchzer, like Commenius, deployed in their work. While the latter paid close attention, in a way that Fludd did not, to the literal citation and then precise line-by-line interpretation of scripture, Fludd adopted a looser, more synthetic approach. Yet his cosmological science was nothing if not a synthesis of Christian theology with natural science. His operation as a theosophist, if we adopt Brucker's label, also gave Fludd a freedom to navigate the relation between Holy Scripture and natural philosophy that was not available to the rigorous Mosaic philosopher, even as his natural philosophy remained Mosaic in the sense of being beholden to the authority of the Mosaic scriptural books of the Tanakh as much as any other source.

The account Fludd offered of the primordial beginning of the cosmos illustrates well the similarities and differences between these two modes of Christian natural philosophizing. As a theosophist, Fludd approached Holy Scripture as a broad corpus of divine texts and not simply as the canonical texts of the Old and New Testaments. This allowed him to think about the complexities of the Hebrew text of Genesis free of its stabilization first by Jerome in his Vulgate and then by modern vernacular translators after 1550. As a Paracelsian Neoplatonist, he was also possessed of a complex natural philosophy that in his eyes agreed with the true gnosis of God even if understanding it required the use of innovative natural philosophical and scientific methods.

To see the possibilities this combination opened up for Fludd, consider this translation of Genesis 1:1–5 as found in The Jewish Study Bible, a modern scholarly translation used by those who want to directly render Jewish scripture into English in a way faithful to the ancient Hebrew in which it was written:

> [1]When God began to create heaven and earth – [2]the earth being unformed and void, with darkness over the surface of the deep and a wind from God sweeping over the water – [3]God said, "Let there be light"; and there was light. [4]God saw that the light was good, and God separated the light from the darkness. [5]God called the light Day and the darkness He called Night. And there was evening, and there was morning, a first day.[57]

Subsequent lines are also grouped in narrative paragraphs like this one, and with this break from the line-by-line approach of paradigmatic Christian translators, a wholly new understanding of the action of creation is revealed, one that challenges the understanding found in the other translations we have seen.

Most important, given our concerns, is the reconfiguration of creation as an event unfolding within a pre-existent world already present as God begins his generative work. No beginning moment is evoked when an act *ex nihilo* brings into being a wholly new cosmos from nothing. Instead, the Hebrew text as translated here brings us into the action *in medias res* as God is beginning to create heaven and earth from the unformed matter and void, together with the water, wind, and a depth of darkness that were also present with him. Into this primordial cosmic substance that includes God but is also something more than him alone, God introduces light, sparking the crucial change that initiates the creation of our world. Subsequent days continue this process, adding sky as an expanse for light separate from the darkness of the deep, and then a separation of earth from water creating terrestrial land separate from oceans, lakes, and streams. With light and sky in place, and earth joined with land, water, and wind, life becomes possible, and a third day is devoted to generating vegetation on earth, followed by a fourth day where lights are cast into the expanse of the sky to regulate the days and nights that shine on the earth. The creation in this telling is a divinely guided natural process, and this is how Fludd narrated it in his natural philosophical explanations. And if *Physique sacrée* suggested an immanent deity unfolding his rational spirit from within the matter of the world, it also pointed to the more orthodox Christian idea of an eternal and immaterial God standing outside of his creation as a providential architect and world-maker. Fludd's theosophy, by contrast, conceives of God as a world-generating alchemist and magician, one whose perpetual transformative presence within all cosmological substance drives the essential transformations that create and sustain the cosmos at every turn and at all levels.

Fludd unfolds his cosmological understanding throughout the two super-folio volumes of *Utriusque Cosmi, Maioris scilicet et Minoris,* using a combination of Latin textual explanations that synthesize scriptural understandings of God's theosophic work with philosophical and scientific accounts of how the divine creation was achieved chemically, physically, and spiritually. At every step, Fludd's textual work as a theosophic natural philosopher is supplemented by Merian's copious and fabulously rendered etchings, which appear throughout the treatise and work to convey a visual argument sustaining and sometimes complicating the textual account offered alongside them. This is also the manner of Pfeffel's engravings as they relate to Scheuczher's explanatory text. No scholarship exists on the actual working relationship between Fludd and the De Bry workshop in Oppenheim, nor on the working methods of Matthäus Merian the artist. No presentation of the book's "scientific team" of scholars, authors, and artists is found at the start of *Utriusque Cosmi, Maioris scilicet et Minoris* either in the manner found at the beginning of *Physique sacrée.* But to judge by the resulting volume that Fludd and Merian produced together, an authorial collaboration is clearly suggested, one that offers a clear precedent for the collaboration of Pfeffel and Scheuchzer over a century later.

Given the knotty problem of its scientific and theological interpretation, the primordial moment of creation can serve as a useful point of comparison between Fludd and Merian's cosmological effort and that of Pfeffel and Scheuchzer. The latter, as we saw, evoked the spectre of Spinoza, conceived either as a philosophical modernizer or as a throwback to heterodox Gnostic Christianity. And while the philosophy of the Jewish apostate was not available as an influence upon Fludd, who died in 1637 just before Spinoza's fifth birthday, the ancient cosmological learning that some readers placed at the source of the scandal provoked in the 1670s by Spinoza's *Tractatus* and *Ethics* were present. Fludd's alchemical and Neoplatonic understanding of the cosmos also had strong ties to ancient Gnostic thought and the so-called oriental philosophy, and even without Spinoza's sceptical and rationalist philosophical presentation, some thought it to be equally heterodox, especially in its immanent explanations of God in nature, and of creation as a living being animated throughout by the divine spirit contained within.[58]

Fludd was certainly not the wilful rebel that Spinoza was, and overall he used complex Latin explanations to accomplish a philosophical synthesis between scriptural accounts of creation and its natural operations as perceived by humans scientifically. As with *Physique sacrée*, the treatise he and Merian authored was ultimately conciliatory in its effort to show the harmony of science and religion, not a work seeking to divide and oppose them. Yet also like *Physique sacrée*, the work of the treatise cannot be understood by reading its text alone, because in many ways the text followed behind the images as the clarifying explanation of what was already visually seen. The images were also not textual illustrations so much as their own visual arguments that were afterwards clarified by accompanying text.

Compare, for example, Merian's first image depicting the overview of cosmological creation (fig. 13.4) with tab. II from *Physique sacrée* (fig. 13.3), which plays the same role at the opening of that assemblage. Both works open with elaborate fold-out images depicting the creation as a *fait accompli*, tab. I by Pfeffel (fig. 13.2) and the image below by Merian (fig. 13.4).

Yet whereas Pfeffel continues in this complex visual mode by working with a combination of naturalist and symbolic imagery and across an ornamental frame that defines spatial zones that serve as boundaries for different cognitive and interpretive registers, Merian visualizes the first moment of creation with a solid black square that has the Latin phrase *Et sic in infinitum*, "and so on to infinity," inscribed on each side, as if each side is an opening to the image (fig. 13.5).[59]

The whole is also depicted as if it is to be viewed as opening in each direction at once. Note also that this image is an etching, meaning that Merian created the black square he desired by first preparing the print-making plate with a wax cover and then carving away the wax of the square he intended to make black so as to make it accessible to an acid bath that would actually create the printable plate. The same square could have been printed without any of this labour by simply inking and pressing a clean metal plate on the page, and in the print copies of Fludd's book the traces of Merian's diligent labour in actually sculpting the black square in all of its substance is evident. The repeated inscription, which serves as the boundary of all four sides of the square, suggests cursive handwriting rather than mechanical type, and while etching allows for an easier rendering of handwriting, in this case it also had the effect of joining the space of creation with the work of the creator in the

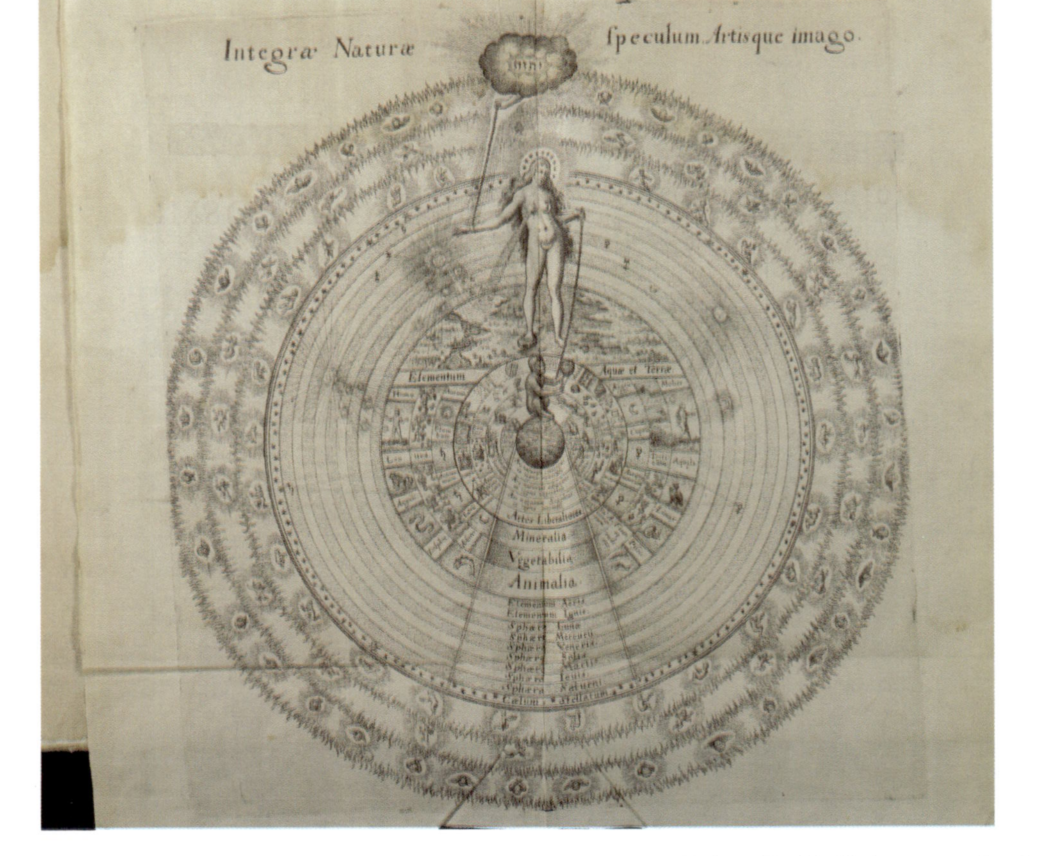


Figure 13.4. Matthäus Merian, *Integrae naturae*, in *Speculum artisque imago*, in Robert Fludd, *Utriusque cosmi maioris scilicet et minoris metaphysica, physica atque technica historia* (Oppenheim: Theodor De Bry, 1617). Etching. Courtesy of the Newberry Library, Chicago

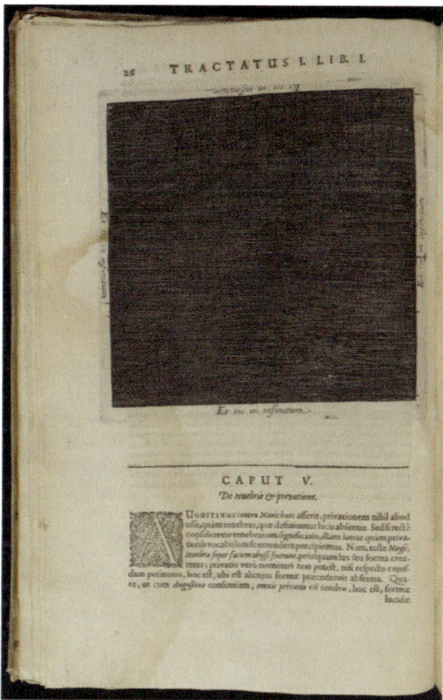

Figure 13.5. Matthäus Merian, *Et sic in infinitum,* in Robert Fludd, *Utriusque cosmi maioris scilicet et minoris metaphysica, physica atque technica historia* (Oppenheim: Theodor De Bry, 1617), 1:26. Etching. Courtesy of the Newberry Library, Chicago

same shared handiwork. All of this effort fits with Fludd's Neoplatonic vision of God as a craftsman and maker moulding the substance of creation to form through divinely rational means.

A clear theme throughout Fludd's treatise is the intricate processes essential to the divine labour immanent in the creative work of God the divine craftsman, and since Fludd's creator is an alchemical maker, his text seeks to show how the material categories found in nature – water, light, earth, the heavens – participated in a dynamic process of physical transformation and transmutation producing the generation of the cosmos. Merian's image has been compared aesthetically with the modernist abstraction of Malevich's twentieth-century *Black Square,* but with the labour of the etcher and its making evident in the black square – its inking bleeds through the page and is visible on the verso, and the scratches of the burin are present in the print itself – this image is not an abstraction like Malevich's, but a material depiction of the beginnings of creation as a dark, unformed *infinitum,* to use the language of the inscription, a body that is both a nothing that precedes the world and the material from which God, the magical artisan, will make it. On the one hand, this depiction accentuates the idea of a creation *ex nihilo* in that it is the nothing, the unformed infinite darkness, that is present "when God began to create," to use the Jewish Study Bible translation of Genesis. At the same time, however, it is not a nothing since this infinite and unformed darkness exists when God in his omnipotence began to work, and it is from this darkness that God creates the heavens and the earth, and all that they contain. Fludd's text performs the usual Christian gymnastics to align his story of creation with Christian orthodoxy, and Merian's image both supports and complicates that account. It does so by stressing the material darkness that precedes God's work, and also the creation of the world from it in a manner figured in Fludd's genius as an alchemical natural philosopher, and Merian's genius as a material artist.

Subsequent images in *Utriusque Cosmi, Maioris scilicet et Minoris* reveal the later interaction of space and matter, darkness and light, and eventually raw matter and its dynamic transformation into the created bodies of our world. The interplay between text and image is crucial to these presentations as well, and while they are not organized, as in *Physique sacrée*, into discrete assemblages isolating precises steps in the march of creation, they follow the same process as narrated in Genesis, albeit with a much more naturalist and physico-chemical presentation of the essential transformations. And yet, while their theosophical presentation of creation is more directly material and alchemical and less strictly scriptural than that found in *Physique sacrée*, Merian's images are more stylized and symbolic than the physical naturalism found in Pfeffel's. This can be seen in Merian's use of the dove and the word "FIAT" to illustrate God's separation of light from darkness (fig.13. 6), different certainly from Pfeffel's more insistent naturalism, but a combination akin to his physical description of imagined natural processes along with his attention through symbols to the invisible divine spirit underlying and driving it.

Overall, both works combine complex textual explanation with dramatic and arresting visual imagery, and each mode works to advance the cosmological project of the treatise as a whole. There are certainly important differences to be noted in the precise cosmological science each presents, and an account of the differences between them would reveal a history of the development of European cosmological understandings

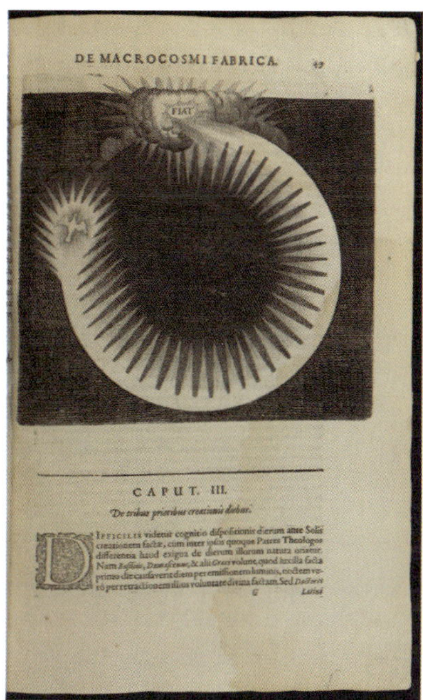


Figure 13.6. Matthäus Merian, *De Macrocosmi Fabrica*, in Robert Fludd, *Utriusque cosmi maioris scilicet et minoris metaphysica, physica atque technica historia* (Oppenheim: Theodor De Bry, 1617), 1:49. Etching. Courtesy of the Newberry Library, Chicago

between 1600 and 1750. But what is also striking is the way that their differences are found within a medialogical mode of cosmological science – the super-folio illustrated book – that is continuous across these centuries.

## A Modern Enlightenment Cosmology?

The synergy between God and nature, the Bible and natural philosophy, and the divine *logos* as scientific *ratio* and holy writ is as central to the alchemical world view present in the *Utriusque Cosmi, Maioris scilicet et Minoris* of Fludd and Merian as it is to the image-text assemblages found in Pfeffel and Scheuchzer's *Physique sacrée*. Brucker's description of Fludd as a "theosophist" rather than a "Mosaic and Christian philosopher" suggests a difference between the two, but his description in 1744 of each group as among the modern philosophers suggests that this is a difference of degree more than one of kind. Others with very different attitudes were certainly present at the same time, but in the similarities we see here across the century that separates Fludd and Merian from Pfeffel and Scheuchzer, we detect powerful continuities in cosmological thinking that cannot be dismissed as retrograde.

To the extent that these patterns can be found to persist and exert power well into the eighteenth century, the labelling of them as Enlightenment cosmology is certainly warranted. But was there an innovative aspect of Enlightenment cosmology as well, a dimension of it beyond the long-standing drive to hold together the Christian religion with natural philosophy and science? In this essay, I suggest that a medialogical stance can allow us to see Enlightenment cosmology as a product of the eighteenth century as an innovative moment in the history of print media. This was a moment, I argue, when the ever-present aspect of human cosmological explanation as imaginative worldmaking found a particular and spectacular outlet in the convergence of new methods of metal-plate image making and sophisticated commercial and technological systems of book making. The result was blossoming of large and sumptuously illustrated treatises that explained the foundations of science in both ancient and innovative terms, books made by authors who placed one hand firmly on the traditions of revealed religion while the other pushed the boundaries of new scientific and philosophical thinking.

This publishing technique was a source of innovation in and of itself, but even more powerful was the way that the new use of images together with printed text in the production of multimedia conglomerates created a powerful new dynamic for the encapsulation and communication of scientific knowledge, with the sciences of theology and biblical philology included in that label. It is sometimes said that empirical picture making with the eye no longer matters in modern astrophysics, having been replaced by the quantitative analysis of the mind's eye as a result of the replacement of the optical telescope and positional astronomy by the quantitative electromagnetic data recorded by radio telescopes. Yet what is our contemporary understanding of the universe, whether held by cosmologists or lay people alike, without the powerful pictures of it provided by the Hubble telescope? And by supporting and complicating in equal measure the data-driven, and data-limited, work of scientific astrophysics, how do the imaginative understandings evoked by these images work to anchor the creative worldmaking present in twenty-first century cosmological theorizing? In this way, Enlightenment cosmology as I have described it here is as much a historical feature of the eighteenth century as it is an illustrative example of the universal features of our scientific cosmological worldmaking, then as now.

## NOTES

1 Neil deGrasse Tyson, *Astrophysics for People in a Hurry* (New York: W.W. Norton, 2017).

2 Nasser Zakaria, *A Final Story: Science, Myth and Beginnings* (Chicago: University of Chicago Press, 2017).

3 John Keill, *An Examination of of Dr. Burnett's Theory of the Earth* (Oxford: at the Theater, 1698). Cited in William Poole, *The World Makers: Scientists of the Restoration and the Search for the Origins of the Earth* (Oxford: Peter Lang, 2010), 15–16.

4 Régis Debray, *Media Manifestos: On the Technological Transmission of Cultural Forms* (London: Verso, 1996); *God: An Itinerary* (London: Verso, 2004).

5 See for example Helge S. Kragh, "Enlightenment Cosmologies," chap. 2.2 in *Conceptions of the Cosmos: From Myths to the Accelerating Universe: A History of Cosmology* (Oxford: Oxford University Press, 2007), 75–89.

6 Thomas Wright Durham, *An Original Theory or New Hypothesis of the Universe: Founded upon the Laws of Nature, and Solving by Mathematical Principles the General Phaenomena of the Visible Creation* (London: Printed for the author, and sold by H. Chapelle, 1750). Immanuel Kant, *Allgemeine Naturgeschichte und Theorie des Himmels oder Versuch von der Verfassung und dem mechanischen Ursprunge des ganzen Weltgebäudes nach Newtonischen Grundsätzen abgehandelt* (Königsberg and Leipzig: Johann Friedrich Petersen, 1755). My citations will be drawn from the English translation, "Universal Natural History and Theory of the Heavens, or Essay on the Constitution and the Mechanical Origin of the Whole Universe According to Newtonian Principles (1755)," found in *Kant: Natural Science. The Cambridge Edition of the Works of Immanuel Kant*, ed. Eric Watkins (Cambridge, UK: Cambridge University Press, 2012), 182–308.

7 For an account of the sources of this legendary conversation between Laplace and Napoleon, see Ted Davis, "Did Newton's God Vanish with the 'Gaps' in his Science?," *BioLogos* (12 April 2015), https://biologos.org /articles/did-newtons-god-vanish-with-the-gaps-in-his-science.

8 Christian Huygens, *Kosmotheoros, sive De terris coelestibus, earumque ornatu, conjecturae* (The Hague: Adriaan Moetjens, 1698). In English, *The Celestial Worlds Discover'd* (London: Timothy Childs, 1698); in Dutch, *Wereldbeschouwer* (Rotterdam: Bernard Bos, 1699); in French, *Nouveau traité de la pluralité des mondes* (Paris: Jean Moreau, 1702); in German, *Weltbetrachtende*

*Muthmaassungen von den himlischen Erdkugeln* (Leipzig: Friedrich Landeschens Erbens, 1703). The Russian title is Книга мірозрѣнія, или, Мнѣніе о небесноземныхъ глобусахъ и ихъ украшеніяхъ.

9	Joas van der Schoot, "Interpreting the *Kosmotheoros* (1698). A Historiographical Essay on Theology and Philosophy in The Work of Christiaan Huygens," *De Zeventiende Eeuw. Cultuur in de Nederlanden in interdisciplinair perspectief* 30 (2014): 31.

10	*The Celestial Worlds Discover'd*, 7.

11	Voltaire, *Micromégas*, ed. Nicholas Cronk and J.B. Shank, in *Complete Works of Voltaire / Œuvres complètes de Voltaire*, 20c, *'Micromégas' and Other Texts (1738–1742)*, ed. Nicholas Cronk et al. (Oxford: Voltaire Foundation, 2017).

12	Lucian, *A True Story*, in *Phalaris. Hippias or The Bath. Dionysus. Heracles. Amber or The Swans. The Fly. Nigrinus. Demonax. The Hall. My Native Land. Octogenarians. A True Story. Slander. The Consonants at Law. The Carousal (Symposium) or The Lapiths*, trans. A.M Harmon, Loeb Classical Library 14 (Cambridge, MA: Harvard University Press, 1913).

13	Written around 1610 and published posthumously. Johannes Kepler, *Somnium, seu opus posthumum De astronomia lunari* (Frankfurt: Sagani Selesiorum, 1634), https://www.loc.gov/item/39010144.

14	Libertus Fromondus, *Saturnalitiae coenae, variatiae somnio sive peregrinatione coelesti* (Louvain: Petri Sasseni, 1616, 2nd ed. 1665). Giordano Bruno, *La Cena delle ceneri* (London: John Charlewood, 1584).

15	Cyrano de Bergerac, *L'Autre monde ou Les États et empires de la lune* (Paris: Charles de Sercy, 1657).

16	John Wilkins, *A Discourse Concerning a New Word and Another Planet in 2 Bookes* (London: John Norton and R. Hearne, 1640).

17	Margaret Cavendish, *The Description of a New World, Called the Blazing-World* (London: A. Maxwell, 1666).

18	Bernard le Bovier de Fontenelle, *Entretiens sur la pluralité des mondes habités* (Paris, 1686).

19	Paul Hazard, *La Crise de la conscience Européene* (Paris: Boivin, 1935).

20	George Minois, *The Atheist's Bible: The Most Dangerous Book that Never Was*, trans. Lyn Ann Weiss (Chicago: University of Chicago Press, 2012).

21	Thomas Paine, *The Age of Reason: Being an Investigation of True and Fabulous Theology* (Boston: Thomas Hall, 1794).

22	On the claim of a tandem development of scientific naturalism and the secular eclipse of religion, see the essays in Peter Harrison and Jon H. Roberts, eds., *Science without God? Rethinking the History of Scientific Naturalism* (Oxford: Oxford University Press, 2017), especially, for the developments in the decades around 1700, Peter Harrison, "Laws of God or Laws of Nature," and J.B. Shank, "Between Isaac Newton and Enlightenment Newtonianism."

23 Martin Mulsow, *Enlightenment Underground: Radical Germany, 1680–1720,* trans. H.C. Erik Midlefort (Charlottesville: University of Virginia Press, 2012), chap. 2, "The Ambivalence of Scholars: A Jewish Anti-Christian Manuscript and its Path into the early German Enlightenment."

24 Genesis 9:16 (NIV).

25 *Kant:Natural Science,* 303–4.

26 Johann Jakob Brucker, *Historia critica philosophiae,* 5 vols. (Leipzig: Bernard Christoph Breitkopf, 1742–4). The Mosaic philosophers appear in 4:610–43.

27 Ann Blair, "Mosaic Physics and the Search for a Pious Philosophy in the Late Renaissance," *Isis* 91 (2000): 32–58.

28 As this chapter was going to press, I was made aware of this new study that I have not yet fully digested: Ann Blair and Kaspar von Greyerz, eds., *Physico-theology: Religion and science in Europe, 1650–1750* (Baltimore: Johns Hopkins University Press, 2020). The review by Thokozani Kamwendo published in *H-Sci-Med-Tech, H-Net Reviews* (August 2021), https://www.h-net.org/reviews/showrev.php?id=55997, suggests that the book may suggest the label "Physico-theology" as a bridge term between seventeenth-century Mosaic physics/philosophy and the thinking of the eighteenth century, but while these detailed distinctions might be worth noting, for my purposes here thinking about "Enlightenment cosmology" as a label that includes both is sufficient.

29 Johann Jakob Scheuchzer and Johann Andreas Pfeffel, *Kupfer-Bibel, in welcher die Physica sacra oder geheiligte Natur-Wissenschaft derer in heil. Schrift vorkommenden natürlichen Sachen deutlich erklärt und bewährt,* 4 vols. (Augsburg and Ulm: Johann Christoph Steinberger and Christian-Ulrich Wagner, 1731–5).

30 Although Kant's precise theory about the cause of the flood stemming from the ancient Saturnine rings around the earth collapsing onto its surface is not found in this text, tabs. XLIV and LXVI both deal with the mathematical-physical dynamics of the flood and the post-diluvian rainbow respectively, and they certainly approach the topic in a manner akin to Kant's speculative reasoning in his universal natural history. See Johann Jakob Scheuchzer and Johann Andreas Pfeffel, *Physique sacrée, ou Histoire-naturelle de la Bible,* 8 vols. (Amsterdam: Pierre Schenk and Pierre Mortier, 1732–7), 1:58–63, 80–5.

31 Ibid. For a sample of the journal commentary, see the discussion of "Scheuczer's" [*sic*] proposal for the book in *Journal des Savants* (1727): 258, and a discussion of it in print in *Journal des savants* (1740): 524.

32 On the idea of the visual artist as author of scientific books, see the case of Willem Goeree (1635–1711), especially the analysis of Wouter de Vries, "'One can't imagine they have ever read the Bible!': On accuracy and knowledge in the prints of Willem Goeree," *Jaarboek voor Nederlandse boekgeschiedenis/Yearbook for Dutch Book History* 26 (2019): 79–100. See also Femy

Horsch, "Goeree, Willem," *Grove Art Online,* https://doi.org/10.1093/gao /9781884446054.article.T032983, accessed 17 November 2020.

33 Johann Jakob Scheuchzer and Johann Andreas Pfeffel, *Physique sacrée, ou Histoire-naturelle de la Bible. Traduite du latin de Mr. Jean-Jaques Scheuchzer, docteur en medecine, professeur de mathématiques à Zurich, membre de l'Académie impériale des Curieux de la nature, & des Societés royales d'Angleterre & de Prusse. Enrichie de figures en taille-douce, gravées par les soins de Jean-André Pfeffel, graveur de S. M. Impériale,* vol. 1 (Amsterdam: Pierre Schenk and Pierre Mortier, 1732), https://gallica.bnf.fr/ark:/12148/bpt6k1512572g/f11.item. Hereafter, *Physique sacrée.*

34 *Physique sacrée,* I-IX.

35 Ibid., X-XXXIV.

36 "Sculptorum palmate decus, PFEFFELIVS, ista, / Qua vultum sculpture, cernitur effigie. / Quem mentis dotes, manum monumenta per orbem / Concelebrant, monstrant Biblia Sacra Tibi." I am grateful for the work of Ian Karp on this Latin translation.

37 Ibid., XXXV-XXXVI.

38 I am grateful to Bronwen Wilson for this suggestion.

39 As an example, see *Figures de la Bible* (The Hague: Pierre de Hondt, 1728), https://repository.ou.edu/uuid/1015dee4–4ea2–58ec-b7ba-d0d89c440800 #page/6/mode/2up. This is a pictorial presentation of the Bible starting with primordial creation that uses full-page engraved images only and no accompanying text whatsoever.

40 The essentially nineteenth-century origins of creation science are made clear in Ronald L. Numbers, *The Creationists: From Scientific Creationism to Intelligent Design* (Cambridge, MA: Harvard University Press, 2006). For those interested in experiencing twenty-first-century creation science in all its depth and sophistication, *il vaut le voyage,* as the Michelin Guides say, to the Creation Museum in Petersburg, KY (https://creationmuseum.org/ about/), and its partner in nearby Williamstown, KY, the Ark Encounter (https://arkencounter.com/about/), a massive re-creation of Noah's Ark as it really was according to precise creation science calculations.

41 Here is the Newberry Library catalogue entry: https://i-share-nby.primo. exlibrisgroup.com/permalink/01CARLI_NBY/i5mcb2/alma996563298805867.

42 Genesis 1:1–5 (King James Version)

43 *Physique sacrée,* 5.

44 *La Sainte Bible interpretée par Jean Diodati* (Geneva: s.l., 1644).

45 Ibid., 3.

46 *Physique sacrée,* 5.

47 Benedict de Spinoza, *Ethica, ordine geometrico demonstrata,* in *B.D.S. Opera posthuma* (Amsterdam: J. Rieuwertsz, 1677). A good summary analysis of

Spinoza's thought, with an up-to-date bibliography of the best scholarship, is Steven Nadler, "Baruch Spinoza," in *The Stanford Encyclopedia of Philosophy,* ed. Edward N. Zalta (Summer 2020), https://plato.stanford.edu/archives/sum2020/entries/spinoza/.

48 The Gospel of John 1:1–2 (King James Version).

49 Citations drawn from the online Latin Vulgate at http://www.latinvulgate.com/.

50 Physique sacrée, 5.

51 Isaac de Beausobre, *Histoire critique de Manichée et du Manicheisme* (Amsterdam: Jean-Fréderic Bernard, 1734). J.G.A Pocock situates Beausobre's work well within contemporary discussion of the history of early Christianity in *Barbarism and Religion,* vol. 5, *Religion: The First Triumph* (Cambridge, UK: Cambridge University Press, 2010), chap. 5, "Isaac de Beausobre: heresy, philosophy, history."

52 Pocock, *Religion: The First Triumph,* 152.

53 Robert Fludd, *Mosaicall philosophy grounded upon the essentiall truth, or eternal sapience, written first in Latin and afterwards thus rendered into English by Robert Fludd, Esq.* (London: Humphrey Mosley, 1659).

54 Robert Fludd, *Philosophia Moysaica. In qua sapientia et scientia creationis et creaturarum sacra vereque Christiana (ut pote cujus basis sive fundamentum est unicus ille Lapis Angularis Iesus Christus) ad amussim et enucleate explicatur* (Gouda: Petrus Rammazenius, Bibliopola, 1638).

55 Robert Fludd, *Utriusque cosmi maioris scilicet et minoris metaphysica, Physica atque technica historia,* 2 vols. (Oppenheim: Theodor De Bry, 1617–21). Michael Maier, *Atalanta fugiens, hoc est, emblemata nova de secretis naturæ, chymica, accomodata partim oculis & intellectui, figuris cupro incisi, adiectisque sententiis, epigrammatis & notis, partim auribus & recreationi animi plus minus 50 rugis musicalibus trium vocum* (Oppenheim: Theodor de Bry, 1618). See the excellent digital presentation of *Atalanta fugiens* directed by Tara Nummedal and Donna Bilak, "Furnace and Fugue: A Digital Edition of Michael Maier's *Atalanta fugiens* (1618) with Scholarly Commentary," https://furnaceandfugue.org/.

56 Blair, "Mosiac Physics," 35–6.

57 Adele Berlin and Marc Zvi Brettler, eds., The Jewish Study Bible (Oxford: Oxford University Press, 2004), 13.

58 On Fludd's natural knowledge, see Bruce Janacek, *Alchemical Belief: Occultism in the Religious Culture of Early Modern England* (University Park, PA: Penn State University Press, 2011); Alan G. Debus, *The English Paracelsians* (New York: Watts, 1961).

59 See https://archive.org/details/utriusquecosmima01flud/page/n3/mode/2up. Note the way Merian's etching of the black square bleeds through the page on 25, an indication of the elaborate inking involved.

# chapter fourteen

# Masked Alliances: Global Politics and Economy in the Art and Performance Rituals of Mexico's Indigenous People

JOHN M.D. POHL AND DANNY ZBOROVER

One of the most enduring forms of Indigenous pageantry performed throughout southern Mexico is the Danza de la Pluma, a festival rooted in pre-Hispanic creation stories, heroic histories, and dynastic accounts originally painted in screenfold books or "codices." The theme of this "feather dance" can be identified in Codices Nuttall (fig. 14.1) and Vienna. It begins with the magical descent from the heavens of priests who bring the first temples, sacred bundles, and other cult objects to earth. After separating the sky from the sea to reveal the land, they establish the first kingdoms and call forth the sun to bring light and warmth. A cosmic war ensues in which personifications of stones rise up from the earth and stars fall from the sky to attack the culture heroes. After much loss of life, the conflict is resolved with the magical appearance of the first ancestors, who marry and engender the first dynasties.[1] By asserting kinship to culture heroes, Mixtec rulers irrefutably fixed their role as society's mediators with the supernatural. By claiming to be literally descended from various parts of a personified landscape, they could maintain proprietary claims by divine right, unattainable to the lower classes, a hegemony that extended from the ninth through the sixteenth century.[2]

This study examines how the Indigenous peoples of southern Mexico have used performance, either through theatrical re-enactment or through encoding dramatic action in representational art like the codices, to document their historical experiences on their own terms. While these records entwine chronicled events with myth, we nevertheless discern from archaeological remains, oral traditions, and sixteenth-century texts that essential elements of these accounts constitute real historical phenomena. A discussion of the social and economic organization of the confederacy of kingdoms, the "Children of the Plumed Serpent"

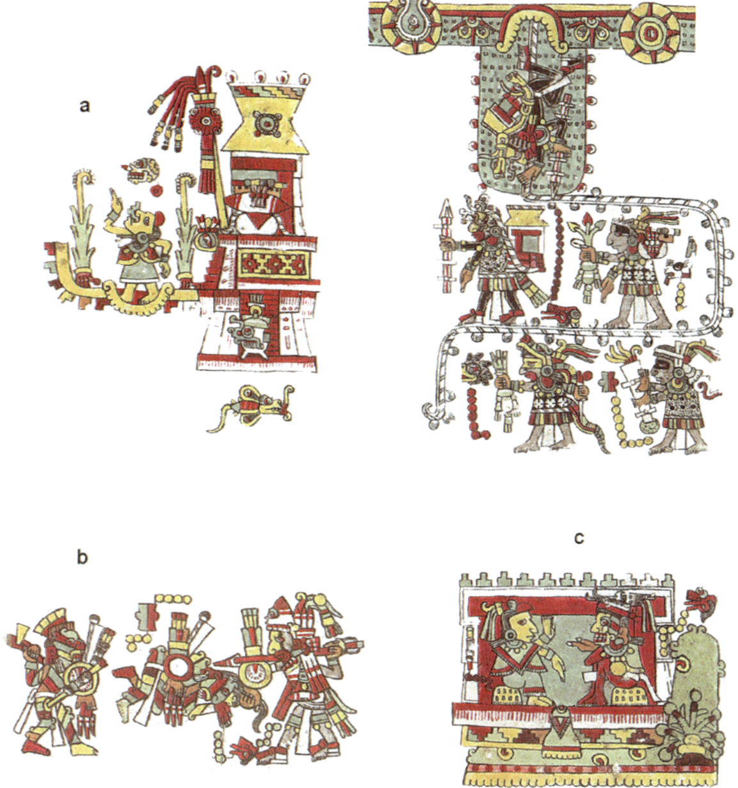

Figure 14.1.  The pre-Hispanic Codex Nuttall is preserved in the British Museum and details the founding of the first Mixtec and Zapotec kingdoms. (a) Priests miraculously descend on a rope from the sky during a rainstorm to establish a temple at Yucu Yoco, or Hill of the Bee, the kingdom where the divine ancestor Lady One Death first emerged from the earth. (b) The cosmic War of Heaven was waged between the dynastic founders and the Stone Men, a primordial race who were turned to stone by the sun when it was brought forth by the priests to bring light and warmth to the earth for the first time. (c) The War of Heaven is resolved with the marriage between the dynastic ancestor Lady Five Reed and the Stone Man Lord Nine Wind. By the sixteenth century these narratives of divine creation, cosmic conflict, and peaceful resolution through marriage composed an "Iliad" of Oaxaca that justified rights to territorial control by caciques, the colonial noble rulers whose ancestral lineages depicted in the codices extended back to the ninth century CE. The paintings were presented in palaces, where courtly poets recited the legends at feasts. The stories also prescribed the dances that were to be performed at the annual festivals together with the markets that were held at sacred sites in the surrounding hills. Illustration by John Pohl

as they called themselves, that dominated southern Mexico during the Postclassic period from 950 to 1521 CE, establishes the setting. We then examine the lucrative partnership that developed between caciques, essentially colonial Indigenous rulers, and the Dominicans. This partnership not only played an instrumental role in the establishment of the Manila Galleon trade together with the silver-mining industry, but simultaneously fostered an equally prosperous contraband economy that incorporated both Indigenous and European peoples who had been disenfranchised by the global Habsburg imperial system.

Written and painted colonial sources indicate that Indigenous and European leaders sought to promote a synthetic identity to promote their political agendas in New Spain. They turned to a shared tradition of historical pageants in which actors used masks and ritual dress to graphically portray different ethnic factions. The goal was to promote a social atmosphere of inclusiveness by conflating multiple historical experiences into a single dramatic event. Many of these dramas continue to the present day. Two variants based on the theme of world creation originally appearing in the pre-Hispanic codices and the colonial fiestas will be compared. One is presented annually by a community of the central valley of Oaxaca and commemorates the origin of the Zapotec people together with giving an account of the Spanish conquest and the apotheosis of Moctezuma as an Indigenous culture hero. The other is presented by a Chontal community located on Oaxaca's Pacific coast. Although it presents a comparable story of creation, it virtually ignores the conquest in favour of celebrating the Chontal engagement with Dutch, English, French, and possibly Islamic corsairs who were invested in the contraband trade, a phenomenon that is under-represented in studies of the economy of the early modern World.

## Historical Background

While many scholars have tended to promote the Aztec empire as the dominant culture during the Postclassic period, others have demonstrated that a confederacy of city-states, dominated by Nahua, Mixtec, and Zapotec nobility in southern Mexico, successfully resisted both Aztec and Spanish subjugation. Calling themselves the "Children of the Plumed Serpent," because of their belief that Quetzalcoatl had founded their royal lineages, this ruling class of caciques resurrected themselves on a new colonial foundation and continued to affect cultural development in Mesoamerica during a dramatic period of social transformation.[3] Southern Mexico had witnessed the introduction of a package of new forms of wealth that included finely crafted works of art manufactured in gold, copper, silver and turquoise, as well as jade and shell jewellery in unprecedented quantities, the feathers of tropical birds, lavish polychrome pottery, and specialized foods like cacao, used to make chocolate. Palaces were production houses where each noble family sought to buy their way into more lucrative alliances through systems of bridewealth, dowry, and other forms of gift exchange. Women not only supplied the lifeblood of the confederacy through exogamous marriage but also became the principal producers of these new forms of wealth.[4] Competition intensified as palace-based traders and craftspeople were driven to seek out the rarest and most exotic materials, fostering trading networks that extended from the greater American Southwest through West Mexico to Pacific coastal Oaxaca. The greater a royal house's ability to acquire these exotic materials and to manufacture exquisite jewels, textiles, and featherwork, the better marriages it could contract. The better marriages it could contract, the higher rank a royal house could achieve within the confederacy and, in turn, the better access it would have to more exotic materials, experienced merchants, and trained artisans. In this way royal marriages promoted exclusive control over access to both rare commodities and the skill sets of highly trained artisans who could transform them into the currency of social relations.

Despite widespread devastation after the Spaniards arrived in the early sixteenth century, not all of Mexico was "conquered." Many kingdoms engaged with the new colonial order peacefully under the leadership of caciques who claimed direct descent from pre-Hispanic lineages appearing in the codices.[5] The evangelization of the Children of the Plumed Serpent was undertaken by first the Franciscan and later the Dominican orders, which sent missionaries to all of the ranking noble houses from the Valley of Puebla to coastal Oaxaca. Before long, factional disputes emerged over the administration of Indian territories between Spanish nobles called *encomenderos*, the church, and the caciques. Acting as mediators between the crown and the caciques who actually controlled the land, the Dominicans eventually succeeded in forming more lucrative partnerships. Southern Mexico became a land of opportunity for this new consociation. Traditional forms of production, marketing, trade, and the institutions of tribute continued. The cultivation of maize, beans, and squash was supplemented with the introduction of European domesticated plants and animals, and the region became integrated into the Habsburg world economy. Textile production thrived as a regional specialization, especially with the introduction of wool and silk alongside native cotton. Dyed with the local scarlet cochineal, garments were unsurpassed in quality and workmanship. At one time, the dye alone rivalled gold on the commodities market. The caciques capitalized on the new economy by engaging in lucrative long-distance trading ventures, gaining monopolies over the transportation of international goods moving from Manila to Spain via overland routes through Mexico.

Caciques were granted positions of authority by the viceroyalty that made them equivalent to Spanish nobles. They dressed as Spaniards, rode horses, carried firearms, and acquired new titles to suit their elevated positions, such as Lord Seven Monkey of Yanhuitlán, who became Domingo de Guzmán, adopting the name of the founder of the Dominican order. The cacique of Tilantongo became Felipe de Austria, adopting the title of the Holy Roman Emperor himself. They expanded their domains, enlarged their palaces, dedicated churches, and yet they were careful to preserve Indigenous traditions, not the least of which was the continuing production of codices, maps, and *lienzos*, remarkable works of art that recorded king lists extending back to the ninth century, making them the longest continuous royal genealogies in the western hemisphere. Hardly a relic tradition, a manuscript such as the Mapa de Teozacoalco is an ingenious fusion of Indian and European international art and iconography, with its pre-Hispanic representations of rulers wearing their traditional pre-Hispanic jaguar helmets juxtaposed with Romanesque-Gothic churches.[6] By the same token, a colonial codex dating to 1535 features an Indigenous portrait of the conquistador Hernan Cortés. Significantly, he appears not as a conqueror but as an elegant lord wearing the quetzal plumes of an Indigenous Nahua ruler who would have been every bit the equal of the four Tlaxcalteca lords who offer him an alliance.[7]

By 1522, many city-states within the confederacy joined the Spaniards by contributing thousands of troops to the conquests of the Isthmus of Tehuantepec, Chiapas, Guatemala, and West Mexico extending as far as New Mexico.[8] Although factional conflict between rival pre-Hispanic noble families within the confederacy ended once viceregal authority was imposed, Dominican friar Francisco de Burgoa recorded a fascinating account of a conflict between the kingdoms of Cuilapan and Zaachila that was taking place when the Spaniards first arrived in Oaxaca. While the nobles involved set aside their differences, their great conflict continued to be commemorated through a ritual dance held at a church-sponsored fiesta at Cuilapan. What especially fascinated Burgoa was how the performance featured ritual combats by dancers dressed as Indigenous warriors representing the Cuilapan and Zaachila factions.

The drama climaxed when the actor who played the Zapotec king of Zaachila was doomed to be executed and acted out his death by hanging with all of the agonizing spectacle of a great theatrical drama.[9] Burgoa goes on to explain why the dance had taken on so much importance for these communities. It had been intentionally adapted to incorporate other major historical events, from the Spanish victory over the Moors at the battle of Clavijo in 834 CE to the conquest of the Aztecs in 1521. A sixteenth-century text preserved in the church of the Soledad in Oaxaca actually credits Dominican friars at Cuilapan with contributing original text and songs for the dance, indicating that they were purposefully participating in the creation of this synthetic history-making that established the original Danza de la Pluma. Celebrated on the feast day of Santiago at Cuilapan, it has continued to be performed as part of that community's annual Guelaguetza celebrations through the present day.[10]

A remarkable representational depiction of the Danza de la Pluma painted in Burgoa's time is preserved on a screen or *biombo* in the Los Angeles County Museum of Art (LACMA).[11] It features a number of details that demonstrate graphically how the Dominicans and the caciques were using church theatre to publicly present a new socio-political ideology of consensus among their Mixtec and Spanish constituents by the recounting of a shared tradition of creation stories during religious celebrations. The screen is nearly 3 metres long and 1.7 metres high. The medium is oil on canvas that was stretched over the wood framework of a series of separate panels. The scene portrays a cacique marriage, with the newly-weds emerging from the church at the right. They are magnificently dressed, with the husband wearing an intricately embroidered *tilmatli* (cape) and broad-brimmed hat, while his wife is wearing a magnificent *huipil* (tunic) with her hair coiled in ribbons and decorated with flowers.

The marriage couple is welcomed into the central plaza by eight dancers who are dressed as pre-Hispanic lords, wearing lace-trimmed tunics, breeches, hose, and slippers. Each holds a panache of quetzal plumes and strikes a choreographed pose that characterizes the Danza de la Pluma, in which each dancer leaps from one foot to the other while bowing, rising, and twirling to emulate the strike and dodge tactics used by ancient Mexican warriors engaged in combat. Musicians playing a harp and a guitar stand behind a larger-than-life figure who wears a magnificent fan of quetzal plumes and holds a *maquahuitl* or pre-Hispanic sword to orchestrate the battle. This lord is a mythic interpretation of Moctezuma, and he is accompanied by a child Malinche, reinterpreted within the dramatic narrative of the Conquest to represent either his wife or daughter (fig. 14.2).[12]

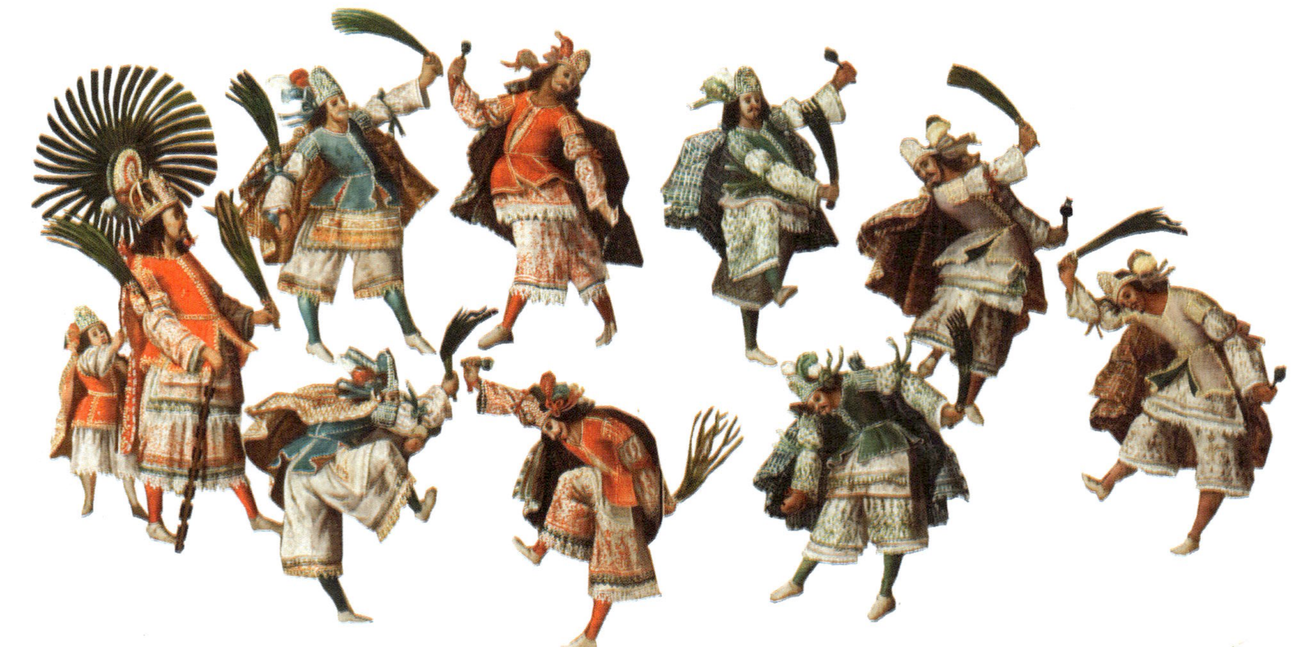

Figure 14.2.  Detail of Folding Screen with Indian Wedding, Mexico, 1690. Oil on canvas, 167.64 x 295.28 x 5.08 cm. Moctezuma, wearing a great quetzal feather radial headdress and holding a macuahuitl (obsidian-edged sword), orchestrates the ritual combat of the dancers in the Danza de la Pluma together with Malinche. Purchased with funds provided by the Bernard and Edith Lewin Collection of Mexican Art Deaccession Fund (M.2005.54). Courtesy of Los Angeles County Museum of Art, Los Angeles

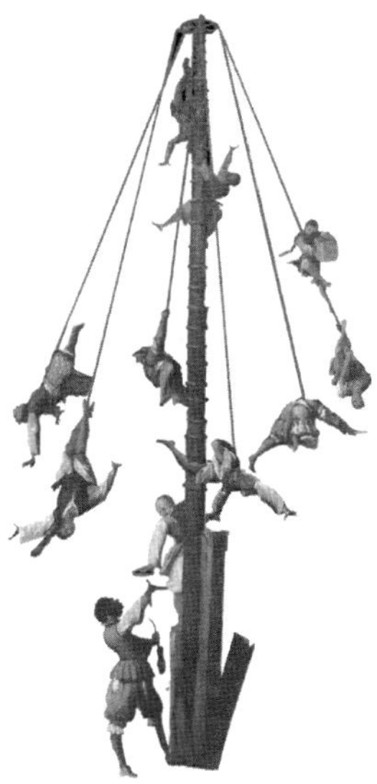

Figure 14.3. Detail of Folding Screen with Indian Wedding, Mexico, 1690. Oil on canvas, 167.64 x 295.28 x 5.08 cm. *Voladores* or "flyers" descend from the top of the pole on ropes tied to their feet. Purchased with funds provided by the Bernard and Edith Lewin Collection of Mexican Art Deaccession Fund (M.2005.54). Courtesy of Los Angeles County Museum of Art, Los Angeles

To the left of the Danza de la Pluma warriors, a crowd of Spanish and Indigenous men and women gather in front of the cacique's residence to gaze in amazement at the acrobatic skills of six *voladores* ("flyers"), who are captured in mid-flight descending by ropes from a central pole. This remarkable aerial dance has been the subject of considerable study among Mexican Indigenous peoples since colonial times.[13] Sixteenth-century testimonials describe the *volador* rituals of Yanhuitlan, while the dance continued to be practised in Cuilapan together with the Danza de la Pluma through the twentieth century (fig. 14.3).[14] Writing of the Zapotec version, the Dominican friar Rios wrote that it was performed in pre-Hispanic times to petition for rain, and this explanation is confirmed by the appearance of both the star warriors who descend through rain storms to attack the heroes during the war of earth and sky in Codex Nuttall 21, and the founder priests who descend on magical ropes to institute the temples and cult objects of the various Mixtec kingdoms after the creation of the sun.

The painted screen emphasizes how fundamental weddings, with all of their investment in noble pageantry, were to the establishment of social order under the caciques throughout southern Mexico during the colonial period. If the early colonial marriage of the *cacica* Doña Ines de Guzmán is in any way reflective, then we may envision ceremonies like these with as many as two thousand persons of royal blood participating in gift exchanges of jewels, featherwork, and textiles to be measured in tonnage.[15] They demonstrate how the same kinds of events – the creation of the world, royal marriage, ethnic conflict, and the appearance of strangers – had become purposefully intertwined, even treated as interchangeable regardless of when their actual historical occurrence took place. The performances emphasize the cyclical, or perhaps better, spiralling, nature of time reckoning among the Indigenous population, of course, but they were simultaneously endowed with the profound significance of directly comparable spiritual, historical, and social phenomena that was equally esteemed among Christians. The Danza de la Pluma continues to be performed by a number of communities in Oaxaca, including Cuilapan, Zaachila, Zimatlan, and Teotitlan del Valle. One of the most impressive is presented over the course of three days in July in Teotitlan del Valle, a Zapotec community renowned for its extraordinarily rich weaving traditions. It coincides with the celebration of Guelaguetza, a pageant originally rooted in ancient systems of Indigenous kinship group reciprocity and bridewealth.[16] An examination of how the performances are conducted today give us a remarkable sense of continuity with the colonial past but simultaneously projects a sense of the profound devotional investment that living theatrical drama is so successful at transmitting.

### The Zapotec of Teotitlan del Valle, Oaxaca

The Danza de la Pluma is organized by groups of men, women, and their families who aspire to advance within the administrative and religious hierarchies or *tequio* of Teotitlan by contributing their time and resources for the greater benefit of the community. Organization takes months and includes not only the preparation of food and beverages to be served during a feast for the entire community but the construction of sets, stages, and fireworks, together with the fashioning of ritual dress for over thirty performers. The dances are structured around a narrative of the Conquest of Mexico and are performed by two opposing sides, with the Spaniards led by Hernan Cortés and the Aztecs led by

Moctezuma. The Spaniards appear in sombre black military uniforms with shakos and perform in simple march steps. The Aztecs, by contrast, wear richly woven and embroidered tunics and short trousers. Their elaborate plumed headdresses feature a great circular fan constructed of cane over a white metal crown, to which is applied elaborate ornamentation in dyed feathers – an investment of labour and resources on the part of the dancer and his family that can exceed several thousand dollars.[17]

The story begins with the arrival of Hernan Cortés at Veracruz, together with the reception of the Aztec emissaries. Moctezuma meets Cortés while Malinche serves as ambassador and translator. The performances are feats of endurance, as the dancers leap and twirl for hours to enact the various battles as Moctezuma invokes the spirit forces of the sacred four directions to destroy the enemy and bring a new order to the world. Moctezuma is imprisoned and the Aztecs submit to the Spaniards. Cortés appears to be triumphant, but remarkably Moctezuma is resurrected, reclaims his authority, and vanquishes Cortés to restore the cosmic order to the world.[18]

The Danza de la Pluma represents a fascinating conflation of events that generally follows the historical record, but with some significant variation in the details of the personages involved. For example, Malinche is played by one young girl who dresses in the manner of the Aztec dancers, while another playing Doña Marina dresses as a Spaniard and sports a broad hat with an ostrich plume. Historically, Malinche and Doña Marina are the same individual, Cortés's consort and translator, but in the performance she is presented as two distinct personalities who play very different roles.[19] Malinche is identified as the wife of Moctezuma, and they perform together as a couple. Despite the fact that Doña Marina is allied with Cortés, she is also addressed as Sehuapila or Cihuapilli, meaning "Royal Woman" in the Aztec language.[20] At the conclusion of the drama, the conflict is resolved not through defeat and death but by a celebration of the fusion of the European and Indigenous cultures, performed through a dance by Doña Marina and Malinche.

The origins of the Danza de la Pluma today lie in the seventeenth-century performance that is represented in the LACMA *biombo*, with its themes of world creation, ritual conflict and resolution with royal marriage, and the Guelaguetza and reciprocal gift giving to re-establish world order. The historical setting of the Conquest of Mexico in which Moctezuma plays such a significant role, on the other hand, is rooted in Iberian traditions of pageants that were celebrated by communities on the occasion of visits by royal dignitaries or of other significant events such as the news of a great victory. Such festivals frequently evoked the triumphs of Santiago Matamoros, patron saint of the Reconquista, and featured ritual combats between performers dressed as Moors and Christians.[21] From the beginning, festivals, dramas, and triumphs were the principal form of public entertainment in Mexico City.[22] Among the earliest recorded are the dramas that were presented to celebrate the Truce of Nice, in which the Holy Roman Emperor Charles V and the king of France Francis I agreed to end their Italian war.

Magnificent sets were raised that featured ritualized hunts through forests and gardens inhabited by wild animals. Jousts and bull fights were performed, but especially popular were mock combats, in which hundreds of masked and costumed performers would play the roles of Greeks, Romans, Christians, Moors, and Turks, as well as the Indigenous peoples of Mexico.[23] In 1539 the city-state of Tlaxcala presented an elaborate spectacle of the Siege of Jerusalem, inspired by the Roman conquest of the city in 70 CE by the emperor Titus, the 1099 conquest by the First Crusade, and the expectation that Charles V would one day reclaim the holy city following his successful 1535 conquest of Tunis, an event in which Cortés had also participated.[24]

The Jerusalem set was enormous and featured camps, villages, and castles. All the roles were played by the Tlaxcalteca, including prominent lords, many of whom had fought for the Spaniards during the conquest of Tenochtitlan. However, the organizers reconfigured the story so that Charles V led the Spanish army under the flag of the viceroy of New Spain, Antonio de Mendoza. The defenders, on the other hand, were led by a "Sultan" represented by Hernan Cortés, at the head of an army of "Moslems and Jews" who were in reality the Tlaxcalteca fitted out in their former glory as Indian warriors, complete with weapons, feather shields, and headdresses.

For all intents and purposes, the Siege of Jerusalem was therefore presented more as an amalgamation of the events surrounding the Conquest of Mexico, together with the ongoing conflicts with the Ottoman empire, than anything from antiquity. While there are no records of how these pageants were planned and what effect was intended by conflating so many historical events, we know that government and religious officials of New Spain had become conscious of the tremendous diversity of the population to whom they needed to appeal. The festivals had to convey a visual impression of cultural pluralism as the foundation of the expanding state while still reinforcing the primacy of the European social order. Political commentary was even accommodated, but tempered with ritual humour. Consequently, the choice of Cortés as the Sultan was more than satire. It reflected a real Tlaxcalteca concern with the conflict in administrative authority that was dividing Viceroy Antonio de Mendoza and the Marqués del Valle de Oaxaca, Hernan Cortés. The Danza de la Pluma at Teotitlan del Valle offers a comparable slippage between the real world of the audience and the fictional world. In reality, Moctezuma's resurrection addresses the tension between the nation of Mexico, symbolized by Cortés and his men wearing the uniforms of Mexican army cadets, and the Zapotec community represented by the Aztecs.[25] The banishment of Cortés is therefore the means by which the world is purified and returned to its Indigenous glory. Moctezuma is invoked as an essential part of the territorial narratives by which Indigenous peoples assert their rights to traditional lands. Scholars can reconstruct the dynastic history of the Zapotecs from the codices and even identify a tomb at Mitla as the resting place of the lords of the paramount lineage of Zaachila, but Moctezuma presides at the ruins today, while the traditional spirit forces like Sus Giber and Etlakwatla that invest the surrounding landscape serve as his agents. Each New Year, Moctezuma returns to perform with his ghostly *danzantes* (dancers) in the palaces and bestow wealth on his petitioners.[26]

Re-enacting the Conquest of Mexico became as much an Indigenous form of documenting historical experience as it was Spanish. The festivals supported the missionizing process, as the friars resorted to these kinds of plays and performances to popularize the Christian religion as well as satisfy the demand for the full calendar of rotating feasts that supported the regional market system throughout the year. If Santiago Matamoros (The Moor Slayer) was going to be presented as Santiago Mataindios (The Indian Slayer) by the Spaniards, then the Indigenous response was logically to promote an "Indio" hero in Moctezuma.

By 1545 the Danza de la Pluma was being performed throughout much of southern and central Mexico, conveyed through the traditional systems of marriage alliance between colonial caciques together with the sponsorship of the church. When silver was discovered in Zacatecas and Guanajuato, the formidable partnership between Eastern Nahua, Mixtec, and Zapotec *cacicazgos* (Indigenous colonial kingdoms) across the Plain of Puebla and Oaxaca began sponsoring expeditions of settlers and miners into Northern Mexico and the greater American Southwest where these and other communities were founded.[27] Having been engaged through trade with the peoples of the Gran Chichimeca since the thirteenth century, they were responsible for acting as intermediaries by negotiating treaties for transport routes, forming militias for protection, and establishing communities to facilitate the permanent settlement of the local hunting and foraging tribal populations. In return the viceroyalty extended rights that were equivalent to those of Spanish colonists. Settlers were entitled to ride horses, carry firearms, own cattle, and manage ox-cart trains. They negotiated their own trade agreements with the Pueblo populations and intermarried while maintaining their own Indigenous identity. Pecos Pueblo also became known as Nueva Tlaxcala, for example.

Eastern Nahuas, Mixtecs, and Zapotecs introduced the European economy to the Pueblo peoples of the greater American Southwest, where sheep raising and wool blanket weaving, as well as metalworking, were combined with the ceramic traditions that extended back to the fourteenth century. Acting as mediators between Spanish and Indian officials, they opened turquoise and copper mines, despite the fact that these materials had little direct contribution to make to the broader imperial economy rooted in silver and gold. What had once been a pre-Hispanic palace-based economy that linked the greater Southwestern United States to Southern Mexico was transformed into the frontier economy of New Spain.

Feasts, so critical to the exchange of goods, continued to be celebrated with an annual ritual calendar shared between Pueblo Indian rituals and Mexican Indigenous rituals like the Danza de la Pluma, reconceived as the Danza de Matachines to include, in addition to the Conquest, the historical experience of the Chichimec Wars.[28] Significant landscape features throughout Northern Mexico and the Southwestern United States were given Nahua names and endowed with the spirit forces of "Moctezuma" and "Malinche," together with narratives associated with legends of origins and conquest performed in the dances – the traditional way of constructing an Indigenous territorial narrative.[29] For example, the Nahua cacique of Cuauhtinchan, Don Alonso Castañeda Chimalpopoca, commissioned the *Historia Tolteca-Chichimeca,* a history written in Nahuatl and accompanied by lavish pictographic scenes that portray the creation of his world and the subsequent migration from Chicomoztoc to found the principal kingdoms of the Valley of Puebla and northern Oaxaca. For Don Alonso, Chicomoztoc was Cerro de Culiacan, a sacred mountain located sixty miles south of the Veta Madre, a seven-mile mother lode of silver that had been identified in 1548 in Guanajuato, New Spain. As an Indigenous territorial narrative, the *Historia Tolteca-Chichimeca* together with the pictographic *Mapas de Cuauhtinchan* that accompanied it demonstrated that what had been a twelfth-century migration route for the settlement of the Plain of Puebla was now the silver road back to the sacred place of origin, with the *cacicazgo* of Cuauhtinchan advocating for the reclamation of its riches for the new viceregal economy.[30]

## Pacific Coastal Networks of Oaxaca: The Chontal

While silver was the primary commodity driving the economy of the north, many more high-value goods, such as cochineal and gold, were flowing through the south by land and sea. Here the acquisition and transport of elite materiel was managed by a network of competitive Chontal, Huave, and Pochutec-Nahua trading specialists who maintained extraordinary long-distance relationships with related "home" cultures elsewhere along the Pacific coast. Ethnohistorical sources suggest that they were engaged in commercial importation of cacao from coastal Chiapas by seagoing canoes. Some even speak of travellers from lower Central America. They were either patronized through mutualistic arrangements or subjugated by city-states within Nahua-Mixtec-Zapotec-dominated confederacies who, in turn, pumped the wealth up from the Oaxaca coast into the highland Mexican economy in quantities comparable to, if not surpassing, overland routes from Veracruz and Chiapas.[31]

In the late fifteenth and early sixteenth centuries, the Pacific coast of Oaxaca was divided between the competing Mixtec kingdom of Tututepec and the Zapotec kingdom of Tehuantepec. The Pochutecs controlled the port of Huatulco, but were largely subjugated to Tututepec. Despite nearly nine thousand miles of shoreline, harbours are relatively few and far between along the Pacific Coast of the Americas. Huatulco is unique in that it possesses a natural inlet protecting the community from the hurricanes that can seasonally devastate southern Mexico. Between 1200 and 1522, Huatulco served as the principal port for the Mixtec kingdom of Tututepec and became a significant base for trade in turquoise, copper, gold, shell, cacao, exotic tropical birds valued for their feathers, hides, textiles, and dye between Central America and West Mexico.[32]

These Indigenous polities played a pivotal role in Pedro de Alvarado's conquest of the Pacific coast in 1522, while often using the Spanish as pawns to settle old scores against each other. Don Juan Cortés, the cacique of Tehuantepec, was a descendant of the twelfth-century Oaxaca dynastic founder and warlord Eight Deer and a member of the royal house of Zaachila that had moved to Tehuantepec following their fifteenth-century conquest of the coast. Don Juan changed his Indigenous name, perhaps stemming from his grandfather Cosijopii, to Cortés following baptism,

appropriating a fictive kinship title to confirm his alliance with the conquistador.[33] It was he who allied early on with Hernan Cortés to subdue the
Mixtec ruler of Tututepec and provide Cortés with easy access to the Pacific.
The cacique supplied the labour, resources, and navigational intelligence
necessary for the construction of the fleets of ships needed to explore the
Gulf of California, using an Indigenous coastal trade route that had linked
coastal Oaxaca to the greater American Southwest. Long before Acapulco,
the Oaxacan Pacific coast played a truly globalizing role in connecting
the Americas, Europe, Asia, and – through the slave trade – Africa. The
Zapotec port of Tehuantepec and later the Mixtec-Pochutec port of Huatulco were transformed into the main hubs in the trans-Pacific Habsbur-
gian commerce. It is from the latter port that Central and South American
goods were exchanged and made their way to New Spain and then Spain,
and where Asian merchants may have first set foot in the Americas.[34]

Positioned in a buffer zone between the competing Zapotec and Mixtec
kingdoms, and later midway between the cosmopolitan ports of Tehuantepec and Huatulco, are the Chontal people who still inhabit that stretch
of the Pacific coast and adjacent highlands. Chontal is a linguistic isolate,
suggesting that their ancestors may have travelled from a distant homeland
and may have strategically chosen this region to settle in. The burgeoning
local factionalism and the Chontal's semi-independent status further allowed several of their caciques to form alliances in the fifteenth century
with the intrusive Aztecs, who were similarly interested in gaining access
to coastal resources. Perhaps it is not surprising then that Alvarado's combined forces of Spanish and Indigenous conquistadors faced their most
noteworthy resistance at the hands of Chontal coastal communities, who
continued to remain semi-independent from any direct hegemonic yoke
for most of the sixteenth century.[35] What is more amazing is how the Chontal, like the Zapotecs, have encoded their historical place in the Habsburg
economy into their own form of Danza de la Conquista ritualism.

### The Festival of San Pedro Huamelula

One of the largest annual festivals on the Mexican Pacific coast is held at
the Chontal community of San Pedro Huamelula from 24 June to 30 June,
and is dedicated to the patron saint. It is a community-wide affair involving
passionate formulaic discourses, theatrical performances, ritual dances,
religious ceremonies, and solemn processions, accompanied by traditional
music. As is the case with many such festivities, those episodes are embedded in convivial domestic and public feasts. Several groups of performers

from the community participate in multiple interweaving narratives; many of these performers are youths who are customarily instructed by an elder well versed in the event sequence and choreography. The performances, be they mythical or historical, mostly revolve around alliances and conflicts between the Chontal people and foreign groups. Notably, and unlike any other known Indigenous festivity that we are familiar with, all of these groups represent seafaring peoples of local or distant origins.[36]

Several narratives take place simultaneously in various parts of the community throughout the week. One of the first acts is the welcoming of Princess Crocodile. Princess Crocodile is an actual crocodile that typically is caught each year in a nearby river by the Huamelultecos or other poachers. She represents a culture hero who is the subject of legends told by the Huave people, who occupy the area surrounding the lagoons of Tehuantepec to the east and who specialize in fishing. Chontal actors dress as the Huave by wearing fishing nets wrapped around their bodies and bring the princess in a procession down the main road to the entrance of Huamelula, where they are greeted by the *presidente*, the town mayor, her betrothed. The princess is then taken to her residence, where she is well cared for and prepared for her special appearances throughout the days leading up to her baptism and the wedding to the *presidente*.

In the meantime, a group of men are busy in another part of the community transforming a massive wooden ox cart into the ship of the "Turcos-Pechelingues," also known as "the pirates," by furnishing it with long poles (representing the masts), ropes, reed mats, and blankets (fig. 14.4). The purple and red hues of the sails symbolize the Chontal natural riches in cochineal and in purpura, a dye made from shellfish. During some aspects of their performances, the Turcos-Pechelingues assume the role of travelling merchants rather than pirates and proclaim that the vessel carries luxury commodities, precious stones and metals, and "high technology." Joining the Turcos-Pechelingues are two characters who are identified as "Rey Mahoma" ("King Muhammad") and his "escribano" ("scribe") although they possess their own sailing craft.

These Turcos-Pechelingues are easily recognizable by their elongated pyramid-shaped red hats decorated with mirrors, flowers, bells, and tassels, the red handkerchief around their heads, and the flowing purple sashes that adorn their bodies. The red and purple colours represent the natural dyes produced from the cochineal insect and the purpura sea shell respectively, the local production of which had enriched quite a few Chontal caciques in the colonial period. The performers also wear wooden masks portraying bearded fair-skinned characters, some with

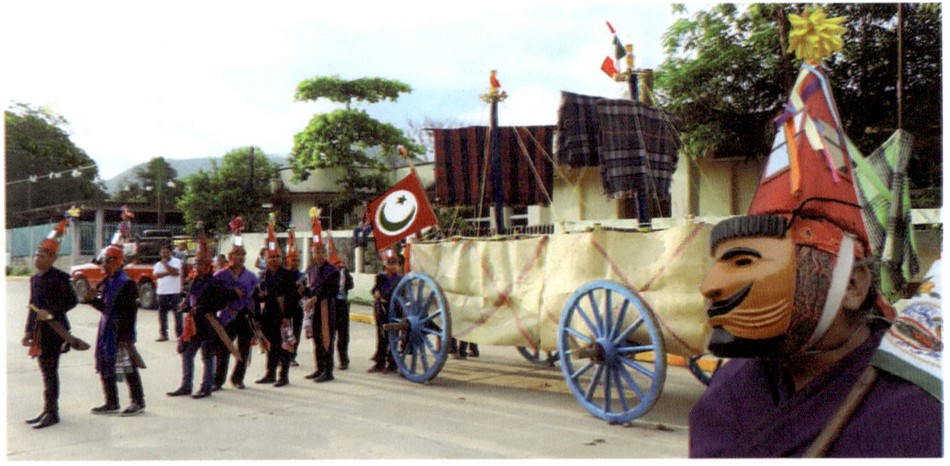

Figure 14.4.  The Turcos-Pechelingues don their masks and prepare to board their "ship." San Pedro Festivity, San Pedro Huamelula, July 2017. Photo by Danny Zborover

moustaches. These facial features are quite uncommon among the Indigenous people of Huamelula and the Pacific coast, and further serve to identify the Turcos-Pechelingues as foreigners. The sharp machetes these characters are all carrying indicate their bellicose intentions.

As they arrive and make their presence known in town, the Turcos-Pechelingues claim that they have sailed from Panama and are searching for the "Negritos," the "'Black Ones," who allegedly stole riches off their boat. The Negritos represent a seafaring faction that claims to come from Jamaica. True to their title, they wear black-painted wooden masks and are dressed in mostly tattered dark cloths. In addition to batons and musical instruments, the Negritos carry with them their "Bonifacia queen," a wooden statue now battered from decades if not centuries of continuous ritual use.

Both the Turcos-Pechelingues and Negritos perform numerous ritual dances in the town plaza, municipality building, streets, and the two town churches. Throughout the festivity, the groups are constantly chasing and accusing one another of being thieves, in choreographed conflicts and public discourses. In one of their major confrontations, interpreted through ritual dancing, the two forces face off against each other in a fierce display of power on both sides of a rope tied tight to both ends of the street, known as "la muralla," that is, "the defensive wall." The climax

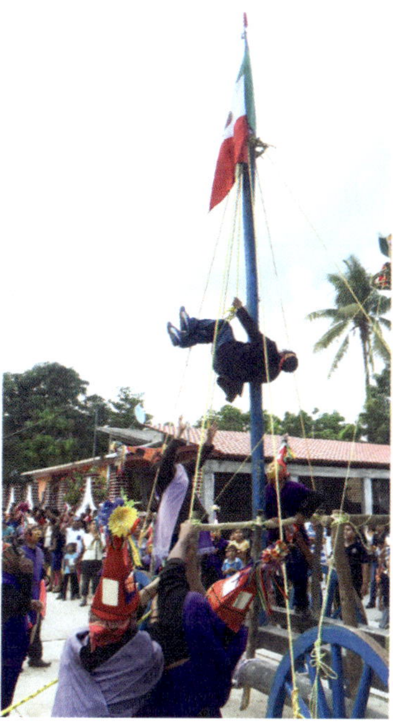

Figure 14.5.  Hanging the Negritos from the ship's mast by their feet. The performance commemorates the defeat and punishment of the Negritos following their ritual battles with the Turcos-Pechelingues, but it clearly evokes the ancient *volador* ritual as well. San Pedro Festivity, San Pedro Huamelula, July 2017. Photo by John Pohl

of another is the submission of the Negritos, in which each in turn is tied by one foot to a rope and suspended from the main mast of the Turco-Pechelingues ship (fig. 14.5). The allusion to hanging as punishment for the capital offence of piracy seems clear.

Comparing the Zapotec-Mixtec Danza de la Pluma with the Chontal Festival of San Pedro, we see a comparable core theme of solar creation and divine descent, conflict, marriage as resolution, and renewal.

### The Ottoman Empire and the Dutch Free States

The Turcos in the Chontal performance are the Ottoman Turks. Europeans named them "Ottoman" for their fourteenth-century leader Osman, who was credited with expanding their hegemony over northwestern Anatolia following the dissolution of the Seljuk Empire.[37] Within a century, an Ottoman army under the command of sultan Mehmed II had expanded across the Bosphorus into Europe and conquered Constantinople, thereby putting the Ottomans in virtually uncontested control of the eastern Mediterranean. Suleiman the Magnificent ultimately ruled a hegemonic empire that extended across North Africa, Egypt, the Middle East, Anatolia, and Eastern Europe, and Ottoman fleets were beginning to move against Portuguese interests in the Indian Ocean and Southeast Asia.

The Pechelingues of the Chontal performance, on the other hand, represent northern Europeans. The prevailing historical interpretation for the term's origins associates it with a Spanish-language corruption of the name of the Dutch port of Vlissingen (Flushing), where merchant fleets recruited their crews before venturing out to distant ports for the wool that fuelled textile manufacturing, along with virtually any product that could turn a profit in the open and highly competitive markets of the first modern global economy, which was emerging in the Low Countries.[38] Calvinism offered tremendous appeal to the merchants of the Low Countries and northwestern France who sought freedom from the heavy taxes imposed by Rome as well as corrupt foreign influence manifested in the papal appointments of Italians. Before long nobles saw distinct advantages in supporting Protestant merchants and even began to initiate wars in their interests, while adventurers from northwestern France, where Calvin himself originated, began to sally forth and attack Spanish shipping.

In 1523, the French corsair Jean Fleury intercepted one of Cortés's treasure fleets off the south coast of Portugal. The take included an astounding three cases of gold ingots, five hundred pounds of gold dust, and nearly seven hundred pounds of pearls and gemstones.[39] Word of the riches of Mexico rapidly spread throughout Europe, and Protestant corsairs from France, the Netherlands, and England were soon venturing into the Atlantic in hopes of equally enriching themselves.

Upon Holy Roman Emperor Charles V's abdication in 1556, the Seventeen Provinces fell under the rule of his son and successor Phillip II, king of Spain. By then the Spanish hold on the northern Netherlands was becoming tenuous. By 1565, resentment of Spanish authority and heavy taxation was openly voiced by the Dutch nobility, who wished to recover much of the autonomous power they had lost to Phillip as their self-proclaimed overlord. Furthermore, Phillip declared all Protestants heretic and therefore subject to trial by the Inquisition. Perhaps the most significant blow to the Dutch economy, however, was occurring on the other side of the world. After Magellan's expedition circumnavigated the globe, its survivors reported to Charles not only the use of gold among the paramount chiefs of the Philippines, but also the demand for silver by the Ming economy of imperial China. The discovery of the vast silver resources of northern Mexico, combined with the navigator Andrés de Urdaneta's 1565 mapping of the northern currents, secured an exclusive Pacific trade route between the Philippines and Mexico. When a Manila–Acapulco galleon transport system was established, Spain found itself in control of the most lucrative economy the world had ever known.[40] The Netherlands, on the other hand, was excluded from any real economic profit in this new global economy. Motivated by Protestant revolts in France, riots erupted in the northern provinces as iconoclasts seized Catholic churches and destroyed holy images during what was called the Beeldenstorm, literally "statue storm" or "war against images." In April 1566, a council of nobles led by Prince William of Orange met to propose a compromise to Phillip's regent in the Netherlands, but it was rejected. Leiden then proclaimed independence from Spanish authority in 1566, and the city was later followed by Haarlem, Rotterdam, and Antwerp among others.[41]

In 1567, Phillip directed a Spanish army to invade the Netherlands. Mass executions soon followed, driving many nobles into exile, where they devised a military strategy to begin what would become the Eighty Year's War for Dutch independence. While fleets engaged the Spaniards in open sea battles from the North Sea to the Iberian Peninsula, corsairs were sponsored by merchant coalitions to attack Spanish ports, seize assets, and divert Spanish resources from the war in the Netherlands itself.[42] Although they were declared to be pirates by Spain, the corsairs established what should more correctly be described as a "forced economy," given that their actions were sanctioned by the nobles and coordinated by city authorities, with their mission being to reopen or even expand global trade after they had been effectively neutralized by the Spanish stranglehold on their commercial enterprises. One of the earliest reports of a corsair action is that of Francisco Chambrio, who attacked the communities of Autla and Acatlan in the Jalisco region of West Mexico in 1565.[43] It is unknown how Chambrio navigated to West Mexico; he could have sailed around South America from the Caribbean, or he could have sailed from Asia, perhaps following the first Spanish ships to use the northern passage from Asia to California and south to Mexico. Among the benefits

of declaring religious tolerance in some of the Dutch cities was that it attracted Jewish Marrano merchant families from Spain and Portugal who
sought to practice their devotional traditions openly. They also brought
with them maps and strategic reports on the overseas logistics of the Spanish empire. One of these Marranos was Joseph Nasi, a friend of Dutch
leader Prince William of Orange, who had fled the Spanish Inquisition in
the Netherlands and began working for the court of the Ottoman sultan
Suleiman the Magnificent. Nasi arranged for a letter in which the sultan
offered a promise of financial and military support to the Netherlandish
cities in revolt.[44] Nasi had doubtless informed Suleiman that during the
Beeldenstorm, crowds had gathered and chanted a song advising the citizens of Antwerp to wear silver medals fashioned as an Ottoman crescent
moon and bearing the slogan "Rather Turk than Pope." The plea was
for religious tolerance, like that believed to be fostered within Ottoman
territories; but before long, Dutch sailors were wearing the medal while
festooning their warships with Ottoman flags and crescent emblems to
terrorize the Spaniards into believing that a military alliance had indeed
been achieved between the "Turcos" and the "Pechelingues."[45]

> The Prince of Orange triumphant
> God will make him wise and understand
> That God's Word from this moment
> May be preached to every corner
> Rather Turk than Pope he has become
> Although the Turk is not called Christian
> He did not burn anyone for the faith
> As the Papists do, every single day
> (After a 16th Century Dutch Song.)[46]

The global political situation would soon draw the Turks and the Dutch
into the Indian Ocean and Southeast Asia. In 1564 the sultan of Aceh in
northern Sumatra sent emissaries to Suleiman the Magnificent to petition for assistance in his conflict with the Portuguese for control of the
vital Malacca Strait and the most lucrative spice markets in the world.
Recognizing an opportunity to expand Ottoman influence by capital-
izing on the ambitions of Indigenous populations disenfranchised by
European expansionism, Suleiman dispatched troops to Aceh. Before
long the Turks were supplying engineers and artillery as well, and Aceh
warships began to fly the Ottoman flag as they attacked Portuguese ships,
just as the Dutch were doing.[47]

Fourteen years later the sultan of Morocco, Abu Abdallah Mohammed II, appealed to King Sebastian of Portugal for military assistance in recovering his throne from a usurper who had seized power with Ottoman backing. Hoping to thwart the Ottoman threat to Portugal's trade with Africa, India, and Asia, Sebastian sailed to Morocco and engaged Abu Abdallah's rival at Alcácer Quibir. The battle ended in disaster when Sebastian was killed, and a succession crisis for the throne of Portugal erupted. When Sebastian's uncle, Phillip II of Spain, assumed the throne in 1581 and unified the Iberian kingdoms, he declared Lisbon's Indian market closed to the Dutch.[48] The Dutch responded by declaring Portugal's colonies in Africa, Brazil, India, and Southeast Asia open to attack as an extension of the war in which they were already engaged with Phillip. By 1600, the Dutch were even negotiating with the Japanese in an effort to open their own trade in silver with China.

Before long Dutch corsairs were regularly appearing off the Pacific coast of Mexico, with sightings of Ottoman ships being reported as well.[49] To what extent the Dutch were collaborating with Ottoman and Aceh ships in these raiding expeditions is unknown and needs further investigation. However, when Queen Elizabeth of England learned of the profits the Turks and the Dutch were reaping from their overseas strategy of "forced" economy, she issued letters of marque to English sea captains, who used their trading ventures to finance predatory expeditions against Portuguese and Spanish shipping. Despite Spanish laws prohibiting the English from entering overseas ports, John Hawkins discovered that many governors and magistrates throughout the Caribbean and Central America were engaged in a contraband economy that enabled him to trade African slaves for gold, silver, pearls, hides, and sugar as long as he was willing to bribe them and discount his human cargo in their markets. Overseas commerce was becoming a complex system of negotiations between buyers and sellers operating in a global social and political atmosphere where the distinction between war, piracy, and trade was becoming capricious. Having served with John Hawkins, Francis Drake became the first Englishman to sail into the Pacific to loot Spanish towns and capture a Manila galleon.[50] His attack on Huatulco, Oaxaca, in 1579, followed by that of Thomas Cavendish in 1587, prompted the Spaniards to identify all such raiders as "Pechelingues" regardless of nationality, and the term became synonymous with "pirate." Although it has not been incorporated into any known festivals performed on the Oaxaca coast, Cavendish's raid is commemorated at Huatulco.[51] According to legend, when Cavendish sailed into the bay he saw a cross that had been an object of

Indigenous veneration, associated first with Quetzalcoatl but later consecrated to Saint Thomas. Believing it to be the work of a devil, Cavendish attempted to destroy the cross by chopping and burning it. Failing at this, Cavendish then secured the cross to his ship with ropes and attempted to drag it into the sea. The cross resisted, and the miracle that the event signified to the local Indigenous people continues to be regarded as a testament to the triumph of the Catholic faith by the Vatican today.

### Conclusions

In 1458, the emerging Aztec Imperial Triple Alliance carried out its first protracted long-distance campaign into southern Mexico and selected the rich highland "port of trade" kingdom of Coixtlahuaca in the Mixteca Alta as its first target for conquest.[52] Its victory severed the primary alliance corridor controlled by the Eastern Nahuas, Mixtecs, and Zapotecs at its most critical link. The Aztecs then turned on other confederacy members by destabilizing internal relationships, such as royal marriages that bound royal houses into systems of mutual obligation, before providing military support to the factions that best served their interests.[53] By 1500 only the Eastern Nahuas of Tlaxcala remained autonomous, while the Mixtecs and Zapotecs reoriented their interests to the Pacific coast, establishing new centres of power at Tututepec and Tehuantepec respectively.

Despite the complexities of the political relationships between Indigenous suppliers and consumers on the coast, Huatulco continued to serve as the principal port for colonial trade until a viceregal decision was made to move the base of the Manila Galleon to Acapulco in 1566. Over the following 250 years Acapulco thrived, of course, but so did Huatulco and Tehuantepec, causing one to wonder, how and why? The answer lies in the deep history of complex relationships between the various ethnic groups and Indigenous political factions who both shared and contested the access that these ports supplied to them. The expansion of mining and the colonization of Northern Mexico and the greater American Southwest by Nahuas, Mixtecs, and Zapotecs among other populations, as well as coastal shipping with Central and South America, continued to be vital. For example, the Huave, occupying the area of the ancient Zapotec port of Tehuantepec, possess an extraordinarily complex vocabulary for shells, suggesting they had been shell acquisition specialists up to recent times.[54] Indeed, ethnohistorical sources describe them as having been accomplished seafarers, travelling as far south as

Nicaragua with the sail-fitted dugout canoes that they continue to use today. The Dominican chronicler Francisco de Burgoa documented a legend in which, in ancient times, a priest arrived at Huatulco from Central America who spoke a language that was understood by the Mixtecs. This is doubtless a reference to the Otomanguean speakers of Nicaragua, with whom the Tlapanecs of Acapulco were also affiliated.

However, there were other equally significant factors, not the least of which was the expansion of a rich contraband trade between the Philippines and Peru after 1565. As early as the 1530s, contraband trading had become a specialty of northern French Huguenot merchants, who discovered that many Spanish Caribbean colonies were more than eager to barter outside the highly restrictive Spanish monopoly over trade within the Antilles.[55] Their attempts to establish trading settlements in Florida and Brazil, however, were dealt with ruthlessly, and thereafter the French resorted to outright piracy. The Dutch, with whom the Huguenots had been allied, soon followed when the war with Spain demanded that they seek out a new source of salt for their herring industry.[56]

While the Indigenous peoples of southern Mexico provided mutual support to one another when faced with any major outside threat to their existing social order, the viceregal pronouncements that coastal communities were largely responsible for their own defence also fostered a volatile atmosphere of alliance, economic competition, and warfare. In some cases communities relocated back into the mountains to make them less susceptible to surprise attack and the seizure of their property. On the other hand, other communities may have actively sought alliances with foreign merchants and corsairs who financed the contraband economy. For example, when Joris van Spilbergen was sailing up the south coast to attack Acapulco, he was informed by his Indigenous navigators that there were peoples with whom they could trade and resupply along the coast of Oaxaca just to the south of his target.[57] These people may have been the Chontal, the Pochutec, or the Huave.[58] The fact is that competition among traditional rivals makes it impossible to entirely determine when any particular area was open to or closed to contraband trade during the colonial period.

What we learn by comparing the embedded histories of Indigenous affairs found in dance festivals is that relationships with the viceroyalty and among the caciques were subject to negotiation. The Zapotec-Mixtec Danza de la Pluma and the Chontal Festival of San Pedro Huamelula are clearly amalgamations of different storylines, some factual while others fictional, some interrelated while others not. They were originally conceived, and documented in the codices, as performances of the pre-Hispanic relationships between ruler and ruled, with the dramatic presentation of the ancestral elite as being responsible for the creation of the world and the distribution of the land. A seventeenth-century *biombo* preserved in the Los Angeles County Museum of Art that summarizes in conflated terms exactly the same ritualism and the same performance order as that diagrammed in the codices indicates a direct continuity, with the incorporation of European events such as a theme of "ethnic" conflict as well as the highlighting of the importance of royal marriages as a way of defining an exclusive Indigenous noble class, separate but equal to the Spaniards.

The viceroyalty conveyed an impression of hegemony through state ceremony, parades, and other rituals that publicly demonstrated the predominant order of social, political, and ethnic ranking within major centres of power. This presentation would be perceived as the official public transcript in social negotiations.[59] The Indigenous population might feign deference while at the same time plotting their own course of empowerment, in which the survival of their customs and the preservation of much of the context of their rituals of authority became a hidden transcript that fostered a secret discourse representing a critique of power presented behind the backs of viceregal authorities. For example, the Danza de la Pluma was remarkably flexible in its ability to sustain multiple historical referents in a single action. The vision of an alternative world drew heavily on expectations that Moctezuma would return to initiate a new cycle of Indigenous rule.[60] However, it is this messianic expectation arising out of the narrative of the conquest that was the fundamental vision of the dance, and any particular application to the relationship between the local community and the state, although pertinent, was secondary. Their strategy relied on the use of anonymity and ambiguity, veiling a mocking or even vengeful tone.[61] They were aided in these endeavours by the Dominican order, who had just as much vested interest in cultural preservation as their own sources of wealth and prosperity were tied to the fortunes of this faction of the Indigenous elite.

Equally, through their interactions with other agents of incipient globalizing tides, the Chontal people contributed directly to the formation of the early trans-Pacific modern world. We focus on their Pacific coastal festival, which features the themes of *voladores* (creation saga), ritual combat between "ethnic factions," and then a royal marriage – the resolution of conflict – which is the transcendent fundamental theme shared with the Zapotec festival. However, in comparing the two, we have discovered that the Chontal of Huamelula have developed a variant that incorporates an "alternate" history relating to the Dutch and Ottomans, versus the standard Spanish and Aztec Danza de la Conquista theme. The opening of the Manila–Acapulco Galleon effectively cut the Dutch merchant cities (otherwise Spanish vassals under siege) out of free trade in the Pacific. The Dutch countered by establishing special trade relationships with those Indigenous peoples antagonistic to Spanish interests, ranging from Brazil to Oaxaca to Japan. The San Pedro Huamelula festival is critical because it helps explain why this greater Huatulco area continued to prosper even after the Manila Galleon moved to Acapulco. It became an essential component of the contraband economy, a shadow economy that in many ways turned out to be just as important to conveying transnational culture globally as the Manila Galleon itself. We use drama and contemporary representation of history through pageantry to open up the Chontal Indigenous engagement with the Dutch/Ottoman forced-trade economy, demonstrating a persistence of historical myth-making that links an Indigenous Oaxaca community with some new insights into the history of the Netherlands.

## ACKNOWLEDGMENTS

The authors would like to thank Byron Hamann, Xochitl Flores-Marcial, Veronica Pacheco, and Aaron Sonnenschein for their advice and assistance in this study. We would also like to acknowledge the help of our collaborators in Huamelula and Huatulco, Oaxaca, and particularly Jaime Zárate Escamilla and Nahui Ollin Vázquez Mendoza. Our Pacific Rim field school students collected much of the ethnographic information presented here.

## NOTES

1  Bruce E. Byland and John M.D. Pohl, *In the Realm of Eight Deer: The Archaeology of the Mixtec Codices* (Norman: University of Oklahoma Press, 1994), 109–27, 237–41; Byron Hamann, "The Social Life of Pre-Sunrise Things: Indigenous Mesoamerican Archaeology," *Current Anthropology* 43, no. 3 (2002): 351–82; Manuel Hermann Lejarazu, "Códice Nuttall," *Arqueología Mexicana* 29 (2007): 14–23, 38–59; Robert Lloyd Williams, *The Complete Codex Zouche-Nuttall: Mixtec Lineage Histories and Political Biographies* (Austin: University of Texas Press, 2013), 35–57, 65–81.

2 John M.D. Pohl, "Creation Stories, Hero Cults, and Alliance Building: Post-classic Confederacies of Central and Southern Mexico from A.D. 1150–1458," in *The Postclassic Mesoamerican World*, ed. Michael Smith and Frances Berdan (Salt Lake City: University of Utah Press, 2003), 61–6.

3 Pohl, "Creation Stories, Hero Cults, and Alliance Building," 61–6; John M.D. Pohl, "Ritual Ideology and Commerce in the Southern Mexican Highlands," in Smith and Berdan, *The Postclassic Mesoamerican World*, 172–7; John M.D. Pohl, "Royal Marriage and Confederacy Building among the Eastern Nahuas, Mixtecs, and Zapotecs," in Smith and Berdan, *The Postclassic Mesoamerican World*, 243–8; John M.D. Pohl, "Ritual and Iconographic Variability In Mixteca Puebla Polychrome Pottery," in Smith and Berdan, *The Postclassic Mesoamerican World*, 201–6; John M.D. Pohl, "Transnational Tales: A Millennium of Indigenous Cultural Interaction between the United States and Mexico," in *The Forked Juniper: Critical Perspectives on Rudolfo Anaya*, ed. Roberto Cantú (Norman: University of Oklahoma Press, 2016), 253–88; John M.D. Pohl, Virginia M. Fields, and Victoria L. Lyall, "Introduction," in *Children of the Plumed Serpent: The Legacy of Quetzalcoatl in Ancient Mexico*, ed. Pohl, Fields, and Lyall (London: Scala Publishers Ltd, 2012), 15–49.

4 Pohl, "Ritual Ideology and Commerce," 177; Pohl, "Transnational Tales," 265.

5 Ronald Spores, *The Mixtec Kings and Their People* (Norman: University of Oklahoma Press, 1967); Ronald Spores and Andrew K. Balkansky, *The Mixtecs of Oaxaca: Ancient Times to the Present* (Norman: University of Oklahoma Press, 2020); Kevin Terraciano, *The Mixtecs of Colonial Oaxaca: Ñudzahui History, Sixteenth Through Eighteenth Centuries* (Stanford: Stanford University Press, 2004).

6 Barbara E. Mundy, "At Home in the World: Mixtec Elites and the Teozacoalco Map-Genealogy," in *Painted Books and Indigenous Knowledge in Mesoamerica*, ed. Elizabeth Hill Boone (New Orleans: Middle American Research Institute, 2005), 363–81.

7 John M.D. Pohl, "Dramatic Performance in the Theater of the State; the Cults of Divus Triumphator, Parthenope, and Quetzalcoatl," in *Altera Roma: Art and Empire from Mérida to México*, ed. John M.D.Pohl and Claire L. Lyons (Los Angeles: Cotsen Institute of Archaeology Press, 2016), 150–1.

8 Laura E. Matthew and Michel R. Oudijk, *Indian Conquistadors: Indigenous Allies in the Conquest of Mesoamerica* (Norman: University of Oklahoma Press, 2007).

9 Francisco de Burgoa, *Geográfica Descripción* (México: Imprenta de Juan Ruyz, 1934 [1674]), 188–9.

10 Elsie Clews Parsons, *Mitla, Town of Souls and other Zapoteco-speaking Pueblos of Oaxaca, Mexico* (Chicago: University of Chicago Press, 1936), 247–8; Eleanor Friend Sleight, *The Many Faces of Cuilapan: A Historical Digest of a*

*Sixteenth-Century Dominican Monastery and Church Complex and Village, Oaxaca, Mexico* (Orlando: Pueblo Press, 1988).

11 Ilona Katzew, *Contested Visions in the Spanish Colonial World* (New Haven: Yale University Press, 2011).

12 Max Harris, "Moctezuma's Daughter: The Role of La Malinche in Mesoamerican Dance," *The Journal of American Folklore* 109, no. 432 (Spring 1996): 149–77; Max Harris, "The Return of Moctezuma: Oaxaca's 'Danza de la Pluma' and New Mexico's 'Danza de los Matachines'," *TDR* 41, no. 1 (Spring 1997): 106–34; Max Harris, *Aztecs, Moors, and Christians: Festivals of Reconquest in Mexico and Spain* (Austin: University of Texas Press, 2000), 237.

13 Marta Ilia Nájera Coronado, "El Rito del 'Palo Volador': Encuentro de Significados," *Revista Española de Antropología Americana* 38, no. 1 (2007): 51–73.

14 Parsons, *Mitla*, 246–8. Sleight, *The Many Faces of Cuilapan*, 128.

15 Pohl, "Ritual Ideology and Commerce," 177.

16 Xochitl Marina Flores Marcial, "A History of Guelaguetza in Zapotec Communities of the Central Valleys of Oaxaca, 16th Century to the Present" (PhD diss., University of California Los Angeles, 2015).

17 Jeffrey H. Cohen, "Danza de la Pluma: Symbols of Submission and Separation in a Mexican Fiesta," *Anthropological Quarterly* 66, no. 3 (July 1993): 149–58; Harris, *Aztecs, Moors, and Christians*.

18 Cohen, "Danza de la Pluma," 152–3; Harris, *Aztecs, Moors, and Christians*, 243–5.

19 Harris, *Aztecs, Moors, and Christians*, 237–8.

20 Ibid., 243, 248.

21 Ibid., 31–63.

22 Linda A. Curcio-Nagy, *The Great Festivals of Colonial Mexico City: Performing Power and Identity* (Albuquerque: University of New Mexico Press, 2004).

23 John M.D. Pohl and Claire L. Lyons, "Introduction," in Pohl and Lyons, *Altera Roma*, 71–2.

24 Toribio Motolonía, *Motolonía's History of the Indians of New Spain*, trans. Elizabeth Andros Foster (Berkeley: The Cortes Society, 1950), 101–20.

25 Cohen, "Danza de la Pluma," 150; Harris, *Aztecs, Moors, and Christians*, 39.

26 Parsons, *Mitla*, 220–1.

27 Pohl, "Transnational Tales."

28 Harris, *Aztecs, Moors, and Christians*; Sean F. McEnroe, "Spain's Tlaxcalan Vassals: Citizenship and State Formation on Mexico's Northern Frontier" (PhD diss., University of California Berkeley, 2009).

29 Michael Dean Mathiowetz, "The Diurnal Path of the Sun: Ideology and Interregional Interaction in Ancient Northwest Mesoamerica and the American Southwest" (PhD diss., University of California Riverside, 2011), 628–54.

30  Paul Kirchhoff, "Se Puede Localizar Aztlan?," *Anuario de Historia, Año 1* (1961); Paul Kirchhoff, Lina Odena Güemes, and Luis Reyes García, *Historia Tolteca-Chichimeca* (México: Instituto Nacional de Antropología e Historia, 1976); Dana Leibsohn, *Script and Glyph: Pre-Hispanic History, Colonial Bookmaking, and the Historia Tolteca-Chichimeca* (Cambridge, MA: Harvard University Press, 2009); Pohl, "Transnational Tales," 275.

31  Pohl, "Transnational Tales," 269.

32  Danny Zborover, "Decolonizing Historical Archaeology in Southern Oaxaca, and Beyond," in *Bridging the Gaps: Integrating Archaeology and History in Oaxaca, Mexico,* ed. Danny Zborover and Peter Kroefges (Boulder: University Press of Colorado, 2015), 279–332.

33  Pohl, "Transnational Tales," 272.

34  Nahui Ollin Vásquez Mendoza, *Pueblo a orilla del mar: Huatulco en el siglo XVI (1522–1616)* (Mexico City: Conaculta, 2012).

35  Zborover, "Decolonizing Historical Archaeology in Southern Oaxaca, and Beyond."

36  Alicia Gonzalez, *The Edge of Enchantment: Sovereignty and Ceremony in Huatulco, Mexico* (Washington DC: National Museum of the American Indian, 2002); Andrés Oseguera, "Relaciones rituales y contradicción en la fiesta patronal de los chontales de San Pedro Huamelula, Oaxaca" *Alteridades* 20, no. 40 (2010): 95–108; Jaime Zárate Escamilla, *Huamelula, Pueblo Danzante* (Mexico City: CDI, 2007).

37  Roger Crowley, *Empires of the Sea: The Siege of Malta, the Battle of Lepanto, and the Contest for the Center of the World* (New York: Random House, 2008).

38  Peter Gerhard, *Pirates of the Pacific* (Lincoln: University of Nebraska Press, 1960), 101–32.

39  Hugh Thomas, *Conquest: Montezuma and the Fall of Old Mexico* (New York: Simon and Schuster, 1993), 568–9.

40  Edgardo J. Angara and Carlos Madrid, *The World of the Manila–Acapulco Galleons: The Global and Human Context* (Quezon City, Philippines: Vibal Foundation, 2017); James S. Olson, *Historical Dictionary of the Spanish Empire 1402–1975* (New York: Greenwood Press, 1992), 614.

41  Peter J. Arnade, *Beggars, Iconoclasts, and Civic Patriots: the Political Culture of the Dutch Revolt* (Ithaca: Cornell University Press, 2008).

42  Jonathan Israel, *The Dutch Republic: Its Rise, Greatness, and Fall 1477–1806* (Oxford: Clarendon Press, 1995).

43  Matías Angel de la Mota, *Historia de la Conquista de la Provincia de la Nueva-Galicia; Volume 3* (Guadalajara: J. Santos Orosco, 1856 [1742]).

44  Zoltán Biedermann, Anne Gerritsen, and Giorgio Riello, *Global Gifts: The Material Culture of Diplomacy in Early Modern Eurasia* (Cambridge, UK: Cambridge University Press, 2018).

45  In 1609, Henry Hudson sailed up the river that bears his name in an effort to find a Northwest Passage from the Atlantic to the Pacific. His ship was named the *Halve Maen* ("Half Moon") and displayed this Ottoman symbol boldly on its stern.

46  Abdul Haq Compier, "'Let the Muslim Be My Master in Outward Things:' References to Islam in the Promotion of Religious Tolerance in Christian Europe," *Al-Islam eGazette* (January 2010).

47  Morris E. Eugene, *Islam and Politics in Aceh: A Study of Center-Periphery Relations in Indonesia* (New York: Cornell University, 1983).

48  E.W. Bovill, *The Battle of Alcazar* (London: The Batchworth Press, 1952).

49  Byron Hamann has identified an account of Turkish or Moorish ships arriving off the Coast of Nueva Galicia (West Mexico). Archivo General de la Nación. JUSTICIA, 1041 N° 2. Año 1574. "Información hecha por la Audiencia de la Nueva Galicia sobre ciertos navíos de turcos o moros que llegaron a aquella costa. Una pieza."

50  Gerhard, *Pirates of the Pacific*; Kris R. Lane, *Pillaging the Empire: Piracy in the Americas, 1500-1750* (New York: M.E. Sharpe, 1998), 33–49.

51  Vásquez Mendoza, *Pueblo a orilla del mar.*

52  John M.D. Pohl, *Aztec, Mixtec and Zapotec Armies* (Oxford: Osprey Publishing, 1991), 21–2; John M.D. Pohl, *Aztec Warrior: AD 1321-1521* (Oxford: Osprey Publishing, 2001), 6.

53  Pohl, "Transnational Tales," 270–1.

54  Ibid., 269.

55  Lane, *Pillaging the Empire*, 28–30.

56  Jonathan Israel, *Dutch Primacy in World Trade, 1585-1740* (Oxford: Clarendon Press, 1989), 137–38.

57  Joris van Spilbergen and Jacob Le Maire, *Oost ende West-Indische spiegel der 2 leste navigatien, ghedaen inden jaeren 1614.15.16.17 ende 18. daer in vertoont woort in wat gestalt Joris van Speilbergen door de Magellanes de werelt rontom geseylt heeft, met eenighe battalien so te water als te lant, ende 2 historien de een van Oost ende de ander van West-Indien, het ghetal der forten, soldaten, schepen. ende gheschut. Met de Australische navigatien, van Jacob le Maire, die int suyden door een nieuwe Streat ghepasseert is, met veel wonders so landen, volcken, ende natien, haer ontmoet zijn* (Leyden: Nicolaes van Geelkercken, 1619).

58  Gerhard, *Pirates of the Pacific*, 114.

59  See James C. Scott's *Domination and the Arts of Resistance: Hidden Transcripts* (New Haven: Yale University Press, 2009) for a broader discussion of the hidden transcripts of resistance and rebellion in the ritual practices of subordinate populations within colonial political systems.

60  Harris, "The Return of Moctezuma," 106–34.

61  Harris, "Moctezuma's Daughter," 149–77.

# chapter fifteen

# Unease with the Exotic: Ambiguous Responses to Chinese Material Culture in the Dutch Republic

THIJS WESTSTEIJN

Around 1650, the market for the applied arts in the Dutch Republic was one of the largest – if not the largest – in Europe. With the Netherlands being the first "true world entrepôt," goods from Asia, in particular China, took up a sizeable share of this market.[1] According to one estimate, the Dutch East India Company (*Vereenigde Oostindische Compagnie* or VOC) imported at least forty million pieces of porcelain in the seventeenth and eighteenth centuries.[2] As listed in an Amsterdam newspaper of 27 June 1634, a single incoming cargo included 219,027 pieces of Chinese porcelain, 52 chests with Japanese and Korean porcelain, 241 pieces of Japanese lacquerware, and 1,155 pounds of raw Chinese silk.[3] Such goods found an easy entrance into Dutch households, through sale at public auctions and in specialized "Indies shops."[4] One of those shops is depicted on a leaf from a Dutch fan, made around 1680, featuring over three hundred luxury objects including porcelain and redware, folding screens, gilded lacquer cabinets, textiles, and East Asian landscape paintings (fig. 15.1).[5] Although its female shoppers, in fanciful Turkish-Persian costumes, demonstrate that this was an imaginary scene, the taste for Asiatica was in fact shared by all levels of Dutch society. Contemporaries noted that the use of porcelain was "in nearly common use with commoners,"[6] that it was a "cheap" fixture in Dutch kitchens that smelled of foreign spices,[7] and that the lowliest of households could afford imitation Chinese Delftware ceramics.

Written sources provide an even more varied impression of this imported material culture. Chinese books, maps, calligraphy, jewellery, weapons, games, and *materia medica* feature in the testimony of the Danish physician Ole Borch, who marvelled at the profusion of exotica in the Dutch homes he visited in the 1660s. One of his hosts was the Leiden apothecary Jan Jacobsz Swammerdam, father of the famous microscopist; he owned a sizeable collection of Chinese porcelain, a material that

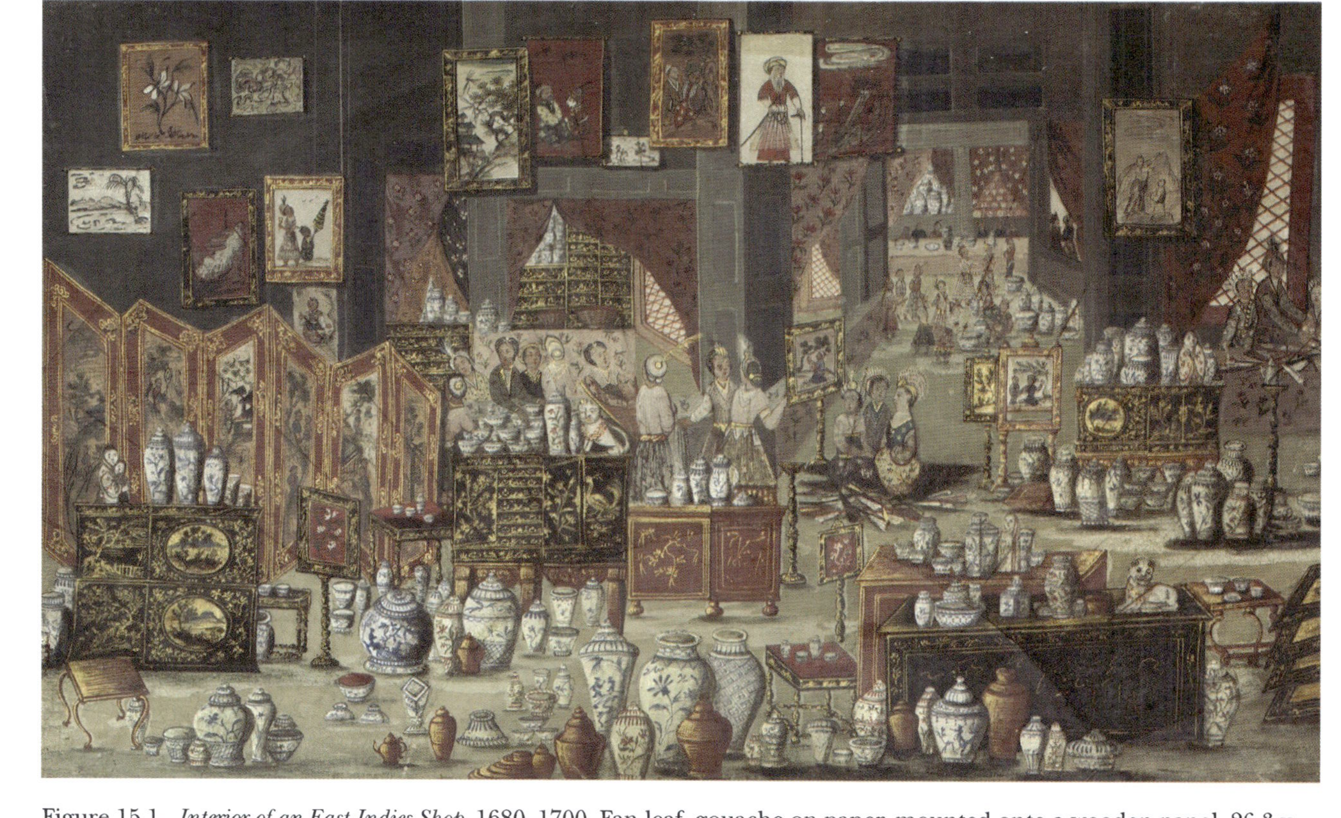

Figure 15.1. *Interior of an East Indies Shop*, 1680–1700. Fan leaf, gouache on paper, mounted onto a wooden panel, 26.3 x 43.6 cm. Victoria & Albert Museum, London. Given by Sir William Lawrence, Bt, inv.nr P.35-1926. © Victoria and Albert Museum, London

was associated with apotropaic and other medicinal qualities due to its foreignness and hygienic surface. He also displayed in his house:

> Various paintings of Chinese soldiers, gods (of which also images of gold were seen), of women, some engraved with a burin ... we saw Chinese books described with a wondrous variety of characters (of which they have sixty thousand), none of them printed on both sides ... various figures in slate stone, of trees, castles, shrubberies, cities, towers, ruins of cities and towers, pentagonal castles with their entrances ... a Chinese bow; very beautiful images of birds made of stones of different colours; silk flowers made artfully by the Chinese; Chinese silver vases without rust; various Chinese silk shoes made of red and blue silk.[8]

This chapter will explore how hearts and minds were affected by such an abundance of imported objects. Most of the visual and written reactions to Dutch maritime efforts glorified the success of their young state on the world stage. The converse, however, was also the case: some texts and images expressed sentiments of cultural anxiety about the foreign influx. The present analysis will therefore return to Simon Schama's famous formula, "the embarrassment of riches": the Dutch urban merchants, often Calvinists, were initially hesitant to showcase their wealth.[9] It was only towards the end of the seventeenth century that this unease made way for a more open kind of bourgeois consumerism, shared by large swathes of society. Embarrassment regarding luxuries from the non-Western world will be the focus here. How were these types of consumer goods received in ideological terms? Focusing on Chinese wares in particular, we will first discuss the celebratory accounts before moving on to the reservations held by others. Unfettered trade, displacing so many objects across continents, seemed to some to run against claims that the global division of commodities had been ordained by the Divinity. As will become clear, sentiments of cultural anxiety were formulated throughout the seventeenth century and, if anything, intensified with the increasingly regular consumption of foreign wares in the early eighteenth century. Ultimately, as we shall see, even the drinking of tea would become associated with the dangerous philosophical radicalism of Benedictus de Spinoza and his followers.

### Celebrating the China Trade

At least a thousand extant oil paintings made in the Netherlands, mostly still lifes, feature Chinese porcelain, testifying to the ubiquity of porcelain and the great esteem in which it was held, in contrast to the disdain that the Chinese themselves bestowed upon these second-rate export wares.[10] Porcelains were the only Chinese artefacts featured prominently in paintings, despite the presence of so many other East Asian goods in Dutch households.[11] This selective interest suggests that paintings with porcelain did not primarily signal the buyers' excitement about a foreign civilization; it was rather included as a reference to the success of the Dutch commercial enterprise. Even the House of Orange came to associate itself rather explicitly with Chinese material culture. Amalia van Solms, wife of the stadtholder Frederik Hendrik of Orange, played a foundational role in the European fashion for porcelain cabinets. In the series of paintings Amalia commissioned to commemorate her deceased husband and to glorify his role in the rise of the Dutch Republic as an independent world power, a sizeable Chinese porcelain vase featured centrally, surrounded by a variety of other arts and crafts from the world the Dutch traded with: West Africa, Brazil, the Moluccas, and Japan (fig. 15.2).[12]

Porcelain could also be combined with oranges imported from East Asia, which in Dutch are still called *sinaasappels* ("China's apples"), as evident in Jan Davidsz de Heem's painting inscribed "Vivat Oraenge" ("Long Live Orange"), probably made on the occasion of the re-instalment of the stadtholder, William III of Orange, in 1672 (fig. 15.3). Elsewhere in Europe, the association of Chinese porcelain with Dutch maritime exploits was reflected in the term "Dutch cabinets," used in Britain and Germany to denote porcelain collections.[13] "By means of a strange circulation, Holland is beginning to become Asian," the medical doctor Cornelis Bontekoe concluded in 1678.[14] The celebrated poet Joost van den Vondel opined that "one does not have to travel to China, to cross so many seas, to speak with the Chinese in Beijing's impressive palaces," since so much splendid art was available in Amsterdam.[15]

Vondel and one of his younger epigones, Johannes Antonides van der Goes, were also responsible for the most conspicuous literary celebrations of Dutch global trade. Both authors presented China as the ultimate horizon of Dutch overseas expansion and as a counterpart, a worthy mirror to Dutch glory. Vondel's *Het lof der zee-vaert* (*In Praise of Seafaring*, 1623), an erudite poem published in a major new nautical pilot book, celebrates worldwide trade as the basis of Amsterdam's prosperity; he also wrote a *Hymnus over de scheeps-vaert* (*Hymn about Navigation*, 1620). Half a century later, Van der Goes emulated Vondel in

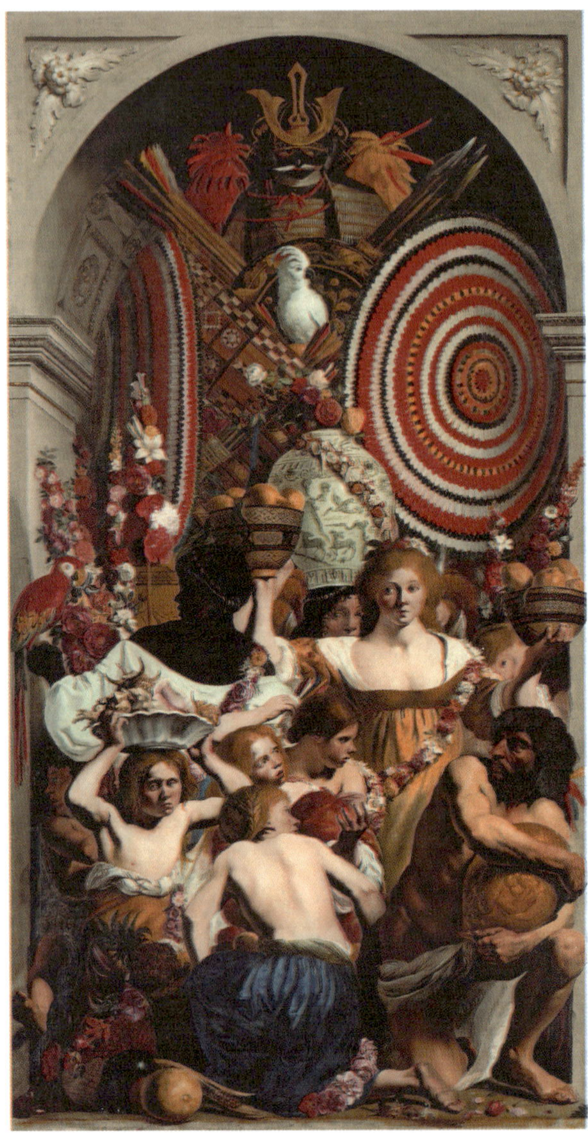

Figure 15.2. Jacob van Campen, *The East and West Indies Present Their Riches*, 1650–1. Oil on canvas, 383.5 x 204.5 cm. Koninklijk Paleis Huis ten Bosch, The Hague. © Image collection Institute for History and Art History, Utrecht University

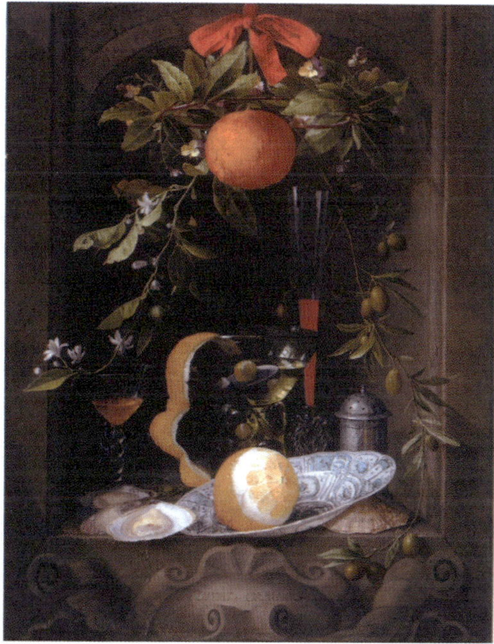

Figure 15.3. Jan Davidsz. de Heem, *Long Live Orange*, c. 1667–72, oil on canvas, 63 x 49 cm, Rijksmuseum, Amsterdam (on loan from Museum Paleis Het Loo, Apeldoorn), SK-C-1794. © Rijksmuseum Amsterdam

*Ystroom* (*The River IJ*, 1671), a poetic account of a walk along the river IJ in Amsterdam, which takes the reader to the institutions, storehouses, and naval carpentry yards of the VOC. The poem ends with a protracted mental voyage across the oceans, from the Cape of Good Hope to the East Indies.

In *Ystroom*, the Dutch capital is presented as a global trade metropolis: one has "every right to be proud of such a capital city, the true staple market of all the world's mercantile treasures." Amsterdam is described as comparable to Beijing, and the poem emphasizes its lucrative trade with the "empire of riches" (*koninkrijk van schatten*) that is China.[16] The Celestial Empire, after the suicide of the Ming emperor and the ensuing civil war, was rearing its head again under Manchu rule:

No naval misfortune will clip the wings of the courage [of Dutch ships]
Since China no longer hesitates to discharge from her lap
And hand over generously the golden fruit of Atlas
Even though the country sighs under a pressing yoke
And the imperial court in Beijing, struck by the Tartar's axe,
Still shows with what a crash giants may fall
From their elevated heights, since the realm, in deepest sorrow, saw
The great Emperor dangling from a tree
And his dying visage, splashed with a deadly pale.
Closed were then the mouths of the Saffran-Yellow and Kiang Rivers
Which, now rearing their heads more freely in the sun,
Discharge their harvest in the forts of Guangzhou
And pay us tribute with an empire of riches.[17]

The fall of the Ming after ruling "a hundred centuries" [*sic*], however, makes Van der Goes conclude that the Dutch capital, having thrown off the Spanish yoke, is a more resilient city than Beijing. After discussing the Great Wall of China at length, he concludes that Amsterdam's bulwarks are stronger: "Your city wall offers a better promise of protection, oh illustrious merchant princess, the market place of Europe!"[18] On *Ystroom*'s frontispiece, China's "empire of riches" is depicted as a submissive maiden ("Maegt van Sina") in a sumptuous dress, who duly empties her coffer in Amsterdam's lap (fig. 15.4). The engraving illustrates the fact that in the Netherlands, China was present chiefly in terms of its material culture.

Van der Goes and Vondel both wrote plays set in China that, if conceived for the stage, may have presented similar displays of foreignness and opulence. The Dutch playwrights seem to have borrowed from the Jesuit school drama that was staged in the Southern Netherlands and German states, which often featured East Asian elements. They may also have been inspired by those Jesuits who returned from China on the ships of the Dutch East India Company.[19] The missionaries fashioned their visits to the Low Countries as elaborate performances to advertise their project, donning the eye-catching silk dress of the Confucian literati (Nicolas Trigault in 1614) or mandarins under Manchu rule (Martino Martini in 1653). They were also accompanied by Chinese assistants, who sometimes demonstrated their calligraphic virtuosity.[20] A particularly strong impression must have been made by the eyewitness images of China displayed via the new contraption of the magic lantern, which may have looked like the lavish illustrations in the well-known books on China by Olfert Dapper and Johan Nieuhof. These were also turned into half-transparent

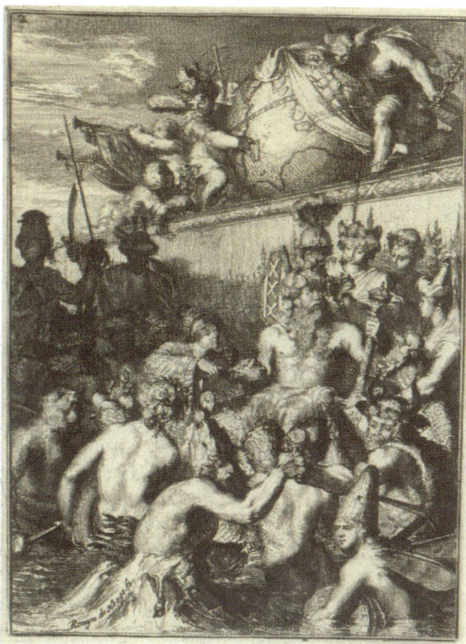

Figure 15.4. Romeyn de Hooghe, *Amsterdam Receives the World's Riches*, in
Johannes Antonides van der Goes, *Ystroom* (Amsterdam: Arentsz, 1671),
Part 2, 33. Etching, 17.2 x 12 cm. Rijksmuseum Amsterdam, RP-P-1965–176.
© Rijksmuseum, Amsterdam

*vue d'optique* images, to be lit from behind or be seen through a convex
lens for an additional impression of lifelikeness and spatiality.[21] In addition, Dutch publications about the East Indies often emphasized the
performative elements of Chinese culture. The author Simon de Vries recounted in 1682 that Chinese actors "greatly excel above the Europeans";
in "costumes and the representation of characters," Chinese plays were
more skilful than even those seen on the English stage. He described how
Chinese performances were accompanied by lavish banquets that might
last for twelve days. A print in his book shows Chinese actors donning
spectacular feathered headdresses and fans while the spectators, covered
in at least as much textile, are being served elaborate dishes and drinks,
with pieces of decorated ceramics at their feet (fig. 15.5).[22] Such reports
of Chinese spectacle must have resonated with the luxuries and artefacts

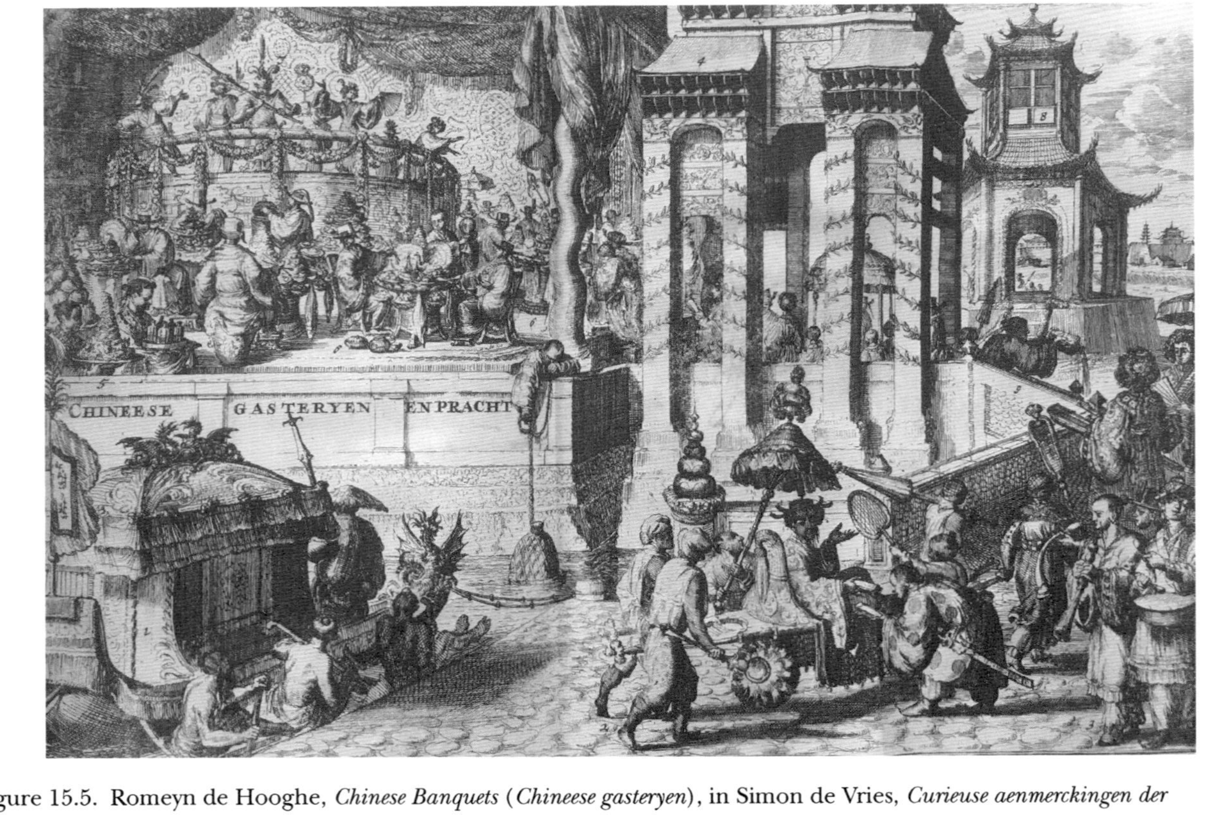



Figure 15.5. Romeyn de Hooghe, *Chinese Banquets (Chineese gasteryen)*, in Simon de Vries, *Curieuse aenmerckingen der bysonderste Oost en West-Indische verwonderens-waerdige dingen; nevens die van China, Africa, en andere gewesten des werelds* (Utrecht: Ribbius, 1682), vol. 3, before page 185. © Image collection Institute for History and Art History, Utrecht University

that were familiar to the Dutch. This connection was certainly made in De Vries's book, which also included lengthy discussions of Asian ceramics, gemstones, gold and silverware, and other precious objects.

A well-documented visual performance of the Asian "empire of riches" was the display organized by the burgomasters of Amsterdam on the occasion of the visit of the French Queen Mother, Marie de' Medici. This event provided a significant opportunity for the city of Amsterdam to showcase its new identity as a global capital, and included many references to its lucrative connections with Asia. The theatrical events staged for this worthy visitor were described in Latin (1638) by the well-known humanist Caspar Barlaeus, while Vondel was charged with the Dutch translation (1639). The text described the artistic displays set up for the Queen Mother, who was placed on a boat to admire a series floating *tableaux vivants*, featuring Amsterdam's City Maiden flanked by Neptune and Mercury, gods of sea and trade. The festivities included a surprising homage to the Jesuit project in Asia. Burgomaster Albert Coenraadsz Burgh presented his royal guest with a bespoke gift: the rosary of Saint Francis Xavier, the "Apostle of the East" who had single-handedly baptized hundreds of thousands in East Asia. Xavier's body parts had been carried around Asia and Europe as relics and were put on display in churches in Goa and Rome.[23] Vondel waxes lyrical about the rosary as a "holy jewel of the Church," caressed by the very hand of the "blessed Xavier, who in the world's Eastern part announced the honour of Jesus."[24] For the Calvinist burgomasters of Amsterdam, this celebration of the Catholic mission may have been redeemed by the fact that the rosary also clearly signalled the rising global dominance of the Dutch trading companies, which had recently captured this rosary from a Portuguese vessel off the Brazilian coast.

In the evening, Marie de' Medici was honoured with an elaborate banquet in the VOC's East India House, stocked with sumptuous Indies wares: porcelain, spices, drugs, weapons, and bundles of woven and unwoven silk. In the central hall, she admired "Chinese and Japanese paintings" and images of "those places, close to China, in which one can see how the Dutch are daily winning the increasing favour of remote peoples."[25] These East Asian artefacts were permanent fixtures, as confirmed by a later description (1683) of the hall as filled with "various curiosities [made] of lacquerwork, such as Chinese screens, Japanese cabinets, along with Japanese silk robes, silk fabrics, textiles, tea and all the like."[26] Indeed, East Asian imagery may have decked the hall from floor to ceiling, in a manner similar to how VOC director Nicolaas Witsen displayed a collection of more than 250 Chinese paintings in his own home.[27]

The queen mother's gaze reportedly lost its focus among so many splendours, and Barlaeus writes that she was under the impression of being received in East Asia rather than the Netherlands.[28] She feasted her other senses on a display of "fruit and vegetables from Persia, Arabia, the Moluccas, Japan, and China, served in large and ample porcelain dishes, which ... pleased the Queen because of their foreignness."[29] Although historians have suggested that this performance was "more theatre than food," the display of imports from Asia in Amsterdam was in fact quite common.[30] Marie de' Medici was apparently enchanted by the city's various East Indies shops and, on the next day, bartered with local shopkeepers to acquire Chinese porcelain, "treating the citizens as a merchant woman rather than a queen," which, to the Dutch, was the highest compliment.[31] The board of directors of the VOC saved her from any mercantile embarrassment by making her a gift of "beautiful porcelain objects and costly Japanese chests, artfully inlaid with lacquer, gold, and mother of pearl."[32]

## An Embarrassment of Riches

In his fulsome account of the festivities Barlaeus apparently succumbed to a bout of *delirium imperialis* ("imperial delirium," to use Schama's term). He described the VOC's "ongoing low and high tides of wares and merchandise," and boasted that it must have been God's grace that ensured that "the Company, from small beginnings, has nowadays ... climbed and risen so high that every investment had doubled many times."[33] At this point in the discussion, he inserted the proviso that, apparently, not all Amsterdammers approved of the new Asian luxuries: "Someone might say about these cargoes, what Pliny once said about the great Pompey's victory over Mithridates: 'this was the cause that the Romans, instead of the ordinary household wares that they imported, began to use jars of mother of pearl and precious stone'."[34] Learned readers would have recognized this reference to the Roman Republic and its condemnation of luxury and decadence. The Roman military leader Pompey (106–48 BCE) had splashed out on oriental refinement after defeating a prince from Asia Minor. This behaviour inspired a rebuke from Pliny, who held up Alexander the Great as a better example: even though Alexander's conquests in Asia had been far more substantial, he had resisted the lure of luxuries. (To be precise: he personally retrofitted an effeminate Persian pearl- and gem-encrusted unguent holder, turning it into a protective case for the virile, unpolished works of Homer.)

Barlaeus's poem thus referenced a paradox found in antiquity's authoritative book on material culture, Pliny's *Naturalis Historia* (first century CE). On the one hand the text showcased the period's fascination with *mirabilia*: exotic animals, plants, and natural phenomena; on the other hand it warned against the Roman Empire being flooded with imported luxuries.[35] In fact Roman writers from Cato the Elder (234–149 BCE) onward had railed against the growing taste for *luxuria*, a negative term that suggested suspicion and disapproval of all things foreign, expensive, and opulent; the poets Horace (first century BCE) and Juvenal (first century CE) specifically deplored the influence of the decadent East on what they characterized as the simple and honest Roman character.[36] A reference to Pliny's "jars of mother of pearl" clearly signalled unease regarding the luxury tableware imported from overseas. This was a criticism that some of the Dutch, at least, shared with the ancients. A similar sentiment was put into programmatic form by the Amsterdam burgomasters themselves (who liked to compare themselves to Roman consuls) when they commissioned Govaert Flinck to decorate the new Town Hall with a sizeable painting of *Marcus Curius Dentatus Refusing the Gifts of the Samnites* (1656, fig. 15.6). The scene highlights the moment when Dentatus, the republican consul, chooses an honest meal of raw turnip above imported fare. Lifting a turnip, the consul turns away a luxurious bribe that Flinck clearly marked as foreign: the gold and silver is carried by an African boy, and the shiny fabrics worn by the visitors contrast starkly with Dentatus's simple clothes.

Native turnips above foreign luxuries: this message must have gone down well with puritan moralists. Calvin himself had condemned trade with Asia in his commentary on Isaiah 2:12–16, "And upon elegant pictures":

The Prophet condemns navigation, which had brought many corruptions into the land. It is too frequent and common that riches are followed by luxury, effeminacy, and a superfluity of pleasures, which we commonly see in wealthy countries and commercial cities; for those who trade by sea in distant countries are not satisfied with the commodities obtained at home, but carry away new luxuries which were formerly unknown. Since, therefore, wealth is usually the mother of superfluity, the Prophet here mentions costly furniture, as if he had said that the Jews, by adorning their houses at great expense, draw down upon themselves the judgment of God; for he employs the word pictures, by a well-known figure of speech, to denote rich tapestry, and the productions of Phrygia, and vessels framed with consummate skill.

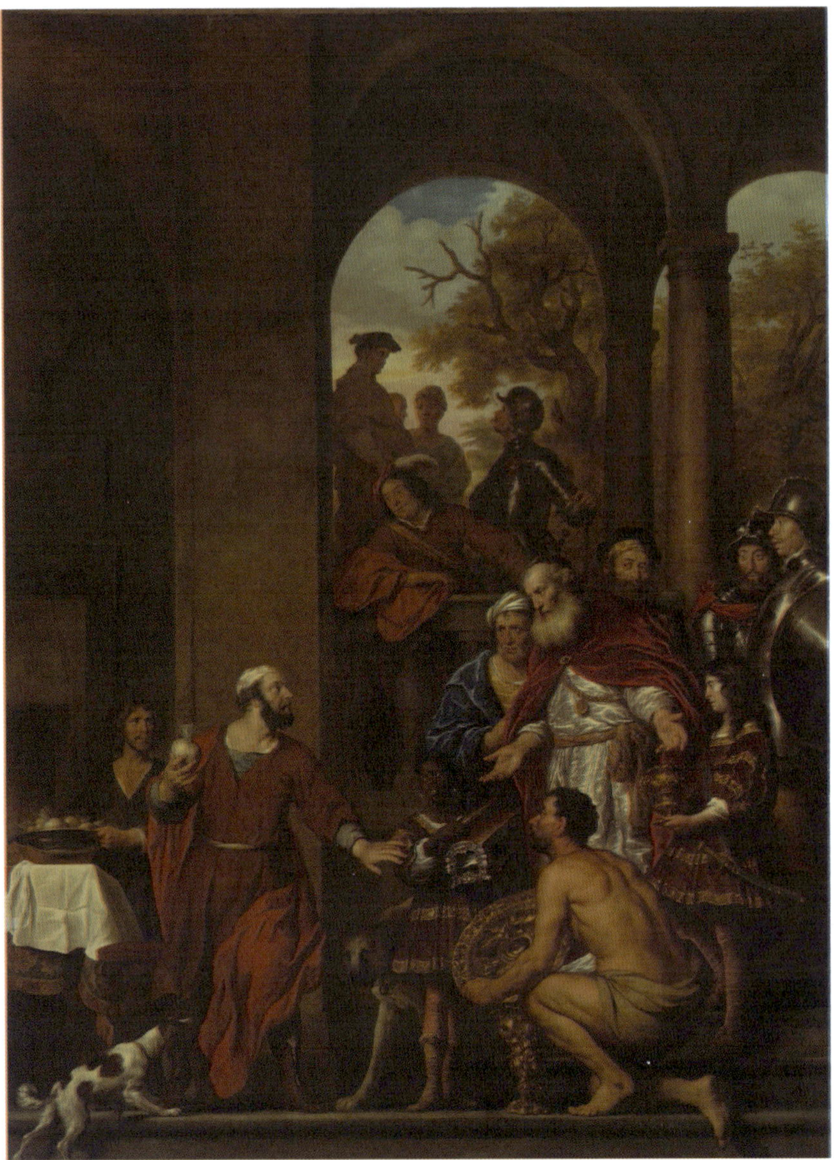

Figure 15.6. Govaert Flinck, *Marcus Curius Dentatus Refusing the Gifts of the Samnites*, 1656. Oil on canvas, 485 x 377 cm. Royal Palace, Amsterdam. © Image collection Institute for History and Art History, Utrecht University

It is certain that the manners of men are corrupted, when they eagerly pursue, in every direction, superfluous enjoyments.

"Phrygia" denotes a region in present-day Turkey, the region that the Romans associated with "Asian" exuberance in opposition to "Attic" (Greek) purity. Calvin's warning that empires fall because of imported luxuries would have had an ominous ring to any reader involved in the Dutch East India Company's proto-colonial ambitions on a worldwide scale:

> And we see how destruction was brought on the Roman Empire by delicacies of this nature; for before they traveled into Greece, the greatest moderation prevailed among them; and no sooner had Asia been vanquished than they began to grow soft and effeminate; and when their eyes were dazzled by pictures, furniture, precious stones, and tapestry ... all their senses were immediately overpowered, and, by imitating the luxury of the East as a higher form of civilization, they began gradually to indulge in every kind of debauchery."[37]

The cultural anxiety expressed by Calvin must have resonated strongly with those Dutch men and women who had second thoughts about the import of Asian goods.

Other works of moralistic intent, such as emblem books, emphasized, for instance, the lack of practical usefulness of beautiful but fragile porcelain, which was – in line with Calvin's warning – described in terms of the lure of female deceit and luxuriousness. The frontispiece of a book by Mennonite artist Jan Luyken, *Het leerzaam huisraad* (*Edifying Household Wares*, 1711) features a sizeable number of vases and plates; the cupboard on the left is a *Pronkkast* or showcase with porcelain or its Delftware imitations. Luijken writes:

> These are jars, but they are of no use
> To carry food to that table
> Which is the support of our life;
> They merely provide gratification,
> Enjoyment to the eye, and decoration.
> These will always be empty barrels:
> Therefore, Need passes them by
> And Necessity sweeps them to the side.[38]

Luyken's sentiment echoes the cultural ambiguity about Chinese porcelain that had been evident from the first decades of the seventeenth

century. For Dutch moralists, the material's combination of sheen, hardness, and fragility evocatively lent itself to meditation about the paradoxical allure of the most fleeting details of the visible world.[39]

In the many still lifes that depict porcelain, such references to im-
permanence are usually present implicitly in the manner in which
plates are balanced precariously on the edge of a table, displayed
alongside flowers and fruit prone to wither and rot, or presented in
a mirroring ensemble where the reflective surface of the porcelain
might itself be reflected in a mirror. One example is Pieter Claesz's
1627 work featuring spots of rot on the apples in a Wanli bowl.[40] Particularly explicit is a sumptuous still life by an anonymous Dutch master, known as the *Paston Collection*: an hourglass, clock, and pocket
watch emphasize the temporal nature of the riches displayed (fig.
15.7). Here, the porcelain is placed next to an Amsterdam-made
globe turned to display China,[41] and in proximity to other exotic objects such as shells, which could symbolize the idleness of collecting
(according to the well-known emblematist Roemer Visscher).[42] Shells
and porcelain were deemed to be closely related in terms of their reflective surfaces. The "secret" of porcelain manufacture allegedly consisted of the use of ground seashells that had matured for a century
underground, according to *Pseudodoxia* (first ed. 1646) by the chemist
Thomas Browne, who was a close collaborator of the commissioner of
the *Paston Collection*.[43]

The transience and reflective sheen that were associated with otherwise unfathomable imports from the East could inspire gendered
appreciation: these qualities underscored Calvin's take on "soft and
effeminate" superfluous enjoyments. Traditionally women had been
associated with mirrors in terms of their mutual vanity and fragility;
in the words of Shakespeare, "women are [as] frail ... as the glasses
where they view themselves, / Which are as easy broke as they make
forms."[44] Yet the lure of Asia in general was also explained in gendered terms. Among the Dutch travelogues, Jan Huygen van Linschoten's account of his voyage to India, which was spiced with reports
about realms further East, was the first to connect the Orient to the
lasciviousness of seductive women, claiming that Asia had corrupted
the Portuguese overseas empire and brought about its fall. This gendered approach, needless to say, later developed into a common
trope of European orientalism.[45] Of all non-European women, as de
Vries emphasized to his readers, the Chinese were by far the most
alluring.[46]

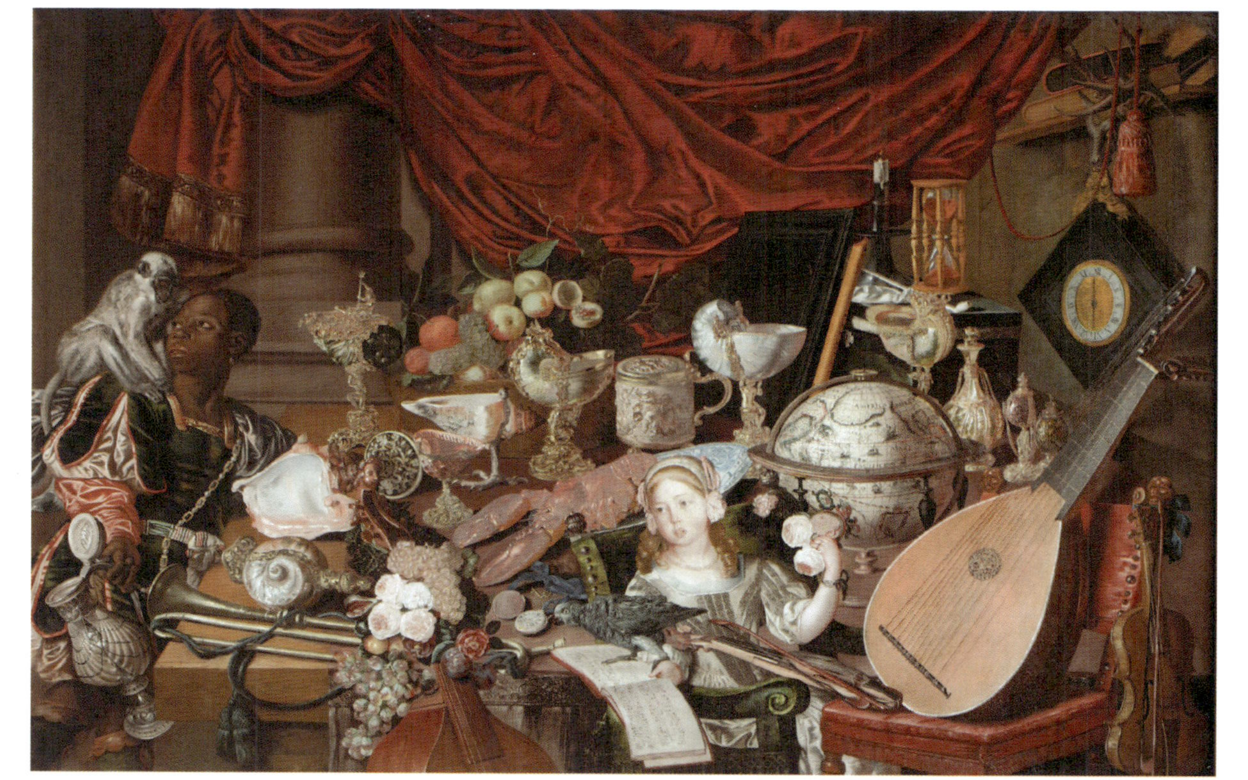

Figure 15.7.  *The Paston Collection*, 1665. Oil on canvas, 165 x 246.5 cm. Norwich Castle Museum and Art Gallery. © Image collection Institute for History and Art History, Utrecht University

The fact that the European craze for porcelain began with Amalia van Solms and her daughters, who married German and English aristocrats, and that it remained a predominantly female predilection, may have contributed to the criticisms of women needlessly spending their husbands' money on fungible, essentially worthless Asian trinkets that were "as easy broken as they make forms."[47] As the author of *De Gedebaucheerde en betoverde Koffy en Thee wereld* (*The Depraved and Enchanted World of Coffee and Tea*) complained in 1701, "women's craziness" to waste money on fragile porcelain "is so highly pernicious, especially in a country like Holland, which solely consists of commerce."[48] Similarly in *Het groot ceremonie-boek der beschaafde zeeden* (*The Great Book of Ceremonies of Civilized Behavior*, 1735) "some burgher women" are portrayed "who ruin their men by establishing cabinets with old porcelain," in contrast to the honourable, masculine predilection for collecting paintings, books, and antiquities. "It is much nobler to contemplate the art in a beautiful work of painting, than in the scribbles of the Japanese and Chinese on a few pieces of glazed earth, which perishes when it falls."[49] In 1725 the English poet John Gay went so far as to compare noblewomen in general to ancient Chinese pottery on the basis of their shared beautiful, but highly impractical, sheen: "Vessels so pure, and so refin'd / Appear the types of woman-kind: / Are they not valu'd for their beauty, / Too fair, too fine for houshold duty? / ... How white, how polish'd is their skin, / And valu'd most when only seen!"[50] In this light it is unsurprising that all the shoppers in the painted "China Store" mentioned at the outset of this chapter are women (fig. 15.1). In spite of such mockery, female collectors like Van Solms took pride in their ability to acquire and display foreign luxury goods. Catharina Copal, for instance, had herself portrayed (by Agnes Hoeufft) with her right hand draped elegantly over a sizeable Chinese (or Delft-made) vase.[51]

Men would do well to buttress themselves against the lure of foreign ceramics, wrote Jan Six van Chandelier in 1657. The poet may have been attempting to redress his own guilty pleasures (he addressed many of his poems to Calvinist pastors, in particular Johannes Hoornbeeck, whom we shall discuss shortly). He echoed the time-honoured example of Horace's virile and rustic Roman farmer who remained immune to exotic seduction. "If one is able to live at home in peace / what would one care for the rich sea?" asked Six in a poetic rant against luxury goods from foreign lands, *Necessity is Sufficient* (*Nooddruft is genoegh*).[52] Happiness lies in being satisfied with one's local surroundings:

He is happy, who enjoys plowing
The land as if he has borrowed it ...
A simple citizen lives much happier
Never afraid of the harsh and jealous.
The nightmare of sleepless money
Assaults him in vain, for he is tired;
The addictive curse of the golden shards
Does not doom him: Remember you must die,
O stingy fool, in this night
What use are riches and splendour?[53]

The "splendour" of imported "shards" of tableware apparently feeds a cultural anxiety that is best remedied by sticking to local produce.

## Protestant Sensibilities towards Unfettered Global Trade

Dutch ministers were not unanimous in sharing Calvin's embarrassment with imported riches from Asia. One of the most orthodox ministers and a leader of the hardline Counter-Remonstrants, Petrus Plancius, was himself a governor and shareholder of the VOC.[54] Proselytization in Asia could even benefit from an affective involvement in the trade and collecting of porcelain, as was demonstrated by the success of the Jesuit missionaries.[55] The Jesuits' extremely positive stance towards Chinese civilization clearly left its mark on many Dutch publications about China.[56] In a Protestant context, however, a sceptical attitude towards the figurative arts, and towards the display of wealth in general, made admiration for Chinese material culture more equivocal. Such ambiguities may have played a role in the foundation, in Leiden in 1622, of the Seminarium Indicum, a "College of the Indies" whose aim was to prepare Calvinist ministers for the mental and material challenges of proselytization in Batavia (the capital of the Dutch colonial project in Asia, now Jakarta in Indonesia) and Formosa (now Taiwan).

Two publications related to the Seminarium are *De conversione Indorum et gentilium* (*On the Conversion of Indians and Heathens*, 1669) by Johannes Hoornbeeck and *'t Geestelijkck roer van het coopmans schip* (*The Spiritual Helm of the Merchant Vessel*, 1638) by Godfried Udemans. Both painted very positive pictures of Chinese civilization, repeating the Jesuit claim that Chinese moral virtues often put Europeans to shame and extolling the unmatched qualities of products such as porcelain. This point of view was more, however, than an unthinking echo of the Jesuits' stance, as it was informed directly by the authors' knowledge of East Asia. Hoornbeeck had received from his "special friend" Justus Heurnius, a minister in Batavia, a translation of Confucius's Analects that he had made with the help of a Chinese schoolteacher from Macao. Manuscript copies survive in Leiden, London, and Oxford and are testimony to the early Dutch attempts at translating Confucius, which would culminate in the first printed Western translation of the Analects, by Pieter van Hoorn in 1675.[57] Udemans also reported on a Chinese boy who had travelled to the Netherlands with the very first Dutch expedition to reach the East Indies, which had returned in 1597. It is not impossible that he personally met this boy, who apparently learned to speak Dutch and could illuminate his hosts about his homeland.[58] The minister went on to paint a very positive image of China as a "very happy and pleasant land, like a paradise," producing enough silk to clothe the whole world and other admirable goods such as porcelain (allegedly made from shells, snails, and eggs).[59] The two ministers' statements on Chinese material culture must have been informed by the actual goods that were omnipresent in Dutch households; these, indeed, would have offered the students of the Seminarium their most direct cultural acquaintance with East Asia before their departure.

The import of foreign material goods posed moral and theological challenges. Apparently the mere quality, worth, and presence of these wares begged the question of *why* they were made and *how* it was possible that they were shipped in such large quantities over such large distances. Hoornbeeck and Udemans concluded that God had compensated the heathens' state of ignorance about Christ with the material abundance of their countries. To Hoornbeeck, therefore, the Dutch should pay for the material goods they took away by bringing the Protestant faith:

> [T]he hidden corners of the East and West ... were occupied, tamed and taken into possession by the Dutch some time ago, in my opinion not so much to promote the interests and glory of the Republic as of that of Christ and the church. ... For who would believe that by the singular providence and gift of God these things happened to our people only to make them ... take away the riches of the earth or for a larger or superfluous quantity of material things, to the glory and the idle triumph of the Dutch name, instead of, what is more likely, to bring knowledge and worship of God the Maker of Everything to lands that so far have been strangers to the community of humanity and religion[?][60]

Hoornbeeck evidently clung to the biblical notion that the postlapsarian world is in a fallen state, and that its paradisiacal resources have ended up in different parts of the world, separated by cultural chasms after the destruction of the Tower of Babel. This diffusion of materials has resulted in global inequalities, which a good Christian should seek to redeem:

> Can it then be the case that we, who owe a very great deal, if not all, of our commerce and wealth to the heathens and Indians, never think about remunerating them with that type of goods which does not belong to us but only to God, and that is handed over not only without cost but even with great profit, by which means those people will shortly become the most fortunate instead of the most miserable of all, because they become the best, because they become Christians?[61]

The new trade routes thus heralded global conversion. Although Hoornbeeck depended on many Jesuit sources, here his optimistic outlook diverged from their perspective. The Jesuit authority on China, Athanasius Kircher, saw God's plan in strategic terms: since the Divinity "provide[d] such richness and opulence to the kingdom [of China] immersed in the darkness of errors and contamination of luxury," one must conclude that He, knowing of "the eternal punishment which awaits the natives, wished to compensate them for the good morals which they cultivate, and for the discipline by which they live"; material luxuries were their temporary consolation for their damnation in the afterlife.[62] The Calvinist Udemans drew on a similar insight to conclude that the luxuries of Asia are proof that spiritual riches are only to be found in Europe:

> [T]he riches and goods of this world are commonly possessed by those people who do not know God or do not serve him according to his will. ... From this follows that true wealth does not consist in an abundance of gold, silver, diamonds, pearls. ... Let the rich not go proud of their temporary and transient wealth, as the Asians, who are mere heathens, are much richer in silver and gold, land, and sand: but let them gather their treasures in Heaven, where moths and rust can do no damage and where thieves cannot dig or steal.[63]

Since the Dutch themselves, states Udemans, had originally been converted to Christianity by Anglo-Saxon missionaries who did not receive any material recompense, they, who now acquired so many material riches, should be all the more prepared to bring the Gospel to the Indies. Udemans is sure that it is no coincidence that the discovery of new shipping routes to the Indies coincided with the Reformation. Once the overseas heathens have been converted to Protestantism, the Jews will follow suit, and the Day of Judgement will come:

> Meanwhile we need to be concerned to bring these poor pagans to Christianity, like the Saxons and the English have been concerned with our ancestors in the past.... We have all the more reason to do this as the Indians are so liberal in sharing their goods of the flesh with us such as silver and gold, diamonds, gems, pearls.... The Reformation in Europe, and the discovery of the Indies, have certainly happened around the same moment, by which the Lord has wished to show that now the time has come for the Gospel of the Kingdom to be preached throughout the entire world to be witnessed by all peoples, so that the fullness of heathendom will join in.[64]

Hoornbeeck's and Udemans's fervour in regard to a spiritual recompense for imported "silver and gold, diamonds, gems, pearls" can, at least in part, be explained by the fact that they were reacting implicitly to a radical idea and cultural phenomenon, related to the growth of early modern capitalist economies and their competition as imperial powers. The lawyer Hugo Grotius had notoriously argued, in connection to the Dutch interest in Chinese goods, that trade was one of the necessities of nature. On the first page of his manuscript text *On the Indies* (*De Indis*, written 1603–8), he wrote that the Creator has distributed the world's resources "in accordance with the design of divine justice," in order for "human friendships [to] be fostered by mutual needs and resources, lest individuals, in deeming themselves self-sufficient, might thereby be rendered unsociable."[65] What was so remarkable about this position was its claim that trade was not simply a human right but something demanded by God and nature: "We hold that, by the authority of that primary law of nations whose essential principles are universal and immutable, it is permissible for the Dutch to carry on trade with any nation whatsoever."[66] Consequently,

> anyone who abolishes this system of exchange, abolishes also the highly prized fellowship in which humanity is united. He destroys the opportunities for mutual benefactions. In short, he does violence to nature herself ... In Seneca's opinion, the supreme blessing conferred by nature resides in these facts: that by means of the winds she brings together peoples who are scattered in different localities, and that she distributes the sum of her gifts throughout the various regions in such a way as to make reciprocal commerce a necessity for the members of the human race.[67]

As a modern legal historian has argued, this reasoning about global trade as a "necessity" ordained by nature allowed Grotius to make "the first systematic effort to subordinate the entirety of the early, or mercantilist, modern world-system to an international rule of law derived from 'naturalism,' or natural law."[68] It was this defence of the opening of the whole world to free trade in legal terms that Hoornbeeck and Udemans contrasted in religious terms.

What is more, in reality the ideal of removing all boundaries on the global exchange of goods was completely utopian in the early seventeenth century. When the VOC made its first trade embassy to the imperial court in Beijing and argued Grotius's point of view, the sovereign of the Middle Kingdom is likely to have raised an eyebrow. The Emperor received this assertion from the Dutch:

> The omnipotent God ... hath ordained by eternal wisdom, that no one place should be stored with all manner of things; but whatsoever is either necessary for the life, or convenient for the ornament of mankind, whether production of nature, or invention of art, should be found partly in one country, and partly in another; Divine providence so disposing it, that the wants of this land should be supplied by that, and the defects of that retributed by another, that so by means of commerce, men might enjoy society, and the common wants of all nations might, by receiving mutual relief, knit themselves together in the bonds of friendship.[69]

Not surprisingly, this Dutch plea for free trade fell on deaf ears in China, which did not conceive of other countries as equal counterparts, but as bearers of the tribute that was the Emperor's due. Moreover, the Dutch message did not match the goods they brought. These were not, in fact, home-produced (*fang wu*, 方物), as was essential for a tribute to be valid, according to the complex rules of courtly ritual. As Johan Nieuhof narrated in his account of the embassy, the Imperial magistrates asked:

> whether all the presents which were thus packed up, came directly out of Holland? The embassadours thereupon told them, that some of those goods came out of Holland, as the cloths, looking-glasses, corral, perspective-glasses, all manner of arms, and the furniture of horses; but the rest were added by the Governor-General at Batavia, by order of the high Indian Government in Holland.[70]

The Dutch had to admit that their most impressive gifts had been procured from their extensive trading network in India and South-East Asia, which might explain the failure of their embassy. In China, tribute from foreign sovereigns was typically brought by a ruler's immediate relatives, not by private merchants from the East Asian headquarters of a joint-stock trading company.[71]

To many in the Netherlands as well, the Grotian notion of an unfettered capitalist and globally interconnected world was unpalatable, as the statements by Hoornbeeck and Udemans testify. They may have noted that Grotius could find many classical arguments in favour of his thesis, but fewer biblical ones. They may also have known that, from the start, the composition of Grotius's *On the Indies* was not motivated by ideology (let alone by clear ideas about divinely ordained trade). It was rather a feat of juridical sophistry in defence of a specific act of piracy: the Dutch capture of the Portuguese carrack *Santa Catarina* in the Strait of Malacca on 25 February 1603. The commanding admiral, Jacob van Heemskerck, was Grotius's cousin.[72] Upon its arrival in the Netherlands, the *Santa Catarina* was condoned as "a good and just" prize by the Dutch Admiralty Court.[73] The auction of its Chinese objects in Amsterdam attracted great international interest. The cargo included 1,200 bales of raw Chinese silk; chests filled with coloured damask and silk; large amounts of gold thread or spun gold; cloth woven with gold thread; silk robes and bed canopies spun with gold; "an innumerable quantity of porcelain vessels of all kinds"; and a "thousand other things that are produced in China."[74] Grotius's defence of the seizure and sale of the *Santa Catarina*'s goods, which were worth in excess of three million guilders, confirmed the necessity of the formation of the VOC to coordinate the smaller and less efficient privateering operations of provincial companies. The legality of the Dutch commercial empire in East Asia thus rested on the shaky foundation of a stolen cargo of Chinese porcelain and silk.

As is evident from the above-quoted ministers, not everyone agreed with a full-fledged defence of global capitalism and the legitimacy it sought to provide to the new trading company (sometimes dubbed "the world's first multinational"). In this context, Ronny Spaans has recently described the disapproval of practices such as the importation of foreign medicine.[75] A good example is Johan van Beverwijck's *Inleydinge tot de Hollandtsche geneesmiddelen: ofte kort bericht, dat elck landt ghenoegh heeft tot onderhoudt van het leven, ende de gesondtheydt der inwoonders* (*Introduction to Dutch Medicine: Or Short Notice That Each Country Holds Enough for Its Inhabitants' Livelihood and Health*, 1642). In stark contrast to Grotius, Van

Beverwijck argued that God provided each nation with the natural resources to cope with the illnesses prevalent in that area. Business should therefore be limited to homegrown produce, and not be misdirected to enriching traders or middlemen. Van Beverwijck railed against "foreign and far-fetched drugs ... that served better to make the apothecaries rich than to make the ill healthy."[76] The Latin edition of his book *Autarkeia Bataviae* (*Dutch Autarchy*, 1644) signals how Van Beverwijck saw foreign luxuries as incompatible with the mentality of the ancient Batavian people, forefathers of the Dutch, which was based on the values of equality, humility, and sobriety. This stance stood in explicit contrast to Grotius, who championed international trade as a quintessential "Batavian" accomplishment.[77]

Van Beverwijck mobilized a classic economic argument against international trade: the high prices of imported spices would undermine the national economy, which led him to conclude that importing foreign spices was just as great an evil as the slave trade and the exploitation of natives in the colonies. Echoing this sentiment, the apothecary Lambert Bidloo concluded in his *Dissertatio de re herbaria* (*Treatise on Herbs*, 1683): "Because of the foreigners' wares, our people are assailed by weakness, luxury, and gluttony, like in the days of the Romans."[78] Bidloo's reference to the role of foreign luxuries in undermining the Roman Empire clearly echoed the earlier critiques of Calvin and Barlaeus.

### Asian Material Culture and Philosophical Radicalism

A trope in the Dutch debate on East Asia, in particular China, was an association with radical ideas that, since the impact of Cartesianism from around 1650, had come to shape public intellectual debate as least as much as had the increased contact with the non-Western world. The new information from foreign lands sparked philosophical doubts about the literal truth of the Bible and the universal validity of revealed wisdom. Conversely, the Dutch climate of philosophical scepticism and experimentation resulted in a greater openness towards the potential validity of non-Western religion and philosophy. The insight that the five millennia of continuous Chinese civilization undermined the authority of the Bible as a historical source (according to the Hebrew Bible, the Universal Flood had taken place in 2349 BCE) may have given Chinese cultural artefacts an exciting "radical" tinge. This association may also have been true for the highly original plays set in China by Vondel and Van der Goes. Whereas the former has been seen as a critic of Spinoza, the latter, younger playwright had attended the same Latin school as Spinoza and was acquainted with various "Spinozists." By the end of the century, the association of China with radical new ideas inspired the popular comparison of Confucius with Spinoza. Most explicit was the "Philosopher of Rotterdam," Pierre Bayle, who defined Chinese and Japanese philosophy as varieties of Spinozism.[79]

This comparison was elaborated in various ways. Spinoza's purported atheism and republicanism were paired with Confucianism and with the Chinese "Platonic Republic." Moreover, the Dutch "New Philosophy" was often associated with women, who, as we have seen, were also portrayed as the prime consumers of Chinese material culture.[80] What has been largely ignored in recent discussions on this philosophy is the material substrate – the uniquely ubiquitous place of Chinese material culture in Dutch society – that made discussions about the Celestial Empire so prominent in the first place. A libertine thinker from Spinoza's circle, Isaac Vossius, famously criticized the Hebrew Bible on account of China's greater antiquity. Not only did Vossius praise the superiority of Chinese politics, philosophy, and medicine, but he also extolled Chinese visual arts, especially ceramics, above those of the West.[81] In a general sense, the images on porcelain – and on many Delftware imitations – of peaceful Chinese figures strolling in paradisiacal gardens confirmed an idealized image of utopian tranquillity, in contrast to the ills of contemporary Europe, riven by philosophical upheaval, religious dissent, wars, famine, and illness.

As I have discussed elsewhere, the ubiquity in Dutch everyday life of Chinese porcelain stands in curious contrast to the relative paucity of written statements that explain (or condemn) this taste for a foreign material culture.[82] There was, however, a related commodity that inspired a more heated debate: tea, which had arrived in the Netherlands in 1634. Initially popular among the Dutch in Batavia (where, in 1643, 1400 pounds of tea together with 7635 cups were ordered from China), by the middle of the century tea was sold by many apothecaries in the Dutch Republic.[83] The most eloquent proponent of tea was the medical doctor Cornelis Bontekoe, who ran a chemical laboratory in The Hague and wrote two treatises in defence of Chinese tea and its alleged medical properties. Apparently he advised his clients to consume extraordinary amounts. His texts provide a rare glimpse into how material and intellectual dimensions of the Dutch fascination with China overlapped. As a modern scholar has argued, Bontekoe was "convinced most people's ideas about virtually everything – society, politics and religion, no less than philosophy, science and medicine – were wildly wrong, his writing provides some of the most revealing evidence of the linkages between systematic philosophy, religious controversy and the medical reformism of the age" – which extended, one might add, to non-Western *materia medica* such as tea.[84] His *Tractaat van het excellenste kruyd thee* (*Treatise on Tea, the Most Excellent Herb*, 1678) defended this drink for a variety of reasons including its contribution to longevity, in a chiliastic spirit that foreshadowed Vossius's utopian view of China as a philosopher's republic in which most of the arts and sciences had come to greater fruition than in Europe.[85] As incontrovertible proof, Bontekoe pointed to the sizeable population of China and Japan, where people drink tea all their lives. The popular treatise's first impression (1678) sold out in a few weeks and a second (1679) and third (1685) printing followed.

Detractors, however, accused Bontekoe of having been sponsored by the VOC.[86] The virulence with which the doctor was attacked was not so much due to his Chinese taste, but rather to his being suspected of Spinozist leanings, despite his often-professed dislike of Spinozism. In 1675 Bontekoe was ordered to desist from teaching at the university of Leiden or attending any meetings there. He may have been the medical doctor who tended to Spinoza on his death bed in 1677, if one is to believe an anonymous pamphlet, *Dialogue van een groote thee en tobacq-suyper* (*Dialogue of a Fervent Tea and Tobacco Boozer*, 1680).[87] There is no proof for this allegation, but it confirms Bontekoe's reputation as the controversial "tea doctor." His defence of tea as a panacea resonated with his desire "to reform almost everything [in medicine], fiercely condemning blood-letting, purging and all the usual remedies of traditional medicine, lambasting the apothecaries and most of the rest of the medical profession."[88] He promised that his experimental treatment with Chinese tea would prolong life, convinced that one's hour of death was not prearranged by God or Nature, but depended in large measure on one's lifestyle and diet, an idea that was close to heresy.

In public, however, Bontekoe took care to decry radical thought as a very dangerous "poison," claiming to be actively combating the "monster" Spinoza.[89] This official stance against novelties also characterizes his treatise on tea. He balances his lengthy praise of tea as beneficial to a long and healthy life with a condemnation of the vain interest in Chinese luxury goods. These extravagances seem to have corrupted religion in the Netherlands, which, perhaps not in its doctrines, but in its everyday practices, has returned to heathendom:

> During the last few years tea has, in our country, already found so many
> devotees that in most houses of some standing it is considered a shame not
> to drink it. Vanity and pride which blow up the hearts of nearly all people,

till they almost burst, has introduced a fashion in tea-drinking and its implements, the same as in all other things. People here are indistinguishable
from the Chinese in the costliness of their pots, cups, saucers, basins, tables
of lacquer and of mother-of-pearl, and so on. Our work-masters have also
shown their art in imitating the China and earthenware of that country, and
by means of a strange circulation Holland is beginning to become Asian,
even in dress, and may the Lord prevent it from becoming so in religion,
which, if not in words, has certainly in the practical part of life, almost entirely become heathen again.[90]

The trope that the Dutch were about to turn Asian through their luxurious taste and ability to recreate the sheen of the Chinese wares, a transformation that Vondel had praised, could apparently be interpreted
negatively. Delftware imitations of Chinese themes and styles, and the
fashion for dressing in Asian gowns, were only two symptoms of the Dutch
disease of revelling in transience. Bontekoe was undoubtedly referring
to the *Japonsche rokken* or "Japanese robes" that were popular among students and scholars in an effort to appropriate the learned reputation of
Confucian literati (fig. 15.8). Leiden's professor Jacob Gronovius may
have had Bontekoe in mind when, in 1691, he delivered a festive oration
on the occasion of the return of the victorious stadholder William III.
He proclaimed that "by superior authority, entrance to the university is
forbidden to all those who are not dressed in a civilized manner but in
Asian attire, sustaining a dishonourable public perception."[91]
    More exceptional was Bontekoe's reference to "heathen" religion
shared by the Dutch and the Chinese. This was an explicit reference
to the increasing role of the New Philosophy and its perceived danger:
Spinozism was associated in particular with pantheism (because of Spinoza's identification of God with nature) and with Epicureanism, the
classical teaching that the greatest good is to attain a state of tranquillity
through seeking modest pleasures. Dutch texts about China often compared ideas from Confucianism and Taoism with pantheism and Epicureanism, in an attempt to understand foreign ideas in familiar terms.[92]
Bontekoe's belief that the Dutch had adopted Chinese material culture
to such a degree that they were at risk of embracing a Chinese world view
took this comparison to an extreme.
    Bontekoe's ambiguous stance made him an easy target of ridicule. He
moved to Berlin, where he was reported to have died of an overdose
of his preferred Asian beverage. In 1698, the Dutch satirical journal
*Haegse Mercurius* (*The Hague's Mercury*) made fun of the fashionable taste

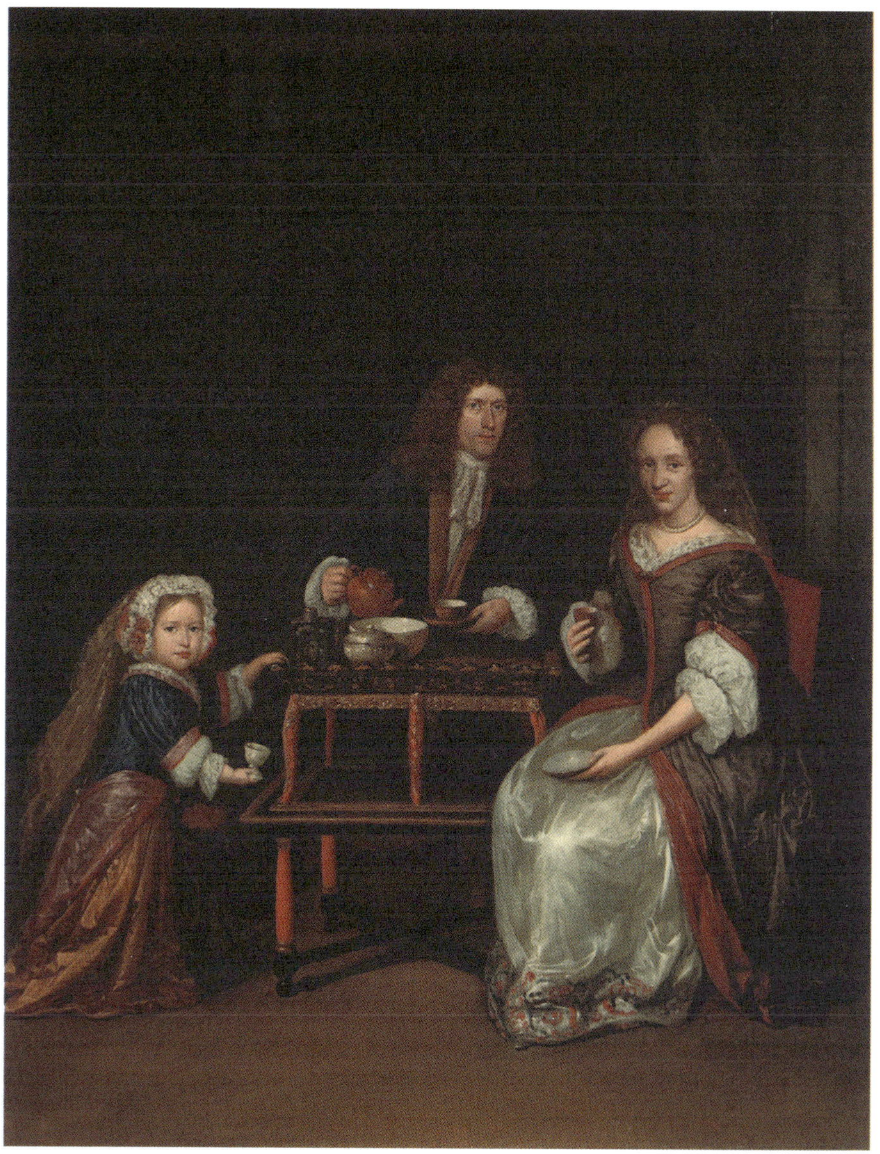

Figure 15.8.  Roelof Koets II (attr.), *Family Taking Tea,* 1680. Oil on canvas, 78.5 x 63 cm. Private collection, England. © Image collection Institute for History and Art History, Utrecht University

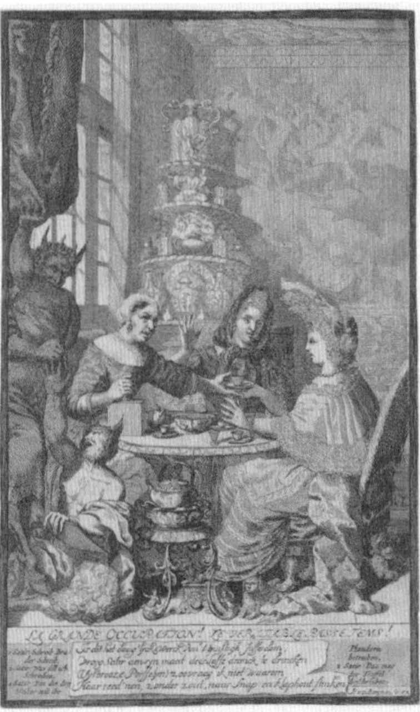

Figure 15.9. Pieter van den Berge, *Ladies Taking Tea ("La Grande Occupation")*, 1694–1737. Etching, 27.3 x 17 cm. Rijksmuseum, Amsterdam, RP-P-1908–4729. © Rijksmuseum Amsterdam

for "pieces of [Indian] chintz, on which were printed in lively colours the grand ideas about tea of Doctor Bontekoe," alongside long lists of VOC cargoes with items such as "delicate bird's nests," a "painting of twelve mandarins with a single brushstroke," or even the "register of the Pre-Adamites" – taking aim at the purported age of Chinese civilization as well as at its esteemed "culture of the brush."[93] Around the turn of the century, Chinese material culture had clearly become *gesunkenes Kulturgut* (a cultural preference that has "sunk" from high to low culture), so popular that the well-known satirist Jacob Campo Weyerman ridiculed the importation of tea and ginseng.[94] Most explicit in its satirical intent was the frontispiece of the aforementioned treatise on *The Depraved and Enchanted World of Coffee and Tea*. It features a smiling satyr who lifts the mask with which he has apparently just beguiled his fashionable audience, and points out with finger and hoof that drinking from the tea set on the floor – presumably porcelain – is a laughing matter. Similar satyrs appear in an illustration of the "grand occupation" of tea drinking, made around the same time by Pieter van den Berge (fig. 15.9). Three ladies sit around a tea table, against the backdrop of a bulging porcelain vase and a bespoke display stand with China dishes, bottles, vases, and statues. To the left, one satyr assures another that the empty chatter of today's "spendthrift damsels" stems from their continuous consumption of such an insipid drink from such fragile tableware.[95]

One way of interpreting such satire is, of course, as a means for the Dutch to deal with the cultural anxiety that had accompanied the import of foreign goods and that had informed the condemnations of vanity by authors such as Six van Chandelier, Bidloo, and Luyken, as well as the interrogations of the Dutch capitalist conscience by Udemans and Hoornbeeck. Towards the end of the century, this condemnation culminated in the equation of China with the radical philosophy that was upsetting beliefs in revealed wisdom and traditional intellectual authority. Humour was one means to dispel the unease that the celebratory accounts of the globalized world of the VOC – by Barlaeus, Vondel, and Van der Goes – tried to repress a little bit too emphatically. The need for ironic self-reflection, however, also indicates the extent to which Chinese material culture had become an integral part of everyday life as well as intellectual debate in the Dutch Republic: Holland was beginning to become Asian.

## NOTES


1 Jonathan Israel, *Dutch Primacy in World Trade, 1585–1740* (Oxford: Oxford University Press, 1989), 414.

2 Robert Finlay, *The Pilgrim Art: Cultures of Porcelain in World History* (Berkeley: University of California Press, 2010), 258.

3 *Courante uyt Italien en Duytschland*, 27–28 June 1634, quoted in Simon Schama, *Overvloed en onbehagen: de Nederlandse cultuur in de Gouden Eeuw* (Amsterdam: Atlas Contact, 1987), 352.

4 Jaap van der Veen, "East Indies Shops in Amsterdam," in *Asia in Amsterdam: The Culture of Luxury in the Golden Age*, ed. Karina Corrigan et al. (Amsterdam: Rijksmuseum; Salem: Peabody Essex Museum, 2016), 134–41.

5 Cf. Suet May Lam, "Fantasies of the East – 'Shopping' in Early Modern Eurasia," in *The Mercantile Effect: Art and Exchange in the Islamicate World during the 17th and 18th Centuries*, ed. Susan Babbaie and Melanie Gibson (London: Gingko Library, 2017), 14–26; and Lam, "Fantasies of the East and

Beyond: Unfolding Early Modern Curiosity about the Unknown" (MA diss.,
Courtauld Institute, 2016).

6 "[A]engaende de Porcelleynen ... dese Oost-Indische handelinghen een
groote menichte der selver inde Nederlande ghebracht hebben ... der
welcker overvloet daghelicx meer ende meer aenwast, ... by de onse by na to
het ghebruyck des ghemeenen volcks ghemeyn gheworden sijn." Johannes
Pontanus, *Historische beschrijvinghe der seer wijt beroemde coop-stadt Amsterdam*
(Amsterdam: Hondius, 1614), 146.

7 "[S]peceriën daervan haer keuckens riecken, Oost-Indische confituren
in porcelainen goetcoop." Arnoldus Buchelius, *VOC-dagboek 1619–1639:
aantekeningen van Arnoldus Buchelius over zijn bewindhebberschap van de
kamer Amsterdam van de VOC (1619–1621) en over de WIC*, transcribed by C.
Smit, 2011 (original at National Archive of the Netherlands, The Hague,
1.11.01.01, nr. 1882 A VI 8, 1 & 2), fol. 142v, undated (fol. 142v describes
a meeting that took place in 1623). See Anne McCants, "Exotic Goods,
Popular Consumption, and the Standard of Living: Thinking about Globalization in the Early Modern World," *Journal of World History* 18, no. 4 (2007):
433–62, and "Asiatic Goods in Migrant and Native-Born Middling Households in Eighteenth-Century Amsterdam," in *Goods from the East, 1600–1800:
Trading Eurasia*, ed. Maxine Berg (Basingstoke: Palgrave MacMillan, 2015),
197–215; and "Modest Households and Globally Traded Textiles: Evidence
from Amsterdam Household Inventories," in *The Birth of Modern Europe:
Culture and Economy, 1400–1800: Essays in Honor of Jan de Vries*, ed. Laura Cru-
zand and Joel Mokyr (Leiden: Brill, 2010), 109–32.

8 Picturae Sinensium variae militium, Deorum (quorum etiam visa ex auro sim-
ulacra) faeminarium, quaedam etiam acu pictae, qualis erat quaedam imago
elephantis cui insidens gubernator hamo illam frontis partem pungebat, quae
ossium expers cerebrum ostendit, ut bestiam pro arbitrio regeret; visi libri
Sinensium admiranda characterum (quos habent ad sexaginta millia) varie-
tate descripti, nulli eorum opistographi ... variae in lapidibus Lydiis figurae
arborum, castellorum, fruticum , urbium, turrium, ruinarum urbium et turrium, castelli pentagoni cum suo exitu ... arcus Sinensis, ex varii coloris lapidibus junctis pictae elegantissmae avium imagines ... flores sericei a Sinensibus ex
arte confecti, Sinensium argentea vasa sine ferrumine, calcei varii Sinensium
serici ex serico rubro et coeruleo. O. Borch, *Olai Borrichii Itinerarium, 1660-1665:
The Journal of the Danish polyhistor Ole Borch, ed. with Introduction and Indices by H.
D. Schepelern*, 3 vols. (Copenhagen: Reitzel, 1983), 2:79-81 (original entry dated
21 March 1662).

9 Simon Schama, *The Embarrassment of Riches: An Interpretation of Dutch Culture
in the Golden Age* (Los Angeles: University of California Press, 1988).

10  According to a card catalogue made by the late Hessel Miedema, now kept at Utrecht University.

11  See the overview (appendix 5) in Thijs Weststeijn, *Foreign Devils and Philosophers: Cultural Encounters between the Chinese, the Dutch, and Other Europeans, 1580–1800* (Leiden: Brill, 2020).

12  Beatrijs Brenninkmeyer-De Rooij, "Indische Exotica auf einem Gemälde des Jacob van Campen im Oraniensaal des 'Huis ten Bosch," in *So weit der Erdkreis reicht: Johann Moritz von Nassau-Siegen, 1604–1679*, ed. Guido de Wird (Kleve: Städtisches Museum Haus Koekkoek, 1979), 57–60; B. Dam-Mikkelsen and T. Lundbaeck, eds., *Etnografiske Genstande i det Kongelige Danske Kunstkammer, 1650–1800* (Copenhagen: Nationalmuseet, 1980), 50, 144. Prince Maurits of Orange was given at least one suit of Japanese armour by the Shogun Tokugawa Hidetada, and it may be this suit that is represented; K. Zandvliet, *The Dutch Encounter with Asia: 1600–1950* (Amsterdam: Rijksmuseum, 2002), 101–6.

13  Three examples: the Countess of Arundel's "Dutch" cabinet in London contained Chinese porcelain; August the Strong built a "Holländische Palast" in Dresden to house his East Asian ceramics; the *Trianon de Porcelaine* at Versailles seems to have been torn down in 1687 because its blue-and-white-pottery-covered exterior was associated too much with France's enemy, the Dutch Republic. Andrew Zega and Bernd H. Dams, *Palaces of the Sun King* (New York: Rizzoli, 2002), 102–3.

14  Cornelis Bontekoe, *Tractaat van het excellenste kruyd thee: 't welk vertoond het regte gebruyk, en de grote kragten van 't selve in gesondheid, en siekten: benevens een kort discours op het leven, de siekte, en de dood: mitsgaders op de medicijne, en de medicijns van dese tijd, en speciaal van ons land. Ten dienste van die gene, die lust hebben, om langer, gesonder, en wijser te leven, als de meeste menschen nu in 't gemeen doen* (The Hague: Hagen, 1678), 309.

15  "Men hoeft voortaen naer China niet te reizen, / Te ploegen zoo veel zees, / Om in Pequijns geweldige pallaizen / Te spreecken den Chinees." Joost van den Vondel, *Op de toetssteene feesttafel der Goden bevlochten met den kunstrijcken parlemoerkrans door D. van Rijswijck* (Amsterdam: De Wees, 1660), quoted in *De werken van Vondel, deel 9: 1660–1663* (Amsterdam: Maatschappij voor goede en goedkope lectuur, 1936), 266.

16  "Met welk een recht magh 't y op zulk een Hoofstad pratten, / De ware stapel van al 's werrelts koopmanschatten." Joannis Antonides van der Goes, *De Ystroom* (Amsterdam: Arentsz, 1671), 125.

17  "Geen wateronheil zal hun moet te wieken korten, / Nu Sina haeren schoot niet weigert uit te storten, / En Atlas gouden ooft met onbekrompen hand / Te schenken, schoon het zucht in een' benauder

band, / En 't ryxhof te Peking, van 's Tarters byl getroffen, / Nog tuigt met wel[k] een smak de grooten nederploffen / Uit hun' verheeven top, daar 't ryk in diepen schroom, / Den grootsten Keizer zagh gehangen aan een boom, / En 't stervende aengezicht, met lootverf overgooten, / Des ryxsaffraenstroom en Kiang den mont geslooten, / Die, vrijer nu het hooft verheffen in de zon, / Hun oegst ontlaeden in de vesten van Kanton, / En met een koninkrijk van schatten ons vereeren." Van der Goes, *Ystroom*, 38.

18 "De muur van Sina ziet nu vry haer aenzien breeken ... Peking draegt op zyn' muur vergeefs zoo grooten moet, / Wanneer het bloedig heir des Tarters, als een vloet, / Die afschiet met gedruisch, en schuurt door steile rotsen, / Ter muurbresse ingestormt, 't Sineesch gezag komt trotsen, / En schokt het stamhuis van Taiminga in den gront, / Dat hondert eeuwen pal op Sinaes troonen stont. / Uw ringmuur geeft tot uw bescherming grooter hoope, / Doorluchte Koopvorstin, en koopmerkt van Europe." Van der Goes, *Ystroom*, 30–1. Marginal note: "De Stad magh zich op haeren muur beter verlaeten, als Sina op haeren ringmuur."

19 Goran Proot and Johan Verberckmoes, "Japonica in the Jesuit Drama of the Southern Netherlands," *Journal: Bulletin of Portuguese-Japanese Studies* 5 (2002): 27–47.

20 On the Jesuits' use of silk, see Liam Brockey, "Authority, Poverty, and Vanity: Jesuit Missionaries and the Use of Silk in Early Modern East Asia," *Anais de História de Além-Mar* 17 (2016): 179–222.

21 Noël Golvers, "De recruteringstocht van M. Martini, S.J. door de Lage Landen in 1654: over geomantische kompassen, Chinese verzamelingen, lichtbeelden en R.P. Wilhelm van Aelst, S.J.," *De zeventiende eeuw* 10, no. 2 (1994): 331–50; Johan Nieuhof, *Het Gezantschap der Neêrlandtsche Oost-Indische Compagnie, aan den grooten Tartarischen Cham ... beneffens een naukeurige beschryving der Sineesche steden, dorpen, regeering* (Amsterdam: Van Meurs, 1665); Olfert Dapper, *Gedenkwaerdig bedryf der Nederlandsche Oost-Indische Maetschappye op de kuste en in het keizerrijk van Taising of Sina: behelzende het tweede gezandschap ... en het derde gezandschap ... beneffens een beschryving van geheel Sina* (Amsterdam, 1670); Athanasius Kircher, *Toonneel van China: door veel, zo geestelijke als wereltlijke, geheugteekenen, verscheide vertoningen van de natuur en kunst, en blijken van veel andere gedenkwaerdige dingen, geopent en verheerlykt* (Amsterdam: Van Waesberghe, 1668). Cf. Georg Balthasar Probst, *Vue d'optique of an inner courtyard of the Imperial palace, 1766–90*, hand-coloured etching and engraving, J. Paul Getty Museum, Los Angeles; discussed in M. Reed and P. Demattè, *China on Paper: European and Chinese Works from the Late Sixteenth to the Early Nineteenth Century* (Los Angeles: Getty Research Institute, 2007), 13.

22 Simon de Vries, *Curieuse aenmerckingen der bysonderste Oost en West-Indische verwonderens-waerdige dingen; nevens die van China, Africa, en andere gewesten des werelds* (Utrecht: Ribbius, 1682), 4:879–80.

23 Liam Brockey, "The Cruelest Honor: The Relics of Francis Xavier in Early Modern Asia," *Catholic Historical Review* 101, no. 1 (2015): 41–64.

24 "O heiligh Kerckjuweel / Van Zaligen Xaveer, / Die in het Oostersch deel / Der weerelt, Jesus' eer / Verkondigende, u streeck / Met zijn gewijde hant." Joost van den Vondel, "Op het Pater Noster des zaligen Vaders en Apostels van OostIndien, Francois Xaveer" (1642), in *Verscheidene Gedichten* (Amsterdam: Hartgers, 1644), 223.

25 "Chineesche en Iaponsche schilderyen. ... Daer hangen uitgeschildert die plaetzen, dicht by China gelegen, waer aen men speurt, wat een gunst de Nederlanders by veergelege volcken dagelijcx meer en meer vinden." Caspar Barlaeus, *Blyde inkomst der allerdoorluchtighste koninginne, Maria de Medicis, t'Amsterdam*, trans. Joost van den Vondel (Amsterdam: Blaeu, 1639), 37; Latin original: *Medicea Hospes, sive descriptio publicae gratulationis, qua Serenissimam, Augustissimamque Reginam, Mariam de Medicis, excepit Senatus Populusque Amstelodamensis* (Amsterdam, 1638).

26 "Curieusheden van lackwercken, als Chinesche schutten, Japansche comptoiren, vort Japansche zyde rocken, syde stoffen, lywaten, thee en diergelycke." Visit by the Prince of Orange, 18 November 1683 (National Archive The Hague, VOC Archief Resoluties Heeren Zeventien, 18 November 1683, 1.04.02, inv.nr. 154); I thank Willemijn van Noord for this reference.

27 W. Jeeninga, *Het Oostindisch Huis en het St. Jorishof te Amsterdam* (Zwolle: Waanders, 1995).

28 "De oogen van MEDICIS verdwaelden; en zy beelde zich in, ziende en aentastende 't uitheemsche en ongewoone bancket, datze by den Indiaenen, Molucken, Persiaenen Arabiers, Iaponesen, en Chinesen te gast was." Barlaeus, *Blyde inkomst*, trans. Vondel, 40.

29 "[D]e vruchten en 't gewas van Persiaenen, Arabiers, Molucken, Iaponesen, en Chineesen, aengerecht in groote en ruime porceleine lampetschotels, die, op een lange tafel in orden gestelt, om haer vreemdigheid, de Koningin vermaeckten." Barlaeus, *Blyde inkomst*, trans. Vondel, 41.

30 Elmer Kolfin, "Omphalos mundi: The Pictorial Tradition of the Theme of Amsterdam and the Four Continents, circa 1600–1665," in *Aemulatio: Imitation, Emulation and Invention in Netherlandish Art from 1500 to 1800. Essays in Honor of Eric Jan Sluijter*, ed. A. Boschloo et al. (Leiden: Primavera, 2011), 382–92, especially 387.

31 "[G]ing in verscheide winckels naerstigh vraegen na den prijs van waren en porceleinen, en bejegende de winckeliers vriendelijck, bood en dong na

koopers wijze. ... Dus geliet ze zich by de burgers als een koopwijf, en niet als een Koningin." Barlaeus, *Blyde inkomst*, trans. Vondel, 69.

32  "[E]enige fraeyigheden van porceleinen, en kostelijcke Iaponsche kisten, kunstigh met lack, goud, en parlemoer ingeleit." Ibid., 70.

33  "Het is 'er met waren en koopmanschappen altijd eb en vloed ... Deze Compagnie, van kleen opgekomen, is heden ... zoo hoogh geklommen en gesteigert, dat elcx ingeleide hoofdzom menighmael verdubbelt is." Ibid., 38.

34  "Yemant moght met recht zeggen van deze vaert, 't geen eertijds Plinius zeide, van des grooten Pompejus zege over Mithridates, dat deze meest oirzaeck was, dat de Romeinen, in plaets van hunnen gewoonen dagelijckzen overzeeschen huisraed, vaten van parlemoer en kostelijck gesteente begonnen te gebruicken." Ibid., 38.

35  E.g., Pliny, *Naturalis Historia*, XXII, 118.

36  Karl-Wilhelm Weeber, *Luxus im alten Rom: Die Schwelgerei, das süße Gift* (Darmstadt: Primus, 2003); Paul Freedman, *Out of the East: Spices and the Medieval Imagination* (New Haven: Yale University Press, 2008).

37  John Calvin, commentary on Isaiah 2:12–16, "And upon elegant pictures," in *Commentary on the Book of the Prophet Isaiah, by John Calvin*, trans. William Pringle (Edinburgh: Calvin Translation Society, 1850–3), https://www.ccel.org/ccel/calvin/calcom13.ix.i.html.

38  "'t Zyn Vaten, doch zy doen geen nut, / Om Spyze op den Dis te draagen, / Daar't leven meê word onderstut, / Maar dienen enkel't welbehaagen, / Tot Oogen lust en Pronkery: / 't Zyn Leege Vaten, t'allen tyde; / Dies gaat behoeven haar voorby, / En Nooddruft schuift haar aan een zyde." Jan Luijken, *Het leerzaam huisraad* (Amsterdam: Arentz & Vander Sys, 1711), 119–20, fig. XXXIV.

39  See Thijs Weststeijn, "Cultural Reflections on Porcelain in the Seventeenth-Century Netherlands," in *Chinese and Japanese Porcelain for the Dutch Golden Age*, ed. Jan van Campen and Titus Eliëns (Amsterdam: Rijksmuseum, 2014), 213–29, 265–8.

40  Pieter Claesz, *Still Life with Turkey Pie*, signed and dated (on the knife) "A° 1627 PC," oil on panel, 75 x 132 cm, Rijksmuseum, Amsterdam, SK-A-4646.

41  Globe by Pieter van den Keere and Petrus Plancius (four editions of the globe, dating to between 1614 and 1645, are extant). See Andrew Moore, Nathan Flis, and Francesca Vanke, *The Paston Treasure: Microcosm of the Known World* (New Haven: Yale University Press, 2018).

42  "Het is te verwonderen datter treffelijcke lieden zijn die groot gelt besteden aen Kinckhorens en Mosselschelpen, daer niet fraeys aen en is als de seltsaemheyd." Roemer Visscher, *Sinnepoppen* (Amsterdam: Blaeu, 1614),

emblem IV; Sam Segal, *A Prosperous Past: The Sumptuous Still Life in the Nether-lands, 1600–1700* (The Hague: SDU, 1989), 77–9.

43 Thomas Browne, *Pseudo-doxia epidemica, dat is: Beschryvinge van verscheyde algemene dwalingen des volks,* trans. J. Grindal (Amsterdam: Van Goedes-bergh, 1668), 87–8; English original, *Pseudodoxia Epidemica: Or, Enquiries into Very Many Received Tenents, and Commonly Presumed Truths* (London: Ekins, 1656), 72–3. Nieuhof, *Het gezantschap,* 90–1.

44 Shakespeare, *Measure for Measure,* ed. A R Braunmuller (Cambridge, UK: Cambridge University Press, 1991 [1623]), 2.4.126–31.

45 Jan Huygen van Linschoten, *Itinerario, voyage ofte schipvaert, naer Oost ofte Por-tugaels Indien inhoudende een corte beschryvinghe der selver landen ende zee-custen* (Amsteredam: Claesz, 1596).

46 "[E]en heerlijcke Natuerlijcke Schoonheyd, en uytgeleesene Gestalte; in lieflijckheyd, vriendelijckheyd en aenlocklijckheyd alle Heydensche Vrou-wen des gantschen Werelds overwinnende." De Vries, *Curieuse aenmerckin-gen,* 3:413.

47 Each of Amalia's four daughters designed and installed porcelain rooms in their homes, evocative of their mother's. C. Willemijn Fock, "The Apart-ments of Frederick Henry and Amalia of Solms: Princely Splendour and the Triumph of Porcelain," in *Princely Patrons: The Collection of Frederick Henry of Orange and Amalia van Solms in The Hague,* ed. Marlies Enklaar (Zwolle: Waanders; The Hague: Mauritshuis, 1997), 76–86, especially 84; cf. Cordula Bischoff, "Women Collectors and the Rise of the Porcelain Cabinet," in *Chi-nese and Japanese Porcelain for the Dutch Golden Age,* ed. Jan van Campen and Titus Eliëns (Zwolle: Waanders, 2014), 171–89. On the gendered appreci-ation of porcelain, see: He Feng, "Embodied Beauty: Feminising Chinese Ceramics in Eighteenth-Century China and Europe," in *Exchanging Gazes: Between China and Europe 1669–1907,* ed. Matthias Weiß et al. (Petersberg, Imhof; Berlin: Staatliche Museen zu Berlin, 2017), 98–114; Susan Broom-hall and Jacqueline van Gent, "Gendered Strategies of Porcelain as Power in the Early Modern House of Orange-Nassau," in *Gender and Political Culture in Early Modern Europe,* ed. James Daybell and Svante Norrhem (London: Routledge, 2016), 49–67; David Porter, "Gendered Utopias in Transcultural Context," in *The Chinese Taste in Eighteenth-Century England* (Cambridge, UK: Cambridge University Press: 2010), 57–77; Stacey Sloboda, "Porcelain Bod-ies: Gender, Acquisitiveness, and Taste in Eighteenth-Century England," in *Material Cultures 1740–1920: The Meanings and Pleasures of Collecting,* ed. Alla Myzelev and John Potvin (Burlington, VT: Ashgate, 2009), 19–36; and D.M. Mitchell, "The Influence of 'Tartary' and the Indies on Social Attitudes and Material Culture in England and France, 1650–1730," in *A Taste for the*

*Exotic: Foreign Influences on Early Eighteenth-Century Silk Designs*, ed. A. Jolly (Riggisberg: Abegg-Stiftung, 2007), 11–43.

48 "Dese dwaasheid en uitzinnigheid der vrouwen … is dan ten hoogsten schadelyk, en wel in 't bysonder in een Land als Holland, alleen door de koopmanschap bestaande." Anonymous, *De gedebaucheerde en betoverde koffy en thee wereld* (Amsterdam: Ten Hoorn, 1701), 483.

49 "[Z]ommige Burgers Vrouwen … door het oprechten van Cabinetten met Oud Porcelein; … het is nog een veel Edeler Liefhebbery de Kunst in een schoon Stuk Schildery te bespiegelen, als het gekrabbel der Haanepooten van de Japoneezen en Chineezen, op eenige stukken verglaasde Aarden, het geen verloren is als het vald." Jan Claus Willem van Laar, *Het groot ceremonie-boek der beschaafde zeeden* (Amsterdam: Mourik, 1735), 415.

50 John Gay, *To a Lady on Her Passion for Old China* (London: Clarendon, 1725).

51 Agnes Jeannette Hoeufft, *Portrait of Catharina Copal (1644–1723)*, 1675–99, oil on canvas, 52.5 x 45.5 cm, private collection, location unknown. Image at https://rkd.nl/nl/explore/images/130766.

52 "Wie leeven kan te huis, in vree, / Wat jaaght hy naa de ryke zee?" J. Six van Chandelier, "Nooddruft is genoeg," in *Poëzy* (Amsterdam: Pluimert, 1657), 165–6, especially 166, lines 5–6. For more on Six, see R. Spaans, *Dangerous Drugs: The Self-Presentation of the Merchant-Poet Joannes Six van Chandelier (1620–1695)* (Amsterdam: Amsterdam University Press, 2020).

53 "Luksaaligh is hy, die genoegen, / In land, schept, als geleent te ploegen: … Een simple borger leeft veel blyder, / Nooit schroomich voor den bitsen nyder. / De nachtmeer van 't ontslaaprigh geld / Doet, hem vermoeit, vergeefs geweld. / De suchtvloek van de goude scherven / Verdoemt hem niet: gedenk te sterven, / O gierge dwaas, in deesen nacht. / Wat baat hem rykdom dan, en pracht?" Six van Chandelier, "Nooddruft is genoeg," 166, lines 19–34.

54 Schama, *Overvloed en onbehagen*, 345.

55 S. Broomhall, "'Such Fragile Jewels': The Emotional Role of Chinese Porcelain Early Modern Jesuit Missions," in *Changing Hearts: Performing Jesuit Emotions between Europe, Asia and the Americas*, ed. Y. Haskell and R. Garrod (Leiden: Brill, 2019), 261–83.

56 T. Dijkstra, "The Chinese Imprint: Printing and Publishing Chinese Religion and Philosophy in the Dutch Republic 1595–1700" (PhD diss., University of Amsterdam, 2019), especially chap. 1.

57 Johannes Hoornbeeck, *De conversione Indorum et Gentilium*, trans. Ineke Sloots (Amsterdam: Van Waesberghe, 1669), 49; Trude Dijkstra and Thijs Weststeijn, "Constructing Confucius in the Low Countries," *De zeventiende eeuw* 32, no. 2 (2017): 137–64.

58 Weststeijn, "Just Like Zhou," 106.

59 "[S]eer lustigh ende playsantigh landt, als een lust-hof." Godfried Udemans, 't Geestelyck roer van 't coopmans schip (Dordrecht: Boels, 1655; first
pub. 1638), 94; on porcelain, 93; on Chinese inventions, 111.

60 Johannes Hoornbeeck, On the Conversion of Indians and Heathens: An Annotated Translation of De conversione Indorum et gentilium (1669), ed. and trans.
Ineke Loots and Joke Spaans (Leiden: Brill, 2019), 39.

61 Hoornbeeck, On the Conversion of Indians, 40–1.

62 Atahanasius Kircher, China Illustrata: Translated by Dr. Charles D. Van Tuyl from the
1677 Original Latin Edition (Muskogee: Indiana University Press, 1986), 160.

63 "[D]en rijckdom ende de goederen deser wereldt, gemeynelijck in den
meesten overvloedt worden beseten an sulcke menschen, die Godt niet en
kennen, oft niet en dienen naer synen wille.... Hier uyt volght, dat den rech-
ten rijckdom niet en bestaet in den overvloedt van gout, silver, diamanten,
peerlen ... Laet dan de rijcke niet hoovaerdigh zijn op haren tijdtlijcken
ende verganckelijcken rijckdom, want de Indianen, die maer Heydenen en
zijn, zijn van silver en goudt, landt en zandt, al vele rijcker: maer laetse hare
schatten vergaderen in den Hemel, daer de motte ende den roest niet en
schendet, ende daer de dieven niet door en graven noch stelen." Udemans,
Geestelyck roer, 102.

64 "Onder-en-tusschen moeten wy met dese arme Heydenen bekommert zijn, om
haer tot Christum te brengen, gelijck de Saxones, ende de Engelschen, eertijdt
met onse Voorouders zijn bekommert geweest.... Te meer, moeten wy dit doen,
overmits dese Indianen soo liberael zijn, om ons mede te deelen van hare vlees-
schelijcke goederen, als silver ende gout, diamanten, gesteenten, peerlen....
De reformatie in Europa, ende de ontdeckinge van de Indien, zijn dan vast
ontrent eenen tijdt geschiedt, daer mede de Heere heeft willen toonen, dat nu
den tijdt gekomen was, dathet Euangelium des Koninghrijcx door de geheele
wereldt soude gepredickt worden, tot getuygenisse allen volckeren, op dat de
volheydt der Heydenen soude inkomen." Udemans, Geestelyck roer, 104–5.

65 De Indis was published as De iure praedae commentarius; modern edition, Hugo
Grotius, Commentary on the Law of Prize and Booty, ed. and intro. Martine van
Ittersum (Indianapolis: Liberty Fund, 2006), https://oll.libertyfund.org/
titles/1718, 182, thesis 1. Cf. Hugo Grotius, Mare liberum sive de iure quod
Bavavis competit ad Indicana commercia dissertatio (Leiden: Elzevier, 1618), 2.

66 Grotius, On the Law of Prize and Booty, 182.

67 Ibid., 183.

68 Eric Wilson, "Making the World Safe for Holland: De Indis of Hudo Grotius
and International Law as Geo-Culture," Review of the Fernand Braudel Center
32, no. 3 (2009), 239–87.

69 Gabriel de Magalhães, "A Narrative of the Success of an Embassage sent by John Maatzuyker de Badem, General of Batavia, unto the Emperour of China & Tartary," in Johan Nieuhof, *An Embassy from the East-India Company of the United Provinces to the Great Tartar Cham, Emperour of China* (London: Macock, 1669), 12. Cf. M. Keevak, *Embassies to China: Diplomacy and Cultural Encounters Before the Opium Wars* (Basingstoke: Palgrave Macmillan, 2017), 82.

70 Nieuhof, *Embassy from the East-India Company*, 116.

71 Keevak, *Embassies to China*, 74.

72 Martine van Ittersum, "Hugo Grotius in Context: Van Heemkerck's Capture of the Santa Catarina and its Justification in *De Jure Praedae* (1604–1606)," *Asian Journal of the Social Sciences* 31, no. 3 (2003): 511–48.

73 J.H.W. Verzijl, *The Law of the Maritime Prize* (Dordrecht: Kluwer, 1992), 10, and Van Ittersum, "Grotius in Context."

74 Levinius Hulsius, *Achte Schiffart oder kürtze Beschreibung etlicher Reysen so die Holländer und Seeländer in die Ost Indien von Anno 1599. biß Anno 1604. gethan* (Frankfurt, 1605); quoted in Teresa Canepa, *Silk, Porcelain and Lacquer: China and Japan and their Trade with Western Europe and the New World 1500–1644* (London: Holberton, 2016), 89–91.

75 R. Spaans, "Exotica, Ornaments and Idolatry in the Poetry of Jan Six van Chandelier (1620–1695)," *De zeventiende eeuw* 32, no. 2 (2017): 115–36.

76 "Vremden en ver-gehaelde Drooghen ... die meerder streckten om de Apothekers rijck, dan om de Krancken ghesont te maken." J. van Beverwijck, *Inleydinge tot de Hollandtsche genees-middelen: ofte kort bericht, dat elck landt ghenoegh heeft tot onderhoudt van het leven, ende de gesondtheydt der inwoonders* (Amsterdam 1651; first pub. 1642), 8.

77 Marijke Meijer Drees, *Andere landen, andere mensen: de beeldvorming van Holland versus Spanje en Engeland omstreeks 1650* (The Hague: SDU, 1997), 41.

78 Lambert Bidloo, *Dissertatio de re herbaria* (Amsterdam: Boom, 1683), 34.

79 Thijs Weststeijn, "Spinoza sinicus: an Asian Paragraph in the History of the Radical Enlightenment," *Journal of the History of Ideas* 68, no. 4 (2007): 537–61; Jonathan Israel, "Admiration of China and Classical Chinese Thought in the Radical Enlightenment (1685–1740)," *Taiwan Journal of East Asian Studies* 4, no. 1 (2007): 1–25; Jonathan Israel, "The Battle over Confucius and Classical Chinese Philosophy in European Early Enlightenment Thought (1670–1730)," *Frontiers of Philosophy in China* 8, no. 2 (2013): 183–98; for the French situation, Virgile Pinot, *La Chine et la formation de l'esprit philosophique en France, 1640–1740* (Paris: Geuthner, 1932).

80 One example is the ideal of a women's university, which Hendrik Smeeks in 1708 associated with a Chinese-style utopia under the benevolent rule of

Confucius's favourite student. See A. Agnes Sneller, "Utopia of een vrou-
wenuniversiteit omstreeks 1700," *Literatuur* 5 (1988): 141–8.

81  Isaac Vossius, "De artibus et scientiis Sinarum," in *Isaaci Vossii variarum obser-
vationum liber* (London, 1685), 69–85; Thijs Weststeijn, "Vossius's Chinese
Utopia," in *Isaac Vossius (1618–1689): Between Science and Scholarship*, ed. Erik
Jorink and Dirk van Miert (Leiden: Brill, 2012), 207–42.

82  Weststeijn, "Cultural Reflections."

83  Pim van Oostrum, "Trammelant rond de theestoof: over de sekse van thee
(en koffie)," *Mededelingen van de Stichting Jacob Campo Weyerman* 29 (2006):
49–66, especially 52.

84  Jonathan Israel, "Enlightenment, Radical Enlightenment and the 'Medical
Revolution' of the Late Seventeenth and Eighteenth Centuries," in *Medicine
and Religion in Enlightenment Europe*, ed. Andrew Cunningham (London:
Routledge, 2017), unpaginated e-book.

85  Weststeijn, "Vossius's Chinese Utopia."

86  He defended himself in the treatise's second edition (The Hague: Hagen,
1678), containing an *Apologie van den Autheur tegens sijne Lasteraars*.

87  Anonymous [possibly Adriaan van Beverland], *Dialogue van een groote thee en
tobacq-suyper, over het wonderlijck hart gevecht voorgevallen in den Haag tusschen
[...] Johan Fredericq Swetser, alias doctor Helvetius, en mennoniste Kees alias Dr.
Cornelis Bontekoe* (s.l.: 1680). The only surviving copy is in The Hague, City
Archive, Gemeentearchief Hgst 5361.

88  Israel, "Medical Revolution," unpaginated.

89  Ibid.

90  "Onse Thee heeft alrede in ons land zedert enige Jaren soo veel liefhebbers,
dat men in de meeste huysen van enig aansien, voor schande houd geen
Thee te drinken. De vaniteyt en de hovardye, die't hert van meest alle de
menschen tot berstens toe opblaast, heeft een Mode gelijk in alle dingen, soo
ook in Thee drinken, en gereetschap daar toe, ingevoerd. Men wijkt geen
Chinesen in kostelijkheyt van potten, kopjens, schoteltjes, bakjens, tafels van
lak, en paarlemoer, en wat dies meer is; onse werkmeesters hebben ook haar
kunst getoont, en nageb[o]otst 't Porceleyn en aard-werk van China, en door
een wondere circulatie begind Holland Indiaansch te worden tot de kleding
toe, en gave God! selfs ook niet tot de religie toe, die indiense niet met
woorden, sekerlijk sy is met de praktyk van leven, by na geheel wederom Hey-
densch geworden." Bontekoe, *Tractaat van het excellenste kruyd thee*, 308–9.

91  "Ex auctoritate superiorum interdicitur ingressus Academiae omnibus
illis, qui non civili more vestiti Asiatico habitu, conspectum publicum
dedecorare sustinent." Molhuysen, *Bronnen tot de geschiedenis der Leidsche
universiteit 1574–1811: Part IV (1682–1715)* (The Hague: Nijhoff, 1913–24),

87. Cf. A.M. Lubberhuizen-van Gelder, "Japonsche Rocken," *Oud Holland* 62 (1947): 137–51, and *Oud Holland* 64 (1949): 25–38; Wybe Kuitert, "De Japanse watten van Constantijn Huygens," *Spiegel der Letteren* 56, no. 4 (2014): 539–50; Myranda Hoogen, "Japonse rocken en andere zeldzaamheden: de handel van Bartel Jansen Bruijnvis, koopman en Oostindisch winkelier in de Amsterdamse Warmoesstraat," *Amstelodamum* 101, no. 2 (2014): 78–101; Anne Gerritsen, "Domesticating Goods from Overseas: Global Material Culture in the Early Modern Netherlands," *Journal of Design History* 29, no. 3 (2016): 228–44.

92 Olfert Dapper, *Atlas Chinensis ... Englished by John Ogilby* (London: Johnson, 1671), 575, compares the philosopher "Xexia" to Democritus, "Fe" (the Buddha) to Pythagoras and the Stoics (579), and the "Taokiao" sect to the Epicureans (592).

93 "[E]enige Citsen, daer men met levendige couleuren op gedrukts iet de *idées* van Doctor Bontekoe over de Thè." Hendrik Doedijns, *Haegse Mercurius* 69 (2 April 1698); "In de Carga of lading van de Oost-Indische Retour-Schepen zyn eenige delicate Vogel-nesjes ... Eenige Schilderyen, daar onder 12 Mandaryns met eene streek gemaakt." *Haegse mercurius* 97 (9 July 1698), [3]; "'t Geslagt-register der Praeadamiten." *Haegse Mercurius* 103 (30 July 1698), [1–2]. All quoted from Edwin van Kley, "Qing Dynasty China in Seventeenth-Century Dutch Literature 1644–1700," in *The History of the Relations Between the Low Countries and China in the Qing Era (1644–1911)*, ed. W.F. Vande Walle and Noël Golvers (Leuven: Verbiest Instituut, 2003), 217–34, especially 230.

94 *Den Amsterdamsche Hermes* 2, no. 4 (20 October 1722), 25–30. Ginseng was discussed seriously in Johannes Breynius, *Dissertatio botanico-medica de radice gin-sem* (Leiden: Elzevier, 1700), and Nicolaes Witsen, *Noord en Oost Tartarye* (Amsterdam: Halma, 1705), 45–6. Ginseng was brought to the Netherlands in large quantities by, among others, Johan van Hoorn; its cost in Amsterdam ran to 18 guilders per 100 grams.

95 "Is dit het daag'lycks werck van 't quistigh Jufferdom,/ Vroeg Satir aen syn maat dees laffe dranck te drinken / Uyt brooze Porsseleyn, zoo vraag ik niet waarom / Haar reed'nen, zonder zout, naar Snap en klaphout stinken."

# Contributors

**Angela Vanhaelen** is Professor of Art History at McGill University, Montreal. Her research focuses on the art and culture of the Dutch Republic. Her most recent book is *The Moving Statues of Seventeenth-century Amsterdam: Automata, Waxworks, Fountains, Labyrinths* (Pennsylvania State University Press, 2022).

**Bronwen Wilson** is the Edward W. Carter Chair in European Art and the Director of the Center for 17th- and 18th-Century Studies and William Andrews Clark Memorial Library at the University of California, Los Angeles. Her current book project, "Otherworldly Natures: Lithic Formations, In-Between Spaces, and Early Modern Italian Art," probes artistic engagement with quarries and riverbeds.

**Kristopher W. Kersey** is Assistant Professor of the Arts of Japan at the University of California, Los Angeles. His research focuses on the intersecting histories of Japanese art, design, and aesthetics. His article "The Afterlife of the Western Canon: Archive and Eschatology in Contemporary Japan" recently appeared in *The Art Bulletin.*

**Carrie Anderson** is Associate Professor of Art History at Middlebury College, Vermont. Her primary area of research is the art of the seventeenth-century Dutch Republic, within which she focuses on themes related to inter- and intracultural diplomacy and gift exchange. Her current book project, *The Art of Diplomacy in the Early Modern Netherlands: Gift-Giving at Home and Abroad,* is forthcoming from Amsterdam University Press.

**Elisa Antonietta Daniele** received her PhD in Art History from Ca' Foscari University of Venice in 2018. She has been an Ahmanson-Getty postdoctoral fellow at the Center for Seventeenth- and Eighteenth-Century Studies at the University of California, Los Angeles, and a Berenson Fellow at Harvard University – Villa I Tatti. Elisa is currently a Marie Skłodowska-Curie Postdoctoral Fellow at the University of Bologna and UCLA, with a project on the Baroque ballets staged at the court of Savoy in Turin.

**Benjamin Schmidt** is the Costigan Professor of History at the University of Washington, Seattle. His current work explores various ways early modern Europeans engaged with Asia through material technologies and material things. His most recent book, *Inventing Exoticism: Geography, Globalism, and Europe's Early Modern World* (2015; paperback, 2019; Chinese trans., 2020), was selected as a finalist for the Kenshur Prize.

**Helen Smith** is Professor of English Literature at the University of York, UK. She is author of *Grossly Material Things: Women and Book Production in Early Modern England* (2012) and co-editor of *Renaissance Paratexts* (2011), *The Oxford Handbook of the Bible in Early Modern England* (2015), and *Conversions: Gender and Religious Change in Early Modern Europe* (2017). Her current monograph project is an ambitious account of early modern matter and its shifting forms.

**Daniela Bleichmar** is Professor of Art History and History at the University of Southern California. Her research and teaching address the history of images, objects, and texts in colonial Latin America and early modern Europe, focusing particularly on the histories of science, knowledge production, cultural encounters and exchanges, collecting, and books. Her current work on *Codex Mendoza*, an illustrated manuscript produced in early colonial Mexico, traces the extraordinary life of this transcultural object from Mexico City in the 1540s to London in the 1830s.

**Ting Chang** is Associate Professor of Art History at the University of Nottingham, UK. Her monograph *Travel, Collecting, and Museums of Asian Art in Nineteenth-Century Paris* was published by Ashgate in 2013 and is available in paperback with Routledge. She is currently working on a book project on European maps, games, optical devices, and spectacles from the seventeenth to the nineteenth century.

**Emine Fetvacı** is the Norma Jean Calderwood University Professor in Islamic and Asian Art at Boston College. Her research focuses on the arts of the book in the early modern Islamic world. Her latest monograph, *The Album of the World Emperor: Cross-Cultural Collecting and Album Making at the Ottoman Court* (Princeton University Press, 2019), focuses on an imperial album created for the Ottoman sultan Ahmed I (r. 1603–17), and examines the art and architecture produced during the sultan's reign.

**Patricia Badir** is Professor of English at the University of British Columbia, Vancouver. She is a specialist in Renaissance drama and poetry with a particular interest in religious writing. The first of her current two book projects, *Shakespeare from Here*, is a place-based study of Shakespeare and the West Coast. Her second project, *The Design of Theatrical Wonder*, considers the theory and practice of theatre director Roy Mitchell and the matter of the theatrical archive.

**Lyle Massey** is Associate Professor of Art History and Visual Studies at the University of California, Irvine. She is author of *Picturing Space, Displacing Bodies: Anamorphosis in Early Modern Theories of Perspective* (Penn State University Press, 2007), editor of *The Treatise on Perspective: Published and Unpublished* (National Gallery of Art, Center for Advanced Study in the Visual Arts/Yale University Press, 2003) and co-editor with James Nisbet of *The Invention of the American Desert: Art, Land, and the Politics of Environment* (University of California Press, 2021).

**Gavin Hollis** is Associate Professor in the Department of English at Hunter College, City University of New York. He specializes in Shakespeare and early modern drama. He is the author of *The Absence of America: The London Stage 1576–1624*, published by Oxford University Press in 2015. He is working on a book project tentatively titled *Shakespeare's Mappery*, which explores the deployment of the cartographic imaginary across a range of cultural fields (architecture, the decorative arts, drama, and poetry).

**J.B. Shank** is Professor in the Department of History and Scholar of the College of Liberal Arts at the University of Minnesota. He is the author of two books on the eighteenth-century French reception of Isaac Newton's mathematics and physics, and has edited a special issue of the *Journal of Early Modern History*, 21.5 (2017), entitled "After the Scientific Revolution: Thinking Globally about the Histories of the Modern Sciences."

More recently, he published "Between Isaac Newton and Enlightenment Newtonianism: The 'God Question' in the Eighteenth Century" in *Science without God? Rethinking the History of Scientific Naturalism,* ed. Peter Harrison and John Roberts (Oxford University Press, 2019), a work that stems from his current research project, "Enlightenment Cosmology, or Understanding All That Was and Is before the Advent of Astrophysics."

**John M.D. Pohl** is Adjunct Professor in the Department of Art History at the University of California, Los Angeles. His research focuses on the pre-Columbian civilizations of southern Mexico and the roles they played in a Pacific coastal exchange system that extended from Oaxaca through West Mexico to the greater American Southwest. He has enjoyed a prolific career as a writer, designer, and curator for museums and exhibitions across the country, including the Getty Villa, the Los Angeles County Museum of Art, and the Princeton University Art Museum.

**Danny Zborover** is Head of the Americas Section at the British Museum. As an anthropological and historical archaeologist, he specializes in the interdisciplinary study of literate societies. He is a co-director and instructor at several projects and field schools in Mexico and Peru, collaborating with descendent communities in the study of colonialism, territoriality, mobility, social memory, mining, and pirates. His co-edited book, *Bridging the Gaps: Integrating Archaeology and History in Oaxaca, Mexico,* was published in 2015.

**Thijs Weststeijn** is Professor of Art History before 1800 at Utrecht University, where he chairs the project "Histories of Global Netherlandish Art, 1550-1750." Weststeijn's research focuses on the Dutch seventeenth century and the global connections that shaped it, as well as the opportunities that artworks from beyond Europe provide to look back at the Netherlands. In 2015 he published *Art and Antiquity in the Netherlands and Britain: The Vernacular Arcadia of Franciscus Junius (1591-1677),* a study of the revival of classical antiquity in countries around the North Sea.

# Index

Page numbers in *italics* refer to illustrations. An "n" following a page number indicates an endnote.